THE
LAZARUS
FILES

THE LAZARUS FILES

A COLD CASE INVESTIGATION

MATTHEW McGOUGH

Henry Holt and Company   New York

Henry Holt and Company
Publishers since 1866
175 Fifth Avenue
New York, New York 10010
www.henryholt.com

Henry Holt ® and 🏢® are registered trademarks of
Macmillan Publishing Group, LLC.

Distributed in Canada by Raincoast Book Distribution Limited

Library of Congress Cataloging-in-Publication Data

Names: McGough, Matthew, author.
Title: The Lazarus files : a cold case investigation / by Matthew McGough.
Description: First Edition. | New York : Henry Holt, [2019]
Identifiers: LCCN 2018037256 | ISBN 9780805095593 (hardcover) |
    ISBN 9781250245779 (international edition)
Subjects: LCSH: Lazarus, Stephanie. | Rasmussen, Sherri—Death and burial. |
    Murder—California—Los Angeles. | Cold cases (Criminal investigation)—
    California—Los Angeles.
Classification: LCC HV6534.L7 M354 2019 | DDC 364.152/3092—dc23
LC record available at https://lccn.loc.gov/2018037256

Our books may be purchased in bulk for promotional, educational, or business
use. Please contact your local bookseller or the Macmillan Corporate and
Premium Sales Department at (800) 221-7945, extension 5442, or by e-mail at
MacmillanSpecialMarkets@macmillan.com.

First Edition 2019

Designed by Meryl Sussman Levavi

Printed in the United States of America

1 3 5 7 9 10 8 6 4 2

To Kathryn, Hudson, and Declan,
for lighting my way

Penetrating so many secrets, we cease to believe in the unknowable. But there it sits nevertheless, calmly licking its chops.

—H. L. MENCKEN, *Minority Report*

Contents

PART TWO
THE MURDER OF SHERRI RASMUSSEN

PART THREE
THE MURDER OF CATHERINE BRALEY

PART FOUR
EPILOGUE

PART

Sherri, John, and Stephanie

ONE

The Aftermath

(February 24, 1986)

Sherri Rasmussen, a twenty-nine-year-old hospital nurse, was just one of 831 people murdered in Los Angeles in 1986.

Sherri's husband, John Ruetten, came home from work at six p.m. on Monday, February 24, and discovered her lifeless body. Sherri and John had been married for only three months. The young newlyweds lived in the Balboa Townhomes, a well-kept but nondescript condominium complex in the Van Nuys section of Los Angeles.

Van Nuys was a middle-class community in the heart of the San Fernando Valley. As late as the 1940s, Van Nuys was mostly sunbaked farmland. After World War II, its orange and walnut groves were uprooted for vast tracts of single family homes. Practically overnight, the character of Van Nuys changed from rustic to suburban. Major companies like General Motors and Anheuser-Busch built massive plants in Van Nuys that employed thousands. Prosperity fueled more development, until few traces remained of the once bucolic landscape. The streetscape that supplanted it was flat and unglamorous, with broad boulevards lined by all manner of businesses. The 1970s brought more change to Van Nuys. Many single family homes were torn down and replaced by higher-density apartment buildings. Violent crime increased. From 1970 to 1975, the LAPD's Van Nuys Division averaged about a dozen homicides per year. Over the next five years, the Van Nuys murder rate doubled.

The Balboa Townhomes, built in 1980, were well secured compared to other residences nearby. A six-foot wall surrounded the entire condo complex, which spanned the 7100 block of Balboa Boulevard, a major north–south thoroughfare through the Valley. The only gaps in the wall were a locked pedestrian gate, which opened by key or from inside by buzzer, and an electric car gate. Past the car gate was a paved interior driveway bordered on each side by rows of three-story condos.

John sensed that something was wrong as he pulled up in his car that night. Their unit's garage door was open, which was highly unusual, and no cars were parked inside. John knew Sherri had called in sick to work that morning, so there was no reason for her car to be gone. The pavement in front of the garage door was strewn with broken glass. To John it looked like auto glass. It reminded him of a minor driving mishap Sherri had a few months before, when she clipped her car while backing out of the garage. John wondered if she might have done something similar, like broken her taillight or side mirror. John figured maybe she took her car to get fixed and forgot to close the garage.

John and Sherri had had a burglar alarm system installed just two months earlier. They typically armed the alarm only when they were both out, and before they went to sleep. When John left for work at 7:20 that morning, Sherri was still in bed. John had not thought to set the alarm, or to make sure that their front door was locked. The front door unlocked automatically when opened from inside. If they didn't manually lock the door afterward, it remained unlocked. John and Sherri rarely used the front door, mostly only to let the cat in or out, or when they had guests. Their friends tended to use it because it was closest to the condo's visitor parking.

Sherri's younger sister, Teresa, and her husband, Brian, had visited with Sherri and John the day before, a Sunday. Teresa was five months pregnant with her and Brian's first child. During the visit, Sherri gave her a present, a maternity bathing suit and swim cap she bought to encourage Teresa to exercise during her pregnancy. Sherri, Teresa, and Brian also took a drive in Sherri's BMW to a pet store to look at saltwater aquariums. Sherri's car was stylish and still new. She let Brian drive. Sherri and John had bought the BMW 318i for Sherri nine months earlier, the same weekend they got engaged, in lieu of a diamond ring. Sherri decided having a car was more practical. After Teresa and Brian went home, a friend of John's, Mike, also visited John and Sherri at home.

On his way to work the next morning, John dropped off some clothes at the dry cleaner's. He arrived at his office at about ten minutes to eight. John had started work about six weeks earlier as an engineer at a company named Micropolis, which made computer disk drives. Around 10:00 a.m., he called home, to see how Sherri was feeling, but got no answer. A little later, he tried again. The phone rang and rang. John then called the hospital and spoke with Sherri's secretary, Sylvia. Sylvia told him that Sherri was out of the office, teaching a class. Unbeknownst to John, Sherri's sister Teresa also tried calling her at home and left a message on the answering machine. Sherri did not return the calls. John finished work around five o'clock. On his way home, he ran a few errands, stopping to collect their dry cleaning plus a package at the UPS store.

John drove past the broken glass and parked in his usual spot in the garage. He took the dry cleaning and started up the short staircase inside the condo. John's unease deepened when saw that the door at the top of the stairs was wide open. He was certain he had closed and locked that door when he left that morning. As John walked upstairs, he did not see that the wall alongside him was flecked with bloodstains.

The stairs up from their garage opened onto a tiled entryway near the front door. John saw Sherri lying in the middle of their living room, which was in disarray. A shelf of their entertainment wall unit had collapsed. A corded telephone and pieces from a broken vase were strewn on the carpet around her. A drawer from a nearby end table had been pulled out and its contents dumped in a heap. In the entryway, right at John's feet, two video components were stacked on the floor. John stepped past them into the living room, where, amid the detritus, Sherri lay motionless on her back.

Sherri was dressed in a short rust-colored robe, which she wore over a sleeveless undershirt and panties. Her right arm appeared frozen in place, with her hand raised to the ceiling. Her left hand, with its wedding ring, rested on her chest.

John couldn't understand why Sherri would be on the floor. He wanted to believe she was sleeping. He draped the dry cleaning across the back of their living room sofa and approached her body with trepidation.

I hope she's okay, John thought. But one look told John that she was not. Sherri's face was badly bruised, and her complexion the wrong color. Her left eye was open and unblinking. Her right eye was swollen shut and crusted with blood. More blood was smeared across her forehead. Sherri's lips were parted slightly, as if in midgasp.

Tentatively, John touched his wife's calf. Her leg felt stiff and cold. John tried to find a pulse and couldn't. But it was her face, so beautiful just that morning, that most unnerved him. He could tell from her eyes that she was gone. Sherri's facial injuries were so disturbing to John that he did not notice the three gunshot wounds in her chest, or the bite mark on the inside of her left forearm.

John picked the phone handset up off the floor and dialed 911. Ten or fifteen seconds later, a dispatcher came on the line.

"I think my wife is dead," John said. The operator took the address and told him not to call anyone else. "Just wait there, somebody is on the way," the operator promised. John set the phone down and paced the living room. If it even occurred to him to call Sherri's parents and notify his in-laws of her death, he could not bring himself to make the call.

John didn't know what to do with himself while he waited. He went back to Sherri and looked at her again, which only made him feel worse. He took a hand towel and draped it over Sherri's face, less for her dignity than to spare himself the distress of seeing her injuries. Even with Sherri's face covered, John still felt too upset to stay in the living room with her body. He walked back down to the garage and looked around to make sure no one else was there. He considered waiting by the front door to meet the authorities and let them in. Then he decided he should stay near the phone in case someone called. The wait was only a few minutes but seemed interminable. John felt he couldn't take it, being there alone. He wanted someone else to be there with him and Sherri's body.

The 911 operator had routed the call to the Los Angeles Fire Department, which dispatched an ambulance. Two firefighter-paramedics arrived at the condo at 6:08 p.m. John was standing near the front door, crying, when they came inside.

The paramedics removed the makeshift shroud that John had placed over Sherri's face. Her blunt force trauma was so extensive that the paramedics, like John, did not initially notice her gunshot wounds. Sherri had no pulse or respiration. It was obvious that there was nothing they could do. They pronounced her dead at 6:10 p.m.

The paramedics saw the broken vase on the floor as they checked her vital signs. Once it was clear she was dead, they stepped back from the body, so as not to disturb any potential evidence. The paramedics' responsibility had shifted from saving a life to keeping everyone away until the LAPD showed up. The paramedics led John to the kitchen, one flight up from the living room and out of view of Sherri's body, and assured him the police would be there soon. John felt like he was in shock. John kept telling the paramedics, "I didn't think this could happen here."

The paramedics ceded control of the scene at 6:20 p.m., when the first LAPD patrol unit arrived. LAPD officer Rodney Forrest, a training officer assigned to the Van Nuys Division, and his partner, an LAPD reserve officer, were on patrol when they heard the radio call for a possible homicide at 7100 Balboa.

One of the paramedics was waiting outside by the ambulance when Forrest drove up. The paramedic said that a husband had come home and found his wife dead. The paramedic led the officers to the front door. The second paramedic stood in the entryway. Past him, Forrest could see into the living room, where the victim's body lay with a towel over her face. The paramedics explained that the husband had placed it there before they arrived, and they replaced it after their examination, because he could not bear to see her face that way.

Forrest and his partner set about clearing the condo, which entailed checking room by room for any suspects. They found John sitting upstairs at the kitchen table, distraught, with his head in his hands. Forrest told John that he needed to leave the premises. Forrest watched John and the paramedics walk out the front door.

Once the condo was cleared, Forrest radioed the watch commander, the officer on duty at the Van Nuys station responsible for managing police response. Forrest informed him of the homicide and requested a supervisor at the scene. He then instructed his partner to stand at the front door and start the crime scene log. The log, the first document in any homicide investigation, is intended to record everyone who enters and leaves the crime scene. Without one, it would be impossible to determine later whether a fingerprint or other trace evidence came from a potential suspect or was left inadvertently after the murder by authorized personnel.

Forrest's report to the watch commander was relayed to Leslie "Al" Durrer, the commanding officer of Van Nuys detectives. Durrer was a Lieutenant II, among the highest-ranked officers in the division. The detectives who worked under Durrer were assigned to various "tables," each dedicated to investigating a different species of crime: homicides, robberies, burglaries, auto thefts, and so on. Detective work was organized along the same lines in all of the LAPD's geographic divisions.

Durrer in turn notified Roger Pida, the detective in charge of the Van

Nuys homicide table. Pida was a Detective III, the LAPD's highest detective rank. As the Van Nuys homicide coordinator, Pida was responsible for allocating cases among his detectives, supervising their investigations, and signing off on their reports.

By 6:30 p.m., half an hour after John discovered Sherri's body, Pida had assigned the case to two detectives, Lyle Mayer and Steve Hooks. Pida called and gave them the address.

Mayer was by far the more seasoned of the two detectives. Mayer had more than twenty years on the job, and more than a decade's experience as a homicide investigator. He had worked homicide in Van Nuys for five years, since 1981, and had cut his teeth as a detective, earlier in his career, on the homicide tables at the LAPD's Hollywood and Rampart Divisions. Mayer's rank in 1986 was Detective II. In addition to working cases, detectives of Mayer's rank were expected to train and supervise lower-ranked detectives. Mayer's assertive personality reflected the great pride he took in his investigative experience and his status as a homicide detective.

Hooks in 1986 was eight years into his LAPD career, and still a Detective I. Along with being younger, less experienced, and lower ranked than Mayer, Hooks was also more reserved. Although Hooks later joined the Van Nuys homicide unit, he was assigned to the burglary table when Pida tapped him to work with Mayer on Sherri's case. It was standard LAPD practice whenever the homicide table was overloaded or short-staffed to pull detectives off other tables and loan them to homicide. Sherri's case was the first time Mayer and Hooks had worked together as partners.

According to the crime scene log, the first from the detective bureau to arrive was Lt. Durrer, the commanding officer, at 7:24 p.m. Hooks logged in at 7:48, Mayer at 7:52, and Pida, their supervisor, at 8:04 p.m. Forensic personnel from the LAPD crime lab started to arrive around the same time. By nine o'clock, three hours after John called 911, nearly twenty LAPD personnel had responded to the crime scene.

John remained outside the condo amid all this activity. The detectives' initial impression, based on the crime scene, was that Sherri was killed during an attempted burglary. Still, in order to eliminate John as a suspect, the detectives would need to interview him. In addition to being the victim's husband, John was also the last known person to see her alive. John agreed to go to the Van Nuys station to be interviewed.

Mayer, the lead investigator, would question John. Mayer left for the station at 9:00 p.m. Hooks remained behind to monitor the forensics team's search for clues and physical evidence. Durrer and Pida, the detectives' supervisors, logged out from the crime scene at 9:25.

As John was driven to the station, the LAPD's investigation had only just begun. No one at the time could have predicted how many years the truth would remain hidden, and at what cost to all involved.

2

Sherri Rasmussen

(1957 to 1984)

Before Sherri and John met, the condo had belonged to Sherri. Sherri's parents, Nels and Loretta Rasmussen, had purchased it for her six years earlier, in 1980.

Back then, Sherri was in her early twenties and studying for her master's degree in nursing at UCLA. She also worked at the time as a staff nurse at UCLA Medical Center, to help pay her way through school. Her hours were irregular and long, and often required her to commute to work late at night. The crime rate in Los Angeles was far higher then than it is today.

Sherri was young and beautiful and planned to live alone. Her parents were naturally concerned for her safety. Nels and Loretta lived in Tucson, Arizona, where they had raised Sherri and her two sisters. Coming from Tucson, Nels regarded Los Angeles warily. He and Sherri had looked at countless places for Sherri to live before they chose the condo in Van Nuys, largely because it felt safe.

Although Nels loved all three of his daughters, he was especially close to and protective of Sherri. Sherri was the middle child, but the last of the three to get married. Because Sherri was single, she was more available than her sisters to spend time with her parents. After Sherri moved into the condo, she and Nels talked nearly every night, sometimes for hours.

The Rasmussens had always been a loving and tight-knit family. Nels was a dentist with a thriving practice in Tucson. Loretta worked full time as Nels's office manager. They had been a couple since they were teenagers, in the early 1950s, growing up in rural Washington State. Nels and Loretta met at Columbia Academy, a Seventh-Day Adventist high school, where they dated briefly but broke up before graduation.

Nels lived with his parents, older sister, and younger brother on a small farm in Amboy, about twenty miles from Mount St. Helens. Amboy had one gas station, one grocery store, and four beer parlors. Everyone in town knew Nels as Junior.

Nels Senior was a logger with a reputation as an expert timber faller. Nels's father's work regularly took him into the woods and away from his family for weeks at a time. Being the de facto man of the house at a tender age shaped the younger Nels's character and work ethic.

Nels never gave much thought when he was young to what career he wanted. No one in his family had been to college or talked to him about how to plan for the future. After high school, Nels followed his father's example and became a logger. Logging jobs were transient. Nels and his father sometimes had to drive hundreds of miles to find work. On one such trip in 1952, when Nels was eighteen, he dozed off behind the wheel and flipped their truck. Nels's father escaped injury, but Nels's left leg was badly broken.

Nels was in a full body cast for months. Being laid up and unable to work made him miserable. His thoughts returned to Loretta, who by then had left for college. Nels's mother wrote a letter to Loretta and told her, "If you still care for Junior, he's now in a weakened condition." Loretta visited when she came home for Thanksgiving. Nels and Loretta married less than a year later, in 1953. Nels was nineteen and Loretta eighteen. Loretta soon became pregnant.

Nels resumed logging after his leg healed. When Loretta went into labor, he was at a camp fifty miles away and could not be contacted. A neighbor took Loretta to the hospital, where she gave birth to their first daughter, Connie, in 1954.

The young family lived with Loretta's mother and father, also a logger. Nels came home as often as he could. One night, Loretta asked Nels, "Why don't you go to school?"

"What would I do? I have no idea what I'd be interested in."

"You should be a dentist."

"Why would I want to be a dentist?"

"Well, my dentist gets a new car every year."

Nels thought, "Gee whiz. I like cars. That sounds good." When Connie was six months old, they moved to Walla Walla, Washington, where there was a Seventh-Day Adventist college. Nels started classes at Walla Walla University in the fall of 1954. In addition to his studies, Nels worked full-time hours at the school's dairy to pay his tuition and the family's living expenses. To supplement the meager food that they could afford to buy, Loretta canned fruit and vegetables from her mother's garden.

In summer 1956, Loretta became pregnant with their second child. Nels resolved that he would not miss this birth, as he had Connie's. "When I take you to the hospital, I'm going to stay until you have the baby," he promised her.

Nels majored in chemistry. His faculty mentor was an old, distinguished professor, Dr. George Bowers. Bowers was the chemistry department chairman and a former president of the university. Bowers enjoyed a reputation as a harsh grader. Nels had heard that he needed a GPA between 3.5 and 3.8 to be admitted to dental school. Early in the year, Nels went to see Bowers, who told him, "In my class, I give you a test every day. That's 40 percent of your grade. I give four tests during the quarter. That's 60 percent of your grade." Nels needed an A.

On February 7, 1957, Loretta delivered a baby girl, whom they named Sherri Rae. Nels was true to his word and accompanied Loretta to the hospital. In doing so, he missed a day of classes, and one of Bowers's daily tests.

A few months later, at the end of the school year, Nels received his grades. Bowers had given him a B in chemistry. At home that night, Nels told Loretta he had kept close track of his marks and felt certain he had earned an A.

At Loretta's suggestion, Nels went to see Bowers. "If you look at my record, I have an A, but I got a B," Nels told his professor. Nels said that he needed an A to get into dental school.

Bowers checked his own grade book. "You got a B. You missed one day."

Nels explained that he was at the hospital that day for Sherri's birth. Nels wondered aloud what his average was otherwise. "I'm not asking for any gifts, but what do you have me down as percentagewise for the whole quarter?"

"95.4 percent," Bowers answered. "96 is an A. That's a B. I explained to you at the beginning of the year how my grading is."

"If you believe it's a B, it's a B," Nels said. He got up and walked out. Graduation loomed. Nels knew he was out of time to raise his GPA. Before his final grades were in, he applied to the dental school at Loma Linda

University, also a Seventh-Day Adventist institution, sixty miles east of Los Angeles.

Nels and Loretta interviewed at Loma Linda while his application was pending. The admissions officer showed Nels his college transcript. Nels saw that Bowers had changed his grade to an A.

Nels enrolled at Loma Linda's School of Dentistry in 1957. In 1960, Loretta gave birth to their third daughter, Teresa. While Nels attended school, Loretta ran a day care center out of their home, which had a small fenced-in yard. This allowed Loretta to care for Sherri and baby Teresa while also helping to support the family.

Sherri was a "Momma's girl" as a toddler. Nels could never persuade Sherri to join him and Connie on their trips to the store unless Loretta came with them. Nels would put Connie and Sherri in the car, but as soon as he slid behind the wheel, Sherri would look around and ask, "Is Mommy going?"

"No," Nels would explain. "Mommy has to stay with the kids, because their mommies haven't come picked them up yet." Sherri would flee the car faster than Nels could stop her. Nels even tried to bribe Sherri with promises of ice cream to get her to come. Nothing was enough to convince Sherri to leave her mother's side.

When Nels completed dental school in 1961, Loma Linda gave Loretta and all the other graduates' wives a mock diploma for a Ph.T.—Putting Hubby Through. Soon after graduation, when Sherri was four years old, Nels and Loretta moved their family from California to Tucson, Arizona.

Nels opened his dental office in a working-class neighborhood in South Tucson. Loretta was Nels's full-time office manager and receptionist. To save money, Nels did all of his own lab work. Each day at five o'clock, after his last appointment, Nels and Loretta would come home. Loretta would cook dinner for their family and put the children to bed. After he ate and spent time with his daughters, Nels would go back to the office to cast crowns, wax dentures, or whatever else his patients needed done. Nels worked in the lab many nights until three o'clock in the morning.

With Loretta's help, Nels's dental practice blossomed. Within a few years, he was able to fulfill a dream that he had harbored since high school: owning his own boat.

Nels chose a 19-foot ski boat with a powerful Chevy engine and a top speed of 40 miles per hour. In summer, the family would head to Lake Apache outside Tucson almost every weekend. Nels and Loretta would work

Rasmussen family photo, November 22, 1963
(clockwise from top: Nels, Loretta, Sherri, Teresa, Connie)

late, load their camper, and haul it and their boat to the lake. The next morning, Nels would wake the girls at sunrise. "Daylight's burning. Let's get up. Let's go," was Nels's usual wake-up call. Then they'd get out on the lake, smooth and inviting in the early morning.

All three girls learned to water-ski on Lake Apache. Teresa, at age three and a half, was so light the rope stayed on the surface of the water as it pulled her along. The boat could tow as many as eight skiers at once. Nels issued a standing challenge that he would give $25 to any boy who could stay up longer than Connie and Sherri. Connie, Sherri, and a challenger would grab a tow rope, and Nels would gun the big Chevy engine. Nels never had to pay up, not even once. The girls were his pride and joy. Nels wouldn't have traded a daughter for five sons.

For school, Nels and Loretta sent the girls to Tucson Seventh-Day Adventist Elementary. It was a tiny church school, with fewer than a dozen students per grade. The campus consisted of two rectangular buildings in an L shape, alongside a large cement slab used for recess. Each building held two classrooms. Each classroom held two grades, and one teacher.

The school's principal, a pastor named Carl Groom, lived with his wife, Ruth, in a home on the school grounds. Pastor Groom taught seventh and eighth grades, and Mrs. Groom some of the younger grades. Groom was athletic and well liked by the students. Some days, if a class completed its lessons early, Groom would let them play sports all afternoon. Years later, Groom would perform Sherri and John's wedding ceremony.

Sherri was an eager and naturally disciplined student. Nels and Loretta never had to get after Sherri to study. She was organized and planned out how much time she spent on this or that subject. Her intelligence and competence were evident to her teachers, who sometimes relied on her in class to make their jobs easier.

In fourth grade, Sherri had a math teacher, Mrs. Mapara, who was visiting from overseas and not fluent in English. Because the students had difficulty understanding her, Mrs. Mapara eventually delegated math lessons to Sherri. One day when Sherri was at the blackboard explaining a math problem to her classmates, Mrs. Mapara criticized how Sherri held the pointer. After publicly scolding Sherri for holding the stick wrong, she told the class, "Everyone laugh at Sherri." Everyone laughed. Sherri held the stick the way Mrs. Mapara wanted and resumed the lesson. When Sherri finished the math problem, she set the pointer down and said, "Everyone laugh at Mrs. Mapara." Mrs. Mapara kicked Sherri out of class and sent her to the principal.

Groom called Nels and Loretta and explained the situation. "I've got a problem," Groom said. "I have a teacher whom I have to please, and I have a student that I know has been mistreated. What do I do?"

"Follow your best guidance," Nels replied. "Sherri's young. She'll recover."

Groom explained to Sherri how she might have handled the situation better. After Groom spoke with Sherri, he told Nels he greatly respected Sherri for listening and accepting his advice.

Sherri's role within her family, as she grew older, was the peacemaker. Sherri got along equally well with her sisters and her parents, so it didn't matter which member of the family was ticked off. Sherri could smooth it over and, more often than not, turn their frustrations into laughter.

When Sherri was finishing sixth grade, Groom went to Nels and Loretta and told them, "I think we're wasting Sherri's time. I think she should do seventh grade during the summer and graduate next year. She's bored. She's ready for high school."

That summer, working with Groom, Sherri completed the coursework for seventh grade. Sherri's eighth grade class was two boys and five girls, including her friend Emily Hindman, whose family lived a few miles from the Rasmussens. Although Sherri was a year younger than her classmates, she earned the top marks in her grade. To keep Sherri engaged, Groom had her write independent research papers on topics in science, history, and other subjects and then present them to the class.

Nels and Loretta considered Groom's academic demands good for Sherri's development. Sherri always had the drive to do well in school, but Nels sensed she sometimes seemed uncomfortable being at the top of her class. Some of her friends weren't doing as well and didn't feel school was important, as Sherri did. Groom helped Sherri understand that she should not be ashamed of her gifts. Before Sherri skipped the seventh grade, she would bring home her schoolwork to show her parents but wouldn't talk about it with great pride. In eighth grade, this changed.

Because of Sherri's modest demeanor, her intelligence and achievements provoked no resentment among her older classmates. Sherri was voted the class president, and she delivered a speech at graduation.

Sherri's closest friend in adolescence was her classmate Emily. Emily saw Sherri as happy and extremely intelligent, but serious-minded. Sherri shared with Emily her worries that she could be doing more than she was. Emily never knew what to say when Sherri expressed her feelings of inadequacy.

ABOVE: *Sherri Rasmussen's eighth grade school photo*

LEFT: *Sherri's eighth grade graduation, with Pastor Carl Groom*

From Emily's perspective, she felt awed that Sherri was so intelligent that she could skip a whole grade. Emily had never heard of anyone skipping a grade before.

Sherri and Emily both participated in their church's youth ministry, a scouting-like program called Pathfinders. One night after Pathfinders, Sherri and Emily were sitting in the backseat of Emily's parents' car. That night's sermon was about the coming return of Jesus, which would precipitate the end of the world. Sherri and Emily were pious girls. The sermon left them convinced that Jesus would appear before they reached adulthood. The two friends sat in the car and cried together. Emily would never forget how Sherri looked that night, dressed in her white fur coat. Emily thought Sherri looked so beautiful in the dim light, her eyes brimming with tears. Sherri loved Jesus. But like any young person, Sherri wanted to grow up first.

For high school, Sherri followed her sister Connie to Thunderbird Adventist Academy, a coed boarding school located on an old military airfield in Scottsdale, Arizona. Connie was three years older but, because Sherri had skipped a year, only two grades ahead. Sherri's roommate her freshman year was Donna Hancock, a sophomore who had roomed with Connie the year before. Donna initially thought of Sherri as Connie's shy little sister. Although Sherri was younger than everyone else at the school, she was taller than many other girls, even as a freshman. Donna wondered if Sherri was quiet in part because she didn't want to draw attention to herself.

Relations at Thunderbird between male and female students tended to be regimented, consistent with the school's Christian ethos. Girls and boys lived in separate one-story dormitories across campus. There were two grassy hills on campus, which students referred to as "the boys' hump" and "the girls' hump." At certain times of day when intermingling was discouraged, the girls would lie out on the grass in view of the boys, and vice versa. Once a month, students were permitted to go to the mall together. The girls typically went in a pack. Sherri was popular among both the girls and the boys but related to the boys mostly as friends. Sherri went out on a few dates but never had a serious romance or a steady boyfriend in high school.

For illicit thrills, students sometimes sneaked out of the dorm late at night to walk to the nearest Tastee Freez, a few miles away. When the urge for ice cream seized them, Sherri and Donna would jimmy the screen on their dorm room window. The screens had locks, which were checked from time to time but weren't hard to repair before the next check. Once they were outside, and certain the dorm monitors had not heard their escape, Sherri and Donna would set off on foot for the Tastee Freez. Rather than use the roads around the old air base, they trekked straight through the desert, as the crow flies. Neither gave much thought to rattlesnakes, coyotes, or other perils they might encounter walking through the desert, in darkness, to get ice cream. Sherri and Donna saw it as an adventure and always made it safely.

Every six weeks, Thunderbird students were allowed to go home for four days. Donna's family lived in Bullhead City, Arizona, close to the California and Nevada state lines. Some breaks Sherri went home with Donna. Other breaks Donna went with Sherri to Tucson. Donna thought the Rasmussens were a wonderful family. She especially loved Nels, whose generosity seemed limitless. Whenever Thunderbird took school outings to Tucson, Nels always treated everyone to lunch.

Sherri continued to excel academically. By the end of her junior year of high school, she had completed all the classes required to graduate. The old familiar feelings of boredom began to gnaw at her. In fall 1973, for the second time in four years, Sherri skipped a grade.

Donna had already graduated from Thunderbird and enrolled as a freshman at La Sierra College in California. La Sierra was affiliated with Loma Linda University, Nels's alma mater for dental school. La Sierra agreed to accept Sherri's credits. Within weeks, Sherri and Donna became roommates again, this time on the La Sierra campus. When Sherri began college classes in September 1973, she was just sixteen years old.

Sherri's high school photo, circa 1973

Sherri's older sister, Connie, was also at Loma Linda, studying nursing. Connie had planned on becoming a nurse since she was four years old. A great-aunt on Loretta's side of the family was an accomplished nurse who had devoted her life to improving public health standards on the island of Guam. She was greatly admired within the family, and Connie had resolved to follow her example. Sherri looked up to both her older sister and her aunt. During Sherri's freshman year of college, she decided she also wanted to pursue a career in nursing.

Donna marveled at Sherri's precociousness as a college student, and the ease with which she mastered coursework that Donna found challenging. As freshmen at La Sierra, Sherri and Donna had many of the same prerequisites. Sherri studied hard for her classes, although it seemed to Donna that she didn't need to. Donna thought Sherri was capable of memorizing anything. La Sierra did not allow students to keep cars on campus unless they achieved a certain grade point average. Sherri qualified to have a car in January of her freshman year.

Sherri had had her driver's license for less than a year. Nels had taught her to drive in the family's four-wheel-drive Toyota, a car the Rasmussen girls nicknamed Herbie. Soon after, returning from a family trip to Lake Apache, Sherri was behind the wheel when Nels corrected her driving somewhat harshly. Sherri didn't appreciate the advice and announced, "I'm not driving anymore."

"Well, pull it off the road, then," Nels replied. "We'll wait."

Sherri pulled onto the shoulder and placed Herbie in park. The family sat by the side of the road, in silence, as minutes passed. Nels adjusted the passenger seat and leaned back, as if he was about to settle in for a long nap. More minutes passed in silence. "Okay, I'll drive," Sherri finally relented.

Sherri was growing up in other ways as well. By that spring, Sherri and Donna had both started to date boys. Donna's romance, with a classmate named Lynn Robison, was more serious. Sherri had an on-and-off relationship with a sophomore named Paul. Connie had also fallen in love. During her sophomore year, Connie and her fiancé decided they didn't want to wait any longer to get married. At the time, Loma Linda had a policy that discouraged nursing students from marrying before graduation. Connie got married anyway. The school stripped Connie of her academic honors and forced her to take a year off.

Near the end of Sherri's freshman year, she applied to enter the nursing program at Loma Linda. Sherri was admitted and switched campuses as a sophomore in the fall of 1974. The move ended Sherri's brief relationship with Paul. Donna, who was studying education, stayed at La Sierra. Although Sherri and Donna lived on different campuses twenty miles apart, they remained close friends. Almost every weekend, Donna stayed at Sherri's place, or vice versa.

During their summers, Sherri and Connie worked as student nurses at the school's teaching hospital, Loma Linda University Medical Center. Their work shifts were eight hours long, and often overnight. Connie and Sherri had always been close, as sisters and as friends, but never colleagues. The sisters worked in different departments but sought each other out on their breaks.

Sherri was assigned to the hospital's Surgical Intensive Care Unit, where she gained her first experience of caring directly for patients. Connie was impressed that Sherri knew how to use the ICU's computer, which monitored patients' conditions and relayed information to the nurses. The computer was so enormous that it took up an entire wall. It was not just the size and complexity of the computer that intimidated Connie, but the high-stakes nature of nursing in an ICU, caring for patients who were gravely ill. Connie liked interacting with patients, getting to know them as people and comforting them, but Sherri was unfazed by the high-tech, fast-paced atmosphere in the ICU. Connie didn't know how she did it. Sherri was still a teenager who wore her hair in a ponytail, but she demonstrated a preternatural ability to handle life-and-death decisions. Anyone who worked with Sherri could tell she had a special gift, which she tried to use to help other people.

Sherri and her sisters had lots of fun times, too. Sherri and Connie went home to Tucson often. The family went to football and basketball games at the University of Arizona, everyone decked out in red and blue. Nels and Loretta sold the family ski boat, which had figured so prominently in their girls' childhoods, and bought a bigger boat, a 36-foot motor trawler, which they christened *The Tucson Queen*. Nels kept it at a marina in San Diego, the nearest oceanfront city to Tucson. Sherri and Connie would drive down from Loma Linda to meet their parents and Teresa for family cruises up the coast to Catalina Island.

Teresa, four years younger than Sherri, was in eighth grade at the time. When it came time for Teresa to get braces, Nels sent her to a dental school classmate whose practice was in Loma Linda. Teresa flew in monthly for her appointments. Sherri and Connie would pick her up at the airport and take her to the orthodontist and then home with them for the weekend.

On one of Teresa's visits, Sherri confided to her sister that she felt torn between becoming a nurse and going to medical school. Nels had told Sherri on many occasions that she would make a phenomenal doctor. Sherri believed she might, but also felt she could accomplish so much in nursing. Sherri did not want Connie to feel overshadowed if she left nursing and pursued medicine instead. Sherri also aspired to start a family one day and worried that if she became a doctor, she would have to sacrifice a family life. Sherri did not want to miss out on being a mother.

In the fall of 1975, Connie, her husband, and Sherri moved into a two-bedroom trailer home near the Loma Linda campus. Connie and her husband took the larger, back bedroom. Sherri's front bedroom had an extra pullout bed. Teresa started high school that fall at Thunderbird, the same boarding school her sisters had attended. Compared to her older sisters, Teresa had a bit of a wild streak. Teresa was unhappy at Thunderbird from her first day of freshman year.

In mid-September, Donna married her boyfriend, Lynn. Donna asked Sherri to be a bridesmaid. The entire Rasmussen family was invited to the wedding. Teresa was looking forward to it because she had a crush on Donna's brother.

Freshmen were not allowed to leave the Thunderbird campus without permission. The school initially approved Teresa's request. Donna's parents and brother were traveling from Scottsdale to the wedding and offered Teresa a ride. Just before the trip, the school told Teresa she could not leave unless one of her parents signed her out in person. Teresa knew that was impossible. When Donna's mom came to pick her up, Teresa neglected to mention that she was going AWOL from campus.

After Teresa arrived at the wedding with Donna's family, and it became clear what she had done, Nels and Loretta gave her an ultimatum: return to Thunderbird, or move back home and go to public school in Tucson. Teresa had only attended small church schools. The idea of being a new student at a big school terrified her.

Sherri offered Teresa a third option, to come live with her and Connie and enroll at Loma Linda Academy, the university-affiliated high school on campus. The school year at Loma Linda Academy had not yet begun, so Teresa hadn't missed any classes. Nels and Loretta agreed.

Teresa never went back to Thunderbird. Two weeks later, Sherri went to Scottsdale, packed up her little sister's dorm room, and moved her into their two-bedroom trailer in Loma Linda. Teresa spent the next two years sleeping on the pullout couch in Sherri's bedroom.

Because Sherri had twice skipped a grade, and Connie took a year off from nursing school to get married, the sisters ended up as classmates their junior year at Loma Linda. Although Connie was nearly three years older, she was not uncomfortable that Sherri had caught up to her in school.

Connie believed Sherri had a special intellect that she tried to keep secret. As smart as Sherri was, she wasn't the type to make anyone around her feel stupid.

The sisters shared their joys, problems, and sorrows with one another during the time they lived together. Teresa and Connie never forgot the emotional impact one patient made on Sherri, a teenage boy about her own age. Sherri was still a student nurse assigned to the ICU at Loma Linda. The boy was a motocross rider, and had been racing his motorcycle out in the sand dunes when he crashed and suffered a serious head injury. By the time he was brought to the ICU, he had slipped into a coma.

For weeks on end, Sherri came home from work and told her sisters about him. Sherri said caring for the boy was one of the toughest things she'd ever done. She described how she sat and talked to him, even though she wasn't sure he could hear her. Sherri cried as she recounted their one-sided conversations.

In June 1977, Sherri and Connie graduated together from Loma Linda. Sherri's grades earned her an invitation to Sigma Theta Tau, a nursing honor society, but she declined because Connie was not also selected.

Nursing school graduates traditionally receive a pin to signify their admission into the profession. Loretta's great-aunt, who had inspired them to become nurses, attended their pinning ceremony. Loretta got Teresa a pretty floral headband to wear for the occasion, so she wouldn't feel less important than her sisters.

In July 1977, at the age of twenty, Sherri was granted her nursing license by the State of California. She continued to work as a staff nurse in the ICU until August. Over the summer, she visited schools with master's in nursing programs, including the University of Houston, Tulane, and UCLA. Sherri liked UCLA the most.

In September, Sherri was hired as a nurse in the Coronary Care Unit at UCLA Medical Center. Teresa, meanwhile, was starting her junior year of high school. Sherri and Teresa got an apartment together in Van Nuys. Teresa enrolled at San Fernando Valley Adventist Academy. The following June, Sherri was admitted to the master's in nursing program at UCLA. Soon after Sherri got the news, Nels handwrote her a letter to congratulate her and offer his encouragement for the next stage of her career:

> *The sacrifices you will have to make over the next two years will be considerable but it will be the most rewarding experience of your young life.*

Sherri and Connie at Loma Linda graduation, June 1977

Let your leadership abilities surface and step out and make your way to the top. Remember the world waits for no one. The contributions you make to nursing will make a better person out of you and you will enjoy your profession so much more if you give of yourself . . .

To be a leader you must be an expert in your field. Learn while you're young to motivate others to guide and influence, but listen to others as well. Maintain your honesty and humility and be ready to experience some lonely times. To be a leader you give a lot but in time the hidden rewards are seen and you are accepted by your peers. This brings great pride and sense of accomplishment. I want you to always remember I'm as close as the nearest phone. We all need a friend from time to time to talk to. I hope I will always qualify . . .

Congratulations & Good Luck. Your Dad, Nels Jr. Love ya.

Sherri entered the master's in nursing program at UCLA in September 1978. She and Teresa, by then a senior, moved into an apartment in Westwood, close to the UCLA campus. Teresa drove herself daily to and from her high school in the Valley.

Sherri's workload included a full slate of classes, as well as intensive clinical training in the form of nursing shifts at UCLA Medical Center.

Sherri's clinical focus was cardiac care, treating patients with serious heart problems.

Sherri often came home from her clinical rounds bone-tired. Teresa attributed Sherri's exhaustion partly to her physical exertions on the job, such as performing CPR on multiple patients during a single shift. Teresa thought Sherri's fatigue also reflected the emotion that she could not help but bring to her work and invest in her patients, knowing that she held their lives in her hands.

Her social life took a backseat to her schoolwork and clinical responsibilities. Sherri went on a handful of dates, and was asked out on many more, but she was more intent on finishing her master's degree than finding a boyfriend. When Sherri socialized, it was usually with classmates, or nurses and residents she knew from the hospital. Sherri joined a study group of half a dozen nursing students. Sherri was the only nonsmoker in the group. By the time they graduated, she had persuaded all but one of them to quit smoking. It wasn't her style to lecture, badger, or scold. Sherri was respectful and encouraging in a way that got to people in their quiet moments. She made people around her want to be better.

Teresa, despite being in high school, had a more active social life than her older sister. Nels nicknamed her two boyfriends Pencil Neck and Snake Charmer. Sherri felt responsible for Teresa and sometimes called Donna to ask for advice—for instance, if Teresa wanted to go out on a date and Sherri didn't think it was a good idea. She worried about Teresa and didn't want to disappoint her parents or have anything happen to her younger sister on her watch. During Teresa's senior year, Snake Charmer gave her a kitten. It was supposed to be a gift, but because he had no money at the time, Teresa paid for it. Sherri and Teresa named the kitten Bozo, to honor its supposed benefactor.

After Teresa graduated from high school, in 1979, she left Bozo with Sherri. Teresa moved back to Tucson and enrolled at the University of Arizona. Halfway through her freshman year, Teresa visited Donna's parents and reconnected with Donna's brother and a friend of his, Brian Lane. Teresa and Brian had gone on a few dates at Thunderbird Academy before Teresa moved to Loma Linda. Teresa had an extra ticket to the Arizona State basketball game in Phoenix that night and invited Brian to come along. Three months later, Teresa and Brian got engaged.

Sherri was awarded her master's degree by UCLA in March 1980, at age twenty-three. Even after Sherri was officially credentialed as a Cardiovascular Clinical Nurse Specialist, Nels tried to persuade her to consider medical school. "Look at your understanding of the heart's problems, and your abilities," Nels told his daughter.

Sherri heard her father out. When he finished, she put her arm around him and said, "No, Dad. I'm going to stick with nursing. But I'm going to make you proud."

That summer, Nels and Sherri set out to find a new place for her to live in Los Angeles. It seemed to Nels that they drove from Long Beach to Northern California looking at options. Nels purchased the condo in Van Nuys in August 1980, the same year the Balboa Townhomes complex was built. He liked that the neighborhood seemed safe and that the condo complex was relatively secure. Because the unit had a drive-in garage, Sherri would be able to come home from work at all hours and not have to worry about walking alone on the street.

The condo was a split-level unit, and quite spacious, especially for one person to live in alone. Above the two-car garage was the first floor, with the front entryway and living room. The second floor, up a short staircase from the living room, had a dining area with a built-in bar, and the kitchen. Next to the kitchen was a small breakfast room fronted by a balcony with a sliding glass door. The balcony, large enough for a charcoal grill and a few chairs, was directly over the unit's garage door and overlooked the interior of the condo complex. Stairs from the second-floor dining area led to the top floor, with the master bedroom, a guest bedroom, a small den, and a laundry room.

Although the deed to the condo was issued in Nels's name, Sherri wrote a rent check to her father every month equal to the mortgage payment. Sherri had come of age in the 1970s, amid increasing social consciousness of feminism and equal rights for women. Being financially independent from her parents was very important to her.

On November 23, 1980, nine months after they met, Teresa and Brian married. Teresa didn't want to choose between Connie and Sherri as her matron of honor, so she asked both sisters. Soon after the wedding, Sherri and Bozo moved into their new home, unit 205 of the Balboa Townhomes in Van Nuys.

Sherri's master's degree helped her earn a promotion at UCLA Medical Center, to head nurse of the Coronary Care and Coronary Observation Units. The two units, both on the fourth floor of the hospital, had ten and twenty-two beds, respectively. Sherri had previously worked in the CCU

as a staff nurse. In her new position, Sherri had round-the-clock responsibility for nursing care in both units. In addition to her clinical and administrative duties, Sherri had to manage a staff of nurses, several of whom were
former peers. Nearly all the nurses who Sherri supervised were older than
her. Despite the potential pitfalls, Sherri was liked and respected by the doctors and her fellow nurses. In the hierarchy at UCLA Medical Center, head
nurses reported to nursing supervisors. When the hospital was short-staffed
for nursing supervisors, Sherri was one of the head nurses often tapped to
fill the role.

Among Sherri's best friends she met at UCLA Medical Center were two
staff nurses, Jayne Ryan and Anita Kramer, who were also in their twenties.

Jayne had worked part time at UCLA for four years, since 1976, while
she earned her bachelor's degree at Cal State Los Angeles. The youngest
child and the only girl in a family of seven kids, Jayne grew up in Harrow,
Ontario, a small town twenty-five miles over the border from Detroit. When
she met Sherri, Jayne lived with another nurse, Nancy, in a small house in
West Los Angeles.

Anita enjoyed a reputation among her fellow nurses as a matchmaker.
She had introduced a friend of hers to a classmate of Jayne's, and the couple
fell in love and got married. A few years later, Anita would introduce Sherri
to John Ruetten, who was a childhood friend of Anita's boyfriend, Matt
Gorder.

Nursing shifts at the hospital were long and unpredictable. Sherri was
known for her ability to remain calm under pressure, whatever was happening. Jayne was walking one day through the CCU, past the beds for their
most critically ill patients, when she heard Sherri call out, "Excuse me,
Jayne, can you give me a hand for a minute?" Jayne sensed urgency but no
panic in Sherri's voice. Jayne turned to see Sherri standing over a patient
who had gone into cardiac arrest. Sherri was doing one-person CPR. "Yeah,
I can!" Jayne said, rushing over to help. Sherri was always focused and
unflappable in such moments.

Sherri told Nels about another incident that occurred while she was a
nurse at UCLA, which might have ended tragically had she not been there
that day. Sherri had a patient in her unit, a woman with advanced heart
disease, who was in critical condition. Sherri had been treating her for some
time, long enough to become familiar with her husband. One day, when
Sherri was on duty, the woman suddenly went into cardiac arrest. A team
of cardiologists rushed to her side, along with Sherri and other nurses. They

were able to resuscitate her, but only briefly, before her heart gave out. There was nothing more anyone could do.

Sherri was in the patient's room afterward cleaning up when another nurse rushed in, panicked. The nurse told Sherri that the woman's husband was in the waiting room with a gun, demanding to see the doctors who had failed to save his wife. The doctors within earshot had fled, which had left the nurse to seek help from Sherri. Sherri went out to the waiting room and calmly approached the husband. Sherri put her arm around him and told him nothing would be accomplished by doing anything with the gun. Sherri asked him to give it to her, and he complied.

In other situations, when she felt the circumstances warranted it, Sherri did not shrink from confrontation. She strongly believed that nurses played just as important a role as physicians in caring for patients. It bothered her when doctors treated nurses as less than their equals.

One afternoon, Sherri was on her way to the hospital's pharmacy when two doctors came down the hallway from the opposite direction. Both doctors, a cardiac surgeon and the chief resident, had self-important personalities. The two men were deep in conversation and oblivious to everyone in their path. Sherri later recounted to Jayne what happened. As the doctors approached, Sherri thought, "Well, I can either walk between them, which is rude, or I can get up against the wall until they go by." Then she thought, "I have as much right to walk down this hall as they do. How dare they take up the entire hall? I'm not going to flatten myself against the wall for them." Sherri kept walking and refused to yield. When she bumped into the chief resident, he shot her a look. Sherri held her ground. "You're taking up the entire hall," she said. "You're not God." Sherri then continued on to the pharmacy.

Sherri expected everyone she worked with to meet the same standards of patient care to which she held herself. One day when Sherri was working with Jayne, Nels and Loretta called to tell Sherri her grandmother had been taken to the hospital in Tucson. Sherri immediately left work, went to LAX, and caught the first flight home. From the airport in Tucson, she went straight to the hospital where her grandmother was admitted. Sherri still had her UCLA nursing uniform on. She walked right up to the resident on duty and said, "I need a report on my grandmother's condition. What's going on? What are you doing?" The resident didn't have the answers she demanded. Sherri asked to speak with the attending physician. The resident looked at her name tag, which read HEAD NURSE,

CORONARY CARE UNIT. That her uniform was from a hospital five hundred miles away was beside the point. Sherri could be very assertive when necessary. She wasn't going to accept a vague report on her grandmother's condition.

Sherri's friend Jayne had a physical education requirement for her bachelor's degree at Cal State L.A. One of the options was a self-defense class. Jayne and Sherri were both safety conscious. After a series of rapes on the UCLA campus, the hospital issued rape whistles to all the nurses, to keep on their key chains. For nurses whose shifts ended late at night, UCLA provided shuttles and escorts to the parking lot. The warnings were drummed into them: "Don't walk out there alone. Take the shuttle. Call an escort." Jayne went to her self-defense class weekly. After each class, Sherri asked Jayne, "What did you learn this week?"

Jayne related to Sherri the lessons the instructor had imparted: "If you think someone's following you, turn around and look at them. Let them know you're aware of them. Walk in another direction. If somebody attacks you, drop everything that you're carrying."

One time, Sherri asked Jayne, "What do you do if that person has a gun?"

Jayne said she didn't know and would ask the instructor.

Next class, the instructor advised Jayne, "Well, you either need to talk your way out of it, or you need to run away. Sometimes it's better to try to talk your way out of it. You need to be very careful, because you're at a disadvantage."

Around the same time, Sherri had a frightening experience at home. Her friend Donna was visiting Los Angeles and staying with her. Sherri and Donna came home late one night from Knott's Berry Farm, where they had met Connie and her husband for dinner. Sherri wanted to show Donna the swimming pool at the condo complex, so Donna could swim while Sherri was at work the next day. When they entered the house, Sherri took Donna straight upstairs to show her the guest bedroom where she would be sleeping. Sherri left Donna in the guest room and went to her own bedroom, just steps away. Donna kept chatting, but noticed Sherri was silent.

"Sherri?" Donna called out.

"Oh my gosh," Sherri said. "Someone's been in the house."

Donna rushed to Sherri's bedroom and saw that her dresser drawers had been yanked out. Sherri said her first thought was that Bozo had got into them, before it occurred to her: How can a cat open a drawer? Sherri didn't own any expensive jewelry, but a few costume pieces were tossed about, along with some of her lingerie.

There was no phone upstairs to call the police, and they didn't know whether the intruder was still inside. Sherri and Donna armed themselves with the only weapons at hand, two cowboy boots in Sherri's closet. Each clutching a single boot, they crept downstairs. Garbage was strewn across the kitchen floor. The intruder had for some reason dumped the contents of the kitchen trash can. As Sherri came out of the kitchen, she could see into the living room and the front entryway, one floor below. Her unit had a small outdoor patio off the living room, with a sliding glass door. The glass door was wide open. Sherri and Donna hadn't noticed that when they came in.

Sherri called the police, and then her parents, who naturally were very concerned. Sherri and Donna were afraid to go out on the patio while they waited for the police. Nothing like this had ever happened to them before.

Sherri and Donna waited for more than an hour for the LAPD to show up. When the officer arrived, he went through the condo and asked Sherri what had been stolen. The lock on the patio door was flimsy and appeared to have been jimmied or shaken until it disengaged. The officer told them it was probably a teenager from the neighborhood. The cop's theory on the garbage in the kitchen was that the guy probably wanted the trash bag to use as a sack. The officer seemed untroubled by their close call. The patio door wasn't broken. Nothing of value was missing. Sherri and Donna got the sense that the case was a low priority as far as the LAPD was concerned.

Sherri and Donna were too spooked to sleep alone that night, so they shared Sherri's bed and slept with the lights on. The next morning, Nels explained on the phone what type of replacement lock to buy at the hardware store. "You go down and you get that sliding door fixed," Nels told Sherri. Sherri and Donna bought a drill and installed the new lock in the frame of the patio door.

Nels was a gun owner and had been for most of his life. On at least one occasion, he offered to buy Sherri a gun for her to keep at home for her protection. Sherri told her father she didn't need or want one in the house. She did not think she was capable of pointing a gun at another person and pulling the trigger.

Sherri did not earn a big salary as a staff nurse at UCLA Medical Center. Nels and Loretta helped her with money from time to time, but she valued her financial independence. Early in 1982, her friend Jayne asked if she would consider sharing her condo with a roommate. Jayne needed a place to live. Sherri had a spare bedroom, and a roommate would offset some of her living expenses. Sherri agreed.

Sherri and Jayne were very compatible roommates. Neither had a serious boyfriend at the time, so they spent a lot of time together. Jayne often worked the overnight shift so she could go to school during the day. Sherri, as a head nurse, worked fairly regular hours. UCLA was an easy commute from Van Nuys, right down the 405 freeway. Whenever they worked the same shift, they would race each other home. Whoever lost had to make dinner. Sherri and Jayne developed the sort of routines and bargains that roommates do, to make both their lives easier. Because Jayne was around during the day, she handled Sherri's laundry, dry cleaning, and banking. Sherri in turn typed Jayne's term papers for her. Living with Sherri, Jayne became as familiar as anyone with her daily habits, as well as the layout of the condo.

Sherri and Jayne's unofficial third roommate was Bozo, who had matured into a lively cat with a black-and-white coat and bright blue eyes. Bozo always bounded downstairs to greet them when they got home. At night, when they watched TV, he would sit on the living room sofa with them. They both became quite attached to Bozo.

Jayne noticed one day that Bozo seemed listless. Sherri took him to the vet, who delivered bad news. Bozo needed surgery that cost $400, money Sherri didn't have. The vet sent Bozo home with Sherri to sleep on what she wanted to do. Sherri told Jayne she wasn't sure she could justify spending $400 on a cat, even Bozo.

"I think I might have to put him down," Sherri told Jayne, crying.

"Oh, no, no, no," Jayne said. "I'm not living with you if you put Bozo down, because you'll be miserable. If he needs surgery, we'll split the cost." Bozo had the surgery and made a full recovery.

As Sherri's roommate for more than two years, Jayne saw firsthand how close Sherri was with her parents, especially Nels. Sherri and Nels spoke on the phone almost every evening. It was not uncommon for their father-daughter chats to go on for hours.

If Sherri needed to go to the bathroom or get a drink, she would hand the phone to Jayne and say, "Here, you talk to him." Jayne could talk to Nels easily for an hour herself. Jayne and Nels often sparred good-naturedly about politics. Jayne was Canadian and liberal, qualities that Nels teased her were redundant. Nels was a self-made man, deeply religious, and a proud political conservative. Sherri refused to talk politics with her father, but Jayne was always up for it. Nels liked to debate politics, especially with liberals. In Nels's experience, most liberals didn't have the spine to debate him for very long. Jayne was an exception. Jayne's intelligence and feistiness endeared her to Nels instantly. He could tell Jayne that she was a pinko or a socialist, and Jayne would give it right back.

Jayne had grown up with six older brothers, so she admired Sherri's close bond with her sisters. Jayne's family was tight-knit, like the Rasmussens, but lived far away. In time, Jayne came to think of the Rasmussens as her West Coast family. She felt Nels and Loretta treated her like a fourth daughter.

Sherri's career continued to flourish. She was appointed assistant clinical professor at UCLA's School of Nursing and lectured to undergraduates and graduate students. Although it was an unpaid position, Sherri saw it as a stepping-stone to advance her career. Sherri spoke at several professional conferences, including a national convention of critical care nurses in New Orleans. The topics Sherri lectured on ranged from artificial pacemakers to how to best evaluate the implementation of higher nursing standards.

In January 1983, Sherri was nominated by UCLA Medical Center as its Outstanding Management Nurse of the Year. The next month, Sherri's nursing director, Rebecca Hathaway, awarded her bonus pay and wrote her a glowing letter of commendation. That November, UCLA promoted Sherri to nursing supervisor. Sherri's new position was evening supervisor of the Critical Care Division, which had eighty beds. Sherri was responsible for all nursing issues from 3:00 to 11:30 p.m.

Sherri was just twenty-six years old, exceptionally young for her résumé. She had worked at UCLA Medical Center for more than six years. Despite her latest promotion, by late 1983, Sherri was contemplating moving on. UCLA's hospital was a huge institution with lots of competition to get promoted. Sherri thought she might have better luck advancing within the smaller Adventist health care system. There was an Adventist hospital in the San Fernando Valley, Glendale Adventist Medical Center. Sherri applied for a nursing director position there.

Sherri's application crossed the desk of Althea Kennedy, Glendale Adventist's vice president of clinical services. In early 1984, Althea was several months into a search for a director of critical care nursing. The Critical Care Division at Glendale Adventist included the Emergency

Department, Surgical Intensive Care Unit, Medical Intensive Care Unit, Coronary Care Unit, and Definitive Observation Unit, for patients who required long-term care. Collectively, the units had more than fifty beds and were the most high-pressure and technology-intensive in the hospital. Althea had interviewed half a dozen candidates and found all of them lacking.

Althea liked Sherri's credentials on paper and invited her in for an interview. The day of the interview, Sherri was waiting outside Althea's office when an acquaintance from college, Peggy Daly, walked by. Peggy was head nurse of Glendale Adventist's emergency room. Peggy had graduated from Loma Linda the year after Sherri. Peggy did not know Sherri personally but they had mutual friends. Peggy had no idea that Sherri was applying for a job at the hospital.

Peggy told Sherri, "Oh my gosh, I know you." They chatted until Althea's secretary, Vera,* called Sherri in for the interview. Peggy wished Sherri luck. Peggy did not realize until later that Sherri was interviewing to become her boss.

Althea and Sherri hit it off immediately. For Althea, meeting Sherri felt like a breath of fresh air. Althea thought, "My goodness gracious, not only does she have all these skills, she's so personable." At the end of the interview, Althea invited Sherri back to meet with the head nurses and key physicians. Althea considered it a no-brainer to offer Sherri the position. Althea felt extremely fortunate to entice Sherri away from UCLA, a much bigger hospital. In early 1984, Sherri was hired as director of critical care nursing at Glendale Adventist.

Sherri started her new job on February 27, 1984, a few weeks after she turned twenty-seven. Sherri was likely one of the youngest nursing directors in the country. Although her responsibilities no longer included direct patient care, she continued to wear a lab coat over the business clothes she wore to work each day.

Sherri's office was on the ground floor of the hospital, on the same hallway as Althea and the rest of Glendale Adventist's senior leadership. Sherri was also assigned a secretary, Sylvia Nielsen, an older, red-haired woman with a shy personality. Sylvia's demeanor toward Sherri was reserved but motherly. Sylvia reported informally to Althea's secretary, Vera, the lead secretary for the nursing division.

---

* A pseudonym, at her request.

Sherri was one of several directors who reported to Althea. Every week, Althea held a team meeting with all the directors, and also met with each one individually. Althea expected Sherri and the other directors to deal pro-actively with issues in their units. Directors who ignored problems, and failed to deal with the root causes, risked losing the respect of their staff. If a director had a problem, Althea wanted them to come to her and say, "Okay, this is the problem, and this is what I think we can do to fix it." In Althea's experience, not all directors had the necessary initiative, problem-solving ability, and management skills to do the job well.

Unlike the hospitals where Sherri previously worked, Glendale Adven-tist was not a teaching hospital. Most physicians at Loma Linda and UCLA were also medical school faculty, and thus accountable to the university. Doctors at Glendale Adventist were independent contractors, free to leave or threaten to leave for a competitor hospital if they were dissatisfied with the medical technology, staff, or other accommodations. As director of crit-ical care nursing, Sherri had to work with some of Glendale Adventist's most intense and demanding doctors.

Sherri surpassed all of Althea's lofty expectations. She carried herself professionally. She was a natural leader. She was strong clinically. She could mentor. She was respectful and kind in her interactions with everyone, no matter their station. Sherri did not erect barriers between herself and the nursing staff. She communicated well with the physicians, and with her colleagues in the hospital's administration. Even when a sit-uation at hand might be unpleasant, Sherri always had a smile. Althea believed Sherri was a rising star in the nursing profession.

Among the half dozen head nurses who reported to Sherri was Peggy, her college acquaintance. All the other head nurses were years older than Sherri and Peggy. Because of their similar ages and backgrounds, Sherri and Peggy became fast friends. Both women had grown up in families active in the Adventist church, and attended Adventist schools. Their upbringings had instilled in them a shared belief in the value of education and a commitment to service as a moral imperative. Peggy credited that foundation for the success she and Sherri enjoyed early in their careers.

Sherri's employee benefits at her new job included a life insurance pol-icy, the premiums for which were paid by Glendale Adventist. Sherri ini-tially planned to list both her parents as the policy's beneficiaries. But when Sherri mentioned it to Nels, he told her, "No way."

Sherri got upset with her father. "Dad, I want you to be on it."

"No," said Nels. "I'm not going to take a benefit from the death of my child, number one. Number two, you have sisters, and you have your mother, but you just keep my name off it." Nels was emphatic. When Sherri submitted the life insurance form to Althea's secretary, Vera, only Loretta was listed as her beneficiary.

Around the time Sherri started her new job, her friend Donna visited for a weekend, and stayed with her and Jayne in Van Nuys. Donna lived in Utah with her husband of a few years. One night, Sherri mentioned that her parents had sent her tins of salmon, fish that Nels caught off their boat and Loretta canned. Sherri and Jayne weren't adventurous cooks and didn't know what to do with the salmon, so they kept it in the freezer. Donna thawed the tins and proceeded to whip up a gourmet meal. After dinner, Donna cleaned up in the kitchen. When Donna finished, Sherri and Jayne marveled that they had never seen their kitchen sink so gleaming.

"No wonder we're not married," Jayne said. "Look at what a clean sink that is. We never clean the sink like that. That's why she's married and we're single." All three of them laughed.

Jayne and Sherri did not know that within a few months, both would meet their future husbands.

3.

John Ruetten

(February 1984 to May 1985)

In May 1984, Sherri's friend Anita, the matchmaker, invited her to a party. Anita was recently engaged to Matt Gorder, a UCLA graduate from San Diego. Anita also invited one of Matt's closest friends, John Ruetten, to the same party. Anita promised John, "There'll be girls there."

John and Matt were best friends as adolescents, growing up in San Diego. After they graduated from high school in 1977, they enrolled at UCLA, where they were dormmates for two years. John, tall and handsome, was looking to meet someone new. Anita thought John might be a good match for Sherri.

John fell for Sherri at first sight. Sherri was standing outside on the patio, talking with other people. She was dressed that night in blue jeans, a white blouse, and dangling earrings. In her high heels, Sherri was six feet one, almost as tall as John.

John was startled by Sherri's beauty and presence. Although he was athletic and good-looking, John had never been much of a ladies' man. Somehow he summoned the nerve to approach Sherri and say hello. To his great relief, John managed to get through their first conversation without saying anything idiotic. After the party, he told Matt and Anita, "You've got to get me her number." Matt had never seen his friend so excited about a girl. John called Sherri and asked her out.

For their first date, Sherri invited John over for dinner. She planned to make beef Stroganoff. The evening of the date, Sherri came running in from work with a bag of groceries, which she thrust into Jayne's hands.

"I'm making beef Stroganoff," Sherri said. "Here's the recipe. I'm going to go shower and put on fresh makeup. Make this food and then get lost. John's coming over for dinner."

When John drove up to the condo, Sherri was waiting outside on the balcony off the kitchen. She could see a car approach from there. The sight of Sherri waving from the balcony put John at ease and made him feel welcome. Later that night, over the beef Stroganoff Jayne had surreptitiously prepared for them, John and Sherri fell in love. John's heart raced every time he looked at Sherri.

John's feelings for Sherri deepened the more time he spent with her. As lovely as he found Sherri's appearance, he came to believe her most remarkable qualities were on the inside. Sherri was joyful and a kid at heart. She loved exercising and being outdoors, whether swimming, skiing, biking, or playing tennis. Sherri was a bona fide star professionally, a hospital's director of nursing at age twenty-seven. She had held people's lives in her hands, literally, and proved her mettle and grace under pressure. Since John had graduated from UCLA in 1981, he had held down the same job, as a computer engineer at a company called Data Products. It made him feel good about himself to be with someone as beautiful and accomplished as Sherri.

John liked being able to call Sherri his girlfriend, which happened soon after they met. He wasn't accustomed to saying that he was part of a couple. But he couldn't help but brag about Sherri. John felt it was impossible to ignore her when she walked into a room. Being with Sherri fueled his ego. Sherri was advanced in a way that matched John's perception of himself. It was one of the reasons John felt so attracted to her.

Early that same summer, Sherri's roommate, Jayne, was feeling less than satisfied with her own love life. Jayne worked nights at UCLA, which made it hard to plan dates with men who had regular jobs. Jayne had noticed a pharmacist around the hospital who she thought was handsome. She usually saw him in the hallway on his way to or from the pharmacy, at the start of his shift, so she began to time her breaks to bump into him. Jayne would rush to the ladies' room to freshen her makeup so that when he walked by, she didn't look as if she'd been up all night. Colleagues used to tell Jayne, "Boy, how do you do it? You look great in the morning!" She wanted to say, "Well, I put new makeup on, because this pharmacist might walk by." Jayne knew his schedule by heart before she knew his name.

One night after work, Jayne went out for drinks with some friends from the hospital. The pharmacist Jayne liked happened to walk into the same bar. "Oh, look," one of Jayne's friends said. "There's Mike Goldberg. We should invite him over."

"Great, I'll finally get to meet this guy," Jayne thought. Mike came over and sat with them for a while, but Jayne sensed he was completely uninterested in her. "Well, this is a bust," she thought. Jayne did not realize that Mike had a terrible hangover. The night before, Mike had gone out drinking with two friends to drown their sorrows. All three had been dumped by their girlfriends that same week.

Soon after, Jayne's friends from that night invited her to a Roaring Twenties costume party they planned to throw. Jayne told Sherri she might go. In late June, a few days before the party, Jayne drove up to Santa Barbara to have lunch with a different guy she liked. The guy lived with another woman, but had assured Jayne that relationship was over. During lunch, he asked Jayne for her opinion on his living situation. He told Jayne, "I don't want to live with her. She moved in."

Jayne said, "Well, I wouldn't give you my opinion, except you asked."

The guy insisted he wanted Jayne to be honest.

Jayne told him, "I'm through with men like you. You tell me I'm wonderful, but you're living with someone else? I'm done." Jayne cried the whole drive back from Santa Barbara. When Jayne got home, she told Sherri, "I'm done with men. That's it. Over. Done."

The Roaring Twenties party was that Saturday night, June 30, 1984. Jayne had worked the overnight shift at UCLA on Friday and gone to bed when she came home. Late Saturday afternoon, Sherri went into Jayne's room and woke her.

Sherri asked Jayne, "Hey, aren't you going to that party?"

"No, I told you, I'm done with men," Jayne said.

"Well, isn't that pharmacist going to be there?"

Jayne was exhausted and didn't feel like going out to a party. Furthermore, she told Sherri, she didn't have a costume. Sherri said she had a costume Jayne could wear and insisted she get out of bed. Sherri dressed Jayne in a fringed dress and a flapper's headband. Out the door Jayne went.

Jayne arrived late to the party. She immediately saw Mike across the room. He wasn't wearing a costume. Jayne also spotted her UCLA clinical adviser, who stood near the kitchen. Unbeknownst to Jayne, Mike saw her and followed her to say hello.

"How's your love life going?" Jayne's adviser asked her.

"I'm done with men," Jayne said. "I'm not giving my number to any more men. They say they'll call but they never do."

Mike walked up just in time to hear the exchange, although he didn't acknowledge Jayne's comment at first. They talked for the rest of the party and were the last to leave. At the door, Mike handed Jayne his phone number and said, "I heard you're not giving out your number to men these days."

Jayne was reluctant to call Mike. Sherri again intervened. Jayne's birthday was the following weekend, and she had no plans. Sherri suggested they host a barbecue for her birthday. Sherri made Jayne call Mike and invite him. When they spoke on the phone, Jayne gave Mike the address, but she did not mention that the barbecue was to celebrate her birthday.

The night of the party, Mike parked on the street outside the condo complex. Mike was buzzed through the pedestrian gate and was trying to figure out which direction to walk when he noticed several people carrying gift-wrapped presents. Mike thought, "These people must be going to a birthday party." Not until Mike reached the door of Jayne and Sherri's unit did he realize that he, too, was going to a birthday party. The condo was full of people. Jayne greeted him at the door.

"You didn't tell me it was your birthday," Mike said. "I didn't bring anything." In truth, Mike had brought three bottles of wine.

Jayne took the bottles and said, "Wine is great. Don't worry about it." She led Mike into the party, where she introduced him to her roommate, Sherri, and Sherri's boyfriend, John.

When the party finally wound down and everyone else went home, it was just the four of them: Sherri and John and Jayne and Mike. Mike thought Jayne and Sherri were a lot of fun, best friends but almost like sisters. Sherri and John had been dating for only about a month. The two couples stayed up late that night, talking and getting to know one another better. Before Mike left, he told Jayne he would call her Tuesday at eight o'clock. That Tuesday at eight, the phone rang in the condo. After that, Jayne and Mike started dating.

Once Sherri and John had dated for a few months, she told her parents she wanted them to meet him. Nels and Loretta sailed up from San Diego and docked at a slip in Marina del Rey. Sherri brought John to the boat and the Rasmussens welcomed him aboard.

The boat the Rasmussens then owned was a 49-foot sailboat with a teak hull and three staterooms. Sherri, John, and her parents chatted on deck and looked out on the water for a little while, then went ashore to a restaurant

Sherri and John at Jayne's birthday party, July 1984

for dinner. Nels could tell that Sherri was head over heels for John. He wanted only the best for his daughter, as any father would. Nels knew Sherri was smart and strong. He thought John seemed like a nice guy. But Nels was also mindful that she had not had many serious romances before John.

Around the same time, Sherri met John's mother, Margaret, and his father, Richard, who was a history professor at San Diego State. John had three siblings: his brother, Tom, and two sisters, Gail and Janet.

Nels and Loretta's first contact with John's parents came when they all went to a basketball game in San Diego. Richard and Nels's relationship was tense and distrustful from the start. Richard was a liberal Democrat, while Nels was a conservative Republican. Nels considered Richard to be an extreme leftist who constantly brought up politics and went out of his way to point out how the left was more thoughtful than the right. Richard may well have felt similarly about Nels. Politics seemed to infect every moment and interaction between them. Nels had never been someone to shrink from a political debate. On some level, Nels enjoyed arguing with John's dad. Nels sensed that Richard saw him as a considerable foe. For whatever reason, they couldn't leave politics alone. Sherri and John and their parents would meet for dinner, and everyone wanted it to be a good time. But from Nels's perspective, once Richard had a few cocktails, he would be raring to go, and Nels would always oblige. Their arguments over politics were so bitter they would end up ruining dinner. It must have been mortifying and torturous for John and Sherri.

The young couple did their best to tune out the discord between their fathers. The Los Angeles Summer Olympic Games were set to begin at the end of July, and enthusiasm was building across the city. Sherri and Jayne auditioned to be banner carriers during the opening ceremonies. The try-outs were fun, but they weren't selected. They heard later that David Wolper, the opening ceremonies' producer, had cast only women with long hair.

Sherri and Jayne watched the opening ceremonies together on the television in their living room. Later during the Olympics, they got tickets to see diving and two days of track and field in person. Mike bought tickets to see rowing, because he had rowed in college. Mike took Jayne to that event. Jayne and Sherri were inside the Los Angeles Coliseum the day of the first ever Olympic women's marathon and witnessed Joan Benoit's triumphant gold medal finish. The other track and field day, Jayne and Sherri had four tickets and invited Mike and John to come with them.

It was a perfect day for the two couples, right up until the end.

Everyone dressed patriotically for the outing. Sherri wore white shorts and a red-and-blue-striped shirt, and John a polo shirt with narrower bands of red, white, and blue. Jayne dressed in white and carried a small Canadian flag. Sherri had her own small American flag. John, Sherri, and Jayne also had sweaters, red, white, and blue, respectively, which they tied around their shoulders by the sleeves.

Early in the morning, they parked at Valley College in Van Nuys and took a bus to the Coliseum. Sherri and Jayne had taken the same bus trip earlier in the Olympics, so they knew the lay of the land.

Both new couples were still in the flush of just having met and fallen in love. When they arrived, the four of them strolled around the Coliseum and Exposition Park, which had been transformed for the Olympics. It was still morning, and the summer sun was not yet at full intensity. They stopped in front of a wall-sized mural of a hurdler in midstride, so Mike could take a snapshot.

Later, inside the monumental stadium, they watched the men's 100-meter dash. Carl Lewis won the gold, the first of his four gold medals that year. Jayne's countryman Ben Johnson, four years prior to his disgrace at the following Olympics, took the 100-meter bronze. The weather was brilliantly sunny that day, and it got progressively hotter as the day went on.

Jayne, Sherri, and John at the Summer Olympics, August 1984

The summer sun beat down on them mercilessly in the Coliseum. They had brought hats for the sun, but even Sherri and Jayne's wider-brimmed ones provided little shade, and no respite from the heat.

After the last events, the four of them left the Coliseum and explored Exposition Park some more. They found a grassy, shaded area to relax and people-watch. The hours in the hot sun had taken their toll. John and Sherri stretched out side by side, closed their eyes, and took a nap.

Eventually, the crowds began to thin out, and they decided to head home to the Valley. It had been a fun, even glorious, day together, but long and tiring. On top of the early morning start, and the effects of the sun and heat, they had eaten nothing but junk food all day.

Sherri and Jayne led the way to the buses. Sherri was much taller than Jayne, and could see over the crowd. She pointed to a bus and they went to board it. Just as Sherri put her foot on the step of the bus, John said, "Oh, no, Sherri. There's another bus over here. Let's go over here."

Sherri, Jayne, and Mike followed John to the bus he saw, but when they got there, they discovered it wasn't going to the Valley. In the meantime, the first bus left. The next bus to Valley College, where they had parked, wasn't for an hour. Jayne knew the bus ride would take another hour at least. Jayne was furious with John. "You jerk," Jayne wanted to say to him. "Would it bother you to let a woman lead the way? We had a bus, but no, you've got to . . ." During the hour they waited, Mike tried to make light of the situation, but Jayne was in no mood to be mollified.

Jayne was so annoyed at John that she didn't speak to anyone the whole bus ride home. When they finally got back to the condo, Jayne marched up to her bedroom and slammed the door. Mike turned to Sherri and said, "Is she like this often?"

"No. Actually, this is the worst I've ever seen her," Sherri said.

"Well, if this is the worst, it's not that bad," Mike joked. Mike went upstairs to Jayne's room and sat on the end of her bed.

"I'm so angry," Jayne said. It wasn't that Jayne disliked John. But she felt her relationship with him change when he stopped Sherri from boarding the right bus. Jayne's anger at John dissipated within a few days, but for a while after, whenever she saw him, Jayne sensed that he looked at her as if to say, "Stand back. You never know when she's going to implode." Jayne's takeaway was, "Is this guy for real?"

Donna, Sherri's best friend from high school and college, first met John during the Olympics as well. Sherri had called Donna earlier in the summer and told her that she had met someone. Sherri invited Donna to come visit and stay at the condo so she could meet John. When Donna did, John told her the story of how he met Sherri. John said he was at a party and saw Sherri from a distance. John said he thought, "Whoa, I need to meet her. She seems so self-assured, and what a beautiful smile." Donna was so happy that somebody was in love with Sherri.

Later in the summer, Donna came back for another visit. John and a friend of his wanted to go surfing, so the four of them drove to the ocean. Sherri and Donna sat on the beach and talked while John and his friend surfed. Sherri talked about John and told Donna, "I think this is the one." Donna could tell Sherri was serious, so much so that it scared Donna a little. She thought to herself, "Man, he better love her. If he breaks her heart, I'll scratch his eyes out."

Around the same time, Nels was also trying to make up his mind about John. The more time Nels spent with John, and the better he got to know him, the more wishy-washy John seemed to him. Nels sensed that John couldn't make a decision, which was the opposite of how Sherri was. Nels and Loretta discussed their daughter's relationship. Sherri was obviously in love with John, and he seemed equally in love with her. Nels and Loretta decided there was nothing they could do but trust Sherri's judgment. John was her choice. Sherri was a grown woman.

In September, John and Sherri attended the wedding of their friends Matt Gorder and Anita Kramer, who had introduced them a few months earlier. John served as one of Matt's groomsmen. Jayne and Mike also attended the wedding. So did John's parents, Richard and Margaret, since Margaret and Matt's mother Bonnie were best friends. The Ruettens and Gorders had watched their sons grow up together. Now John and Matt were men, seemingly on the cusp of starting their own families.

Sherri wore a turquoise dress to the wedding. Jayne loved the dress on Sherri. During the reception, John's father, Richard, asked Sherri to dance. John thought it would be awkward for Sherri, and for him, for her to dance with his dad. But Sherri had poise. Sherri accepted the invitation and went to the dance floor with Richard. John could see them talking as they danced, but the music was loud. When Richard came back to the table, he told his son, "Well, that one has got it together."

The following month, October 1984, Nels and Loretta invited Sherri, Jayne, and their boyfriends to go sailing in San Diego. The three couples spent a weekend sailing to Catalina Island and back.

Sherri and John at Matt and Anita Gorder's wedding, September 1984

The Rasmussens' sailboat had a small Boston Whaler dinghy suspended off its aft. The dinghy's outboard motor was acting up, and Nels wanted to fix it. Nels got his tools out, and he asked John and Mike to get in the dinghy with him in case he needed their help. Sherri and Jayne watched from the deck as Nels tinkered with the motor while John and Mike looked on. Nels yanked repeatedly on the motor's pull cord, but it refused to start.

Nels was a physically imposing man, six feet tall and brawny. Although Nels was no longer as spry as when he was a teenager, logging in the woods, he had retained much of his strength. Jayne sensed that John was a little intimidated by Nels.

Nels yanked the motor's pull cord again. Still nothing. Just as Nels went to try once more, a motorboat sped close by. The motorboat's wake rocked the Rasmussens' sailboat and the small dinghy. As the dinghy rose and fell with the waves, the motor Nels was working on toppled into the water.

Jayne and Mike thought it was hilarious and burst out laughing. Sherri covered her mouth with her hand and ran belowdecks to spare her dad the indignity of seeing her, too, laugh at his misfortune. Nels hauled the motor back into the dinghy, but it was completely waterlogged. Jayne thought John looked as if he wanted to jump overboard. Mike looked at John, standing awkwardly beside Nels, and thought, "That's your father-in-law, not mine."

It was apparent by then, at least to Mike and Jayne, that John and Sherri were on the wedding track. Mike and Jayne's relationship was serious too. It was natural to envision a future in which both couples got married and remained friends forever. Mike thought, "This is the way it's going to be. This is her best friend. These are fun people. We're going to have a lifetime of enjoying each other's company, doing things as two couples." During the weekend sailing trip, they discussed taking an even more ambitious voyage. The boys—Nels, John, and Mike—would sail to Hawaii, while the girls— Loretta, Sherri, and Jayne—would fly to Hawaii to meet them there.

One night after they returned home, Jayne and Sherri talked about the strangeness of their having met their boyfriends so close in time. Jayne told Sherri, "One minute we're going along single, thinking we'd be single forever, and we meet these two guys. What happened?"

"Oh, Jayne. The Lord decided it was our time," Sherri replied.

Sherri wasn't the type to proselytize, but she was quietly virtuous. Jayne could swear like a sailor, and sometimes couldn't help it. If Sherri had something bad to say about someone, she would say things like, "That guy is such a horse's patoot."

John and Sherri aboard the Rasmussen family's sailboat, October 1984

Christmas 1984 was John and Sherri's first as a couple. As a little girl, Christmas was Sherri's favorite holiday. She and her sisters watched the Bing Crosby film *White Christmas* together every year, among other Rasmussen holiday traditions. Christmas 1984 was also Sherri and Jayne's third as roommates. They had always gotten a tree and decorated for the holidays. Sometimes they invited friends over to help. That year, Sherri bought a nice tree and brought it home. Sherri and Jayne decided to have a tree trimming party. John and a few other friends came over. Sherri was stringing lights on the tree and stepped back to get a better view. "I think it needs more lights," she announced.

Had Jayne and Sherri been home alone, they would have grabbed their purses, run to the store, and picked up more lights for the tree.

John replied, "I think it's fine. Do we need more lights? We don't have to go get more lights, do we?"

Jayne thought, "The woman loves Christmas, John. Go get more lights."

John didn't offer. His reaction bugged Jayne. Sherri was so much fun, so easy to be with, and she made so few requests. Sherri was a doer. She didn't rely on other people a lot. It bothered Jayne to see John squander a chance to do something for Sherri. On the heels of the Olympics bus fiasco, the Christmas lights exchange crystallized Jayne's impression of John as a little self-centered and immature. That Sherri was herself so giving and mature only heightened the disparity in Jayne's eyes.

Sherri and Jayne sometimes spent nights at their boyfriends' places. One time that Jayne planned to stay at Mike's, she changed her mind and returned home instead. Jayne came in through the garage and went upstairs. Their bedrooms were on the top floor of the condo, two flights of stairs up from the first floor, where Jayne had entered. As she turned to go up the second staircase, she was startled by Sherri, who stood with her back to the wall, holding a bedpost like a baseball bat. Sherri didn't swing but looked as if she was about to.

"Oh my God, what are you doing?" Jayne said.

"I didn't know it was you. I heard a noise and I thought you were staying at Mike's. I thought there was somebody here." Sherri said it was her biggest fear, to come downstairs and discover a stranger in the house. Even so, Sherri occasionally let her own vigilance slip. If Sherri was just coming home briefly to get a few things before she went to John's, she sometimes parked in a visitor's spot and came in and out through the front door instead of the garage entrance. One night, Sherri came home after work and told Jayne she was going to stay at John's. Jayne said okay and went back to the book she was reading. Later, Jayne thought, "I wonder if she locked that front door." Jayne went downstairs to check. Sherri had neglected to lock it. Jayne thought, "Thanks a lot, Sherri. Here I am home alone with the front door unlocked."

Sherri's sisters, Connie and Teresa, both owned guns. Sherri always said she wasn't interested, but during one trip home to Tucson, in November 1983, Sherri told her parents she had changed her mind. Nels and Loretta took Sherri to a gun shop. Sherri purchased two handguns that day, a .22 revolver and a .45 semiautomatic. Before her flight back to Los Angeles, Sherri asked Nels to hold both guns for her in his gun safe in Tucson. She still did not think she could fire a gun at a person.

Another reason Sherri may have felt she didn't need a gun at home was because her condo and the Balboa Townhomes complex seemed relatively safe. If Sherri had wanted a burglar alarm system installed, Nels would have paid for it, but she never asked. When her parents visited, if they arrived at the condo before Sherri or Jayne got home from work, they had to wait outside on the street. The management company would not give the Rasmussens a key, even though Nels's name was on the condo's deed, since they were not residents. Nels and Loretta didn't mind. To the contrary, they found the policy reassuring.

John and Sherri's romance continued to deepen into the spring of 1985, as they neared one year as a couple. Sherri's friend Donna visited and stayed with Sherri and Jayne. John was over the evening Donna arrived. Later that night, Donna was unpacking when she saw John getting ready for bed. Donna knew Sherri's upbringing, and still thought of her as innocent. That Sherri had a boyfriend who spent the night told Donna that Sherri was serious about John. The next evening, John came over for dinner. While Sherri was away from the table, Donna put John on the spot and quizzed him about his intentions with Sherri. John seemed taken aback, and Donna wondered if her pointed questions came across as harsh. John assured Donna, "No, I'm serious. I'm very, very serious about Sherri."

In May, John and Sherri called their parents and made plans to go sailing together on the Rasmussens' boat over Memorial Day weekend.

John and Sherri announced their engagement to their parents at midday on Saturday, May 25, while sailing on San Diego Bay. The engagement was hardly a surprise to the Rasmussens and Ruettens. Since John and Sherri first met, just a year earlier, it had been clear to their families that they were madly in love. The weather that day was overcast, with temperatures in the low sixties. But there appeared to be no dampening the celebratory mood aboard the Rasmussens' sailboat following John and Sherri's announcement. Nels expected they would sail into the early evening, then go onshore for dinner.

The water was crowded with dozens of pleasure craft, befitting a Saturday afternoon on a holiday weekend and the traditional start of summer. As Nels navigated the channel between San Diego Bay and the Pacific Ocean, they sailed past the North Island Naval Air Station, a U.S. naval air base. Military planes on training flights circled over the Rasmussens' sailboat.

Suddenly, from the sky above, they heard a loud pop. They looked up and saw a fighter jet coming in for a landing. Flames spewed from the back of the jet. The pilot steered for the airstrip, but the plane could not make it. The pilot banked sharply and aimed for empty water. A flight officer ejected from the cockpit and deployed a parachute. Moments before impact, the pilot also ejected, but at too low an altitude for his parachute to open. The plane hit the water about 75 feet from the Rasmussens' sailboat. An eyewitness later told the *Los Angeles Times*, "There were a lot of boats in the

area. I can't believe it didn't hit one of them." A second eyewitness told the
Times, "I saw one parachute. It was barely high enough for it to open, but
it did. The plane barely missed two sailboats."

In the moments after the crash, Sherri wanted to dive into the water
and assist in the rescue. Nels had to stop her. Nimbler boats than theirs were
already on the way to where the two aviators bobbed in the water. A Coast
Guard boat rescued the one whose parachute had opened. The pilot was
pulled onto a fishing boat.

The Rasmussens and Ruettens were understandably shaken by what
they had witnessed. They agreed it was best to return to shore. Nels piloted the
sailboat back to the marina. Later that afternoon, they learned the pilot
had succumbed to his injuries. The following day's newspapers identified him as Lt. Matthew C. Hawley, a twenty-six-year-old navy pilot from
Chesterfield, Missouri. The flight officer, Lt. Kathryn Ann Cullen of South-
hold, New York, survived the crash with minor injuries.

Sherri and John tried to make the best of things, despite the somber
turn of events. They still had family and friends with whom they wanted
to share their news. When Sherri called Donna, John also got on the phone.
"Are you happy now, Donna?" John asked her, a teasing reference to how
Donna had interrogated him over dinner.

In lieu of an engagement ring, John and Sherri decided that Sherri
would trade in her Toyota for something nicer. Sherri agreed it was more
practical to spend money on a better car than on a diamond. Later that
Memorial Day weekend, John and Sherri went to a BMW dealership and
picked out a silver 1985 318i sedan. John cleaned out his savings, and they
made a down payment of six or seven thousand dollars on the new car. John
and Sherri took out an auto loan to finance the cost of the BMW beyond
the down payment and trade-in value of Sherri's Toyota.

Sherri called the BMW her "engagement car." Sherri told Jayne she
loved it and planned to drive it forever. At the hospital, her friend Peggy
was surprised to see Sherri in her sleek new car. Sherri was excited, and
Peggy wanted to be excited for her, but to Peggy, such a fancy car was just
not Sherri. Peggy thought Sherri would never have bought a BMW for
herself if not for John. When Sherri called Nels and told him she and John
had traded in her Toyota, Nels was also surprised. Sherri had gotten the
Toyota so recently that it had less than ten thousand miles on it. Sherri
told Nels it was John's dream to have a BMW. Nels did not sense that
Sherri was disappointed, or that she would have preferred a traditional

engagement ring. Nels had to accept that Sherri was free to make her own decisions.

Nels and Loretta knew that Sherri valued her financial independence. Not taking money from her parents afforded her a measure of freedom in her personal life. Money for money's sake was never a big motivator for Sherri. She lived by five-year goals she set for herself each year: where she wanted to be in five years, and what she wanted to accomplish in that time. For Sherri, there was always a hill to climb. Her highest priorities in life were her friends and her belief in the future. She didn't care very much about material things, and she was careful not to spend more than her income. Sherri didn't have credit card problems because she didn't put things on her credit card. All the furniture in the condo, for instance, Sherri bought with cash after she saved up for it. If Sherri didn't have the money, she wouldn't buy it. Nels's impression of John was that he had the opposite financial philosophy: if John could put something on a credit card, it meant he could buy it. Nels thought if John could have charged it or been able to get a loan, he'd have bought the state of California. Nels worried how Sherri and John were going to manage their finances as a couple.

Whatever doubts Nels had about John, he knew that Sherri had made her choice. Sherri picked November 23, 1985, as their wedding date because her sister Teresa was married on the same day in 1980.

A few weeks after the engagement, Sherri told Jayne that John would be moving in. Sherri and John thought it was foolish for both of them to continue to pay for housing when they were going to be married in a few months. Sherri assured Jayne that she could take her time finding a new place and there was no rush for her to move out.

Jayne knew she didn't want to still be living in the condo when John moved in, so she started looking for a new place right away. Almost immediately, she found a room with a UCLA nursing colleague who lived in Culver City. Jayne liked the area, which was closer to UCLA and Mike's place in Venice than Van Nuys was. Jayne's new lease started July 1.

When Jayne told Sherri that she had found a new place to live, Sherri was concerned that Jayne felt kicked out. Sherri said she was welcome to stay longer. Jayne sensed that Sherri hadn't expected her to move out so quickly. Later, in hindsight, Jayne wondered if Sherri had been counting on her paying rent for a few more months and did not envision John moving in until closer to the wedding.

Living together before marriage was not as common or socially accepted in 1985 as it is today. Sherri and John talked to Nels and Loretta about their decision. Sherri explained to her parents how much money it would allow her and John to save before the wedding, and they did not try to talk her out of it.

In July, John gave up his apartment in Canoga Park and moved in with Sherri in Van Nuys. On July 25, Nels filed a quitclaim deed with the Los Angeles County Recorder's Office, which transferred ownership of the condo from himself to John and Sherri as joint tenants. Although the wedding was still four months away, John and Sherri were officially co-owners of the condo, which Nels had purchased for Sherri in 1980. For the first five years that Sherri lived in the condo, she sent her father a check each month to cover the condo's mortgage. Nels did not want to get caught between Sherri and John if they had problems in their marriage, so he asked them to refinance in their own names the amount that remained on the mortgage.

Not long after John moved in with Sherri, there was a major reorganization at Glendale Adventist Medical Center. The hospital was going through a turbulent period financially. Numerous positions were consolidated, and a few nursing directors were let go. Among the nursing managers promoted to take their place was Sherri's friend Peggy, who went from reporting to Sherri to a peer relationship at work. Sherri was made director of critical care nursing for all of the hospital's surgical units.

When the dust settled, Sherri and Peggy felt lucky to have made it through the reorganization. Both also felt a little daunted by the scope of their new responsibilities. Glendale Adventist's management mantra was "Hire for attitude, train for skill." If someone had good leadership skills, and demonstrated they could meet the hospital's high standards, they had the opportunity to be promoted very quickly. Sherri and Peggy did not doubt their abilities, but there was so much they didn't know and had to figure out as they went along.

The challenges Sherri and Peggy faced together as nursing directors made them even closer friends. Sherri and Peggy played off each other's strengths. Although Sherri no longer treated patients directly, she remained a clinician at heart. Peggy was more interested in the business side of health care. Sherri leaned on Peggy for help with budgets, which Sherri dreaded. Peggy relied on Sherri for clinical advice. If one was out of the office, the other covered her daily rounds. Having a supportive friend and colleague to work with made the bad days bearable, and the good days fun.

As part of the reorganization, Sherri's office was moved to the second floor of the hospital, closer to the surgical units. Sherri's secretary, Sylvia Nielsen, moved with her. Sherri's new office was considerably smaller than her former one. Peggy inherited Sherri's old office. Every time Sherri came to see Peggy, Sherri would say, "You took my office. I can't believe you took my office." It became their running joke.

Sherri and Peggy team-taught a class on the public image of nursing, which all nurses at Glendale Adventist took. The class explored how nurses were portrayed in the media. They used clips from popular TV shows and movies to illustrate the negative stereotypes that were out there: nurses as sex objects, nurses as doctors' handmaidens, Nurse Ratched. The message Sherri and Peggy tried to impart was that it was up to all nurses to change the public perception. Nurses were professionals. To be seen as such, nurses had to act professionally at all times, and also insist on being treated professionally. Sherri led by example. Peggy believed that Sherri was on a mission to change how the world perceived nurses.

Sherri taught another class at the hospital, by herself, called "The People Difference," which focused on conflict resolution. Sherri stressed the importance of being proactive when confronted with a problem. "People's biggest mistake in dealing with conflict is they let conflict control them, as opposed to them controlling the conflict," Sherri said during one videotaped class. "When we react positively or proactively, we have control over the situation, and we can start to implement some of our problem-solving techniques."

Sherri walked her colleagues through various hypothetical conflicts and how to resolve them by following a series of steps: listening; demonstrating empathy; identifying solutions; and acting on the solutions. When Sherri got to the point about identifying solutions, a woman taking the class asked her, "Does every problem have a solution?"

Sherri thought for a moment, then answered, "Good question. A lot of times I think we see a solution as completely resolved and over with, versus ongoing and still there. I think a lot of times we need to say, here's the conflict. What we need to do is everything possible to minimize it. It may not go away completely. But what can we do to minimize the problem, the conflict, the situation?"

The woman replied, "Sometimes somebody sees something as a problem, where we really have no control over it. I mean, maybe their expectations are way out of line."

Sherri opened the floor to everyone in the class. After a few minutes' discussion, Sherri returned to the woman who posed the original question, and asked her, "Does that help answer the question of, are all problems resolvable?"

The class laughed. The woman could have just said yes, to be agreeable and allow Sherri to move along. Instead, the woman said, "Sherri, I think sometimes, especially in our personal lives, we just need to agree to disagree. That's a solution in itself, too. There are those cases where the outcome is completely appropriate that we're never going to come to resolution but we need to move on, so let's agree to disagree."

The idea of an "unresolvable problem" seemed to strike Sherri as a theoretical dilemma rather than a situation she might encounter in the real world. Sherri's upbringing and education had conditioned her to trust in the essential goodness of people, and to have faith that hard work and ingenuity could solve most any problem, even one that appeared intractable. Peggy, who was also Adventist educated, attributed her and Sherri's professional success to their dedication to these values.

Only later did Peggy realize there was a huge blind spot in her and Sherri's worldview at that point in their lives. Despite the positive aspects of their educations, Peggy felt she and Sherri were ill prepared to deal with the world's uglier realities. They had no sense of the evils that existed beyond their own sheltered experience. They trusted that everything was going to work out for the best for them in some magical way.

How could Sherri have known there were people and situations in the world too dark and volatile to be tamed by conflict resolution techniques? Nothing in Sherri's history ever gave her any reason to doubt her own problem-solving abilities. To the contrary, Sherri was known at the hospital for her track record at solving problems and her ability to get along with difficult people. The fact that Glendale Adventist tapped Sherri to teach its class on conflict resolution speaks for itself.

As the summer of 1985 wound down, Sherri's career was at its apex. Her wedding was only a few months away.

Sherri did not know that her conflict resolution skills, and her relationship with John, were about to be tested in ways she could never have imagined.

Stephanie Lazarus

(1960 to March 1984)

Following their engagement in May 1985, John and Sherri's news spread quickly among his family and friends. John and Sherri first told his brother, Tom, because they were so excited and felt they had to tell someone right away. John later called a few friends and told them he was getting married. Other friends learned John's news by word of mouth. Among those who heard secondhand, rather than directly from John, was a college friend of his, Stephanie Lazarus.

John and Stephanie initially met as UCLA students in the fall of 1978, when John was a sophomore and Stephanie a freshman. Both lived on the top floor of Dykstra Hall, a ten-story dormitory located on "the Hill," the elevated northwest part of campus. The views from the tenth floor of Dykstra were majestic. Rooms on one side of the hall looked out over Westwood Village, and on the other side to the Pacific Ocean. On clear days, it was possible to see Catalina Island and as far south as the Palos Verdes peninsula.

The rooms and hallways of Dykstra were painted in bland, institutional colors like gray, white, and yellow. It was Dykstra's residents, a mix of upperclassmen and incoming freshmen, who brought the dorm to life each year. Every fall, a new mix of about eight hundred young men and women moved in. Although the dorm's architectural layout was not especially conducive to group socializing, the shared bathrooms and laundry facilities on each floor ensured that residents became well acquainted.

John Ruetten and Matt Gorder, John's best friend from high school and a UCLA classmate, were dormmates at Dykstra as freshmen, and then again as sophomores. The two friends were both engineering majors. Although John's focus was mechanical engineering and Matt's was electrical engineering, they took many of the required core classes together. John and Matt were basketball teammates in high school and played intramural basketball at UCLA. On school breaks, John and Matt often traveled back and forth to San Diego together.

Stephanie Lazarus was one of the more outgoing and assertive students on the tenth-floor hallway, according to another resident of the floor that year. Steph, as most people called her then, was very athletic and into sports, interests which helped her blend in at Dykstra. Although Dykstra was not exclusively a dorm for UCLA athletes, many lived there, and it had a reputation among students as the "jock dorm."

Stephanie was also known for her acerbic sense of humor, especially toward men, whose egos she seemed to enjoy deflating. If a guy said something pompous or otherwise left himself open to it, Stephanie rarely passed up an opportunity to cut him down to size. Most guys just rolled their eyes or ignored her teasing. If someone took offense, Stephanie would dismiss it as a joke, and the offended guy as oversensitive. Among her friends on the tenth floor, Stephanie's verbal barbs became an endearing quality. Some friends thought she relied on her sense of humor as a defense mechanism, a way to assert psychological control over others and create a zone around herself where she held sway.

Stephanie came to UCLA from Simi Valley, a bedroom community northwest of Los Angeles. She was born in Santa Monica on May 4, 1960, the eldest child of Shelton and Carol Lazarus. A sister, Judi, followed two years later, and then a brother, Steven, the next year. The family was living in Norfolk, Virginia, Shel-

Stephanie outside her Dykstra Hall dorm room, circa 1978–79

ton's hometown, by the time Steven was born in 1963. Carol's childhood was spent in Venice Beach and Culver City, in west Los Angeles. The Lazarus family was Jewish but nonobservant. Religion was not a big part of the children's upbringing.

In 1965, Carol told Shelton that she couldn't tolerate the humidity in Virginia and wanted to move the family back to Los Angeles. The family lived briefly in an apartment in Culver City, followed by a two-bedroom apartment in Inglewood. The three children slept together in one bedroom, and their parents in the other. There were lots of other kids around the neighborhood to play with. The family lived in Inglewood until Stephanie was about ten years old.

In 1970, Stephanie's parents bought a new home under construction in Simi Valley. In the prior decade, Simi Valley's population had grown from a few thousand to nearly sixty thousand. Despite the proliferation of tract housing, Simi Valley retained a sleepy, Old West feel into the early 1970s. Hollywood westerns were still being filmed in town at the Corriganville and Big Sky movie ranches.

For several weekends before they moved in, the Lazarus family drove to Simi Valley from Inglewood to watch their house being built. Their new neighborhood seemed to the kids like it was on another planet. They chased lizards around the yard and marveled at their home in progress. The freeways that serve Simi Valley today did not exist in 1970, so the only way to drive there was on winding canyon roads that Carol dreaded. Their route through the Simi Hills also took them past the Spahn Movie Ranch, notorious since the previous summer, when Charles Manson and his followers were based there. The Manson Family trials took place in Los Angeles the same summer that Stephanie's family moved to Simi Valley.

Lots of other kids lived in the same subdivision as the Lazarus family. The neighborhood felt safe and wholesome enough that Stephanie and her siblings were free to play outside without adult supervision. When it rained, they made little boats and raced them in the gutters against other kids. In summertime, they roamed the neighborhood with friends until late in the evenings. All three children attended Simi Valley public schools. Stephanie went to Garden Grove Elementary.

Almost every Sunday, the family went to see Carol's mother and extended family. On a typical Sunday morning, Stephanie, Judi, and Steven woke up, did their chores, got cleaned up, and piled in the family car for the drive to Culver City. They would spend all day with their grand-mother and uncles and then eat Sunday dinner as a family. It was usually dark out by the time they drove back to Simi Valley.

Throughout Stephanie's childhood, to the same extent that Sundays were for family, Saturdays were for sports. Stephanie's lifelong love of sports began early. Even as a little girl, she was a gifted athlete and naturally com-petitive. Stephanie played in a softball league for girls called Little Miss Softball. Her favorite baseball player as a kid was the slick-fielding Orioles third baseman Brooks Robinson.

Stephanie's interest in sports took after her father. Shelton had been an athlete and was an avid sports fan. He sometimes took sports a little too seriously. Whenever Steven went to her softball games with their dad, he cringed anytime the ump made a bad call, because he knew his father might lose his temper and embarrass him. "Oh God, my dad's going to go off," Steven thought. "There he goes . . ."

Stephanie's play on the softball diamond made her a perennial on the league's all-star team. The all-stars got to compete in a postseason tour-nament called the Jamboree. The tournament took place in Buena Park, southeast of Los Angeles, and attracted teams from across Southern Cali-fornia. The softball fields were adjacent to a small-time amusement park called Japanese Deer Park. The landscaping, food, and attractions were all designed to evoke traditional Japanese culture. Visitors could watch mar-tial arts demonstrations and hand-feed deer imported from Japan.

The Lazarus family didn't vacation often when the kids were young, apart from a few trips to Las Vegas, so Stephanie's softball tournaments were a big deal to her siblings. The first year they went, the family camped overnight in the parking lot of Japanese Deer Park. While Stephanie played in the tournament, Steven hung out with other boys his age, the younger brothers of Stephanie's teammates. The pack of boys could sneak into Japa-nese Deer Park easily. They went around the park and collected bottles to cash in for a nickel apiece, then spent the proceeds on candy. Carol usually chauffeured the family to Stephanie's softball tournaments. Steven recalls that Shelton traveled to fewer than half.

All three Lazarus children attended Sequoia Junior High School in Simi Valley from seventh to ninth grade. Stephanie grew out of playing softball and took up basketball and tennis.

Simi Valley High School began in tenth grade. Stephanie continued to excel at sports. She made the varsity girls' basketball and tennis teams as a sophomore and lettered in both sports all three years of high school. Stephanie also demonstrated a willingness to tackle goals and projects that would have intimidated most teenagers. Soon after she was old enough to drive, she saw an old Chevy Nova for sale. The price was low because the car's engine needed work. Stephanie couldn't afford to both buy it and take it to a mechanic, and her parents weren't going to pay for any repairs. Stephanie heard that her high school taught auto shop and devised a plan. She had taken shop class in junior high and already knew how to weld. She bought the car and rebuilt the engine herself at the school's auto shop. Although she did it mostly for the car and to save money, it was also a point of pride for her to do something a lot of guys didn't know how to do.

Around the time Stephanie entered high school, her parents announced they were getting divorced. The divorce became official in October 1975, when Stephanie was fifteen. Steven was so devastated and embarrassed that he lied about it for a year to his friends at school. He has no recollection of him or his sisters ever going to counseling or talking with a psychologist at the time. Their parents let them choose whom they wanted to live with. Judi and Steven picked their dad. Stephanie chose to live with her mom. Carol and Stephanie moved out of the family home and into a two-bedroom condo across town. Stephanie saw her siblings only rarely while they lived apart.

Stephanie graduated from Simi Valley High School in 1978. The summer before college, she and a girlfriend went backpacking in Europe, something Stephanie had always wanted to do. The experience cemented her lifelong love of traveling.

It was a big deal within her family for Stephanie to be admitted to UCLA. She cobbled together some of her tuition by applying for small grants and scholarships. Her attitude was, fill out every application, even if it was for $20, because that was tuition money she didn't have. Stephanie took the Chevy Nova with her to college.

Early in her freshman year at UCLA, Stephanie and John became part of a group of about a dozen friends who lived on the

Stephanie's senior year Simi Valley High School yearbook photo, 1978

tenth floor of Dykstra Hall. The friends were a mix of men and women of different class years. Nothing in particular defined the group other than the fact they lived on the same hallway and liked to hang out together. If it was the weekend, and someone said let's go see a movie, they would go around knocking on doors to see who else wanted to go. John and Stephanie's common interest was sports. She and John would go on runs together and shoot hoops on the outdoor basketball court behind Dykstra Hall.

Although a handful of people who lived on the hall paired off into couples, most of the dating that took place was casual, as was normal in a college dorm in the late 1970s. Some of John's close friends noticed that Stephanie seemed to want more than a platonic relationship with him. John's friend Matt Gorder got that impression once while he, John, and Stephanie were playing basketball together behind the dorm. Stephanie had the ball and John was defending her. Stephanie posted John up, with her back to the basket. Stephanie initiated a lot of body contact with John as she backed him down under the hoop. Matt thought that it looked like Stephanie wanted John to guard her even closer. Matt observed that John and Stephanie spent a lot of time together, but he never saw them kiss or hold hands. As far as he could tell, John and Stephanie's relationship was platonic, just a very close friendship. Matt's impression was that John was not physically attracted to Stephanie. John once told Matt, "Steph has a great body, but the face just doesn't cut it."

John was six feet three and handsome but relatively inexperienced romantically. He had had only one relationship of any significance before college. John and Stephanie made out a few times but never had sex during college, according to John. From his perspective, his relationship with Stephanie was in the gray area between dating and a close friendship, but definitely not boyfriend and girlfriend.

Neither John nor Stephanie seriously dated anyone else at UCLA. Stephanie didn't act outwardly as if she was looking to be anybody's girlfriend. Most guys on the hall thought of her as a good friend who was fun to be around, but not girlfriend material. Other women in the dorm attracted more suitors than Stephanie.

Some guys may have been put off by Stephanie's brash sense of humor. One male friend from the tenth floor took a class with her in Jewish history. Their class took a field trip to the Holocaust museum at the Simon Wiesenthal Center. The center also had a yeshiva, the cafeteria for which was next to the entrance to the museum. As the class waited by the museum's doors for their tour to begin, Stephanie turned to her friend and loudly announced, "Hey, I'm getting a little hungry standing here. I wonder if I could go in there and get a ham and cheese sandwich." It was clear to Stephanie's friend that she had not made the joke naively or innocently. He believed Stephanie said it purposefully, for impact, and loud enough for everyone to hear.

Stephanie also had a reputation as an inveterate prankster. Once when John was using the showers, Stephanie ran into the bathroom, made eye contact with him for a split second, then snatched his clothes and took off down the hall. Another time, Stephanie sneaked into John's room and took a snapshot of him in his underwear while he slept. Stephanie kept a print of the photo and wrote on the back: *"John Ruetten, 1979, Dykstra Hall. I snuck in room and took the picture."* John later saw the photo.

John and Stephanie both returned to Dykstra Hall in the fall of 1979, when John was a junior and Stephanie a sophomore. John's roommate that year, David Neuman, also became friends with Stephanie, and the three of them spent a lot of time together. David sometimes hung out with them individually as well, John more often than Stephanie. David thought of Stephanie as an upbeat person. It was rare for him to see her sad or serious. When it was time to study, Stephanie got down to work, but as soon as the work was done, it was time to close the books and have some fun.

One day during Stephanie's sophomore year, she and David shared a meal in the Dykstra dining hall. Stephanie's demeanor was awkward and uncharacteristically sad. Stephanie shared with David that she was romantically interested in John, but John didn't feel the same way about her. Stephanie said John just wanted to be "buddies." She seemed resigned to John's feelings and the limits he'd placed on their relationship. It wasn't what Stephanie wanted, but it was the way it was.

During Stephanie's sophomore year, she, John, and David took a road trip together to San Francisco for a friend's wedding. Although David was aware of the feelings Stephanie had confessed to him, his impression of John and Stephanie's friendship was that it remained platonic. As far as David knew, John didn't date anyone seriously while they were at UCLA.

John and Stephanie also took a few trips to San Diego, where John's parents lived. Stephanie visited John's home and met his family many times. Stephanie struck up friendships with John's mother, Margaret, his brother, Tom, and his sister Janet. John's other sister, Gail, was already married.

Tom's impression at the time was that John and Stephanie were

Stephanie and John in San Francisco, circa 1979–1980

boyfriend and girlfriend, but the relationship seemed casual. John did not share any intimate details with his brother, so Tom did not know how serious it was. Tom sensed that Stephanie liked John more than he liked her, but he never talked about it with either of them. John did not describe Stephanie as his girlfriend to his sister Gail. Her impression was that John and Stephanie were friends and were also dating. John brought no other women from UCLA home to San Diego to meet his family.

In the fall of 1980, Stephanie, by then a junior, tried out for UCLA's junior varsity women's basketball team and made the roster. John attended several of Stephanie's basketball games. Although Stephanie was only five feet seven, short for a basketball player, she compensated for her lack of height with tenacity. Her strength and physical fitness had only improved since she had arrived on campus as a freshman.

For John's senior year, he moved into an off-campus apartment with David and two other friends, but he and Stephanie continued to see each other. Among some of their friends, it was an open secret that she pined to be John's girlfriend. John, for reasons he did not discuss with his friends, did not want to be known as Stephanie's boyfriend.

John graduated from UCLA in 1981 with a degree in mechanical engineering. A computer company in Woodland Hills, Data Products, hired John out of college. He rented an apartment in nearby Canoga Park. According to John, it was during the summer after he graduated that he and Stephanie had sex for the first time, which further muddled their already ambiguous relationship.

That summer, Stephanie did an internship for college credit at the Inglewood Juvenile District Attorney's Office. Stephanie completed two research projects, one on prosecutorial discretion and the other on juvenile recividism.

Stephanie received her degree from UCLA in political science and sociology in June 1982. John went to Stephanie's graduation and posed for photos with her afterward. It was not the first time John had met Stephanie's family. A month earlier, John had attended Stephanie's twenty-second birthday party, which her mother, Carol, hosted.

John and Stephanie continued to see each other after they graduated. John thought of Stephanie as a great person, and he considered the two of them good friends. According to him, it wasn't the type of relationship in which they saw each other daily. It was more on and off, two to three times a month. Sometimes when they got together, they ended up in bed. A few

John and Stephanie at her UCLA graduation, June 20, 1982

times, Stephanie spent the night at John's place. Occasionally, they took trips together: water-skiing on Lake Mojave once, and to Catalina Island. They also took a trip to Palm Springs with a group of friends. On both the Catalina Island and Palm Springs trips, they had sex. Thirty years later, in sworn court testimony, John estimated that he and Stephanie slept together approximately twenty-five to thirty times between 1981 and 1984.

It seemed clear to John, at least in his own mind, that he and Stephanie were friends having fun together and were never going to get married. The idea that they were just friends but also sleeping together sometimes made John feel uncomfortable. When those feelings got to him, he would draw back and try not to see Stephanie for a while. He never really broke it off with her, or vice versa. Because John did not consider them a couple, it did not occur to him to talk with Stephanie about the status of their relationship, their future together, or their lack of one. During these cold periods, John went on dates with other women, and he didn't feel obliged to tell Stephanie when he did. There was no time during his entire relationship with Stephanie that he wouldn't have considered dating someone else, but none of his dates with other women led to anything serious. Inevitably, John and Stephanie drifted back together.

Stephanie's first job after college was as a file clerk at a law firm, Fine, Perzik & Friedman, which represented pro athletes and sports teams, including the Lakers and the Kings. Most of her friends assumed she was headed to law school and eventually a career as an attorney. According to one UCLA classmate, Stephanie initially wanted to be an attorney, but quickly realized it was too much work. It came as a surprise to many of her friends when in February 1983, she applied to the LAPD to become a police officer.

At the time, relatively few UCLA graduates, and even fewer women, pursued careers in law enforcement. In many ways, Stephanie's choice of a police career suited her personality. She was strong and in excellent physical shape. She was naturally assertive. The idea of entering a male-dominated work environment did not intimidate her. Like most women of her generation joining the workforce at the turn of the 1980s, Stephanie believed that women deserved equal rights and career opportunities. Another UCLA friend interpreted Stephanie's choice of police work as her way of declaring, "Yeah, this is typically a male career, but I'm going to do it. I'm going to show them up."

The LAPD has a surprisingly long history of female officers in its ranks. For most of the department's history, the LAPD treated its female officers differently than its policemen, who were overwhelmingly white men. Progress toward equality occurred fitfully, and often only as a result of protracted legal battles. Today's LAPD recognizes that to effectively police Los Angeles, its force of nearly ten thousand officers should reflect the diversity of the city's population. But for decades, the department's leadership resisted changes to the LAPD's hiring and promotion policies, until the courts forced the department to reform.

The determined policewomen who made it through the LAPD academy long endured resentment, discrimination, and harassment on the job. Complaints to superiors invited retaliation and further humiliation. The price of incomplete acceptance seemed to be silence and acquiescence to the status quo. Over the decades, many policewomen and minority officers decided it wasn't worth it and ended up quitting the LAPD in disgust. The high attrition rate reinforced the belief within the department that only certain types of people were fit for police work. Not until the early 1980s, when Stephanie came on the job, did the LAPD start to accept large numbers of women into its ranks.

Until the 1970s, female LAPD recruits trained separately from the men. It was presumed women didn't have the physical strength and were too injury prone to train alongside men. Recruits had to be at least five feet eight, which excluded many women. Because most LAPD policemen could not abide being supervised by a female, policewomen were never promoted beyond the rank of sergeant. Many desirable assignments within the department were restricted to male officers only. Throughout the 1960s, perhaps partly in response to social upheaval outside the LAPD, its culture grew progressively more macho and inhospitable to female officers.

In 1971, Chief of Police Ed Davis stunned the department's approximately two hundred policewomen by announcing that "women are no longer wanted or needed by the LAPD." Davis also declared policewomen couldn't be trusted with guns "during that time of the month." Between 1970 and 1973, no new female officers joined the LAPD. Many policewomen who were already on the job were reassigned to secretarial roles within the department. Asked when the department would allow women officers in patrol cars, Davis replied, "When the Los Angeles Rams have women football players."

In 1973, a veteran LAPD policewoman named Fanchon Blake upended Davis's plans. Blake was one of 159 women on the LAPD in 1973, barely 2 percent of the total police force. Blake had joined the LAPD in 1948. Prior to the LAPD, Blake had served in the U.S. Army and attained the rank of major. During her LAPD career, Blake worked a variety of assignments available to policewomen, including the juvenile detail, a downtown foot beat, and jail matron for female arrestees. Blake loved being a cop and considered herself a loyal officer. Blake believed the LAPD was the best police force in the world. Her paramount interest was what was good for the department.

Blake believed strongly that women should have equal rights. Throughout her army and LAPD careers, Blake never tolerated sexist treatment. Blake learned that not standing up for herself when she was treated disrespectfully did something to her inside that she couldn't abide. Unlike many policewomen, Blake talked openly about her views. The indignities endured by Blake and other policewomen of that era were both day-to-day and systemic. Male officers routinely made rude and sexist comments without fear of reproach. The notion that a policewoman could be promoted above sergeant and command male officers was considered bizarre.

By the late 1960s, twenty years into her LAPD career, Blake had climbed the ranks to detective sergeant. In 1969, Blake applied to take the exam for lieutenant, a rank no LAPD policewoman had ever held. The department repeatedly denied Blake permission to take the exam. For four years, Blake petitioned the City Council and the Police Commission to force the LAPD to let her take the test. Nothing changed. Blake knew the department would never reform its culture voluntarily.

In 1973, Blake filed a sex discrimination lawsuit against the LAPD. Blake's decision ultimately cost her her own career, but it also paved the way for the largest influx of female and minority officers in the history of the LAPD. Blake did not know at the time how consequential her lawsuit would be. Before news of its filing broke, she called and tipped a reporter friend at the *Los Angeles Times*.

"You know what you're doing?" he asked her.

"No, but I'm tired of doing what I've been doing, accepting it," Blake replied.

Blake's courage astonished and terrified her fellow policewomen. The president of the Los Angeles Women Police Officers' Association later recounted to the *Times*, "We panicked. I was afraid for her and for us. It was like going up against God, only God doesn't wear a gun, so it was worse."

The morning the story hit the papers, Blake felt scared to death to walk into the police building. When she finally summoned the nerve to go inside, she found her desk cleaned out. Blake, a detective sergeant, was informed that her new desk was in the reception area. Blake was also told she could no longer perform any investigative casework. Then came the silent treatment. No one at work acknowledged Blake was alive, even when she stood right in front of them. Blake had worked with many of the officers for years. The experience was emotionally devastating for her.

Media outlets all over the world flocked to Blake and her story. Despite her ostracism at work, Blake granted many interviews and continued to be outspoken about her views. To blunt criticism of the department, Chief Davis announced the LAPD would abolish the ranks of policeman and policewoman in favor of a single rank: police officer. Along with the unisex rank, the LAPD introduced its first unisex uniform. Female LAPD officers would no longer be required to carry their firearm in a department-issue purse, but could wear a holster on duty, as male officers always had.

Amid the unfolding legal and PR battles, Blake kept reporting to work. She heard the department was organizing a task force to target rapists and volunteered for a role. Blake was assigned to walk a foot beat. Two male officers were supposed to tail her and provide backup. Late one night, Blake was alone on her foot patrol when a Cadillac pulled up alongside her. Her backup team was nowhere in sight. The guy behind the wheel told Blake to get in. She told him to shove off. The Cadillac went around the block and came back. Again, Blake received no backup. Blake told the driver, "Bug off, buster," and eventually he drove away. When she got back to the station, her lieutenant was laughing up a storm.

"What'd you do out on the beat tonight?" he asked her.

She told him what happened, and how her backup officers had abandoned her.

The lieutenant replied, "Well, I just had a report from a snitch that the main pimp in the area is really upset because he thinks you're taking over his territory."

Blake decided to retire from the LAPD that same night. After her retirement became official in 1974, Blake's lawsuit continued to wend its way through the courts. In 1977, the U.S. Department of Justice joined Blake's case with its own lawsuit against the LAPD, which alleged discrimination against black and Hispanic officers. In 1980, to settle both cases, the LAPD agreed to a federal consent decree. Under the agreement, the LAPD committed to increase its proportion of women officers to 20 percent, and its share of black and Hispanic officers to match their representation in the broader Los Angeles workforce. The minimum height requirement for entry into the LAPD academy was reduced from five feet eight to five feet.

In 1980, when the Fanchon Blake consent decree went into effect, the LAPD had 6,574 male and 178 female officers, 2.6 percent of the force. Thanks to higher percentages of women in each new academy class, the share of women in the LAPD grew to 4.1 percent in 1981 and 4.8 percent in 1982. By 1983, the year Stephanie entered the academy, the LAPD had 431 female officers, 6.2 percent of the force, which still left the department 93.8 percent male.

It would take more than a court decree, and 250 new female officers over three years, to change the culture of the LAPD. Sexism remained ingrained in the attitudes of many LAPD officers. A common complaint was that the department had lowered standards to get more women into the academy. Male officers complained that their safety would be endangered if they had a woman for a patrol partner. One female officer who joined the LAPD in 1980, Sandy Jo MacArthur, recounted to the *Los Angeles Times* in 2010 that when she worked patrol at the start of her career, wives of other officers called the station to say, "Don't let my husband work with her." MacArthur spent ten years working patrol and later rose to assistant chief, one rank below chief of police.

Female LAPD officers who came on the job in the early 1980s were in a no-win situation. If a female officer acted assertively in a case or on the street, their male partners would accuse them of having "Jane Wayne syndrome." If they held back, they risked being seen as passive and incompetent. Stories about female officers' screw-ups, some of them fabricated, circulated widely at LAPD stations.

The chauvinists found confirmation for their beliefs in the high dropout rate for female recruits at the LAPD academy. Unlike in the past, male and female recruits trained together and had to meet the same standards in order to graduate. From 1976 to 1980, 55 percent of female recruits who entered the academy failed to graduate, versus 17 percent of men. Because the LAPD had committed to increase sharply the share of women in its ranks, the attrition rate for female recruits posed an acute problem. Rather than lower the standards for academy graduation, which would have fueled the rank and file's perception that women couldn't cut it, the LAPD introduced a program to help prepare female recruits for the rigors of the academy.

Beginning in 1980, female LAPD recruits were offered eight weeks of paid, specialized preacademy training through the Crime Prevention Assistant program. The CPA curriculum was highly regimented. Recruits received three hours of physical fitness training daily. The workouts were supervised by academy instructors and included long-distance runs, weight lifting, and wrestling. The CPA program also aimed to provide female recruits with "psychological preparation" for the academy and life as a police officer. Recruits in the CPA program spent fifteen hours per week on work assignments at LAPD divisions across the city.

Among the realities female recruits had to be prepared for psychologically was disrespectful treatment by their fellow officers. Dr. Robin Greene, an LAPD psychologist, described the LAPD's culture at the time in a scholarly paper on the CPA program. Greene wrote, "It is not uncommon for male officers to resent women as law enforcement officers. They may feel that women are not skilled in street-wise logic, are too frail to subdue male offenders, and are not above using their femininity to gain special favors. In many instances this motivates a display of unwarranted antagonism, lack of cooperation, intemperate language, or sexist behavior of no practical utility except to demean."

In 1980 and 1981, the first two years the LAPD offered the CPA program, more than half of the women who completed the CPA training nonetheless dropped out of the academy before graduation. Not until 1982, the year before Stephanie joined the LAPD, did the attrition rate for female recruits begin to improve. More than 70 percent of the women in the CPA class of 1982 made it through the academy. Encouraged by the results, and still under pressure to increase the number of women in its ranks, the LAPD in 1983 lengthened the CPA program from eight weeks to six months.

In March 1983, Stephanie was hired by the LAPD and entered the CPA program, which was then in its fourth year. As at UCLA, where one of Stephanie's friends thought of her as "her own icebreaker," she was outgoing and collegial with the other women in her class. As training intensified and the women were tested individually and collectively, the bonds between them intensified as well. Stephanie

Stephanie's LAPD photo during the CPA program, April 28, 1983

forged lasting friendships with some of her fellow recruits, including Jayme Weaver, a future confidante and patrol partner, and Kim Dittbern. Stephanie excelled at the physical training aspects of the CPA program. Her athleticism and friendly demeanor led Dittbern and others to consider Stephanie the student leader of their CPA class.

Stephanie, like all prospective LAPD officers, was required to pass a psychological screening exam prior to her admission to the academy. The examination consisted of two parts, a written test and an interview with a department psychologist. The purpose of the exam was to identify and weed out candidates who had a propensity for violence or criminal thoughts. Stephanie evidently raised no red flags, and she passed with flying colors.

In September 1983, as part of her official application to the LAPD academy, Stephanie submitted a three-page, handwritten personal essay, in which she recounted her education and employment history, her hobbies and love of sports, and her motivation to become a police officer. Stephanie ended her essay, "*I view my role as a police officer as first, an enforcer of the laws. As a police officer I must also help people and be a mediator of their problems. One of the most important aspects of a police officer is as a role model. If people see that I am honest, trustworthy and do a good job, they will respect me, the job and the department.*"

That fall, Stephanie and her classmates who had completed the CPA program entered the LAPD academy. The schedule was grueling for everyone, men and women alike. Classes began most days before 6:00 a.m. The training ran the gamut. Recruits received academic instruction in subjects like law and Spanish, and technical training in driving, firearms, and self-defense. The biggest challenge for most recruits was the physical training, which included endless runs on the academy grounds and the surrounding hills. One physical requirement, introduced after the department lowered the minimum height to five feet, was that all recruits be able to climb over a six-foot wall. Because getting over the wall required height and upper body strength, the obstacle was particularly intimidating for many female recruits.

Another element of their physical training was "combat wrestling," which involved fighting and trying to pin an opponent. One combat wrestling drill the recruits practiced was the "gun retention drill." Two recruits paired off. One played the officer, who started with a dummy gun in hand. The other played the suspect and tried to take the gun away. The recruits were instructed to do whatever was necessary—punching, kicking, scratching, biting—to win the fight. Ever since 1963's Onion Field murder case, in which an LAPD officer was killed after his partner surrendered his gun to two criminals, officers were taught never to give up their weapon, no matter what. Retaining control of your gun at all times and at all costs was a cardinal rule and responsibility for LAPD officers.

By the end of their academy training, all the recruits, male and female, had faced each other in the gun retention drill at least once. One classmate, Brian McCartin, recalls that Stephanie was among the toughest combatants in their class. Although Stephanie was only five feet seven and 130 pounds, McCartin found she was by far the strongest, most aggressive, and most persistent fighter of all the female recruits. Stephanie would go crazy to get out of a hold or escape if she was cornered. When McCartin wrestled Stephanie, he had to put her in a full nelson hold in order to control her.

Once during combat wrestling training, Stephanie requested to wrestle a different male classmate, who was five feet nine and 175 pounds at the time. When he and Stephanie began wrestling, he was losing, which was very embarrassing to him, as the whole class was watching. He attributed Stephanie's wrestling prowess to both strength and skill. He considered her very physically fit, vocal, and in the forefront of their class.

Another male classmate, who was six feet two and about 200 pounds, also remembers Stephanie as a very good wrestler. She was slender but strong for her size and very athletic. When he wrestled Stephanie, he was able to overpower her, but she was strong and elusive. Off the wrestling mat, his impression of Stephanie was that she was outgoing and very talkative, with a "type A+" personality.

Shooting was another facet of training at which Stephanie excelled, unlike most other female recruits. Kim Dittbern, Stephanie's CPA classmate, observed at the academy that whatever training Stephanie did, she tried her hardest and did it well. Dittbern considered it part of what made Stephanie a natural leader in their class.

The intensity of the academy experience and the long hours the recruits spent together fostered some tight-knit relationships among the classmates. This was especially true of the female recruits, who knew one another longer from having gone through the CPA program together. Some recruits were more open than others about their personal lives. Stephanie mentioned John Ruetten to at least a few of her academy classmates. Stephanie described John to them as her college boyfriend.

Stephanie made some time to relax despite her rigorous academy schedule. Her relationship with John continued as before, on and off. During the summer of 1983, while Stephanie was in the academy, she was asked to house-sit for a family named the Kaplans. The Kaplans lived in Brentwood, an affluent neighborhood in West Los Angeles. Their home was nicely landscaped and had a backyard swimming pool with a diving board.

Stephanie had previously house-sat for the Kaplans during college. One night, when she was a junior or senior at UCLA, she was home by herself when a burglar entered the Kaplans' home. The intruder encountered Stephanie and tied her up. Little else is known about the incident and what impact it may have had on Stephanie's outlook at the time, her eventual choice of career, and later events, including how Sherri Rasmussen was killed.

Although John was among Stephanie's closest friends when the home invasion occurred, it is unknown what she told him about it, or when. A few years later, when Stephanie house-sat in 1983, John sometimes came over to go swimming. Stephanie liked to lie out in her bikini and work on her suntan. Thanks to her academy training, she had never been more fit. Stephanie took some photos and posed for others while she and John hung out by the pool. On the back of one print, a snapshot of her reclining in her bikini, Stephanie handwrote, *"House Sitting, Kaplans—Summer '83."*

Stephanie poses in her bikini, summer 1983

In late 1983, around the time Stephanie completed the LAPD academy, she purchased a two-bedroom condo in Granada Hills, in the northern San Fernando Valley, about twenty miles east of her hometown of Simi Valley. The condo was located close to the 405 freeway and a hilltop restaurant, the Odyssey.

Stephanie told her LAPD friend Jayme Weaver that John helped her move from her apartment in Santa Monica. John's brother, Tom, helped Stephanie paint her new condo. John's sister Janet also visited Stephanie at her new place. Tom was in school at Cal State Northridge, where he played on the basketball team. Stephanie went to some of Tom's games and took photographs. John spent some nights at Stephanie's condo.

In December 1983, John invited Stephanie to his company's Christmas party. John's employer, Data Products, hired a portrait photographer for the party. John and Stephanie posed for a photo together. Stephanie kept a copy of the print.

Stephanie's first full year as an LAPD officer began auspiciously. On January 20, 1984, before she had even been assigned to a geographic area, Stephanie received her first official commendation from the department. The commendation read in full: *"Excellent appearance during formal inspection."*

In early February 1984, when John turned twenty-five, Stephanie threw

ABOVE: *LAPD photo of Police Officer Stephanie Lazarus, circa 1983–1984*

LEFT: *Stephanie and John at his company's Christmas party, December 1983*

a surprise birthday party for him at her new place. In sworn court testimony in 2012, John could not recall whether or not he spent the night with Stephanie after the party.

A few weeks later, on February 29, Stephanie stopped by the Los Angeles Police Revolver and Athletic Club, which operated a gun shop on the LAPD academy grounds exclusively for police officers. Stephanie had received extensive firearms training at the academy. Six months earlier, when she completed her academy training, she was issued her LAPD duty gun, a Smith & Wesson six-shot revolver with a four-inch barrel. Most LAPD patrol officers in the 1980s also carried a backup weapon on duty. In anticipation of her imminent deployment to the field, Stephanie had decided to purchase a backup gun.

The backup gun Stephanie selected and bought that day was a .38 Smith & Wesson model 49 revolver with a dark blue steel finish. The model 49 is a very compact revolver, with a snub-nosed two-inch barrel and a swing-out cylinder for five .38 cartridges. It uses the smallest gun frame manufactured by Smith & Wesson. The size of the model 49, small enough to be worn in an ankle holster, made it a common choice of backup or off-duty weapon for LAPD officers in the 1980s.

Stephanie presented her California driver's license to the gun shop clerk, who instructed her to fill out the top half of a 4473 form, the firearm transaction record required by the federal government. She printed her name and address in block letters, along with her date of birth, height and weight (five feet seven and 128 pounds), and other personal details. She signed and dated the form. The clerk filled out the bottom half, which noted the gun's make, model, and serial number: ACM6890.

After Stephanie took her new weapon home, the clerk filed the completed form. Federal law requires sellers to retain gun transaction records for a minimum of twenty years. The Los Angeles Police Revolver and Athletic Club gun shop stored its 4473 forms chronologically in cardboard file boxes. Stephanie's 4473 would sit in a file box on the grounds of the LAPD academy for more than twenty-five years before anyone looked at it again.

The following day, March 1, Stephanie took her new revolver to the LAPD's armorer. LAPD policy required officers to present a firearm to the armorer for inspection and registration with the department before it was used on duty or worn concealed while off duty. The armorer pulled Stephanie's official Firearm Inspection Card, a preprinted black-and-white card. The first entry on Stephanie's card, below her name and LAPD serial number, listed her duty weapon, the Smith & Wesson revolver with the four-inch barrel, which was issued to her six months earlier. On the line below that, Firearm No. 2, the armorer recorded the date, make, barrel length, model, and serial number of Stephanie's new backup gun.

On March 2, Stephanie graduated from the LAPD academy ranked twenty-third in her class of sixty-six men and women. Her mother, Carol, and brother, Steven, attended the graduation ceremony. It is unknown whether John was also there to see Stephanie complete her transformation into a full-fledged Los Angeles police officer.

The 1983 CPA class that included Stephanie was the most successful in the history of the program. Ninety percent of the women in Stephanie's CPA class graduated from the academy.

The unprecedented influx of female officers was the subject of a *Los Angeles Times* story headlined LAPD WOMEN PIONEER TOUGH NEW TERRITORY, on March 30, 1984, just a few weeks after Stephanie graduated. The story described the cultural headwinds women officers faced within the department, and the stress many felt as a result. An LAPD psychologist, Susan Saxe, told the *Times* that some women officers encountered difficulties in their personal lives as they transitioned from civilian life: "For many policewomen, stress isn't limited to the job arena, Saxe noted . . . 'Often women change dramatically after they join the force. Their self-image and self-confidence improve. Some men get real uncomfortable with that . . ."My wife carries a gun, she has permission to take away freedom, to put someone in jail, to kill.""

No one but Stephanie can say authoritatively how becoming a police officer changed her. Only she and John know how their relationship changed in the spring of 1984, as she prepared to start her LAPD career. Twenty-five years later, in an interview with LAPD detectives in 2009, John was unable to recall for certain how often he saw Stephanie that spring, the last few months before he met Sherri.

5

"Admit Nothing. Deny Everything. Demand Proof."

(March 4, 1984, to March 30, 1985)

When Stephanie graduated from the LAPD academy in March 1984, she started on the same rung as all of her classmates. Few of her academy classmates, however, shared her instinct and talent for ingratiating herself up the chain of command. By the end of her LAPD career, more than a quarter century later, the department's culture and inner workings would be second nature to her. But back in March 1984, everything was brand new for Police Officer I Stephanie Lazarus, who at the time was just another boot.

After graduation from the academy, LAPD officers spend their first year on probationary status. Probationary officers carry the rank of Police Officer I, P-1 for short. P-1s who successfully complete their probation are automatically promoted to Police Officer II. Unlike in New York, where the NYPD refers to its newest officers as "rookies," the traditional term used in Los Angeles is "boot," a legacy of the LAPD's historical ties with the U.S. Marine Corps, whose recruits must endure boot camp.

On March 4, two days after her academy graduation, Stephanie reported for her first field assignment to an LAPD geographic division, the Hollywood station.

Hollywood has always been one of the most high-profile and exciting areas of Los Angeles. For a hundred years, the neighborhood's unique blend of glamor and seediness has lured generations of revelers, tourists, and ne'er-do-wells. The prevalence of transients in Hollywood has always made it a challenging section of the city to police. Along with the transient population, the Hollywood Division is one of the LAPD's most diverse. Its jurisdiction includes the nightclubs and tourist traps along Sunset and Hollywood Boulevards; breathtaking movie star mansions nestled in the Hollywood Hills; and the deceptively placid Hollywood flats, where most of the street crime, drug sales, and prostitution occur.

Like Times Square in New York, Hollywood has experienced dramatic gentrification over the last several decades. The area's current renaissance is the latest chapter in a boom-and-bust cycle that began during the silent movie era. In his 1992 autobiography, *Chief: My Life in the LAPD*, no less an authority than Chief of Police Daryl Gates offered this nutshell history of Hollywood, and the neighborhood's character in the early 1980s:

> *The area had its heyday in the thirties and forties, when the studios were churning out glamorous stars and movies that somehow seemed magical. The streets reflected that magic. All along Hollywood Boulevard were elegant theaters: Grauman's Chinese, with its legendary footprints, and the Egyptian, where on any night of the week the klieg lights might have signaled a star-studded premiere of a new film. There were restaurants like the Brown Derby, and nightclubs with big-band music, where celebrities dropped in to be noticed. But that Hollywood began to disappear in the fifties.*
>
> *In time, the area deteriorated into one of the sleaziest, slimiest parts of the city. The theaters and businesses had slipped, replaced by porn palaces and prostitutes—male and female—and the people on the streets were largely thieves, robbers, con artists, wierdos, drug dealers, and tourists who didn't know any better. Car thefts were among the highest in the city. No woman could walk Hollywood Boulevard without being accosted. A woman fifty-five years old with grocery bags would be hustled, since it was automatically assumed that any woman on the street was a hooker.*

This was the Hollywood that awaited LAPD probationary officer Stephanie Lazarus in 1984. In March, when she first arrived in Hollywood, Gates had been LAPD chief for almost six years. His national profile was on the rise. Los Angeles was poised to host the upcoming Summer Olympics. A new program Gates called DARE, for Drug Abuse Resistance Education, had started to send uniformed LAPD officers into local schools to warn kids about the dangers of drugs. Within a few years, the DARE program would spread to countless other police departments across the country. Nationally, the LAPD was still probably best known for its association with the TV show *Dragnet*. The LAPD's serial scandals of the 1990s—Rodney King, O. J. Simpson, Rampart—were still years away, although the seeds were already planted.

Among Stephanie's first field training officers was James Tomer, a Hollywood Division veteran. Tomer was in his midthirties and had been an LAPD officer for more than fifteen years, since the late 1960s.

There were only a handful of female officers assigned to Hollywood station when Stephanie arrived. One of the few women already there was a fellow probationary officer, Nina Greteman. Greteman had been at Hollywood for six months, since September 1983, when she graduated in the academy class before Stephanie's.

Later in life, Greteman would look back on her experiences as a probationary officer in Hollywood and see it for what it was: "a frickin' wild ride," in her words. Because the LAPD was required under the Fanchon Blake consent decree to sharply increase the percentage of women in its ranks, half of her academy classmates were female. When Greteman got to Hollywood, however, the ratio was jarringly different. Of the 150 to 200 patrol officers who she estimated worked at Hollywood when she started her probation there, Greteman was one of only four or five women.

Greteman's consciousness of her minority status and her eagerness to assimilate made her particularly attuned to the various cliques and subcultures that existed among her fellow officers. The proximity of the other, more glamorous Hollywood—the film and TV business, flush with money and other temptations—uniquely impacted the culture at Hollywood station. Sightings of movie stars were commonplace, since the stars and the cops shared the same turf. Some Hollywood officers even hung out with celebrities of the era, among them O. J. Simpson.

According to Greteman, several Hollywood officers had side businesses or part-time jobs that catered to the entertainment industry. Years later, when she saw the film *L.A. Confidential*, the moonlighting detective character Jack Vincennes, played by Kevin Spacey, reminded her of some of the officers she worked with at Hollywood. During roll call, officers openly discussed this or that lucrative sideline, which they seemed to prefer to police work. Greteman got the impression from some that the only reason they were cops was because it was their "in" for their off-duty gigs, which was their higher priority. Greteman thought, "Why are you even doing this job, if it's not that important to you?"

Another subculture at Hollywood station Greteman became aware of as a probationary officer was among those officers who worked narcotics. James Tomer, Stephanie's training officer, was part of that clique, Greteman recalls. Like the officers who leveraged their LAPD credentials into access, status, and money from the other Hollywood, some of the guys who worked narcotics seemed to Greteman to have their own special interests that motivated them.

In other areas of the city, the drug market was perceived as comprised of junkies and hypes, people who were downtrodden and socially undesirable. In Hollywood, by contrast, all different sorts of people were involved in the drug trade. The neighborhood was a magnet for young, attractive women, drawn by the ephemeral Hollywood but ill-suited for the real thing. Inevitably, some fell into the drug scene and ended up in a compromised position with the police.

Greteman imagined it would be easy in Hollywood for a narcotics cop to tell a girl, "I'll do you a favor and let you off, if you do me a favor later." As a female probationary officer, Greteman was not privy to any such exchanges of favors. But she would not have put it past some of the guys who worked narcotics at Hollywood, including Tomer, who struck her as shady and creeped her out. She thought it was strange that Tomer was always working narcotics, as if he liked it too much. Just being around him made her feel nervous, like she might get in trouble herself.

Greteman never really bonded with the few other women officers already at Hollywood when she began her year-long probation there. Six months later, when Stephanie arrived, Greteman was happy to see a fresh face, someone actually newer than her. Greteman and Stephanie were both assigned to PM watch, the patrol shift from midafternoon to midnight. Because they were both probationary officers, they never worked together as partners, but they often talked at the station during roll call or at the end of watch. Sometimes they also crossed paths in the field. If Stephanie and her partner took a radio call, and Greteman and her partner were out on patrol and not busy, they might show up as backup, or vice versa.

Greteman and Stephanie had a lot in common. They were the same age, about to turn twenty-four. Both were college graduates. Both were excellent, avid all-around athletes. Greteman played basketball at Santa Clara University, as Stephanie had at UCLA.

Greteman and Stephanie both graduated from high school in 1978, the same year American high schools and colleges were required to comply with Title IX, a landmark federal law that barred sex discrimination in athletic programs at federally funded schools. In practice, Title IX compelled schools to field female athletic teams. Equality for women athletes was just one prong in the larger national movement, ascendant in the 1970s, that demanded equal rights for women.

Women born too early for Title IX in high school, as Greteman and Stephanie were, had paltry opportunities to play organized youth sports, compared to boys their own age. At the time, girls were rarely encouraged to play team sports. When Greteman was growing up and wanted to play basketball, the only way she could play was with and against boys. Based on Stephanie's athleticism, Greteman figured they probably had very similar experiences growing up, roughing around and playing sports with guys.

Title IX ushered in a new era for women's sports just as Greteman and Stephanie began college, so they were part of the first wave of women to benefit from the sweeping changes. Athletic scholarships for women, formerly almost nonexistent, started to become more available. Women's college teams proliferated. Many more women than ever before got to learn what it was like to play sports competitively, be on a team, and be a good teammate, all stereotypically male experiences at the time. For Greteman and Stephanie, sports were more than an activity they excelled at and enjoyed. Sports were an environment in which they thrived.

When Greteman joined the LAPD, she discovered there were many women like her and Stephanie, former athletes drawn to police work. Greteman thought they enjoyed the excitement of the job. Women athletes were also less intimidated by the LAPD's fitness requirements and better conditioned to meet the physical rigors of the academy. Via team sports, they already understood partnership, teamwork, and the importance of having your teammates' backs, principles also fundamental to police work. During Greteman's academy training, she promptly internalized the imperative to always look out for her partner and fellow officers. Greteman felt the women in her class who had no background in team sports did not grasp that mentality as easily.

Greteman thought she and Stephanie were a lot alike when they met at Hollywood. Greteman saw that Stephanie got along well with guys, a prerequisite for success on the job, given the LAPD's culture at the time. Greteman believed Stephanie's athletic background helped her acclimate to police work. Stephanie did not act competitively with other women officers, as far as Greteman ever saw. Greteman thought Stephanie wanted to be accepted, to feel as though she belonged. Greteman believed all female officers felt that way. There were so few women at Hollywood that it was only natural to want to fit in.

Stephanie had a good reputation as a street cop, Greteman recalls. She had no doubt that Stephanie could do the job and would have trusted her in a dangerous situation, although they were never in one together, since they were never partners.

Greteman could tell the job was important to Stephanie and that she took it very seriously. Stephanie was interested in always looking sharp and having the best gear. The LAPD, for instance, issued ballistics vests to all officers that were of poor quality. The vests, supposedly unisex, were in fact designed for men's bodies. Greteman felt women officers looked like sacks of potatoes in them. Stephanie said she was going to buy her own, because she wanted to look good in uniform. She chose an expensive vest form-fitted for a woman's figure. Greteman thought it probably cost her two or three hundred dollars. Everyone wanted to look good in uniform, but Greteman felt Stephanie took it to another level.

To boost officers' physical fitness and morale and promote cohesion within the department, the LAPD fielded recreational teams in many sports. By the mid-1980s, as more women joined the force, this included a growing number of women's teams.

Greteman was already playing on the LAPD women's basketball team when Stephanie arrived at Hollywood. Unlike the men's team, which played traditional full-court, five-on-five basketball, the women's team played half-court, three-on-three. In 1984, most police departments interested in fielding a women's basketball team did not have enough female officers to play five-on-five.

The coach of the women's team was Jerry Stokes, an LAPD officer and academy instructor. Stokes had played high school and college basketball. After Stokes joined the LAPD, he played for several years on the men's team. A few years later, Stokes agreed to be the inaugural LAPD women's team coach.

Stephanie tried out and made the team. In the eyes of her coach, Stokes, her biggest strengths on the court were that she played tough defense and good team basketball. She hustled and had some offensive skills but was not a high-scoring player.

Greteman also regarded Stephanie as a good basketball player, very aggressive but also skilled and able to handle the ball. Some teammates struggled with their conditioning, but Stephanie was always in excellent shape. Greteman ranked Stephanie's athleticism in the top echelon of all female LAPD officers at that time. The team's games often got physical, which Greteman attributed to the players no longer being girls, as during college, but grown women and police officers.

Stokes's impression of Stephanie off the court was that she had a great personality and was always upbeat. Stokes thought she was well-liked and was considered a good teammate. He never had a problem with her during the time he coached her.

Stephanie did not share much with Stokes about her personal life. At least once or twice, she showed up to practice with a guy who Stokes assumed was her boyfriend. The same guy also came to their games some-times to watch her play. Stephanie introduced the guy to Stokes once, but other than his impression that it was her boyfriend, Stokes has no recol-lection of him. It may have been John Ruetten. In the early spring of 1984, when Stephanie joined the LAPD basketball team, John was still seeing Stephanie on and off and had not yet met Sherri.

The largest and most prestigious competition for LAPD athletes was the California Police Olympics, held annually in June. Only sworn police were eligible to participate. Law enforcement agencies statewide sent teams of athletes to represent them and compete for medals in more than forty different sports, from archery to wrestling. In men's basketball, the LAPD had long been the dominant team, gold medal winners at six straight Police Olympics from 1978 to 1983. The 1984 games were to be the first time that women's basketball was an official medal event as well. Naturally, Stokes and the LAPD women's team wanted to do as well as they could. They prac-ticed hard and ended up winning the silver medal that June.

Stephanie and Greteman often went on lunchtime training runs together. As they ran, they talked about work and their experiences at Holly-wood. Greteman was already halfway through her year-long probation, and six months closer to promotion than Stephanie. But in rank, and most other respects, they were in the exact same boat. Women police officers in the 1980s had to put up with a lot of crap and casual sexism. Greteman's time as a female probationary officer was often painful. Greteman believed it was something she and Stephanie both experienced, and bonded over.

It was during one of their runs that Stephanie confided to Greteman about a dilemma involving her training officer, James Tomer. Stephanie called Tomer an asshole and told Greteman, "He keeps saying he wants to sleep with me." Tomer was about ten years older than her. Stephanie said she told Tomer, "Hey, that's not me," but he continued to volunteer constantly that he wanted to have sex with her. Stephanie described him as relentless. She asked Greteman what she should do. Avoiding Tomer was not an option, since he was her training officer and they worked together as partners daily. Stephanie was unsure if she should go to her sergeant and report Tomer, her own training officer, or if that would just make things worse.

Greteman advised Stephanie to ignore Tomer's come-ons, finish her probation, and get the hell out of Hollywood. Tomer was a P-3 + 1 training officer. The +1 meant he was a senior lead officer, a rank higher than most other training officers at Hollywood. Despite Greteman's low opinion of him, it seemed to her that everybody at the station loved Tomer. She and Stephanie discussed what good it would do for her to initiate a personnel complaint against him. What would that really accomplish?

There was an axiom Greteman heard repeated by other officers at Hollywood, which Stephanie presumably heard as well: *Admit nothing. Deny everything. Demand proof.* It was a credo some LAPD officers lived by whenever allegations of misconduct arose. The saying reflected the "us against them," LAPD versus the world mentality that permeated the culture of the rank and file in the 1980s.

Greteman believed Stephanie's story about Tomer. At the same time, she worried that Stephanie would put her probation at risk if she reported him. She thought Stephanie would probably be reassigned to a new training officer, but from then on, her name would be mud. Greteman advised her, "Don't give in, just stick to your guns."

In the same conversation, Stephanie said she heard a rumor was going around the station that she was gay. The rumor may have been sparked by her rejection of Tomer's sexual advances. In the eyes of at least some of their fellow officers, refusing to sleep with this guy or that guy apparently meant you had to be a lesbian. What other explanation could exist for a female probationary officer to pass up the chance to have sex with her training officer? Stephanie and Greteman laughed about that.

Later during Greteman's probation at Hollywood, she also had occasion to work with Tomer. He told her as well, "I really want to sleep with you." Greteman thought, "Wow, he's hitting on everybody." She replied to Tomer, "Great, but it ain't going to happen. I appreciate the compliment." After that, she took to warning female officers newly assigned to Hollywood about him, "Hey, watch out for this guy."

With the exception of the one training run when Stephanie talked about Tomer, she was not very open about her personal life with Greteman. The women on the LAPD basketball team got along well and spent a lot of time together traveling to tournaments, but they did not delve much into each other's love lives. One reason was that some women on the team were gay. Greteman thought people knew but didn't talk about it. Within the LAPD back then, being gay was not something that was openly acknowledged, let alone discussed. Most conversations about romantic relations stayed superficial. Topics like messy breakups were avoided.

Stephanie was particularly guarded about her love life, Greteman felt. To the extent that Stephanie discussed it at all, she would say things like, "I just wish I could meet somebody nice," or "I'm going through a hard time," without going into specifics.

Greteman knew Stephanie had dated someone who wasn't a police officer, but little else about him. Stephanie did not mention John Ruetten by name to Greteman during the time they played basketball and worked at Hollywood. Nor did she go into detail with Greteman about the relationship, and why things hadn't worked out.

That the guy Stephanie had dated was not LAPD stuck in Greteman's memory because it seemed so unusual to her at the time. Most female LAPD officers who were single dated other cops, because that's who they were around.

Greteman got the impression Stephanie was looking for something different than the type of guys they worked with at Hollywood. Stephanie wanted to meet someone, be in a serious relationship, and get married. She was looking for her knight in shining armor, someone who would take care of her but was also her equal. Stephanie was athletic, strong-willed, and very independent. That she considered it beneath her to date cops, the same pool of men many of the women she worked with dated, made her seem a bit aloof to Greteman. Only later, in hindsight, did Greteman realize that despite all the time they spent together, she never really saw Stephanie develop meaningful relationships with other people, male or female.

Greteman visited Stephanie at home only once, for a housewarming party at her new condo in Granada Hills. Greteman was surprised and impressed by how nice Stephanie's place was, as well as the neighborhood it was in. Greteman thought, "This is a really cool place for someone so young." The condo made Greteman feel a little blue-collar compared to Stephanie. Most cops their age Greteman knew rented unremarkable apartments. That Stephanie already owned a nice place of her own made her seem more mature and accomplished. Greteman thought, "Look at you, Stephanie, you've got the world by the tail. Nice place, you're making good money . . . You go, girl."

In June 1984, Hollywood officers were rattled by the surprise arrest of one of their own. James Tomer, Stephanie's onetime training officer, was accused by LAPD Internal Affairs of narcotics theft and taken into custody at Hollywood station. It is unknown whether Stephanie was still assigned to Tomer at the time of his arrest or if she had a different training officer by then.

Unlike an ordinary citizen arrested for narcotics theft by the LAPD, the allegations against Tomer did not land him in a criminal courtroom. Because Tomer was a police officer, his arrest prompted a quasijudicial LAPD disciplinary trial known as a Board of Rights hearing.

The LAPD's disciplinary system was modeled after military justice, which is why a Board of Rights hearing resembles a court-martial. Internal Affairs conducts the proceedings. The allegations against the officer are itemized in a written complaint similar to a criminal indictment. Board of Rights panels consisted at that time of three LAPD command staff ranked captain or above. The accused is entitled to representation by a fellow officer or a private attorney hired at their own expense. A department advocate, also a sworn LAPD officer, serves as prosecutor and presents the department's case. Both sides can call witnesses and cross-examine them.

Because the Board of Rights is considered an administrative tribunal and not a court of law, the rules of evidence are looser and burden of proof lower than in a criminal proceeding. For a finding of guilt, the department must prove the truth of the charge by a "preponderance of the evidence," meaning more likely than not, much lower than "beyond a reasonable doubt," the standard for a criminal conviction. Officers found guilty can appeal the decision to the Los Angeles Superior Court.

Tomer's Board of Rights hearing was held in November 1984, five months after his arrest. Stephanie was among the witnesses called to testify. Because transcripts and other records from Tomer's board are no longer publicly available, it is unknown which side called Stephanie as a witness, the LAPD or Tomer. Also lost to time are the details of what she testified about and whether her testimony was favorable or adverse to her former training officer's case. In the end, according to the *Los Angeles Times*, Tomer was acquitted on all charges.

In June 1985, seven months after Tomer's departmental acquittal, he filed a federal lawsuit against LAPD Chief Daryl Gates, the City of Los Angeles, and four other officers including Raymond Lombardo, the Internal Affairs sergeant who had led the investigation against him. Tomer alleged in the lawsuit that he was framed for narcotics theft by the LAPD. Tomer sought damages of $10 million. Another two years passed before Tomer's case went to trial in federal court, in 1987.

The court file for *Tomer v. Gates* was apparently destroyed in the mid-2000s, in a scheduled purge of old court records. The only record that survived is the docket, a bare-bones list of all the court filings and proceedings in the case. Stephanie's name does not appear in the docket, nor is she listed among the witnesses who testified at the trial. Tomer prevailed in court and was awarded $55,000 by the jury, $5,000 in actual damages for the "humiliation and degradation" produced by his arrest, plus $50,000 in punitive damages. The city also had to pay Tomer's attorney's fees, which totaled $42,000. The *Los Angeles Times* reported that it was the first time an LAPD officer had successfully sued the department's Internal Affairs Division.

The *Times* ran three articles about Tomer's lawsuit, the first in June 1985, when it was filed, and two more in 1987, after the verdict. In February 1987, the U.S. Court of Appeals for the Ninth Circuit issued a decision that included a brief account of "undisputed facts" about the LAPD's investigation of Tomer for narcotics theft.

According to the *Times* reports, and the facts as set forth in the Ninth Circuit decision, Internal Affairs started to investigate Tomer after a tip from another Hollywood officer, Luis Lopez. Lopez said he suspected Tomer was skimming small quantities of marijuana during arrests. In the lawsuit, Tomer claimed Lopez reported him because he had recently upbraided Lopez for using excessive force on duty in Hollywood. A sergeant in Internal Affairs, Lombardo, was assigned to look into Lopez's allegation.

Lombardo's investigative strategy was to give Tomer access to drugs and watch what he did. Lombardo set up a series of stings designed to tempt Tomer. Tomer never took the bait and booked whatever quantities of drugs he found. Lombardo nevertheless felt convinced that Tomer was skimming. The Internal Affairs investigation of Tomer escalated. Twice, Lombardo had undercover officers place a bag of marijuana in a planter on Hollywood Boulevard, where Tomer was on a foot beat. Both times, the sting was ruined when other uniformed LAPD officers arrested the undercover officers before Tomer walked past the planter.

Lombardo still did not give up. The sergeant asked a woman he knew, a receptionist at a TV station in Hollywood, to hold a package for him. Lombardo checked out a small amount of marijuana from police property, put it in a bag, and left it with the woman. Lombardo then had Tomer sent to the TV station to pick up "found evidence." Lombardo and his Internal Affairs team watched Tomer collect the package. After Tomer returned to the station and booked the drugs, Lombardo claimed the amount was six grams less than the amount he had checked out. Tomer was arrested, strip-searched, and jailed for an hour while Internal Affairs detectives searched his locker and truck. No marijuana was found. Nevertheless, Tomer was brought up on departmental charges for failing to book evidence.

Police departments differ from other types of institutions in that they are taxpayer funded. At least in theory, they are accountable to the public. For a police department to function effectively, it must enjoy the public's trust. The terms of the relationship are enshrined in the LAPD's own training manual, which states, *"The police at all times should maintain a relationship with the public that gives reality to the historic tradition that the police are the public and the public are the police."*

The LAPD's code of conduct reminds officers that the public trust, built painstakingly over decades, can be lost through the actions of a single officer: *"The public demands that the integrity of its law enforcement officers be above reproach, and the dishonesty of a single officer may impair public confidence and cast suspicion upon the entire Department."*

The LAPD, like all police departments, jealously guards its responsibility to investigate and discipline its own officers. The culture of the department is reinforced by the conduct of the chief and his top deputies, including the brass at Internal Affairs. If the department is seen as overzealous and uneven in responding to reports of police misconduct, the chief risks losing the support of the rank and file. On the other hand, if serious reports of misconduct come to light and the public begins to perceive the department as tolerant of corruption and excessively lenient in disciplining its officers, no amount of rank-and-file support is likely to save the chief's job. This is the line the chief must walk when confronted with a report of serious police misconduct.

Tomer's arrest at Hollywood station in June 1984, during Stephanie's assignment there as a probationary officer, resurrected uncomfortable memories in the station's squad room of an earlier scandal that had only recently finally subsided.

In December 1981, two Hollywood patrol partners, Jack Myers and

Ronald Venegas, were arrested for burglarizing video stores while on duty. Under questioning by Internal Affairs, Myers and Venegas named other Hollywood officers who they said had committed similar crimes. The press dubbed the scandal the Hollywood Burglars case.

Chief Gates ordered an Internal Affairs investigation that lasted for eleven months. All 250 officers assigned to Hollywood were interviewed. In May 1982, Myers and Venegas agreed to resign from the LAPD and plead guilty to burglary. A dozen other Hollywood officers resigned or were fired after they were implicated in crimes including burglary, receiving stolen property, and solicitation of prostitutes. Fifteen more officers kept their jobs but faced departmental charges for neglect of duty or conduct unbecoming an officer.

Gates addressed the episode in his autobiography. Gates saw a possible link between the misconduct and where the officers were assigned to patrol. Gates wrote, *"If you were to look at the number of officers who have gotten in trouble, either domestically or with the department, Hollywood division would be way up at the top. There is something about the place—an almost carnival atmosphere that suggests 'here, anything goes'—that causes good people to deviate from their normal conduct and their values. So you've got to have officers out there with a great deal of moral conviction and strength, willing to stay on the right track and keep others on the right track. Jack Myers and Ronald Venegas were two who got sidetracked."*

The LAPD fired the last of the twelve officers implicated in the Hollywood Burglars scandal in January 1983. Gates had sent a clear message down the chain of command to the Hollywood officers who survived the housecleaning: first, there would be harsh consequences if the department was embarrassed again; and second, this unseemly chapter of the LAPD's history was closed.

For the Hollywood officers, it was a reminder of another eternal and universal law of police department politics: shit rolls downhill. In February 1983, fourteen months after the scandal broke, an Associated Press story described poor morale at Hollywood. *"For officers in the division, the emotional fallout continues,"* the AP reported. One officer, Jerry Beck, said of his fellow Hollywood officers, "They are walking on eggshells, every one of them. How would you like to go to work after hearing, 'You will have a squeaky clean division,' that any little mistake you make is going to be thoroughly investigated? What he [Gates] is saying is that nothing can go wrong down there. If it does, someone is going to go down." A sergeant, Marco

Gupton, who was new to Hollywood, said of the atmosphere there, "These guys are living in a fishbowl. It puts tremendous stress on the people beyond anything you've ever seen."

Officers throughout the LAPD, not just in Hollywood, resented the taint of the scandal. A representative of the Police Protective League, the LAPD's union, told the AP, "It's all very depressing. It spills all over everyone. They feel sold out. They feel betrayed that they have to pay for some idiot."

Gates's longtime official spokesman, LAPD commander William Booth, meanwhile insisted that morale at Hollywood had fully recovered. "There was a period of time when the morale was exceptionally low," Booth told the AP. "I think it is not that way now. It's like a surgical patient who has just been told the malignancy has been removed and has been told to go about his life like he did before. It's a great feeling."

In March 1984, when Stephanie reported to Hollywood for her probationary assignment, the memory of the scandal was still fresh throughout the LAPD, and nowhere more so than at Hollywood station. The officers who made it through the scandal were ostensibly the lucky ones, but they still saw firsthand how easily lives and promising careers can be ruined by one bad decision. All of the Hollywood officers had risked their lives for one another. Many knew one another's spouses and children. Even the officers who had no knowledge of any wrongdoing and were cleared by Internal Affairs witnessed the implosion of their fellow officers' careers and the strain the scandal had put on their families.

The LAPD's sensitivity at the time to any hint of corruption at Hollywood may explain why Internal Affairs took the tip about Tomer's alleged theft of marijuana so seriously. It may also account for why Lombardo pursued the investigation with such determination, culminating in Tomer's arrest in June 1984.

Whatever Tomer's fellow officers believed of the allegations against him, it was clear to Stephanie and everyone at Hollywood that they were still under the microscope. The opening ceremonies of the Summer Olympics were a month away, and the eyes of the world were on Los Angeles. Gates knew that any allegation of police misconduct, especially in Hollywood, had the potential to blow up into a major scandal and shower the LAPD with negative publicity at the worst possible time.

To the perpetual exasperation of Gates and his spokesman, Booth, the press loved writing about bad cops and never passed up an opportunity to do so. The more salacious and sordid the allegations were, the more intense the media frenzy. Stories about the department's good works—murder mysteries solved, serial rapists apprehended—were underpublicized. Countless acts of kindness, heroism, and bravery by nameless thousands of LAPD officers went unrecognized.

Negative stories provided ammunition to the LAPD's critics and poisoned community relations. The press made it seem that the misconduct of a few officers showed the whole department was rotten. In most police scandals, as in most murders, the media lost interest and moved on to another story before all the facts emerged. Sometimes the accused cop was exonerated, months later, but those follow-up reports rarely made the papers. Meanwhile, the scrutiny and negative publicity made it harder for good cops—the vast majority of the department—to do their jobs.

Through the summer of 1984, life at Hollywood station moved on uneasily. Tomer's Board of Rights hearing was scheduled for November. Stephanie settled into her probationary assignment and found a lot to enjoy in her new job. Her life revolved around her work, which was exciting and different every day. She showed camaraderie with other officers and acted like she belonged.

Stephanie was less content with her personal life at the time. She had not seen much of John Ruetten since early summer, when he met Sherri. After John stopped calling, Stephanie's job kept her busy. Being a police officer made it hard to lead a conventional social life. Her hours were all over the place, not conducive to dating or meeting new guys. There were lots of guys on the job, some of who occasionally made passes at her. None apparently were up to Stephanie's high standards.

On September 4, six months to the day after Stephanie arrived in Hollywood, she received an official commendation: *"Letter of appreciation from citizen who was mistaken as a prowler, was drunk and not cooperating with officers. Officers showed patience and restraint."* On September 15, it was noted in her personnel file: *"Commended for devoting their time and effort to raise money for the Spastic Children's Foundation."* Not quite legendary police work, compared to what cops did on TV. But within the LAPD, Stephanie had started to make a name for herself.

In early November 1984, Stephanie began keeping a diary in which she recorded her day-to-day experiences as a young LAPD officer and, occasionally, more personal thoughts. An instructor at the police academy had encouraged Greteman's class, and possibly also Stephanie's, to write down their experiences in the field. The instructor told them, "Hey, this is an exciting job. You never know what you're going into. Your story may end up in print someplace. You could end up writing a book."

Only Stephanie knows what motivated her to start her diary and stick with it. When Greteman was in her midtwenties and a young cop, she had too many other interests and priorities in her life to want to sit down during her off-duty time and rehash what she did at work that day. Keeping a diary would have felt obsessive to Greteman, a sign that she was overinvested in the job and the LAPD.

Stephanie made the time. The level of detail in her diary entries suggests she wrote them contemporaneously, most likely right after she went off duty. Did Stephanie keep the diary purely for herself, to be able to look back later in life and remember what it was like early in her LAPD career? Did she think she might need it one day, in case questions ever arose about her whereabouts and activities on a particular day? Did she envision herself as destined for a fascinating career, perhaps one even worthy of a book?

Stephanie's diary is an extraordinary document for several reasons. Handscratched in cursive on ruled three-hole paper, the diary is a detailed account, in her own voice, of her on-duty experiences from 1984 to 1986, her first years on the job. Each entry is a snapshot of one patrol watch, told from her unique, privileged perspective inside the department. Stephanie's unguarded asides about her fellow officers paint a vivid picture of the LAPD's culture in the mid-1980s. Her diary also reveals, from one entry to the next, how she developed as a person and a police officer early in her career. More than thirty years after she wrote it, the diary offers a window into what was on her mind at the time, and occasionally even a glimpse at her soul.

Stephanie wrote at the top of each entry the LAPD car number she was assigned to that day; the hours she worked; her partner's name; the LAPD division; and the date. What is believed to be her first entry, on November 4, 1984, is typical:

6A97
1445-0030
BIEZO
HWD
11-4-84

In roll today we saw a film given by Daryl Gates regarding the Olympics. It showed a lot of ofcrs from Hollywood on their job assignments. The film also said we were going to get special Olympic pins.

First thing we did was to take a drunk to Jail Div. This black man was really drunk. Biezo was tapping him with his baton. The guy was so drunk he didn't feel it. So we booked him and that was it.

We were very busy all night. We answered a Landlord Tenant Dispute with this crazy woman. I went to search her and she was real jumpy so I hand cuffed her. I'm being [sic] to feel up on the signs people display when they might have something to hide. She had nothing on her but I didn't trust her.

We answered a call for a 415, man with a poss gun. He was gone.

I wrote a ticket to this Oriental woman who ran 3 stop signs, no lights, U-turn in a business district. She was pathetic.

Biezo one ticket early [sic] to a guy who was raring his wheels.

I ate lunch with Brown and Souza because Biezo brings his lunch.

We also handled a call for a group fight on the Blvd. (Hwd). No susp was found with a gun.

At the end of watch I took a burglary report from a woman on Franklin. The burglar was in her window (Second Story). I got an hour overtime.

<u>*P.S. NOTE*</u> *Tonight I was stopped by the Highway Patrol for going 68 M.P.H. I didn't get a ticket. It was funny because the ofcr had a partner and when he showed her my ID, she said "Oh Shit." I was the second ofcr. they had stopped. This was the second time I have been stopped—no ticket.*

Stephanie had a new partner for her next shift, on November 7, an Officer Chavez who was on a temporary assignment to Hollywood. One of the radio calls they answered was a family dispute. She recounted in her diary: "*The woman only spoke Spanish so we used a little boy to translate. Chavez told the woman if her husband hit her or her child he would come back and kick the guy's butt. I don't [think] Chavez is too well-liked by the Sgts. because he causes them too much paperwork. He is only on loan from Traffic Div. but they say he loves to taze people.*"

Stephanie was learning on the job, soaking it all in. Every day was different. On November 8, she and her partner ended their shift with a 415 call, the California penal code section for disturbing the peace. When they arrived at the location, they discovered the disturbance was a man sleeping in a vacant apartment. Stephanie climbed through a window, woke the man, and told him he had to leave.

On Saturday night, November 10, Stephanie and her partner, an officer Hal Collier, went looking for punk rockers in Hollywood:

> *We were going to search 1525 Cassil for punk rockers. We saw this kid exiting the building so we talked to him and ended up taking him to the Station for a possible warrant. Well the warrant was not for him. So we told him to tell the punk rockers to get out of the house. We went by later and went up in the building. I could hear voices. So we went up to the second story. I would have gotten a back up but Collier said then a Sgt. would come out and they'd all have to be booked.*
>
> *So I took one room, which happened to have about 10–15 kids in the room. I had my gun out and told them let me see their hands. We got them all to lay on the floor and then we let them go. One at a time, of course. The kid we stopped earlier was also in there. Hal was a little upset so we let the kid go last. Hal told him to run down the street to his friends as fast as he could.*

Later that same night, Stephanie and Collier got a 415 call for a group at the intersection of Yucca and Wilcox. Their unit was the second to arrive at the scene. Stephanie was tasked with searching the female suspects: *"The first female I searched must have weighed 220 lbs. She was a big black girl. Well I found a gun in her pocket. I immediately told her to get on her knees and I'd shoot her if she moved. It took me a few seconds to get the gun out. Then we moved into the felony prone position on all of them. This is the first gun I have found. At first I wasn't sure it was a gun. I was surprised I found it. She was so fat."*

Monday, November 12, was supposed to be a day off for Stephanie, before she received a 7:30 a.m. call at home from a lieutenant at Internal Affairs. Tomer's Board of Rights hearing was scheduled to begin that Friday morning. The lieutenant wanted her to come downtown to be interviewed and review her statements in advance of her testimony. At noon, Stephanie met with the lieutenant and an investigator at Internal Affairs. *"They were very nice,"* she wrote in her diary. Stephanie told Internal Affairs that she was scheduled to work late on Thursday, the night before Tomer's hearing. The lieutenant called Hollywood and told them to let her out early. Stephanie ended her diary entry by noting she earned two hours of overtime for going downtown to meet with Internal Affairs on her day off.

The next night, Stephanie was assigned to a task force rather than a patrol unit. She wrote, *"Today was my first night on the Mid PM task force. I was the only female in roll call. Roll call was really lax. First thing we discussed was what time to come into work tomorrow, because the guys are all going to mud wrestling for Robinson's bachelor party."* Later in the watch, over dinner at a Sizzler, Stephanie had to defend her assignment to the task force. *"The guys were asking me how I got chosen for this assignment. I guess it was because they needed a female and they picked me over the other P-I's and even some of the P-II's,"* she wrote.

Near the end of watch, the task force chanced upon a fistfight on Hollywood Boulevard. Stephanie got in the middle of it and ended up hitting one of the guys, the first time on the job she had ever used force. The guy she hit turned out to be a crime victim, rather than a criminal. *"I think I broke his nose if it wasn't already broken,"* she recounted in her diary.

Despite Stephanie's satisfaction with her job, she evidently was still hung up on John Ruetten. Stephanie wrote in her diary on November 14, *"Today we came in early because Robinson was having his bachelor party at the mud wrestling place on Western (Tropicana) . . . We got off work at 2200, we had to deduct 2 hours. I did go with the guys to the Tropicana. I was only going to stay for a while. I ended up leaving at 0100. It was fun. Sgt. Feely oil wrestled and Robinson mud wrestled. They held some dollars over my head so that the referee would kiss me. Then some of the guys would give me a dollar to kiss them. It was all in fun. They kept buying me daiquiris. I must have had 6–7. It was fun. Kept my mind off of John for a while anyway."*

On Friday morning, November 16, Stephanie went downtown to Internal Affairs for the first day of Tomer's board hearing. *"Tomer looked really upset,"* she recounted of her onetime training officer. When the day's proceedings ended at 4:00 p.m., she had not yet been called to testify, and was told to return Monday afternoon. Stephanie noted in her diary that she got almost eight hours of overtime for attending the hearing.

Later that night, John Ruetten's sister Janet stopped by Hollywood station. Stephanie was out in the field at the time and was notified. She returned to the station and met Janet. Stephanie did not reveal in her diary what prompted Janet's visit, nor what they discussed.

On Monday afternoon, November 19, Stephanie returned to Internal Affairs to testify at Tomer's board hearing, but after waiting for three and a half hours, until 4:30 p.m., was told to come back again in two days, on November 21.

Stephanie returned to duty on Tuesday evening, November 20. In her diary, she wrote, *"I took the guys cookies today. They all liked them."* Stephanie appeared eager to endear herself to the other officers on the task force. She was only a week into the assignment, so she was still getting to know "the guys," and vice versa. On the one hand, she seemed determined to act like one of the guys, as on her second night with the task force, when she tagged along to the Tropicana for Robinson's mud-wrestling bachelor party. On the other hand, passing cookies out at the station was a stereotypically feminine gesture, the opposite of the impression she likely made when she joined the bacchanal at the Tropicana.

Stephanie's diary suggests she was not guided by any deep-seated personal convictions or sense of purpose. To the contrary, she comes across as motivated primarily by her desire for acceptance and belonging, almost as if she wanted to be everyone's little sister. True north on her internal compass seemed to point to whatever she figured would make her fellow officers like her more, whether that meant watching mud wrestling or bringing cookies to work.

Beyond what Stephanie related in her diary, it is unknown what the officers she worked with thought of her as a person and a cop. Given social attitudes in 1984, especially within the LAPD, at least some of the officers whom she worked with likely resented her, simply because she was a woman. Since 1980, the number of women in the LAPD had more than doubled, from 178 to 491, and from 2.6 percent to 7.5 percent of officers. Because academy classes in the 1980s were more evenly balanced between men and women, every new class that graduated accelerated the department's transformation.

As in any institution, change threatened the status quo and rankled the old guard. Many officers believed women had no business on the job. Trust was a bedrock principle of police culture, yet at the time Stephanie joined the LAPD, women officers were often assumed to be untrustworthy until they proved otherwise.

Another potential reason for officers at Hollywood to feel threatened by Stephanie was her looming testimony at Tomer's board hearing. LAPD officers subpoenaed by the Board of Rights were required to testify. Officers who refused to provide testimony could be charged with insubordination. Stephanie was still a probationary officer, which meant she had few of the job protections longer-tenured LAPD officers enjoy. Probationers deemed insubordinate can be terminated without much red tape.

While Stephanie's refusal to appear at Tomer's hearing would have placed her in an untenable position with the LAPD, testifying carried other risks for her reputation and career prospects. It was a fraught proposition for any officer to offer testimony that could be used against a fellow cop. Stephanie was a twenty-four-year-old female probationer with barely eight months on the job. The department had ordered her to testify at the disciplinary trial of her former training officer, who had worked for several years at Hollywood station, where she was still assigned. Regardless of how her testimony went, she had another four months at Hollywood to get through.

The dilemma Stephanie faced was the code of silence that officers were expected to honor. Also known as the blue wall of silence, the code was one symptom of the "us versus them" strain of police culture that flourished whenever cops felt persecuted. Despite the power and authority wielded by the LAPD and its individual officers, the department cultivated a collective mentality of being perpetually under siege. It did not matter that there was no meaningful civilian oversight of the LAPD in the 1980s, as there is today. It mattered only incidentally whether the perceived persecutor was a civilian, a city politician, the media, the brass, or, as in Tomer's case, Internal Affairs. The widespread perception among the rank and file was that Internal Affairs often railroaded cops. From this cynical perspective, the Board of Rights was designed to deliver whatever preordained result the department wanted, irrespective of the actual evidence.

The scope of the problem within the LAPD was not exposed to the public until seven years later, in 1991, when the videotaped beating of Rodney King made national news. To quell the uproar, Los Angeles mayor Tom Bradley convened an independent commission to investigate the LAPD, chaired by future U.S. secretary of state Warren Christopher. The Christopher Commission report declared, *"Perhaps the greatest single barrier to the effective investigation and adjudication of complaints is the officers' unwritten 'code of silence.' . . . The code of silence influences the behavior of many LAPD officers in a variety of ways, but it consists of one simple rule: an officer does not provide adverse information against a fellow officer . . . Officers who do give evidence against their fellow officers are often ostracized and harassed, and in some instances themselves become the target of complaints."*

By November 1984, when Tomer's board hearing was held, Greteman had already completed her probation at Hollywood and transferred to a different division. Greteman heard that another female officer at Hollywood, a former roommate of hers, testified at Tomer's hearing and was ostracized for it, to the point that she was reassigned from Hollywood to another division.

Stephanie did not reveal in her diary how the prospect of her own testimony was perceived at Hollywood, or if she felt conflicted about it. She did not betray any concern about potential retaliation at Hollywood for breaking the code of silence. Stephanie may have genuinely believed that her testimony at Tomer's hearing would have no impact, positive or negative, on her career and relationships on the job.

It is also possible that Stephanie was not so naive, and that she sensed more tension around the Tomer case than she let on in her diary. Perhaps her behavior at Hollywood was calculated, a preemptive charm offensive prior to her testimony, to disarm any suspicions about her loyalties. Bringing cookies to work "for the guys" was a supremely nonthreatening gesture. Later in her LAPD career, Stephanie became known for handing out gift bags of chocolate-covered cherries at Christmastime. Her desire for acceptance appeared paramount. Stephanie closed her diary entry on November 20, *"I really like working the task force. I am the only girl. I have the locker room to myself. I hope they let me stay another DP,"* or deployment period.

Stephanie returned to Internal Affairs the next morning. The Board of Rights panel appointed to decide Tomer's case included LAPD captain Steven Gates, Chief Daryl Gates's brother. Stephanie recounted in her diary:

1700-2315
HWD
6Q21
MCDONALD
O'DONNELL
11-21-84

Today at 0900 hrs I was finally interviewed by Internal Affairs. I was interviewed for about 1 hr 15 min.

I sat at the front of a table facing three Captains: Captain Gates, 2 others I don't know. Tomer was sitting on my left w/ his representation and Internal

Affairs on my right. The questioning wasn't that bad even though the
Defense kept repeating questions and the Captains didn't like that they
didn't ask me anything about my personal life. Lt. Salicas thought I did a
pretty good job. Sgt. Lombardo was also doing the investigation on the
affair. I ended up with 13.8 overtime hours.

Stephanie's diary did not explain what possible relevance her "personal life" had to the charges Tomer faced. The nature of the "affair" Sgt. Lombardo investigated is also a mystery. It is unknown whether Stephanie ever reported to Internal Affairs what she told Greteman, that Tomer had pressured her relentlessly to have sex with him. Stephanie did not mention the affair or Sgt. Lombardo again in her diary.

Stephanie continued to chronicle in her diary the nightly circus at Hollywood station. The evening of her testimony at Tomer's hearing, she wrote, *"Sgt. Ferguson told us at about 2100 that we were taking a early out because there was a party in the Valley. The party was supposed to be nurses and officers . . . I did go to the party, and about the only people there were Hwd officers, not too many nurses and no doctors. McDonald bought my drinks. Thank God he was driving. I had about 6 Long Island Ice Teas."*

Stephanie had to work on Thanksgiving night, November 22. In her diary, she noted that she received a positive evaluation from one of her training officers. *"Collier gave me a rating. It was very good,"* she wrote.

Stephanie seemed at ease with the power and authority she wielded as an officer. How she and her partners treated suspects varied from night to night. In her diary for November 30, she wrote, *"We were on Highland south of Hwd Blvd and some guys ran across the street. We were going to write them when we found out they were fraternity brothers from Northridge. There were about 7–8 of them. So I got to decide what their punishment would be. I made them run backwards to the corner and the last person had to do 25 push ups. It was really funny to watch. Better than giving them a ticket. Then towards the end of the night there was a girl standing in the road way. We made her walk heel to toe to the corner, do 3 spins, and run across the street. That was also fun."*

In early December, Stephanie was reassigned from the mid-PM task force to morning watch, the overnight shift. Stephanie wrote that one of her task force bosses, Sgt. Feeley, told her he had tried to hang on to her but it was out of his hands. She later heard that the sergeant on morning watch specifically requested her transfer. Stephanie seemed to have sensitive antennae for department gossip.

On December 4, Stephanie overheard a rumor about Tomer's Board of Rights hearing, the outcome of which had yet to be announced. She wrote in her diary, *"Tomer only got 22 days off. Supposedly the only count they found him guilty of was Hargreaves' count of destroying evidence. I can't wait to see him. He'll be back to work on Friday."*

The next day at Hollywood station, there was a briefing on the Tomer case during roll call. Stephanie wrote:

HWD
1700-2315
Q21
O'DONNELL
12-5-84

During roll call Capt. Brown told us about the Tomer Decision. That he got 22 days. That he would be returning to work and so would Lopez. A lot of the guys were calling Louie a snitch. The Capt. said that Tomer destroyed the marijuana because the woman was an epileptic and he didn't want to add to her problems. This sounds to me like they believed that story. Who knows. The Capt. also brought up the Tropicana, the mud wrestling place, that Organized Crime was investigating it.

After roll call we went to Ah Fongs for Chinese food. It was free.

Mike told me they were going to take an early out which I didn't mind because I was feeling crummy anyway.

We wrote some parking tickets. Went to a rape in progress. No one was there. That was about it.

<u>NOTE</u> I got my rating from O'Donnell yesterday and it was a very good one.

Stephanie's final watch with the mid-PM task force, on December 7, was also the last day of a month-long "contest" with another Hollywood unit. Earlier in her diary, on November 13, she had described how the competition worked: each arrest counted for ten points, finding a gun was five points, writing a ticket was two points, and so on. Of her last night with the task force, Stephanie worked with two partners. She recounted, *"We ended up getting about 30 pts. We had gone back out at 2315 and it was raining so hard. We had asked Sgt. Feeley for an early out, so we could go see Beverly Hills Cop."* Their task force won the contest by several hundred points.

Stephanie loved competition in all its forms. As she and her fellow Hollywood officers watched the midnight showing of *Beverly Hills Cop*, she surely felt pride at their victory and her role in it.

Six months into her police career, Stephanie seemed to feel validated and accepted. Commendations and positive ratings were starting to pile up in her LAPD personnel file. Why wouldn't they? She was enthusiastic, eager to volunteer, seemingly always ready to help. She was in phenomenal physical shape, better than many of the guys on the job. She was a team player, not a complainer. Unlike so many women—and men—who couldn't cut it on the LAPD, Stephanie knew how to follow the program.

Stephanie's reassignment to Hollywood morning watch meant a new cast of veteran cops and training officers for her to get to know. Her real-world education and sense of what it meant to be an LAPD officer expanded partner by partner. Stephanie's diary narrated her daily assimilation into the LAPD and her gradual adoption of its "us versus them" worldview. Her writing is rich in detail but almost entirely devoid of emotion and empathy.

Sex tinged many of Stephanie's nights on patrol, although Hollywood's seediness and the nocturnal hours she worked were contributing factors. She worked Christmas night with a new partner, Russ Kilby. Stephanie wrote, *"I thought it was going to be boring working with Kilby, he was kinda quiet at first but then he got friendlier."* They did a couple of bar checks, first at a disco, Odyssey One, and later at a strip club. *"I didn't know they had totally nude strip places. Most of the men were Orientals. Russ wanted to leave because he was getting too excited . . . Kilby compliment* [sic] *on working w/ me. He said he wouldn't mind having me on the car. Also that I was one of the better probationers he had worked w/,"* she bragged in her diary.

On January 11, Stephanie crossed paths at Hollywood station with James Tomer. She had not seen him since she testified at his board hearing in November. Stephanie wrote, *"I saw Tomer today. Boy did he give me a dirty look. I was walking into the detectives' rooms and I happen to turn around. He was staring at me."*

Stephanie's new hours thwarted her ability to lead a normal social life. Morning watch was notorious for the havoc it wreaked on officers' personal lives. Stephanie was on duty when most people her age were either asleep or out having fun. Dating in Los Angeles was demoralizing enough for any-one who wanted a serious relationship but was not blessed with movie star looks. Working the graveyard shift made it even more difficult for her to meet someone she liked and go out on dates.

On January 27, Stephanie wrote in her diary, *"This was my last night of morning watch. I was pretty glad. Some of the guys mentioned something about going to day watch, just wise cracks. I really don't care, at least I'm off the watch. I really didn't mind the work but the hours just got me so tired."*

Stephanie's evaluations from her morning watch training officers were uniformly positive. Her year-long probationary assignment to Hollywood was due to end in March. At the end of January, she put in her transfer requests, which had to be approved by the captain at Hollywood.

Stephanie continued on morning watch for another few weeks. On February 4, she had a new patrol partner, an officer Wyeth. After midnight, they encountered a gruesome scene at a home in the Hollywood Hills. She recounted in her diary:

Wyeth was showing me around the hills and we got a call to go to a successful suicide. Well the suicide happened at 2200. We got there about 0140. The body was still there. The Vict was a 35 year old woman. She was a inspiring [sic] actress and I guess her husband had been nagging her. Well she put a rifle in her mouth 30/30 ammo and shot herself. Well I couldn't believe the body. She had shot herself on the front porch. Half her head was blown off her left eye was still there. Her brains were on the porch. It looked so unreal. The blood was in a big puddle.

Her husband apparently found her on the front porch. She yelled to him, "Do you want to see something pretty." The husband really upset. After the Homicide Det. (Lt. Proctor) left the man was balling [sic]. I got him something to drink. I felt really bad for the guy. I also washed the porch down because of the blood. The woman was really pretty. It was too bad. You know this really made me realize that none of my problems are as bad as hers. Also it didn't bother me because it looked so phony.

In her diary, Stephanie only superficially acknowledged the darkness she often encountered on patrol in Hollywood. What impact it had on her psyche is unknown. By her own account, the human carnage she witnessed as a young officer seemed unreal to her. Less than a year after she graduated from the academy, Stephanie already appeared desensitized to violence that would horrify most other twenty-four-year-olds.

Whatever her mental state at the time, almost a year into her LAPD career, Stephanie was likely in the best physical shape of her life. Unlike many officers, she was a gung-ho participant in the LAPD's athletic programs. Sports provided a way for young, ambitious officers to distinguish themselves to the LAPD brass. On February 24, she wrote, *"This morning we had a qualifying run for the Vegas run. I ran 5 miles in 37 minutes. There were 8 people, me and 7 guys. I came in 7th. I beat May at the end,"* referring to Dave May, her training officer at the time. To her superiors, Stephanie must have seemed the very image of a fit and enthusiastic female officer with a bright future in the LAPD. At the end of her diary entry that day, her last night on patrol with May, she wrote, *"Dave I think liked working with me and said someday he'd probably be working for me as Chief or something."*

On March 19, Stephanie completed her probation and was promoted to Police Officer II, which meant she was no longer required to partner with a training officer.

Stephanie's first watch as a full-fledged P-2 was on March 20. There was no fanfare at roll call to mark the occasion, but later that day, her captain congratulated her on her transfer from Hollywood. *"I did find out I am possibly going to Devonshire. They call it Club Dev, it's a retirement place. Devonshire was not one of my choices, but it might not be too bad, beats Jail Div or Communications . . . Since I live in Devonshire Div it at least will be only 5 min from my house. Who knows,"* she wrote.

Stephanie learned the following day that her friend and academy classmate Jayme Weaver was also headed to Devonshire. *"Everyone was congratulating me on going to Club Dev,"* Stephanie wrote.

Stephanie's last day at Hollywood was March 30. Although she had only just been promoted to Police Officer II, Stephanie already had her eye on the rank above it. In her final diary entry while assigned to Hollywood, she wrote:

HWD
DESK
0645—1530
3-30-85

I went to roll call dressed in uniform and Sgt. Dena asked who was taking the P3 exam. I raised my hand and had to go change my clothes . . . We got a ride from one of the ofcrs to Hollywood High to take the test . . . The test was 75 questions, multiple choice. One could miss 24, I think I'll come pretty close to that.

. . .

The desk wasn't that bad . . . A few people said good bye, but nothing spectacular.

Let me tell you a whole year has gone by and boy was it quick. I think of some of the things I've done and how did I ever stay awake on AM watch.

I really enjoyed the Supervisors in Hwd. Most of the guys were great.

<u>NOTE</u> I did make the Baker to Vegas run. I was 19th and I'll be running the only 3.7 leg which is a slight up hill.

At first I wasn't too excited about leaving, but things I guess work out for the best and I won't have to deal with some of the real weird, smelly people of Hollywood.

6

Stephanie at Club Dev

(March 31 to June 16, 1985)

Devonshire, and the suburban sprawl of the north San Fernando Valley, could hardly have been more different from the carnival atmosphere Stephanie left behind in Hollywood. Stephanie went from one of the most unpredictable and intense patrol assignments, Hollywood morning watch, to its polar opposite. Devonshire Division policed the upper-middle-class communities of Northridge, Chatsworth, and Granada Hills, which were as sleepy as Hollywood was raucous.

The LAPD's Valley Bureau consisted of Devonshire and four other divisions: West Valley and Van Nuys to the south, Foothill to the east, and North Hollywood to the southeast. Devonshire was the only Valley division without a standing unit dedicated to targeting street gangs. In 1985, Devonshire recorded 10,291 serious crimes, the second fewest among the LAPD's eighteen geographic divisions. The only division with fewer serious crimes that year, Harbor, was half the size and had thousands fewer residents than Devonshire. The neighboring Van Nuys division recorded more than twice as many serious crimes in 1985 as Devonshire did.

Unlike in busier LAPD divisions, where a never-ending stream of incidents meant officers continually bounced from call to call, Devonshire officers were able to patrol at a more leisurely pace. It was a point of pride at Devonshire that its officers' response times to emergency calls were among the fastest in the LAPD. Police relations with community residents, unapologetically antagonistic elsewhere in Los Angeles, were generally good in

Devonshire. A neighborhood watch program organized at Devonshire in the mid-1980s had eight thousand citizens on its rolls.

Roughly 180 officers worked at Devonshire station, a redbrick and concrete building at Etiwanda and Devonshire Avenues in Northridge. The station opened in 1973. Compared to most other LAPD stations in the 1980s, Devonshire was modern and comfortable, even cushy. Amenities for officers, unusual for a police station at the time, included a lounge, overnight facilities, a jogging track, and a weight room.

LAPD officers assigned to neighboring divisions were fully aware of the disparities in crime and working conditions between their own divisions and Devonshire. They often derided Devonshire as a "retirement village" or "country club" compared to their own rougher turf. Another expression of their resentment was the pejorative nickname they bestowed on the division, Club Dev.

The LAPD in 1983 introduced new communications equipment known as MDTs, Mobile Data Terminals, in its fleet of patrol cars. MDTs were small computer terminals with keyboards, which sat between the front seats and enabled LAPD units and dispatchers to exchange short text messages. MDTs promised to transmit information more quickly and securely than two-way radios.

When the LAPD introduced the technology, it planned to monitor the messages to ensure officers used the equipment for official messages only. The huge volume of MDT messages promptly overwhelmed the staff tasked with the monitoring. One month's messages, printed out, made for a tower of paper eleven feet tall. The monitoring was abandoned but the MDTs remained in use. Officers from other divisions who traded MDT messages with Devonshire units sometimes signed off with mild digs like "Keep it up out there in Club Dev," or "Good luck in Club Dev."

Not everyone at Devonshire enjoyed the teasing nickname. A Devonshire sergeant named Mark Krecioch decided to co-opt the label and try to turn it into a morale builder. Krecioch ordered "Club Dev" T-shirts and baseball caps and distributed them at the station. Devonshire officers wore them to golf tournaments, track meets, and other LAPD athletic events. Two young officers who had just completed their probation at Devonshire donated an oversized wooden CLUB DEV sign that was hung on the weight room wall.

Soon thereafter, a new patrol captain, Mark Stevens, arrived at Devonshire from the West Valley Division. Stevens was a big proponent of physical fitness. He believed exercise fueled officers' motivation and reduced on-the-job injuries. Stevens knew about the Club Dev moniker that Krecioch had co-opted to rally the division. The new captain decided to embrace the nickname as well. Stevens established a new perk he called the Club Dev Athletic Association. He decreed that three days a week, Devonshire officers could elect to work out—jogging, lifting weights, or practicing self-defense—for the first forty-five minutes of their shift instead of attending roll call.

Devonshire's laid-back pace and the captain's affinity for physical fitness made for a soft landing for Stephanie from Hollywood. Devonshire station was also a far shorter and less stressful commute for her than Hollywood. Her condo was only a few miles away. Around the time Stephanie began her new assignment, she rented the spare bedroom in her condo to Mike Hargreaves, an officer she knew from Hollywood. Hargreaves was single, but their relationship as roommates was platonic. Like Stephanie, Hargreaves was a dedicated athlete, into working out and lifting weights.

Of her first shift at Devonshire, Stephanie wrote in her diary:

0730—1630 (got out 1545)
DEVONSHIRE
DESK
3-31-85

Well today was my first day at Devonshire.

Lt. Finn welcomed me in roll call. Which was nice of him. He seemed a little friendlier. Block from my class was there. Roll call was real short, they didn't read off wanted susps just extra patrols.

This division has a lot of Burglaries from Motor Veh.

I worked the desk with a P-I. The P-I's at this division get to work one man cars, report cars, a little different than Hollywood. I took about 5 reports today. Lt. Finn just told me that I needed to put 'unknown' in the space for brand and serial number. He had to correct all of mine.

It was kinda fun at the desk. You could read the newspaper. I ate lunch there and then sat in the sun for Code 7. The phones don't ring off the hook and you don't have a lot of people coming into the Station.

I think I'll like it here for a while. Kinda a rest from Hwd.

Stephanie was learning that some standard operating procedures varied between divisions and supervisors. On April 5, she wrote, *"Today in roll call I got a report back which should have been titled Plain Theft (Petty). I had put Theft Plain. So Lt. Agedo sent me a form to notify me. One thing at Devonshire, they are very picky about their reports. Lt. Finn is particularly picky. But I think he kinda likes me because I work out during roll call. He mentioned this in roll call today, that more people need to work out."* Although Stephanie had worked at Devonshire less than a week, she already felt comfortable enough to step away during the workday when it suited her. She recounted, *"Today I took a car out for lunch and ran a few errands and came home for a few minutes . . . The difference between Hwd and Dev Desk is that at the Desk in Dev, we really try to help the people. In Hwd all you had time to do was transfer them."*

The following week, Stephanie applied to the department for an off-duty work permit, so she could work *"movie jobs,"* she wrote in her diary. Her new sergeant approved the request. Stephanie also submitted her application for the California Police Olympics, the 1985 edition of which would be held in June. Stephanie signed up to represent the LAPD in women's basketball, tennis, and track.

Over the weekend of April 13 and 14, Stephanie ran in the inaugural Baker to Vegas Challenge Cup relay race, an annual LAPD tradition to this day. Teams of officers from each of the LAPD's geographic divisions ran in stages, day and night, more than 120 miles through the Mojave Desert. The competition for the best time was intended to foster camaraderie within and between LAPD divisions. Captains, lieutenants, and sergeants trained and ran alongside patrol officers and detectives. Chief Gates attended the postrace award ceremony, held on a dirt roadside in Nevada.

Stephanie ran for the Hollywood team, rather than Devonshire, her current assignment. In her diary, she recounted of the race, *"It was fun. I went up Saturday with the Hollywood team . . . We got to Baker where the run started at about 1200. It was hot so I got my bikini on and laid in the sun . . . We started at 1830 . . . We were in first place for the first 5 legs. I ran at about 0430 on Sunday. By now we were in about 4th place. I had to run 3.7 miles slight uphill. I ran it in about 28:37. That was a good time for me. Central Div came in 1st . . . Hwd fourth . . . Devonshire came in 13th place. I was glad I didn't run with them. I think Devonshire was kinda mad at me for not running with them. The guys from Dev kidded me."*

Stevens, the Devonshire captain, took to calling Stephanie a "traitor" when he saw her at the station, for having run with Hollywood, she wrote in her diary.

Stephanie's first day in the field at Devonshire was April 18. She wrote, *"I went to Fuddrucker's and met another unit that was already there. It was 2 guys that I don't really know. But they were somewhat nice. I could tell not real thrilled. This place went 1/2,"* meaning she paid half price. As she left the restaurant, she noticed a parked car that she recognized: *"After lunch I was leaving the lot and I saw John Ruetten's car. Just my luck. I put a note on it and watched the car for 1/2 hour and checked up on it a few times. Well I find out from him later that he had gotten into Fuddrucker's at about 1210. Just about 5 minutes before I left."* At the time, in April 1985, John and Sherri had been a couple for nearly a year and were only a month from getting engaged. It is unknown when, and how, Stephanie found out from John what time he was at Fuddruckers.

Stephanie also noted in her diary that day an exchange she had with another female officer at Devonshire, Malena Heissel. Stephanie wrote, *"Heissel today said something about my tan. I said, 'Yeah, I was wearing my bikini at the run.' She said, 'Yeah, I heard.'"*

Stephanie worked the desk at Devonshire on April 20. In her diary, she made note of a rumor circulating about her role in Tomer's case. *"Here is an interesting piece of gossip which followed me from Hollywood. Sgt. Setty who used to work for Internal Affairs asked me if I had burned a Sgt. in Hollywood and I said no. He was the Sgt. in charge of the investigators in the Tomer case. I guess he had heard from some of the guys I burned a Sgt. in Hollywood. He said he would set the rumor straight,"* she wrote.

For lunch, Stephanie went to John Ruetten's brother Tom's apartment. Two days had passed since she saw John's car and left a note on his windshield. She wrote of her lunch at Tom's, *"His mom and Janet were there. I picked up some burgers at In and Out and took that over."* Stephanie did not elaborate in her diary about what was discussed during her lunch with John's mother and two of his three siblings.

The gossip she heard about the Tomer case, and what other officers were saying about her, was still on Stephanie's mind when she went to work the next morning, April 21. Her patrol partner was an officer named Jerry Smith. *"Smith drove. He didn't seem to be talkative, I think he must have heard the rumor,"* she wrote. After they went for coffee and doughnuts, Stephanie sensed a slight improvement in Smith's demeanor. *"I think Sgt. Setty must have talked to Smith about the rumor because he seemed more talkative,"* she wrote. At the end of her diary entry, she revisited Tomer's case again and noted the latest scuttlebutt: "<u>NOTE</u> *SGT. SETTY—The reason the Tomer Investigation was blown was because Louie Lopez opened his mouth in a bar and everyone at Hwd knew before it was announced.*"

On April 27, Stephanie was assigned to patrol by herself, which she had never done before. She recounted, "*I was working a L car which is a 1 man car. This is my first time working a L car. It's weird. You have to do everything yourself. Fix the car, do the log, use the computer. It was kinda neat. So for the first 2 hours we worked the street intersection of a parade for the little leaguers. That was fun. We'd go from intersection to intersection playing leapfrog. Then after the parade I did whatever I wanted. I stopped by the house, checked the car bazaar lot for Corvettes. My first call was a Code 30. Well I was at home and the call was on Dearborn & De Soto. It took me 25 minutes to get there.*" Stephanie also wrote that she visited two friends that day while on duty.

Stephanie's diary suggests she treated the responsibility of patrolling alone as a license to do as she pleased. On May 2, she worked an L car, and wrote, "*Work out day today. First call that came out was a child abuse invest. I bought the call and was on my way when I got flagged down by a motor ofcr. They were filming a movie so I went in and they gave me some orange juice. The movie was being filmed at Devonshire & Owensmouth at the lumber yard. I hung around about 1/2 hour. My call was cancelled.*"

Stephanie was off duty on May 4, her twenty-fifth birthday.

Although still a patrol officer, Stephanie showed an early interest in detective work. On May 7, she wrote, "*No roll call today. It was work out day. I worked by myself today. First thing I did was to get about 10 traffic warrants from Detective Dillard. I wanted to arrest some people so he gave me some of his warrants. I'd be doing his work but that's ok. It gave me something to do. I went to 3 different addresses and of course no one was home. But it was interesting going to the addresses because I'd get different answers for where the people were at. If anything it kept me busy.*"

Stephanie was assigned to an L car again on May 10, which enabled her to visit more friends while on duty. Stephanie went by John Ruetten's apartment, where she met Sherri Rasmussen, apparently for the first time. In her diary, Stephanie wrote, "*I worked by myself, which I didn't mind. I went and visited Russ Kilby. I use [sic] to work in Hollywood with him. I also visited Herb Kraus. I really can't remember if I did anything else work wise. I did visit John Ruetten, but his girlfriend was over.*"

Stephanie did not mention in her diary her impressions of Sherri, nor whether she thought they might meet again.

On Sunday, May 12, Stephanie wrote, "*Roll call was real short because it was Mother's Day. I worked by myself, which was alright with me. I could do what ever I wanted. First thing I did was to check out the cars at the Car Bazaar. No Corvettes for me. Then I went across the street to visit Tom and Jerry. Then I went and visited Smita Patel. Her dad recognized me. They had some family from India, so when Smita's cousin opened the door, I told her Smita was under arrest. She looked scared to death. Smita's mom gave me some OJ and I sat for about 1/2 hour and talked with her family. Then I had to make a death notification. The Station had the wrong name, but I found the guy, great detective skills.*" Stephanie took lunch at home, time she also used to pack for her upcoming vacation, a four-night party boat cruise to Ensenada, Mexico.

Stephanie's cruise was aboard the *Azure Seas*, a faded ocean liner advertised as "a floating fiesta." The ship's amenities included a disco, multiple bars, and a movie theater. Stephanie was joined on the trip by two female friends, one of them her cousin, and her roommate, Mike Hargreaves. The four friends embarked from Los Angeles on Monday evening, May 13. The cruise's ports of call included Catalina Island and San Diego before it returned to Los Angeles on Friday, May 17. Stephanie did not describe the cruise in her diary, but her photos suggest she enjoyed her vacation.

In addition to traditional pastimes like sunbathing, shuffleboard, and Ping-Pong, the *Azure Seas* offered passengers some novel activities, including skeet shooting. Stephanie and Hargreaves both tried it, firing shotguns at clay pigeons launched into the air over the Pacific Ocean. As LAPD officers, they had far more firearms experience than the typical passenger. Stephanie's accuracy with the shotgun impressed Hargreaves. Based on her skeet shooting he witnessed, Hargreaves considered her an expert-level shot.

Stephanie and Margaret Ruetten in front of the Azure Seas, *May 1985*

When the *Azure Seas* docked in San Diego, John Ruetten's mother, Margaret, came down to the harbor to see Stephanie. Stephanie took her aboard and they posed for photos together. It is unknown whether Stephanie mentioned to John's mother that she had visited him just a few days earlier, while his girlfriend was over. Nor is it known whether they talked about John, his and Stephanie's relationship, or his relationship with Sherri. Less than two weeks after Stephanie and Margaret's rendezvous in San Diego, John and Sherri announced their wedding engagement to their parents on a sailboat in the same harbor.

On May 20, after she returned from the cruise, Stephanie got the results of the Police Officer III exam she took at the end of March. In her diary, she wrote, *"I found out that I didn't pass the P3 exam. I got a 43 and one needed a 48. Oh well next year."*

Stephanie had three days off for Memorial Day weekend, Friday to Sunday. It was on Saturday, May 25, that John and Sherri announced their engagement to their parents. Over the weekend, other family and friends learned John and Sherri's news. Stephanie did not hear about John's engagement until later.

On June 4, Stephanie recounted, *"I was supposed to work with Kirk, but when Sgt. Reihm called roll I was working with Heissel. I guess the guys really don't like working with females. Before roll call I talked to Sgt. Rebhan and I'm in charge of organizing a run against Foothill. The run is on June 22 just before the Police Olympics. So I'm not going to run. I drove. First thing we did was to get some coffee. Then Heissel wanted to see one of Sgt. Rebhan's Rottweilers so we went up to his house. We went by the hospital. I saw Mark Currie again."*

Currie was a doctor friend whom Stephanie visited often over the next year, according to her diary. Although the June 4 mention of Currie is the first of many in her diary, Stephanie never described the nature of their relationship or what it entailed, beyond her frequent visits to the hospital where Currie worked. Her diary is vague as to whether her interest in Currie was strictly platonic, or if she desired something more with him, as in her similarly ambiguous relationship with John.

Stephanie's long-standing dream of herself and John as a couple was dashed the same day, June 4, when she learned of his engagement to Sherri. Stephanie did not reveal in her diary how she heard the news. Of her watch with Heissel, she wrote, *"We really didn't do much. I really didn't feel like working. I found out that John is getting married. I was very depressed, this is very bad. My concentration was –10."*

Mike Hargreaves, her roommate, never forgot how upset Stephanie was when she came home, late one night, after she first learned of John's engagement.

Stephanie had mentioned John to Hargreaves about a half dozen times since he'd moved in with her in March, a few months earlier. They never sat down for a discussion where Stephanie poured her heart out, but she did tell Hargreaves that she loved John, and that John was her idea of a perfect guy. Although Hargreaves had never met John or seen him come pick up Stephanie for a date, his understanding from her was that they had dated for quite some time through college, and that they were still dating. Stephanie had also told Hargreaves that John had another girlfriend, who worked as a nurse at a hospital. Hargreaves had told Stephanie that it seemed to him that John was using her, trying to go out with two women at the same time.

Hargreaves himself was single. Once or twice while they lived together, he had made a pass at Stephanie. She had politely rebuffed him, and he had taken it in stride. There was no lasting damage to their relationship as roommates. Like Stephanie, Hargreaves worked irregular hours and spent a lot of his free time working out. Sometimes they trained together and went to the Cal State Northridge track to run intervals. Hargreaves considered Stephanie a friend and felt she was open with him, but he had never thought of himself as one of her close confidants.

Hargreaves was asleep in his bedroom, well after midnight, when Stephanie came home and woke him up. He saw her in his doorway crying. Through tears, she told him that John had broken up with her.

Hargreaves had seen Stephanie become emotional about John before, and even cry on occasion, but never this upset. He could tell she wanted someone to console her, so they talked for twenty or thirty minutes. Stephanie said she had been out with John and he wanted to end the relationship definitively because he was going to marry someone else. Hargreaves tried to comfort her as best he could. Talking through it seemed to help.

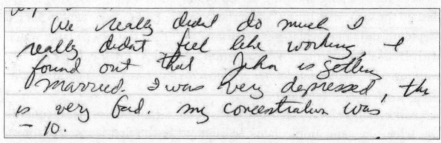

Stephanie's diary excerpt on learning of John's engagement, June 4, 1985

Stephanie suggested they do some buddy sit-ups to burn off energy. Hargreaves got out of bed and they sat across from each other on the floor. They interlocked their shins to brace themselves and alternated sit-ups. After fifteen minutes of buddy sit-ups, it seemed to Hargreaves that she had calmed down.

Amid the turmoil in her love life, Stephanie continued to make her patrol rounds. On June 9, she recounted in her diary, "*We got a call at Roscoe and Winnetka, that there was a blk man with a knife. Well we got there and all these blk women were screaming. It turned out to be a neighbor dispute and the blk woman had a knife . . . One of the neighbors did shoot off a shotgun, which we confiscated. I had to guard this big fat man while everyone got interviewed. The man said, 'They leave a woman like you with me.' I said if you try anything I'll shoot you.*"

Of her watch the following day, June 10, Stephanie wrote, "*We were supposed to patrol Bryant St and Vanalden and write all kinds of tickets to the Mexicans because they have been creating so many problems.*"

The casual disrespect that Stephanie and other officers doled out to the public, as chronicled in her diary, stood in stark contrast to their thin-skinned reaction to insults and provocations. On Saturday night, June 15, she and her partner, Terry Kibodeaux, spent most of their watch breaking up parties. She recounted in her diary, "*We went to one on Rayen and Andasol. There were probably 400–500 kids. Everything was going smoothly until some kid yelled 'Fuck You' to the Police. Terry saw the kid and we took off after him. He ended up having a $850.00 misd. warrant from Santa Monica. So we took him to jail. Then we handled a few more party calls.*"

The next day, June 16, news broke of the incendiary civil suit filed by James Tomer, Stephanie's former training officer, against the LAPD. The *Los Angeles Times* reported, "*A Los Angeles police detective filed a $10-million lawsuit in federal court Friday accusing fellow officers of trying to 'frame' him on charges that he 'habitually stole' narcotics during drug investigations. James Tomer, 37, a 17-year veteran now assigned to the Hollywood Division, named Police Chief Daryl F. Gates as a defendant along with Officers Luis Lopez, Raymond Lombardo, Michael Ranshaw and Jerry Bova.*"

Tomer's attorney was Stephen Yagman, a forty-year-old civil rights lawyer originally from Brooklyn. Yagman's specialty was suing Southern California law enforcement agencies. His personality was brash and unrelentingly pugnacious, whether he was in the courtroom, conducting a deposition, or addressing a cluster of press microphones. Yagman portrayed

his clients to juries and the media as victims of brutal and corrupt authorities, and presented himself as fighting tooth and nail for justice and
accountability. By the mid-1980s, Yagman had become the leading legal
bête noire of the LAPD brass and the Los Angeles City Attorney's Office,
which had the often unenviable responsibility of defending the LAPD
against lawsuits.

Yagman was also widely detested by the LAPD rank and file, despite
the fact that he sometimes represented individual officers, like Tomer,
against the department. Stories circulated among officers about Yagman's
rapacity and underhanded tactics. According to LAPD lore, Yagman would
subpoena officers to appear for sworn depositions at his office, an expen-
sively appointed spread high above Wilshire Boulevard. Officers had to sit
in a chair that faced a video camera. Hung on the wall behind the camera
was an oversized framed oil painting of a uniformed police officer. The
depiction was true to life, except the officer in the painting had a Pinoc-
chio nose. Officers had to look straight at it while they answered Yagman's
questions. Before he started the deposition, he sometimes liked to ask officers to look around at how nicely furnished his office was. Yagman would
inform them that all of it was paid for by the LAPD and Los Angeles police
officers. Only then would he begin the deposition.

In the *Times* report on Tomer's lawsuit, Yagman explained that he had
named Chief Gates personally as a defendant, "mainly because he is the
head man in a department whose custom and policy is to have an Internal
Affairs Division that is overzealous in making cases against officers who are
accused by fellow officers without respect to the likelihood of guilt."

If Stephanie read the news about Tomer's lawsuit, or heard about it at
work, she made no mention of it in her diary. She seemed preoccupied with
her personal life. On June 16, the same day Tomer's lawsuit hit the papers,
she wrote in her diary, *"I really didn't feel like working, too stressed out about
John. I have had a real hard time concentrating these days. So I called up
and said I didn't feel well, could I have a T.O. They gave it to me."*

7

The Hospital Confrontation

(June to August 1985)

One evening a few weeks after Stephanie learned of John's engagement, he received a phone call from her at his apartment. John was in his last month of living alone. He and Sherri had already decided he would move into her condo after her roommate, Jayne, moved out on July 1.

John recounted Stephanie's call during a tape-recorded interview he gave LAPD detectives in 2009. Three years later, in 2012, John also testified in court about their interactions that night in early summer 1985, weeks after he asked Sherri to marry him.

According to John, Stephanie was crying when he answered the phone. "I want to see you," Stephanie told him. She asked him to come over to her place so they could talk in person. John went to see her that same evening, without telling Sherri.

When John arrived, Stephanie was still crying. He had known her for almost seven years, and although they were best friends for much of that time, John had never seen her so upset.

Stephanie confessed to John feelings that she had never expressed to him before. She said she loved him and wanted to be with him, not as friends but in a real relationship. She was upset that John had decided to marry someone else. She said this was her last shot before he got married to tell him how she really felt about him.

John felt that he had always been very clear with Stephanie about their relationship. In John's mind, they were just friends and had no future together. Years earlier, Stephanie had once told John, "I don't necessarily want to get married. I'm not that into kids." Even back then, John already knew he wanted to get married and start a family. John believed that was why people got married, to have kids. He always knew that was what he wanted.

As John listened to Stephanie pour her heart out to him, he wondered if she assumed he didn't already know her true feelings. She had never bared her feelings to him so directly, but John had known for some time that Stephanie wanted a more serious relationship than he did. But from the moment John met Sherri, about a year earlier, he knew it was Sherri he wanted to be with and start a family with.

John told Stephanie they could not be together as a couple because he was going in a different direction. John thought she seemed more upset than angry. He wanted to console her but had trouble finding the right words. Stephanie told him more than once that she wanted to have sex with him, one last time.

John later rationalized that he didn't know how else to calm Stephanie down. He could tell that she had had no closure and felt bad about his role in that. He wanted to make her feel better. As so many times previously in their protracted, ambiguous relationship, one thing led to another. John relented, and they ended up in bed.

Afterward, John dressed and went home to his apartment. When he next spoke with Sherri, he did not tell her he had visited Stephanie at her place, or about the feelings Stephanie had confessed to him, or that they had had sex, one last time.

Within a few weeks, John moved in with Sherri in Van Nuys. Nels Rasmussen signed a quitclaim deed in Tucson on June 25 that transferred ownership of the condo to "JOHN A. RUETTEN, a single man, and SHERRI R. RASMUSSEN, a single woman, as joint tenants." The deed also noted: THIS IS A BONAFIDE GIFT AS THE GRANTOR RECEIVED NOTHING IN RETURN. As part of the real estate transaction, John and Sherri obtained a new mortgage to replace the one Nels took out when he bought the condo for Sherri in 1980. According to Nels, when Sherri and John refinanced in 1985, the condo's value had appreciated about $30,000 from what Nels had paid for it five years earlier.

Stephanie's work served most days to distract her from John and her broken heart. The California Police Olympics were also coming up. Stephanie trained religiously, noting in her diary every time she hit the gym at the Devonshire station.

Stephanie ran into Tom Ruetten, John's brother, while out on patrol Friday night, June 21, with her partner Terry Kibodeaux. She wrote, *"Tonight was pretty slow. There were a few parties. In fact I saw Tom Ruetten at one. The party he was at was real quiet but a guy opened the door and then closed it, so Terry got all huffy and wanted to go break up the party. I really didn't see any problems with the party. So we walk up and he tells this guy and girl sitting on a car to break it up. Well I noticed it was Tom. I said Tom, Be cool, so he left. We talked a bit."* Stephanie did not reveal in her diary whether she and Tom discussed John or his wedding plans.

From June 25 to 30, Stephanie represented the LAPD at the California Police Olympics. The 1985 games were held in Oxnard, an hour from Los Angeles. Most of the players on the inaugural LAPD women's basketball team, which won silver in 1984, returned for 1985, including Stephanie and Nina Greteman, her friend from Hollywood. The team also benefited from two new additions, officers Pam Roberts and Anita Ortega, both former college basketball players. Ortega was an All-American at UCLA and played professionally before she joined the LAPD.

Ortega considered Stephanie a friend but they were not particularly close outside of basketball. Ortega never socialized with Stephanie or visited her at home. Her impression of her was that she was a fun, nice, outgoing person who laughed a lot and always seemed upbeat. She never suspected Stephanie to be the type of person who would hurt someone intentionally. Ortega never saw her lose her temper or use profanity. Stephanie seemed to get along well with everyone else on the team.

What Ortega enjoyed most about playing basketball with Stephanie was how feisty and competitive she was. She wasn't the best offensive player, but she played tough, aggressive defense and her energy level was super high, verging on hyper. Whoever she guarded, she was always up in their face, giving 110 percent. Stephanie did not talk trash, but her intensity frustrated opposing teams. She was exactly the type of player Ortega loved to have as a teammate but would have hated to play against.

Although Ortega knew little about Stephanie's personal life at the time, she recalls Stephanie mentioned having a boyfriend from UCLA whose name was John. Ortega never learned any other details about John or the relationship. Based on how Stephanie talked about him, Ortega believed the relationship was ongoing. She never got the sense Stephanie was sad or upset about her love life, or that there were problems in the relationship. To the contrary, Ortega thought Stephanie and John were looking forward to getting married.

Greteman was not as close with Stephanie as she had been a year earlier, when they were both at Hollywood. Greteman had since been reassigned to Hollenbeck, and Stephanie to Devonshire, which meant they saw much less of each other. Stephanie did not discuss her personal life with her at the 1985 Police Olympics, as far as Greteman can recall.

The team's opening game in Oxnard was against the Alameda County Sheriff's Department. According to Stephanie's diary, the LAPD won 110 to 48. Their next opponents were their crosstown rivals, the Los Angeles County Sheriff's Department. Jerry Stokes, the LAPD coach, recalls it was always a tough game when they played the sheriffs because both teams had good athletes. In Greteman's opinion, the sheriffs were a very physical, mean, dirty team. The game grew so heated that a benches-clearing fistfight erupted. Greteman recalls the fight broke out while the sheriffs were shooting a free throw. Greteman said something under her breath to one of the sheriffs to goad her. Whatever she said worked, because the player responded by taking a swing at her. Greteman recalls that Stephanie jumped in, and possibly threw a punch at somebody herself, before order was restored.

Greteman was shocked because she always thought of Stephanie as goofy and bubbly, not quick to fight. She glimpsed that Stephanie was a tough cookie under the surface. It was not one of Greteman's prouder moments, to have played a role in instigating a fistfight at the Police Olympics, but she appreciated that Stephanie was fiercely loyal and defensive of her teammates. Greteman chalked the incident up to Stephanie's being very competitive, as they all were.

Stephanie mentioned the game against the sheriffs in her diary. *"One of their players punched me in the lip, I guess I was guarding her too closely or something like that. She got thrown out of the game. We played them again for the Championship and beat them for the gold,"* she recounted.

In addition to basketball, Stephanie also competed in women's doubles tennis. Stephanie and her doubles partner lost in the finals to a team from the Escondido Police Department.

Despite the two medals she won, Stephanie wrote in her diary that the Police Olympics *"weren't that great."* She was surprised and disappointed to have been passed over for the LAPD's track and field team. Stephanie blamed the snub on racial politics within the department: *"I was supposed to run track but somehow L. Brown told Coach Banks that I wasn't running and he scratched me from the team. I knew things were political but I didn't think they were that political, in the meaning of blacks. So I told him fine and walked away."* Without Stephanie, the LAPD women's track team won gold in the 100-meter, 200-meter, and 400-meter races, and both gold and silver in the 400-meter and 1600-meter relays. Stephanie's roommate, Mike Hargreaves, won gold in the decathlon. Stephanie made no reference in her diary to her fellow officers' achievements.

Another disappointment Stephanie noted in her diary was the lack of socializing she did with the other athletes. The fact that Stephanie had stayed with a friend in Camarillo, ten miles from Oxnard, may have been a factor, she wrote. Of her experience at the Police Olympics, she recounted, *"Overall it was OK. I didn't do anything at night because I didn't have anyone to do things with. No good parties."*

Stephanie partnered with her friend Jayme Weaver on July 3. In her diary, she wrote, *"In roll call tonight Sgt. Flores was talking about how chicken shit Devonshire is about statistics. It's really a joke. Also we can't get off early at 0230 anymore. Lt. Finn found out and he's a real stickler for rules."* To begin their watch, they handled a few burglar alarm calls. *"Then we went to a fire at Louise and Andasol, very close to Mark Currie's parents' house,"* she wrote, referring to her doctor friend. Stephanie mentioned Currie in her diary more often starting in July 1985. Over the next few months, according to her diary, Stephanie sometimes visited Currie at the hospital where he worked multiple times a day.

Had Stephanie been assigned to a busier, grittier area of Los Angeles, she might not have had the time to visit friends and do whatever she pleased while she was ostensibly on patrol. Her diary laid bare the languid tempo she enjoyed at Devonshire and the trifling nature of much of the police work she performed while on duty.

On July 5, the only radio call she received on patrol was a noise complaint. Stephanie wrote in her diary, *"We went to a party and told all the kids to keep quiet. Well, we went back about 15 minutes later and saw 3 boys were drinking and because they had such bad attitudes, one kid kicked over a bottle after I told him to put it down on the ground, that we arrested them and took them to the Station."*

On July 17, Stephanie wrote, *"We were going to take an early out tonight. Everyone on the unit because Sgt. Flores brought beer to celebrate the Juvenile raid last week. I invited them all over . . . All the guys came over to my house and we drank and ate some appetizers until about 0545. It was nice to have them over."*

Stephanie appeared to want to move past her relationship with John. On occasion, she went out of her way to flirt with other guys, as on July 18, when she was assigned to patrol with her friend Jayme Weaver. Stephanie's style of flirting was juvenile and reminiscent of how she acted toward John, back when they were dormmates at UCLA and she used to play pranks on him. She recounted in her diary, *"We had work out day today. I drove. First thing we did was go to the Academy to qualify for the Shot Gun . . . After shooting we stopped by the Fire Station in Van Nuys and I visited Walt Wilmington. The firemen were funny. They jumped in our car. I went inside and Jayme grabbed everything removable. Then as we left the fire station it sounded like tin cans were tied to our car. Well they had put bolts in our hub caps. It was funny. Well we took out some of the bolts. Then they got called away to a fire. We went to their room and put all the helmets and Playboy magazines on their beds and some toilet paper."*

Two days later, on July 20, Stephanie wrote, *"I went and visited the Fire Station. Wilmington was there again and again the guys put bolts in my hub caps and also grease on my handle."*

After a few apparently downbeat days off, Stephanie returned to work on July 25. She wrote in her diary, *"Kirk drove. It was fun to come back after 4 days off and see Kirk. I really looked forward to seeing him, because he cheers me up."* Near the end of their watch, they answered a radio call for a robbery at a McDonald's. They drew their weapons as they left their car, which seemed to thrill Stephanie. *"Kirk had the shotgun. False alarm. When I handle calls like this it reminds me of the movies, us sneaking up with guns drawn,"* she recounted.

The next night, July 26, she partnered with two officers, Pelt and Pond: *"First thing we did out of roll call was to go by the hospital. I had to see Mark. The guys were giving me a real hard time because he's married. Then we went and picked up Pelt's check from the Winnetka drive in. Note—Pelt is a weird guy, but he was nice and he brought me some fresh eggs."*

On July 28, Stephanie wrote in her diary, *"NOTE I have kinda been kidded about having so many days off this month. I don't really mind because it's true because I have been."* Stephanie also wrote of her doctor friend, cryptically, *"I gave extra patrol to Mark Currie's pad."*

Stephanie did not mention it in her diary, but it was likely on one of her days off in July or August that she visited Glendale Adventist Medical Center, where Sherri Rasmussen worked. Stephanie had met Sherri in person at least once before, on May 10, an encounter she had documented in her diary.

On the day she went to Glendale Adventist, Stephanie wore skimpy athletic shorts and a tank top. She showed up around lunchtime. Sherri's secretary, Sylvia Nielsen, a shy, older woman, was at her desk outside Sherri's office.

Stephanie asked to see Sherri but did not identify herself. Sylvia told her Sherri was at lunch. Stephanie said she would wait, and took a seat in front of Sylvia.

After a few minutes, Stephanie got up and walked out into the hallway. When she came back, Sherri was with her, having returned from lunch. Sylvia watched them go into Sherri's office. Sherri closed the door behind them.

Minutes later, the door opened again and Stephanie left. Sherri came out a little while after that. Sylvia could see that she had been crying. Sherri was so upset that she decided to go home, although it was the middle of the day. Sylvia apparently never reported the incident to hospital security, nor discussed it with anyone else at the time.

Sherri called her parents in Tucson that evening. She recounted to Nels how John's ex-girlfriend had come to her office uninvited. Sherri said the woman had told her that if she couldn't have John, then no one could, "including you." Sherri said that John's ex was dressed in a tight top and shorts that barely had a leg. She described the outfit as "very provocative" and said she thought the woman wanted to show her she worked out and was in top shape. This was the first time Sherri ever mentioned John's ex-girlfriend to her parents or gave them any indication that there was a problem. Nels could tell Sherri was devastated.

Sherri confronted John when he got home from work. She told him that Stephanie had visited her at the hospital and what Stephanie had said. Stephanie had claimed to Sherri that John went to see her and that she and John were still having sex. Stephanie said she had known John for a long time and that she knew what he wanted. She told Sherri that if the marriage failed, she would be waiting to pick up the pieces. Sherri had responded, "Don't worry. We won't be needing your services."

John admitted his infidelity to Sherri. He explained that Stephanie had called him crying, and that he had gone to her place, where they had sex. John said he had made a terrible mistake and begged for Sherri's forgiveness. He pleaded with her not to let his mistake ruin what they had, or keep them from where they wanted to go together.

According to John, he could tell Sherri was very upset with him, but he did not sense that she felt endangered by Stephanie, either physically or as a threat to their marriage. Sherri seemed to him more disappointed that he had gone to see Stephanie without telling her than fearful or conflicted about their future.

Begging Sherri for forgiveness made John realize how deeply in love with her he was. John felt surprised how certain he was that he wanted to be with Sherri. He wasn't sure why it surprised him, but he knew that Sherri was the one. He told her that he wanted nothing more in the world than to be married to her.

John was adamant with Sherri that there would be absolutely no more contact with Stephanie. In his mind, whatever romantic relationship he once had with Stephanie was over. For that reason, John considered it unnecessary to contact Stephanie and discuss what had happened. He would not ask Stephanie why she had gone to Sherri's workplace and tried to wreck his engagement. He would not call and tell her that she had acted inappropriately and to please leave his fiancée alone. He would not ask her not to contact him or his parents and siblings since he was getting married to someone else. John believed going back to Stephanie and confronting her would only fuel the whole situation and make things worse. He told Sherri he did not want to risk perpetuating any more drama related to Stephanie. John insisted that it was the best way to handle the situation. He told Sherri, "Look, let's just let this lie. It's done."

John and Sherri talked for a while that night. By the time they went to bed, John felt it was clear that they were moving forward and that the wedding was still on.

Sylvia did not learn who the aggressive visitor was until the following morning, when Sherri returned to work. Sherri told her that it was John's ex-girlfriend. Sherri said the ex-girlfriend was very angry and agitated as they talked in her office. Sherri also told Sylvia that the ex-girlfriend had threatened her. Sherri was ordinarily a very private person, a quality she shared with her secretary.

In 2009, during a videotaped interview with LAPD detectives, Stephanie was asked whether she had ever met Sherri in person.

"I may have," Stephanie said.

"Do you remember her name or anything or what she did for a living or where she worked or anything about her?"

"Well, I think she—I'm going to say I think she was a nurse."

Later in the interview, Stephanie was asked, "You said you thought his wife was a nurse. Do you have any idea where she was working at the time, or did he ever mention that to you? Was it a hospital or a doctor's office?"

"I'm sure he must've mentioned it. I mean, now that you're bringing it up, I think she worked at a hospital somewhere. And yeah, I may have met her at a hospital. I may have talked to her once or twice—"

"At a hospital?"

"—or more, you know?" Stephanie said.

Later, the detective asked her, "Do you remember her first name?"

"Shelly, Sherri. I don't know. Something. You know, like I said, it's been so many years and—"

"But from all the years, as far as you can remember, you don't—do you remember ever talking to her just—"

"Well, it's just—I said earlier, you know—I—I mean, I may have. You know, I may have talked to her. I—"

"You mentioned a hospital maybe. You may have talked to her at a hospital?"

"Yeah, yeah, I may have. You know, I'm thinking back, now that you guys are bringing back all these old memories . . . I'm thinking that—because, I mean, we would date," Stephanie said, in reference to herself and John. "He would date other people. I would date other people. And I think, you know, at that point, I mean, he may have been dating her or—I don't know. Maybe he was married. I don't even remember. And I'm, like, you know what? Why are you calling me if you're either dating her or living with her or married to her? 'Cause I honestly don't remember the time frame. And I'm like, come on. Knock it off. And I'm—and now, I'm thinking I may—I may have gone to her and said, hey, you know what? You know what? Is he dating you? He's—he's bothering me. And so I'm thinking that we had a conversation about that, one or two. You know, I—it could've been three. I don't want to say I had three conversations with her. I don't even—"

"But like at her work or at their house or—"

"No, I'm thinking that I'm—you know, he obviously must have told me where she worked. I'm thinking it was a hospital somewhere in L.A. . . . So I could've said, okay, well, you know, and I went and talked to her and just said, hey, you know what? You know, if he's dating you, he's—he keeps calling me. Why don't you tell him to knock it off or whatever and—no, because I probably would've told her to knock it off, you know?" Stephanie told the detectives.

Later in the interview, Stephanie was asked, "When you say that you may have, you know, that you talked to his wife and said, hey—or, you know, I don't know if it was his wife at that time, girlfriend or whatever and said—"

"Yeah, I don't know if it was his wife or his girlfriend. I—I mean, quite honestly I don't even remember."

"When you said, like, hey, you know, he's calling me, he needs to knock it off or what have you, I mean, was that—was that civil? Was there—I mean, did—"

"Oh, yeah, no, there was not—I don't think there was anything—it was—it—the conversation lasted a few minutes. I can't even remember. It wasn't like, you know, we went out to lunch or anything."

"Right. But there was no, like arguments or fight or—"

"I don't—I don't think so."

"It didn't get heated or anything like that?"

"Not that I recall, no. I mean, I would think that would stand out, I would think. Now, again, that's not standing out in my mind."

"So you didn't have any problems with her then?"

"No," Stephanie replied.

"You didn't have any issues with her?"

"No, I mean—"

"But let me ask you. It seems like you didn't have any issues. Now, did she have an issue with you, as far as, because now you're telling her, hey, you know, have him stop calling. Now, you know, she's, like hey—you know, you figure she'd be threatened by you . . . From what you remember as far as when you talked to her, maybe you didn't take it as serious but maybe, you know, did she, if she was bugged by it?"

"You mean, like, was she throwing things at me or something or—"

"Well, no, just—as far as you're trying to explain, like, hey, have him stop calling, you know, stop playing games and—"

"You know—I tell you if the conversation—I couldn't even tell you how long the conversation—if you said did it last a half an hour, did it last three minutes, did it last twenty minutes. I can't even remember. It's been so long ago."

"You just remember talking to her, telling her that—"

"Yeah, and that's why when you said how many times you talked to her, I don't know how many times I've talked to her. Maybe it was once. Maybe it was twice. Maybe it was three times. You know, I honestly don't know. I don't know what year it was. If you—if he said I met her in such and such year, I'd go, okay. Well, I don't even know what year he met her."

Later, the detectives asked Stephanie, "When you went to see her, do you remember if it was at her house or at the place she worked at?"

"No, I'm thinking that—I'm thinking that it was probably—for some reason I want to say that the hospital seemed that—you know, if you say she got married in eighty-five or something, I'm thinking that, you know, maybe the hospital was on my way to work in Hollywood. I mean, that's sounding familiar," Stephanie said.

Stephanie was in fact assigned to Devonshire, not Hollywood, in mid-summer 1985, when she confronted Sherri in her office. Stephanie also lived at the time within Devonshire's boundaries. Glendale Adventist Medical Center was not on the way to work for Stephanie, but rather a twenty-minute drive in the opposite direction.

The detectives asked Stephanie, "Would you have gone on duty?"

"Oh, no. I'm sure I wouldn't have. I—"

"No?"

"No, I'm—I'm pretty good about not doing stuff. You know, I mean, now, I'm not saying that, you know, you haven't done stuff on duty, but I—I would've—I mean, I would've been working with somebody. You know, so I wouldn't—I wouldn't think—I mean, I try to avoid doing stuff on duty."

"Okay. So you would've gone—if it was en route to work, you—more than likely you would've gone to her work and had this discussion with her?"

"I mean, that's—now that you guys are bringing this stuff up, I mean, it sounds—that sounds familiar."

Stephanie denied to the detectives that her conversation with Sherri was contentious, or even memorable. Stephanie was asked, "When you guys met at the hospital, I mean, you guys talked, but it wasn't, from what you recall, confrontational?"

"I don't think so," Stephanie replied.

"From either side?"

"I—I mean, I'm trying to, you know, turn my memory back, you know, and I'm trying—I can't even—can't even picture the, you know, picture the conversation. I mean, I can't even picture the conversation."

"Well, let me ask you, I mean, at the hospital it never got to the point where people were going, hey, hey, you know, go—everybody go to your own corner type of thing?"

"I don't think so."

"Nothing like that?"

"I don't think so. I mean, I really don't. If you—you know, if you say people said that, that's not ringing a bell to me at all. I mean, it's not. I mean, that—that's not ringing a bell to me at all," Stephanie told the detectives in 2009.

Back in 1985, Stephanie had mentioned to her roommate, Mike Hargreaves, that she went to see John's fiancée at the hospital where she worked and that they had an argument about John. Hargreaves had noticed that Stephanie's demeanor had changed since she learned of John's engagement. Stephanie seemed sad more often, upset a little more often. She had started to leave Hargreaves notes about household issues like dirty dishes—wash this, clean that—whereas before, they would have just talked about it. Hargreaves believed her moodiness was related to her breakup with John. Stephanie did not go into great detail with Hargreaves about the confrontation at the hospital. Stephanie did say that she thought John's fiancée wasn't that good-looking.

Stephanie's diary also revealed her state of mind around the time she visited Sherri. On August 2, she wrote, *I really have headaches the last few nights. It's not work at all. It's just worrying about my personal life. I really have to stop this because otherwise it's really going to kill me.* The same watch, Stephanie noted that two of her sergeants at Devonshire commented she had *a great personality and they like my legs. They were teasing me tonight but it was all in fun.* The next night, Stephanie's patrol partner was Bill Wolleck. She wrote in her diary, *Wolleck told me that he didn't mind working with women and he thought I was too hyper, but that I had a lot of enthusiasm.*

Stephanie was off for eight days, from August 4 to 12, to compete in the first ever World Police and Fire Games in San Jose. The games were modeled after the California Police Olympics. By virtue of the two medals she had won at the Police Olympics that June, gold in women's basketball and silver in women's doubles tennis, she automatically qualified for those events at the games in San Jose.

On August 4, Stephanie sat down to write a letter she had been putting off writing. Margaret Ruetten, John's mother, had mailed her some photographs, and she had been unable to bring herself to reply. The photos Margaret sent may have been from when Stephanie's cruise stopped in

San Diego in mid-May, less than two weeks before John and Sherri's engagement. What sentiments Margaret expressed to Stephanie, if any, when she sent her the photos are unknown. Only John knows how much he shared with his mother about his most recent interactions with Stephanie. Presumably, it would not have been an easy conversation for John to tell his parents that he and Stephanie had had sex after his engagement to Sherri, and that Stephanie had later gone to see Sherri at the hospital and told her about it.

What is known for certain is what Stephanie wrote in her two-page, handwritten letter to John's mother:

8-4-85

Dear Mrs. Ruetten,

I wanted to thank you for the pictures. The reason it has taken me so long to respond is because I had to build up my courage.

For now I don't know when or if I'll ever see you and your family again. I do want you to know a few things though.

I'm truly in love with John and this past year has really torn me up. I wish it hadn't end [sic] the way it did and I don't think I'll ever understand John's decision.

I do want you to know that your family has meant so much to me. I really have learned a lot from your family, and I hope someday I can find someone that I care for as much.

I hope if you ever need anything you'll contact me.

Love always,
Stephanie

P.S. Say hello to your husband and Janet.

Stephanie addressed the envelope to Mrs. Margaret Ruetten. She mailed it on August 6 from San Jose to John's parents' home in San Diego.

Although Stephanie was certain about her feelings for John, and John was certain about his feelings for Sherri, Sherri apparently harbored at least some doubts about her and John's future together. Sherri was too private, even with her close girlfriends, to air John's dirty laundry and the issues they were working through as a couple. It was humiliating enough that John had been unfaithful. Sherri's friends suspect that she didn't want them to think less of John, whom she was still engaged to marry. Telling her friends would only have invited questions about why she lacked the fortitude to

8-4-85

Dear Mrs. Ruetten,

I wanted to thank you for the pictures the reason it has taken me so long to respond is because I had to build up my courage.

For now I don't know when or if I'll ever see you and your family again. I do want you to know a few things though.

I'm truely in love with John and this past year has really torn me up. I wish it hadn't end the way it did and I don't think I'll ever understand John's decision.

I do want you to know that your family has meant so much to me. I really have learned a lot from your family and I

over

-2-

hope someday I can find someone that I can care for as much.

I hope if you ever need anything you'll contact me.

Love always
Stephanie

P.S. SAY HELLO
TO YOUR HUSBAND
AND JANET

Stephanie's letter to Margaret Ruetten, August 4, 1985

break up with him. Sherri had accepted John's explanation and apology and had forgiven him. Sherri evidently wanted to handle the situation herself and believed herself capable of that.

Sherri did not even tell Peggy Daly, her closest friend at Glendale Adventist, about Stephanie's visit to the hospital and what prompted it. Peggy considered herself Sherri's "bread-and-butter friend." Some lifelong friendships are sparked at a party, or on a vacation, or over drinks. Sherri and Peggy's close bond was forged going to work every day. They rarely socialized together at night or on weekends.

Peggy had met John only a few times. The first was at a party at John and Sherri's condo, a rare occasion when Peggy visited Sherri at her home. Peggy's brief interactions with John had left her feeling vaguely unimpressed. Peggy thought John was fine and didn't dislike him, but he seemed to her like the type of man who did the minimum to get by. Peggy never got the feeling that John was somebody who was going to take care of Sherri, truly cherish and protect her. At the same time, she knew that Sherri had chosen John, and she had to respect Sherri's choice. She never shared with Sherri the ambivalence she felt about John.

During the summer of 1985, while Sherri and John were engaged, Peggy noticed one day at work that Sherri seemed upset. Peggy assumed it was something involving John. Sherri didn't volunteer what was bothering her, and Peggy didn't ask. Not long after that, Sherri mentioned to Peggy a formal event that she and John were planning to attend. Sherri said she didn't have a dress to wear and was thinking of buying a new one. Sherri had seen Peggy in a dress she liked. It was black and white, cut straight and tight at the hip, with the puffy sleeves that were fashionable at the time. Peggy told Sherri she got it at Nordstrom.

"Go to Nordstrom and get one. It doesn't bother me," Peggy said.

"I can't spend that money. I don't even know if we're going to stay together," Sherri told her friend.

"If you break up, you can always take it back," Peggy said. "It's Nordstrom."

Sherri bought the dress, and Peggy's line about Nordstrom became a running joke between them. A few months later, on the night before she married John, Sherri wore the Nordstrom dress to her rehearsal dinner.

Sherri's impending wedding and her concerns about Stephanie were not the only stressors in her life during the summer of her engagement. There were also personnel problems within Sherri's nursing unit at

Glendale Adventist. The hospital had just completed a major reorganization. Sherri and Peggy's responsibilities both increased within the nursing
division. Some nurses lost their jobs. Others were passed over for promo-
tions they felt they deserved.

Among the personnel changes Sherri made was to promote one of
her staff nurses, Cheryl Starling, to manager of critical care nursing. A
different nurse, Deborah Putnam, had held the position on an unofficial
basis before the reorganization. Putnam believed the job should have been
hers.

Putnam was dating a cardiologist who was also Glendale Adventist's
medical director, a powerful post within the hospital. He and Putnam later
married, but at the time, he was married to someone else. When he
attempted to intervene on Putnam's behalf, Sherri held her ground. The situation became progressively messier and more divisive within the Critical
Care Unit.

Sherri told her parents about the drama and her perspective. Nels and
Loretta remember the conversation because it was strange for Sherri to
complain about conflict at work. Sherri thought Putnam believed, mistakenly, that Sherri denied her the promotion because of her affair with the
married doctor. Sherri told Nels the affair had nothing to do with her decision. "Their moral responsibility is not mine. Dad, she wasn't a good nurse.
She wasn't thorough. I have to have people that, when I leave the room, I can
rely on."

Peggy had known Deborah Putnam since high school. Both had
attended Sacramento Adventist Academy. Peggy knew back then that
Putnam had a reputation as a hothead. Peggy thought Putnam got along
better at work with male than female colleagues, but most nurses were women.
Sherri wearied of Putnam's pot-stirring and the medical director's interference and unwanted telephone calls. Some of the calls Sherri received
were threatening and obscene. The hospital launched an internal investigation and determined that Putnam and the cardiologist were responsible
and should be disciplined. Putnam could have been terminated but retained
her job. The cardiologist was stripped of his title as Glendale Adventist's
medical director.

Around the same time the situation with Putnam arose, Sherri reported
to the hospital's security director, Jim Feldman, that her car was keyed in
the parking lot. Who was responsible, and whether Sherri was a random
victim or the target of a message, is unknown. In response to this and other

incidents, Feldman arranged for the nurses to be able to call security for an escort to their cars.

Feldman also spoke about parking lot security with Glenn Crabtree, Glendale Adventist's director of design construction. Feldman asked Glenn to install extra lighting where Sherri parked. Feldman said it was a precaution they were taking because somebody was harassing Sherri. Feldman did not tell Glenn who he or Sherri suspected might be behind the harassment. Glenn did not know enough at the time to ask Feldman whether the new lighting was prompted by the situation with Putnam and the cardiologist, or by the uninvited visit John's ex-girlfriend paid to Sherri's office.

As part of Glendale Adventist's disciplinary investigation into Putnam and the cardiologist's conduct, a written report was produced which recounted the conflict over Starling's promotion and blamed Putnam and the cardiologist for the calls Sherri had received. The report apparently made no reference to John, his ex-girlfriend, or her confrontation with Sherri at the hospital.

The World Police and Fire Games concluded in San Jose on August 11. Stephanie returned to Los Angeles with two more medals for the LAPD, silver in women's basketball and bronze in women's doubles tennis. She did not write about the games in her diary, so it is unknown whether she was proud or disappointed with the medals she won. In sports, as in life, Stephanie was intensely competitive, and loath to settle for less than first place.

8

Night Stalkers

(August 12 to October 12, 1985)

Stephanie returned from her week away at the World Police and Fire Games to a city on edge. Los Angeles residents, the media, and the police were struggling to make sense of a series of horrific murders and sexual assaults, which detectives believed to be the work of a single unidentified man.

The attacks began in the San Gabriel Valley, east of Los Angeles, but eventually spread across the city, north to San Francisco, and south to Orange County. There was no geographic pattern apparent in where the killer struck. The victims also defied easy categorization: various races, men and women, young and old. The seeming randomness of his attacks heightened the collective sense that anyone could be next. The most terrifying aspect of the killing spree was the sole link that connected the disparate cases. The assailant, whoever he was, tended to attack people in their own homes, very late at night, while they were sleeping.

Not since the summer of 1969, when the Manson Family was on the rampage, had such a sense of fear and dread blanketed Los Angeles. The foreboding mounted with the revelation of each new attack, along with the media frenzy and police response.

At the time, the authorities believed the first murders had occurred the night of March 17, 1985, in two separate confrontations. A thirty-four-year-old woman, Dayle Okazaki, was shot and killed inside her condo in Rosemead, on the eastern outskirts of Los Angeles. Okazaki's roommate, twenty-five-year-old Maria Hernandez, was also shot, but she survived after the bullet deflected off the car keys she raised to her face to protect herself. An hour later, a few miles away, Tsai-Lian Yu, a thirty-year-old student, was dragged from her car, shot twice, and left for dead.

Ten days later, a married couple, Vincent and Maxine Zazzara, were murdered in their home in Whittier, southeast of Los Angeles. Police believed their assailant entered the home through an unlocked door. Vincent was shot in the head while asleep. Maxine was tied up, shot, stabbed, and her body mutilated.

On May 14, the assailant crawled through an open window into the home of another married couple, Bill and Lillian Doi, in Monterey Park, east of downtown Los Angeles. Bill was fatally shot while trying to protect his wife and call 911. Lillian, who had recently suffered a stroke, was bound and raped.

Two weeks later, on May 29, two elderly sisters, Mabel Bell and Florence Lang, were beaten and tortured in their home in Monrovia, northeast of the prior attacks. The sisters' small house was located on a dark, winding road. Few neighbors lived nearby. The assailant, wearing gloves, let himself in through an unlocked door. The sisters were sleeping when he attacked, this time with a hammer. After raping Florence, he drew pentagrams with red lipstick on the walls and on Mabel's thigh. A gardener who came to the home two days later discovered the sisters, who miraculously were still alive.

In early July, there were more disturbing unsolved murders and assaults. On July 2, a widowed grandmother of five, Mary Louise Cannon, was killed inside her home in Arcadia. A neighbor who noticed a window screen had been removed from the front of the house discovered her body, throat slit. On July 5, in Sierra Madre, a sixteen-year-old girl asleep in her own bedroom was beaten with a tire iron and strangled nearly to death with an electrical cord while her parents slept down the hall. Late at night on July 6, the assailant climbed through an open window of a home in Monterey Park and attacked Joyce Nelson, a sixty-one-year-old grandmother, who was asleep on her couch in front of the television. Nelson was punched and kicked to death so viciously that a footprint of the assailant's sneaker was imprinted on her face. Hours after Nelson's murder, another Monterey Park woman, sixty-five-year-old Sophie Dickman, was beaten and raped by a home intruder.

The shocking violence of the murders, combined with the killer's terrifying modus operandi of entering victims' bedrooms in the dead of night, stoked fears across the region. The press began referring to the suspect as "the Valley Intruder." In Monterey Park, where the attack on Bill and Lillian Doi in May was still a fresh memory, the proximity of the most recent crimes panicked residents. More than six hundred crammed a Monterey Park Neighborhood Watch meeting on July 11. Two days later, on July 13, more than two thousand showed up at a public meeting called by the Monterey Park Police Department. A police lieutenant assured the overflow crowd that undercover officers were patrolling the community around the clock. He also advised residents to sleep within arm's reach of a telephone and to practice dialing 911 in the dark.

The authorities were not yet ready to reveal to the public, or confirm to the media, that detectives were searching for a suspected serial killer. The Los Angeles County Sheriff's Department established a task force led by a veteran homicide investigator, Sgt. Frank Salerno. Six years earlier, Salerno had led the search for the Hillside Strangler, who had raped and murdered ten young women in late 1978 and early 1979, dumping their bodies in the hills overlooking the city. The Hillside Strangler task force grew to include more than 160 investigators from the sheriff's department, the LAPD, and the Glendale Police Department. That case ended with the arrests of cousins Angelo Buono and Kenneth Bianchi, after Salerno's task force pieced together that the Hillside Strangler was not one killer but two working in tandem.

As in the Hillside Strangler case, the Valley Intruder's trail of violence spanned multiple police jurisdictions. In addition to Salerno's team of sheriff's homicide investigators, the LAPD, Monterey Park police, and other law enforcement agencies also assigned detectives to work the Valley Intruder case. The Hillside Strangler investigation had been plagued by poor coordination and sharing of information among the many detectives and agencies on the case. Kenneth Bianchi, for instance, was interviewed by investigators on three separate occasions before his arrest. None of the investigators were aware of the prior interviews. Similar communications problems threatened to hamper the search for the Valley Intruder.

In addition to the fatal attacks, several victims survived their encounters with the Valley Intruder. Eyewitnesses described him as tall and lanky, with longish hair and bad teeth. Invariably, they said he dressed entirely in black clothing. He warned his victims not to look him in the face. He was careful always to wear gloves, which deprived investigators of fingerprints. There were two promising forensic leads. Ballistics experts examined the slugs recovered after several of the murders and determined they were fired from the same .22 caliber gun. The most intriguing clue was the distinctive waffle footprint of the assailant's sneakers, which had been left at multiple crime scenes. Forensic examination of the footprint determined the sneakers were an uncommon brand, Avia, size 11½. Investigators contacted Avia and learned that only 1,354 pairs of that particular model were manufactured, of which only six pairs were sold in Los Angeles. Of the six pairs sold, only one was size 11½. The Valley Intruder was wearing those sneakers. The footprint took on the import of a fingerprint. A photo of the Avia sneakers was distributed to police and sheriff's stations throughout Los Angeles.

The killings continued unabated. Between 2:00 and 4:00 a.m. on July 20, the assailant struck at a home in Glendale, just a block from Glendale Adventist Medical Center, where Sherri Rasmussen worked. The victims were a couple in their late sixties, Max and Lela Kneiding. The Kneidings were asleep in bed when they were attacked with a machete and then shot to death. After killing the Kneidings, the assailant drove north to Sun Valley, which was part of the LAPD's Foothill Division. He broke into the home of Chainarong and Somkid Khovananth, a Thai immigrant couple with two children, an eight-year-old boy and a two-year-old girl. He shot and killed Chainarong, the husband, and bound, beat, and raped his wife, Somkid. He also bound their son and placed a sock in his mouth to muffle his cries. Somkid and both children survived. Somkid's description of the man resembled the Valley Intruder. Crime scene evidence confirmed what investigators suspected. The distinctive Avia footprints were found both outside and inside the Khovananths' home. In the Kneidings' bedroom, a .22 caliber slug was recovered and examined. Ballistics tests revealed that the Kneidings were shot with the same gun used to kill Dayle Okazaki and Tsai-Lian Yu on March 17.

The murders of Max and Lela Kneiding devastated the congregation at the Glendale Seventh-Day Adventist Church, a mile from their home. Max was a deacon at the church and a regular at Saturday services. The couple had been married for forty-seven years, and left behind three children and thirteen grandchildren. Their pastor, the Reverend Arthur Torres, struggled to answer his congregation's questions about why God would allow something so terrible to befall such good people. The Los Angeles Times quoted a line from Rev. Torres's sermon: "To try and give a rational explanation for an irrational act is to legitimize it."

Although the police refused to confirm that a serial killer was on the loose in Los Angeles, they could not stop the media from speculating. On August 1, the *Times* ran a story headlined "SIMILARITIES" STUDIED IN SERIES OF KILLINGS. The paper reported: *"The Los Angeles County Sheriff's Department and Glendale police are investigating a possible connection between the July 20 murders of an elderly Glendale couple and a string of five killings and four attacks in the West San Gabriel Valley."* The police declined to release any details apart from a physical description of the suspect: white, age twenty-five to thirty, six feet tall, 160 pounds, and curly brown hair. A Glendale police captain told the *Times*, "At this point, it is vital we maintain the integrity of the investigation and not compromise the nature of any evidence we may have."

The sheriff's department increased its task force to twenty-five detectives, a third of its homicide squad. Salerno called the FBI's Behavioral Sciences Unit and asked them to produce a psychological profile of the suspect based on the evidence collected to date. Somkid Khovananth, still distraught over her husband's murder, worked with an LAPD sketch artist to produce a composite of the suspect, which was distributed to police stations across Los Angeles. Photocopies were handed out at roll call and taped to patrol car dashboards.

The sketch was also released to the news media, to be splashed across TV screens and the front page of the papers. CNN and even international news outlets picked up the story and ran with it. Along the way, the media abandoned the suspect's first nickname, the Valley Intruder, for a new epithet: the Night Stalker. Public alarm escalated with the increase in media attention. Many residents across Los Angeles sought protection. Gun stores and alarm companies were inundated with new customers. Locksmiths had to work around the clock to meet demand.

On August 6, while Stephanie was away competing in San Jose, the Night Stalker struck in the Devonshire Division. The victims were a young family in Northridge, Chris and Virginia Peterson and their four-year-old daughter. It was after two in the morning when Virginia awoke to the sound of a gun being cocked. The black-clad man's first shot hit Virginia below her left eye, but at a downward trajectory that spared her brain and her life. Incredibly, she never lost consciousness. Chris woke at the gunshot. Before he could get his bearings, he was shot in the temple. Again, miraculously, the shot was not fatal. The bullets were old ammunition, with degraded gunpowder. The bullet struck Chris with sufficient force to stun him and draw blood, but not enough to penetrate his skull. The slug ended up lodged in his neck.

Chris emitted a growl, like a wounded bear, and scrambled to his feet. As Chris charged, the man fired at him but missed. They grappled over the gun. More shots were fired in the struggle, but none landed. Chris chased the man down the hallway to the living room and out of the house. Their daughter, who stayed in her bedroom during the assault, was unharmed. Unwilling to wait for paramedics, Chris managed to drive his wife and daughter to Northridge Hospital.

The first LAPD detectives to respond to the Peterson home found no telltale Avia footprints at the crime scene. Still, there were enough similarities to the previous Night Stalker attacks for the task force to take control of the case. The morning after the assault on the Petersons, the news was relayed to the LAPD academy, where a meeting of fifty detectives was already under way. Sgt. Salerno of the sheriff's task force had convened the summit, inviting detectives from every police agency in Los Angeles County. Representatives of the LAPD, the L.A. County Sheriff's Department, the FBI, the Glendale Police Department, the Monterey Park Police Department, and several other agencies participated. Everyone in attendance promised to cooperate and share tips and leads.

The next night, August 8, the Night Stalker struck again. This time it was in Diamond Bar, thirty miles east of Los Angeles, and farther east than any prior attack. After 2:30 a.m., he jimmied open the back door of the home of Elyas Abowath, his wife, Sakina, and their two young boys, a three-year-old and a two-month-old. Elyas was shot point-blank in the head and died instantly. Sakina was beaten, handcuffed, and sexually assaulted. The three-year-old was also bound but unharmed. The infant, having just been breastfed by Sakina at 2:30, slept through it all. Elyas Abowath was buried at Rose Hills Memorial Park in Whittier, the sixth victim of the Night Stalker interred at the cemetery in less than five months.

The attacks on the Peterson and Abowath families galvanized ever more intense media attention. L.A. BOLTS ITS DOORS, WINDOWS: RESIDENTS BRACE FOR NEW ATTACK BY NIGHT STALKER was the banner headline across the front page of the August 10 *Los Angeles Herald-Examiner*. The same day, the *Times* reported that detectives believed a "curly haired, gapped-tooth man" was responsible for at least six and possibly as many as twelve or thirteen murders. At a press conference on the case, L.A. County Sheriff

Sherman Block was asked if he expected the Night Stalker to attack again. "There's nothing to think that he won't," Block replied.

Public fear of the Night Stalker was especially acute in the San Fernando Valley, and nowhere more than in the Devonshire Division, where the Peterson family lived. In less well-off areas of Los Angeles, violent crime was numbingly common. Devonshire was sleepy and suburban, but the Peterson attack was an unwelcome reminder that terrible things can happen anywhere. Residents were unaccustomed to thinking of themselves and their loved ones as potential murder victims. The community was deeply rattled. On August 14, under the headline FEAR OF "INTRUDER": POLICE CALLS SURGE WITH CRIME SPREE, the *Times* reported:

> San Fernando Valley residents, frightened by the brutal attacks of the so-called "Valley Intruder," are phoning police with false sightings of prowlers and with questions about forming neighborhood watch groups and securing their homes, Los Angeles police said Tuesday.
>
> Several Valley gun shops also reported increased handgun sales prompted by fear over the attacks, although most said the increases were slight, and some saw no change at all.
>
> The Police Department's communications division, which processes emergency crime calls throughout Los Angeles, said the number of daily crime reports jumped to 4,200 calls last weekend, about 600 more than the usual 3,600 . . .
>
> Authorities believe the Intruder may have been the man who shot Christopher and Virginia Petersen [sic] in the head last week as they lay in bed in their Northridge home. The couple survived the attack and were released from a hospital the next day. Christopher Petersen dodged other bullets to chase the man from the house, then drove his wife and unharmed 4-year-old daughter to a hospital.
>
> The shootings seem to have triggered the sharpest response in the West Valley area around Northridge, which is served by the Police Department's Devonshire Division.
>
> The number of queries to that division regarding home security and watch groups has risen an estimated ninefold, with 40 to 50 calls coming in daily since publicity about the attacks became widespread last week.
>
> "People are really scared. They want to know about locking up, about securing their residences," said Sheila Bell, a police service representative

at Devonshire Division. "People are asking if it's all right to shoot some-
one in their home."

Stephanie had returned to duty at Devonshire on August 12. Her diary entries reflect the social panic that, in her absence, had suddenly gripped the community. Stephanie's diaries also capture her distinctly nonchalant attitude toward residents, despite their rising fears.

Stephanie's patrol partner her first night back was Don Bailey. She drove. Stephanie counted five calls on their car's MDT, the most she'd had in a single watch since she was at Hollywood. In her diary, she wrote, *"The calls started coming out with a burglary susp in 9000 block of White Oak. Well the air unit came. No susp was found. Then all the other neighbors started putting out calls that they saw someone. We were driving around like we're a chicken with our head cut off. Going from 1 call to the next and accomplishing nothing. By the time we got to all our calls the susp were gone."* Of her new partner, Stephanie wrote, *"Bailey wasn't that bad to work with. I had a good time. He was talkative. Not what I expected since Wolleck told me that he didn't like working w/ women. We had stopped earlier at Cupids for a hot dog. Then we ate about 1230. I also wrote a ticket for the no left turn at the Mall. Bailey thought it was chickenshit, but so do I. But it was a ticket."*

Stephanie worked with Bailey again on August 13. They answered a 459 call, a burglary that had just occurred. *"The vict said that her stereo was taken, but nothing else was taken. They were also moving so I'm sure some-one moved it to her new location,"* she wrote. She took a report. *"Then we went by the hospital to see Mark,"* referring to Mark Currie. She also noted, *"Sgt. Rebhan is a funny guy. He was joking w/ me and said, 'I'll leave my wife for you.' Lately a lot of the guys have been saying comments to me. More like sexual jokes really."*

Late that same night, there was a new Night Stalker attack, this time in San Francisco. The victim was sixty-six-year-old Peter Pan. He and his sixty-two-year-old wife, Barbara, were asleep when the intruder climbed through a window and crept into their bedroom. Pan was shot in the head and died instantly. His wife was beaten, sexually assaulted and shot, yet somehow survived. The killer used lipstick to draw an inverted pentagram on the bedroom wall before he fled.

The Night Stalker task force in Los Angeles learned of the Pan case the day after the murder. All previous known attacks were clustered around Los Angeles, hundreds of miles south, so investigators were initially unsure if it was their suspect or a copycat. Four detectives, two each from the LAPD and the sheriff's department, were immediately dispatched to San Francisco. All the hallmarks of the earlier crimes were present: entering a home in the dead of night through an unlocked door or window; shooting the husband in the head before sexually assaulting the wife; footprints from the correct size Avia sneakers. The detectives returned to Los Angeles with slugs recovered at the Pan crime scene. Within a few days, ballistics tests confirmed the bullets were fired from the same gun used in two of the Los Angeles murders. The Night Stalker was still active. Even more troubling, with each new attack, the suspect seemed to expand the area where he might strike next.

On August 21, Stephanie and Wolleck were assigned to patrol in a plain car. Wolleck drove. If they were on heightened alert for the Night Stalker, Stephanie made no mention of it in her diary. *"First thing we did was go to the donut shop at Mason and Devonshire. Wolleck met some lady there and they talked for about 30 minutes or so. It was rather rude of him but I didn't say anything. It felt like I was listening to their conversation but there was not much I could do about that,"* she recounted.

Two nights later, on August 23, Stephanie, Wolleck, and a probationary officer, Paul Robi, were assigned to work in plainclothes as a three-officer team. Stephanie wrote in her diary, *"Well tonight was going to be fun . . . We went to Denny's to discuss our game plan for our undercover deal for tonight. We also ate. Wolleck and I wore shorts and of course shirts. We drove Wolleck's convertible Tiger and went to Dearborn Park. When we drove up there were a few people there. We walked arm / arm to the park, set out our blanket and talked for a while. Then I rubbed his back for about 20 minutes. No one was really doing anything. Then Wolleck rubbed my back. Then the sprinklers came on. We didn't arrest anyone."*

At the same hour Stephanie was out on undercover park patrol, Sheriff Block held a rare Friday night press conference. Earlier in the day on August 23, the mayor of San Francisco, Dianne Feinstein, had announced at her own televised press conference that ballistics tests had definitively linked the recent murder there to the crime spree in Los Angeles. She urged San Francisco residents to be vigilant. "Somewhere in the Bay Area, someone is renting a room, an apartment or a home to this vicious serial killer. I am hoping that people will look at this composite drawing," Feinstein said, holding the sketch up to the cameras.

While Mayor Feinstein's intent was to calm the public, her impromptu disclosure of the confidential ballistics information stunned and infuriated the police in both San Francisco and Los Angeles. The Night Stalker task force organized by the L.A. County Sheriff's had worked sixteen-hour days for weeks chasing down tips and leads. The ballistics link was among the best evidence the task force had. The fact that one gun was used in multiple murders was closely guarded information, not least because investigators hoped to arrest the suspect with the gun in his possession. The frustrated detectives saw Feinstein's remarks as tantamount to encouraging the Night Stalker to get rid of the murder weapon.

Hours later, at his hastily called 10:00 p.m. press conference in Los Angeles, Block condemned the disclosure and other media leaks, some of which were untrue. "That information has not only jeopardized the conduct of our investigation, but in reality it places this community in jeopardy," he said. Block announced that with the latest attack in San Francisco, "We have now definitely tied fourteen murders to this individual and possibly as many as thirty-three individual cases that have occurred." Fourteen was double the number of murders investigators had publicly attributed to the Night Stalker suspect just days before. Block cautioned residents to lock all doors and windows, especially during the overnight hours, when the suspect was most active. Sgt. Salerno told the *Times* he expected more attacks. "Most serial murderers don't stop. They might relocate. They will kill again," Salerno predicted.

The weather in Los Angeles the following day, August 24, was sweltering. Nevertheless, countless people throughout the city slept with their windows shut, sacrificing a nighttime breeze for a semblance of security in their own bedrooms. Outside Los Angeles and San Francisco, residents were less vigilant. After 2:00 a.m. on Sunday, August 25, the Night Stalker struck again, this time in Mission Viejo, fifty miles southeast of Los Angeles. As in the prior cases, the suspect entered a home through an open window, crept into the bedroom, and attacked the sleeping victims. Twenty-nine-year-old Bill Carns was shot in the head multiple times but survived. Carns's twenty-nine-year-old girlfriend was tied up, beaten, and raped.

Mission Viejo was within the jurisdiction of the Orange County Sheriff's Department, whose investigators contacted the Night Stalker task force in Los Angeles early Sunday morning. Salerno and his partner, Gil Carrillo, drove down to Mission Viejo to examine the crime scene. The pattern was disturbingly familiar, with the male immediately shot and then the female attacked. Based on the crime scene and what Carns's distraught girlfriend was able to tell detectives, they returned to Los Angeles certain their suspect was back in Southern California. By midafternoon on Sunday, both the L.A. and Orange County Sheriff's Departments confirmed to the media that the Night Stalker was responsible for the latest attack.

It was the first suspected Night Stalker attack in Orange County, in the opposite direction than San Francisco from Los Angeles, where the crime wave had started. The geographic focus of the investigation, already sprawling, expanded once again, this time southward. The Night Stalker task force had received more than two thousand tips from the public, and dozens of reported sightings. But despite months of dogged detective work, investigators were still unsure of their elusive suspect's identity. Up and down the Pacific Coast, law enforcement agencies were inundated with prowler calls. On a typical night, the Orange County sheriffs received three or four calls to report prowlers or suspicious behavior. On Monday night, August 26, they received seventy-six. The Night Stalker case became national news. The suspect's composite sketch was ubiquitous on TV and in the papers.

The blanket media coverage further stoked public alarm. The fourteen murder victims ranged in age from thirty to eighty-three, a demographic that included most adult Californians. On August 27, the *Los Angeles Times* reported, "*In the wake of Sunday's attacks in Mission Viejo—the 34th and 35th linked to the serial killer—Orange County residents, like those in the San Fernando and San Gabriel valleys and San Francisco before them, were buying guns and dead bolt locks to fortify their homes and protect themselves.*" The Orange County Humane Society received multiple calls from people who wanted to adopt dogs, specifically pit bulls, German shepherds, and Dobermans. Hardware stores sold out their stocks of window locks and bars. Home alarm companies, accustomed to making appointments and giving estimates, received walk-in customers willing to pay for an alarm system on the spot. Across the Southland, to deprive the Night Stalker of cover, homeowners cut back the foliage around windows and screwed brighter lightbulbs into outdoor fixtures. Before getting into bed, people double-checked their locks and wedged broomsticks into the base of sliding patio doors. Many slept with firearms at their bedside.

The tip that finally broke the Night Stalker case came from an observant thirteen-year-old boy, James Romero, who lived with his parents and sister in Mission Viejo, about a mile from Bill Carns's home. The night Carns and his girlfriend were attacked, James was up past midnight fixing his motorbike in his parents' garage when he heard rustling outside in the yard. James initially thought it was an animal, but moments later, he heard the distinctive crunching sound of footsteps on gravel. James hid in the garage behind his parents' car until the prowler passed. After the footsteps stopped, James went and woke his father. While his parents called 911, James went back outside just in time to see a man, dressed all in black and a black baseball cap, get into an orange Toyota station wagon. As the car made a U-turn and sped away, James caught the first three digits of its license plate, 482. Police responded to the 911 call within ten minutes. James showed the officers where in the yard he heard the footsteps. Nearby, his parents' bedroom window was open. On the ground under the window was a dead bird. The officers took a report and left, unaware of what was happening inside Bill Carns's house a mile away.

The significance of the information James Romero provided was not apparent to the police until the next day, after the Carns attack. The description of the orange Toyota was relayed to the Night Stalker task force, which released it to the media. The resulting news publicity prompted a call from a man who said the description resembled his car that was stolen off the street in Los Angeles's Chinatown on Saturday night, a few hours before the attack in Mission Viejo. The license plate of the stolen car was 482RTS, which matched the partial plate James saw. Within hours, police officers throughout Southern California were on the lookout for the orange 1976 Toyota station wagon.

On Tuesday morning, August 27, the orange Toyota was found abandoned at a shopping center parking lot in the Wilshire district of Los Angeles. The car was put under surveillance in the hope that the suspect would return to it. The same day, the sheriff's task force received a call from a woman, Pauline Perez, who said her father was certain he knew the Night Stalker. Two sheriff's detectives went to the Perez home in East Los Angeles, where her father, Jesse Perez, nervously told them about an acquaintance of his, a burglar he knew only as Rick. Jesse's physical description of Rick resembled the composite sketch. Jesse said Rick had once told him about killing an Asian couple in Monterey Park. Jesse also said Rick had sold him a .22 caliber gun, which he had since given to a female friend for protection. It was the same caliber gun used to kill some of the victims. Jesse didn't know Rick's last name, address, or phone number. He did tell the detectives he believed Rick had been arrested by the LAPD in December 1984, after he crashed a stolen car into the bus terminal in downtown

Los Angeles. The information was relayed to the task force, which asked the LAPD to search its reports for any such incident involving a Rick, Ricardo, or Richard. The LAPD informed the task force they could find no record of the arrest.

Stephanie returned to work at Devonshire on Tuesday evening, August 27, after three days off duty. While the rest of Los Angeles was consumed with the Night Stalker, Stephanie appeared preoccupied with other matters. Her on-duty visits to Mark Currie, her married doctor friend, continued to increase in frequency. Stephanie recounted in her diary, "*Tonight was work out. I got to work by myself which was nice. That way I could go by the hospital to visit Mark. Lt. Malen gave me a call to go on. I had to meet Sgt. Johnson. Some police officer's ex-wife was beating up on his girlfriend. It took me forever to get to 23022 Mayall. The first car I had the computer didn't work, nor did the radio. So I had to switch cars. It never fails. You get the first car all set up and something doesn't work.*" By the time Stephanie finally got there, Johnson had arrested the suspect. She wrote, "*Well I went to search her and she got all pissed off at me. So I twisted her wrist. She worked for Santa Monica Police Dept. So I twisted her wrist a little so she'd stop. She was a real bitch. The cop's girlfriend made a citizen's arrest. I had another unit transport because of the way she was acting. Acosta and Rost booked her at Van Nuys jail for me.*"

Later that same watch, Stephanie wrote, "*I went by the hospital to visit Mark. Then I went to the Station. I didn't get much of the report done, because I went to dinner. After dinner I had to go take a 459 report but of course I stopped by the hospital to visit my buddy, Mark. I went and took the report. Then I went over to Mark's in-laws. His wife was there and boy was she watching us like a hawk. I think she must think something is up.*" Stephanie did not say whether Mark's wife's suspicion was warranted. Stephanie's efforts to cultivate a relationship with the Currie family are reminiscent of how she tried to secure a future with John by ingratiating herself with the Ruettens. Stephanie worked on her reports at Mark's in-laws', then went to a doughnut shop to finish them. Before she turned in her reports, Stephanie went back one more time to Granada Hills Hospital, where Mark worked, and dropped off some doughnuts for the nurses.

Detectives staked out the Night Stalker's orange Toyota, in the hope that the suspect might return to it, until dawn on Wednesday, August 28. He never did. The station wagon was transported by flatbed truck to the LAPD's Newton Division station, and then to the Orange County sheriff's garage in Santa Ana. Beginning Wednesday evening, inside a lightproof shed, Orange County sheriff's criminalists thoroughly examined the Toyota for latent fingerprints using two different methods, the best available to investigators in 1985.

The first method relied on the controlled fumigation of superglue. When heated under proper conditions, the glue released fumes that bonded with the oils in fingerprints. The chemical reaction turned the ridges white and rendered any prints visible. The second method took place in total darkness and used an argon-ion laser beam projected from a handheld wand. When the beam was swept over a surface, it illuminated fingerprints otherwise invisible to the naked eye. The Orange County Sheriff's Department had purchased its argon-ion laser a year earlier for $35,000. It was the first law enforcement agency in California to own one. The device was the envy of other police departments. An LAPD spokesman told the *Los Angeles Times*, "Orange County has the best, most sophisticated equipment on the West Coast. We don't have a laser or anything like it."

Stephanie reported for duty at Devonshire at about the same hour the forensic examination of the Night Stalker's Toyota got under way in Santa Ana, sixty miles away. Stephanie's patrol partner the evening of August 28 was a probationary officer, Liz Tate. Although Stephanie at that time had less than two years on the job, she had already begun to carry herself as a veteran officer. She did not hesitate to criticize Tate for her inexperience. *"Thank god I don't always have to work with her. Her tactics are really poor,"* she wrote of Tate in her diary.

The painstaking examination of the Night Stalker's Toyota for fingerprints lasted until early Thursday morning, August 29. No latent prints were found inside, which suggested the suspect had either worn gloves or wiped down the steering wheel and door handles. Just before the forensic tests were completed, a female criminalist found a single fingerprint on one of the car's rearview mirrors. In contrast with the high technology used to find it, the print was dusted with black fingerprint powder and removed with ordinary lifting tape.

In San Francisco, police released to the media photos of jewelry stolen during the Pan murder on August 17, in case the suspect had pawned, fenced, or given away a piece and someone recognized it. A photo of a gold bracelet reminded a man, Earl Gregg, of a bracelet his mother-in-law recently gave his wife. Gregg called the Night Stalker tip line and reported that a man he and his wife knew only as Rick gave the bracelet to his mother-in-law. He also said Rick resembled the suspect sketch in the papers. Two San Francisco detectives went to interview Gregg and his wife in person. The Greggs told the detectives that Rick was a professional burglar originally from El Paso, Texas, who was obsessed with Satanism. The detectives' next interview was with the mother-in-law, Donna Meyer. Meyer didn't know Rick's last name either. She explained that she met Rick through a man she used to live with, Armando Rodriguez. It was Rodriguez who finally provided a full name to the detectives: Rick Ramirez.

The San Francisco detectives passed the name on to the Night Stalker task force in Los Angeles. Along with the description of Rick provided by Jesse Perez, the tip seemed to fit like a puzzle piece. Although the detectives were confident they were narrowing in on the right suspect, computer searches of police records returned thousands of men named Richard, Rick, or Ricardo Ramirez who had come into contact with the California criminal justice system. Any of their fingerprints might well match the exemplar lifted from the Toyota's rearview mirror.

In the mid-1980s, computerized fingerprint databases were brand new and just beginning to revolutionize how homicides were investigated. Previously, crime scene fingerprints could be compared only to the prints of a known suspect rather than to a pool of many potential suspects. As of the early 1980s, the California Department of Justice had about six million fingerprint cards on file, but no easy way to search their characteristics. If detectives did not have a suspect's name or print card on file, crime scene prints had limited investigative value. This began to change in California in 1985 with the introduction of Cal-ID, a program that stored fingerprint images and identified latent prints. The unidentified fingerprint from the Toyota was flown to Sacramento to be fed into Cal-ID and compared to all the Ramirez fingerprints on record.

The Cal-ID database spat out a potential fingerprint match for twenty-five-year-old Richard Munoz Ramirez, originally from El Paso, Texas. Ramirez's lengthy rap sheet included past arrests for drug possession, petty theft, and operating a stolen vehicle—the incident the LAPD initially found no record of—but nothing as serious as murder. A visual comparison of the fingerprint lifted from the Toyota and Ramirez's fingerprints on file confirmed they matched.

Contrary to popular belief, obtaining a fingerprint match does not mean a case is solved and the investigation is complete. Unless the suspect is already incarcerated, a fingerprint match tells detectives nothing about where the suspect might be, nor how long until they might commit another crime. In the case of the Night Stalker, who had already murdered at least fourteen people and was still on the loose, the stakes were especially high. The LAPD pulled the booking photo for Richard Ramirez from his December 1984 arrest. His resemblance to the Night Stalker composite sketch was uncanny. Sheriff's detectives showed the mug shot to Jesse Perez, who confirmed it was the Rick he knew.

For weeks, police officials had repeatedly assured the public that there was no higher law enforcement priority than apprehending the Night Stalker. The countless man-hours devoted to the investigation by the fifty detectives on the multiagency task force attests to the truth of those assurances. Throughout the day on Friday, August 30, the task force intensified its focus on Richard Ramirez. All the pieces seemed to fit that Ramirez was the Night Stalker.

The evidence implicating Ramirez was swiftly passed up the chain of command to Sheriff Block. Block promptly alerted LAPD Chief Daryl Gates, Orange County Sheriff Brad Gates, and San Francisco Police Chief Cornelius Murphy. The task force wanted more time before Ramirez's name and mug shot were released to the public, but as in any case as high profile as the Night Stalker, the top brass would make the call. The detectives believed that they would find Ramirez soon, and that their chances were better if he was unaware he was the most wanted man in California. By publicizing his identity, they increased the risk that Ramirez would flee and go further underground. On the other hand, waiting to do so would leave the public vulnerable to another attack, possibly even that night. Into Friday evening, Block discussed his options with his high-ranking counterparts.

Notwithstanding the grim pros and cons being weighed at headquarters, and the abject fear that continued to grip the city, the mood was decidedly light that evening at Devonshire station. Stephanie recounted in her diary, *"In roll call today, they held Kangaroo Court on Wolleck, because he missed court, and he was on a Code X (which is he tells his wife he's working but he's with his girlfriend). So Kibodeaux and I were his defense rep, Sgt. Flores was the Judge, and Kirk was the prosecutor. The jury (other officers) found him guilty, so he had to buy a case of beer for the guys after work . . . We ate about 2200, then Wolleck went to Hughes. He took off his gun belt and shirt and went and bought a case of beer and then we took it back to the Station. We arrested 1 guy at Dearborn Park for having an open container . . .*

Nothing else happened. Most of the guys went to the park after work to drink the beer, but I went home."

At roughly the same hour when Stephanie and Wolleck were on their beer run, according to her diary, hundreds of reporters, cameramen, and photographers jockeyed for space inside the press room at the Hall of Justice, the sheriff's headquarters downtown. For the second consecutive week, Sheriff Block had called a late Friday night press conference. Seated with him behind a table full of microphones were LAPD Chief Daryl Gates and Orange County Sheriff Brad Gates. "We are satisfied that we now know the identification of the individual known as the Night Stalker," Block told the cameras. He announced that an all-points bulletin had been issued for Richard Ramirez, who should be considered armed and dangerous. Block defended his decision to release Ramirez's name and mugshot as a matter of public safety. Addressing Ramirez himself, the sheriff said, "You cannot escape. Every law officer and every citizen now knows exactly what you look like and who you are."

Indeed, television networks across the country interrupted their programming to broadcast the press conference and photo. Lead investigator Frank Salerno ordered thousands of copies of Ramirez's mug shot printed. In an age before fax machines and email, Salerno requested that every area law enforcement agency pick up hard copies to distribute to all their officers. Salerno then worked until 4:30 a.m., coordinating surveillance on places Ramirez was known to frequent. Salerno went home to sleep more than an hour after the Devonshire officers cracked open their case of beers at the park. Stephanie did not note in her diary whether it was the same park where, earlier that night, she and Wolleck had arrested a man for an open container.

The next morning, Saturday, August 31, Richard Ramirez's mug shot was on the front page of all the Los Angeles papers, including a Spanish language daily, *La Opinion*. Around 8:00 a.m., Ramirez walked into a liquor store near the bus terminal downtown and saw his own photo on the front of *La Opinion*. Until that moment, Ramirez had not realized that he had been identified and was the subject of a police manhunt. He fled the store, but not before drawing stares and then shouts from other customers as they recognized him. The liquor store's owner called 911.

Ramirez fled on foot, jumping fences and crossing the Santa Ana Freeway through traffic. He boarded a bus, but felt people staring at him and quickly got off. He then saw a car with a woman in it idling outside a grocery store. He ran up and tried to carjack it. The woman's screams alerted her boyfriend, who ran out of the store and fought him off.

Ramirez fled through alleys and backyards looking for another car to steal. A short distance away, on a residential block of Hubbard Street, he saw a red Mustang that was up on jacks with its engine running. The car was parked in front of the home of Faustino Piñon, who was fixing its transmission. Ramirez was able to get the Mustang into gear, but Piñon grabbed the wheel and steered the car into the side of his house. The Mustang stalled out.

Ramirez ran across Hubbard Street and tried to carjack a third car, parked outside a neighbor's. Inside the car was a young mother, Angela De La Torre, who was going to the store to buy a piñata for her daughter's fourth birthday party. As Ramirez approached, she recognized him from his photo and began screaming. When she refused to hand over her car keys, Ramirez punched her in the stomach and grabbed them from her.

The commotion drew the alarm of more neighbors on the tight-knit block. Several men, including Angela's husband, Manuel, came running to her aid. Manuel grabbed a two-foot steel rod and prepared to defend his wife with it. He also recognized the stranger's face from the papers. Ramirez bluffed that he had a gun but was pulled from the car roughly anyway. Manuel swung the rod and struck Ramirez on his head. Ramirez took off on foot, with a swelling crowd of Hubbard Street residents in pursuit. Initially, their anger stemmed from seeing Ramirez punch a woman and try to steal a car. Faster than Ramirez could run, word spread through the neighborhood that it was the guy on the news, the Night Stalker. *"El maton, el maton!"* they shouted, Spanish for thug or bully. A few men caught up to Ramirez half a block away and tackled him. By now, he was slick with sweat, bleeding from the head, and exhausted. They sat Ramirez on the curb in the hot sun while somebody called the cops. Ramirez begged the men to let him go. Manuel stood over him with the steel rod, ready to swing if he tried to bolt again.

The first police officer at the scene was Andres Ramirez, a twenty-five-year-old sheriff's deputy, who responded in his patrol car to what he thought was an ordinary 415 call. By chance, Deputy Ramirez had grown up four blocks from Hubbard Street. When he approached, he saw a group of people, including one with a metal pipe, guarding a bleeding man. Everyone was talking at once, trying to tell him what happened. More people streamed from their homes, some waving copies of *La Opinion*. "You got the guy! You got the Night Stalker!" people shouted.

Deputy Ramirez stood the bleeding man up and searched him, then handcuffed him. The deputy asked his name and the man replied, "Ricardo Ramirez." All the while, the size of the crowd continued to grow, along with the intensity of its anger. To prevent mob justice, the deputy put Ramirez in the back of his patrol car. A scrum of agitated people surrounded the vehicle. Everyone wanted to see with their own eyes if the suspect really was the Night Stalker. Just as the crowd was threatening to overwhelm the lone deputy, other sheriff's and LAPD units arrived on the scene. Reporters and TV news crews also descended en masse on Hubbard Street. The decision was made to transport the Night Stalker suspect to the LAPD's Hollenbeck Division, east of downtown, to be interrogated.

All morning and afternoon, people thronged Hollenbeck station. The *Times*, in its story on the arrest, described "*a carnival-like atmosphere*" outside. "*As soda and ice cream street vendors did a brisk business under the scorching sun, spectators gathered five and six deep on the curb and watched from windows to commend the police and condemn the suspect. Police eventually had to seal off the area in front of the police station because the crowd, estimated at more than 400, had grown so loud and boisterous in waiting for a glimpse of the Stalker suspect,*" the *Times* reported. A handcuffed suspect brought into the station on an unrelated case was mistaken for Ramirez, which caused the crowd to surge forward as the detectives rushed the suspect inside. Forty uniformed officers came out to push back the throng and clear the street alongside the station.

Throughout the day, detectives from the Night Stalker task force arrived at Hollenbeck station to try to get their own peek at the man they had hunted for months. Much of the top brass of the LAPD and Sheriff's Department showed up as well, less to see Ramirez than to bask in the reflected glory of the arrest. The mayor of Los Angeles, Tom Bradley, came to the station to congratulate and thank the police. "California can breathe a sigh of relief tonight. A very dangerous man is off the streets," Bradley told the *Times*.

The waiting crowd finally got to see Ramirez at 3:30 p.m., when he was led from Hollenbeck station and placed in the backseat of an unmarked police car. The crowd cheered as the car left for the Central Jail downtown. The *Times* reported, "*One teenage boy, who had stood on a wall for almost two hours to get a glimpse of Ramirez, said, 'He sure doesn't look mean. He just looks like everybody, doesn't he?'*"

Stephanie reported for duty at Devonshire a few hours later, at 6:15 p.m.

She wrote in her diary, "*They caught the Night Stalker, which has relieved everyone's minds. I was so glad to work by myself. First I went and got a malt at Tiffany's . . . I then went and visited Mark's parents' house . . . I had to go take care of a parking violator in a apt complex. Luckily I found the owner of the Veh and told him he shouldn't have parked there. I also ran him in case he had a warrant. I could have arrested him, because he was inconsiderate. Then I went by the hospital. Mark was sick so he wasn't there.*" After the hospital, she wrote some tickets and visited another friend. Her last call of the night came while she was running another errand. "*I was flagged down on Lassen & De Soto because I was going to the Donut Shop to get a donut for John Weaver, Jayme's husband who was working an off-duty job,*" she wrote.

Stephanie was assigned to patrol with an officer named Kirk on September 11. She wrote in her diary, "*We visited Kirk's relatives in the Knollwood and I visited Brian.*"

"Brian" was Brian Brase, a fitness instructor Stephanie met at Mid Valley Athletic Club, a gym in Reseda. In the mid-1980s, before the fitness boom and proliferation of gyms across Los Angeles, Mid Valley was the nicest, most modern workout facility in the San Fernando Valley. Brian's job was to give new members an hour-long orientation and fitness assessment. Members also received three follow-up training sessions, to ensure they felt comfortable working out on their own.

Stephanie was assigned to Brian for her briefing and fitness assessment when she joined Mid Valley. During their initial meeting, she mentioned to him that she was an LAPD officer. The first thing he noticed about her, after spending just a little time with her in the gym, was that she really didn't need his help. Unlike most new female members, Stephanie was already conversant with the techniques and equipment that he went over with her. Her fitness level was advanced, especially compared to most women then. Brian could tell she was in excellent physical shape. Stephanie's body was lean and attractively muscular. He thought she looked great.

Brian had moved to Los Angeles from Indiana a year earlier, in August 1984. In addition to his job at Mid Valley, he worked as a track and field coach and physical education instructor at Cal State Northridge. He lived by himself in a studio in an apartment building a short bike ride from both the gym and the Northridge campus. Unlike most Valley residents, Brian chose not to have a car. He preferred to bike the familiar triangular route between his apartment and two jobs.

Over the course of their initial meeting and three follow-up sessions, Stephanie and Brian chatted and became friendly. He was single but avoided dating clients, which he considered an occupational hazard. Still, Brian thought Stephanie seemed fun and had a unique look. Most women who were into fitness at that time wore leotards to exercise. Aerobics classes at Mid Valley sometimes felt like fashion shows. Stephanie always wore high-cut gym shorts, usually with a UCLA T-shirt. Her personality had an impish quality that made an impression on Brian. When Stephanie was happy, which was her normal mood during their appointments, Brian saw a mischievous glimmer in her eyes.

On September 13, Stephanie wrote in her diary, *"I also saw Tom Ruetten behind his apt complex and at the market on Zelzah."* Stephanie did not indicate whether she and Tom spoke, and if so, whether John's name came up.

Despite everything Stephanie had done so far that summer to break up John and Sherri's relationship, from sleeping with John after she learned of his engagement to confronting Sherri at the hospital and informing her of John's infidelity, nothing had seemed to have any impact on John and Sherri's future plans.

In mid-September, Nels and Loretta visited from Tucson to spend time with John and Sherri, who were in their third month of living together in what had been her condo. Sherri and John seemed to her parents every bit as in love as when they announced their engagement in May. Nels and Loretta gave Sherri and John some housewarming presents. Sherri was grateful to her parents for accepting her and John's living arrangements, even though they weren't getting married until November. Sherri was already immersed in planning the wedding. There were decisions to make about her dress, the rehearsal dinner, and the reception. Sherri had picked up several bridal magazines, which she paged through for advice and inspiration.

Sherri also brought her parents to Glendale Adventist Medical Center to show them where she worked, and gave them a grand tour. Sherri took them by her old office to meet Peggy. "This is the lady who stole my office" was how Sherri introduced her. Peggy had never met the Rasmussens before, but she found them warm and wholesome, like Sherri. Nels and Loretta's affection for Sherri, and their pride in what she had already accomplished in her young life and nursing career, were palpable to Peggy.

Stephanie was assigned to patrol with Bill Wolleck on Saturday,

September 14. Not long before, on September 4, she had written in her diary, "*It's been okay working with Wolleck. He really does know a lot and he has a very good way of talking with / to people. He is very well spoken.*" Only ten days later, she seemed to have soured on him, writing, "*Thank god tonight was my last night working with Wolleck on a permanent basis. He is so cynical and boring to work with. I don't think I could have put up with it anymore.*"

During their patrol watch, she and Wolleck assisted at a location with a barricaded suspect: "*Since 2300 we directed traffic and put flares up for 4 hours. Real exciting. It wasn't that bad. We had a few people just run over the flares like they didn't know why they were placed there,*" she recounted. The barricaded suspect situation attracted news crews from the local TV stations. The police put up yellow tape to close off the street to vehicles and pedestrians. Stephanie was tasked with keeping the media in line.

Stephanie caught the eye of a freelance news cameraman named Rodger. Rodger recalls Stephanie was dressed in her LAPD uniform top but, instead of uniform pants, in jeans. Rodger introduced himself and tried to strike up a conversation by asking about her attire. Stephanie explained she was on park patrol when she was called to the location. Rodger was a few years older than Stephanie and newly single. At the end of the conversation, he asked her for her phone number. In her diary, she wrote, "*I met this cameraman, Rodger, who was asking Kirk and Rost about me. He asked me for my number. I told him try the Station.*"

On September 16, Stephanie was assigned to patrol with her academy friend Jayme Weaver for the first time since July, almost two months earlier. Stephanie wrote, "*It was so nice to work with Jayme. I drove.*" After roll call, they answered a robbery call and wrote a few traffic tickets. Stephanie recounted, "*We then wrote some parking tickets over near the fraternities. The neighbors have been complaining about the frat boys. We then went and visited Mark at the hospital. I also visited Brian but he wasn't home . . . Mark saw us on his way home and stopped. It was nice to see him.*"

Stephanie and Weaver had been friends since March 1983, when they entered the preacademy Crime Prevention Assistant program together. More than two years later, they were still close enough that Stephanie talked with Weaver about her love life. In more than one conversation with Weaver, Stephanie had described John Ruetten as her boyfriend during college. Weaver got the impression that Stephanie's relationship with John was rocky before their breakup. Stephanie also told Weaver about some of the newer guys she liked, including her doctor friend Mark Currie, and Brian Brase from the Mid Valley Athletic Club. Stephanie wanted Weaver to meet them.

Although Brian was not home when Stephanie and Weaver visited him on September 16, they tried again some days later. The exact date is unknown, because Stephanie made no note of the return visit in her diary. Brian, however, never forgot the strangeness of that encounter, which began with an unexpected knock on his apartment door. Although his building had a buzzer and intercom system for visitors to announce themselves before they could enter the building, Brian heard no buzz or other warning before the knock on his front door.

Brian was home alone and wasn't expecting company. In fact, he had just finished smoking a joint, the scent of which lingered inside his studio apartment. Worse, when Brian opened his door, he found himself face-to-face with two uniformed LAPD officers, Stephanie and her partner, an attractive young blonde, a description that matches Weaver's appearance. Stephanie's surprise appearance at his front door startled Brian for more than one reason. It was not only that Stephanie hadn't told Brian she might come by his place, and that he hadn't invited her over. Brian had never given her his home address. He had no idea how she found out where he lived. All Brian could think at that moment was, "Oh my God, a surprise visit, the place smells like pot, and there are two cops at my door."

Brian felt he couldn't invite them inside, because if they came in, they would basically all be standing in his bedroom. Stephanie and the other female cop stayed for about ten minutes, chatting with Brian in his doorway. Brian thought it was strange that Stephanie had somehow found out his address, but he didn't feel threatened by her. At the time, Brian took Stephanie's visit as a clear indication that she was romantically interested in him. "Wow, that's kind of neat," Brian thought. He was twenty-seven, two years older than Stephanie, and unattached. Later on, after they left, Brian wondered how things might have unfolded differently if he hadn't smoked just before her surprise appearance and acted so standoffish. The thought crossed his mind, "What if I had invited them inside? Did they want to get freaky?" Brian imagined playing Cops and Robbers with the two attractive female officers. "Frisk me," Brian pictured himself telling Stephanie and her partner, had their visit gone another way.

Stephanie was open with Weaver about more than just her love life and where her crushes worked and lived. Once, some months earlier, while they were alone in the women's locker room at Devonshire, Stephanie showed Weaver a small pack of tools. Stephanie explained that it was a lock-picking kit and that she had received some training in how to use it. It was unclear to Weaver whether the training was a class Stephanie took or a book she read. In February 1985, Stephanie noted in her pocket date-book the names of two textbooks on the esoteric subject of locksmithing: *Practical Course in Modern Locksmithing*, by Whitcomb Crichton, and *Complete Course in Professional Locksmithing*, by Robert L. Robinson.

To supplement her income from the LAPD, Stephanie took a part-time job working security at Pierce College in Woodland Hills. Stephanie remained on the lookout for better opportunities, both within the LAPD and moonlighting. At the bottom of her diary entry on September 17, she noted, *"On 9-18-85 while working at Pierce I met a Sgt. and ofcr from Valley Narcotics. I think the ofcr liked me because he called back and told me he arrested this student they were looking for and I told him I was interested in Narcotics. He said he'd look into it for me. Also he offered me a part time job $13.00 / per hour to deliver jewelry. I told him I was interested."*

Stephanie and Weaver got to work in plain clothes on Friday evening, September 20. Their assignment was to infiltrate fraternity parties at Cal State Northridge and find out which houses were charging for entrance, had unpermitted live music, or were serving alcohol to minors. Stephanie recounted in her diary, *"Tonight we got to work with Vice undercover at the Fraternity parties . . . About 2130 Lt. Malen dropped us off . . . The first frat we go to 9934 Zelzah is not charging, does not have a band. So the only violation we had was serving to minors. This girl recognized me. We had arrested her boyfriend a few months ago and she said, Hi Stephanie, don't you work for the LAPD? I said no, I go to UCLA. She was very apologetic and walked away. We did have a few wine coolers and beer. Then I went outside and told the vice guys who were sitting in a Corvette across the street that we had no violation. We went to the party next door, same thing. Then we went over to the Halsted frat. Nothing there either."* Stephanie wrote that she and Weaver returned to the station at 11:00 p.m., having made no arrests.

A few days later, on September 23, Stephanie brought a birthday cake to work for Rick Rashi, a fellow Devonshire officer. After roll call, she dropped the last piece of cake off at the hospital for Mark. She and Weaver then drove to the academy to qualify in shooting. Stephanie qualified on her first try. From the academy, they visited a family friend of Stephanie's, Marilyn.

On September 25, Stephanie wrote of her and Weaver's watch, *"I drove* tonight. In roll call Sgt. Smith brought in some ice cream cake to celebrate the capture of the 211 susps. We went by the hosp to visit Mark. He was busy filling out insurance papers w/ his wife. We then went by Marilyn's at about 1945 for dinner. Mom was there." The reference to her mother was one of only a few times Stephanie mentioned either of her parents in her diary. She also noted, "I got my first rating at Devonshire. It was a good rating. Sgt. Flores told Jayme we were doing a good job."

On the same day that Stephanie saw her mother, Sherri and John wrote to Nels and Loretta, thanking them for their housewarming gifts:

9/25/85

Dear Mom & Dad:

Had a great weekend. Was so nice to have you over. A special thanks for so many things:

- *Meals (left-overs which are being utilized this entire week as dinner)*
- *For not questioning my current living situation*
- *For the lovely Bridal Shower gifts (dustbuster, pillows, bathroom & bedroom goodies)*
- *For the very special "John & Sherri" poem.*
  I appreciate it all & love you both.

Thanks–
Sherri & John

John wrote his own note to his future parents-in-law. In his card, John told Nels and Loretta, "Thank you for the leather shaving kit & hat. Most of all thanks for a fun weekend. John."

On Saturday night, September 28, Stephanie went out on a date with Rodger, the news cameraman who two weeks earlier had asked for her number. Stephanie had told Rodger to call the station, and he did. For their first date, they went to see the Manhattan Transfer, a jazz group, at the Greek Theater. After the concert, they stayed out late talking. Rodger, being newly single, felt his dating skills were rusty. Stephanie seemed to him like a nice girl. Although she was a few years younger than him, she didn't seem naive. Rodger enjoyed her sense of humor and that she seemed eager for new experiences. He was also impressed that Stephanie spelled his name correctly, with a *d*, right off the bat. He had friends he had known for years who still got it wrong. Although Rodger wasn't looking to jump into a relationship right away, he liked Stephanie enough to call her again.

Despite the serial overtures Stephanie had made to several guys she seemed to like, no romances had blossomed to make her forget about John. Whatever the nature of her interest in Mark Currie, their relationship seemed to have evolved into a platonic friendship with him and his wife, Pam. Between June and October 1985, Stephanie noted in her diary more than a dozen visits to the hospital where Mark worked, not including her visits with Mark and Pam at home and to Mark's parents' and Pam's parents' homes. During that entire five-month span, she never once mentioned Mark visiting her.

Things between Stephanie and her fitness instructor Brian Brase had cooled as well, before they even went on a first date. The next time Brian saw Stephanie, after her and Weaver's surprise visit to his apartment, was at the Mid Valley Athletic Club. Stephanie asked him out and he agreed. They made a plan to go out, but before the date, Brian had second thoughts. At the last minute, he called Stephanie and canceled.

Brian did not give it much thought until the next time he saw her at Mid Valley. When they made eye contact, Stephanie shot him a vengeful look that shocked him. Brian could sense her rage from across the gym. "She looks like she could kill me," he thought. Stephanie never confronted Brian directly. After that day, he steered clear of her. The few times he saw her later, working out, he thought, "There she is. She's pissed at me."

Stephanie eventually stopped frequenting Mid Valley. She could get her workouts in at the station, thanks to the policies instituted by Captain Stevens as part of his "Club Dev" fitness push. Not all officers made use of the station's weight room, or took advantage of "work out days," when they were allowed to skip roll call and hit the gym instead. Stephanie's diary suggests she worked out at the station every chance she got.

Midday on Tuesday, October 8, Stephanie met up with Rodger. They planned to go bike riding in Santa Monica. Rodger lived far from the beach but had a bike rack on his car. That day, Rodger carried his bike out to his car, then realized he needed a wrench for the bike rack. He leaned the bike against his car and went to get one. When he came back, minutes later, his bike was gone. No one had cellphones in 1985, so he couldn't call Stephanie and cancel their plans. Rodger got in his car and drove to Santa Monica.

Rodger met Stephanie where they had agreed and explained to her that his bike had just been stolen. Stephanie walked her bike along the board-walk with Rodger and they talked. Rodger recalls that Stephanie was nursing an injury that day, a big gash across the bridge of her nose. The wound was red and noticeable. Rodger asked her how she got it. Stephanie told him she had been wrestling with a suspect and got hit with a pipe. She made no reference in her diary to any such incident or injury, so beyond what she told Rodger that day in person, no other details are known.

Throughout the fall of 1985, when Stephanie and Rodger were spending time together and casually dating, she never seemed to him forlorn or heartsick. Rodger does not recall that Stephanie ever mentioned John Ruetten or talked much about her ex-boyfriends. Nor did she ever pay an unexpected visit to Rodger's home or office, as she did with other men.

Stephanie did tell Rodger what type of guys she was uninterested in dating, specifically "cops and nerds." Ironically, Rodger had come close to joining the LAPD himself. While training to become an officer, an accident cost him some of the vision in his left eye. Forced to consider other lines of work, he pursued photography, which led to his job as a news cameraman. Stephanie had never been involved with someone in the news business before. Rodger thought she got a charge out of it. When they compared their workdays, nine times of out ten, Rodger's escapades in his news van were more exciting than what Stephanie did on patrol in Devonshire. A typical anecdote for her was "Some guy thought he heard something outside his house, but it turned out to be nothing." Rodger, by contrast, was all over the city, chasing whatever stories of the day would lead that evening's local newscasts. A normal day for Rodger was "I went to a car crash today. There were four people killed. They found some dope in the car." Rodger recalls Stephanie would marvel, "Wow, that's exciting!"

On the evening of October 8, after Stephanie met Rodger in Santa Monica, she was assigned to patrol with Weaver. In her diary, Stephanie wrote, *"First thing we did after work out day, we had to make a death notification on Vanalden and Roscoe. First we dropped some film off for Jayme at the Mall."* Later, *"We stopped by to visit Mark and Pam at Pam's. Then we ate at House of Pancakes."* They spent the rest of their watch handing out tickets. Stephanie recounted, *"I wrote a Mexican man for crossing against the don't walk . . . I wasn't going to write him but he acted so dumb like he didn't understand English so I wrote him a ticket."*

She partnered with Weaver again on October 12. *"This was a night I hope I never forget and that it will last forever,"* Stephanie wrote in her diary. For dinner, she and Weaver went to a restaurant called Solley's. Stephanie narrated, *"I saw this guy that I couldn't keep my eyes off of . . . Well, he and his group left."* She and Weaver thought the guys were going to a show, so they drove around looking for them.

Outside a movie theater, two of the guys from the restaurant, Gene and Andy, spied their patrol car. Stephanie wrote in her diary:

> *We were cruising the parking lot and Gene and Andy came over and wanted to know if we were following them. We talked for a while and they asked us to meet up after the show. We answered a few radio calls. We met them at 0045. We talked some more. I found out that Andy and Gene have a Corvette. Andy a '60 convertible, Gene a '59 convertible. Gene seems like such a nice guy and his body is in perfect condition. Gene lives around the corner from me and he said he has a Jacuzzi. We followed them over to Bob's Big Boy. They ate and we talked a little more. Well that ended our work night.*
>
> *I went after work by myself to Gene's. We drank wine. Andy was there. We all talked, we jacuzzied. Then Andy left. We drove over to my house and got Twilight Zone tapes. I got some Carrot Cake & Pop Corn. We had a really nice night. I got very sick from the wine. I think we went to sleep around 0700 and got up about 1230. I went home and got my bikini to lay in the sun w/ Gene.*

Stephanie worked with Weaver again two nights later, on October 14. Stephanie wrote, *"Tonight was my last night before my 23 day vacation. Jayme drove. We went over to visit Gene, but he wasn't home."* Later, after they took a report from a woman whose purse was snatched, she and Weaver went and ate. *"Luckily because we got very busy after dinner. We did stop by and visited Gene for a few minutes,"* she noted in her diary.

Time would tell whether Stephanie's romantic endeavors would lead to the committed relationship she desired.

9

Tying the Knot

(November to December 1985)

By all outward appearances in the fall of 1985, John and Sherri looked forward to their upcoming wedding. The date was set for November 23, the Saturday before Thanksgiving. Sherri juggled her responsibilities at the hospital with the myriad decisions, big and small, that she and John had to make before their wedding day.

The couple decided to hold the wedding in Pasadena at the First Congregational Church. The large, stately gray stone church had a dramatic Gothic arch entrance, stained glass windows, and a vaulted ceiling.

Sherri found her wedding dress with her mother, Loretta, at a bridal boutique in San Diego. Connie and Teresa, her sisters, agreed to be her matrons of honor. Sherri chose floor-length pink dresses for her sisters to wear. She asked Donna Robison, her best friend from high school and college, to be her bridesmaid. Sherri's girlfriends Jayne Ryan, her former roommate, and Nancy Tankel, a nursing friend from UCLA Medical Center, were included in her bridal party as candlelighters.

John asked his brother, Tom, to be his best man, and his two friends Mike Boldrick and Matt Gorder to be groomsmen. John's sister Gail agreed to do a reading at the ceremony, and his other sister, Janet, to handle the guest book.

Sherri's first choice to officiate the wedding was Charles Cook, the pastor of the Adventist church the Rasmussens belonged to in Tucson. Sherri had known Cook since she was a little girl. Cook and Nels were friends dating to the early 1960s, when they had both settled in Tucson around the same time. The Rasmussens had long been one of the most active and generous families in the congregation. Yet when Sherri asked Cook if he would marry her and John, he said he couldn't, because Sherri and John were not of the same faith. Sherri explained that she and John had worked out their religious differences and didn't expect it to be a problem in their marriage. Cook was unmoved. He cited to Sherri a line from Paul the Apostle's second letter to the Corinthians: "Do not be unequally yoked with unbelievers."

Sherri told her father about the disappointing conversation. Nels could tell that her feelings were hurt, but she had nothing bad to say about Cook. Sherri said, "I respect him, because he explained it." Nels believed Cook had an eye on advancing within the Adventist Church. The yoking of unbelievers might be a black mark on his record, and Cook wouldn't risk it. The way Nels saw it, asking someone to marry you is a compliment from the couple-to-be. Nels thought he wouldn't have handled it as well as Sherri did. Sherri tried to understand, even if she didn't agree with the family pastor.

Sherri next approached Pastor Carl Groom, her elementary school teacher in Tucson. Five years to the day before Sherri and John's wedding, Groom had married Sherri's younger sister, Teresa, and her husband, Brian. Groom had also taught Teresa as a girl. Teresa's childhood personality was more mischievous than Sherri's. Teresa considered Groom to be a tough, old-school teacher who did not let kids get away with anything in class. More than once when Teresa was his student, Groom told her, "You are nothing like Sherri." Teresa never disagreed, since she knew it was true. Years later, the Rasmussen girls were all grown up. Sherri would be the last of the three to marry. Groom did not object to Sherri and John's religious differences, and he agreed to come to Pasadena to perform the ceremony.

Amid all the wedding planning, Sherri shared with hardly anyone the shadow Stephanie had cast over her and John's engagement. Even Sherri's closest friends—her sisters, Connie and Teresa; her best friend at work, Peggy; and her three girlfriends in her bridal party, Donna, Jayne, and Nancy—were mostly unaware of Stephanie's intrusions that summer. Sherri told no one at all that John had been unfaithful to her during the engagement, which Sherri had learned only because Stephanie came to her office and informed her. Sherri was too private, and too protective of John, to tell her friends about his infidelity. It would have been humiliating for Sherri to admit. She had forgiven John for his mistake. She loved him and still intended to marry him.

Sherri and Donna spoke on the phone every week or so, and also wrote each other letters, their habit since college. During one phone conversation before the wedding, Sherri told Donna, "I never thought relationships could be this difficult." When Donna asked what was wrong, Sherri said, "Oh, there's an ex-girlfriend in the picture." Donna urged Sherri to discuss it with John and tried to be encouraging. "You're marrying him. Talk about it ahead of time," Donna suggested.

Sherri also spoke on the phone regularly with her parents in Tucson. Her older sister, Connie, was living in Seattle with her husband and their infant daughter, Rachel. Her younger sister, Teresa, and her husband were expecting their first child. In part because Sherri had less on her plate at home than her sisters, she kept closest in touch with their parents. Earlier that summer, the day Stephanie came to Sherri's office, she had called her parents, upset, and told them what happened. Sherri left out the worst of what John's ex-girlfriend had told her.

Later in the fall, Sherri mentioned to her parents that she and John were having a problem with their home phone. Sherri said the phone often rang, but when they picked it up, it was a dead line. The phantom calls had started that summer, around the time John moved in, and continued, once a week or so, for months. Had someone been on the line and said "Wrong number," the calls would have been easier to ignore. John felt the hang-up calls were bizarre but figured it was something with the phone line. John was not alarmed. The source of the persistent hang-up calls was never investigated or determined, either before or after Sherri's murder.

As the wedding approached, tensions continued to linger, just below the surface, between Nels and John's father, Richard. But that had been a constant throughout Sherri and John's relationship. Although Nels felt less than completely impressed with John, he respected Sherri's prerogative and would not stand in her way.

Even Bozo, the cat Sherri adopted from Teresa and raised with her roommate Jayne, seemed to accept John. Prior to John, Sherri and Jayne had seen Bozo display only antipathy to men. Yet Bozo and John got along remarkably well. One time, while they were hanging out in the kitchen, Bozo climbed up on John's lap and stayed there. Bozo was never the type to perch on a man's lap until John came along. The sight was so surprising and adorable that Sherri was inspired to take a snapshot.

Stephanie returned to duty at Devonshire on November 8, following her lengthy vacation. *"This was my first night back after 24 days off. My vacation was not that relaxing and it was nice to go back to work. When I first heard the radio it sounded like a TV show,"* she wrote in her diary.

Days later, Stephanie came down with the flu and missed several more days of work. On November 18, she wrote in her diary, *"I had 3 days of Advanced Ofcrs training at the Academy . . . I really didn't mind the school at all. It actually allowed me to get rid of my cold and relax. We got out everyday at 1500. It was nice having my nights off."* Stephanie completed her training on November 20, and was off until November 23, the day of John and Sherri's wedding.

A few days before the wedding, Sherri's friend Donna came to Los Angeles to help her get ready, and stayed with Sherri and John in their spare bedroom. Sherri and Donna went to a neighborhood nail salon the day before the wedding. During their manicures, Sherri announced, "I'm going to get my toenails done red." Sherri said it as if it was a crazy thing, which for her, it kind of was. "So when I take off my shoes, you'll see red toenails," she added impishly. Sherri got married with clear polish on her fingernails, and secretly, red toenails.

Some minor drama erupted at the wedding rehearsal, when John's mother, Margaret, saw the programs a print shop had delivered to the church. John's surname was spelled correctly on the front of the program, but inside, in the wedding party list, John's siblings' last name was misspelled "Reutten." Margaret went through the box of programs and confirmed they were all misprinted, which only made her more upset. There was no time, the night before the wedding, to print new programs. Margaret threw a fit while everyone in the wedding party looked on, including Jayne and Loretta. Loretta said to Jayne, "If that's the worst thing that ever happens to us, we'll be lucky." Loretta's casual remark stayed with Jayne. From then on, whenever Jayne found herself getting upset about something, she tried to remind herself, "Wait a minute. If this is the worst thing, we're lucky."

John and Sherri's rehearsal dinner, on the eve of their wedding, was held at the Castaway, a hilltop restaurant in Burbank with sweeping views. Donna's husband wasn't due to arrive until the next day, so she sat at a table with another high school friend of Sherri's. Donna was surprised that she

Sherri and John at their rehearsal dinner, November 22, 1985

didn't know more people at the rehearsal dinner. Donna assumed the unfamiliar faces were new friends of Sherri's, from her life in Los Angeles, and friends and family of John. Donna had not met John's parents before. Donna's impression, based on how Margaret doted on John at the rehearsal dinner, was that he was still his mother's baby. During the dinner, Donna made a toast to Sherri and John: "To love, laughter, and happily ever after."

After the rehearsal dinner, the Rasmussen family joined Donna, Sherri, and John back at the condo. The men—John, Nels, and Teresa's husband, Brian—gathered downstairs in the living room to talk. The women—Sherri, Loretta, Teresa, and Donna—sat around the dining room table upstairs. Sherri said, "Okay, today's my last day. Give me any advice about being married." They went around the table and, one by one, each gave Sherri her best advice, earnest, funny, or both. Donna saw on Sherri's face how happy and excited she was to get married.

On the morning of the wedding, Donna thought Loretta seemed more a bundle of nerves than Sherri. Donna enjoyed being a bridesmaid because she could observe more than Sherri and her family could. Donna knew from her own experience as a bride how hard it was to focus on anything except making it down the aisle.

The Rasmussens at Sherri's wedding (left to right: Teresa, Nels, Sherri, Loretta, Connie)

John and Sherri on their wedding day, November 23, 1985

When the ceremony began, Donna watched as Nels escorted Sherri into the church. Sherri was never the type to seek the spotlight. Her wedding was the one time that Donna saw her comfortable being the center of attention. Donna thought Sherri glowed as a bride. Everything about the wedding seemed regal to Donna, from the big, elegant church, to how beautiful Sherri was in her dress, to how handsome and happy John looked to marry her. When Nels and Sherri reached the altar, Nels could barely give Sherri away, because he couldn't stop crying.

Following the ceremony, everyone moved to the church parlor for the reception. The Rasmussens and Ruettens made the rounds of all the tables and accepted their guests' congratulations. All of Sherri's closest friends were there except her work friend Peggy, who had a family wedding the same weekend. There was no drinking or dancing at the reception, except for Sherri and John's first dance as a married couple. The song they chose was a 1980 country-western hit by Anne Murray, "Could I Have This Dance."

Stephanie spent the evening of November 23 on duty at Devonshire. She did not acknowledge in her diary that it was John's wedding day.

In early December, Stephanie was reassigned from mid-PM watch to day watch at Devonshire. She seemed relieved at the prospect of working more normal hours. In her diary on December 4, she wrote, *"Jayme drove. This was our last night working together. This was my last night for at least 6 months . . . All I can say is that I'm glad I won't be working nights for a while. I really need to improve my social life before I go crazy. I still really like the job and I think if I didn't have such a good job, with a lot of neat people at work, I would definitely go crazy."*

Stephanie's workday on December 12, like so many others, began in the gym at the Devonshire station. Later, she received a card in the mail that deeply upset her. Stephanie wrote in her diary, *"Work out day today. I didn't get done until about 0830. Then I had to take court papers to San Fernando Court. Then I went and picked up my mail. Unfortunately I got a card from Mrs. Ruetten! This made me very very very sad."*

Stephanie did not reveal in her diary what sentiments John's mother expressed to her. At the time, John and Sherri had been married less than a month and had yet to take their honeymoon, which they decided to delay until closer to the holidays.

Later that day, perhaps to get her mind off John and the card from his mother, Stephanie went looking for Greg and Mark, two other guys she had

DEV
0730-1615
Pc
U-1

12-12-85

Work out day-today. I didn't
get done until about 0830.
Then I had to take court papers
to San Fernando court., then I went
and picked up my mail. Unfortunately I
got a card from Mrs. Linette's, this
made me very very very sad.

Stephanie's diary excerpt about a card from John's mother, December 12, 1985

met. "*I went and drove over by Business Center Drive to see if the guys I had met at Chili's were in their offices (Stereo). They weren't so I went and ate at Fuddruckers, full price,*" she wrote.

Stephanie worked alone on December 16. In her diary, she recounted, "*First thing I did was to go see if Gene was at work. No his car wasn't there. I then drove by his house and he was out in his yard. I talked with him for a while. In the meantime I answered a few Code 30's at various locations. Nothing too exciting . . . I then stopped by Greg and Mark at their bus [sic] on Bus Center Drive. I then went to lunch w/ them and they bought.*"

The same day that Stephanie went out of her way to visit Gene's house and Greg and Mark at work, John and Sherri upgraded their home's security with a burglar alarm system. The system was installed by a local company, Locktronic, on December 16, days before they left on their honeymoon. When the technician was done, he affixed a white LOCKTRONIC sticker to the glass panel next to the front door, so anyone who approached knew the premises were protected by an alarm system.

Sherri called her parents and told them about their new alarm system. Nels was surprised, because Sherri had lived for years in the condo, first by herself and then with Jayne, without one. Had Sherri ever told her parents she felt unsafe and wanted an alarm, they would have made sure she had one. But Sherri had never mentioned it, or suggested she needed one, until after she and John were married. Sherri didn't tell her father what prompted her and John to decide to get a burglar alarm installed when they did, and Nels didn't quiz her on it. The impression he got from Sherri was that John insisted on having the alarm system installed.

Based on Sherri's description of the alarm system, it sounded to Nels like no toy. Sherri said it cost $2,000, and that she and John had the money to pay for it. In addition to the main alarm panel mounted on the wall alongside the front door, the system included two handheld panic controls, which were about the size of a garage door opener, small enough to slip in a pocket. Sherri explained they got two so that she and John could each have one. If they were in different rooms, and there was a problem, either could set off the alarm without having to reach the main panel. At the time, Nels found it amusing to imagine Sherri and John at home, toting their panic controls from room to room.

Sherri asked her friend Jayne to care for Bozo while she and John were on their honeymoon. Jayne stopped by the condo to pick up keys. Sherri taught Jayne how the burglar alarm worked so she wouldn't trigger it when she came to feed the cat. Sherri showed Jayne the wall panel inside the front door, and punched in the secret code to disarm the alarm: 1-1-2-3.

Jayne remarked of the simple code, "Well, that's not very clever."

"Jayne, it's our wedding anniversary," Sherri replied.

"Oh, I guess that makes sense," said Jayne.

Although Jayne was one of Sherri's dearest friends, she knew only a little about John's ex-girlfriend and the degree to which she was still in the picture. Sherri never told Jayne why she and John had the alarm installed, and whether it was related to the situation with the ex-girlfriend or just a more general fear of crime. Jayne knew that John had been in an on-again, off-again relationship with a woman before he met Sherri; that it was off when he and Sherri met; and that at some point, John had had to tell his ex-girlfriend that it was off permanently, because he planned to marry Sherri.

Sometime in late fall 1985, possibly the same evening Sherri showed Jayne the new burglar alarm system, Sherri told her that the ex-girlfriend had come to Glendale Adventist and confronted her. Sherri said that John's ex was dressed "provocatively" and told her, "If this marriage fails, I'm going to be waiting to pick up the pieces." Sherri said she had replied, "Don't worry, we won't be needing your services." The way Sherri told the story,

Jayne thought it seemed that Sherri had laughed it off. Sherri never told Jayne anything about what else John's ex-girlfriend said at the hospital.

Jayne and her boyfriend, Mike, had been a couple for almost as long as Sherri and John. Jayne had long assumed that she and Mike were going to get married too. Jayne was getting impatient waiting for him to propose. Sherri used to tease Jayne about the fact that Mike hadn't yet popped the question. After a while, Jayne complained to their friend Anita that Sherri's teasing was starting to get on her nerves. Sherri got the message. Jayne had her own concerns about what was taking Mike so long. Jayne hoped it would finally happen over the holidays. Sherri told Jayne she was saving her bridal magazines for her.

John and Sherri honeymooned at a Sandals beach resort in Jamaica. After their return home, they planned to celebrate Christmas in Tucson with the Rasmussens.

Despite all their travel, John and Sherri made time to decorate their condo for the holidays. For their first Christmas as a married couple, Sherri and John got a cute little tree, which they decorated and placed on a table in their living room. Two Christmas stockings hung from the mantel were the finishing touch.

Sherri made a fire to enhance the holiday spirit while they trimmed their tree with ornaments and wrapped presents for Tucson. Bozo watched them decorate, then made himself comfortable on the living room floor midway between the fireplace and the Christmas tree.

When Sherri and John finished decorating, she changed out of the clothes she had been wearing, jeans and a dark blue sweater, and put on a sheer white robe she thought John would like. The robe was short, only to her thighs, but Sherri had a roaring fire to keep her warm in the living room, and John for the rest of the night.

Stephanie wrote in her diary on December 18, *"I received a box of candy at the Desk from Rodger."* Despite Rodger's romantic gesture, and her flirtations with

Sherri and Bozo in front of the living room fireplace, December 1985

him and other men, she was still looking to meet the special guy who would
make her forget all about John, their history together, and the future she had
imagined with him.

At the top of her diary entry on December 20, Stephanie jotted down
a draft of a personal ad she was considering placing in the newspaper. On
the one hand, she seemed to want to move on from John. But to whatever degree Stephanie believed she had gotten over him, the ideal man her
draft personal ad described sounded uncannily like him:

> *25 yr UCLA GRAD, VERY*
> *ATHLETIC, LOVES TO TRAVEL.*
> *SEEKS TALL ATHLETIC*
> *MALE (25-31) WHO LIKES TO*
> *TRAVEL, HAS GOOD SENSE OF HUMOR.*

Stephanie's diary excerpt of draft personal ad, December 20, 1985

Warning Signs

(December 1985 to January 1986)

The year 1985 had been full of blessings and milestones for the Rasmussen family. In August, Nels and Loretta became grandparents for the first time when Connie and her husband's daughter, Rachel, was born. Soon after Rachel arrived, their youngest daughter, Teresa, and her husband, Brian, announced they, too, were expecting a baby. In November, Sherri and John married.

Christmas 1985 was the first time Nels and Loretta hosted all three daughters and their husbands at their home in Tucson. Including baby Rachel and Nels's and Loretta's parents, four generations of the family would be together for Christmas. Because Sherri and Connie were nurses and did not always get Christmas Day off work, the family decided to celebrate a few days early, on Sunday, December 22.

Christmas had always been a favorite holiday for the Rasmussens. One family tradition, dating from the time Sherri and her sisters were little girls, was to watch the classic film *White Christmas* together. Sherri, Connie, and Teresa had seen it so many times over the years they knew all the songs and lyrics by heart. Along with the title song, famously performed by Bing Crosby, their favorite was "Sisters," sung in the film by Crosby's costar, Rosemary Clooney. Irving Berlin's lyrics begin, *"Sisters, sisters / There were never such devoted sisters / Never had to have a chaperone, no sir / I'm there to keep my eye on her."*

In anticipation of everyone's arrival, Loretta hung a dozen red-and-white-striped Christmas stockings from the mantel above their fireplace.

Loretta also went out and bought a video camcorder. Consumer video cameras had only recently come on the market, and the idea of being able to conveniently capture memories in one's own home was still novel. The main reason Loretta wanted a camcorder was to record Rachel's first Christmas for posterity. Loretta never could have imagined at the time that Rachel's first Christmas might be Sherri's last. In later years, for an entirely different reason than when she bought the camera, Loretta thanked God she had.

When it came time for the family to open the many gifts piled around the Christmas tree, Connie's husband, Bill, set up the camcorder on a tripod to record the festivities. The scenes captured on tape were an assortment of heartwarming and occasionally awkward moments, a typical American family's holiday gathering.

Four-month-old Rachel was naturally the center of attention. Nels sat in a leather armchair with Rachel on his lap. Nearby was a gift already opened for Rachel, a Teddy Ruxpin animatronic teddy bear, which that Christmas season was the top-selling toy in America. The bear, slightly larger than Rachel herself, had a cassette tape deck and speaker hidden inside its torso. When Teddy Ruxpin told stories or sang lullabies, its big eyes and bulbous muzzle moved in sync with the words. Rachel was transfixed by the singing bear. She reached out to touch it with her tiny hands. "Typical high-tech baby," Nels said proudly.

After a few minutes, Bill panned the camcorder over to where John and Sherri sat on the floor beside the Christmas tree. "You're on," Bill warned them. "Be exciting!"

Once Nels had watched everyone open their gifts, he stood up with Rachel, who was beginning to fidget, and walked off camera. John and Sherri moved to where Nels had been sitting. John sat in the armchair, and Sherri on the floor in front of him, her back resting between John's legs. With his hand on Sherri's shoulder, John pointed to a present under the tree and asked Bill to pass it to Sherri.

Sherri unwrapped John's gift to find a smaller clamshell box inside. John looked over Sherri's shoulder as she opened his present, a bracelet. Sherri leaned her head back and she and John kissed. Sherri draped the bracelet over her wrist to admire how it looked. Connie helped Sherri with the clasp. Sherri reached up and caressed John's face. John wrapped his arms around Sherri's shoulders to hug her from behind, and kissed her under her ear. No one in the family took offense at their open displays of affection. John and Sherri were newlyweds. They appeared very much in love.

Three identical large gift-wrapped boxes from Nels and Loretta were under the Christmas tree for the three young couples. Sherri and her sisters rearranged themselves so they could open their presents on camera at the same time. The three sisters knelt on the floor with their gifts to face the camera. Their husbands sat in leather armchairs behind their wives, three in a row.

"Forty-pound box of chocolate," Brian guessed, while Teresa kneeled next to Sherri. Teresa was three months pregnant but not yet showing. Sherri started to untie the ribbon on her and John's gift, without waiting for her sisters.

"Sherri's already cheating," Teresa protested. Teresa insisted Sherri wait before she went any further. Sherri shook the box and playfully lifted a corner of the gift wrap, as if to sneak a peek. "Hey, you cheat!" Teresa shouted. Sherri laughed at her little sister. Nels said, "Try to guess. Make one guess each. One guess what it is."

Sherri said, "Escape ladder. To get out of a fire."

Teresa hoped not. "I don't have two stories! A lot of good that's gonna do me."

Sherri urged her sisters to guess, so they could get on with opening the boxes.

"I don't know, you guess," Teresa told Sherri.

"It's a pool table," Sherri said.

Teresa laughed. "A miniature pool table. Some kind of furniture junk."

Nels feigned offense. "Furniture junk?"

"I don't know, some kind of furniture," Teresa said.

"A bookcase," Connie guessed.

"A bookcase. That's the consensus," John chimed in.

Nels and Loretta's Christmas gifts to the three couples were wood-and-glass serving carts. Nels explained they were handmade in Sorrento, Italy, where he and Loretta had been on vacation that summer. The quality and craftsmanship of the carts was apparent from their gleaming parts. As Sherri repacked their box, John pulled on the new sweater he had received from Sherri's parents.

Nels and Loretta also gave their three sons-in-law matching tan zip-up jackets. Teresa made them all wear the jackets right away.

John, Brian, and Bill posed for a photo together. "We're the Pips," John joked.

"Where's Gladys Knight?" Nels said.

Nels and Loretta also gave Teresa and Brian a folding high chair for the baby they were expecting. The family referred to the child as Baby Lane, Brian's last name.

The high chair was a fashionable Japanese brand. Sherri asked Teresa to take it out of the box so she could see it.

"Now you've got the official yuppie high chair," John said.

"What did Baby Ruetten get?" Bill asked. John grinned but didn't answer. Bill persisted, "Sherri, where's Baby Ruetten at?"

"Oh, a little here, a little there," Sherri demurred.

While Teresa and Brian assembled Baby Lane's new high chair, Connie continued to open presents for Rachel. John said, "Well, Rachel, you think you got enough Christmas presents this Christmas?"

Sherri got down on the floor on her stomach, with her face close to Rachel's, and made silly noises to entertain her. Rachel reciprocated by giggling back at her aunt. "So cute!" Sherri blurted. Sherri found another of Rachel's presents, a panda teddy bear, and tipped the panda's nose to Rachel's until they touched. Rachel clamped her gums around the panda's nose. Sherri squealed in mock pain. Nels chuckled at his daughter and granddaughter playing together.

Sherri and John later received more gentle ribbing from her family about Baby Ruetten. The pressure may have been inevitable, given that both her sisters were already well on their way to starting their own families.

Later that day, Loretta cradled Rachel in front of the Christmas tree. "I need a break," Loretta said. John volunteered to hold the baby. Loretta went to get a toy for Rachel and left her with John.

"We're on camera," John told Rachel. One of Sherri's grandmothers was also there in the living room. It was unclear whether John was speaking to her, to Rachel, or to whoever in the Rasmussen family might eventually watch the videotape. As if pretending to confide in Rachel, John went on, "Everybody here thinks there's going to be a Baby Ruetten soon. I think they better talk to Sherri." John glanced at the camera and laughed. "I don't think she's ready for a baby, and I don't think I am either. I think we've got to get to know each other. Even as cute as you are, Rachel, we can't. We still have to wait a little."

Sherri's grandmother chimed in, "I think it's your decision to make. Not somebody else's."

"We'll wait until . . . We desperately need to increase our popularity with the family," John said. He laughed, but the comment was revealing.

In truth, it was not "we," meaning Sherri and John, nor Sherri whose "popularity" was in question. John knew Sherri was beloved by her sisters and parents. It was John who felt insecure about where he stood, especially with his father-in-law, Nels.

Despite the thoughtful Christmas gifts John had received from his in-laws, and the veneer of holiday cheer, John still seemed self-conscious about whether Sherri's family liked him. The fact that John and Sherri were husband and wife was not enough for John to feel fully accepted. Being married to Sherri did not make John and Nels's personalities more simpatico than they were prior to the wedding. Nor did it make John feel less intimidated in Nels's presence. John may have sensed that Nels thought he lacked the same qualities Nels most prided himself on: frugality, decisiveness, forthrightness. Deep in his heart, Nels believed John had no backbone. The ring on John's finger did not change Nels's perception of him.

If John genuinely wanted to endear himself to the Rasmussens, he had a peculiar way of going about it. The camcorder was still rolling when Loretta returned to the living room with a rattle for Rachel. Nels and Sherri were somewhere else in the house, but several family members, including Loretta, Teresa, and Rachel's father, Bill, were there or nearby, within earshot of the camcorder.

John resumed his pseudo-dialogue with Rachel, which was actually a soliloquy, fully aware of the rolling camera. John said, "Now I want you to tell me truthfully, Rachel, do you consider yourself a granddaughter first and then a daughter, or a daughter first and then a granddaughter?" Even if Rachel had been older than four months, and able to speak for herself, it would have been an awkward question for her to answer in front of her father and grandmother.

John nevertheless persisted with the bit. "Whisper it in my ear," John said. John lowered his head to Rachel as if to listen for her answer, then announced, "Aw, she said daughter. Tough luck, Grandpa." Teresa laughed in the background. John went on, "He's not here to see that, but he'll get to watch it on tape, so he'll know that's what you said." John pointed to Rachel's bib and said, "Even though you've got your 'I Love Grandpa' thing on." John seemed unconcerned that whenever Nels watched the family's Christmas video, he would know it was not his baby granddaughter but John who was talking. Nor did John appear to consider whether it was inappropriate for him to project his insecurities onto his baby niece and use her as cover to subtly needle his father-in-law.

If Loretta heard what John said, she didn't acknowledge it. Loretta focused instead on Rachel, poking at her tummy with the panda bear. "Ahh-boo-boo-boo-boo," Loretta said.

Nels came into the living room moments later. John kept pretending to speak for Rachel. "Oh, there's Grandpa. Say hi," John said. John waved Rachel's tiny hand to greet Nels. If John had been more tactful, he would have said nothing else, or at most, "Don't tell Grandpa what we were just talking about." Instead, John said aloud, "Don't tell him that you like to be a daughter better than a granddaughter, okay?"

Loretta looked at Nels, who said nothing, then went back to Rachel. "Ah-boo-boo-boo," Loretta said, as if to change the subject a second time.

"And here comes Aunt Sherri," John narrated, as Sherri rejoined him and her family in her parents' living room. Sherri apparently missed the entire conversation.

The remainder of the Christmas videotape, a series of vignettes recorded later that day, depicted the same dynamic: warmth and affection between Sherri and John, and an undercurrent of tension between John and Nels.

John and Nels had another exchange, not recorded on video, which bothered Nels. It happened when John and Sherri were sharing their honeymoon photos with her family. John showed Nels a photo of Sherri in her swimsuit and said, "What guy wouldn't like to be able to say, that's my wife walking there." Nels considered John's remark indelicate but did not say so at the time. Nels thought to himself, "I hope that's not the only thing he likes about her." Nels knew that beauty inevitably fades. Nels wondered if John was unprepared for that. Nels worried about the depth of John's commitment to Sherri, and what truly motivated his love for her.

While Sherri and John celebrated Christmas in Tucson, Stephanie was stuck working in Los Angeles over the holidays. Her diary suggests she was not particularly in the holiday spirit. On December 21, she partnered with a female officer named Laskowski. Stephanie recounted, "*Work out today. Laskowski drove. We took a call to meet this motor ofcr . . . The woman had a warrant. The motor ofcr let her use her car phone to call her husband to bring the 75.00 bail. She was on her way to church. So we took her to the Station. The warrant was a misdemeanor warrant for not having her dog on the leash. She was the upper middle class and her husband was a real snob. He knew a Sgt. from West Valley. The Sgt. called our station and I let the motor ofcr talk to him. The Sgt. wanted to make sure she was ok. Her husband had the money. The woman was pretty funny. She had to go sing at a church in Glendale. I took my wood to Arrow lumber. We went over to the Webbs."* The Webbs were friends of Stephanie's.

Stephanie's diary reflected her routine penchant for running personal errands and visiting friends while on duty. She seldom received criticism from her superior officers about her work habits and job performance. On those rare occasions when Stephanie was reprimanded for doing something wrong, she seemed to resent it.

On December 27, Stephanie wrote in her diary:

Today was a rather bad day. Sgt. Flores wanted to see me after roll call. Before I saw him I walked by past Sgt. Wonders and he mentioned something about not putting booking slips with our daily reports. He didn't say anything to me just made the statement loud enough so I could hear it. Then I saw Sgt. Flores and I had no idea what this was about. Well I found out soon enough. When I was working mid PMs with Weaver, we arrested the juveniles for GTA in San Fernando. Det. Roberts had sent me a note asking me some questions about the report. Well I had sent him a note back saying I couldn't answer them but the San Fernando PD ofcr could. Well apparently Capt. Stevens saw my note and wanted a Notice to Correct Form filled out on me. Sgt. Flores was not going to do this. He just counseled me. He said I was too good an ofcr for that. To say the least I was surprised and mad. I couldn't believe Capt. Stevens was that Chicken Shit. I think he knew me better than that, to want to make a notice to correct on me. I didn't write the note in any derogatory manner. I then went and talked to Roberts . . . He told me I should have gotten statements from the juveniles. Which he was right. Because he questioned them and got a few stolen vehicles from the boys' statements.

Near the end of her watch that day, Stephanie tried to cultivate an informant on a burglary case. *"I talked to this guy at 10331 Lindley about some info regarding 459 susps. I'm going to start working on how to get informants and crime info,"* she wrote.

Stephanie was off work from December 28 through New Year's Day 1986. She did not indicate in her diary if she celebrated New Year's Eve with anyone in particular, or anyone at all. On the front of her new 1986 pocket datebook, she jotted a note that suggests she did at least some celebrating: *"Captains Morgan Spiced Rum."*

In late December or early January, shortly after John and Sherri returned home from Christmas in Tucson, Sherri called her parents and informed them that John's ex-girlfriend had come to their condo uninvited.

Sherri had mentioned John's ex-girlfriend to her parents only once before, almost half a year earlier, after Stephanie went to the hospital and confronted Sherri in her office. Nels and Loretta knew John's ex-girlfriend was a police officer, but Sherri never told them the woman's name.

Sherri told her parents she and John were at home when the ex-girlfriend appeared at their front door. At least for Sherri, the visit was completely unexpected. Sherri said the ex-girlfriend had with her a pair of snow skis, which she said she wanted John to wax for her.

Sherri said the ex-girlfriend had stayed for a while, longer than Sherri wished. Sherri eventually let her know she was not welcome to hang out, she told her parents. Nels's impression was that it was Sherri who finally spoke up, because John lacked the nerve to stand up to his ex-girlfriend. Sherri told her parents she asked John not to take the skis, but he took them anyway.

Sherri said she let John know she was angry after the ex-girlfriend left. Sherri wanted John to give the skis back unwaxed. Sherri told her parents John went ahead and waxed them, over her objection. Sherri said John's attitude was, "Oh, I'll just wax them and that will take care of her." John seemed to believe that once he gave the skis back to his ex-girlfriend, she wouldn't bother them anymore.

The ex-girlfriend returned one evening about a week later, Sherri told her parents. This visit was less of a shock to Sherri than the first, if only because she knew she'd have to pick up her skis sometime. Sherri had made clear to John he was not to deliver them to her. Sherri said the ex-girlfriend again did not call ahead or buzz for entry to the complex. As on the day she dropped off the skis, she appeared at their front door without warning.

Nels knew from experience that security was tight at the condo complex. Sherri had lived there for nearly five years, first alone, then with Jayne, and finally with John. Although Nels's name was on the condo's deed for most of the time Sherri lived there, he and Loretta were not considered residents by the management. Neither parent was ever issued a key to the pedestrian gate or a clicker for the electric car gate. More than once when they visited and Sherri was stuck at work, Nels and Loretta had to park on the street and wait until Sherri came home and let them in. Nels thought it was odd that on at least two separate occasions, John's ex-girlfriend managed to bypass security and reach their unit's front door without buzzing for entry or otherwise announcing her presence.

Sherri told her parents she and John were both at home when the ex-girlfriend came to pick up her skis. Sherri did not describe the second visit in detail to her parents, except to say it was shorter than the first. Sherri said she had asked the ex-girlfriend to take her skis and leave.

Stephanie made no reference in her diary in December 1985 and January 1986 to asking John to wax her snow skis for her. At no point during the same period did Stephanie mention in her diary visiting John and his wife at their home in Van Nuys.

In 2012, more than two decades later, John testified in court that he had no recollection of Stephanie's ever showing up at the condo with snow skis. Nor could John recall waxing her skis at her request, or arguing about it with Sherri. In John's memory, and his sworn testimony, his only contact with Stephanie after his engagement was when she called him in tears and asked him to come to her place. Stephanie confessed her love to John that night, and they wound up having sex. John testified that other than that one night, he could not recall seeing Stephanie, or even speaking with her on the phone, after he and Sherri started dating. John also testified that once he moved in with Sherri, Stephanie never visited his and Sherri's condo while he was there.

Sherri never told her parents that John had been unfaithful to her during their engagement. Sherri gave her parents no indication that she felt fearful or threatened. Nels and Loretta never suspected their daughter might be trapped in an ongoing love triangle. The impression they got from Sherri was that John would not cut off contact with his ex-girlfriend the way he should. Now that she and John were married, Sherri wanted his ex to leave them alone.

It was only later, in hindsight, that Nels wondered whether the true purpose of the ex-girlfriend's visit was not to get her skis waxed, but to confirm where John and Sherri lived and to see their place for herself. In the 1980s, long before the advent of social media and online maps, it was not yet possible, let alone easy, to snoop on an ex from a distance. Back then, keeping tabs on someone meant doing it in person.

Since John's graduation from UCLA in 1981, he had worked for one company, Data Products, for more than four years. Shortly after Christmas

1985, John left Data Products for a new job at Micropolis, a computer disk drive manufacturer. Micropolis's offices were in Chatsworth, a twenty-minute drive from Van Nuys. John's hours for his new job were officially 8:00 a.m. to 5:00 p.m., but Micropolis did not require its employees to clock in or out.

Around the time John started his new job, he and Sherri planned their own skiing getaway. They booked a room at Mammoth Mountain, a ski resort north of Los Angeles. The trip, however, did not go as expected.

Sherri called her mother when she and John got home. Sherri told Loretta, "I can't believe it, but John and I fought all the way up to where we were going skiing." The drive to Mammoth was five hours long. Sherri said that when they finally arrived, they never even put their skis on. Sherri said they stayed only long enough to use the restrooms, then got back in the car and drove the five hours back to Los Angeles. Sherri said she and John also argued on the way home. "We weren't talking to each other by the time we got back," Sherri told her mother.

Sherri told her parents the dispute was over their finances. Sherri felt John was spending too much and not saving enough. For Sherri, it had always been a priority to stay out of debt. Prior to meeting John, Sherri rarely purchased anything on credit. Sherri preferred to save and pay cash. Early in Sherri's nursing career, Nels offered to cover half of her mortgage payments on the condo if she was ever short of money. Sherri insisted on making the full payment every month, no matter what, and never missed one. Sherri tried to save as much of her income as possible every month. She had savings but didn't flaunt it. Nels thought Sherri often talked as if she was dead broke, but she always had money.

Nels and Loretta knew it was common for newlyweds to experience friction in merging their finances. Sherri wasn't asking her parents for help. Nels thought John didn't know how good he had it with Sherri. After John and Sherri became engaged, he had moved out of his rental apartment and in with her. John didn't need to bring much with him, since Sherri's place was already fully furnished. Sherri had paid for all the furniture herself, up front. Nels believed the only thing John brought with him when he moved in with Sherri was his student loan debt for his UCLA tuition. Sherri told Nels she thought it would probably take John two or three years to pay off what he owed.

Sherri was unaccustomed to making monthly car payments, since she had always owned her cars outright. Sherri and John had celebrated their engagement by trading in her Toyota for a silver 1985 BMW 318i. Sherri and John financed the difference in price between the Toyota and the BMW. After their wedding, John traded in his old car for a nicer one, a 1986 Mazda RX-7, which they also financed.

The financial implications did not fully dawn on Sherri until after John got the Mazda. Whereas a year earlier, she had no monthly car payments, they now had to write two checks every month. Sherri told her parents it wasn't that they couldn't afford the payments. Sherri said she felt she and John shouldn't be working for nothing. Sherri believed they should have something left at the end of every month to show for their efforts. She disliked how their money was flowing out and not coming in at the same rate. Sherri wanted to continue saving for the future, whether or not it was a priority for John.

Sherri lowered the financial boom on John during their long drive home from Mammoth, she told her mother. Sherri said she told John she was going to the bank the next day to change all of her accounts. She planned to take everything in her savings and checking accounts and transfer it to a joint checking account, out of which they would pay their bills. Sherri also told John she would open two separate savings accounts, one for each of them. Sherri said she would set things up so a certain amount of her income every month went into her savings account. She told John he would be responsible for putting a set amount into his own savings account, though she didn't tell her parents how much.

During the same conversation with her parents, Sherri talked with her mother about what documents she would need to present at the bank to set up her and John's joint checking account. Since the wedding, Sherri had started to go by "Mrs. Ruetten" in her personal life. But because Sherri had published articles using her maiden name, she decided to keep using it professionally. Loretta suggested that Sherri show her marriage certificate to the bank to establish her identity as both Sherri Rasmussen and Sherri Ruetten. Sherri told her mother she would keep the marriage certificate in her purse in case she had any trouble at the bank.

John testified in court in 2012 that he had no recollection of his and Sherri's taking a ski trip to Mammoth in January 1986. John also testified he could not remember driving up into the mountains with Sherri and back to Van Nuys without their going skiing. Nor could John recall arguing with Sherri during the long round-trip drive. According to John's testimony, similar to the incident involving Stephanie's snow skis, it was as if his and Sherri's ski trip and argument never happened.

Sherri, however, mentioned the ruined ski trip to at least one other person in addition to her parents: her friend Donna Robison. Shortly after Sherri and John returned home, Sherri wrote Donna a letter. They had exchanged letters for years. Donna received Sherri's letter in mid-January.

Donna no longer has the letter, but she recalls it was written on plain paper and folded inside a small envelope. The letter proved to be the last Donna ever received from her friend. Donna recalls that Sherri described in her letter how she and John had planned to go skiing but their trip was soured by an argument.

Sherri told her parents she and John had argued over their finances. Sherri never mentioned to them that the subject of John's ex-girlfriend had come up. Sherri's letter to Donna suggested the argument was about John's ex-girlfriend and made no reference to fighting about money or anything else. Donna recalls that Sherri wrote, early in the letter, *"We are being harassed by John's ex-girlfriend."* Sherri confessed to Donna that she felt frustrated and did not know marriage would be so hard. Sherri's letter then moved on to other topics, Donna recalls. Sherri never told her the name of John's ex-girlfriend or what she did for a living.

Stephanie patrolled alone in an L car on January 3. Between sporadic radio calls, she was unfettered and was able to run personal errands and visit friends. She wrote in her diary, *"First thing I did after roll call was I went and got 3 donuts. I went by Greg and Mark's work. They weren't there so I went by their house."* After lunch, she answered a call about a possible burglary suspect on a bench. *"I think someone called in because the man was black. I couldn't find him,"* she wrote. Her last errand, before she went off duty, was to drive to the Cal State Northridge campus to talk with a dean about classes there. She did not indicate what discipline she planned to study. Stephanie also noted in her diary that a fellow officer seemed interested in dating her. *"Schmid keeps hinting at wanting to take me out,"* she wrote.

Stephanie worked an L car again the next day. While on duty, she visited with some friends, which caused her to miss a radio call. She wrote, *"I guess while I was in there I got a call to back someone up. But I didn't hear it. So Schmid took the call. Then he started looking for me. What a pain he's becoming."* Nonetheless, according to her diary, she went out to lunch with Schmid later that day.

Despite Stephanie's professed disinterest in dating other cops, she still chronicled in her diary who was dating who among her fellow officers. Stephanie was dismissive of their romances, which she painted as one-sided and beneath her. On January 6, she wrote, "*New gossip. Debbie Cruz and Bob Kirk are hot and heavy. Now Kristin Kiesling is going out with Bailey, and Melissa Mayer is going out w/ Jim Becker. I don't see what these women are getting out of these relationships. I would definitely want more.*"

On January 11, Stephanie noted in her diary, "*Sgt. Rebhan told me that some lady called and complained that I was driving on the Fwy too fast, fluffing my hair and making eyes at some guy. He didn't take a complaint and I told him I really didn't know what she was talking about.*"

Stephanie's patrol partner on January 15 was Mike Alexander. She recounted in her diary, "*I drove. Alexander had been out drinking last night for his birthday and he sure smelled like it. We stopped for coffee first.*" Their first call was at an elementary school, for a nine-year-old girl who had reported sexual abuse by a relative. "*The girl was real cute and smart. It was fun interviewing her because she seemed real special,*" Stephanie wrote. Next they handled a dead body call, which turned out to be a man who had had a fatal heart attack. "*Then we went and ate. Didn't really do much the rest of the day. We did get a call at about 1515—Family Dispute and I didn't want to work O/T. So it ended up being a boy/girlfriend dispute. So I talked w/ the girl. Mike talked w/ the boy. The girl lived in the apt and didn't want the boy around. So I came out and told the boy she doesn't want you here you'll have to leave. I did it firmly because I didn't want to work late,*" she wrote.

It was precisely the type of firm demand that John never made to Stephanie, on behalf of Sherri.

Three years as a cop had conditioned Stephanie to expect compliance when she issued a command. She did not have to tell the boyfriend what would happen if he refused to leave. The authority conferred by her badge and gun meant people did what she told them to, or else. In her professional life, she was accustomed to getting her way.

Stephanie had always been assertive, even before she joined the LAPD. By January 1986, she had been immersed in the LAPD's "us versus them" culture long enough to have internalized some of its worst qualities. Among the fundamental lessons she had learned was that cops live by different rules than everyone else. Stephanie's close observation of her fellow officers, as detailed in her diary, reinforced that lesson daily.

Only John knows what kept him from telling Stephanie, once and for all, to leave him and Sherri alone. John may not have imagined that Stephanie, once among his closest friends, could be capable of violence. Maybe it was the opposite. Perhaps John was scared of Stephanie and could not find the nerve to stand up to her. John's plan of action, if it can be called that, was to hope that the problem, namely Stephanie, would go away on its own.

The Month Before the Murder

(Mid-January to February 23, 1986)

One weeknight in mid-January, Sherri called her parents in tears. She recounted another strange and alarming encounter, earlier that same day, with John's ex-girlfriend, whose name Sherri never told them.

Sherri said that she had stayed home later than usual that morning before going to the hospital. Most workdays, Sherri was the first out the door and left John behind to get ready for work. Since John had started his new job, he tended to leave earlier, sometimes before Sherri. Sherri said that on that particular morning, John left for work first. Sherri was preoccupied with a lecture she had been asked to deliver at an upcoming nursing conference. She decided to get a few hours of writing done at home, where she expected she would face fewer interruptions than at work.

Sherri told her parents that around ten o'clock, a few hours after John left for work, she was shocked to discover his ex-girlfriend standing in their living room. Sherri said she did not hear her enter and had no idea how she got into their home. Although Sherri did not explicitly say the ex-girlfriend was dressed in her police uniform, Nels got the impression she was, because Sherri told him, "She had to have been on break, because she was on duty."

Sherri recounted that when she confronted her in the living room, the ex-girlfriend said she was there to see John. Sherri told her to get out, and that she didn't want her coming by to see John ever again. The woman left after Sherri told her to go, another reason Nels believed she was likely in uniform. Nels thought if she was off duty, she might not have felt compelled to leave.

The startling visit and its peculiar timing, midmorning on a weekday, made Sherri uneasy. Sherri told her father she thought it wasn't the first time John's ex had done this, come to their home and somehow gotten inside, while Sherri was at work. Later, Nels wondered if the officer had mistimed her visit and shown up when Sherri was home but not John, due to John's having just started his new job with earlier hours. Nels suspected she might have intended to surprise or rendezvous with John while Sherri was at work.

Sherri told her parents she didn't know what to do. She and John had been married for almost two months, but his ex-girlfriend was still imposing on their life. Nels thought Sherri was understandably disturbed and frustrated. Nels said, "You've got to get John's help on this, and let her know that she's not invited."

"John doesn't have the will to stand up to her," Sherri replied.

Nels told Sherri that if she needed his help, he would come to Los Angeles and talk with John's ex-girlfriend himself. Sherri declined her father's offer.

Sherri and Nels briefly discussed whether she should report the incident to the police, but Nels did not encourage it. Nels believed that realistically, if Sherri went to the LAPD or any police department to report she was being harassed by an officer, she would be laughed out of the station.

Sherri told her parents she didn't want to go to the police because she didn't want John to think she didn't trust him. The way Sherri described her predicament, it was as though she was fighting for her marriage on two fronts. Sherri felt suspicious of what might be going on between John and his ex-girlfriend. At the same time, John had promised Sherri that that relationship was over. Sherri wanted to trust John.

Sherri also wanted to avoid provoking the ex-girlfriend. Sherri thought that if she reported the encounter to the police, it could inflame the situation rather than resolve it. Sherri wanted to handle it in a professional manner, calmly, so as not to make things worse. Sherri never told her parents that she felt physically threatened.

Still, it was very unusual for Sherri to call her parents in tears. Sherri wasn't the type to cry easily. As a critical care nurse, she was accustomed to defusing crises and handling challenging personalities. Sherri's self-confidence and calm under pressure were hallmarks of her personality.

Her life experience had conditioned her to believe she could reason her way out of any situation, and to look for the best in people. It would have been inconceivable for Sherri to think her own happiness might be someone else's problem.

Sherri made clear to her parents that John did not know that she had called them, and that she was talking to them in confidence. At the time she spoke to them, she had not yet told John about finding his ex-girlfriend in their living room that morning. Sherri's insistence on confidentiality made Nels believe she wasn't telling John everything on her mind.

All Nels and Loretta knew was what Sherri had told them herself. In a span of six months, it was the third time Sherri had mentioned John's ex-girlfriend to her parents and reported a disturbing encounter with her. The first was during the engagement, when she showed up at the hospital and confronted Sherri. The second was after Christmas, when she dropped off her snow skis for John to wax. Just a few weeks after that was this latest incident, the most invasive to date. It seemed that John's ex-girlfriend did not intend to let it go. To the contrary, she appeared increasingly emboldened to show up wherever and whenever she wanted.

It is unknown what, if anything, Sherri told John when he got home the day she found Stephanie in their living room. More than twenty years later, in 2009, John insisted in police interviews that he could not recall Stephanie ever visiting him and Sherri at their condo, nor any incident in which Stephanie surprised Sherri inside their home. If what Sherri told her parents in 1986 was true, John was adamant that Sherri never told him about it.

Stephanie wrote nothing in her diary during January 1986 about visiting John's place or unexpectedly encountering his wife there. Her diary entries do suggest that beyond showing up on time for roll call, and answering sporadic radio calls, she felt entitled to do whatever she wanted while she was ostensibly on patrol. What Stephanie seemed to enjoy most about being an officer was the casual power and status afforded by the badge. The fact that Stephanie chronicled on a daily basis her many diversions while on duty is itself revealing of her character. Ordinarily, someone ashamed of their behavior would not memorialize it in a quasiofficial work log.

Notwithstanding the liberties Stephanie routinely took while on duty, she continued to rack up positive ratings from her LAPD supervisors. On January 23, she wrote in her diary, *"I worked by myself and the first thing I did was go to McDonald's and get Wally Cook some breakfast. I also got something. Then I met Sgt. Rembold and picked lemons at his house. I got 2 bags. Then I went to visit Pam's Mom. I gave her a few lemons. Then I had to go to the Station to see Sgt. Flores to discuss my monthly report. This was the first time I had ever had a monthly report. He said I was doing a good job. Then I went to my PO Box, got my mail. Went to the Toyota dealer and got a blinder for my car. Then I dropped off everything at my house. Pam's Mom had given me some wood pieces for my fireplace. Then I went by Greg and Mark's to say hello. It was now about 1115. I haven't done a thing all morning. Of course I've got to put something on my log."* Whether Stephanie's patrol log, her official account of her activities and whereabouts on duty, matched what she wrote in her diary that day is unknown.

It was on January 28, shortly after 8:30 a.m. in Los Angeles, that the space shuttle *Challenger* exploded off the coast of Cape Canaveral, Florida. All seven astronauts on board were killed. The planning of the *Challenger* mission had generated significant national interest, in part because the crew included the New Hampshire schoolteacher Christa McAuliffe. Across the country, millions of people witnessed the catastrophe unfold on live television. In the ensuing wall-to-wall news coverage, footage of the explosion looped endlessly.

Sherri had lunch that afternoon with Peggy, her closest work friend. They met at Jax Bar and Grill, a pub in Glendale. Their lunch turned out to be the last meaningful conversation Peggy ever had with Sherri. Live news coverage of the *Challenger* tragedy played on all the televisions in the restaurant as they caught up over lunch. Sherri and Peggy discussed how unbelievable it was that the astronauts' lives were lost in an instant, and the terrible impact on their families. Despite the sadness in the air, Peggy and Sherri were happy to reconnect and be able to talk for a little while away from the hospital.

During lunch, Sherri told Peggy about feeling harassed by John's ex-girlfriend. Sherri told Peggy that day the ex-girlfriend's first name, Stephanie, and said she worked as a police officer. Otherwise Sherri did not confide as much to Peggy as to her parents. Peggy knew nothing about Sherri's confrontation with Stephanie at the hospital, six months earlier. Nor did Sherri tell her about Stephanie's dropping off her snow skis for John to wax, or their most recent unsettling encounter in her living room.

Sherri told Peggy that John's ex kept showing up in unexpected places, like when she went to the gym or dry cleaner's. Sherri said she felt she was being watched and followed. Sherri seemed to Peggy more unhappy and frustrated with the situation than fearful. Still, Stephanie's behavior bothered Sherri enough for her to bring it up with her friend. Peggy told Sherri she thought John should deal with it.

Sherri also mentioned to her parents sometime in January that she sensed someone was shadowing her and John in public. More specifically, Sherri described a Friday night when she and John were at a neighborhood restaurant. It had been a hard week at work, and they decided to go out for a drink to begin the weekend. Sherri said the restaurant had an open layout, with seating at slightly different elevations. Sherri said she noticed someone unfamiliar watching her from across the restaurant. At some point, the person realized that Sherri had spotted them and moved to a different place. A short time later, Sherri saw the person leave, she told her parents.

Sherri did not tell her parents who she suspected the person might be. Nels thought Sherri knew, but didn't want to say it, because she wanted to trust John. Sherri did tell her father, "The person that was following me was dressed as a boy." Nels thought Sherri would not have described someone as "dressed like a boy" unless she believed the person was a woman. Sherri also shared with him another vivid detail about the person's appearance, which Nels never forgot: "This person had eyes that looked like they could see right through you."

On January 28, the same day as Peggy and Sherri's lunch, Stephanie went out on a date with Rodger, whom she had dated casually for about three months. Rodger got them tickets to see the Lakers play the Milwaukee Bucks at the Forum in Inglewood. The Lakers were the reigning NBA champions at the time and at peak popularity. In front of a sellout crowd that included Stephanie and Rodger, Kareem Abdul Jabbar scored 32 points to lead the "Showtime" Lakers to victory. After the game, they went out to a coffee shop, Tiny Naylor's. Stephanie seemed to Rodger her usual self throughout their date, he recalls.

John's and Sherri's birthdays were two days apart, on February 5 and 7. John was turning twenty-seven and Sherri twenty-nine. Before her birthday, John called her parents and told them he wanted to take Sherri home to Tucson for her birthday weekend. Nels tried to talk John out of it. Nels suggested they meet in San Diego and go sailing instead.

Nels recalls he told John on the phone, "Listen, it's just as easy for us to go to the boat. I get out of town, I don't have to worry about phone calls and stuff. We'll meet you at the boat and you kids can save the money on the plane fare. We'll just have a great time all weekend on the boat." Nels and Loretta had hosted John and Sherri on the boat many times previously.

John was unswayed. Nels recalls John told him, "No, I told Sherri I was going to take her home, and I'm going to take her home for her birthday."

As far as Nels knew, John had no idea that Sherri had been calling her parents and confiding to them about her marriage. Nels and Loretta never discussed with John any of the incidents Sherri shared with them about his ex-girlfriend: the three uninvited visits to their home in the weeks since Christmas; her sense that she was being followed in public; nor her suspicion that John had not completely cut ties with his ex-girlfriend, despite his promises. Sherri had requested that her parents do nothing, and say nothing to John, about what she had told them. Nels and Loretta wanted to respect Sherri's independence and boundaries. They felt it was not their place to interfere in Sherri and John's marriage, nor would Sherri have tolerated it.

Nels told John that he and Sherri were welcome to come to Tucson for Sherri's birthday, if that's what they wanted to do. John and Sherri planned to spend the weekend at the Rasmussens' home, and booked their flights.

Later, after they got off the phone, Nels could not get out of his head something John had said. John's insistence and the way he talked about wanting to take Sherri home bothered Nels. It was unimportant to Nels whether they met in San Diego or Tucson. He would look forward to seeing Sherri either way. But John's phrase kept ringing in Nels's ears. He was tempted to ask John, but didn't, "What do you want to take her home for? You've only been married three months. You can't be tired of her already."

Stephanie wrote in her diary on February 6, "*Detective Robertson asked me what I was doing next week. I said nothing. Later he let me know that I might get to go to Salt Lake City, Utah on an extradition.*"

Stephanie worked alone in an L car on Friday, February 7. She recounted, "*Nothing was going on in the morning. I stopped by the Webbs and Mark was there. Mark and I went to Bob's for breakfast. It was weird going so early but it was nice. Then I got called into the Station to talk to Sgt. Knapp. He told me I had to give up my work permit at Pierce or else the Captain was going to revoke it. There is some government section that makes it a conflict to work there. I said no problem and called Pierce up. I told them I couldn't work there anymore.*" Stephanie also noted, "*I found out that I am going to Utah. We leave Tuesday morning at 0530.*"

John and Sherri pose in Old Tucson's jail cell, February 1986

Sherri and John flew to Arizona that same Friday, on Sherri's twenty-ninth birthday. Over the weekend, Nels and Loretta took John and Sherri sightseeing around Tucson. Sherri wanted John to like her hometown. They went to the Desert Museum, dedicated to the appreciation of Tucson's natural landscape. They also visited Old Tucson Studios, a movie set and theme park where Hollywood actors like John Wayne and the current president, Ronald Reagan, once filmed westerns. One tourist attraction at Old Tucson was a fake frontier town, complete with a saloon, jail, and one-room schoolhouse, where mock gunfights and stunt shows were staged. Between performances, visitors could walk around and take photos. John and Sherri posed for several playful snapshots, including one inside the Old Tucson jail cell.

Nels and Loretta also wanted John to like Tucson. Sherri had lived in Southern California for more than twelve years, since she left for college at age sixteen. Nels and Loretta wished Sherri lived closer to them. Over Sherri's birthday weekend, Nels tried to persuade her and John to consider moving to Tucson.

"If you guys move home, I'll help you buy a house," Nels told John and Sherri. Nels also offered to help John find a good job. Nels explained that one of his dental patients was head of hiring for Hughes Aircraft. Hughes had a plant in Tucson and was always hiring engineers. "One phone call,

I can get you an interview," Nels said. Nels thought John seemed interested. Nels's sales pitch was persuasive enough that John and Sherri drove around the Tucson foothills with her parents and looked at some houses.

Ultimately, Sherri told Nels no. Nels recalls Sherri said, "Dad, I want to do some things on my own. Give me five years." Sherri planned her life in five-year increments, always mindful of the personal and professional goals she wanted to accomplish by then. Instead of waiting five years to set new goals, Sherri would revisit her list every year and reevaluate what else she might squeeze in. Sherri was not yet thirty, but because she had graduated from college so young, she was almost a decade into her career. Sherri said, "In five years' time, I'll be established to the point to where I can teach and lecture and probably make more than I can working in the hospital. I'm in the position right now where I can do a lot that will add to my résumé."

"Well, gee whiz, five years, that's fine," he replied. Five years didn't seem to Nels that long to wait.

That Saturday night, Nels and Loretta took Sherri and John out to dinner. The restaurant played country-western music and had a small dance floor. The two couples had spent the entire weekend together. At some point during dinner, John and Loretta both went to the restroom and left Sherri and Nels at the table, the first time they were alone all weekend.

Sherri said, "Dad, let's dance." They got up and went to the dance floor, where Sherri knew they could not be overheard. While they danced, Sherri told Nels, "I need to tell you, I've got a problem. I can't tell you what it is, but I'll call you if I can't handle it." Sherri would not say what the problem was or how she planned to resolve it.

"Sherri, I'll come and help you," Nels told her.

"That won't work," Sherri said.

Sherri also said, "What I'm telling you, you cannot discuss in front of John. I don't want to ruin or weaken my marriage, if nothing of what I've surmised is true." Nels believed Sherri kept the problem veiled because she was protecting John, but at the same time, she didn't know where John stood.

Sherri made Nels promise not to tell Loretta anything until she and John were on the plane home. Sherri said she didn't want her mother to worry about her.

It was the only private conversation Sherri had with her father while she and John were in Tucson. By the time their dance was over, John and

Loretta had returned from the restroom. Nels and Sherri went back to the table and spoke no more of what they had discussed on the dance floor.

Nels later regretted not questioning Sherri more aggressively. Although Nels kept his word not to confront John, he was convinced that John knew more than he let on about Sherri's problem. Nels couldn't fathom how Sherri could notice someone watching her and John at a restaurant but John could be unaware of it, let alone all the other incidents Sherri had shared with her parents. Nels believed the reason John had insisted on taking Sherri home for her birthday was that John knew the problem was serious. The threat of violence never crossed Nels's mind, however. Nels knew Sherri wasn't the type of person to do anything violent. Sherri was trusting John, and Nels saw no alternative for him and Loretta but to trust Sherri.

Stephanie was on duty at Devonshire while John and Sherri were in Tucson. On Sunday, February 9, the morning after Sherri and Nels talked on the dance floor, Stephanie's patrol partner was her friend Jayme Weaver. Their first call was a reported suicide. She wrote in her diary, *"A 22 yr old boy had hung himself. His face was purple and his eyes were rolled back. The weather was very cold, 52°. The coroner came and Jayme and I had to help the coroner get the body down. It wasn't our call but Sgt. Wonders I'm sure thought it would be neat for us to help . . . We then went and had hot chocolate and a cinnamon roll."*

Sherri and John flew home that same day. Nels and Loretta offered to drop them off at the airport. On the way, they stopped to eat at a Fuddruckers restaurant. Sherri found a quiet moment to reassure her father she would be okay. "If I can't settle this problem, Dad, in two weeks, I'll give you a call," Sherri told Nels.

At the airport, Nels and Loretta parked the car and walked Sherri and John into the terminal. They said goodbye to Sherri and John at the gate as their flight to LAX was boarding. Before Sherri reached the boarding door, she turned and looked over her shoulder at her father. When their eyes met, Sherri smiled. Forever after, whenever Nels thought to himself, "I can see Sherri right now," the first image that came up for him was his daughter looking over her shoulder and smiling at him, right before her and John's flight home. It was the last time he and Loretta saw Sherri alive.

Stephanie and Robertson, the detective who had invited her to accompany him to Utah for the extradition of two car theft suspects, flew to Salt Lake City early on Tuesday morning, February 11. The suspects, one male and one female, were jailed in the tiny town of Castle Dale, a few hours' drive from Salt Lake City. Stephanie wrote, *"It was cold and snowed in Salt Lake on our way to Price, biggest city near Castle Dale."* They visited the jail where they would collect the suspects the next day, then booked rooms at a hotel in Price. *"Real nice hotel about 50.00 per night. We had a drink at the bar. You must buy your own liquor and then you buy the mixer. It's crazy in Utah. We had a few margaritas. I was buzzed. Then we went and ate. Then we went out on the town . . . Then we went to the Jacuzzi and sat and drank. I went to bed after that."*

The next day, she wrote, *"We got the suspects about 1300. I stripped [sic] searched her. She was a real bitch. Her name was Annette . . . We could only handcuff them as far as the rent-a-car place. Western Airlines doesn't allow prisoners to be handcuffed . . . We got on the plane and had to sit at the rear of the plane. The plane ride wasn't bad. The susps sat against the window, with each one of us next to them . . . Annette and I talked. I kinda felt sorry for just a little. I don't know why."*

Stephanie was off duty on Valentine's Day 1986, a Friday. Although she did not mention it in her diary, her roommate, Mike Hargreaves, moved out the same day. In court testimony in 2012, Hargreaves described his year living with Stephanie as cordial and mostly drama free. The major exception was the night in June 1985 when she came home in tears about John's engagement. Hargreaves had not discussed John with Stephanie since that night.

It is unknown how John and Sherri celebrated their first Valentine's Day as a married couple. The following night, Saturday, February 15, they attended the wedding of Matt Gorder's sister. At the reception, Sherri and John sat at the same table as Matt and his wife, Anita. Matt thought John and Sherri seemed like newlyweds that night, which they still were. The wedding was the last time Matt and Anita saw Sherri.

The next evening, Sunday, February 16, Sherri and John were at home when she got a call from her friend Jayne. Jayne and her boyfriend Mike had just returned from skiing in Mammoth.

"Is it okay if we come over for a minute?" Jayne asked. Sherri said sure.

Jayne and Mike had been a couple nearly as long as Sherri and John. Soon after Sherri and John's wedding, Mike hinted to Jayne that he planned to propose. Jayne was certain Mike would by Christmas, but the holiday passed uneventfully. Jayne shifted her expectations to New Year's Eve. Once again, her hopes were dashed. Jayne had to wait two more months, until

Valentine's Day in Mammoth, when Mike redeemed himself with a proposal and engagement ring.

Jayne wanted to share her news with Sherri in person, so she and Mike drove out to Van Nuys. When Sherri opened the front door, Jayne held out her hand so Sherri could see the ring. Once the friends' squealing and hugging ended, Jayne and Mike came inside to talk in the living room. Sherri's happiness was equal to Jayne's excitement. They talked about how the proposal happened, and early plans for the wedding. John wanted to show Mike his new Mazda RX-7, so the guys went down to the garage for a look. Sherri reached into a magazine rack next to the living room sofa and pulled out the pile of bridal magazines she had saved for her friend.

Sherri told Jayne, "My wedding day was the happiest day of my life. Enjoy this time."

Jayne and Mike stayed for a while, but it was a Sunday night, and everyone had to be at work in the morning. When they left, and Jayne said good night to Sherri, Jayne could never have imagined that she would never again see her best friend.

Sherri's friend Donna spoke to her for the last time in mid-February. Donna had missed her birthday on February 7. One night a week or two later, Donna called with belated birthday wishes. Donna and Sherri chatted and caught up. Sherri said her work at the hospital had been stressful lately. "I have to lay off some people," she explained. Sherri also told Donna that she felt she was being followed in public. Sherri did not mention John's ex-girlfriend on the phone. Donna did not think of the letter Sherri wrote her, a month earlier, about arguing with John about his ex and feeling harassed by her.

Stephanie's patrol partner on February 19 was Jayme Weaver. In her diary, she wrote, *"Jayme drove. The weather was horrible. It was raining. First thing we did was to go over to Demi's restaurant on Balboa Nordhoff. I had left my wallet there from last night. I was lucky it was there."* Although Stephanie made no note of it in her diary, Demi's was only a five-minute drive, straight up Balboa Boulevard, from where John and Sherri lived in Van Nuys.

Stephanie worked the front desk the following day, February 20. She recounted in her diary, *"It was work out day today but I didn't work out. We usually have self-defense but not today . . . I was so glad I worked the desk today. I made a lot of personal calls. I talked with Paul Tree from Narcotics Van Nuys. He's going to talk to Sgt. Helm (Dev) to see if I could get on loan* soon. *The desk was pretty busy. I took about 5 reports. I'm telling you if I worked that desk everyday I'd probably stress out. People call up with the most stupidest questions.*" Stephanie did not divulge in her diary why she wanted to work in Van Nuys.

Stephanie indicated in her datebook that she was off duty from Friday, February 21, through Sunday, February 23. During the 1980s, the LAPD used a form called a Daily Work Sheet to document the duty status of all officers assigned to a particular division on a particular day and watch. Devonshire's Daily Work Sheets from 1986 confirm Stephanie had scheduled days off on February 21 and 22, and took a "holiday" day on February 23.

Sunday, February 23, was John and Sherri's three-month wedding anniversary. To mark the occasion, John gave her three red roses in a slim glass vase, tied with an oversized red bow. Sherri placed the flowers on their dining room table, which they walked past several times a day. The dining room was right outside the kitchen, on the second floor of their split-level condo. When Sherri had work or reading to do at home, she often sat at their dining room table to do it.

Sherri and John spent most of Sunday with family and friends. Sunday morning, Teresa and Brian drove up to Van Nuys in his Porsche two-seater.

John's three-month anniversary roses for Sherri (crime scene photo #19)

Brian parked in a visitor's space across from Sherri and John's garage. Sherri opened the garage door for them so they could enter via the interior staircase. Teresa and Brian seldom used the front door, which was on the opposite side of the condo and would have required a longer walk from their car. Teresa was five months pregnant at the time.

Although Teresa had been married five years longer than Sherri, she was forever the little sister in their relationship. Sherri, always the nurse, quizzed Teresa about her pregnancy and how she was feeling. Sherri's nurturing relationship with her sister dated to Teresa's teenage years, when she lived with Sherri during high school. Sherri's attentiveness reminded Teresa of a mother hen, always making sure that everything was okay.

Sherri encouraged Teresa to go swimming for exercise during her pregnancy. Sherri said a new YMCA with a pool had opened nearby. She and John had joined and enjoyed swimming there. In advance of Teresa's visit, Sherri looked up the address of the YMCA with a pool that was closest to Loma Linda, where Teresa and Brian lived. Along with that information, Sherri gave her sister a bathing cap and maternity swimsuit she had bought for her.

Teresa and Brian were into saltwater aquariums and had heard there was an impressive one at a pet store in Van Nuys. Sherri agreed to come along. Because Brian's car was a two-seater, they took Sherri's BMW instead. Sherri's car was less than a year old and still looked brand new. John had washed it the day before. Brian asked to drive.

On their way to the pet store, Sherri persuaded Brian to drive past the Van Nuys YMCA so Teresa could see it. The vaunted aquarium was underwhelming, and they returned home within half an hour. Sherri suggested they get lunch at an Italian restaurant nearby. It was a warm, sunny day, so the two couples decided to walk to lunch. Teresa noticed that Sherri and John held hands as they strolled to the restaurant. Sherri and John seemed to Teresa very happy, both individually and as a couple.

Teresa and Brian stayed awhile longer at the condo before they said their goodbyes. Brian had studying to do, and Teresa had work on Monday. Everything seemed completely normal to Teresa when she and Brian left.

Later on Sunday, Sherri went for a long run. One of John's friends from UCLA, Mike Boldrick, visited with them as well. Mike came and left through the front door, which John and Sherri rarely used themselves. After Mike left, John did not think to check the front door to make sure it was locked.

Sunday evening, John and Sherri went to the movies and saw *Down and Out in Beverly Hills*. They tried to do something fun together every Sunday night, to buck themselves up for the workweek ahead. They picked a showing at a movie theater in Simi Valley, which was a bit of a drive from Van Nuys, but the weather was nice, and traffic would be light on a Sunday evening. John wanted the feeling of driving his new Mazda on the freeway, with Sherri beside him. They returned home around ten. As they were accustomed to doing, John parked in their two-car garage and they entered via the interior staircase rather than their front door.

Before they went to bed, John made a brown bag lunch for work on Monday. By the time he finished brushing his teeth, Sherri was already in bed. Sherri mentioned to John that she was scheduled to teach a class at the hospital on Monday. The class, called "The People Difference," taught conflict resolution techniques. She had taught it for the hospital several times before. She told John she was dreading having to teach it the next day. John said, "Sherri, just go in. Get it over with. You'll feel better if you just do the class." John got into bed about 10:30 p.m. Side by side, they soon drifted off to sleep, oblivious to Sherri's fate the next day.

The Murder of Sherri Rasmussen

12

Sherri's Final Day

(February 24, 1986)

John and Sherri woke on Monday, February 24, a little before seven o'clock, their usual time on a workday. Unlike most days, however, she stayed in bed while he showered, shaved, and dressed for work. When he asked why, Sherri said she was thinking of calling in sick to the hospital. She asked John to call her later in the morning. She was still in bed when John left home, at about 7:20.

John left for work through the garage, as he did every day. The wall panel for their new burglar alarm was just inside the front door, at the top of the garage staircase. They usually armed the alarm system only when they were out, and at night, while they slept. When they were home, they sometimes left the alarm off to avoid tripping it accidentally. John did not arm the alarm when he left Sherri at home that Monday morning. The door at the top of the garage stairs had a push-button lock that John depressed so that the door locked behind him when he closed it.

John backed his new Mazda out of the garage and watched the garage door close, leaving Sherri's BMW parked inside. All the units in the Balboa Townhomes complex shared a common driveway. The driveway was closed off from the street by an electric car gate. John drove his Mazda past the gate and into Monday morning rush hour traffic. On his way to work, John stopped at the dry cleaner's and dropped off some clothes. John arrived at his office around 7:50.

Roughly half an hour later, two neighbors of John and Sherri's, Gus and Anastasia Volanitis, set out for their daily morning walk. The Volanitises were a retired married couple who had lived in unit 301 for six years, about a year longer than Sherri. Their unit was across the common driveway from Sherri and John's unit, 205, such that their garage doors opened onto opposite sides of the same stretch of driveway. Any time the Volanitises drove in or out, they necessarily passed by John and Sherri's garage door. Anastasia knew Sherri well enough to say hello—for instance, when they saw each other getting their mail—but that was the extent of their relationship as neighbors. Anastasia did not know Sherri's last name.

Gus and Anastasia liked to stroll around a municipal golf course a few miles away, so they usually drove to their morning walk, like true Angelenos. When the Volanitises left home that morning, around 8:30, the garage door for Sherri and John's unit was closed. They returned about an hour later, at 9:30. Gus dropped off Anastasia so she could collect the newspaper at unit 203, a favor for another neighbor who was out of town. Unit 203 was two units west of John and Sherri's. Anastasia retrieved the newspaper and walked back to her own unit by way of the shared driveway. As she passed unit 205, she noticed its garage door was open, unlike an hour earlier. The garage, which had room for two cars, was empty. It was 9:45 a.m.

According to John, he tried calling Sherri at home around ten. Sherri didn't pick up. John tried again about a half hour later, but again there was no answer. John thought it was strange he couldn't leave a message, since Sherri normally turned on the answering machine if she went out. John wondered if she had rallied and decided to go in to work after all. He called Sherri's office and spoke to her secretary, Sylvia Nielsen. Sylvia told John that she believed Sherri was teaching her class. Sylvia said that when Sherri taught, she usually went directly to the class, not to her office.

Teresa also tried calling Sherri at the hospital on Monday. The sisters touched base by phone several times a week. Teresa's job allowed her to make personal calls only on breaks and her lunch hour. Her first call to Sherri that day was during her morning break, at ten o'clock. According to Teresa, Sylvia answered and told her that Sherri had called in sick. Teresa then called Sherri at home. Sherri did not pick up, but the answering machine did. Teresa left her a message.

The factual inconsistencies between John's and Teresa's recollections of what Sylvia told them, and whether the answering machine at home was on or off that day, have never been resolved. The answering machine tape, and any messages that were on it, were not preserved.

Gus and Anastasia Volanitis did not hear any alarming noises from

John and Sherri's unit that morning. Someone in another unit, however, did. Sherri and John's next-door neighbor in unit 206 had a housekeeper, Evangelina Flores, who worked there on Mondays. On February 24, Evangelina came to work at 8:30 a.m., about a half hour before her employer, John and Sherri's neighbor, left for work.

All the condos in the Balboa Townhomes had the same layout, with a living room on the first floor, dining room and kitchen on the second, and bedrooms and a laundry room on the top floor. It usually took Evangelina until two o'clock or two thirty to finish her cleaning. Evangelina had worked there every Monday for about two years, so she was well acquainted with her surroundings and their daily rhythms. Most residents of the complex worked regular hours and were not at home on weekdays. Normally, it was very quiet while Evangelina went from room to room tidying up.

Evangelina was a few hours into her work that morning when she heard a loud, violent thud that sounded as if it came through the shared wall of the condo next door, John and Sherri's unit. She went to a window to look outside and saw nothing amiss. As she left the window, she heard the same loud thud again. Evangelina thought it sounded like people fighting. Both thuds sounded to her as if they came from the second floor, possibly near the kitchen. The second thud was followed by a loud scream. Evangelina couldn't tell if the voice was male or female, and there were no words in it, just a long, continuous scream, followed by total silence. Evangelina went to a different window and looked out. Again, everything seemed normal, and she went back to cleaning.

Around noontime, Anastasia Volanitis was at home in her condo across the driveway when two men came to her front door. The men wore work clothes and spoke only Spanish. She assumed they were gardeners. One of the men had a brown leather lady's purse that he extended to Anastasia. The men did not strike Anastasia as nervous or suspicious.

Anastasia opened the purse and found a wallet inside. She recognized the photo on the driver's license as her neighbor Sherri. Anastasia gave the purse back and pointed the men to Sherri and John's unit. Anastasia watched them walk off in that direction. Five minutes later, they came to her door again, with the purse still in hand. No one had answered the door at unit 205. Anastasia agreed to take the purse from the men. She planned to return it to Sherri later in the day.

John stayed at work throughout the morning. He ate his brown bag lunch at his desk. During his lunch hour, he ran one quick errand, to make a bank deposit. John was back at his desk before one o'clock. John tried calling Sherri again at work that afternoon but was unable to reach her or her secretary, Sylvia.

John never imagined something might be terribly wrong. To the contrary, he felt a little piqued at Sherri for not calling back and letting him know what was going on. John thought it was possible Sherri had called him back while he was away from his desk. He figured she probably went into work late.

The rest of the afternoon, John was busy with his own work. Quitting time at Micropolis was officially five o'clock. John was not too worried about Sherri, so he ran two errands on his way home.

Teresa, by contrast, was very concerned about Sherri. It was unusual for her to be unable to reach her sister, and for Sherri not to return her calls. Teresa had tried calling Sherri at home again during her lunch hour but could not reach her. When Teresa got home from work at 5:30 p.m., she called her mother in Tucson.

"Have you talked to Sherri?" Teresa asked. Loretta hadn't.

Very little is known about Stephanie's whereabouts that Monday, except that it was her fourth straight day off duty. Stephanie's day off on Monday was not an impulsive decision but planned, what LAPD officers called a "regular" day off. Regular days off had to be scheduled prior to the start of that deployment period. On the Devonshire Division's Daily Work Sheet for day watch on Monday, February 24, Stephanie's name was listed under her official status, DAY OFF.

LOS ANGELES POLICE DEPARTMENT
DAILY WORK SHEET

15.26.0 (7/82)

AREA/DIV.	AREA COMMANDING OFFICER	DIV. COMMANDING OFFICER	UNIT (IF OTHER THAN PATROL)	WATCH COMMANDER/OIC	DAY OF WK.	DATE	WATCH
DEV	CAPT FRIED	CAPT MCBRIDE		SGT RENDON	MON	2-24-86	DAY

ASSIGNMENT	ROVER	SHOP	NAME(S)	EOW	SUPV. UNITS.	STATION DETAIL/SPECIAL DETAIL	DO/SICK/IOD/VACATION/ETC.
						DESK	DAY OFF
AW7C			SGT SETTY			COOK P3	FLEMING, P2 SS
						TATE P1	JUDD P2
L20			SGT WONDERS (SUBPOENA)			BELL, S. PSR	DASILVA ORD
							TODD, C. P3
L30			SGT REMBOLD(LOG)				LAUER P3+1
						JAIL	LEWIS, R. P1
L70			SGT JOHNSON(CW)			BRUMETT S/O	LAZARUS P2
						NOONAN S/O	WEAVER, J. P2
A49			HENDERSON, G. P2				HOLIDAY
			ALEXANDER P2			ORDERLY	SGT HABERMAN
						BESSETTE ORD	SGT FLOREZ
A55			RASHI P3				MASCOLA P3
							SCIARRILLO P2
			HENDERSON, S. P2			LN VICE	
						RENNER, G P2	
L77			POGUE, W. P3 TASER				VACATION
L83			TODARO P3 TASER			LOAN DETS	WHITMAN P2
						QUEEN P3	BETANCOURT P1
A91			STIEGLITZ P3+				
			CHERRY P2 FPO			JURY DUTY	
						KOCHAKJI SR ORD	TO DAY OFF
18X53			KEESLING, K P1 FPO				WARCZAK P2
17Z29			BECKER, J. P3+1				
			VOLLMAN P1				SICK
							ORNDORFF P2
			STORM				
17I11			DURNING, B. P2			CERTIFIED TO BE AN ACCURATE REPRESENTATION OF DEPLOYMENT: ____	
						POSTED BY: _____	

LAPD Daily Work Sheet for Devonshire Division Day Watch, February 24, 1986

13

The Chrono and Crime Scene

(February 24, 1986, 6:30 to 9:00 p.m.)

The single most important document in any LAPD homicide investigation is the "chrono," short for chronological log.

The primacy and significance of the chrono are reflected by its prominent place at the front of every LAPD murder book, the three-ring binder of investigative reports that detectives begin to assemble whenever a person is killed in Los Angeles. Many decades ago, the LAPD standardized the organization of its murder books, so any detective could pick up any case and find the information laid out the same way. Section one is the chrono, two the crime scene log, three the crime report, and so on. In Sherri Rasmussen's case, the murder book eventually spanned several three-inch binders. The Rasmussen chrono ultimately ran well over a hundred pages.

The chrono is intended to document all investigative activity, day by day and sometimes minute by minute, conducted by the detectives assigned to work a homicide case. The chrono starts immediately, when the phone rings at the homicide table, and it's as though a timer is running. If the case is eventually solved, and an arrest made, the chrono continues through the jury's verdict, after which time the murder book is archived. If the case is unsolved, the chrono has no end, regardless of how much time elapses between entries. Because the crime of murder has no statute of limitations, there is always the possibility, however more attenuated as years pass without an arrest, that the victim will one day receive justice.

For cold case detectives working an unsolved murder, the chrono is what allows them to trace the history of a case back to its very beginning and follow how the investigation progressed from day one. The chrono recounts all the legwork performed by earlier detectives, down to the date and time every investigative action was taken. It shows the investigation's pace, which typically is fast at the start and then tapers off, and its direction over time. Although the evidence in a murder case does not change, detectives' investigative priorities rise and fall according to the information they learn along the way. By reading between the lines of the chrono, it is sometimes possible to discern the detectives' theory of the murder, and who they suspect committed it, at various points in time.

The chrono documents which witnesses were interviewed, their contact information, and often a brief summary of what they said. Any forensics analysis performed in a case—for instance, of fingerprints, ballistics, or biological evidence collected at the crime scene—is logged in the chrono. If someone calls the police with a tip on an unsolved homicide, the information is customarily recorded in the chrono. If the tip is not logged, it is unlikely ever to have a meaningful impact on the investigation. It is not always apparent at the time of the tipster's call how crucial that information might be to solving the case in the future. In homicide work, as much as any other profession, hindsight is twenty-twenty.

The chrono does more than document. As detectives explore or ignore different leads, and the chrono grows in length, it gradually assumes more authoritativeness in the eyes of whoever reads it later. This is confirmation bias at work. Confirmation bias is the psychological tendency of people to overvalue information that confirms their beliefs and to dismiss contradictory information, irrespective of the truth. In the world of homicide detectives, the phenomenon has another name, "tunnel vision." The more detectives who look at a case, and the longer it goes unsolved, the more difficult it becomes for a new detective to imagine the possibility that all their predecessors misread the evidence. Theories and suppositions left unchallenged for so long calcify and take on the aura of fact. The chrono inevitably becomes the lens through which subsequent homicide detectives perceive and understand the case.

The more detailed the chrono, the more information any detective who picks up the case later will have at his or her fingertips. Nearly all LAPD murder investigations begin at the homicide tables in one of the department's various geographic divisions, for instance the Van Nuys homicide unit. High profile and politically sensitive murder cases likely to attract media attention are sent downtown to the LAPD's vaunted Robbery-Homicide

Division, RHD for short. RHD's jurisdiction is citywide, and its detectives are by reputation the best and most experienced in the department. In the 1980s, the RHD squad room was on the third floor of LAPD headquarters, Parker Center, three floors below the office of the chief of police.

Open homicide cases, particularly those that languish unsolved for years, can be reassigned from the division where the murder occurred to RHD for a second look, and later back to the original division. For unknown reasons, the specific date and rationale for why a case is transferred between divisions is not customarily recorded in the chrono itself. Detectives, like cases, may also be transferred unexpectedly. Detectives retire, leaving behind open cases that are inherited by other detectives they may not know. Whoever picks up the case next must rely on the chrono to get up to speed on the history and status of the investigation.

Some detectives are more thorough note takers than others. Time pressures can affect the quality of the chrono, as when a detective's investigative progress on one murder is interrupted by a fresh case. Because the murder rate in Los Angeles was so much higher in the 1980s than it is today, LAPD homicide detectives back then frequently had to juggle multiple cases. Given the sheer number of detectives over the years, the differences in their individual writing styles and abilities, and their varying degrees of conscientiousness and professionalism, not all detectives' chronos live up to the Platonic ideal.

LAPD homicide detectives often say, when confronted with an unpleasant reality, "It is what it is." Whether the chrono provides a clear or a clouded lens onto a case, the last detective must accept the chrono in the condition it comes to them. There is no practical alternative but to assume that all the work completed up to that point was done in good faith. The detective's primary responsibility is to advance the investigation, not to "Monday morning quarterback" other detectives. The ethos of the department is to move forward, not dwell on the past, particularly with regard to its own mistakes. When the LAPD pauses to reflect on its proud and complicated history, it tends to do so nostalgically, in soft focus.

For many detectives, it does not come naturally to question the theories and actions of those who preceded them on a case. The longer the history of an unsolved case, the slimmer the odds would seem that something important was missed. Detectives are not hardwired to doubt that the chrono is an accurate and complete account of the investigation to that point. The LAPD does not train or prepare its detectives to lose faith in a chrono, or to begin to wonder what else should be in the murder book but for murky reasons is nowhere to be found. Questioning the validity of the chrono is tantamount to questioning the integrity of the detectives who wrote it.

Nor would the LAPD's top brass likely welcome any such inquiry without knowing in advance what else the reinvestigation might uncover. The chief of police's public image and the reputation of the entire department rest on the perceived integrity of the rank and file. This is why the department so jealously guards its power to discipline its own officers, and why it strives to tightly control publicity and information about alleged police misconduct. It also begins to illuminate how Sherri Rasmussen's murder went unsolved for so many years.

The LAPD has a long-standing policy in homicide cases that if a murder is not solved within a certain time, detectives are required to complete a follow-up report on the progress and status of the investigation. In the 1980s, the deadline was two months, so detectives back then referred to it as the "sixty-day report." The often lengthy report typically included a narrative account of the murder, along with a rundown of all the important developments to that point in the investigation. Standard addenda were copies of the chrono, crime scene log, autopsy, and other reports produced in the first two months of the investigation.

Today, LAPD detectives make chrono entries directly on their computers, using word processing software and standardized templates. Back in the 1980s, detectives generally handwrote their chronos, particularly in the fast-moving early stages of an investigation. Before the follow-up report became part of the murder book, it had to be reviewed and approved by the unit's homicide coordinator and the division brass, typically a lieutenant. The brass was regarded, mostly by themselves, as too busy to waste time deciphering the scrawlings of various detectives, so the follow-up report and attached chrono were expected to be typed.

For homicide detectives who lacked the innate motivation to solve a case, disliked writing, or both, the prospect of having to complete a sixty-day report served as added incentive to make an arrest within that time. Some detectives typed up their own handwritten chronos. Most left the tedious task to a clerk-typist, a civilian LAPD employee who assisted with clerical work.

Needless to say, the typed chrono is supposed to be one hundred percent true to the original handwritten version. The two, read side by side, should correspond verbatim. The only reason the chrono is typed is for the convenience of the reader. Although it is not unprecedented for LAPD detectives to work a homicide "off the books"—that is to say, not recording all of their activities in the chrono—it is a risky practice. If an arrest is made and a defendant goes to trial, the detectives can be forced to defend in court how they conducted their investigation. Any deviation from policy and custom can expose the detective, and the department, to embarrassment.

Once the follow-up report is approved, it is incorporated into the murder book, along with all the other reports already compiled in the case. Customarily, this includes the original handwritten chrono, if any part of it was retyped. Similar to physical evidence in unsolved homicide cases, official records are supposed to be retained indefinitely. The original handwritten chrono is by definition the most reliable contemporaneous account of the initial detectives' activities in a case. It should remain part of the murder book for as long as the case is unsolved.

Inexplicably, at some point between May 1986 and March 2008, the original handwritten chrono pages for the first three months of the LAPD's investigation of Sherri Rasmussen's homicide went missing from the murder book for the case.

Among the countless LAPD personnel who enjoyed unfettered access to the Rasmussen murder book during that twenty-one-year time span was Stephanie Lazarus, who was assigned to the Van Nuys Division for several years in the 1990s. By that point in her career, Stephanie had graduated from patrol duties. In 1994, she was promoted to Detective I. Stephanie was assigned to Van Nuys detectives from March 1995 to March 1996, during which time she worked on at least one open murder case. In 1996 she was promoted again, to Detective II, and was reassigned to the Internal Affairs Division. For eighteen months in 1996 and 1997, she was a full-fledged LAPD Internal Affairs investigator. In August 1997, she left Internal Affairs and returned to Van Nuys. Stephanie's second stint at Van Nuys lasted until January 1999. The murder book for the Rasmussen case was stored at the Van Nuys Division throughout the time Stephanie was assigned there. Colleagues from her years at Van Nuys recall that Stephanie frequently volunteered to work morning watch, the overnight hours when the station was mostly empty of personnel, particularly supervisors.

It may never be known when the original handwritten chrono pages went missing from the Rasmussen murder book, who removed them, or, most vexingly, why. Without the handwritten chrono, and being able to compare it to the typed version, it is impossible to know how faithful the transcription was, and whether any information was intentionally omitted. For now, all that can be said for certain about the original handwritten chrono for the Rasmussen case is that the LAPD insists it no longer has a copy.

A close examination of the typed version of the chrono indicates that it dates from May 1986, three months after Sherri's murder. A handwritten note at the bottom of the first typed page designated it as Addendum #1 to the follow-up report. The last typed chrono entry was on May 19, two days before the follow-up report was approved. The thirteen typed pages cover three months' time, from February to May 1986. All the typed entries are evenly spaced and share the same typeface, which suggests that the document was produced in one sitting, three months of entries typed up at once. In June 1986, immediately after the follow-up report was completed, the chrono for the Rasmussen case reverts to handwritten entries.

The surviving typed version of the chrono contains several peculiar typos. The first typo is at the top of page one, where the lead investigator's last name is misspelled. Curiously, John Ruetten's last name is misspelled "Ruetter" throughout the typed chrono. The misspelling may have been an innocent typo, but it was made consistently across several entries, dates, and pages. It is the sort of error that, in 1986, could have made it harder for a detective unfamiliar with the case to locate John as a witness. It may also be a coincidence that John was the primary linchpin, the person in common, between Sherri Rasmussen and Stephanie Lazarus. Nowhere in the thirteen typed pages is there any reference to "John Ruetter" as having an ex-girlfriend. Nor does the name Stephanie Lazarus appear anywhere in the typed chrono.

The typed version of the Rasmussen chrono begins: *"2-24-86 | 1930 | Notified @ home by Pida 7100 Balboa #205."* Pida is Detective III Roger Pida, the Van Nuys homicide coordinator who supervised the unit's case-carrying detectives. The second typed entry, at 8:00 p.m., reads, *"Arrived at scene. S. Hooks #22175 and Mager [sic] #12772 began crime scene investigation. Obtained prelim info on GTA and 459."* S. Hooks is Detective I Steve Hooks. "Mager" is Detective II Lyle O. Mayer of the Van Nuys homicide unit, the original lead investigator on the Rasmussen case. GTA refers to the theft of Sherri's BMW, her onetime engagement present, which was missing from the condo's garage. The number 459 refers to the California penal code section for burglary.

The responsibility for keeping the chrono typically belongs to the lead

LAPD 03.11.6 (1/82)		CHRONOLOGICAL RECORD	
INSTRUCTIONS: This form is used to document any past or future investigative events deemed necessary to control or develop this case.			DR 86-09 10480
DATE	TIME	INVESTIGATION	
2-24-86	1930	Notified @ home by Pida 7100 Balboa #205.	
	2000	Arrived at scene. S. Hooks #22175 and Mager #12772 began	
		crime scene investigation. Obtained prelim info on GTA	
		and 459.	
	2030	Mager to sta to interview John Ruetter. (Husband)	
	2030	Obtained info from owner at 7100 Balboa #206. Maid poss	
		lead about crime. Contacted maid. Evangeline Flores,	
		768-7000, notified her that car would pick her up.	
		Made arrangements to have patrol officer pick up maid and	
		bring her to station.	
	2140	Had stolen vehicle report tatken on victim - vehicle	
		license #1MJK 850.	
		Interviewed John Ruetter and Evangeline Flores.	
	2300	Notification to family, also family in Tuscon, Arizona.	
-25-			
2-25-86	0015	Administrative desk - Collins #15756 notified.	
	0400	Van Nuys Reports and teletypes.	
	0800	Called lady with purse.	
	0900	Called the alarm guy.	
	1000	Re-interviewed deceased husband.	
	1030	Took John R. on walk through of house.	
	1100	Took alarm guy to check alarm.	
		Had location reprints by Ames - obtained lifts. Had loc.	
		ninhydrin.	
	1130	Completed rotator notice on vehicle.	
	1345	Called John Ruetter. Victim poss received threatening	
		phone calls at work.	
		Dr. Vale - LA C Coroner call bite marks good for comparison.	
			CONTINUE ON REVERS

Addendum #1

LAPD typed chronological log for the Sherri Rasmussen case, page 1 investigator, who in Sherri's case was Mayer. Mayer retired from the LAPD in September 1991, more than three years before Stephanie began her first assignment at Van Nuys. According to Mayer, he has never met Stephanie Lazarus and did not know who she was in 1986. To this day, Mayer maintains that during his time as the lead investigator on the Rasmussen case, he never considered Stephanie Lazarus as a suspect in Sherri's murder.

When Sherri was killed, Mayer had been with the Van Nuys homicide unit for about five years, since 1981. He had been an LAPD officer much longer, since 1965, which made him, at the time, a veteran of more than twenty years with the department.

Lyle Mayer always wanted to be a detective. Growing up in the San Fernando Valley in the 1950s, young Lyle discovered he had a knack for communicating with people. He could talk fast and was a quick learner. Lyle's father was an automobile mechanic who worked for a car dealership in the Valley. At the age of fifteen, Lyle took a part-time job in the service department of the same dealership. It was while working there that he first developed his sense that he had a special talent for getting answers and information from people.

In 1968, after three years on the job, Mayer was transferred to the Hollywood Division. Mayer at the time considered Hollywood the most fascinating place in the world. His beat was Hollywood Boulevard, where it seemed like anything could happen at any time around the clock. That November, Mayer was on routine patrol in Hollywood when he saw flames from the fourth-floor window of a hotel. Mayer stopped his car and rushed upstairs to the room, the door of which was locked. Mayer broke down the door and rescued the occupant. For his role in saving the man's life, Mayer was awarded the Medal of Valor, the LAPD's highest honor.

In 1972, Mayer was promoted to detective and later assigned to the Rampart Division. It was at Rampart that Mayer first received the opportunity to work homicide cases. Mayer later transferred to the Northeast Division's homicide table.

Mayer understood that in homicide work, the stakes were very different than in most civilian jobs. In an interview in 2014, Mayer said, "If you make an error or a mistake or misread something, you can be affecting someone's court case, someone's life, someone's family's life. It's demanding, but it's also fun." For Mayer, what made being a homicide detective fun was the camaraderie and teamwork within the unit, and the close friendships he developed with several of his partners.

Detectives are picked to work homicide because of their skill set—for instance, being a great report writer, or interviewer, or trainer of other detectives. Mayer thought of himself as having all of those qualities. Mayer believed a homicide detective had to do two things to be successful: learn to listen and listen to learn. According to Mayer, detective work came very easy for him. If a murder suspect was willing to waive their rights and talk, Mayer found he could usually find a way to solve the case.

In 1981, Mayer was recruited by the homicide coordinator at Van Nuys, Roger Pida, to come work for him there. Pida and Mayer had worked together earlier in their careers at North Hollywood and Hollywood. Like Mayer, Pida had been on the job since the mid-1960s and had worked his way up to investigating homicides.

Mayer discovered that working homicide in Van Nuys was lovely compared to the other LAPD divisions he had worked. Van Nuys had a beautiful, modern station right across the street from the old county courthouse, where criminal proceedings were held. He no longer had to spend hours getting to court every time he had to testify or wanted to file a case. Mayer was used to waiting in line at the courthouse downtown, where there was a vast pool of deputy district attorneys. He never knew which one he and his case might get shuttled to. In Van Nuys, by contrast, there were just a few prosecutors who handled homicide cases. As a detective in Van Nuys, he could call up and make an appointment to bring in his case. Mayer felt his word had much more weight there than it did downtown. His experience working homicide in Van Nuys was that it was heaven, a totally different world than he was accustomed to.

Within the LAPD, working homicide in Van Nuys did not confer the same status as flashier assignments like Hollywood or Robbery-Homicide. At the same time, those higher-profile assignments came with headaches the Van Nuys detectives rarely had to worry about. Unless a murder was particularly horrific or had a celebrity angle, most Van Nuys cases did not attract sustained media attention. Less media attention meant less scrutiny from the department brass. The endless stream of tragedies and crises elsewhere in the city ensured that the Van Nuys detectives were able to run their investigations largely free of distractions and interference.

When Mayer arrived in 1981, the Van Nuys homicide unit had only five detectives, including the homicide coordinator, Pida. Mayer recalls there was a good rapport within the unit. Because of its small size, everyone was accustomed to pitching in on cases, no matter who the lead detective was officially. When there was a spate of murders, and multiple cases to investigate simultaneously, it was all hands on deck. Everyone's individual abilities were utilized as the caseload required.

The four detectives worked in pairs, under Pida's supervision. On weekends, one team or the other was on call to handle any homicides in Van Nuys from 5:00 p.m. Friday to 8:00 a.m. Monday. During the week, which team was assigned to a new case was Pida's call. When a murder occurred, Pida dispatched the team that was "up" to the location. One detective was designated as the lead investigator and the other as his assistant, in part because it was impossible to know when the next homicide might occur. If the same team caught a fresh case, the assisting partner on the first case took the lead on the second case, while the lead detective on the first case continued to focus on that investigation and assisted his partner on the second case.

Mayer viewed his partners as more than colleagues. He considered his partner his protector. Partners had to be able to understand each other intuitively, he believed. Mayer needed to know that what he said, his partner would say. In turn, whatever his partner said, he said. It wasn't that there was no room for disagreement. When there was a difference of opinion about what happened in a case, or how to proceed with an investigation, Mayer believed partners had to communicate and make a decision. The two detectives had to act as a team, almost as though they were actually a single detective. It was important to Mayer that if a superior asked him and his partner for their thoughts on a case, they would agree all the time in what they said.

Mayer got along well with his boss, Pida. Pida was also good friends with another Van Nuys homicide detective, Mel Arnold. Arnold was already part of the unit when Mayer arrived in 1981. Pida and Arnold had such a tight bond that their friendship was profiled in the *Los Angeles Daily News* in June 1985, eight months before Sherri Rasmussen's murder. In mid-1986, a few months after Sherri was killed, Pida left the unit and Arnold succeeded him as the Van Nuys homicide coordinator. Arnold remained in charge of the Van Nuys homicide unit until 1991.

The burglary and robbery units at Van Nuys served as the farm teams for the homicide unit. Not all young detectives had the experience and qualifications to assist on homicide cases. According to Mayer, they had to be a good report writer, able to interview witnesses, and capable of all the different tasks the lead detective might ask of them. Some detectives had the intellectual ability but couldn't deal with dead bodies. For detectives with the ambition, skill set, and intestinal fortitude to work homicide, the surest way to get a foot in the door was to assist more experienced investigators.

It was under these circumstances that Steve Hooks, a young Van Nuys burglary detective, came to assist Mayer on the LAPD's investigation of Sherri Rasmussen's murder. At that point in his career, Hooks had been the lead investigator in about a hundred fifty burglary cases. Hooks had previously assisted on other homicide cases, but the Rasmussen case was the first time he and Mayer worked together as partners. Mayer's impression of Hooks was that he was very sharp. According to Mayer, Hooks seemed to him and Pida like someone they wanted to bring into the homicide unit. On February 24, the day Sherri was killed, Mayer's regular partner was off duty. Hooks was tapped to be Mayer's "partner on call."

In 1986, Hooks had been an LAPD officer for eight years, at least a dozen years less than Mayer and Pida had on the job. Hooks's rank at the time was Detective I, one rank below Mayer and two ranks below Pida. Mayer and Pida's responsibilities included supervising and training lower-ranked detectives. Two years later, in 1988, Hooks officially joined the Van Nuys homicide unit.

Hooks testified in 2012 that over the course of his career, he investigated more than a hundred murders as the primary detective, and another hundred as the secondary. According to Hooks, he solved most of the homicide cases he worked on. Hooks retired from the LAPD in 1998, after twenty years on the job.

According to Hooks, he worked full time on the Rasmussen case for only the first month of the investigation, and then assisted on it intermittently for the next year or two. Notwithstanding the short time Hooks worked on the Rasmussen case, and his limited control over the direction of the investigation, it was a case he never forgot. Sherri's murder didn't fall into the typical categories of murders that Hooks handled during his career. It wasn't a case in which the suspect was already in custody, or a gang homicide, or a domestic violence case. The Rasmussen case stuck in Hooks's mind as much for what it wasn't as for what it appeared to be.

The LAPD crime scene log for Sherri's case indicates that Hooks was the first detective to arrive at the condo, at 7:48 p.m. Lt. Al Durrer, the commanding officer of Van Nuys detectives, preceded Hooks to the location by more than twenty minutes. Other LAPD personnel already on the scene when Hooks arrived included several patrol officers and supervisors, as well as a fingerprint analyst from SID, the LAPD's Scientific Investigation Division. Mayer arrived a few minutes after Hooks, followed by an SID crime scene photographer. Pida logged in to the crime scene at 8:04. About two hours had passed since John came home from work and discovered Sherri's body.

Once all the detectives and the SID photographer were present, they began the crime scene walk-through, the initial step in any homicide investigation. The purpose of the walk-through was to document the state of the victim's body and other aspects of the crime scene before any evidence was disturbed or collected by personnel from SID and the coroner's office.

The crime scene photographer started outside, with the back exterior of the condo, the same way John had come home earlier that night. The garage door remained open but had been taped off, with John's car parked inside. The parking spot for Sherri's BMW was empty. Shards of broken glass littered the pavement in front of their garage, directly under the condo's balcony.

The detectives started their walk-through on the other side of the unit, at the condo's front door. Hooks took handwritten notes during the walk-through. His fourteen pages of notes were later incorporated into the Rasmussen murder book.

Hooks noted that the front door faced southeast, and that it *"was open when the walk-through began. There are (3) locks on the front door. A key activated (inside/outside) deadbolt, an inside latch deadbolt, and a basic key activated bottom lock. No tampering appears with the locks themselves. Small pry marks do appear to the inner door jambs."* Hooks saw no evidence that the door had been forced open, such as splintered wood or bent hinges.

Mayer agreed, based on the undamaged condition of the door and locks, that there was no indication of forced entry. John and Sherri's condo reminded Mayer of a condo he owned, which was not in the Balboa Townhomes complex but had a very similar layout. According to Mayer, the similarities helped him begin to formulate in his mind what might have happened prior to the murder.

Mayer left the other detectives to continue the walk-through while he went to speak with the victim's husband. John was still at the condo, awaiting transport to the station for a formal interview. If the husband had any information about a suspect, Mayer wanted to know that before the interview so he could get the description out to patrol units without delay.

John was extremely distraught when Mayer introduced himself, Mayer recalls. Mayer had to get John to focus, and bring him back to reality a little bit, to get him to answer his initial questions. John seemed heartbroken and close to throwing up as he told Mayer what time he had left home, his whereabouts that day, and so on. John's emotional demeanor, expressions, and physical reaction to his wife's death convinced Mayer right then and there that John had no involvement in her murder.

According to Mayer, John recounted how he came home from work, parked in the garage, and came upstairs to find Sherri's body. Mayer recalls he specifically asked John about the front door, and if it was locked when he left for work that morning. John said a friend had visited the day before and had gone in and out through the front door, which he and Sherri rarely used themselves. John also said he and Sherri went to see a movie later in the evening. John didn't remember checking whether the front door was locked after his friend left, or when he and Sherri got home that night, or in the morning before he left for work. Mayer thought of his own condo, and how its front door did not lock automatically when he closed it but had to be dead-bolted. Mayer knew how easy it was to leave the door unlocked accidentally.

Mayer recalls that he thought, "Okay, what happened here? What are the possibilities? This young couple allowed their friend to come in through the front door. After the friend left, they went downstairs to the garage, got in their car, and exited out the garage as usual. When they returned home from the movie, they drove back into the garage, came upstairs, and went to sleep. The husband never checked whether the front door was locked." Based on the initial information he received from John, and no evidence of forced entry, Mayer theorized the suspect or suspects must have come in through the front door, either because it was unlocked or because the victim let them inside.

John also gave Mayer a description of Sherri's stolen BMW and its license plate. Mayer left John in the company of some patrol officers and rejoined the walk-through in progress. Mayer relayed to the other detectives what John had told him. Mayer recalls he then went back to John again and verified that all the couple's activity in and out of the condo the day before was through the garage.

The detectives' walk-through resumed in the front entryway. Hooks wrote in his notes, "*Two ligature type items (small white rope with blood, and a speaker wire) lie on the entryway tile floor and partially on the living*

Detectives Steve Hooks and Roger Pida (LAPD crime scene photo #18)

room rug." The presence of a bloodstained rope suggested an attempt was made to tie up the victim. Additional evidence of an intense physical struggle was also nearby. Hooks wrote, *"Two fingernails lie on the entryway tile floor near the front door. To the right (East Wall) is a closet door with blood smeared a foot or so from the floor. Continuing inside, the wall protrudes slightly and more smeared blood appears near the light socket on the wall. West from the light socket on the brown tile floor (entry area) blood is smeared on the floor. Just past the light socket is a door, leading to the downstairs garage, partially ajar. Blood is smeared approx. halfway up this door."*

Beside the door leading to the garage was a short, carpeted staircase up to the condo's second floor. At the base of the staircase, two video components were stacked on the floor, trailing their power cords. Hooks noted that the bottom component was a Philco VCR. On top was a Sony digital disc player. Hooks also noted, *"A bloody fingerprint appears on top of the disc player."* The detectives could see into the living room from the front entryway. Against the far wall, past Sherri's body, was a large wooden wall unit with a television and shelves for other electronics. One of the shelves above the television was collapsed, apparently pulled down during the struggle.

The proximity of the video components to the front door, and the way they appeared to have been hurriedly abandoned, suggested to the detectives that the victim may have interrupted a burglary in progress. Despite their collective experience, it apparently did not occur to the detectives that the bloody fingerprint was evidence that the components were moved and placed there after the confrontation turned bloody, rather than before, as one would expect if it were an interrupted burglary.

The detectives' walk-through proceeded to the living room, where Sherri's body still lay on the floor. Hooks wrote on his notepad, *"Turning left and stepping down into the living room area a brown phone is lying on the floor, pulled toward the tile area. To the right is a brown chair containing a multicolored blanket. This blanket was placed on the victim's head by the paramedics prior to detectives' arrival due to the hysterical state of the husband."*

Hooks was slightly mistaken. It was not the blanket but a hand towel that John had placed over Sherri's face while he awaited the paramedics. The multicolored blanket Hooks saw on the chair was a handmade quilt Sherri had received from her grandmother, Loretta's mother, as a Christmas gift one year. The quilt had two armholes and sleeves sewn into it so that Sherri could wear it like a jacket around the house when she was cold. Years later, the style became known as a Snuggie blanket, but the one Sherri had was her grandmother's own homespun design. In the days after the murder, the quilt was examined and found to have several bullet holes and gunpowder residue on it. Subsequent forensic testing supported that the quilt was wrapped around the murder weapon before the gun was fired, as a makeshift silencer to muffle the sound of the fatal gunshots.

The detectives moved farther into the living room, to within a few feet of Sherri's body. Hooks wrote, *"Continuing in a westerly direction is a single end type table with a lamp. The drawer to this table has been completely pulled from the table, and the contents have been partially dumped on the floor with the drawer leaned against the table."* It was the same table on which John and Sherri had placed their miniature Christmas tree not two months before.

Entryway and blanket on living room chair (LAPD crime scene photo #16)

At first glance, like the video components left in the front entryway, the way the drawer was dumped on the floor suggested a ransacking, as if the person who did it was searching for valuables. The detectives apparently failed to notice, however, that whoever emptied the drawer never bothered to rifle through its contents. Resting on top of the pile of papers was a matchbox-sized, clear plastic box of straight pins, which had been inside the drawer. When the drawer was dumped, the lid of the box jostled open. A few pins had spilled out, but most came to rest in a tight radius atop the papers. Had the drawer's contents been rummaged through, the pins would have been scattered and strewn across a wider area.

Nor did the detectives apparently question what a burglar might have expected to find worth stealing inside a living room end table. In most homes, drawers in common areas are more often used as junk drawers than to stash valuables. It was an unusual place for a burglar to focus attention, at least compared to more typical quarries, like a bedroom jewelry box. In hindsight, it made little more sense than why a burglar would bother to carry two video components across the room, but rather than steal them, leave them by the front door. Hindsight, the clearest of lenses, was not available to the detectives at the crime scene on the night of Sherri's murder. Homicide detectives don't often get the benefit of hindsight, especially in the most consequential period of any murder investigation, the first forty-eight hours. When it comes to the first forty-eight hours, there is no such thing as a do-over.

On top of the end table with the yanked-out drawer was the Calendar section of the day-old Sunday *Los Angeles Times*. The headline emblazoned across the front page read HORRIFIC, for a story about a new Rutger Hauer slasher film. The rest of the Sunday paper was in a neat pile across the room, on the living room coffee table.

Coincidentally, the lead story in the section on top of the pile involved a decades-old murder case, the 1955 death of Evelyn Throsby Scott, a wealthy Los Angeles socialite. Evelyn's younger husband, L. Ewing Scott, was convicted of her murder in 1957, although his wife's body was never found. The headline in the paper, memorialized in the Rasmussen crime scene photos, read 30 YEARS LATER, A CASE OF MURDER IS ADMITTED—BUT QUESTIONS LINGER.

The detectives continued their walk-through of the living room. Hooks wrote, *"Moving now south against the west wall, a speaker has been knocked forward, lying on its face. The speaker wire has been removed. This item is lying up flush against the victim's head."* The stereo speaker toppled close to Sherri was large and heavy. The missing speaker wire was one of the two "ligature type items" left on the floor in the front entryway, roughly ten feet away. Hooks also noted the damage to the wooden wall unit. A high shelf with a receiver and cassette deck was collapsed onto the television.

Having documented the perimeter of the living room, the detectives moved closer to the area around Sherri's body. Hooks wrote, *"Moving N/W from the coffee table to the victim, pieces of a porcelain statue type item lie scattered across the center of the living room."* The shattered item was in fact a heavy ceramic vase. Hooks noted that the largest intact piece was about two and a half feet from Sherri's upper torso. Smaller shards, some jagged, littered the carpet nearby. Next, Hooks wrote, *"Moving closer to the victim's*

Living room from second-floor landing (LAPD crime scene photo #17)

body is a blood soaked white cloth"—the towel John used to shroud Sherri's face before the paramedics arrived.

Hooks described Sherri's injuries dispassionately: "*The victim is lying in a supine position with her left leg slightly crossed over her right leg. Rigor is apparent in the victim's right hand which is pointed slightly upward. The victim is wearing a red bathrobe with two obvious holes over the left breast area. Under the robe the victim is wearing a pink nightshirt pulled up around the stomach area, bloodsoaked in the middle. A pair of black panties (string bikini type) appears to be intact. The victim has a small gold necklace on, as well as a single wedding band (left ring finger). The victim has no shoes on. Smeared blood appears on both the left and right wrist of the victim. The victim's right eye is bruised shut, and blood is partially covering the victim's face.*" It was unnecessary for Hooks to document Sherri's injuries in greater detail, given the crime scene photos, and the autopsy to come.

The detectives did not need to wait for the autopsy to begin to piece together what happened. The trauma to Sherri's face, the broken vase near her body, and the trail of evidence from the front entryway into the living room suggested the fight was protracted and ferocious, before it culminated in the fatal gunshots.

The gunshot wounds to Sherri's chest and her facial injuries were so conspicuous that the detectives overlooked on their initial walk-through another injury Sherri suffered: a bite mark on the inside of her left forearm.

The fact that Sherri was bitten during the fight was more evidence of how vicious and unrestrained the struggle was as she fought for her life.

The detectives had to step over the video components stacked at the base of the staircase to reach the condo's upper floors. Hooks wrote, *"Moving up the stairs to the dining area the room appears to be undisturbed. Paperwork appears on the table of the dining room."* Also on the dining room table were the three red roses John had given to Sherri the day before, to mark their three-month wedding anniversary. The detectives were unaware of the roses' significance, and Hooks made no reference to them in his notes. Moving from the dining room to the kitchen, Hooks wrote, *"Into the kitchen area no lights are on. This area itself is clean and undisturbed."*

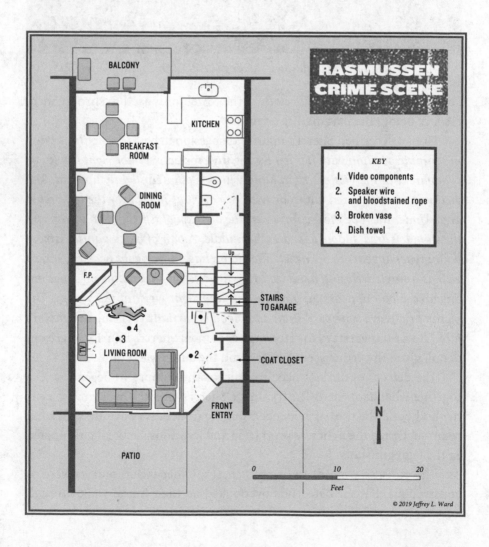

BALCONY

KITCHEN

BREAKFAST
ROOM

DINING
ROOM

F.P.

Up

Up   Down

•4

•3

TV

LIVING ROOM

•2

FRONT
ENTRY

PATIO

RASMUSSEN
CRIME SCENE

KEY

1. Video components
2. Speaker wire
    and bloodstained rope
3. Broken vase
4. Dish towel

STAIRS
TO GARAGE

COAT CLOSET

N

0   10   20

Feet

© 2019 Jeffrey L. Ward

The breakfast nook outside the kitchen had a sliding glass door that opened onto a small outdoor balcony. The glass door was covered by a floor-length white drape. Hooks noted there were two holes in the drape. Most of the broken glass had fallen on the balcony, but some had landed on the driveway below, in front of the garage. The blown-out glass was an indication that the two bullets that pierced the drape and shattered the glass door were fired from inside the condo, near the kitchen. The upper of the two bullet holes in the drape was six feet off the floor, roughly Sherri's height.

The detectives found little else disturbed on the condo's upper floors. Hooks noted, *"Up the stairway to the master bedroom the door is open, and medical books and some type of canvas bag lie on the floor to the left of the door . . . The room itself does not appear ransacked as the jewelry box on top of the dresser drawer has not been tampered with. The drawers to all cabinets are shut . . . The left side of the bed has been slept on, with the covers from this side turned toward the middle of the bed. The bathroom appears to be intact with nothing unusual apparent."*

The final area the detectives examined on their walk-through was the garage. Hooks wrote, *"Returning back down the stairs to the first floor and out the garage access door. Down the stairs to the garage, the husband's vehicle is now parked in the east portion of the garage. The other side is empty. The garage itself appears clean and organized. Two tool boxes and a file cabinet do not appear to have been disturbed."*

It took the detectives about an hour to complete the walk-through. Mayer recalls that when they finished, he, Hooks, and the other detectives present discussed what they thought had happened. The foremost question for the detectives was how the suspect or suspects had gained entry. According to Mayer, his belief that the killer came in through the unlocked front door was not his theory alone, but the consensus of every detective in the unit, along with their supervisors. Mayer recalls that everyone there thought it was the most plausible explanation for how the suspect got inside, based on the crime scene and the limited information they had at that time.

The LAPD's typed version of the Rasmussen chrono stated, *"2030 | Mager [sic] to sta to interview John Ruetter [sic]. (Husband)."* Despite the shorthand and misspelled names, the clear meaning of the chrono entry was that Mayer left at 8:30 p.m. for Van Nuys station to interview John Ruetten there. A second chrono entry at 8:30 referenced the neighbor in the adjacent condo: *"2030 | Obtained info from owner at 7100 Balboa #206. Maid poss lead about crime. Contacted maid. Evangeline Flores, 768-7000, notified her that car would pick her up. Made arrangements to have patrol officer pick up maid and bring her to station."*

The crime scene log indicates that Mayer left the condo at 9:00 p.m., slightly later than the typed chrono indicated. According to the log, a Van Nuys patrol unit arrived at 9:15 to transport John to the station. Pida and Durrer, the Van Nuys supervisors, both logged out of the crime scene at 9:25. John was treated not as a suspect but as the husband of the victim, and he rode to the station unhandcuffed. Hooks remained behind at the crime scene to oversee the collection of evidence.

The LAPD's investigation of Sherri's murder was barely a few hours old. Mayer knew nothing about John, or Sherri, or their history as a couple, beyond what John told him in their initial conversation at the crime scene. Mayer had yet to interview John formally, or to verify that the information John had given him was true. Mayer planned to retrace John's steps that day, to eliminate him definitively as a suspect. John seemed to Mayer genuinely disconsolate, an expected and appropriate reaction to his wife's murder. Mayer had no reason to suspect that John was less than completely forthcoming or had anything to hide.

At the time Mayer left the crime scene, no physical evidence had been collected yet, let alone analyzed. Unlike in television crime dramas, forensic testing in real life can take days, weeks, or even longer to complete. On any given day, the LAPD crime lab has evidence from countless murder cases in the pipeline, all of them competing for the same limited pool of human and scientific resources at SID. Mayer knew it could take two days just to get a ballistics expert to come to Van Nuys and run string lines to determine where inside the condo the gunshots had been fired that shattered the balcony door. Without more information, Mayer could not answer many important questions about how the murder unfolded. Was there one suspect, or more than one? Where did the confrontation begin? Did Sherri try to run away, or did she decide to fight?

As the lead detective, Mayer couldn't well walk out of the crime scene and say, "I have no clue what the hell happened here." It was his responsibility to try to come up with answers. Despite all that he did not know, and could never have known that early in the case, a picture had already started to form in his mind.

Based on the crime scene walk-through, and his initial impression of John, Mayer had already concluded that Sherri was murdered in a burglary gone wrong. Mayer believed it was a very, very good investigative conclusion.

John's Interview

(February 24, 1986, 9:00 p.m.)

Mayer escorted John into an interview room at the Van Nuys station.

John didn't know where he stood with Mayer when the interview began. John had never imagined himself being interviewed by a homicide detective. That was something that happened on TV or in the movies, not in real life. John could barely comprehend that his life had taken this horrific turn, and that Sherri was truly gone.

Mayer set his tape recorder running and shuffled some papers. "To begin with, John, what is your last name, John?" Mayer asked. Mayer spoke quickly and assertively, in a nasal voice. John spelled his last name for Mayer and provided his date of birth, address, and phone number.

"Now, John, what is your wife's name?" Mayer asked.

"Sherri."

"S-H?"

"S-H-E-R-R-I."

"Ruetten?"

"We just got married in November. It's still Rasmussen officially."

"R-A?"

"S-M-U-S-S-E-N," John finished.

"What is her date of birth?"

"Two-seven-fifty-seven." John's voice wavered as he stated Sherri's birthday, which they had celebrated with her parents in Tucson just a few weeks before.

"She's a nurse?"

"She's director of nursing at Glendale Adventist Hospital. She had everything going, I mean she—" John started crying.

"Hey," Mayer said. John was inconsolable. "Hey, hey, hey. John? For a couple of minutes, I need you to be tough for me, buddy. Now, John, I'm going to ask you two quick questions. I need you to listen carefully. Because this will probably help us a great deal."

"Okay," John said.

"Number one, did you have a gun in your home?"

"No."

"There is no gun whatsoever? John, who lived there first? Did you live there or Sherri lived there first?"

"Sherri lived there since 1980."

"Did Sherri ever talk to you about a gun?"

"We talked about guns and it bothered her dad that we didn't have one. So, as far as I know, we didn't have one," said John. It was the first of several times John mentioned Nels in response to a question from Mayer about guns.

"How long have you stayed or lived there, John?"

"I've been living there since the beginning of June."

"June of 1985?"

"Right."

"So, as far as you know, there was no gun in the house at that time?"

"I have no knowledge of any gun either."

"Now, John, in your master bedroom upstairs, on the bathroom side, there's a chest of drawers that is opened about four inches. Is there a possibility a gun could have been in that chest of drawers?"

"I have absolutely no knowledge of a gun in the house."

"Where your tennis shoes are sitting on the floor in your bedroom area, is there any possibility of a gun there?"

John reflected for a moment. "I have no knowledge of a gun, anywhere. I really don't."

"I really appreciate that," said Mayer. The fact that John and Sherri did not keep a gun at home suggested the suspect was armed when they came into the condo, rather than found a gun there. "Okay, next question, John, that's very important. Your wife has a vehicle. What kind of car is it?"

John told Mayer that Sherri drove a silver BMW 318i. Mayer was eager to get a complete description of the vehicle out over the radio, which he could not do from the interview room.

"John, I'm not leaving you alone," Mayer said. John evidently needed the reassurance. "John, I'm walking next door to the computer room. I'm going to get the license number of this car so that I can put a broadcast out on this car, because it's obviously taken and stolen. I'm going to call my partners back at your apartment building to show that there was no gun in the apartment. Okay?"

"Okay."

"You're going to come with me. You're going to be with me all the time to see what's going on. You're not going to be sitting here by yourself."

"Okay."

"Okay, John?"

John had not moved. "I'm coming with you?"

"Yeah. Come on."

Mayer and John came back to the interview room about twenty minutes later. Their return was announced by the sound of their shoes clacking down the hard hallway floor. Mayer closed the door behind them.

"Okay, John, let me explain what I just did, so that you'll understand. What I was just doing there is I was calling an agency that put your wife's and your car in a computer system that shows it's been stolen and taken without permission. So if anybody is driving down the street in your car, and they check or they find it parked somewhere, it comes back and shows that it's stolen and used in a crime. And that they know to hold it for fingerprints, and hold all the occupants in it, and back and forth, and they know that those persons are armed and dangerous. Okay? Do you understand that?"

"Yeah, I do."

Mayer asked to see John's driver's license. "Great, thank you. Phone number at home is seven eight five . . ."

John told Mayer the last four digits of what had been their home number, and his number at work. John did not know it yet, but both phone numbers were already history. John could not bear to live again in the condo, after Sherri was killed there. John was also too devastated by Sherri's murder to return to his job. Mayer asked John for his work address.

"I've just been there like six weeks. It's 21123 Nordhoff," John said. John told Mayer that the name of the company was Micropolis.

"Micropolis," Mayer repeated. The veteran detective made some notes in silence, then handed John back his driver's license. Mayer stated the time and date. He reminded John, "We're at Van Nuys station, in case you're a little confused back and forth. And we're investigating a crime that occurred out at your home. Okay? The young lady that is out there is your wife. Is that correct?"

"Yeah," John said. John's emotion made his voice crack like an adolescent boy's.

"Okay, and her name is Sherri Rasmussen Ruetten?"

"Yeah."

"You haven't had your names changed since you've been married?"

"She's professionally—"

Mayer interrupted. "Hey! John, John? My wife does the same thing. She does the same thing," Mayer said. During interviews, detectives often try to build rapport by highlighting commonalities, however trivial. "Okay, now, John? Something I want you to understand and realize back and forth, I'm going to ask you one question. And it's going to seem right at this time a real, real harsh, or insignificant, or weird question. But you didn't harm your wife, did you, John?"

"No, I did not harm my wife." As John said the last few words, his emotions overwhelmed him, and he dissolved into tears again.

"You didn't harm your wife? Okay, very good. The reason I asked that question is because this conversation is tape-recorded. Okay? And it's just a formality."

"I understand completely," John said, in a stronger voice.

"Now, so let's begin, if we can, to piece together the sequence of events that you were involved in last night, this morning, and when you came home. Okay, John?"

"Okay."

"All right, last evening, that would have been on the twenty-third, which would have been Sunday evening, were you at home with your wife?"

"No. We went out."

"Okay. What time did you return home?"

"We must have returned home approximately ten o'clock p.m."

Mayer jotted some notes. "Okay. When you came home, were there any harsh feelings, or were there any problems, or were you at a dinner engagement, or seeing friends, or what were you doing last evening?"

"We both, both of us get a little Sunday night blues before the week starts. So we plan to go out every Sunday night. We went to Simi Valley and saw a movie."

"Okay. What did you see?"

"We saw *Down and Out in Beverly Hills*."

"Why did you go all the way to Simi to a movie? Was that the closest place where it was playing?"

"I have a new car and I like to drive it. We get a chance to go out on the freeway and it was the right time. It was early."

An unidentified police officer stopped by the interview room. Mayer asked the officer to call Hooks with the DR number, or LAPD case number, that Sherri's murder had already been assigned. Mayer also told the officer to have Hooks call the LAPD's Communications Division and put a broadcast out on Sherri's stolen BMW. The officer confirmed that the suspect would be described as armed and dangerous.

"Okay," said Mayer, returning his attention to John.

"We had been out there one time before and I like the drive on Sunday night. You come up over the hill, you see the view in the Valley."

"Sure, great," Mayer said. Mayer knew the view. "Okay. When you got home, was there anything unusual at your home?"

"No, not that I noticed. We made my lunch for today, which I bring, and then we went to bed."

"About what time was that?"

"Ten thirty."

"Okay. Did anything unusual happen during the evening? Anybody call, or any damage to your condominium or anything like that?"

"Not that I know of."

Mayer asked John whether he owned the condo, or his wife.

"Sherri and I both own it."

"Okay." Mayer made some notes. "All right. This morning, what time did you get up, John?"

"I got up about ten to seven." The wail of patrol car sirens outside, other Van Nuys units responding to unrelated crimes, was audible in the interview room.

"Okay. Does Sherri normally work on Mondays?"

"Yeah, she normally does. Today was one of her days she had to give a class all day, and she was supposed to go in early. So she's normally up before I am. But she called, and I noticed that by the time I got up she still wasn't up. I said, 'What's wrong?' And she says, 'Well, my stomach. I'm not feeling well.' And I said, 'Did you call in to make sure that somebody's doing your class for you?' And she says, 'Yeah, I talked to them.' I said, 'Okay.'"

The sound of sirens again carried into the interview room as John recounted his last moments with Sherri, just that morning.

"Okay. She said she's not feeling well, and she said she had already called in?"

"She told me that she had talked to somebody there. I didn't overhear her talking in the morning or anything, so I'm not positive. But that's what she told me." John's voice quavered with emotion.

"Okay. Do you know if she did that from the bedroom or from downstairs?"

"If she did it from the bedroom, I didn't hear. She was pretty groggy. Maybe she wasn't sure, and I was just waking up. But what I remember is that she said, 'Yeah, I talked to somebody.' Because it's one of the few days that if she doesn't go in, she has to have somebody there to teach the class for her. Normal day—"

"She is the director of nursing?"

"She's the director of critical care nursing. She handles six critical care units. I believe six."

Mayer wrote some notes. "Okay. When you got up, did you shower and shave in the bathroom right by the bedroom?"

John stifled a sob. "Mm-hmm," he managed.

Mayer jotted more notes in silence for half a minute. "Okay. Your closet is at the foot of your bed?"

"Mm-hmm."

Mayer asked John several questions about the closet, and how he and Sherri kept their clothes organized. John explained his were on the left and Sherri's on the right.

"Okay. When you got up this morning and you got dressed back and forth, did you give Sherri a kiss before you left for work or anything? Did she fix you breakfast? Did she stay upstairs in bed?"

"When I left she was in bed, but she was awake."

Mayer asked John what side of the bed Sherri slept on. John said Sherri always slept on the side by the bathroom. "And she told me to call her, that's what she said at home," John told Mayer.

"Okay. Now, your house appears to be very neat. Is Sherri a very neat housekeeper?"

"I wouldn't say she's . . ." John grasped for the right word.

"Meticulous?" Mayer offered.

"She's not a dust freak or anything. We keep it straightened up."

"When you got up this morning, did Sherri kind of fix your side of the bed?"

"When I got out of bed I sort of moved the covers back and she moved them back over, to keep her warm. That's all I remember."

"Okay. So in other words, the covers were sort of over . . ."

"It would be over my side, too."

"Over your side, too?" Mayer wrote more notes.

"God, I don't know why I remember that," John said, almost to himself.

"Okay," said Mayer. "Is Sherri a light sleeper or a heavy sleeper?"

"It depends. If she's thinking about something for work or something, she's very restless. If not, she's . . . I don't think she's a real light sleeper."

"Who hears whatever happens downstairs?"

"She does," said John. "She hears it when the cat tries to get in, which the cat is somewhere, roaming." As Mayer took notes, John muttered aloud, "Why would she hear something downstairs and not push that dumb damn button?"

"Okay. Do you have an alarm in your house?"

"We just had it installed."

"Okay," said Mayer. Mayer did not ask John any follow-up questions about what prompted him and Sherri to get an alarm system. Nor did John volunteer an explanation.

Instead, John said, "It wasn't armed when I left."

"You mean the alarm wasn't armed?"

"No, normally, if she's awake, we keep it armed all night, on instant. Then during the day we run it . . . If she was awake, I normally don't turn it on, because the carpet pad will go off if she forgets and runs down and hits it. You know, sets off the alarm," John said, meaning accidentally. The carpet pad was an undercarpet sensor installed as part of the alarm system John and Sherri had purchased little more than two months earlier.

"Has that been a problem?"

"Yeah. I've done it a couple of times. I don't know if Sherri's ever done it. It's so rare—she's usually gone before I am. It's so rare—"

"What alarm company do you have?"

"It's Locktronic. We haven't had it that long. I think we've had a couple of false alarms."

"Okay. Where is the panic button?"

"There's two panels, one downstairs by the door, and one right by where she sleeps, and she knows how to use the dumb thing." John's composure wavered again. "All she has to do is hit two keys and it's instant. Goes off."

The police officer from earlier returned to tell Mayer the stolen car report had been broadcast. Mayer thanked him.

Mayer asked John, "What if the front door is opened? Does it automatically go off? Does an alarm—"

"If it's armed. If it's armed."

"Okay. But it wasn't armed?"

"I did not arm it when I left." The thought that he might have prevented Sherri's murder, but didn't, seemed to push John's emotions to the brink. "Oh, God, why didn't I plug it in?" John started crying. "I'm going to have to deal with that the rest of my life."

"Hey. Hey. John? You know what? That's just a set of circumstances that happened." John struggled to stifle his sobs as Mayer comforted him. "You know what? That may have not assisted or anything, back and forth. I'm sure it didn't. I'm sure it didn't." John wanted to believe Mayer's assurances and managed to compose himself. "Okay? All right, now you say there's another alarm panel downstairs somewhere?"

"It's right on the wall in between the door to the garage and the front door." John answered some more questions about the location of the alarm panel.

"Okay. Now if you touch that alarm, or if you try and activate it, does it show on the key panel that you may have tried to activate it?"

"If it's not armed—"

"Nothing will show?" Mayer interrupted.

"—the only thing that will show is what door is currently opened." The alarm system included five magnetic door and window sensors. John explained that a red light indicated whenever a door was opened, even if the alarm was unarmed at the time. Once the door was closed, the light instantly turned green. Opening a door did not trigger the alarm unless the system was armed. "If it's not armed, it's worthless," John said.

"Okay. All right. What time did you leave for work? What time did you walk out of the house? Did you have breakfast downstairs?"

"I never eat breakfast."

"Same like me," Mayer said.

"Gets my stomach going weird."

"Me too," Mayer said. His tone suggested he and John had a lot in common.

"Seven twenty is when I left," said John.

Mayer wrote the time down and circled it. "At seven twenty a.m., was your BMW in the garage?" Mayer asked with rising intensity.

"Yes, it was."

"Okay. Normally, your wife keeps your keys to the BMW where?"

John said Sherri usually kept her keys on a bar counter near the dining room.

"All right. Where is her purse normally kept?"

"Same area. The purse she's currently got her junk in."

"Okay. What kind of purse does she normally have her junk in right now?" Mayer's voice was now softer, more compassionate. "It's okay, just take your time."

John said Sherri had a brown leather purse.

"Does she keep the purse close to where the keys are?"

"Yes, sometimes the keys may even be in the purse."

"All right. Seven twenty, you left, went down to the garage, got in your car, Mazda? What kind of Mazda is it?"

"It's an RX-7," John said. "Eighty-six." John had had the car for only a few months.

"It's red, right?"

"Maroon is the official color."

"Okay. And then you back out of the garage. You close the garage door with your garage door opener?"

"This morning, I don't know why, but I remember distinctly watching the garage door. I close it every morning. I think I've forgotten once since I've lived there. I remember distinctly the garage door going down. And I always lock. What happens is, I go out through the garage door to the stairs. That door is always locked, because that's the door I go out. And then the front door, I never even check the front door, because we always keep it locked."

"You really don't use the front door. Just like me in my condo, right?"

"The only thing the front door gets used for is to let the cat in and out, once in a while."

"Now, your door to your garage, just like in my condo, do you lock it with a key, or do you have the little push lock to lock it?"

"I push-lock it. I normally don't dead-bolt it because it's inside the garage."

"Did you push-lock it this morning?"

"Yes, I lock it every morning. It's something I never forget, especially if Sherri had been by herself."

"Did you let the cat in or out last night?"

"I'm sure the cat was let in or out last night."

"Do you remember locking the front door when you go to bed? Do you have a habit of checking the front door?"

John said their typical routine was to double-lock the front door.

"Who normally locks that, Sherri or you?"

"It's a combination. Depends on who's the last one down."

"What it really depends upon is where your keys are, doesn't it? If your keys are upstairs, you don't go all the way upstairs to get your keys, do you? You go over to Sherri's and get hers."

"It's possible that I might go up and grab hers, depending on where my keys are, or she might grab hers. We don't have a set routine on that. We haven't been living that long together," John said. His voice again quavered.

"Okay. You don't remember letting the cat in or out?"

"If I were to guess, I would say that the cat was probably let in or out last night at some time."

"Okay. Was the cat in when you went to the movies?"

"Yeah, I believe the cat was in when we went to the movies. To the best of my knowledge." John said he couldn't guarantee whether they checked the front door was locked after they came home from the movies.

Mayer asked John how long his morning drive to work took.

"I would say twenty minutes, normally, depending on the traffic."

John explained that on his way to work that morning, he'd dropped off some dry cleaning at Pine Hill Cleaners on Topanga and Roscoe, then gone to the office. "I got to work about ten to eight."

"Do you have to punch in?"

"No." .

"Did anybody see you arrive at work?"

"The only reason I remember exactly when I got in is because Paul came in, who's a designer who works right in my area. I noticed that, and I go, 'Paul's in a little before eight.' That's why I remember knowing what time I was in."

"Did you stay at work all day today, or did you go out to lunch?"

"I ate my lunch at my desk. I ate my lunch until about twelve twenty, and then I got in the car, and I went and deposited my check at the bank, which is about five miles away." John told Mayer the name of the bank and described where it was located.

"What time do you get off work?"

"That's very flexible too, but my official hours are eight to five. I left early tonight because I had to pick up the cleaning and pick up some shoes from UPS. So I left about five after five."

"You picked up the cleaning."

"Right."

"How'd you pay, by check or cash?"

"I paid cash. The amount was twenty-six dollars, I believe. I remember that because I couldn't believe how much it was."

John also told Mayer the location of the UPS store. "As far as I know, I left the UPS at about ten to six."

"And from there you went straight home?"

"I went straight home. I must have been there within five or ten minutes."

"Okay. When you came home, what was the first thing you noticed?"

"That the garage door was open. And the garage was empty of cars."

"Did you think that was unusual?"

"Yeah, I did."

"Why?"

"Because if Sherri was gone, she would've always closed the garage door."

"Did you notice anything out in the street or in the parking area?"

"I noticed right away windshield glass."

"Right or left?"

"Right, at the entrance to our garage. At that time, I started going, 'What's going on here?' My first reaction was that Sherri did something on accident. She's very into her profession, but she's absentminded. She plowed into the garage door once and knocked the mirror off the BMW. I'm going, 'Oh God, what did she do? She must have been upset and did something, and forgot to close the garage door.' So—"

"John, this is a little detective technique that we use back and forth, but you said you were going to do something when you got to work today. What was it, when you first got to work?"

"I don't remember. I don't remember anything specific I had to do at work."

"Sherri was home, there was something you were going to do."

"Oh, I was going to call Sherri."

"Did you call her?"

"Yes, I did."

"What time did you call her?"

"I remember in the morning going, I shouldn't call too early 'cause I don't want to wake her up. She's sick and she's resting at home. I can't give that the best time. Best time I can say is between anywhere from ten to eleven, the first time. There was no answer at that time."

"There was no answer at ten or eleven this morning?"

"No, and that's when I got . . . I started feeling a little strange. I go, 'Why would there be no answer?' Because normally, Sherri puts on the phone machine if she goes someplace. I thought to myself, you know how you are. You start to worry, and then you say, 'Aw, it's nothing.' So—"

Mayer interrupted, and said, "John, this is a little difficult, but I want you to do this as best you can. All of us have little routines. You are a newly married couple."

"Okay," said John.

"What was Sherri wearing this morning when you left?"

"She was in bed. We both went in late. We both were tired. Sherri was really tired. She got in bed before I was. She was all covered up. She was tired, she'd gone out for a run. I just crawled into bed."

"She went for a run after you went to the movies?"

"No. She ran earlier and she was tired through the whole movie."

"Oh, okay."

"And so when we got home, I was brushing my teeth. I came in and she was already halfway zonked out, when I got into bed at ten thirty. She maybe got in five minutes before me. So I don't remember."

"Okay. When you crawled into bed, did you touch her?"

"Normally I give her a kiss and tell her I love her and say good night." John's emotions welled up as he said it.

"Was she wearing anything, do you recall?"

"She wasn't naked, I don't think. She doesn't normally sleep naked."

"Okay. Does she normally sleep in a nightgown?"

"It can be either a long flannel nightgown or something with panties and a short top."

Mayer asked John several more questions about what Sherri wore to bed, and where in the bedroom she kept her nightclothes. John answered to the best of his recollection. "Okay," Mayer said. "I know this is a little tough for you. But it's something that, as best you can, try to remember." Mayer's tone of voice was lower now, almost intimate.

"Okay. Now, does Sherri normally wear her brassiere to bed?"

"No."

"Does she normally wear panties to bed?"

"Yes."

"If she was wearing brassiere and panties, would she take them off and place them on the floor? Is that unusual for her? Or would she place them in the hamper, the clothes hamper?" It is unclear what Mayer was driving at with his line of questioning about Sherri's underwear habits. In the LAPD's crime scene photos of the master bedroom, no bra or panties are visible anywhere on the floor.

"It depends. I'm not there a lot. When I'm not there, she may do things differently than when I am."

"I understand. I understand."

"It's possible that they could be on the floor for a short period of time."

"Okay." Mayer made some more notes, then asked, "Is Sherri an inquisitive type of aggressive person, or is she a docile, meek type personality?"

"With regard to her profession, she's very aggressive. But with regard to a lot of personal things, she's very shy. It's a real . . . She's got an interesting combination. So, if it's a personal type thing, she can be very shy. But if it has to do with her profession, she is usually aggressive. She is assertive enough that she has become a director of nursing for critical care. But she is sort of a shy person with personal relationships."

"Okay. Is she afraid to stay home by herself?"

"I don't think she likes it. But I don't think she would be afraid. She's not afraid," John said emphatically.

"Okay. If she heard noises downstairs, do you think she would go down and investigate?"

"I would think she'd hit the goddamn panic button. I mean that's what we bought the dumb thing for." John sounded frustrated and miserable.

"Okay."

"I mean, maybe she thought it was Bozo or something, or I don't know what it was. Bozo's the cat."

"Sure," said Mayer.

"We even talked about it, if we were both there, what would we do if we heard something downstairs. Would we hit the panic button first? Would we lock the door? And, you know, the problem, I hope . . . I don't know. She would be afraid, I think."

Mayer did not ask John any follow-up questions to find out what prompted this conversation with Sherri, about what to do if they heard something or someone downstairs. Nor did John say more about what or who made Sherri feel afraid. Just a few moments earlier, John had said the opposite, that Sherri would not be afraid.

"Okay," Mayer moved on, instead. "Has she had any problems at work?"

"Her work is tough every day. She's got a hard job."

"No, but I mean has she had any problems with—"

"Nothing unusual," John said, without hesitation. "In fact, this wasn't even one of her tougher weeks. She had, you know, things go up and down. But it's just a high-tension job and it takes a lot of responsibility. That's why we both liked to go out on Sunday nights."

"Your VCR is located above the television in your wall unit?"

"Mm-hmm."

"When you came into your residence this evening, you unlocked the door, or was the door—"

"The door was ajar."

"The door was ajar?"

"That's when I was really scared." John's emotions welled again as he relived his walk upstairs from the garage. The same stairs he and Sherri used every day. John whimpered at his memory of what was through the door.

"Okay. It's okay. All right, now, John, this is going to be a little tough part. But here's where I need your help. All right? You opened up the door. When you went into the house, what was the first thing you saw?"

"Well, I saw Sherri right front of me. When I walked in the door, I saw her lying on the ground."

"Okay. What was the first thing that you noticed?"

John spoke briskly at first, his voice brimming with fear and heartache. "Well, the first thing that I thought was maybe she was sleeping or something, and then it just, slowly the data starts to come in. You start to see that things are torn up. There's a broken thing on the floor. And then I started thinking, 'Oh God, I hope she's just okay.' That was my first inclination. So I went up and I looked at her. I noticed her face had some . . ."

John paused as he pictured Sherri's face when he found her, just a few hours earlier. John continued, "It definitely had been . . . something had been done to her. What I did was, first I didn't even . . . at that time I didn't notice fully what was in the room. I don't even think I noticed the two pieces of stereo equipment right front of me."

"Okay," said Mayer.

"I went straight to her and, as soon as I grabbed her leg, I knew it, and saw her face, I knew we were in trouble, because I could feel that she had already, you know . . ." John grasped for a euphemism for Sherri's state, but there was no getting around it. "I knew right away that she was dead. I could tell she . . ." John pulled up, seemingly unable to say aloud again that Sherri was dead. John returned to talking around it. "I don't know what these things do, but I could tell she had been for a while, because I couldn't move her leg or anything. I grabbed her calf. That's really the only portion of her that I touched. I looked at her eyes at that time and I walked away. I just couldn't believe it. I don't know whether it was thirty seconds or forty-five seconds. I was walking around and I realized that she wasn't going to get up."

"Mm-hmm," said Mayer.

"So I dialed 911 right off."

"What phone did you use?"

"The one right by the lamp downstairs."

"The brown one?" Mayer asked. Crime scene photos taken that night show a brown telephone on the living room carpet, midway between Sherri's feet and the video components stacked by the front door.

"Right," John answered. John did not mention whether the phone was on the floor when he went to call 911, and Mayer did not ask. John recounted of the call, "They said something about all operators being busy or something like that. So I just sat there for however long it took. Then the operator came on ten or fifteen seconds later."

"Okay. What did you tell them?"

"I said, 'I think my wife is dead,'" John recalled, his voice breaking.

"Okay. Did you stay in the apartment at that time?"

"At that time they said, 'Don't call anybody else. Just wait there and somebody is on the way.' So I set the phone down and I stood there, pacing back and forth on the thing. Then, at some point, I rechecked and looked at her eyes. She was, you know, she was . . ." John couldn't bring himself to say the word. "Then, I couldn't take it. I was standing there. So I just took the blanket that was right next to her—"

"There was a blanket next to her?" Mayer asked. John's voice was racing, but Mayer's was calm. It seemed to slow John down.

"Right. There was a blanket right—"

"Where is that normally kept, that blanket?"

"I believe those blankets were in the chair, right next to the fireplace. They are folded up usually. They were folded up last night."

Mayer jotted some notes. "Was that blanket physically laying next to her, or was it in the chair?"

"No, it was . . ."

"Was it all unfolded and crumpled?"

"I didn't even really move it. I just sort of flipped it over," John said, meaning onto Sherri's face. John misspoke about what he had used to shroud Sherri, to spare himself the sight of her battered visage. John had in fact covered her face with a towel, not a blanket. John's voice trembled as he recalled his wait after he called 911. "I had to, so I could stand it. I didn't want to leave the place."

"Okay."

"I did . . . It did seem to take forever for the paramedics to get there. I was getting really upset. I couldn't . . . I wanted somebody to be there, because I couldn't deal with being in there by myself."

"Okay."

John spoke faster as he recounted the panic and helplessness he felt, being alone with Sherri's body. "So I walked down into the garage once. I looked around and made sure . . . I was thinking about walking out front to let anybody in and get them in. But I said no, because if they called I had to walk back up. So I just stood there and waited." John sighed deeply.

"Okay. The paramedics got there, did you happen to notice what time it was or anything like that at all? It's not that important, but I just—"

"What I remember, and it may be from what they said or how long it took them, I think it was about six fifteen."

"Okay. All right. The police officers arrived pretty close to the same time, I would imagine?"

"When the paramedics first got there, I thought, 'Are the police coming?' They knew right away that this was not a job, you know . . ." John paused, again unable to say it. "Then I don't know whether they called the police or not at that time. But I heard somebody mentioning calling the police. I thought . . . I don't know. That's all I remember. The police, I think, were there ten minutes after or five minutes after."

"Did you ever go upstairs?"

"No. Not that I remember. I mean, I was out of it."

"I understand."

"But not that I remember. I went to the kitchen and I looked in the kitchen. The only thing I had in my hand, when I came in, was the cleaning. I couldn't carry in the box of shoes and everything, my briefcase and everything, all at once."

"Where is your briefcase?"

"It should be left in the Mazda. I never took it out of the Mazda, as far as I remember."

"Okay. Did your wife normally keep a lot of money at home?"

John seemed to cringe at the senselessness of Sherri losing her life over money. "She never has any money. She never has any cash. She makes tons of money. She never has any cash."

"Does she have credit cards, and a checkbook and all that type of stuff?"

"Yeah, she would have a checkbook, a few gas cards, a Visa card."

"Okay," Mayer said.

Another Van Nuys homicide detective, Sherry Santor, stopped by the interview room. At the time, Santor was one of very few female homicide detectives on the LAPD. "How is it going?" she asked Mayer. They exchanged pleasantries and Santor left.

Mayer returned to John. "Okay. Your wife has a briefcase, I would imagine. Where does she normally keep her briefcase?"

"Normally, it's, as you walk in the kitchen, we both keep them there. There is a little space, down to the right, that we keep them."

"Okay. Does she always keep hers locked?"

"I would doubt it."

"Okay. What does she keep in there?"

"Stuff that she is currently working on and she may have to work on at home. She does work at home quite a bit. In fact, she mentioned before, really quickly, before I left, that she might work on her lecture today. She's working on a lecture."

"Okay."

"That was in the morning."

"As best you can remember, John, when you tried to call Sherri this morning, you said it was between ten and eleven. What time do you take a coffee break?"

"I normally don't. It's a new job. I'm humping it. So I normally don't take a coffee break."

"What time does everybody take a coffee break?"

"About ten."

"Did you call her around coffee break time?"

"Some people in my area . . . The other guy doesn't normally take a coffee break. So it's hard to identify, with that number. The only way I can identify that number is that I didn't want to call her too early and wake her up."

"When did you call a second time?"

"I might have called a half an hour later, after the first time, because I figured she might have run out and done something real quick."

"Did she answer the second time?"

"She never answered all day. I called four or five times. Now, what I did additionally, I think after I called the second time, and I really don't remember when this was . . . Her secretary is named Sylvia." Mayer's pen scratched notes as John recounted his call to Sherri's secretary. "I called Sylvia. I think it was probably after the second time I called. I felt a little stupid, because I was thinking that maybe she got up and decided to go into work and just turned off the phone machine. At this time, I was getting a little concerned that she was sick. I thought she might be really sick, and have gone to the doctor, or who knows what the heck was going on."

"Sure."

"So I called Sylvia. The dumb problem was, she is supposed to teach the PSA. It's a 'People Difference' program that she teaches at the hospital, on Mondays every now and then. When she teaches that, she never goes in to her normal office. So, when I called Sylvia, I said, 'Is Sherri there?' Sylvia said, 'Well, she teaches the People Difference today.' I said, 'Well, then, she did go in to teach it?' This is the frame of the conversation. Sylvia said, 'Well, she never comes into this area when she goes to teach the People Difference.' I said, 'Okay. I'll try again at home.' I just figured she was out or something."

"Okay."

"Then I believe I called . . . I may have gone to lunch. I don't know exactly how many times I called before lunch. Then I called after lunch and I couldn't get her again. Then I tried to get Sylvia back, to make sure that Sherri hadn't come in, and Sylvia knew about it. I couldn't get Sylvia again.

Well, by the time this happened, the work was normal work. You just get back into work, and you start going. By the time I called the last time, she still wasn't there. But I still hadn't been able to get back to Sylvia. So I figured maybe she was at work, had gone in late and taught the program or something. So then I left work early, because I had some things to do before I got home. You know the sequence on that."

"Okay."

"So I was really . . . I was concerned. But I was in this mode where I was saying, 'All right. Nothing's wrong. She's just out.' I was getting a little mad at her for not calling me and telling me what was going on. But I am away from my desk a lot, and sometimes I'm hard to get ahold of."

"So far as you know, there was no gun in your residence whatsoever?"

"No. As far as I know. Sherri knew that I didn't think that it's a good idea to have a gun around the house. If she had one, I don't know about it. Her dad has guns and I think her dad would have liked her to have a gun. But as far as I know, there was no gun in the house."

"Where do her parents live?"

"In Tucson." John did not mention that he had not yet called the Rasmussens and informed them of Sherri's murder.

"Where do your parents live?"

"San Diego."

"Do you have relatives here, anywhere?"

"My brother lives up here. He goes to Northridge right now."

"Where is your brother now?"

"We tried to get ahold of him. He's not at home. He might be over at the fraternity, or I don't know where he is at. I haven't talked to him since this whole thing has happened. The only people I've talked to is my parents."

"Do you know where he lives at?"

"He lives on Devonshire Street in Northridge."

"Okay," Mayer said calmly. "All right, John. What I'm going to have to do this evening, and I hope you can understand this, is I'm going to have to have you go over to someone's house this evening. I will take you over to your brother's house or wherever you can go. Do you have a best friend?"

"Well, my parents are supposed to be coming up here. I called them—"

"From San Diego?"

"—I think about two hours ago."

"Where did you call them from?"

"Here."

"Where are they going to come to? Are they going to come to your residence?"

"Well, I told them what happened and they're coming here."

"To this police station?"

"Yeah."

"Okay. Here's what I'm going to need done. In that case, we are going to let you stay here for a little while, until they arrive here. Then, this evening, I'd like you folks to get yourself a room somewhere. Okay?"

"Okay," said John.

"Tomorrow morning, I would like you to meet me at ten, here, tomorrow morning, okay? Because what I'm going to have to do is, I'm going to have to take you back over to your residence tomorrow morning for a walk-through of your residence with me, so that you can show me a couple of different things, and you're going to be able to point out a couple of different things. And I'm going to ask a couple of different things back and forth so that we can help each other piece this out."

Mayer had talked with John for less than an hour. The walk-through of the crime scene with John did not take place until the following morning. Mayer had not interviewed any other friends or family of Sherri about her habits, her schedule, her fears, or if there was anyone who may have wished her harm. Nevertheless, by the end of Mayer's initial interview with John, only a few hours after Sherri's body was found, Mayer claimed to have the case figured out.

"Now, John, here's what I think happened. I'm usually a pretty good judge of character. I'm fairly certain that you have absolutely nothing to do with this, okay? I believe your house was burglarized today, sometime before ten a.m. I believe they got in your front door by prying open the front door. I don't think it was locked. Okay? If it was locked, maybe just the bottom lock was locked. Once those persons, or that person, or whoever was inside, I believe they were trying to steal your stereo and probably some other items."

John began to cry. "Why would they do anything to her, though? Why wouldn't they just run?"

"I don't know, John. I don't know," Mayer said calmly and evenly. "John, things happen, okay? Here's what I think happened. I think Sherri came downstairs, and I think she surprised them, and she was hurt. You'll be able to see from tomorrow, and you'll be able to see back and forth, I'm not telling you anything out of school. You'll find out anyhow. She was shot—"

"Oh God," John reacted.

"—and the glass out of the window where a couple of . . . That glass wasn't from the windshield of your car, that glass was because two shots went through your sliding glass window in the kitchen." John whimpered as Mayer continued his narrative of what he believed happened to Sherri. "They probably took her down and held her down in the living room. Now were her hands . . . You didn't untie her hands or anything like that while you were there, did you, John?"

John's voice trembled as he recounted, "The only part of her body that I touched was her leg, just to see if she was—" Then John recalled more. "Oh, actually, no. You're right. Her hands were not tied, because I checked her pulse. I'm sorry. I didn't remember that. I checked her pulse. When I grabbed her leg, I knew that it was . . ." John trailed off.

"Okay, John, do you have a family priest or pastor or something that you do? Are you a religious family?"

"Sherri and I don't go to church a lot, but we're pretty religious, I think. I don't have a priest that I go to a lot."

"Is there someone I can call for you?"

"Just my parents. I just want to see my mom and dad." John was twenty-seven years old, but at that moment, he sounded much younger.

"Sure, sure."

"That's it," said John.

"Yeah, okay. How about your brother? Maybe we can give your brother a call and he can come over and be with you here until your mom and dad get here?"

"You can try him again. His roommates know that he's supposed to . . . I don't know what they know. My mom called them after I called them. They had tried to get ahold of my brother and he was gone. I don't know whether he was at work. Usually they know when he's at work. So he must have been at a fraternity thing or something."

"John, are you happy, you were not having any family problems, or marital problems, or anything?"

"We were having the best time. We just got married," John said, crying.

"No financial problems? She's not having any problems with an ex-boyfriend? Or you with an ex-girlfriend?"

"No," John said, without hesitation. John did not mention his long, hard-to-define relationship with Stephanie Lazarus, apparently since in John's mind, at least, they were never boyfriend and girlfriend. John did not volunteer that he last had sex with Stephanie six months earlier, soon after he and Sherri got engaged. Nor did John inform Mayer that Stephanie had gone to Sherri's work and told her about John's infidelity.

John may or may not have known at the time about the letter Stephanie had written to his mother, six months before Sherri's murder, in which Stephanie said she would never understand his decision to get married. Sherri may not have told John, in the months leading up to her murder, about all the unsettling experiences she confided to her father concerning the woman she referred to as John's ex-girlfriend.

John had not paid much attention to Stephanie, or her feelings, since he fell in love with Sherri. From his perspective, Stephanie was history, like the mistake he made in sleeping with her the summer before. Sherri had forgiven him, and they had moved on. When Mayer asked John if he was having any problems with an ex-girlfriend, it was as if Stephanie did not even cross John's mind.

In John's defense, Mayer did not give him very long to dwell on the matter. Mayer seemed to take John at his word, asked him no follow-ups, and moved on to his next question. "Have you had any unusual visitors or any crank phone calls? Or hanging up? Or anything like that?"

Again, John did not volunteer to Mayer any of the stories Sherri had told her parents about his ex-girlfriend's uninvited visits in the preceding months: the confrontation at the hospital; the two visits to the condo, after Christmas, to ask John to wax her skis; or the time Sherri encountered the ex-girlfriend in their living room.

John told Mayer, "The only thing that we get is we get this bizarre thing where the phone rings and there's nothing, it's a dead line, and we've had it for six months. It's something that's a phone line thing. That's what we figured. It happens maybe once a week, or something like that." The hang-up calls were in fact so persistent and annoying that Sherri complained about them to her parents and friends. John had lived in the condo for only about eight months, so the hang-up calls started soon after he moved in. But John did not draw that connection for Mayer, and the veteran detective changed the subject.

Mayer went on, "You get your wallet stolen or your car stolen or anything like that recently, or lost your wallet, or your wife lost her wallet, or anything like that at all? Do you have health insurance on both of you, or life insurance on either one of you? Do you have a life insurance policy on your wife or you, she on you or—?"

"As far as I know, she has no life insurance. I have fifty thousand, I believe, that I get with my company. We don't have any kids. We didn't make a lot of money together." John became emotional as he recalled the life he and Sherri were building.

"Okay. Where did you go to school, John? Are you from here? Are you from San Diego, or—"

"I'm from San Diego but I went to school at UCLA, and I just ended up staying up here. After UCLA, I worked at Data Products for four and a half years, approximately, and I just changed about six weeks ago to this new company, started working on different things."

"Okay. Has your wife experienced any problems at work? Guys hitting on her, or anything like that? I mean, she's an attractive young lady. Has anybody been hitting on her, following her home, or anything like that at all?"

"I would say nothing out of the . . . I don't think there was anything out of the ordinary. She's a nurse, a nursing director, and I think she gets . . . She's an attractive lady. She gets comments from doctors, and sometimes she mentions them to me, but I don't think there was anything out of the ordinary happening." Unbeknownst to John, Sherri had told her parents and friends that she felt she was being watched and followed in public. John volunteered nothing more to Mayer on the subject.

Mayer told John, "All right. Well, I gave you my card. I'm going to give you another one, put it in your wallet there, so in case you forget it or lose it, and then give one to your mom and your dad." John began crying again.

"Did you call Sherri's mother and father?"

John whimpered at the thought of having to inform Nels and Loretta that Sherri had been murdered. More than four hours had passed since John had discovered Sherri's body. John had immediately called 911 and later his own parents, but not the Rasmussens. "No, I haven't," John said. "I feel like I should have protected her, that's the problem. Their family, they're all so close. I don't know if my mom's called them, or what's happened. So I don't know what the status is on that."

Mayer seemed unconcerned. "It's very important, John, that you meet me tomorrow at ten o'clock, okay? I know it's going to be tough, but I'm going to be over there with you, okay? I'm your detective. I'm going to be working with you a million miles an hour. You and I are going to become very close for a while, all right?"

John exhaled audibly. Mayer said, "I'm going to be doing everything possible for you, all right? Let me tell you what we've already done. We've conducted a crime scene investigation at your residence. We have been recovering evidence out there. We'll have taken photographs and fingerprints. Tomorrow we will be taking some more fingerprints out at the location. We will allow you to get whatever you need out of your place there tomorrow. But for this evening, I need you not to go back there."

"I don't want to go back to that place," John said. John sounded as if he had just awoken from a nightmare.

"That's okay, John. In addition to that, in the morning—"

"Oh God," said John, understanding he would in fact have to go back there, whether he wanted to or not.

"—you can have your mom and your dad drop you over here, and then I'll take you over there, and we'll do a little walk-through as to what we're going to do. I'll be right with you and everything will be all taken care of, and you can get out whatever you need for a day or so, all right? Because you won't be able to go back into your apartment for about three days, because we're going to have to do some things on the walls, to lift some fingerprints off of the walls. It's called the ninhydrin process, and it's a little caustic chemical activity, so you won't be able to go in for a couple of days after that. I'll allow you to get some clothes out and everything so everything will be all set."

Mayer prided himself on being a good judge of character, and he trusted his intuition as a detective. He had sized up John for a few hours, long enough to satisfy himself that John's emotional devastation was genuine. Mayer felt bad for the poor guy. He told John so, and also made him a promise.

"I know how you feel. I know what you're going through. We're going to catch these persons, or this person, all right? You've got to have a little faith in me. I know it's tough. We've just met. It's been a tough situation. But we're very successful at what we do. Very, very successful. And we're going to find—"

"That's not going to bring Sherri back, though," John said, crying. John was right.

"I know. But John, we're going to find these persons. Okay? She would want that. Okay?"

"I want it too. I just . . ." John trailed off.

Mayer collected his notes and the rest of the Rasmussen case file, which, that early in the investigation, was still folder thin. Mayer told John, "Let's go out and see if your mom's here. If not, we'll see if we can't get in touch with your brother. The keys to your residence, do you have some keys with you?"

"Yes, I do."

"Okay. I would like to have those keys, John. Now, the reason I need those keys is that I want to lock up and secure the place this evening."

"Okay. This contains the keys to the car and everything."

John's keys clattered as he placed them on the table.

"All right. You wouldn't be needing any of these this evening, would you?

"That's just the house keys and—"

"The two cars."

"This is, yeah, the BMW and the Mazda."

"All right, you won't be needing those this evening and I'll give you them back in the morning. Okay, John, come on with me."

John sobbed quietly as he followed Mayer out into the hallway to wait for his parents. The running tape recorder picked up the ambient sounds of Van Nuys station, late on a Monday night in February 1986. Radio dispatchers relayed a never-ending stream of calls, codes, and addresses to assorted patrol units. Phones rang on desks until whoever was calling gave up and hung up.

Mayer left John alone to wait for his parents. Five hours had elapsed since John had arrived home and found Sherri dead on their living room floor. Sherri's family still had not been informed of her murder.

Despite all the phones ringing within earshot, John could not bring himself to call Nels and Loretta and personally give them the terrible news. John waited for his parents, driving up from San Diego, to come get him at the Van Nuys station.

15

The Bite Mark Swab

(Early Morning of February 25, 1986)

No parents are ever prepared to learn their son or daughter is dead, no matter how grown up the child may be.

In the typed version of the LAPD's chrono for the Rasmussen case, the final entry on the day of Sherri's murder was made at 11:00 p.m. The entry reads in full, "2300 | *Notification to family, also family in Tuscon [sic], Arizona.*"

The typed chrono was prepared in May 1986, three months after Sherri's murder, as an addendum to the Unsolved Murder Investigation Progress Report, the follow-up report required within sixty days. The report, written by Lyle Mayer, the lead detective, included a slightly more detailed account about how the Rasmussen family was notified. It stated, "*On 2-25-86 at 0100 hrs., Detective Mayer made death notifications to the family of Sherri Rasmussen at phone number 626-296-1012. The family of John Ruetten had been notified and arrived at Van Nuys station. John Ruetten left with his family and was instructed to return on 2-25-86 at 1000 hrs. for a second interview. In addition, Detectives Mayer and Hooks informed John that they wished to see if anything was missing from the residence. Ruetten agreed and was cooperative.*"

Nels and Loretta Rasmussen have a very different recollection, not reflected in the LAPD's official records, of how they found out Sherri was murdered.

Nels and Loretta recall they were sound asleep when the phone rang at their home. It was close to 1:00 a.m. on Tuesday morning, February 25. Nels got out of bed and answered the phone.

The caller was not Mayer but Richard Ruetten, John's father. Even in the best of times, Nels and Richard had a strained relationship. John's father told Nels that Sherri had been killed. Nels felt as if the world stopped.

Nels asked what time Sherri was found.

Richard said about six o'clock. Tucson was an hour ahead of Los Angeles, but even with the time difference, that was more than six hours ago.

Nels couldn't understand why no one had contacted him and Loretta earlier. Nels was already thinking about how to get to Los Angeles as soon as possible. Tucson had a small regional airport, with few flights late at night.

Nels wanted to know what took so long for them to be notified.

Richard said when he and Margaret first got to the police station, they spoke with the detectives. The detectives then had talked with John. Richard said he had not called until John and the detectives were done talking.

It also bothered Nels that John's father delivered the news, rather than John. Nels felt John had not only delayed telling them about Sherri's death, but when he finally did, he wasn't man enough to call them himself. Nels told Richard he wanted to speak to John.

Richard said John was too upset to come to the phone. It may have been true that John was too distraught to talk. It's also possible Richard may have wanted to spare his son another wrenching conversation, on top of those John had already had that evening. John may have had other reasons, unknown even to his parents, why he could not bring himself to call the Rasmussens for hours after Sherri's murder.

Eventually, after Nels insisted, John got on the line briefly. Nels recalls that John was too broken up to say much, beyond conveying to Nels he was sorry it happened.

Only John knows why he waited so long to inform his in-laws; why he had his father call instead of calling himself; and why he was reluctant to get on the phone with Nels. To this day, Nels has never received an explanation from John for his actions the night Sherri was killed. How the Rasmussens learned of their daughter's murder set the tone for the next chapter of their relationship with John and his family.

As soon as Nels hung up with the Ruettens, he called the airlines. The last flight of the night from Tucson to Los Angeles had already left, which made Nels even more upset and angry. Had they been notified earlier, they might have been in Los Angeles already. Instead, the Rasmussens could not leave until the morning.

Nels then called his eldest daughter, Connie, in Seattle.

Connie had tried calling Sherri at home earlier that evening, only a few hours before Nels broke the awful news. Connie had thought about calling Sherri several times that day. It had been a few weeks since the sisters last connected. Connie knew that Sherri and John had gone to Tucson for her birthday, but they hadn't spoken about it yet. At lunchtime, Connie was about to call Sherri when a colleague walked in. Connie got busy with work and didn't get a chance to call again before she left the office. When she got home, Connie had to take care of her infant daughter, Rachel, who was sick with an ear infection. Connie's husband, Bill, was out of town.

The first chance Connie had to call was around 7:30 p.m. She dialed Sherri and John's home number.

An unfamiliar male voice answered.

"John?" Connie said.

"No."

"Is Sherri there?"

"No," was all the man said.

"Maybe I dialed the wrong number," Connie said, and hung up.

Connie thought it was weird the man didn't ask who was calling, or offer to take a message. Connie figured she must have dialed wrong. Right after she hung up, Nels called from Tucson. He and Connie had a chat, both of them completely unaware of what had befallen Sherri. Then Connie went back to caring for Rachel. By the time she thought of trying Sherri again, it seemed too late to call.

It was just past midnight in Seattle when Nels called Connie for the second time that night. Connie was still awake because of Rachel's ear infection.

Nels told Connie they had gotten a call, and that Sherri was dead.

Connie said, "That's a sick joke. That's not even funny, Dad."

"I'm dead serious," Nels said. "This is it."

Connie started screaming.

"Get your act together," Nels told his eldest daughter.

Connie could only think, "Okay, I'll get emotional later."

Nels told Connie she had to go to the Seattle-Tacoma airport and book a flight for them to Los Angeles, because the Tucson airport was closed.

As soon as Connie collected herself, she called her boss at home. Connie said she had an emergency and wouldn't be at work the next day, because she had to fly to L.A. Connie wanted to take Rachel and get on the next available flight, whatever time it was.

After Connie booked flights for herself and Rachel from Seattle, and for Nels and Loretta from Tucson, she got herself and Rachel together for the trip. Connie paced the floor until it was time for their 6:00 a.m. flight. Rachel turned six months old that day.

In Tucson, Nels and Loretta could not go back to sleep either. They stayed up all night calling family. Loretta couldn't get a sentence out without dissolving into tears, so she placed the calls, then passed Nels the phone. Nels couldn't do much better but somehow got through the calls.

The loss Nels and Loretta felt most acutely the night they learned of Sherri's murder was of what might have been. They had always anticipated that Sherri would have children one day. Nels and Loretta felt certain Sherri's kids would have been excellent students, like Sherri herself, and gone on to impressive, important careers like their mother's. The realization that Sherri would never be a mom devastated her parents.

In the remaining hours before their flight, Nels tried to think of people, based on his knowledge of what was going on in Sherri's life, who might have wished her harm. Nels came up with only two possibilities.

One was the nurse Sherri had declined to promote at the hospital, over the objections of the nurse's cardiologist boyfriend. Sherri had told her parents about that messy situation. Sherri had received some nasty phone calls that she attributed to the dispute. Around the same time, her car was keyed in the hospital's parking lot. As far as Nels knew, that culprit was never identified.

The other possibility Nels came up with was John's ex-girlfriend. Nels recalled the stories Sherri had told him about her in recent months, both before and after the wedding. Nels knew John's ex-girlfriend was a police officer in Los Angeles. But Sherri had never told her parents the officer's name.

At the Van Nuys station, meanwhile, Mayer interviewed Evangelina Flores, the housekeeper of John and Sherri's next-door neighbor. The interview was tape-recorded. Mayer had a Spanish-speaking patrol officer sit in as an interpreter.

Evangelina described to Mayer the loud thuds and screams she had heard through the wall earlier that day. She was certain she had not heard any gunshots. Mayer thanked Evangelina for the help and asked the officer to drive her home.

As the officer escorted her from the interview room, he asked Mayer, in English, "She's asking me what happened. Can I tell her?"

"Yeah, you can tell her."

"Fine. Okay, sir," the officer said. The question was a nod to Mayer's authority as the lead detective on the case. In addition to steering the investigation, the lead detective controls what information about the case should be released to the public. Homicide detectives are professional hoarders of information, not sharers, particularly when it comes to open murder investigations. If the intimate details of a homicide become widely known, detectives lose some of their leverage over potential suspects. Witnesses may tailor their statements, intentionally or inadvertently, to what they heard elsewhere rather than what they recall. By tightly controlling information about a case, detectives empower themselves and minimize the risk of a tainted investigation.

Mayer put out a Teletype message that contained a description of Sherri's stolen BMW and stated that it was sought in connection with a burglary-murder. Mayer returned to John and Sherri's condo at 12:50 a.m., according to the crime scene log. Mayer's supervisors, homicide coordinator Roger Pida and Al Durrer, the lieutenant in charge of Van Nuys detectives, logged back into the crime scene at the same time.

Three and a half hours had passed since the detectives' initial walk-through. The collection of evidence was already under way, overseen by Hooks. Based on Sherri's injuries and the state of the living room, it was obvious that an intense struggle had preceded her murder. There was reason to be optimistic the suspect or suspects may have left behind fingerprints, blood, or other bodily traces that could help identify them.

When a suspicious death occurs in Los Angeles, forensic science personnel known as criminalists are dispatched to the location by both the Los Angeles County Coroner and the LAPD's Scientific Investigation Division, SID. Criminalists may work in the field, the crime lab, or both, depending on their training and expertise. Responsibility for collecting and preserving physical evidence at homicide crime scenes is divided between the LAPD and the coroner. Any evidence not touching the victim's body—for instance, nearby fingerprints or bullet casings—is the responsibility of the LAPD and SID. The body and anything in contact with it, such as the victim's clothing or blood on their skin, is the province of the coroner.

In 1986, when Sherri was killed, forensic science was on the verge of a sea change that, at the time, still had the aura of science fiction. Automated fingerprints and ballistics databases had already started to revolutionize detective work by allowing the comparison of evidence from one crime scene with that from many other crimes and potential suspects. When the databases first came online, they seemed to work like magic, producing leads out of thin air. Only the advent of DNA analysis, in 1987, had a greater impact on how detectives investigate murder. The new technologies promised to save police incalculable time, labor, and other limited resources. Most importantly, for the families of homicide victims, they increased the chances, and their hopes, that a suspect would be identified and brought to justice.

On the night of Sherri's murder, no one present at the crime scene realized that the science of forensic identification was about to enter a new epoch. Nor could anyone there have anticipated that one day, decades in the future, their contributions to the LAPD's investigation of Sherri's murder would come under intense scrutiny.

The SID latent fingerprint expert assigned to Sherri's case, Gilbert Aguilar, arrived at the condo at 7:15 p.m. Aguilar did not know until he got there that it was a homicide. At an ordinary residential burglary, Aguilar typically printed only for point of entry and any items the suspect may have touched. Homicide crime scenes required much more extensive print work. At murders, Aguilar was trained to print almost everything at the location that could potentially yield a fingerprint. Once he saw the body, and that things appeared to have been removed from the condo, he knew he would be casting a wide net.

Aguilar had to wait to start his work until the SID photographer finished documenting the undisturbed crime scene. Fingerprint powder was inherently messy. Wayward powder could contaminate physical evidence, like blood or saliva, before it was collected. For that reason, Aguilar also had to wait for the criminalists to finish their work in an area before he could dirty it in search of fingerprints.

Aguilar finally got access to the condo around 9:30 p.m. He started in the kitchen, one floor up from the living room and Sherri's body. Aguilar recovered five latent prints on the wall telephone in the kitchen. Each lift was preserved on its own print card. A different SID fingerprint expert would later examine the cards in the lab to determine which ones were identifiable. "Identifiable" meant only that the print was clear and complete enough to compare it to other identified prints on file. Partial or smudged fingerprints that lacked sufficient clarity to make a comparison were deemed "non-identifiable." Of the five prints Aguilar took from the kitchen phone, only one was identifiable. It was later determined to be Sherri's.

Aguilar recovered an additional thirteen fingerprints on the first floor of the condo, including three from the video components stacked in the front entryway. He focused on the bottoms and sides of the components, the surfaces most likely to have been touched by whoever moved them. He found one fingerprint on the Philco VCR, the bottom component, later identified as John's. Two latent prints were found on the Sony disc player, which also had a bloody fingerprint on top. Both latent prints lifted from the Sony component proved to be non-identifiable. Aguilar noted on the print cards the serial numbers of the video components.

Of the eighteen prints Aguilar collected on the night of Sherri's murder, eight were deemed non-identifiable. Nearly all the identifiable prints were eventually matched to either John or Sherri. Since they lived there, the presence of their fingerprints all over the condo and their possessions was unsurprising. It is impossible to tell from a latent fingerprint how long ago it was left.

Bloody prints were different. Whether a bloodstain was wet or dry could help determine when the murder occurred. Unlike ordinary latent prints, the presence of bloody prints can also illuminate how the murder unfolded, moment by moment. In Sherri's case, for instance, several bloodstains were found in the front entryway, more than ten feet away from her body on the living room floor. Blood that distance from the body suggested that the struggle had started somewhere other than where it ended. It also suggested that blood was drawn during the fight, prior to the fatal gunshots. Whether the blood came from Sherri or the suspect was an open question.

Aguilar was careful to steer clear of any bloody fingerprints he saw. If Aguilar noticed a bloodstain, he alerted his colleague from SID, criminalist Alison Ochiae. Ochiae arrived at the condo at 10:30 p.m. It was Ochiae's responsibility to collect any blood, saliva, or other evidence not in contact with the victim's body.

The first blood evidence Ochiae noted was a smear on the inside of the front door, a few inches off the floor. She placed down a small numbered placard, "1," below the bloodstain before it was photographed. Ochiae took a sample from the stain and made a blood swatch, which became item 1 on the LAPD's property report.

Ochiae collected samples from four other bloodstains in the front entryway. These evidence swatches were designated property items 2 through 5. Item 2 was from a bloodstain on a closet door just inside the front door, below the wall panel for the burglar alarm. Item 3 was from a bloody handprint, low on the wall between the closet and the door to the garage staircase, a few inches from an electrical outlet. Item 4 was from a faint smudge halfway up the door to the garage staircase, and 5 was from several drops of blood that had landed in the center of the brown tile floor.

Ochiae moved to the living room, where she collected the heavy ceramic vase that lay in pieces on the carpet a few feet from Sherri's body. The vase was booked as property item 6. The bloody hand towel John used to shroud Sherri's face after he called 911 was booked as item 7.

Next on the property list were the "ligature type items," as Hooks described them in his walk-through notes—the lengths of speaker wire and white rope found on the front entryway floor. The speaker wire was taken from the stereo speaker toppled over next to Sherri's body in the living room. The white rope, about the thickness of a clothesline, was loosely knotted and stained with what appeared to be blood. John was later shown a photo of the rope and did not recognize it as having come from their home, which indicated it was likely brought to the crime scene by Sherri's killer. The speaker wire and rope were collected by Ochiae and booked as property item 8.

Rope and speaker wire on entryway floor (LAPD crime scene photo #51)

Later, during Sherri's autopsy, the medical examiner noted a "pattern abrasion" on her right wrist, an injury caused when something is pressed against the skin forcefully enough to leave an imprint. The abrasion on her wrist was consistent with the texture and thickness of the white rope. Like the bloody handprint on the wall, the presence of blood on the rope suggested that blood had already been drawn when the attempt was made to bind Sherri's wrists.

Ochiae placed a number 9 placard atop the video components stacked at the base of the stairs. For unknown reasons, Ochiae did not take a sample from the bloody fingerprint on the top component, a Sony disc player. Also inexplicably, neither video component was ever booked into property by the LAPD. None of the crime scene photos taken the night of Sherri's murder captured the bloody fingerprint in sufficient detail to identify who left it.

The last items Ochiae collected were the two torn fingernails on the entryway floor. She marked the location of one fingernail with placard number 10 and the other with placard number 11. After the fingernails were photographed in place, Ochiae sealed them inside separate evidence envelopes. The envelopes were booked as property items 9 and 10. Both nails were later determined to be Sherri's.

Any potential evidence on Sherri's body was left for the coroner to gather. Lloyd Mahany, a senior coroner's criminalist, arrived at the condo after midnight with his colleague Walter Rainey, a coroner's investigator. Rainey's job was to assist Mahany with the collection of evidence and then to help transport the body to the morgue, where autopsies were performed. Rainey also wrote a single-page Investigator's Report, which detailed his observations at the crime scene.

Sherri's condo was Mahany and Rainey's second homicide crime scene that night. The first was a woman found dead inside a Ford Pinto in a parking lot in Panorama City. When Mahany and Rainey got to the parking lot, the detectives there told them there was already another body waiting for them in Van Nuys.

The quality that distinguishes the best criminalists from lesser ones is fidelity to procedure. Unlike homicide detectives, who must be creative in their pursuit of witnesses, evidence, and information, the best criminalists never improvise in how they collect and package evidence from one crime scene to the next. When a case goes to trial, any deviation from standard evidence handling procedures can create fissures in an otherwise solid case, as the LAPD was reminded a decade later during the O. J. Simpson trial. The criminalist forges the all-important first link in the chain of custody. The clearer the chain of custody, the more difficult it is to impeach physical evidence at trial. It is rarely obvious at a crime scene which specific piece of evidence will later prove pivotal in the investigation or prosecution. Criminalists who are sticklers for procedure preempt unwelcome surprises down the line.

Mahany was renowned among his colleagues at the coroner's office for his fastidious approach to his work. He always collected evidence in the same order and meticulously documented every step of the process. For each crime scene he visited, Mahany also prepared a written report detailing the evidence he gathered.

Regarding Sherri, Mahany wrote, *"The decedent was observed supine on the living room floor. The decedent was wearing a purple sleeveless shirt, black panties, and a rust colored robe."*

The first thing Mahany always checked for was trace evidence on the body, for instance any loose hairs or fibers that may have been left by the suspect. Mahany's log indicates that the trace evidence he collected from Sherri's body included *"fibers from robe by left thigh,"* followed by *"hair and fibers from robe by left buttock,"* and finally *"hairs from neck."*

Mahany carefully placed the trace evidence in three separate evidence envelopes, each of which he hand-labeled with the decedent's name, the coroner's case number, and the date and time he collected it. He sealed each envelope with red evidence tape, on which was printed in bold type: WARNING—SEALED EVIDENCE—DO NOT TAMPER. To document when he sealed it, Mahany signed and dated the outside of each envelope and wrote his initials across the seal.

The next step in Mahany's crime scene procedure, after trace evidence, was to complete a sexual assault kit. The kits used by the coroner in 1986 contained several swabs and slides for different areas of the decedent's body. Each swab, a tuft of sterile cotton at one end of a thin wooden stick, came prepackaged in its own clear plastic tube. The stem of the stick was permanently attached to the tube's cap. After use, the swab was reinserted into the tube for storage. The hybrid swab tubes were referred to as "swubes." Some swubes had two sticks attached to the cap, side by side. The extra swab was a backup sample, in case one was consumed by lab testing.

Mahany took out a sexual assault kit and a Form 81, the coroner's sexual assault evidence checklist. He opened the cardboard box and arranged the various swubes and slide envelopes neatly on the carpet close to

Sherri's head. As he used each swab, he checked a box and initialed on the form that he had collected it. When he finished, he put all the pieces of the sexual assault kit back in the original box, sealed it with tape, and signed and dated it.

It was while Mahany was completing the sexual assault kit that he and the detectives first noticed the bite mark on Sherri's left forearm. The kit did not include a swab specifically intended for bite mark evidence. Mahany carried with him several spare swubes for when he encountered other types of evidence he needed to collect. If Mahany saw a bite mark on a victim, he swabbed it automatically, because there was a good chance of getting saliva. Unlike blood at a crime scene, which might be from either the victim or the suspect, it was a safe bet that saliva collected from a bite mark on a victim's body was not their own.

By the 1980s, police crime labs had already for several decades been able to determine some identifying characteristics from biological evidence, typically blood, saliva, or semen. Collecting such evidence from homicide crime scenes became standard practice in the 1950s, when the field of forensic serology gained a foothold in crime labs. Serological analysis revealed the source's ABO blood type, as well as the presence of enzymes and proteins carried by known subsets of the overall population. The results were nowhere near as precise as DNA analysis, which would eventually supplant serology as the gold standard for forensic identification. But at the time Sherri was murdered, serology was the best science available, and it had useful applications in homicide investigations.

If detectives knew that foreign blood or saliva came from someone of a certain blood type, they could leverage that information to include or exclude suspects. At trial, prosecutors routinely introduced serological results as circumstantial evidence, to show the defendant had the same blood type as the blood found at the crime scene. In cases where the defendant's blood type was common, serology was hardly a smoking gun. Given a rare enough enzyme or blood type, however, a talented prosecutor could make a lab report seem like one to a jury.

Mahany appraised the bite mark on the inside of Sherri's left arm. In a photo taken a day later, during Sherri's autopsy, the bite mark appears as a reddish oval on otherwise unmarred skin. The bite was forceful enough to leave individual teeth impressions both top and bottom, where the skin was slightly broken.

Mahany reached into his equipment kit for one of his utility swubes.

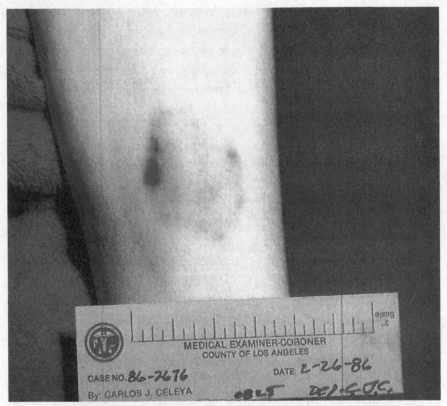

Bite mark on Sherri's left forearm (February 26, 1986, autopsy photo)

The one he used for Sherri's bite mark was six inches long and had a red screw-on cap, with two cotton-tipped wood applicator sticks attached. The clear plastic tube, about the thickness of a cigar, had a few tiny holes drilled into the bottom. The holes allowed the swabs to air-dry, so that over time, only the telltale evidence remained.

Mahany unscrewed the red cap and squirted some distilled water onto the swabs to moisten them. He brushed the swabs across both halves of the bite mark, using one side for the bottom teeth impression and the other side for the top. This technique maximized the amount of evidence collected and gave the crime lab more material to test. When Mahany was done, he replaced the cap and screwed it shut.

On the label on the outside of the tube, Mahany wrote LEFT ARM and BITE MARK, along with his initials, the date, and the coroner's case number. He placed the swube inside a new, crisp 5-by-7-inch evidence envelope, which had on its front several preprinted fields for the criminalist to complete.

On the line above Decedent's Name, he wrote RASMUSSEN, SHERRI. Next to that, he filled in the coroner's case number for Sherri's case, 86-2676. For Evidence Description, Mahany wrote SWABBED BITE MARK, and for Evidence Location, LEFT ARM. He initialed the envelope to indicate that he had collected the bite mark swab and wrote the date and time, February 25, 1986, at 2:06 a.m. Mahany sealed the envelope across its back with a piece of coroner's evidence tape.

Sherri had three gunshot wounds in her chest, in addition to the bite mark and her facial injuries. Two entry wounds were above her left breast. The third, in the center of her chest, had the hallmarks of a contact gunshot wound, meaning the gun's muzzle was pressed to her body when the trigger was pulled. The tank top Sherri had on when she was killed was soaked with blood, front and back, from her gunshot wounds. Earlier, when Mahany had inspected Sherri's body for trace evidence, he had gently rolled her onto her side to check for any evidence underneath. At that time Mahany noticed a small lump on her back, which he recognized as a bullet lodged under her skin. He left it alone for the medical examiner to collect during the autopsy.

According to his evidence log, the last thing Mahany did at the crime scene was swab Sherri's hands for gunshot residue, GSR for short. In homicides involving a firearm, it was standard practice for criminalists to use a GSR kit on the victim's hands, to help determine whether they, too, might have fired a gun.

Mahany unpacked a GSR kit and examined both of Sherri's hands. He noticed soot on her right index finger. The presence of soot suggested that she may have held her hand up to the gun's barrel as it was fired. Her wedding band was still on her left ring finger. Mahany documented each swab he took on his GSR kit checklist, coroner's Form 82. When he finished, he repacked the swabs in the original box, sealed it, and labeled it, as diligently as he had all the other evidence he collected.

For each and every item of evidence Mahany collected at a crime scene, he made a corresponding entry on his evidence log. The purpose of the evidence log was to document the chain of custody. The coroner's 1987 Physical Evidence Policy and Procedures Manual stated, "In order for physical evidence to be of value, it must be: 1) recognized; 2) documented; 3) properly handled; 4) secured and packaged; 5) establish and maintain chain-of-custody; 6) transfer through proper channels."

The evidence log form used by the coroner's office in the 1980s had three columns, left to right. The left column was completed by the criminalist, and recorded the date and time the evidence was collected, and by whom. The middle column documented when each item was received at the coroner's evidence room, and who received it. The coroner's procedures at the time mandated that the information be recorded by hand and not typewritten.

The rightmost column on the evidence log was reserved for when the coroner released evidence. According to the coroner's physical evidence manual, *"It is the Department's objective to release evidence to the agency having analytical responsibility as soon as possible, and to retain evidence not released for the longest period possible, consistent with potential need and storage facility constraints . . . Facilities for storage of all evidence and evidence records shall be secured against unauthorized access at all times."* Under the coroner's procedures at the time, whenever evidence was released, the person who picked it up was required to sign their name and write their law enforcement agency and badge number and the date and time they took custody of the evidence.

Coroner's evidence log for the Rasmussen case, Lloyd Mahany copy
(February 25, 1986)

After Mahany completed the GSR kit on Sherri's hands, he took all the individual items of evidence he had collected and placed them in a brown paper bag, to separate them from the evidence items from the Ford Pinto case they handled earlier that night.

The LAPD's crime scene log indicates Mahany and Rainey removed Sherri's body from the condo at 2:51 a.m. Mayer and Pida also logged out of the crime scene at 2:51. Aguilar, the latent print expert from SID, was not yet done looking for fingerprints. Hooks remained at the condo until Aguilar finished. Hooks and Aguilar eventually left at 4:00 a.m.

Later that night or early the next morning, Pida completed a Preliminary Investigation Report, the one-page typed form that LAPD detectives fill out when they are assigned a fresh case. The preprinted form had several fields for information about the victim, location of the crime, and other basic details. In his report on the Rasmussen case, Pida classified the crime as a *"Burglary/Murder"* and listed the time of occurrence as between 7:30 a.m. and 6:00 p.m. In the box for *"Narrative,"* Pida wrote, *"Between the above times on 2-24-86, Unknown suspects entered victim's residence. Front door was poss unlocked. Once inside suspects burglarize the location. Suspects surprised by Vict during the burglary. Suspects become involved in a physical altercation. Suspects shoot victim and kill her. Suspects leave the location via the sub-garage. Suspects take Victs vehicle, a 1985 BMW 318i, Lic #1MKJ850 Calif. and her purse."*

Mahany and Rainey had additional work to complete on the case as well, after they transported Sherri's body to the coroner's morgue downtown. Mahany collected more evidence from the body, including fingernail clippings and hair standards. He also alerted the coroner's forensic dentist that he had a victim with a bite mark, in case a plaster impression could be made.

Rainey typed out his coroner's Investigator's Report, which described Sherri's visible injuries. Among the injuries Rainey noted was a *"bullet type wound . . . under the decedent's right eye with no indication of an exit wound."* Sherri's autopsy later determined that all her facial injuries were in fact the result of blunt force trauma, not a bullet. That an experienced coroner's investigator mistook the trauma to Sherri's eye for a gunshot wound was itself an indication of how savagely she was beaten.

The coroner's office maintained a drop box, similar to a locked mailbox, where criminalists could securely leave evidence, day or night. The criminalist's original evidence log went into the drop box along with the items of evidence submitted. During working hours, evidence custodians periodically fetched everything in the drop box and took it to the coroner's evidence room. Each item listed on the log had to be accounted for by the custodian before it was recorded as "received" in the log's middle column. The custodian also wrote the date, time, and who had received the evidence on the outside of each individual evidence envelope or package.

Biological evidence considered at risk of degradation was stored in one of several freezers in the basement of the coroner's office. Only coroner's evidence custodians were allowed access to the room with the freezers. The coroner's manual decreed: *"Swabs from bite marks shall be stored frozen in the evidence room in sequence by coroner's case number with other biologically degradable evidence in similar sized packages."* The coroner also stored sexual assault kits in the same freezers.

Before Mahany deposited the physical evidence from Sherri's case in the drop box, sometime after 6:30 a.m. on February 25, he made a photocopy of the original evidence log for his records.

Coroner's evidence custodian Richard Heath collected the evidence from the drop box a few hours later. Heath completed the middle column on the evidence log, certifying that the evidence from coroner's case 86-2676, the murder of Sherri Rasmussen, had been received and secured.

The trace evidence Mahany gathered from Sherri's body on the night of her murder—hair and fibers from two places on her robe, and loose hairs from her neck—was boxed and stored on a shelf in the coroner's evidence room. The evidence log indicates that the Rasmussen trace evidence remained in the coroner's custody from 10:32 a.m. on February 25, 1986, when Heath received it, until the fall of 1993, more than seven and a half years later.

Early in the afternoon of Monday, October 11, 1993, an LAPD detective assigned to the Van Nuys homicide unit, Phil Morritt, visited the evidence room at the coroner's office downtown, about a thirty-minute drive from the Van Nuys station. The evidence custodian on duty that day in 1993 was a student worker whose last name was Patino. Morritt signed in the rightmost column of the coroner's evidence log for all the trace evidence in the Rasmussen case to be released to him. Patino recorded the time, 12:25 p.m., when he signed the evidence log and handed over the evidence to Morritt.

The LAPD's chrono for the Rasmussen case contains several entries in October 1993, following more than eighteen months with no recorded activity in the investigation. According to the chrono, detectives in the Van

Coroner's evidence log for the Rasmussen case, Det. Phil Morritt entry
(October 11, 1993)

Nuys homicide unit were actively working on the Rasmussen case that month, ordering runs on latent fingerprints, reviewing lists of parolees from California state prisons during 1985 and 1986, and performing other investigative tasks.

No entries were recorded in the chrono on October 11, the day Morritt signed out from the coroner's office all the trace evidence in the Rasmussen case. In the entire month of October 1993, the chrono inexplicably made no reference to Morritt, the coroner's office, or the trace evidence he signed out on October 11, according to the coroner's evidence log. Reading the LAPD's chrono for the Rasmussen case, it is as if the coroner's release of the trace evidence to Morritt in October 1993 never happened. Morritt's signature on the coroner's evidence log, however, leaves no doubt that it did.

To this day, no one knows what may have prompted Morritt to decide, more than seven years after Sherri's murder, to go to the coroner's office and sign out all the trace evidence in the case. Nor is it known what pur-

DATE	TIME	INVESTIGATION	DR
LAPD 03.11.6 (1/82)		**CHRONOLOGICAL RECORD**	
		INSTRUCTIONS: This form is used to document any past or future investigative events deemed necessary to control or develop this case.	
10·4·93	0900	CONTACTED DEBBIE @ IRD REQUESTED FI RUN FROM JAN 85 – THROUGH MAY 86 FOR RD's 934, 935, 936, 944 ≠ 945 (IRD 485-6567)	
	1030	CONTACTED SGT LIZENBEE IRD (485-6565) FOR PACMIS RUN IN RD's 934, 35, 36, 44 ≠ 45 FOR JAN 86 - DEC 86.	
	1300	SPOKE WITH AVARDO (SID PRINT SPEC) WHO PULLED PRINT LIFT CASE PACKAGE AND WILL REVIEW SAME FOR ANY FURTHER LEADS.	
10·6·93	0700	Rec'd FAX FROM PRINTS - AVARDO - CHECK OF AFIS DONE IN WIN SYSTEM - (WESTRN ID NETWORK) - NO HITS	
10·25·93		RCD FI RUN FROM REQ ON 10-4-93.	
10·28·93	0700	Rec'd LIST OF '85/86 PAROLEE'S FROM CDC.	
10·28·93		LEFT LIST OF POSS SUSP.S FROM F.I. RUN WITH AMES SID. (C-LIST #1-#11 IN '85/'86 FI RUN BOOK) FOR PRINT COMP.	
11·29·93		PRINT COMP. ON FI's '85/'86 #1-#11 RETURNED NEGATIVE.	
12·13·93		LEFT REQ FOR PRINT COMP. ON '85/86 PAROLEE'S WITH AMES - SID - (NEXT PGE)	
			CONTINUE ON REVERSE

LAPD chrono for the Rasmussen case, page 21 (October 1993)

pose Morritt may have had in mind for the trace evidence when he carried it out of the coroner's office that day.

Morritt retired from the LAPD in 2002. In 2009, he was interviewed by LAPD detectives regarding the evidence he had signed out from the coroner's office fifteen years earlier. During the interview, Morritt was shown a copy of the coroner's evidence log from 1993. Morritt acknowledged that it was his signature on the evidence log, but stated that he did not recall picking up the evidence from the coroner's office or ever working on the Rasmussen case.

The Van Nuys homicide coordinator in 1993 was Detective III Steve Fisk. Fisk had assumed the role from Mel Arnold in 1991.

According to the Rasmussens, it was sometime in 1992 or 1993 that Nels, Loretta, and Connie traveled to the Van Nuys station to discuss Sherri's unsolved case with detectives in person. Since Sherri was killed, six or seven years earlier, the Rasmussens had done all they could to support the LAPD's investigation and keep it alive.

Nels and Loretta initially funded a reward for information, which was publicized in October 1986 and again in November 1987. Nothing came of the reward offer.

Around 1988, Connie was inspired to reach out to Ann Rule, the best-selling true crime author and a fellow Seattleite. Connie thought Rule might want to write a book about Sherri's case. Connie got Rule on the phone and told her a little about her sister's unsolved murder. Connie said her parents were willing to fly up from Tucson to talk with Rule in person, if she was interested. To Connie's surprise, Rule agreed to meet.

Nels and Loretta flew up from Tucson specifically for the meeting. They and Connie met Rule for Sunday brunch at an upscale hotel near Sea-Tac Airport. Rule reserved a private room in the hotel's restaurant, so she and the Rasmussens could talk freely. The brunch lasted two and a half hours, which Nels and Loretta took as a sign her interest was genuine. Nels told Rule about John's police officer ex-girlfriend and the troubling incidents with her that Sherri had described to her parents before her murder. Nels was impressed that Rule asked many questions about John, such as whether the police had checked him for bruises after the murder. Rule said it was not uncommon, in cases like these, for the husband to be involved. Nels did not think John killed Sherri, but he thought Rule was sharp and asked good questions.

Rule also keyed in on the fact that Sherri's cat, Bozo, was in the condo during the murder. Rule said she thought it would be neat to tell the story through the cat's eyes, and what it may have witnessed. Nels thought that was a little weird, but amusing. It mattered to him and Loretta much more that Rule seemed interested, even gung ho, about shining a light on Sherri's unsolved case.

Before they parted, Rule told the Rasmussens that she had a private investigator in Los Angeles, a retired LAPD detective, who assisted her with research for her books. Rule said she would ask him to look into Sherri's case. When Nels and Loretta boarded their flight back to Tucson, they felt optimistic.

A few days later, Nels received a phone call from Rule. Rule said that she had spoken with her private investigator in Los Angeles. Rule said her investigator told her he wouldn't touch Sherri's case because it was "too hot to handle." Rule told Nels that she had to take her investigator's word for it. Rule said she was unable to go down to Los Angeles to do the research herself, so there was nothing more she could do. Nels told Rule he understood. Ann Rule died in 2015.

Also in 1988, around the same time the Rasmussens met with Ann Rule in Seattle, Nels wrote a letter to LAPD Chief of Police Daryl Gates. In the letter, Nels implored Gates to intervene in Sherri's unsolved murder case and ensure that his detectives had not neglected any promising leads.

Thirty years later, the Rasmussens no longer have a copy of the letter that Nels sent to Gates in 1988. The LAPD has never made public its copy of the letter, so what exactly Nels wrote is unknown. The Rasmussens did retain a handwritten rough draft of Nels's 1988 letter. The rough draft, addressed to "*Daryl F. Gates, Chief,*" reads:

Questions to Ask:

- *Were ex-girlfriend & phone threats subject spoken to.*
- *Teeth marks—were they checked against anyone's dental work.*
- *If Burglary, why was marriage license only thing taken.*
- *BMW taken, but keys used and car left several miles away.*
- *Is it a closed investigation. If it is, why can't we be informed of its findings.*
- *Was the possibility of someone following Sherri ever checked out.*
- *No forced entry—possible she knew suspect.*
- *Phone records checked.*
- *Hand print on wall—FBI compare.*

Nels received no reply from Chief Gates, nor any acknowledgement from the LAPD that Gates had received his letter about Sherri's unsolved murder.

In addition to his direct appeal to Gates, Nels also sought help in

Tucson, where he and Loretta were pillars of the community. A patient of Nels's, a Tucson police detective, connected him with a man high up in the local coroner's office. He agreed to review Sherri's autopsy report, the only document from the LAPD's investigation that Nels had been able to obtain. Nels met with the man in his office and explained the situation. The man was very gracious and asked Nels to leave the autopsy report behind. "Let me have this for two or three days. I'm sure I can find something," he told Nels.

Early the next morning, a Tucson police car pulled up outside the Rasmussens' dental practice. The officer asked to see Nels. When Nels came out, the officer handed him an envelope. "I'm just delivering this," the officer told him, and left.

Inside the envelope was Sherri's autopsy report and a short note from the man Nels had met with at the coroner's office. *"Nels, I can't help you. I'm too close to retirement,"* was all he wrote, Nels and Loretta recall.

Another time, Nels walked into the Tucson Police Department and asked to speak with a detective. Nels explained that his daughter had been murdered in Los Angeles. Nels waited and eventually a detective came out to the lobby. Nels told him about Sherri's case and his hope the Tucson police could help him. "I can't seem to get anything out of the LAPD about my daughter's murder," Nels said.

Nels recalls the detective brought a phone over and called the LAPD in front of him. "I'd like to talk to the lead detective in Sherri Rasmussen's case," the detective said into the phone. "Nels is here and he's telling us he's having problems communicating and what have you. Is there anything we can do to help?"

Moments later, the call ended abruptly, Nels recalls. The detective told Nels that the LAPD detective had responded, "We think it's wise if you solve your crimes and let us solve ours. Don't get in the middle," and then hung up. The Tucson detective told Nels, "Well, they're not interested in letting us help you, so there's not a lot we can do."

In 1990, four years into the LAPD's investigation of Sherri's murder, the Rasmussens turned to the television program *America's Most Wanted*, which portrayed unsolved crimes and fugitives from justice. In a letter dated August 24, Nels wrote:

> Our daughter Sherri Rae Rasmussen was the victim of a homicide February 24, 1986. On initial investigation the police believed she was the

victim of a robbery but nothing was taken except her marriage license (she had only been married 3 months). From talking to numerous other police officers and investigators I feel it was only made to look like a robbery.

Possible scenario:

(1) *Sherri was threatened by John's prior girlfriend who is a Los Angeles Police officer.*
(2) *Sherri had been threatened at work. Also associated with the threats were obscene phone calls. She alerted hospital security and was awarded special parking privileges.*
(3) *Sherri & John came home to Tucson 4 weeks before her death. At this time she confided in me the last 5 times she & John had gone out they were followed by someone. I offered assistance, she said dad give me 2 weeks to take care of it if I need help I'll call. From my understanding she never mentioned this to John . . .*

We tried to get Ann Rule to help, at first she was interested, but when her detective read the autopsy he said he wouldn't touch it. He is a retired LAPD detective.

We feel this case has not been thoroughly investigated and we would appreciate any help in this matter.

Nothing came of the letter to *America's Most Wanted* either.

Still, despite the fruitlessness of all their efforts to that point, Nels and Loretta refused to give up hope that Sherri's case could be solved. Into the 1990s, they kept looking for new avenues that might deliver them closer to the truth about who murdered Sherri. The Rasmussens noted with interest the latest advances in forensic science, which in the early 1990s included vastly expanded fingerprint databases and something called DNA, at that time not yet a household term.

Around 1992, Sherri's friend Donna Robison mentioned to the Rasmussens that she had a relative who worked in the field and could arrange for DNA analysis. By then, about six years had passed since Sherri's murder, and about five years since the Rasmussens' last face-to-face meeting with the Van Nuys detectives, in November 1987. Throughout those years, Loretta

Nels E. Rasmussen, Jr., D.D.S., P.C
575 W. Ajo
Tucson, Arizona 85713
—
Phone: 889.3958
Aug. 24, 1990

America's Most Wanted
P. O. Box Crime 90
Washington, D.C. 20016

Attention: Bob Walsh

Dear Mr. Walsh

Our daughter Sherri Rae Rasmussen was the victum of a homicide
February 24, 1986. On initial investigation the police
believed she was a victum of a robbery but nothing was
taken except her marriage license(she had only been married
3 months). From talking to numerous other police officers
and investigators I feel it was made only to look like
a robbery.

Possible scenario:
(1) Sherri was threatened by John's prior girlfriend who
is a Los Angeles Police officer.

(2) Sherri had been threatened at work, also associated
with the threats were obscene phone calls. She alerted
hospital security and was awarded special parking privileges.

(3) Sherri & John came home to Tucson 4 weeks before her
death at this time she confided in me the last 5 times
she & John had gone out they were followed by someone.
I offered assistance, she said dad give me 2 weeks to take
care of it if I need help I'll call. From my understanding
she never mentioned this to John.

Nels Rasmussen's letter to America's Most Wanted, *page 1 (August 24, 1990)*

had called the detectives many times to check on the status of Sherri's case. The updates Loretta had received were cursory and often made her feel that the detectives just wanted to get her off the phone.

Sometime in 1992 or 1993, Nels and Loretta requested to meet with the Van Nuys detectives in person, to try to jump-start the LAPD's investigation. The Rasmussens wanted to find out if there had been any new developments in Sherri's case, and to raise the possibility of DNA testing.

Nels, Loretta, and Connie flew to LAX, rented a car, and drove to the Van Nuys station. When they arrived, Nels went in and asked an officer at the desk where they should park. The officer told Nels anywhere on the street outside.

Nels parked, then went upstairs with Loretta and Connie for their meeting. The Rasmussens recall that although Loretta had made an appointment, they had to wait more than an hour, in a small room that looked as if it was normally used to interview suspects, before a detective came to see them. Nels and Loretta had expected to meet with Lyle Mayer, the original lead detective on Sherri's case, but it was a different detective, someone they had never seen or dealt with previously, whom they met with that day.

The detective introduced himself as Steve Fisk. Fisk told the Rasmussens that Mayer had retired and he had taken over the case. "What do you want to know?" Fisk asked them, the Rasmussens recall.

The Rasmussens recall they asked Fisk whether the fingerprints from Sherri's case had been run through the FBI's database. Fisk said they were still working on it. Connie recalls Fisk brought with him to the meeting a thin folder, which sat closed on the table between them as they talked. It occurred to Connie that if the LAPD was actively investigating Sherri's case, Fisk's folder would be thicker. That Fisk didn't show them any documents or take any notes made Connie suspect the folder was more a prop than anything. Connie recalls Fisk told them, "It's a cold case. We haven't had any leads." Fisk said if anything changed, he would let them know. The conversation was socially polite but the Rasmussens felt dispirited by the lack of investigative progress.

Nels recalls he asked Fisk during the meeting, "Have you run DNA?"

Fisk replied that DNA testing was expensive, a true statement at that time. Fisk said the LAPD had a limited budget and couldn't afford to run DNA in Sherri's case.

"Fine, I'll pay for it," Nels responded. "I even have a person who would do it." Nels meant Donna's relative.

According to the Rasmussens, Fisk said that it wouldn't do any good to run DNA in Sherri's case, even if Nels paid for it, because they had no suspect. Fisk said they had to have a suspect in mind before they could run DNA.

Nels replied, "Well . . ." and brought up John's ex-girlfriend. Nels recalls that Fisk then asked him, "Have you changed your opinion as to who you think did this?"

"No, I haven't," Nels said.

"Do you still have suspicions of John?"

"I've said all along I have suspicions of John. I don't believe John had anything to do with the crime itself. But I believe that John had knowledge." Nels pointed to Fisk's folder on the table. "I think it's in your record there, about John's ex-girlfriend."

Fisk ignored Nels's comment, the Rasmussens recall. Connie sensed that Fisk seemed anxious for them to leave. The meeting lasted less than an hour. Afterward, when they went out to their parked rental car, Nels discovered a ticket on the windshield. Nels went back into the station and complained, "The police told me to park there." Nels was informed he'd have to pay it anyway. Nels paid the parking ticket.

In the wake of their meeting with Fisk, the Rasmussens informed Donna that the LAPD had declined their request to perform DNA analysis in Sherri's case, even if they paid for it, Donna recalls.

The LAPD's chrono for Sherri's case, however, contains no record of the Rasmussens visiting the Van Nuys station or meeting with Fisk in 1992 or 1993, the time frame during which the Rasmussens recall the meeting happened.

Fisk had been the Van Nuys homicide coordinator since 1991, the same year Lyle Mayer retired from the LAPD. Fisk ran the Van Nuys homicide unit from 1991 until his own retirement in 2000.

If the Rasmussens' recollection is correct, and they met with Fisk in 1992 or 1993, it was not long after Nels offered to pay for DNA analysis in Sherri's case that one of the detectives Fisk supervised, Phil Morritt, signed out from the coroner's office all the trace evidence in the Rasmussen case. The Rasmussens were never notified at the time.

In 2009, Fisk was interviewed by LAPD detectives regarding the Rasmussen investigation. The detectives showed Fisk a chrono entry from 1997 that stated, in part, "Detective Fisk contacted the victims family" regarding fingerprints. According to handwritten notes taken by one detective during the interview, Fisk told them, "There was no mention of an involved police officer. Absolutely no mention. Bells & whistles would have gone off . . . Never mentioned any info about a police officer being involved. No one ever mentioned a police officer. That would have been a big deal." Fisk also said he had no recollection of ever discussing the Rasmussen case with Lyle Mayer.

There is no indication in the detective's notes that Fisk was questioned in 2009 about his meeting with the Rasmussens at the Van Nuys station in 1992 or 1993, or Nels's offer to Fisk during that meeting to pay for DNA testing in Sherri's case, or about Phil Morritt and the trace evidence he signed out from the coroner's office in October 1993, while Fisk was running the Van Nuys homicide unit.

It is unknown what became of the irreplaceable trace evidence Mahany collected from Sherri's body, after Morritt signed it out. There is no record that the trace evidence was ever booked into LAPD property or returned to the coroner's evidence room. The trace evidence from the Rasmussen case was never seen again. Whatever answers and information forensic science might have extracted from it, not only in 1993 but anytime in the future, were irretrievably lost along with it.

Detective Morritt left behind one item of evidence at the coroner's office. Since the morning after Sherri's murder, when evidence custodian Richard Heath signed in all the evidence Mahany collected, the envelope that held the bite mark swab had been stored separately from the trace evidence. Per the coroner's evidence handling procedures in 1986, bite mark swabs were stored in sequence by case number in the freezers in the coroner's basement.

There are several possible explanations for why the bite mark swab survived October 11, 1993, while other evidence from Sherri's case at the coroner's office did not. Morritt might not have thought to ask for the bite mark swab when he requested the trace evidence be released to him. Patino, the student worker in the coroner's evidence room, might not have known where to find it.

Even if Patino knew to look in the freezers, he might not have been able to identify the envelope with the Rasmussen bite mark swab, among all the other evidence stored there. On any given day, there were hundreds if not thousands of evidence items in the coroner's freezers. As individual items were removed and added to the freezers over time, the 5-by-7-inch envelope holding the Rasmussen bite mark swab would have rubbed up against countless other items from countless other cases.

The coroner's evidence log indicates that the Rasmussen bite mark swab remained in the freezer for another eleven years after the rest of the trace evidence went missing, until December 2004. In 1986, on the night of Sherri's murder, Mahany had sealed the swube inside a brand-new evidence envelope. After eighteen years in the freezer, the swube appeared intact, but the envelope itself was battered and ratty. The ink on the front of the envelope was almost entirely faded. It was still possible to make out Sherri's full name, in Mahany's handwriting. But where Mahany had written

SWABBED BITE MARK and LEFT ARM, it appeared by 2004 that he had written nothing at all.

The evidence tape Mahany used to seal the back of the envelope in 1986 was still intact in 2004, eighteen years later. On the front of the envelope, however, there was a hole near the top right corner. Poking through the hole was the red cap of the swube with the bite mark swab inside.

Coroner's evidence envelope for Rasmussen bite mark swab (2009 photo)

Sometime between 1986 and 2004, the cap end of the stiff plastic tube pierced the paper envelope. The hole may have opened gradually, through wear and tear as other evidence was moved in and out of the freezer around it, or as the result of one careless jostle that punctured the envelope.

Fatefully, the area on the front of the envelope the cap punched through was precisely where Mahany had written the coroner's case number. Because bite mark swabs were stored by case number, an envelope with an illegible number was both easy to overlook and difficult to find. Whenever the hole in the evidence envelope was made, it effectively obliterated the case number. From then on, the Rasmussen bite mark swab was almost tailor-made to slip through the cracks.

What the condition of the envelope was in October 1993 will likely never be known. If the hole in the envelope predated Morritt's visit to the coroner's office, the Rasmussen bite mark swab would have taken Patino considerable time and effort to locate in the freezers. Morritt may not have wanted to wait while Patino rooted around for the elusive envelope. Patino may have had other evidence items to sign in or release, as Morritt's request was just one of many transactions conducted at the coroner's evidence room that day. It is also possible that Morritt was unaware of the bite mark swab, and did not ask Patino to retrieve it.

Whether by fortune, fate, or divine providence, the bite mark swab that one day would lead to the identification of Sherri's killer remained stowed in a deep freezer in the coroner's basement, waiting for forensic science to catch up to it.

16

"The Day Was Boring and Nothing Happened That Was Worth Remembering"

(February 25, 1986)

Stephanie Lazarus reported for duty at 7:30 a.m. on Tuesday, February 25, less than twenty-four hours after Sherri Rasmussen's murder. Sherri and John's condo was just five miles southeast of the Devonshire station, right over the boundary of the neighboring LAPD division, Van Nuys.

Stephanie's patrol partner that day was Mike Alexander, whom she had worked with at least three times previously, most recently on February 3. Stephanie and Alexander were of the same rank, Police Officer II, although he had been on the job five years longer. The Devonshire Daily Work Sheet for day watch on February 25 indicates that they were assigned to patrol unit A49. A units were basic cars, responsible for patrolling a specific area within the division.

LAPD patrol units were required to maintain a log of their on-duty activities and all the radio calls they responded to during their watch. The log was known as the Daily Field Activities Report, DFAR for short. For patrol units with two officers, the log was customarily filled out by whichever partner wasn't driving. On February 25, the day after Sherri's murder, Alexander drove and Stephanie kept the log.

According to their log, their watch began with roll call, which was presided over that morning by a Sgt. Rendon. If any of Stephanie's supervisors or fellow officers, most of whom she had worked with for months, noticed any change in her demeanor, or any scratches or bruises on her face or body, when she reported for duty that day, there is no record of it.

Stephanie and Alexander were out on patrol together for eight hours on February 25, from 8:15 a.m. until 4:15 p.m. Their log indicates that they spent most of that time in their car, seated only a few inches apart. In 2012, more than twenty-five years later, Alexander testified in court that he had no independent recollection of working with Stephanie on that particular day. Nor could Alexander remember, after so many years, whether Stephanie had any visible injuries.

February 25 was Stephanie's first day back at work after four consecutive days off. She and Alexander rolled out to their first radio call, a Code 30 burglary report near the Northridge Mall, at 8:20 a.m. The weather that morning was 60 degrees and sunny. Later that day, the temperature rose into the mideighties, but the sun had yet to burn off the chill that had settled upon the Valley overnight.

For the rest of the city, it was an ordinary Tuesday morning in February 1986. The *Los Angeles Times* ran a "Local News in Brief" squib on Sherri's murder, though the article did not identify her by name. Under the headline VAN NUYS WOMAN DIES IN APPARENT BURGLARY, the *Times* story read in full:

> *A Van Nuys woman who stayed home from work because she was ill was killed Monday during what appeared to be a burglary of her condominium, Los Angeles police said.*
>
> *The woman's husband found her body when he returned from work about 6 p.m., Lt. L.A. Durrer said. The condominium, in the 7100 block of Balboa Boulevard, was ransacked. The woman, who was not identified, appeared to have been beaten, Durrer said. A glass window leading to the balcony had been shattered, he said.*

All across Los Angeles, Sherri's closest friends and her colleagues were getting up and ready for work, totally unaware of her fate. For the rest of their lives, they would never forget the awful day that they learned of Sherri's murder.

Hospitals, like police departments, are around-the-clock operations in which the highest-ranking employees generally work daytime hours. Althea Kennedy, Sherri's boss and Glendale Adventist Medical Center's vice president of clinical services, received an early morning phone call at home from her night supervisor.

"I'm not sure if it's our Sherri," he told Althea. "But I heard on the news that a Sherri Rasmussen was found in her apartment, and we're waiting for confirmation." Althea was about to leave home for an eight o'clock dental appointment. She had scheduled it before work since it was hard to leave the hospital during the day.

Althea hung up with the night supervisor and called Peggy Daly at her apartment. Peggy was Sherri's closest friend at the hospital. As nursing directors, Sherri and Peggy both reported to Althea. Most of the other high-level administrators at the hospital were significantly older than Sherri and Peggy, and married with children. Until Sherri met John, she and Peggy were both single.

Peggy had just gotten out of the shower following an early morning exercise class. "Have you heard from Sherri?" Althea asked Peggy.

Peggy said she had called her the day before and left a message but hadn't heard back from her. Peggy asked Althea why she asked.

On Monday morning, the day before, Peggy had received a call from the hospital's nursing administrator to inform her that Sherri was out for the day and to ask if Peggy could cover her daily rounds. Peggy said she would. It was something they were accustomed to doing for each other. If one was away from the hospital for whatever reason, the other would check in on her units to ensure everything was in order. Peggy made Sherri's rounds on Monday, but she thought it was strange that Sherri had called in sick. Before Peggy left work, she tried calling her at home and left a message on the answering machine. Something didn't feel right to Peggy at the time about Sherri not picking up the phone.

The next morning, on the phone, Althea told Peggy about the call she had just received from the night supervisor. "He said Sherri was killed," Althea said. Peggy burst into tears. Her roommate rushed into her bedroom to see what was wrong. The way Althea had phrased the news, Peggy assumed Sherri had died in an accident. Peggy thought, "Okay, she wasn't feeling well, where did she go? Did she get in a car crash?" It never occurred to Peggy that someone had killed Sherri intentionally. Althea told Peggy, "Just get dressed and get to the hospital. We're going to regroup there."

Althea tried calling the dentist to cancel her appointment, but it was too early to get hold of anyone at his office, so she drove there. Althea felt fortunate that her dentist was a family friend. When he came in to see her, Althea was sitting in the dental chair, shaking. Althea told him what she was dealing with. He said, "Let's reschedule your appointment. You need to go ahead and get to work."

Althea went straight to the hospital. From the moment Althea walked into the lobby, she saw on her colleagues' faces that the worst was true. It was their Sherri. Althea knew she had to start making phone calls to all of Sherri's co-workers and staff to let them know what had happened. Sherri was well liked and known throughout the hospital. The hospital felt to Althea like a morgue that morning. Althea had no information other than what she had been told and what was in the news. She had never been in such a position before. What could she say to people? Some colleagues had heard before Althea reached them, so it was she who had to confirm, "Yes, it is our Sherri."

When Althea's secretary, Vera, got to work that morning, several people were congregated in the hall outside her and Althea's office. "Did you hear Sherri got murdered?" they asked her. Vera hadn't. Later in the day, she recalls, the talk around the hospital was that Sherri had supposedly gone jogging or worked out on Sunday and hurt her back or something. Vera heard that Sherri had called the nursing education department on Monday morning, when she was scheduled to teach a class, to say that she would not be coming in. Monday evening, John came home after work and found Sherri murdered.

Sherri had always impressed Vera as a beautiful person, not just physically but inside as well. Vera felt there weren't enough good things she could say about her. Vera had met John only once or twice, when he visited the hospital. Vera knew that Sherri and John had gotten married in November, but nothing else about their personal life. Vera had no idea whether John had a girlfriend or an ex-girlfriend. On the day she learned of Sherri's murder, Vera had no reason to speculate.

Romelda Anderson, another of Sherri's colleagues at the hospital, was driving to work when she heard a news report on her car radio about someone being killed on the 7100 block of Balboa Boulevard in Van Nuys. "That's where Sherri lives," Romelda thought. It did not cross her mind that the victim might be Sherri. Only when she pulled up to the hospital and saw her colleagues waiting for her outside the entrance did Romelda grasp that something terrible had happened.

Peggy, meanwhile, made it all the way to her office still believing Sherri had been killed in an accident rather than by an act of violence. When Althea came to see her, Peggy was in in the middle of a meeting with an architect and Glenn Crabtree, Glendale Adventist's director of design construction. The meeting was to discuss one of the hospital's wings, which was being remodeled top to bottom.

Glenn, like Peggy and Sherri, was much younger than most of their colleagues. Although his family was Australian, Glenn had spent his childhood in Fiji, where his parents worked as Adventist missionaries. After a strict and sheltered upbringing, Glenn married young, but soon divorced. In 1983, his father Barry was appointed pastor of the Vallejo Drive Church, which was across the street from Glendale Adventist Medical Center. Around the same time, eager to rebuild his life, Glenn was hired by the hospital. His job entailed keeping the medical equipment and physical plant up to date. Glenn's responsibilities frequently brought him into contact with Sherri and Peggy, who were involved in many of the same capital projects and planning committees he was. Although Glenn knew Sherri and Peggy only at work, he could tell they were the closest of friends.

When word of Sherri's death reached the hospital, Glenn felt terrible. Everyone who worked with Sherri was shaken up, but Glenn could not fathom how Peggy must feel. During their meeting, Althea came into Peggy's office and told her, in front of Glenn and the architect, that Sherri had been confirmed as the victim.

"Where was she?" Peggy asked, still thinking it was an accident. "Why was she out driving?"

"No," Althea replied. "She was murdered."

Glenn could tell from the look of absolute devastation on Peggy's face that she was blindsided. At that wrenching moment, which neither of them would ever forget, Glenn's heart broke for Peggy.

Throughout Tuesday morning, across Los Angeles, Sherri's other closest friends learned the sickening news by phone.

Jayne Ryan got a call at work from Nancy Tankel. Other than Sherri's two sisters, Jayne and Nancy had been the only members of Sherri's bridal party. Sherri, Jayne, and Nancy became friends as staff nurses at UCLA Medical Center early in their careers. Sherri left UCLA for Glendale Adventist in early 1984. Two years later, when Sherri was killed, Jayne still worked there.

Jayne was in the cardiac catheterization lab in the hospital's basement, on her morning break, when Nancy phoned her. A young doctor, one of the hospital's cardiology fellows, was sitting nearby at a desk, writing in a patient's chart.

"Are you sitting down? Because I have bad news," Nancy said.

Jayne thought Nancy was going to say her father had died. Jayne thought, "I like your dad, but I'm not going to get hysterical." Jayne didn't bother to sit down.

When Nancy told Jayne that Sherri was murdered, Jayne screamed so loudly that her boss, who was in a lead-lined room two rooms away, came running into the cath lab to find out what was going on. The poor cardiology fellow didn't know what had happened or what to do. Jayne was distraught.

Jayne had never lost a friend to violence before. She grew up in a small town in Canada, the only girl and youngest in a family of seven kids. Her parents and six brothers were all still alive back home. Sherri was Jayne's best friend, the sister she never had.

Jayne would always remember Nancy's phone call as one of the most terrible of her life. Nancy had little information about what had happened, beyond the fact that Sherri was killed at home. Nancy thought another friend of theirs, Anna Gawlinksi, might know more. Anna was also a nurse at UCLA. Anna had coauthored with Sherri an article published in *Focus on Critical Care*, a respected medical journal in their field. Just a few months earlier, Anna had hosted Sherri's bridal shower at her apartment in Santa Monica.

Jayne called Anna, who worked a few floors above the cath lab. Anna came downstairs to the basement. Anna recounted to Jayne that the night before, she was watching the eleven o'clock news and saw a report about a police investigation in Van Nuys, close to where Sherri lived. Although it was late, Anna picked up the phone and called Sherri at home. A man who wasn't John answered.

"Hi, is Sherri there?" Anna asked.

"No," he answered.

"Who is this?"

"LAPD."

"Why are you answering Sherri's phone?"

"Something's happened here."

"Is Sherri okay? Can you tell me? Is she at a hospital?" Anna asked.

"No, I can't tell you that," the man said, and hung up.

That was when Anna knew something had happened to Sherri, she told Jayne the next morning.

Jayne had last seen Sherri less than two weeks earlier, on the night of February 16, when she and Mike visited to announce their engagement. Sherri told Jayne that night that her wedding day was the happiest day of her life. Jayne never imagined a world in which Sherri was not a part of her own wedding day.

Jayne was among the few people to whom Sherri had confided about John's ex-girlfriend. Sherri had mentioned her to Jayne more than once in the year before the murder. Jayne knew that during Sherri and John's engagement, the ex-girlfriend had confronted Sherri in her office at Glendale Adventist and told her, "If this marriage fails, I'm going to be waiting to pick up the pieces."

On the day she learned of Sherri's murder, Jayne immediately thought of John's ex-girlfriend and what Sherri had said about her. Other than the ex-girlfriend, Jayne couldn't think of anyone who knew Sherri and would want to hurt her.

As even armchair detectives know, the most consequential time in any homicide investigation is the first forty-eight hours. The immediate aftermath of a murder is when physical evidence is most abundant and still intact to collect. Witnesses are easier to identify and best interviewed early in the investigation, while their memories are fresh, rather than later, after people have moved on with their lives. If the victim was killed after an intense struggle, as Sherri was, potential suspects must be examined for incriminating injuries before they have a chance to heal.

The initial detectives tasked with investigating a homicide have a privileged perspective on the murder and the people most affected by it. The days immediately following a murder are when detectives form their first impressions about what occurred at the crime scene, and of the people closest to the victim. Impressions beget assumptions, which, if left unchallenged, tend to harden into conclusions. Conclusions block open-minded consideration of alternative theories of the case.

The first forty-eight hours usually set the course for the entire investigation. Because that window opens only once, mistakes made by detectives early in an investigation cannot always be rectified later. Subsequent detectives cannot double back and truly start over from the beginning. They must accept the investigation and murder book the way it is when the case is bequeathed to them. There is no other foundation but the actual investigation to date on which to attempt to build a case.

When an initial investigation is not thorough, or poorly documented, or both, the impact is pernicious and only compounded by the passage of time. Problems rooted in the first forty-eight hours persist and can haunt a murder case for as long as it remains unsolved. If the original detectives document only the information that buttresses their primary theory and neglect to include relevant information about other theories or suspects, later detectives are less likely to know that an alternative theory even exists. These omissions metastasize into blind spots for any detectives who might pick up the case in the future.

The farther a murder investigation proceeds down a particular path, the harder it becomes to recognize and accept that a wrong turn was made somewhere along the way. Among homicide detectives, the reluctance to admit that a theory may be incorrect, and the tendency to resist changing course, is a common enough impediment to solving murders that there is a name for it: "tunnel vision."

Investigative priorities are revealed and expressed nowhere more clearly than through the detectives' actions: which witnesses they interview, or conversely, make no effort to interview; which potential leads they explore, versus those they choose to ignore. However confident the detectives are in their theory of what happened, they have a responsibility to investigate all viable leads and suspects, if only to eliminate them definitively.

By the morning after Sherri's murder, before her parents even arrived in Los Angeles, the commanding officer of Van Nuys homicide, Lt. Al Durrer, had already told the *Los Angeles Times* that Sherri was killed during an apparent burglary.

The LAPD's crime scene log for Sherri's case indicates that Durrer remained at the condo with Pida, the Van Nuys homicide coordinator, and Mayer, the lead investigator, until early Tuesday morning, February 25. Hooks, the young burglary detective tapped to assist Mayer on Sherri's case, was the last to go home, at 4:00 a.m. According to the typed version of the chrono, the detectives were back at work on the case by eight o'clock Tuesday morning.

Because it is common for multiple detectives to work on a murder case, LAPD detectives customarily note their name, initials, or serial number at the end of every chrono entry, to indicate who performed the described action. No identifying information was noted, however, at the end of any of the entries in the typed version of the Rasmussen chrono. The time span covered by these thirteen pages includes not just the crucial first forty-eight hours of the LAPD's investigation of Sherri's murder, but the entire first three months, from February 24 through the end of May 1986.

Nor is there any indication on the face of the thirteen pages of who typed them, one of the Van Nuys homicide detectives or a civilian clerk-typist.

The typed chrono was prepared in May 1986 as an addendum to the Ras-mussen case follow-up report, also known as the sixty-day report for its standard due date. Although the sixtieth day after Sherri's murder was April 25, the follow-up report in the Rasmussen case was not completed until May 21. The last entry recorded in the typed chrono was May 19.

Because the original handwritten chrono was inexplicably removed from the murder book sometime between May 1986 and March 2008, it is unknown whether the typed version omitted any information contained in the original, the only truly contemporaneous record of the first three months of the LAPD's investigation of Sherri's murder. Solely the typed, backdated version of the chrono survives.

According to the typed chrono, the Van Nuys detectives' first investi-gative activity on Tuesday, February 25, the day after Sherri's murder, was at 8:00 a.m. *"Called lady with purse,"* the typed chrono entry stated in full.

Although the typed chrono did not include her name, or any contact information, the lady was Anastasia Volanitis, Sherri and John's neigh-bor. On Monday afternoon, several hours before John discovered Sherri's body, two Spanish-speaking men came to Anastasia's door with Sherri's purse, which they had apparently found nearby and wanted to return. Later Monday, after Anastasia noticed police activity at Sherri's condo, she had her husband walk over and give the purse to the police.

The second thing the detectives did, according to the typed chrono, was an hour later, at 9:00 a.m. *"Called the alarm guy,"* it stated in full. Once again, no name or contact information was recorded. Presumably, "the alarm guy" was the company that had installed John and Sherri's bur-glar alarm system in mid-December 1985, less than a month after their wedding and about two months before her murder. When the system was put in, a sticker with the name of the alarm company, Locktronic, was affixed next to the front door of the condo, as a warning to potential burglars.

The next typed chrono entry, at 10:00 a.m., tersely read, *"Re-interviewed deceased [sic] husband."* The Van Nuys detectives' follow-up report, writ-ten three months later, offered a slightly more detailed account of the inter-view: *"On 2-25-86 at 1000 hrs., John Ruetten came to the station for a second interview. Detective Mayer and Hooks conducted the interview. John went thru his first statement given to Detective Mayer. There were no changes in his account of what happened. It appeared as though John was truthful and he obviously was still in shock over the death of his wife."*

Unlike Mayer's initial interview with John on the night of Sherri's murder, the detectives' second interview with him the next morning was not tape-recorded. The only documentation of the second interview retained in the murder book was the one-line typed chrono entry and the brief summary in the follow-up report.

To be fair, when the detectives conducted their first two interviews with John, all they knew about John, Sherri, and their relationship was what John told them. Nor could the detectives have anticipated at that time the scrutiny their investigation would face one day, decades later. In hindsight, John's conversations with the detectives on the morning of February 25 were perhaps the most pivotal moments in the LAPD's entire investigation of Sherri's murder. Unfortunately, exactly what John told the detectives that morning seems destined to remain a matter of mystery and conjecture.

In an interview in 2014, nearly thirty years later, Mayer described John's state of mind when he and Hooks reinterviewed him on Tuesday morning as "a little less distraught" than during his first interview, on Monday night, but still "very, very distraught, very emotional." According to Mayer, he and Hooks interviewed John at length. Mayer said they went through John's whole alibi and questioned him about his whereabouts throughout the day Monday, from the time he got up and went to the office until he got home and found Sherri's body.

Mayer recalled that he and Hooks then specifically asked John if he had an ex-girlfriend. Mayer said he pressed John, "Is there any other girl? Is there an ex-lover? Is there something that's rocking here? I mean, come on, a good-looking guy like you, you didn't have an ex-girlfriend?" According to Mayer, John's answer was unequivocal: "No. No other girlfriend, no nothing." Mayer said John never indicated in either of his first two interviews that there were any problems in his marriage.

Although John said there was no ex-girlfriend in the picture, Mayer recalled John did mention during their second interview that he had a "former acquaintance," a woman he knew from college at UCLA. Mayer said John identified her as a policewoman and gave him and Hooks her name, Stephanie Lazarus. According to Mayer, John told them that he had not seen Stephanie since he and Sherri got married. Mayer said John led them to believe that he and this "acquaintance" were in classes together in school, and that was it. John didn't refer to her as either a girlfriend or an ex-girlfriend, just as an acquaintance. Mayer recalled he asked John, "Are you sleeping with her, or what's going on?" Mayer said John told them no.

Mayer took pride in his detective skills and ability to read people. Based on their initial interactions, Mayer pegged John as "the All-American, clean-cut, yuppie worker, newly married guy." Mayer thought John was a nice-looking young man, a college graduate, and obviously intelligent. At the same time, Mayer got the impression that John wasn't a strong person. Mayer thought John seemed pretty woozy, an opinion based in part on John's very emotional reaction to Sherri's death. Mayer considered John to be a lightweight. He reminded Mayer of the right fielder on a recreational baseball team: there for every game, stands there and looks good, but if the ball was hit to him, you couldn't be sure whether he'd catch it.

John didn't strike Mayer as the partying type, out there sleazing around. Mayer thought it wasn't John's style. Mayer felt John wasn't street-smart enough to know how to be a player. Mayer believed if John was having an affair, he would have stammered more under questioning. He would have slipped up and gotten caught.

Mayer recalled he and Hooks gleaned as much information as they could from John about whether there was an ex-girlfriend, ex-boyfriend, or anyone who might have held a romantic grudge against him or Sherri. According to Mayer, he and Hooks both firmly believed John was telling them the truth. Mayer also insisted that prior to his second interview with John, he had never before in his life heard the name Stephanie Lazarus. According to Mayer, he couldn't have said at the time who Stephanie Lazarus was if she walked through the door.

Nothing that John told Mayer and Hooks that morning about Stephanie Lazarus—her name, that she was an "acquaintance" from college but not an ex-girlfriend, or that she was an LAPD officer—was documented in the Rasmussen murder book. According to the typed chrono, the Van Nuys detectives' 10:00 a.m. interview with John Ruetten was over within a half hour.

The next typed chrono entry, at 10:30 a.m., also pertained to John. "Took John R. on walk through of house," it stated in full. The detectives' walk-through of the condo with John was not tape-recorded either. The only additional documentation of the February 25 walk-through with John incorporated into the murder book was in the follow-up report written in May, three months after the fact. The follow-up report recounted, "On 2-25-86 at 1030 hrs., Detectives Mayer and Hooks took John Ruetten for a walk thru of his residence in an attempt to ascertain if anything was missing from the residence. John was unable to ascertain if anything was missing from the residence other than Sherri's purse and its contents."

Since Sherri's murder in 1986, the only interviews John has granted have been with the police. In 2009, John recounted for LAPD detectives his walk-through of the condo with Mayer and Hooks on February 25, 1986, and what he told them that day.

John's 2009 interview, unlike the 1986 walk-through, was tape-recorded. John recalled that he brought up Stephanie Lazarus to Mayer and Hooks the day after Sherri's murder. According to John, however, it was not during an interview at the Van Nuys station, but at the condo, after the walk-through. John recalled that his mother, Margaret, was also present when he told Mayer and Hooks about Stephanie.

It must have felt unsettling for John to be in the condo the day after Sherri was killed there. Although by the next morning her body had been removed, the crime scene was otherwise intact. The evidence of her violent death was impossible to ignore. The living room carpet had a large bloodstain where her body had lain for hours. Upstairs, the shattered glass balcony door had yet to be replaced, or even patched.

According to John, it was something the detectives said that inspired him to bring up Stephanie. John recalled Mayer and Hooks were talking burglary when one of them mentioned the bite mark on Sherri's arm, and that it could be used to identify the killer.

Until that moment, John was unaware that whoever killed Sherri had also bitten her. The night before, when John found Sherri's body, her facial injuries were so severe and disturbing that he failed to notice not only the bite mark on her arm, but also the three gunshot wounds to her chest.

According to John, the detective also made the point that during a fight, women are more likely to bite than men. "This could be a female," one of the detectives said, John recalled.

"It could be a male. Males bite, too, when they get in a fight," the other detective replied, again according to John.

The detectives' discussion of the bite mark, and whether it suggested Sherri's killer might be a woman, is what prompted John to bring up "the Stephanie situation," as he called it during his 2009 interview. John said he told Mayer and Hooks, "You know, I've got to talk to you about Stephanie."

According to John, he provided Mayer and Hooks with Stephanie's full name, along with the information that she was a police officer. John also recalled that he told the detectives, during that same conversation in the condo, about Stephanie going to see Sherri at Glendale Adventist. How exactly John characterized the hospital confrontation is unknown, since none of his conversations with the detectives on the day after Sherri's murder were tape-recorded.

In his 2009 LAPD interview, John said of Stephanie, "I know that she went to go see Sherri. I know that she was upset that we weren't going to have the relationship. That's the reason for identifying her. That's the reason I identified her twenty-three years ago"—referring to his conversation at the condo with Mayer and Hooks. "So there was this issue of, did it really mean there was a female or not? But for me, when it got brought up, I just said, you know, 'We got to check this out. You got to know this.'" John said he told the detectives, "Look, you know, you got to check this out."

By John's own account of what he told Mayer and Hooks, he said nothing to them about the events that led up to Stephanie's confrontation with Sherri at the hospital. Most glaringly, John did not reveal to the LAPD's detectives, in his interviews in either 1986 or 2009, what Stephanie had told Sherri in her office that day: that during his engagement to Sherri, John had gone to Stephanie's place, where they had sex. Nor did John inform the detectives about any of the incidents that Sherri had confided to her parents and girlfriends in the months since the hospital visit: how Sherri felt she was being followed by someone dressed as a boy, or how Stephanie visited their home uninvited to ask John to wax her snow skis, or the time Sherri was home alone and discovered Stephanie standing in their living room, just weeks prior to the murder.

John claimed in his 2009 interview, and later testified in court under oath, that he did not recall any of the incidents involving his ex-girlfriend that Sherri found so upsetting. "I can't fathom Sherri not sharing anything like this with me," John told the detectives in 2009, of Stephanie's threatening behavior. John insisted that except for the hospital confrontation, nothing about Stephanie ever suggested to him that she was capable of murder. "I have to say that, because it's the truth," John said in 2009.

John's feelings about his having cheated on Sherri with Stephanie may have made it difficult for him to admit it to Mayer and Hooks on the day after Sherri's murder. Another inhibiting factor for John may have been the presence of his mother, Margaret, who accompanied him to the condo that morning.

For Margaret to know the intimate details of her son's love life, John would have had to tell his mother about his infidelity to Sherri, which seems implausible. Not even John's closest male friends, Matt Gorder and David Neuman, both of whom also knew Stephanie from UCLA, were aware that John and Stephanie had had a sexual relationship that lasted several years. Apparently, the only people who knew John and Stephanie had sex during his engagement to Sherri were John, Stephanie, and Sherri, who found out only because Stephanie went to the hospital and informed her. Sherri had kept that part of the hospital confrontation secret from her parents and close friends.

Even if Margaret knew nothing at all about her son's infidelity, and as little as John about the other incidents Sherri complained about to her parents and friends, there is no question Margaret knew who he was talking about when he gave the detectives Stephanie's name on the morning after Sherri's murder. John and Stephanie had known each other for almost eight years, since the fall of 1978. During that time, she went out of her way to ingratiate herself with John's family. More than once, she visited San Diego with John and spent time at the Ruetten family's home. Stephanie cultivated friendships with John's brother, Tom, and sister Janet, but particularly with Margaret, his mother. Her contact with the Ruetten family continued well after John and Sherri started dating. In April 1985, Stephanie wrote in her diary about bringing burgers to Tom's apartment for lunch with Tom and Janet and their mother. A month later, in May, she took a cruise that stopped in San Diego. Margaret went down to the harbor to see her, and they posed for photographs together, smiling. Less than two weeks later, John and Sherri announced their engagement to their parents.

Nor was Margaret in the dark about how badly Stephanie wanted to be with John. In fact, with the possible exception of John himself, Margaret knew better than anyone how deep Stephanie's feelings ran for her son. In August, three months before the wedding and six months before Sherri's murder, Stephanie confessed to Margaret in a letter that she was truly in love with John and did not think she would ever understand his decision to get married.

Yet on the morning after Sherri's murder, when Margaret heard the detectives speculate whether the bite mark meant Sherri's killer might be female, and John brought Stephanie to their attention in front of her, Margaret apparently said nothing to the detectives. Margaret Ruetten died in 2011, so what her thoughts were at the time and why she remained silent about Stephanie will remain a mystery.

During John's 2009 LAPD interview, he was asked of Mayer and Hooks, "When you explained this to them, that she's an L.A. police officer, what is the response? Do they ask you any other questions about this?"

John replied, with characteristic ambiguity, "That's a good question. I don't recall. I have this feeling that I recall that it didn't thrill them, you know? But I'm very much speculating, you know? So I'll just say, 'I can't remember any real reaction.' They never brought it up to me again, as far as I recall."

John presumed that because he had provided Mayer and Hooks with Stephanie's name and identified her as a police officer, they would look into her as part of their investigation. In his 2009 LAPD interview, John recalled of the detectives, "There was a lot going on when this happened. They were not looking at just two robbers. They were asking me a lot of questions. They were exploring things, so certainly that looked like what it was, and that was probably the conclusion at the end, but it seemed like they were really trying to investigate the thing," meaning his wife's murder.

John believed that if Stephanie was an issue, the detectives would pursue it. When they did not bring up her again, John apparently assumed that they had checked Stephanie out and determined that she had no involvement in Sherri's murder.

John had no idea what, if anything, Sherri had ever told her parents about his ex-girlfriend. Unbeknownst to John, Sherri in fact had talked to Nels and Loretta about his ex-girlfriend several times in the nine months since he and Sherri became engaged. Nels and Loretta knew about the hospital visit and the other incidents Sherri had shared with them: her belief she was being watched and followed; the uninvited visits to their home to ask John to wax her snow skis; Sherri's unsettling discovery of the ex-girlfriend in their living room. Nels and Loretta had never discussed these incidents with John, because Sherri had asked them not to.

In his 2009 LAPD interview, John said he assumed the reason Nels knew anything about his ex-girlfriend was because John had brought Stephanie to the detectives' attention the morning after the murder, before the Rasmussens arrived in Los Angeles. According to John, in the days after Sherri's murder, Mayer and Hooks never said a word to him about Nels saying anything to them about Stephanie. John said that Mayer and Hooks never informed him that they had information Stephanie was in any way threatening Sherri, or even in contact with her. John insisted that his own family knew that he gave Stephanie's name to the LAPD the day after Sherri was killed.

John expressed regret in his 2009 interview that he didn't do more in 1986 to learn whether Stephanie was involved in Sherri's murder. John said that looking back, "I'm kicking myself for not pushing to find out more of what was going on with that," meaning the possibility that his ex-girlfriend murdered his wife. John continued, "You know, it's one of those things that I regret now, because maybe a lot of this could have been taken care of way back then." John's stated reasons for not doing so were self-centered. John said that at the time, "I'm twenty-seven years old, I'm trying to figure out my life ... I'm trying to figure out who doesn't want me to have a life." Only John can explain why, by his own account, he was oblivious to Stephanie as someone who fit that description.

One of John's big questions after Sherri's murder was whether Sherri had a gun in the house that he didn't know about. John recalled in his 2009 LAPD interview that it was something Mayer and Hooks asked him about in 1986. If Sherri had a gun in the condo, John had no knowledge of it. Yet John felt he couldn't rule out the possibility completely. In his mind, he was the one who came from a Democratic, pro–gun control family. His dad was a history professor, not a gun owner like Nels. John had never owned a gun, had never fired a gun, and wasn't a gun person. In John's view, the presence of a gun risked elevating any confrontation. John believed that the moment you bring the gun out, whether the other person is thinking in life-and-death terms or not, now you're in life-and-death mode. John could not imagine that Sherri didn't know his feelings about keeping a gun at home.

John said in his 2009 LAPD interview that he could envision Sherri hearing a noise and walking downstairs with a gun. John recalled, "The things that went around in my head related to this were, 'God, I hope Sherri didn't have a gun and walked down ... She heard something downstairs, and because she had the gun, it elevated it.'"

The reason John felt a sliver of doubt about whether Sherri secretly had a gun was Nels. John knew that Nels owned several guns. John also knew how fiercely protective Nels was of his daughters, especially Sherri. John told the LAPD in 2009, "The only way I can put it is, I wouldn't be shocked if she had a gun, because Nels would have been the type of guy, 'My daughter's living in the city. She should have a gun.' But I don't know.

I always felt like, 'God dang it, Sherri, I hope you didn't have a gun and I hope you didn't elevate. I hope you weren't the one who caused the elevation of this to a life-and-death issue.'"

In reality, Nels never gave Sherri a gun. Mayer and Hooks found no gun in the condo, nor any evidence that Sherri inadvertently supplied her killer with the murder weapon, which to this day has never been recovered.

The typed chrono indicated that Mayer and Hooks's walk-through of the condo with John was over within half an hour, by 11:00 a.m. None of the information John said he provided to the detectives in the condo that day, specifically Stephanie Lazarus's name and that she was a Los Angeles police officer, was recorded in the typed chrono, the follow-up report, or elsewhere in the Rasmussen murder book.

After the walk-though, the next two entries in the typed chrono were at 11:00 a.m. The first stated in full, *"Took alarm guy to check alarm."* The follow-up report included a slightly more detailed account, but an earlier start time, 10:30, the same time as the walk-through with John. The follow-up report also misstated the name of the alarm company, Locktronic. According to the follow-up report, *"On 2-25-86 at 1030 Hrs., Detective Mayer interviewed Leslie Halloran. Address 2285 N. Tracy, Simi, CA 805-583-1275. The interview was at 7100 Balboa Blvd. #205. The substance of the interview is as follows: 'I am the owner of the Lok Tron [sic] Alarm Company. I work out of my house. John and Sherri have a panic button on their alarms. The panic button will override any signal.' Detective Mayer then took Halloran into the residence and asked him to show him how the alarm of the residence works. Halloran did so. Detective Mayer was shown that the alarm was in perfect working condition. Detective Mayer asked Halloran if his company received a broken signal or a panic alarm on 2-24-86. Halloran indicated that his company had not received any signal from the location on 2-24-86."*

Neither the chrono nor the follow-up report noted when the burglar alarm system was installed in the condo, but it was on December 16, 1985, only ten weeks before Sherri's murder. Sherri had lived in the condo for several years before that, first by herself and then with her roommate, Jayne, with no alarm system. Why John and Sherri decided to get an alarm system installed has never been established. Was it a general fear of crime, which in the mid-1980s was on the upswing in Los Angeles? Or was it in response to a specific incident, or person, they felt threatened by? There is no indication in the murder book that the detectives asked Halloran if he knew what prompted John and Sherri to upgrade their home security when they did. If the detectives ever asked John the same question in 1986, there is no record of it.

According to the typed chrono, at the same time that Mayer was interviewing Halloran about the alarm system, an LAPD fingerprint analyst, Mike Ames, went to work in the condo looking for additional prints. The typed chrono recounted, *"Had location reprints by Ames—obtained lifts. Had loc. ninhydrin."* The corresponding account in the follow-up report misspelled Ames's name and advanced the time an hour: *"On 2-25-86 at 1000 Hrs., Detective Mayer caused S.I.D. print expert Aames [sic] to ninhydrate the inside of the location for possible prints."*

Ninhydrin is a chemical used at crime scenes to develop latent fingerprints on surfaces like painted drywall. The ninhydrin reacts with the amino acids present in fingerprint residue, as well as with blood. The resulting chemical reaction turns any latent prints a deep purple. To apply ninhydrin, the crystals were mixed with acetone to make a solution, which was sprayed onto the surface in a fine mist. The color change did not happen instantaneously but could take days or even weeks to develop, depending on the temperature and other conditions. Because the solution was toxic to inhale and highly flammable, spraying ninhydrin was usually the last step taken at an indoor crime scene. Once the ninhydrin was applied, the location was sealed to allow the reactions to develop. The LAPD's fingerprint analysts liked to wait at least seventy-two hours, after which time any ninhydrin-enhanced prints could be photographed.

During their walk-through on Tuesday morning, the detectives discovered some bloodstains they had not noticed the night before. Regarding these, the follow-up report stated:

> On February 25, 1986 Detectives Mayer and Hooks returned to the crime scene with the victim's husband. Detectives noted small blood stains on the west wall leading down to the garage area. A small amount of blood was also evident on the file cabinet at the east (just west) of the stairs. Additionally S.I.D. print expert Aames [sic] lifted a large hand print from the closet door just inside the front entrance to the condo. This print is only a foot or so from the tile floor. It should be noted smeared blood is evident in the palm area of the print lifted. There is a small amount of smeared blood on the door jam [sic] next to the alarm box on the east wall near the front door.

Ames was part of the same SID unit as Gilbert Aguilar, the fingerprint analyst who, the night before, recovered eighteen prints in the condo. Ames knew Aguilar had preceded him at the crime scene, but it was good practice, especially in homicide cases, to look for any prints that may have been missed. Unlike Aguilar, Ames had the benefit of working in daylight.

Ames's primary assignment was to process the crime scene with ninhydrin, but he decided to reprint some areas first. Ames dusted the front door, where Mayer believed the suspects entered, and the door of the nearby coat closet. Ames lifted ten additional prints from the two doors. Ames also found four prints on the banister in the garage stairway, through which the detectives believed the suspects fled, and one more on the bottom of a cassette deck in the living room. To distinguish these lifts from those collected earlier, Aguilar's set of eighteen was designated as print package A, and Ames's set of fifteen as print package B.

Ames then mixed the ninhydrin solution and sprayed it on the walls in the front entryway, where LAPD criminalist Alison Ochiae had noted multiple bloodstains the night before. The next step was to wait for the ninhydrin reaction. Ames left the condo at 2:00 p.m., three hours after he arrived.

Hooks interviewed Anastasia Volanitis, Sherri and John's neighbor, at 11:15 a.m., according to the follow-up report. The interview was not documented in the typed chrono, nor was it tape-recorded. Anastasia's last name was misspelled repeatedly in the follow-up report, which recounted:

> On 2-25-86 at 1115 hrs., Detective Hooks interviewed Anastasia Volianitis, 7100 Balboa Unit #301 . . . The substance of the interview is as follows: On 2-24-86 at approximately 1630 hrs., I was outside washing the windows. Two male Latins approached me and told me they are gardeners. They had some identification. The first Latin was 20/25 years old 5/6, 140 lbs, possible mustache, possible tan baseball cap. They kept saying '205, 205.' I told them to ring the bell. They handed me a purse and then in broken Spanish they wanted it back. They wanted to give it to her by themselves. I let them in. They walked to 205 and knocked. There was no answer so they came back and gave me the purse. I just set the purse in my house. I was going to give it back later. The paramedics came and I found out what happened. I told them to tell you to come here today and pick it up. On 2-24-86, I noticed the garage door to her residence was open at 1120 hrs. My husband, Gus Volianitis, left for work at 1030 hrs and he saw that the garage door

was open. My nephew, Stefanos Volianitis, left for school at 0845 hrs, and
he is sure the door was closed then.

The detectives also prepared a written statement, a summary of Anastasia's interview, which she signed at the bottom.

In 2012, twenty-six years later, Anastasia testified in court about the day the two men brought Sherri's purse to her. On the witness stand, she was shown the interview summary she signed in 1986, the day after Sherri's murder. Anastasia acknowledged her signature but insisted several of the statements attributed to her were incorrect and diverged from her own recollection of the facts.

According to Anastasia's testimony, the two men delivered the purse around noon, not 4:30 in the afternoon. Anastasia recalled she was in her condo when the men came to her door, not washing windows outside. She also disputed the LAPD's account of how and when she noticed Sherri's garage door was open. Anastasia said it was untrue that her husband, Gus, saw the garage door open at 10:30 a.m. on his way to work, because Gus was retired by 1986. Anastasia testified that it was she who noticed the open garage door, not Gus. Anastasia said she saw the garage was open at about 9:30 a.m., when she and Gus returned home from their morning walk, an hour earlier than the time attributed to him in the written statement.

Anastasia's testimony about when she returned Sherri's purse also differed from the statements attributed to her in 1986. Anastasia said she never told the paramedics to have the police pick up the purse from her on Tuesday, but had her husband bring it to Sherri's condo Monday evening, after she saw the police there. Anastasia said she saw Gus walk over with it and come back empty-handed.

The inconsistencies between Anastasia's testimony in 2012 and her original statements as documented by the LAPD in 1986 are impossible to reconcile.

The next thing the detectives did Tuesday morning, after Hooks interviewed Anastasia, pertained to Sherri's missing BMW. According to the typed chrono, at 11:30 a.m., the detectives *"Completed rotator notice on vehicle."* The follow-up report recounted, *"On 2-25-86 Detectives Mayer and Hooks completed a divisional rotator notice concerning the stolen vehicle and murder."*

The purpose of the rotator notice was to alert patrol units to be on the lookout for the stolen car. That Sherri's BMW was stolen during the commission of a homicide, rather than off the street, made it a high priority to locate and recover.

The rotator notice Mayer and Hooks drafted characterized Sherri's BMW as a *"stolen vehicle taken during burglary-murder"* and stated, *"2-24-86 between 0830 and 1030 the vict possibly surprised a 459 susp in her residence located at 7100 Balboa Bl. In Van Nuys Division. The vict was shot with a possible .38 cal revolver. The suspect took the vict's car keys and her vehicle. No additional suspect info at this time. If the vehicle is located stake and notify Van Nuys Homicide. Vehicle info: 85 BMW 318I 2 door silver . . . registered to John Ruetten. Van Nuys Homicide Handling: Hooks or Mayer."*

Mayer requested distribution of the rotator notice to all patrol units in the Valley Bureau, which included the Van Nuys Division, where the murder occurred, as well as the neighboring Devonshire Division, where Stephanie Lazarus was assigned. Stephanie was on duty, and indeed out on patrol, that very same day. Only Stephanie knows whether she saw the rotator notice, or heard any talk about the BMW stolen in Van Nuys during what was believed to be a burglary-murder.

All this happened before noon on Tuesday, the day after Sherri's murder. Sherri's parents and sisters spent Tuesday morning traveling to Los Angeles. Less than twelve hours had passed since a ringing phone woke Nels and Loretta at home and John's father, Richard, informed them of Sherri's murder.

Tuesday morning, after a sleepless night, Nels and Loretta took the first available flight, which had a stopover in Phoenix en route to LAX. The short flight from Tucson to Phoenix was uneventful. More passengers boarded, and the pilot prepared for takeoff. As the plane hurtled down the tarmac and lifted off, Loretta sensed that they had taken off farther down the runway than usual. Once the plane was aloft, one of the engines didn't sound right. The plane banked sharply as the pilot returned to the airport for an emergency landing. It appeared to Nels, as he looked out the window, that he could have reached down and touched the roofs of the houses below them. The plane landed safely. The flight crew announced that everyone had to deplane, but the directive did not register with Nels and Loretta. As all the other passengers exited, they just sat there in shock, less over the near plane crash than over Sherri's death, which had only just begun to sink in.

After several minutes, a stewardess eventually noticed them still in their seats. She came down the aisle and asked if they were all right.

"Yes," Nels replied. "We want to go to L.A."

"Well, you won't be going to L.A. on this plane," the stewardess said. "You're going to have to get off. We're going to have to hurry." The stewardess personally escorted them off the plane and walked them through the terminal to their new gate. Their connecting flight was about to depart without them, but they made it in time.

Sherri's older sister, Connie, meanwhile, caught the first morning flight from Seattle. Connie brought her six-month-old, Rachel, with her. Connie's flight landed before her parents', so she waited with Rachel for them at the airport.

Sherri's other sister, Teresa, and her husband, Brian, drove from Loma Linda to LAX to meet them. Teresa was five months pregnant, and understandably emotional, so Brian drove. Just two days earlier, on Sunday, Teresa and Brian had visited Sherri and John and spent several hours with them. Tuesday morning, the traffic getting to LAX was terrible. As they sat in traffic, Teresa stewed miserably, thinking about Sherri. Teresa felt angry, as if she wanted to get out of the car and fight somebody, right there and then.

Once Nels and Loretta landed, they went with Connie and rented a car to drive to Van Nuys. Everyone in the family was in a state of shock, except baby Rachel, who was blessedly oblivious. The Rasmussens were exhausted from having been up all night trying to figure out how to get to Los Angeles as soon as possible. They had no information about Sherri's murder apart from what John's father had told Nels during their brief late-night phone call. Nels felt the same as Teresa, angry and ready to fight. The Rasmussens drove straight to the Van Nuys police station. They got there around noon, roughly eighteen hours after John found Sherri's body. They knew nothing of what had transpired so far in the LAPD's investigation.

Nels and Loretta went to the front desk and explained to the officer on duty that they were Sherri Rasmussen's parents. The officer called up to homicide and directed them where to wait. The Rasmussens had to pass through a metal detector before they went farther into the station. Nels recalls they waited only a short time before a man came out of what Nels assumed was an office or interview room, with John Ruetten right behind him. John had returned to the station for further questioning after the walk-through at the condo. The man leading John was Detective Lyle Mayer, whom the Rasmussens were meeting for the first time.

According to Nels, when he saw John, he went to shake hands with him but couldn't, because Mayer stood between them. Nels would have had to reach through Mayer's arms, or go around him, to get to John. In that same moment, as Nels approached John, Nels felt Mayer bump up against his hip. Nels thought Mayer did it intentionally, but in a way he could pass off as inadvertent, or that Nels might not even notice. Nels believed Mayer was making sure he wasn't packing a gun. Nels was dressed in slacks and a polo shirt, with no jacket. Nels recalls that he looked at Mayer with disbelief. Nels thought, "Now, he's not stupid enough to think that I'm going to come to the police department, and in the police department, try something funny?" Later, Nels wondered why Mayer felt compelled to frisk him without coming out and saying so. The only explanation Nels could fathom was that before they arrived, John must have told Mayer that Nels owned guns.

John, meanwhile, cowered behind Mayer, Nels recalls. Nels thought John seemed scared to death, as though he expected Nels to smack him. Nels wasn't about to raise hell, because he didn't know enough yet about what had happened to Sherri. According to Nels, after the surreptitious frisk-bump, Mayer let John past him. Nels recalls that when he and John shook hands, John couldn't look him in the face. When Nels met John eye to eye, John dropped his gaze right away.

Connie also sensed that John was afraid of her father. Nels had a forthright and commanding presence that could be intimidating. John knew that Nels had a particularly close and protective relationship with Sherri. John also knew, from having watched his father and Nels argue politics, that Nels was not one to flinch from conflict or back down when he believed he was right. Nels was physically imposing as well, six feet tall and about 200 pounds. Although Nels was fifty-four at the time, and professionally a dentist, he still had the strong build he had developed as a teenage logger.

Later, in hindsight, Connie believed that John's fear of Nels helped set the stage for the LAPD's treatment of her family. Connie felt Mayer had a preconceived notion of her father, based on what John had told him, before they ever walked into the station. Connie thought it explained why the detectives kept her family isolated and gave them no information, because John had made Mayer wary of how her family would react.

The Rasmussens didn't know what to expect when they first got to the station. Sherri's death still felt unreal. They were physically drained from lack of sleep and their desperate rush to Los Angeles. It felt to Nels as though the world was coming apart. Before Sherri's murder, their family had never been touched by violence. As a child, Nels was brought up to trust the police. He had always regarded police officers with great respect. Nels believed they weren't paid enough for the risks they took on the job. He felt the general public did not appreciate police officers as much as it should.

According to Mayer, his first impression of the Rasmussens was that they were very thankful he and the other detectives were working the case, and on top of things. Later on, however, as the LAPD's investigation of Sherri's murder progressed, Mayer became convinced that Nels wasn't a fan of cops.

Connie and Teresa were not privy to every interaction between their parents, John, and Mayer. For most of the sisters' time at the station, while their parents dealt with Mayer, they sat in a waiting area with Brian and Rachel.

Connie recalls that she saw John and her father together only briefly, standing in an open corridor. It appeared to Connie that Nels wanted to ask John a question, but couldn't, because the detectives kept them separated.

Teresa sat in the waiting area wondering when the detectives were going to ask to interview her. Teresa assumed they would, since she and Brian had been with Sherri and John at the condo on Sunday, the day before the murder. According to Teresa, when she first saw John at the station, he didn't say boo to her. Unlike her parents and some of Sherri's friends, Teresa knew nothing at the time about John's ex-girlfriend. Perhaps because Sherri did not want to worry her during her pregnancy, she had never mentioned the ex-girlfriend to Teresa. For that reason, Teresa did not share her father's unease about John, or his suspicion that the ex-girlfriend may have been involved in Sherri's murder. Teresa wanted to tell the detectives about seeing Sherri on Sunday, and trying to call her on Monday. She thought her information could help them piece together Sherri's last days and hours. Teresa was surprised and disappointed when the detectives never asked her any questions whatsoever.

After Mayer took Nels and Loretta into an interview room to talk privately, John went and sat in the waiting area with Teresa, Brian, Connie, and Rachel. Teresa recalls that John said the detectives had made him remove his shirt, to look for scratches, because Sherri had scratched somebody during the fight. John also said the detectives had photographed him with his shirt off, Teresa recalls. The LAPD's typed chrono and follow-up report, however, contain no reference to John's being photographed on February 25, or any other day. Nor were any photographs or negatives retained by the LAPD, unless they were later removed from the murder book.

Teresa recalls that John also said, during that same conversation at the station, that the LAPD gave him a polygraph examination. There is no indication in the typed chrono or follow-up report that John was administered a polygraph exam on February 25, the day Teresa recalls John told her that at the station.

According to the typed chrono and the follow-up report, John was not given a polygraph exam until March 12, more than two weeks later. The follow-up report recounted, "*On 3-12-86 a polygraph examination was given to John Ruetten by Senior Polygraph Examiner Blair Eckert, S.I.D. LAPD. The results of the examination were inconclusive due to the fact that John Ruetten was too emotional to give an accurate reading. There were major discrepancies in the results of the answers. The test may be repeated at a later date after the shock of the events have settled in John's mind.*"

Teresa has no recollection of John's talking about the results of his polygraph during their conversation on the day after Sherri's murder. Teresa is certain, however, that it was that day, February 25, that John spoke of having taken a polygraph exam. There was no other day that she and John were both at the Van Nuys station, where Teresa recalls the conversation took place.

Under the LAPD's procedures in 1986, polygraph exams for homicide investigations were customarily tape-recorded. Prior to the interview, the detective and polygraph examiner worked together to devise a list of ten or so questions, yes-or-no, for the subject to answer. For convenience and consistency across cases, the LAPD had a preprinted form on which to write the questions, each being one of two types, "control" or "relevant." Control questions are typically about the subject's background, and they are intended to elicit a baseline physiological response. The first two questions on the LAPD's preprinted form—"Is your first name . . . ?" and "Were you born in . . . ?"—are control questions. Relevant questions are specific to the crime being investigated and are designed to induce stress. "Did you participate in the murder?" and "Do you know who committed the murder?" are examples of relevant questions.

During the actual exam, the detective typically left the room while the polygraph examiner asked the agreed-upon questions and monitored the machine for indications of deception or truthfulness. The detective usually listened in from a separate room. The subject's answers, affirmative or negative, were often documented in the margins of the form, next to each question. At the top of the form, there were places to write the names of the polygraph subject and the victim, the date, file number, and tape num-

ber. Following the exam, a copy of the tape recording and the list of questions are supposed to be retained permanently as official records.

In Sherri's case, although SID retained a tape recording and the list of
questions that John was asked on March 12, no contemporaneous documentation from John's aborted polygraph made it into the murder book.
The only indication in the murder book that John was given a polygraph
exam on March 12 were a few typed chrono entries around that date and
the brief summary in the follow-up report. The typed chrono and follow-up
report were both produced in May 1986, more than two months after they
indicate John's polygraph took place. Inexplicably, neither noted the SID
tape number, an omission that made it appear that John's polygraph was
not tape-recorded, when it was, and that no tape existed, when in fact
one did.

Mayer, in an interview in 2014, nearly thirty years after the events in
question, recalled that John's polygraph took place not the day after Sherri's murder, but some weeks later. Mayer recounted, "You don't immediately turn around and put the husband on the polygraph the next day to
determine whether or not he's bad, because your investigative conclusions
are this guy is a pretty straight-up guy."

Mayer said he decided to ask John to take a polygraph exam only after
they had thoroughly investigated him. According to Mayer, everyone they
talked to about John told them "shining stories" about him. Mayer said,
"We checked John up every way we possibly could. We looked to see if there
was any financial gain, if there was anything rocking and rolling. We got
down to the end conclusion at this particular time and I said, 'Look, I'm
satisfied but I want to make absolutely certain.' I put him on a polygraph
to determine his credibility."

Mayer described John's state of mind when they put him on the polygraph machine as "tremendously sensitive" and "tremendously anxious."
Mayer said John was "very emotional, but he's not emotionally distraught.
He was very emotional. You could see he was having a difficult time with
this," meaning the polygraph exam.

According to Mayer, the two "key questions" John was asked during
his polygraph were "Are you personally involved?" and "Do you personally know who killed her?" Mayer said, "On those questions, he was credible. In other words, he showed not deceptive, but throughout the whole
questioning, he showed inconclusive. We couldn't determine that he was
absolutely valid in every answer." Mayer could not recall any of the other

questions John was asked during the polygraph exam. Nor could Mayer recall if any of the questions John answered inconclusively involved the state of his marriage, his prior relationships, or the "acquaintance," Stephanie Lazarus, whose name John had provided to Mayer the morning after Sherri's murder.

Mayer said he knew the polygraph examiner well, from many prior cases. Mayer recalled that he asked the examiner, "'Okay, now, why is he inconclusive?' He goes, his answer was just flat out this, he says, 'Lyle, the guy is just too emotional. He's too emotionally wound up. He will never give you a great answer.'"

Mayer said he went to his boss, Roger Pida, the Van Nuys homicide coordinator, and told him about John's polygraph. Mayer recalled he told Pida, "Look, he shows credible on 'Did you personally know . . . ?' But very honestly he's going to be inconclusive. The exam is going to be inconclusive." Mayer said he, Hooks, Pida, and their lieutenant, Al Durrer, all sat down and talked about it. Mayer recalled he told them, "Obviously he passed the 'Were you personally . . . ?' and 'Do you know who . . . ?'—the two key questions. We said, 'Okay, well, we'll just have to live with the inconclusive activity.'" According to Mayer, they made the collective decision that subjecting John to another polygraph was something someone else could do later, at the time of the follow-up report, or six months, or a year, or five years down the line.

Mayer said another factor in their decision was that polygraph results could not be used in court if a suspect was ever arrested and prosecuted. Mayer recalled, "All of us go, 'Okay, well, the polygraph is only an investigative tool. It's not admissible evidence anyhow.'" Mayer felt they didn't have anything on John, apart from the ambiguous polygraph results, to link him to Sherri's murder. Mayer said he and his fellow detectives asked themselves, and ultimately agreed, "What are we doing here? Is this an end to a means, or a means to an end? Are we gaining anything? Are we losing anything? No, it's inconclusive."

Mayer didn't like the fact that John was too emotional to complete the polygraph, but he felt it was something he had to accept. According to Mayer, John's polygraph was "a very, very minor" part of their investigation. In Mayer's mind, John's polygraph results did not detract in any way from their primary investigative theory. Mayer's main takeaway from the inconclusive polygraph was that it confirmed his impression of John as a weak person. Mayer recalled of John, "The guy, to be honest with you,

I always thought the guy was a wuss. I think he's a wuss now. I just thought, 'Hey, the guy just can't handle it,' so we rocked on."

If Mayer's recollection of when John took the polygraph exam is accurate, and the March 12 date in the typed chrono and follow-up report is correct, John's polygraph could not have been a topic of conversation in the days after Sherri's murder, because it hadn't taken place yet. Sherri's sister Teresa, however, is not the only person who remembers hearing about John's polygraph during those few days, the only time the Rasmussen and Ruetten families were both in Los Angeles and dealing face-to-face with the LAPD.

According to Nels and Loretta, on Tuesday at the Van Nuys station, after their inauspicious introduction to Mayer in front of John, Mayer took them back to an interview room. There is no reference in the LAPD's typed chrono or follow-up report to Nels and Loretta being interviewed or briefed by the detectives on February 25, the day they arrived in Los Angeles. The Rasmussens' initial meeting with Mayer was not tape-recorded. If any contemporaneous notes were taken about what was discussed, they either never made it into the murder book or were later removed.

Nels and Loretta recall they met with Mayer alone in the interview room. According to the Rasmussens, Mayer told them that Sherri was killed in a burglary gone wrong. Mayer mentioned the video components abandoned in the entryway as evidence that she had interrupted a burglar or burglars in the act. Mayer ran down his theory that the burglars likely entered through the unlocked front door, thinking that no one was home. Mayer said he believed Sherri heard a noise and came downstairs to the second floor, where she confronted a burglar near the kitchen. There was a struggle and shots were fired. Sherri ran downstairs, toward the front door, with the burglar in pursuit. The struggle resumed in the front entryway and then moved to the living room, where Sherri may have briefly gotten control of the gun. Mayer told Nels and Loretta about the bite mark on Sherri's arm, which drove home for them the intensity of the fight Sherri put up. According to Nels, when Mayer described how Sherri was knocked unconscious before the fatal gunshots, Mayer said, "Sherri wasn't killed. She was assassinated."

The Rasmussens recall Mayer asked them if Sherri had a gun at home. Nels said no. "She'd have to be pushed pretty hard to use a gun," he told Mayer. Sherri had once told Nels she didn't want a gun at home because she didn't think she could ever face someone and pull the trigger. Nels felt Mayer was trying to provoke him to say something to support the idea that

Sherri's actions had caused the fight or escalated it into a life-and-death struggle. He told Mayer, "You don't know Sherri. She's not that way."

According to Nels, from the very beginning, he never bought Mayer's theory that burglars had killed Sherri. Since late the night before, when John's father had called and informed them of Sherri's murder, he and Loretta had racked their brains for any possible explanation. Because of their delayed notification, and inability to get to Los Angeles sooner, the Rasmussens were essentially frozen out of the first twelve hours of the LAPD's investigation, when the botched-burglary theory took root. By Mayer's own account, he and his fellow detectives believed it was a burglary based on the crime scene and what John had told them. Prior to their meeting with Mayer, the Rasmussens had no knowledge of the crime scene, and no access to any of the LAPD's information. John, for reasons they could not understand, was incommunicado. The only clues the Rasmussens had to go on were things Sherri had once told them. Some of the memories that flooded back to them seemed, in hindsight, like missed warning signs.

At some point during their initial meeting, Mayer asked the Rasmussens if they could think of anyone who would want to harm Sherri. It was in response to this question, the Rasmussens recall, that Nels first told Mayer about John's ex-girlfriend. Nels told Mayer that Sherri had been having "trouble" with the ex-girlfriend. Although the Rasmussens did not know her name at that time, Nels informed Mayer that she was a police officer.

Nels recalls "beyond a shadow of a doubt" that he mentioned John's ex-girlfriend to Mayer during their initial meeting on February 25. The Rasmussens are less certain about whether they also informed Mayer that day about the nurse at Glendale Adventist whom Sherri had passed over for a promotion. Sherri had told her parents about being harassed by the nurse and her doctor boyfriend. The Rasmussens knew Sherri had reported the harassment to the hospital.

In Nels's mind, it was John's ex-girlfriend who loomed largest as a potential suspect for Mayer to investigate. Nels asked Mayer "point-blank" during their first meeting whether Mayer had checked out and interviewed John's ex-girlfriend. According to the Rasmussens, Mayer ignored the question and just went on with his story about the interrupted burglary. Nels wanted to tell Mayer about the many troubling incidents involving John's ex-girlfriend that Sherri had recounted to him and Loretta before the murder. Nels felt he didn't get a chance, because Mayer got him off track by going on about the supposed burglary.

Later in the meeting, Mayer told them John had been given a polygraph exam but was too emotional to answer the questions. Nels recalls Mayer said all John did was cry. Mayer informed the Rasmussens that he had physically examined John with his shirt off and found no scratches or injuries, Nels recalls. Mayer also said photos were taken of John. According to Nels, when he heard about John being photographed, it gave him the idea to ask Mayer, "Well, what about the ex-girlfriend? Has she been photographed?" Mayer did not answer the question, or even acknowledge that it had been asked.

By Nels's count, during his and Loretta's first meeting with Mayer on February 25, he brought up John's ex-girlfriend at least three times. Mayer finally told him, "Don't even go there, there's nothing there." It seemed to the Rasmussens that Mayer had already made up his mind about what had happened to Sherri.

Mayer, in his 2014 interview, confirmed that he met with the Rasmussens the day after Sherri's murder in an interview room at the Van Nuys station. Mayer, however, has a very different recollection of the conversation, and of what Nels and Loretta told him during their initial meeting.

Mayer's impression of the Rasmussens, and Nels especially, was unflattering. Regarding Nels, Mayer recalled, "He was obviously a very overbearing personality." Mayer said Loretta was tough for him to get a read on. According to Mayer, "You could tell he was overly sensitive, and he didn't let Loretta interject much into the conversation whatsoever. It was obvious he was the person in the family that was controlling everything." Mayer recalled Loretta "just kind of followed along with whatever he was saying. She was very distraught as well, but there was very little information that we gained from her whatsoever."

Mayer recalled that Nels and Loretta "kind of cried their way through" the interview. "We were talking. We're trying to find out investigative background. It's a normal investigative technique. 'Okay, Dad, tell me what's going on here? What's happening?'" According to Mayer, "There was no indication from anybody that that was happening. There was no indication to us that the marriage was on the rocks. We questioned them, Nels and Loretta and John, 'Is there a divorce here? Is there? What's happening?'"

Mayer said of Nels and Loretta, "We gleaned as much information as we could from them." According to Mayer, the Rasmussens never suggested to him that John and Sherri had any marital problems. Nor was there any indication from them, Mayer said, "that there was an insurance policy, or anything like that. They had no indication that anything was wrong." Mayer said that based on what the Rasmussens told him, his impression of John and Sherri's marriage was that "they seemed to be very happy with one another."

Among the information Mayer recalled he learned from the Rasmussens during their initial meeting was that Nels was less than enamored with his son-in-law. Mayer said, "We did glean from them that he didn't think John was the greatest guy in the world. He wasn't the number one pick, but still went along with it, because it was his daughter's choice." Later in Mayer's 2014 interview, he said, "Nels didn't like the kid from the beginning. He never said he was a gold digger or anything like that, but he just didn't like him. It was a parent's prerogative, I guess. He told Sherri 'I don't really like this guy that much, but if you want to marry him, marry him.'"

Mayer said he felt for Nels. "Sherri was the apple of Nels Rasmussen's eye. She was his tomboy. She was the athlete that he wanted. She was very athletic, very into fitness, which was a little unusual at that time," Mayer said.

That Sherri was in excellent physical shape was, in Mayer's mind, another building block in his theory of how the botched burglary and murder unfolded. Even more significant to Mayer was something else he recalled Nels said during their first meeting. According to Mayer, Nels told him how bad he felt about some fatherly advice he gave to Sherri prior to her murder. Mayer recalled Nels was gutted with regret over what he had told Sherri to do.

Mayer recounted, in reference to his partner, Steve Hooks, "Basically, Steve and I heard this from Mr. Rasmussen, but I was the one he really directed that to. This is very significant in how to explain the murder." Mayer recalled of Nels, "Here's what he said that caused the death of Sherri Rasmussen. He told her, 'Los Angeles is a horrible place to live. There is nothing but a bunch of gangbangers out there, and a bunch of criminals, and every place that you go, there is crime.' He said, 'But if you go there, I understand. Get yourself a nice place, blah, blah, blah, blah, blah. Be safe. But if you ever come into contact in a situation, I want you to fight your way out. I don't want you to be hurt. I want you to fight with all of your might, just like you are an athlete. I want you to fight and go for it and win the fight.'"

According to Mayer, Nels's advice to Sherri to "go for it" lent credence to his theory of the murder. Mayer knew from the crime scene that the fight between Sherri and her killer was long, intense, and violent. Mayer believed, based in part on "that particular father's mantra to his lovely little daughter, here is what occurred. Sherri comes down and confronts this person," the burglar. Mayer continued, "This guy has a gun. He turns the gun at Sherri. Sherri, being this good little athlete, now goes for it, just like her daddy told her. She's fighting with this guy over the gun." In Mayer's theory, several shots were fired during this initial struggle, near the kitchen, but "Sherri is athletic enough, and she gets the gun away from this person. Now she's running down to activate the alarm in the hallway up at the front door."

Mayer saw this as Sherri's moment of truth. Mayer knew that in a fight for a gun, there was only one rule: win at all costs. No matter how physically fit Sherri was, she was a nurse, with none of the extensive LAPD self-defense and firearms training that Mayer had received as a police officer. Mayer believed that Sherri, "being a lovely human being," failed to grasp that "there's a difference between fighting and going for it, and having the gun now and the guy is coming back at you. You either have to make a decision or not, and that decision is to do what? Shoot or not shoot. Sherri had the gun, but she didn't have the moxie to shoot and kill somebody. She's a good guy."

In Mayer's scenario, because Sherri was unwilling to pull the trigger, the burglar confronted her again in the front entryway. Mayer recalled, "My formulation was, the burglar comes down. Now they're in the little hallway right down by the alarm, and another tremendous fight takes place. Sherri still has the gun but the burglar, in my opinion at this point, is struggling so hard, the only thing you can do is tremendously bite her on the arm, full mouth bite on the arm. It becomes so excruciating that she lets go of the gun. She lets go of the gun. It falls to the floor. The suspect at that time, in my opinion, in my original crime scene, now picks up the gun, hits her over the head with a vase, which was in the fighting process, knocks her down, then winds up shooting and executing her."

Mayer reasoned there were two burglars, rather than one, in part because of Sherri's stolen car. In Mayer's experience as a detective, it was unusual for a victim's car to be taken in a burglary. Burglars usually had their own car to load up with stolen property. A burglar who worked alone and had his own getaway car wouldn't need to steal another.

In Sherri's case, Mayer pictured two burglars downstairs in the living room. One burglar had already stacked the video equipment near the front door, their apparent point of entry. The second burglar went upstairs, Mayer thought probably to look for a purse or cash, and encountered Sherri near the kitchen.

Mayer theorized that the first burglar bolted out the front door at the sound of gunshots from upstairs and took off in the car they came in. Mayer said, "That is the method of operation of burglars. They want to split because they don't want to be seen. Once they're seen, they're identified, they get convicted." According to Mayer, "everybody" involved in the investigation, including Hooks and their supervisor Pida, assumed of the first burglar, "What does he do? He splits to get to his car, and splits."

As for the second burglar, Mayer said their consensus theory was that he chased Sherri down to the living room and killed her. The fact that the second burglar was armed, and possibly injured during the struggle, suggested to the detectives that it was unlikely he fled on foot. According to Mayer, the detectives collectively believed the second burglar rifled the keys to Sherri's BMW and used it to get away.

Most of all, Mayer was convinced that Nels's advice to Sherri, however well intentioned, led her directly into a situation from which there was no exit. Mayer said of Nels, "His line of thinking is that he was helping his daughter. It probably did help her. But when she came into a situation where she was to apply that information, guess what? She couldn't shoot the person." According to Mayer, when Nels realized that Sherri had followed his advice, "It killed him and it hurt him so deeply, because how would you like to tell your daughter to do something, and she does it, and it ends up killing her, and not helping her? That's what occurred."

Ironically, had Sherri not fought so tenaciously with her assailant, she might never have been bitten on her forearm. In this alternate history, with no struggle and no bite, there would have been no saliva left behind by the person who bit her, and no bite mark to swab the night of Sherri's murder. Without the bite mark swab as evidence, it would not have existed to analyze for DNA later, using technology that did not exist when Sherri was killed. Without the DNA results, the truth might never have been known that the person who bit Sherri was not a man, but a woman. In effect, had

Sherri not fought and been bitten by her killer, her murder might never have been solved.

According to Nels, however, he never gave Sherri the advice Mayer attributed to him, that if she ever encountered a criminal, she should fight her way out of the situation. Nor did Nels tell Mayer that he gave Sherri that advice, or express regret to Mayer that he did, in their first meeting or any time after, the Rasmussens recall.

According to Mayer, Nels and Loretta never once mentioned John's ex-girlfriend during their February 25 meeting at the Van Nuys station, let alone at any time during the first week of the LAPD's investigation of their daughter's murder.

Mayer also adamantly denied in 2014 that Nels ever told him in 1986 about any specific incidents between Sherri and John's ex-girlfriend prior to the murder. According to Nels and Loretta, Sherri called them in January, roughly a month before she was killed, and said she was home alone and discovered John's ex-girlfriend in their living room. Asked in 2014 whether Nels informed him of that in 1986, Mayer replied, "That is an absolute bullshit lie. He never told me that. No way. We'd have been all over her. We'd have arrested her for burglary. Are you kidding me? Or we would have done an Internal Affairs investigation as to why she's there. I mean, think about that. That would have been the greatest clue going. Why in the world would we not do something about that? It would be totally opposed to what John had told us."

"Never happened," Mayer continued. "Come on, Hooks would have jumped on that, or Pida would have jumped on that. Do you think if I would have had that information, wrote that down somewhere, that Pida wouldn't have looked at this, or Durrer wouldn't have looked at this, our two bosses, and go, 'Are you kidding me? This policewoman was in that house? Let's go get her.' That would have been incompetence. That would have been unfathomable. That would be the biggest sin in the whole wide world. Why would I do something like that, professionally? Are you kidding me? Think about how outlandish that is. He said, 'Oh, yeah, I told the detectives she was in the house.'"

Mayer dismissed Nels's recollection of what Sherri told her parents before her murder, as well as Nels's account of what he told Mayer about John's ex-girlfriend. Mayer attributed Nels's statements to guilty feelings about the advice Nels insists he never gave Sherri. Mayer said, "Do you not think that's a little embellishment on Nels's part, to rid a little bit of his personal anger of telling Sherri to defend herself? It's a little thing he's escaping on. He's saying, 'I told him.' Come on, he's doing anything to deflect his own personal anguish."

Sherri's sister Teresa recalls that she waited at the Van Nuys station with her husband, Brian, and Connie and Rachel, while Mayer met with Nels and Loretta. According to Teresa, when her parents and Mayer were done talking and came out to where they sat, Mayer gave her his business card. Teresa recalls Mayer told her, "If you have any questions about what's going on, or have any insights, give me a call."

Connie remembers her experience of going to the police station and meeting the detectives as "a strange encounter," and different than what she expected. Connie felt frustrated that the detectives did not give them more information.

Loretta, who, unlike her daughters, was in the meeting with Mayer, recalls it as an "ugly encounter."

After they met with Mayer, the Rasmussens drove from the police station to a Travelodge motel nearby. When they got there, they discovered that John and his parents were staying at the same motel. By chance, or fate, the Rasmussen and Ruetten families were given rooms on the same outdoor corridor, just a few doors apart. Both rooms were on the second floor and faced the motel's courtyard.

Connie recalls sitting with her parents and Rachel in their motel room. There, the Rasmussens began to process what Mayer had told them, and what else they knew independent of the LAPD. As they talked, they remembered more bits and pieces of things they knew directly from Sherri. On their own, to best of their ability, the Rasmussens started to try to put the pieces together.

Nels reached out to their pastor from Tucson, Charles Cook, to inform him of Sherri's death. Nels and Cook had been friends for more than twenty years. Cook had known Sherri and her sisters since they were little girls and had watched them grow up as part of his congregation. Sherri had asked Cook to perform her wedding, but Cook had said he couldn't because she and John were of different faiths and scripture forbade him to marry them. Sherri had told her parents she was disappointed at Cook's refusal but did not hold a grudge against him.

Less than a year later, on the day after Sherri's murder, Nels left Cook a message to call him at the motel in Van Nuys. Cook called back and said he was also in Los Angeles, for meetings. Nels told Cook about Sherri's murder and asked if he would speak at her memorial service. Nels recalls that Cook said, "Absolutely. But I want to meet with you." Nels gave Cook the address of the motel and their room number.

Cook came to the motel dressed in a black suit and tie, the Rasmussens recall. Nels thought of Cook as a buddy. Nels had to watch his slang a little around him, but other than that, he could talk with Cook like any friend. He and the Rasmussens spoke in the motel room for a short time, before Cook suggested, "Let's have prayer."

"Just a minute," Nels said.

Nels went outside and walked a few doors down, to the room John and his parents were in. Nels figured they were sharing one room, because when John answered the door, Nels saw the room had two double beds. Nels recalls he asked from the doorway, "Would you like to come over and have prayer at our room?"

John said yes. His parents, Richard and Margaret, came to Nels and Loretta's room as well. Nels led the Ruettens in and introduced Cook as their pastor from home. Cook said a few words, before praying, to try to lighten the moment a little, the Rasmussens recall. As Cook began to speak, Nels noticed he had left the door to their room open after the Ruettens came in. Nels could hear people talking in the motel's courtyard outside, and beyond it, the sound of passing street traffic.

According to the Rasmussens, when Nels went to close the door, John's mother let out a "whoop" and ran from the room so fast she almost knocked Nels over. John and his father went after her. Nels wondered whether Margaret thought Cook, in his black suit, was actually a hit man. Nels recalls that Margaret reacted as if she thought Cook was about to drop the pastor act and kill John or something.

John and Richard eventually came back in, but Margaret never did, according to the Rasmussens. Nels had to leave the door open. Nels recalls that Margaret stood just outside the doorway, close enough so she could hear, but ready to run the hundred-yard dash if need be. John and his father stayed and prayed with Cook and the Rasmussens. As soon as Cook finished leading prayer, the Ruettens left the room.

According to the Rasmussens, their prayer with Cook was the last time John's parents visited their room that week. Nels recalls that John did not come into their room again unless the door remained open. Nels and Loretta never went into the Ruettens' room. Following the mutually unnerving prayer incident, whenever the two families had to talk, they met on neutral ground, the outdoor corridor in front of their rooms.

Nels still felt bothered by John's behavior the night before, in the hours after John discovered Sherri's body. He questioned why John had not called him and Loretta immediately. Why did John wait more than six hours to tell them? Why did he have his father call instead of calling himself? When the Rasmussens got to Los Angeles, midday Tuesday, and saw John briefly at the police station, John's body language did not reassure Nels. He did not doubt John's emotions were genuine. What troubled Nels was his impression that the vast majority of John's emotional moments concerned himself rather than Sherri. Nels believed John wouldn't have acted so guilty around him and Loretta if he didn't have some knowledge of what happened to Sherri. The revelation that John was too emotional to complete his polygraph examination, information the Rasmussens recall they learned from Mayer on Tuesday, during their initial meeting with him, only intensified Nels's belief that John knew more than he was letting on.

According to Nels, he confronted John at the motel sometime on Tuesday. Nels recalls he told John he wanted him to run down everything he did on Monday, from the time he left for work until the time he came home. "I want you to tell me everything," Nels said. According to Nels, John couldn't even do that. Nels recalls he then asked John, "What did you see when you got home?"

John recounted how he drove up to the condo and saw the garage door open, and broken glass on the ground, Nels recalls. John told Nels he parked his car in the garage and started to walk upstairs to the first floor, but stopped when he saw the door at the top of the stairs was slightly open. According to Nels, John told him, "I just couldn't go in. I stood there for I don't know how long, until I had the courage to go in."

"Did you know if she was dead?" Nels asked.

"Not at first," John said, according to Nels.

"How did you know?"

"I put my foot against her, and she was stiff," John said, Nels recalls. Hearing John say that infuriated Nels. Nels wanted to lay John out. Nels thought, "That's how you treat an animal, not a person." It seemed to Nels that John was scared to touch Sherri, his own wife. Nels recalls John told him, "I just lost it for a minute. I went and sat down, and I said to myself, 'What am I going to do?'"

"Timewise, do you have any idea about how long it was before you called?"

"I don't know, but I think maybe five minutes or more. Then I called an ambulance," John said, Nels recalls.

Nels asked John why he had called for an ambulance, when it was obvious Sherri was already dead. John said he dialed 911 and told them he needed help.

John recounted during his 2009 LAPD interview what he told the Rasmussens when he saw them after Sherri's murder. John recalled that his primary focus was whether he had left the front door of the condo unlocked after his friend Mike visited on Sunday. John said, "I can vividly remember telling the Rasmussens, I thought I didn't check it. So I thought it might have been open. So that I remember vividly. That has been my issue: Why I didn't lock the door, or check it? So you can imagine, every day of my life when I lock doors, what I think about."

In the same interview, John said he could not recall whether he told Nels and Loretta about his relationship with his ex-girlfriend, Stephanie Lazarus, after Sherri's murder. "I may have told the Rasmussens about it, but I don't remember that," John told the LAPD in 2009.

According to Nels, he asked John to his face on Tuesday, the day after Sherri's murder, "What's the name of your ex-girlfriend?" Nels recalls that John ignored the question. The fact that John would not even tell him the name of his ex-girlfriend struck Nels at the time as another red flag.

Other things John once said to Nels came back to mind, and retrospectively seemed suspicious. Nels dwelled on the last time he saw Sherri, only two weeks earlier, when she and John visited Tucson for her birthday. Nels had suggested they meet in San Diego and celebrate Sherri's birthday on their boat, so she and John would save the expense of flying to Arizona. Nels recalls John told him, "Nels, I want to take her home." After Sherri's murder, Nels remembered John's remark, and it ate at him. In hindsight, Nels questioned John's insistence. Nels wondered if John wanted to take Sherri home because John sensed something was going to happen to her.

Nels never believed John played any role in the actual crime. At the same time, he could not shake his feeling that John was holding back information that could help solve Sherri's murder. Nels believed that John, as Sherri's husband, ought to be doing what Nels was doing. Fighting on her behalf. Demanding a thorough investigation from the police. Pushing for the truth to come out. Instead, John's behavior gave Nels the opposite impression, that John didn't want the whole story known. Nels believed there must be some reason why. He wanted to say to John, "This is your wife, not some stranger on the street." It bothered Nels that with so many unanswered questions about what happened to Sherri, John seemed incapable of answering simple questions himself.

Nels recalls that after his initial grilling of him at the motel, John stayed close by his parents. Although this made it harder for Nels to speak with John one-on-one, he did not give up. "I worked at him. His dad was there. His dad said, 'It doesn't do any good to quiz him. He didn't have any part in it.'" According to Nels, "John just shut up. It got to the point where, if I so much as just brought up anything in the line of questioning, anything, he would shut up, and he wouldn't talk for an hour. I just figured, 'Well, I'm going to have to let it fester a bit.'"

In the wake of Sherri's murder, the relationship between Nels and Richard Ruetten deteriorated further. Nels recalls that he kept pressuring John but could not get anything out of him. Nels finally confronted Richard. According to Nels, he told him, "Your son has failed a lie detector test. It could be because of his emotions, they're saying," referring to the police. "I think it's about time that he stands up and lets me know what he knows, and what's going on."

"I can tell you that John's not involved in this, and I want you to lay off," Richard replied, according to Nels.

Richard and Margaret were following their own parental instincts, no less than Nels and Loretta. Nels understood it was only natural for John's parents to want to protect him. However, the Rasmussens believed that if the shoe was on the other foot, and it was John who had been murdered instead of Sherri, John's parents would want to talk with Sherri and ask her questions, just as the Rasmussens wanted to question John. Nels thought Richard believed, mistakenly, that Nels was trying to tear down John. Nels and Loretta just wanted to know what happened to their child. Nels told Richard he had no intention of easing up on John until he answered his questions. Nels recalls, "I made no bones about it. I said, 'John needs to get in and help us.'"

The heated exchange produced "hard feelings" between Nels and Richard, Nels recalls. According to Nels, John defended his father. "If you're going to treat my dad like that, I don't want to have anything to do with you," Nels recalls John told him.

Because Richard died in 1996, his perspective on Sherri's murder and what happened in the days afterward will unfortunately never be known. Only John knows what he told his parents, and what they discussed privately after Sherri was killed.

Shortly before Richard's death, Nels received a phone call from him. Ten years had passed since Sherri's murder, during which time communication between the two families had dwindled. For several years after Sherri was killed, Loretta sent a Christmas card to Margaret, but not to John, Loretta recalls. Teresa, who next to Sherri was probably the closest in her family to John, sent him a Christmas card every year. Teresa did not dare tell Nels. Teresa knew her father would not have approved of her keeping in touch with John, even with a Christmas card. Teresa stopped sending John cards after he remarried, in 1993. According to Teresa, she stopped not of her own accord, or at John's request, but at the request of his mother. In her own Christmas card to Teresa that year, Margaret wrote that because John was getting remarried, Teresa should no longer send him Christmas cards. Years later, after Margaret's death, Teresa asked John whether he was aware of his mother's request. John told Teresa he didn't know anything about it.

When Richard called Nels in 1996, Sherri's murder was still unsolved. The two men had not spoken in ten years, since the day of Sherri's burial. According to Nels, Richard told him on the phone that he was dying of lung cancer. Richard asked Nels if he would come to San Diego to talk with him before he died. Richard said he wanted to "resolve" their relationship.

Nels asked Richard, "Are you willing to run down the whole story?"

"No, I just want to resolve our differences," Richard replied.

"You can't resolve our differences if you don't face up to the fact that we need to know what happened, and what John knows."

"I can't do that, even on my deathbed."

"Well, then we have nothing to talk about," Nels told Richard.

It is unknown whether John was aware of his father's overture to Nels, which was the last time Nels and Richard spoke. Nels believes Richard passed away within a week of their phone conversation. Later, Nels regretted his decision not to go see Richard in person. It felt to Nels at the time like a matter of principle, but in hindsight, he realized he had missed out on a golden opportunity. Despite their argumentative history, and the hard feelings that lingered after Sherri's murder, something had motivated Richard, on his deathbed, to reach out to Nels. Nels could only wonder what

Richard died wanting to tell him, and what else might have come out had Nels gone to San Diego and leveled with Richard in person. Nels believes that if he had, Sherri's murder might have been solved sooner.

Back in 1986, on the day after Sherri's murder, no one in the Ruetten or Rasmussen families knew what the future held. The heated argument at the motel between Nels and Richard simmered into a tense, uncomfortable standoff. There was no escape from the situation, or from one another. The LAPD's investigation of Sherri's murder was still in its first twenty-four hours. Nels's many questions for John remained unanswered. Just three months after Sherri and John's happy, picture-perfect wedding day, her murder involuntarily yoked the two families together in a relationship that was ever more painful and mistrustful.

The argument between Nels, Richard, and John had taken place outside, in front of their motel rooms. Teresa was sitting on the motel's outdoor staircase, and couldn't help but hear everything that was said. Teresa was five months pregnant, and heartbroken by her sister's death. Listening to her father and John's father argue, Teresa felt she couldn't take it. She couldn't deal with being around everyone and their emotions. Teresa told Brian she wanted to go home. Teresa recalls that they drove back to Loma Linda on Tuesday night. She and Brian did not return to Los Angeles until Sherri's memorial service on Friday morning.

Mayer recounted in his 2014 interview that he observed no discord between the Rasmussen and Ruetten families in 1986, in the wake of Sherri's murder. Nor did Mayer recall he heard anything, from either set of parents, about the possibility of a love triangle. Mayer said that in his experience as a homicide detective, "Usually you'll get a sense from the parents, somewhere along the line, as to, 'Was there something else involved here? Was there anything rocking?' The sense we got from the parents, it was obviously a lovely little relationship. They were in love and on their way to be little stars. He had a good job and she had a very good job and was being considered for a promotion, like to be in her other job. They were on their way. They were young superstars, good-looking kids."

According to Mayer, if there was any tension between John's and Sherri's parents, long-standing or otherwise, "We were never made aware of that." Mayer attributed the lack of knowledge to something else his experience as a homicide detective had taught him: "People are only telling us what they want us to hear." Mayer said, "You don't let it affect your investigation, obviously. But see, things like that would have been great for us to know early on." Mayer said the "only thing" about the families he picked up on was that Nels disliked John. Mayer recalled, "Nels didn't care for him. He didn't think he was the greatest guy in the whole wide world. I could see he didn't want him to be his son-in-law. About the fact that there is tension around them, we never knew about that. We never knew about that."

The detectives recorded two entries in the typed chrono on Tuesday afternoon, the day after Sherri's murder, both at 1:45 p.m.

John Ruetten's last name was misspelled as "Ruetter" in the first of the two entries. The mistake was repeated throughout the typed chrono, such that John's last name was not once spelled correctly. On each of the first seven pages of the typed chrono, which covered the first month of the LAPD's investigation, there was at least one reference to John "Ruetter," or someone else in the "Ruetter" family. The final six pages of the typed chrono chronicled the investigation from March 20 to May 19. In those six pages, two months of entries, there were zero references to John Ruetten or "Ruetter."

The first typed chrono entry Tuesday afternoon stated in full, *"Called John Ruetter. Victim poss received threatening phone calls at work."* The follow-up report indicated John called earlier, at 1:00 p.m.: *"On 2-25-86 at 1300 hrs., Detectives Mayer and Hooks received a phone call from John Ruetten. John indicated that the only thing he remembered was that Sherri had received some annoying phone calls at work. Glendale Adventist Hospital. John was informed by detectives that they would investigate this information."* John's last name was spelled correctly throughout the follow-up report.

The detectives' second typed chrono entry Tuesday afternoon pertained to the bite mark on Sherri's arm. When coroner's criminalist Lloyd Mahany collected her body late Monday night, he alerted the coroner's chief forensic dentist, Dr. Gerald Vale, about the bite mark. By Tuesday afternoon, Vale had examined the wound. The typed chrono entry read, *"Dr. Vale—LA C Coroner call bite marks good for comparison."* The follow-up report recounted, in more detail, *"On 2-25-86 at 1345 hrs., Detectives Mayer and Hooks received a phone call from LA County Deputy Coroner Dr. Vale. Vale indicated to Mayer and Hooks that the bite marks on victim Rasmussen were so severe and distinctive that they were good for comparison if a suspect was apprehended. This information is included in the autopsy report and is attached as an addendum."*

The call with Vale about the bite mark was the last activity the detectives recorded in the typed chrono on Tuesday, the day after Sherri's murder.

Mayer, in his 2014 interview, recalled he and Hooks spent Tuesday afternoon checking up on John. Mayer said, "We worked the rest of the day very hard on verifying his alibi." According to Mayer, they went to John's office, and the bank John had visited during lunch on Monday, and confirmed what John had told them. Mayer said, "It's a long, long time ago, but in essence, we verified his alibi."

The detectives' elimination of John as a suspect freed them up to focus on the next stage of their investigation. Mayer recalled, "From that point on, we started. Now, let's see what we could find from crime scene evidence. We took prints, blood spatters. I had a great cast made of her arm, took swabs of that, made calls to her work."

Whom the detectives contacted at Glendale Adventist was not documented in either the typed chrono or the follow-up report. Sherri's closest colleagues at the hospital, her friends Peggy Daly and Romelda Anderson, were never interviewed by the LAPD in 1986. Nor was Sherri's secretary, Sylvia Nielsen. Sylvia was the only eyewitness to the confrontation in Sherri's office, the summer before the murder, between Sherri and the woman Sherri told Sylvia was John's ex-girlfriend.

Romelda heard no speculation at the hospital, following Sherri's murder, about a different motive than what the media reported. Romelda recalls the day they got the news, work at the hospital seemed to come to a standstill. Everyone just sat around talking about Sherri, because it was so shocking that she was dead. According to Romelda, "We couldn't do anything else but think of how nice and how great a person she was, and how sad it was that she had been murdered. The whole hospital at that point was just in shell shock, the day we heard. It started with what people heard in the news, and then some more people listened to the news over the radio. I think we just kept wanting more details, and grabbed at anything. It was confirmed that she had died. There wasn't anything we could do but grieve."

Romelda and Peggy both recall that a local television news crew from KABC came to the hospital Tuesday and interviewed them on camera about Sherri and what had happened. The interviews were taped in the hospital's public relations office. Romelda recalls, "I remember them asking how I felt about this event, the incident. I remember saying something like, 'She did not deserve to have this happen to her.'"

Romelda's statement was true, but as soon as she said it, she worried it might come across on television as insensitive. Romelda wondered how it would sound to someone watching the news who didn't know Sherri. Romélda feared it might seem like she thought other people deserved to have this happen to them, but not Sherri.

Romelda made sure to watch the news on KABC that evening, to see how she came off. Romelda watched the entire news program, but for unknown reasons, the report on Sherri never aired. Romelda recalls, "For myself, I was glad it didn't air, because I didn't know that I did a good job of representing the gravity of what happened to Sherri. But for her, I felt it was too bad that she was not honored more." Romelda assumed a bigger news story must have preempted Sherri's.

In a city as violent as Los Angeles was in 1986, with more than eight hundred recorded homicides that year, individual murders were not automatically newsworthy. The LAPD had announced publicly that it appeared Sherri was killed during a burglary. On the surface, there was nothing extraordinary about her case. In the media calculus, it mattered little how beloved she was by her family and friends, or how irreplaceable her colleagues at the hospital considered her. Given whatever else was going on in Los Angeles and the world that Tuesday evening in February 1986, Sherri's case evidently didn't make the cut at KABC. Sherri's family and friends do not recall any other television news coverage of her case in the days and weeks after her murder.

Althea left the hospital after work Tuesday and decided she didn't want to go home. Home was where her phone was. She didn't want talk to anybody or answer any questions. Althea went over to a girlfriend's instead, where no one could contact her. Her friend had also been a nurse at Glendale Adventist, in the hospital's operating room. Her friend knew who Sherri was but did not know her personally. Althea and her friend both sewed as a hobby. Sewing relaxed Althea, and she just wanted to try to unwind, and not be disturbed for a while. She knew she could do that at her friend's place. They didn't have to talk to each other. They could just be. Althea was still processing that Sherri was gone. They sat together and sewed until nine or ten o'clock that night, before Althea finally went home to her family.

Tuesday evening, John's friend Matt Gorder, and Matt's wife, Anita, went to see John at the motel in Van Nuys. Matt had heard about Sherri's death from Anita, who had called him at work that morning to tell him. Matt had not seen John and Stephanie together since college, almost five years before Sherri's murder. Although Matt was one of John's closest friends, John never confided to him about his years-long sexual relationship with Stephanie.

The last time Matt had seen Stephanie was sometime in 1983, after she also had graduated. He and Anita were jogging around the perimeter of UCLA's campus in Westwood. Matt and Anita were heading north on Veteran Avenue, toward Sunset, when they crossed paths with Stephanie, jogging in the other direction. Matt turned around and ran with Stephanie for half a mile or so. They talked as they jogged, just to say hello, and then parted ways.

Matt and Anita last saw John and Sherri together at Matt's sister's wedding, on February 15. John and Sherri had seemed to Matt that night like newlyweds and very much in love.

Ten days later, Matt and Anita drove to the motel in Van Nuys to offer their condolences to John in person. The mood could not have been more different than the last time they saw him, happy and with Sherri. Matt testified in court in 2012 that John seemed to him in shock, and very quiet, at the motel. Matt thought it was an understandable state for John to be in, given the circumstances. Matt told John that they did not have to talk about Sherri's case unless John wanted to. According to Matt, he and John never discussed the details of Sherri's murder or the LAPD's investigation.

Stephanie's Daily Field Activities Report for day watch on Tuesday, February 25, indicates that she and her partner Mike Alexander answered seven radio calls during their eight hours on patrol. In between calls, they assisted a citizen with a locked car and issued one citation, for an unregistered vehicle. Tuesday morning from 9:15 to 9:45 a.m., Stephanie and Alexander performed *"extra patrol"* for *"narco activity"* at a park in Granada Hills. From 11:00 to 11:35, they were back at Devonshire station for "admin duties." They took Code 7, their meal break, from 12:25 to 1:10 p.m.

Later that afternoon, from 2:15 until 3:00, they handled a 415 call, for a group disturbing the peace outside of Northridge Middle School. Although their log did not specify, the group was likely schoolkids just let out for the day. The school was in the southernmost part of the Devonshire Division, close to its boundary with the neighboring Van Nuys Division. During those forty-five minutes, Stephanie was barely two miles from John and Sherri's condo, the scene of Sherri's murder.

According to their DFAR log, she and Alexander spent the last forty minutes of their watch at the station performing additional *"admin duties,"* of which Stephanie noted on the log, *"Info to Sgt. Setty."* The final entry on their DFAR log, end of watch, was at 4:15 p.m.

In her datebook, Stephanie wrote for February 25, *"Hair perm 1730,"* presumably a hair appointment after work, at 5:30 p.m. It is unknown whether Stephanie kept the appointment.

Stephanie's diary entry for the day was uncharacteristically brief. In its entirety, it read:

0730—1615
ALEXANDER
A49
DEV
2-25-86

Mike drove. For work out today we played basketball at Northridge Park.

We didn't do much. In fact I can't even remember what we did. But the day was boring and nothing happened that was worth remembering. Except that I'm going to morning watch for sure.

Stephanie's diary entry, February 25, 1986

17

The First 48 Hours Ends

(February 26 and 27, 1986)

By Wednesday morning, February 26, thirty-six hours had passed since John discovered Sherri's body.

The typed version of the LAPD's chrono for the Rasmussen case noted only one entry on Wednesday morning. It referred to Sherri's autopsy, and it read in full, "*0900—Post at coroners—Dr. Sherry did post—3 shots. Beat with statue.*"

The LAPD's follow-up report, authored by Mayer in May, three months later, recounted, "*On 2-26-86 at 0900 Hrs, Detectives Mayer and Hooks attended the autopsy of Sherri Rasmussen. The autopsy was conducted by Dr. Sherry. The deceased died as a result of gunshot wounds to the chest. Any of the three wounds could have been fatal.*" Later in the follow-up report, Mayer wrote, "*On 2-26-86, Dr. Sherry, M.D., Deputy Medical Examiner, conducted an autopsy on the deceased at the Los Angeles County Coroner's Office. Caused [sic] of death was listed as gunshot wounds to the chest. The bullets entered the chest cavity and literally exploded the heart. Any of the three shots would have been fatal.*"

Although the LAPD's typed chrono and follow-up report both refer to a "Dr. Sherry," the deputy medical examiner assigned to perform Sherri Rasmussen's autopsy was in fact a doctor named Susan Selser. Like the consistent misspelling in the typed chrono of John's last name as "Ruetter," how and why Selser was misidentified in the chrono and follow-up report is a mystery.

It was standard practice when a murder victim was brought to the coroner's office for the body to be photographed. The morning of Sherri's autopsy, the photographer on duty was deputy coroner Carlos Celaya. Autopsy photographs were taken in the forensic photography room, which had a plastic table that could be washed down. Other workers placed the body on the table before Celaya came in.

After Celaya completed the first set of photographs, and Selser observed the body clothed, Celaya removed the clothing, which in Sherri's case consisted of her bathrobe, tank top, and panties. Later, the clothing was hung in a metal evidence cage, which resembled a three-sided closet on wheels. At night, the evidence cage was rolled into the coroner's drying room, across the hall from the forensic photography room, where it was locked and left overnight for the clothing to dry.

While removing Sherri's bathrobe, Celaya recovered a bullet that was wedged between her back and the fabric. Celaya gave the bullet to Selser for safekeeping as evidence. Once the clothing was removed, the body was washed of blood, and a second set of photographs was taken.

The autopsy consisted of an external followed by an internal examination. As the autopsy progressed, Selser documented her findings by hand on a series of preprinted forms and diagrams of a generic body. Later, Selser produced a typed report with detailed descriptions of Sherri's injuries.

Selser diagrammed the location of the three gunshot entry wounds in Sherri's chest. Selser numbered them one to three. The numbers were not intended to suggest the gunshots were sustained in that order. Without additional forensic evidence, it was impossible for Selser to determine in an autopsy the sequence of a homicide victim's injuries. Nor was it possible for Selser to tell what position the victim's body was in when each shot was fired, for instance standing or flat on the ground.

The gunshot wound Selser labeled #1 was in the center of Sherri's chest. It was a through-and-through wound, meaning the bullet passed all the way through the body and exited. The entry wound for #1 was darker in appearance than the other two. *"Blackish soot is noted along the wound defect and wound track,"* Selser wrote in her final report. Selser also noted the skin around the entry wound appeared blistered. This was consistent with a muzzle imprint. Like the soot, it was a hallmark of a contact gunshot wound, meaning the muzzle was up against the victim when the gun was fired. The bullet passed through Sherri's rib cage, right lung, and right bronchus, the airway between the trachea and the lung, before it exited her back. Because a person cannot live long with a hemorrhage in that airway, or with blood in their lungs, Selser considered gunshot wound #1 would have been rapidly fatal.

Gunshot entry wounds #2 and #3 were reddish in color, with none of the black soot and skin abrasions Selser observed around the edges of #1. The absence of these characteristics indicated that the other two bullets that struck Sherri were fired when the gun was some distance from her body. It was impossible for Selser to pinpoint the range, however, beyond the fact that neither appeared to be a contact wound.

The entry wound Selser designated #2 was in Sherri's upper left chest. Selser determined that this bullet pierced Sherri's thoracic aorta. Any hole in the thoracic aorta would cause internal bleeding and rapid loss of blood pressure. The same bullet also passed through Sherri's thoracic vertebrae and spinal cord, injuries Selser believed likely disabled Sherri and left her unable to walk. Selser recovered from Sherri's back, lodged just under her skin, the bullet that had produced gunshot wound #2.

Gunshot wound #3 was through-and-through. Selser documented the bullet's trajectory, from its entry point in Sherri's lower left chest, through both ventricles of her heart, and finally her left lung, before it exited her back. Given the blood loss and internal injuries caused by gunshot wounds #2 and #3, Selser categorized both wounds as fatal.

Selser placed the two bullets recovered during the autopsy in separate evidence envelopes. On each envelope, Selser wrote the coroner's case number, along with the date, time, and location where that bullet was recovered. Selser also described both bullets in her final autopsy report.

The bullet Selser extracted herself from gunshot wound #2 was, she wrote, "*a 9 mm. silvery flattened-nose, gold based missile, recovered from the subcutaneous tissues of the mid back. It is not marked across the base, shows minimal deformity.*" That the bullet was not deformed increased its potential value as forensic evidence.

A fired bullet spins rapidly, like a well-thrown football, down the barrel of the gun. The inside of a gun barrel is not smooth but lined with a spiral pattern called "lands and grooves." As the bullet travels down the barrel, it picks up nicks and scratches that can later help identify what make and model of gun fired it. Different firearms manufacturers have their own distinctive lands and grooves patterns. Individual guns can also have unique rifling characteristics. If the suspected murder weapon was recovered by the police, ballistics experts could compare the impressions on a test-fired bullet to the one Selser recovered during the autopsy. A match would prove it was the same gun used to kill Sherri.

About the bullet Celaya recovered earlier that morning, Selser wrote, *"The photographer reports that the missile dropped from the posterior aspect of the body upon removal of the clothing. It therefore is consistent with the missile from Gunshot Wound #1 or #3,"* meaning either of the two through-and-through wounds.

Selser noted in the autopsy report that she kept the two evidence envelopes in her pocket until 2:00 p.m. that afternoon, when she placed them in an evidence safe. Richard Heath, a coroner's evidence custodian, retrieved the envelopes the next day. For chain of custody purposes, Heath hand-wrote on each envelope his name, the date and time, and where he received it, before the evidence was stored.

While the official cause of Sherri's death was multiple gunshot wounds, Selser documented several other injuries. These included the oval-shaped bite mark on the inside of Sherri's left forearm. The coroner's chief forensic dentist, Dr. Gerald Vale, had already examined the bite mark and had a cast made of it the previous day. Vale had also discussed the bite mark wound with the detectives. Vale informed them that *"the bite marks on victim Rasmussen were so severe and distinctive that they were good for comparison if a suspect was apprehended,"* according to the LAPD's follow-up report. Forensic science experts now question the reliability of bite mark analysis. In 1986, however, it was still accepted as good science that a bite mark on a victim's body could be matched definitively to a specific suspect's teeth.

To determine when Sherri was bitten in relation to her time of death, Selser cut a small piece of skin from the area of the bite wound. Selser sent the tissue sample to the histology lab, which prepared a microscopic slide. Under the microscope, Selser saw in the tissue some hemorrhaging and bleeding but no inflammation, an indication that the bite was inflicted close to the time of Sherri's death.

Selser also noted pattern abrasions on both of Sherri's wrists. The pattern was most perceptible on her right wrist. Selser observed on the back of her right wrist two parallel lines, more than an inch long but just a quarter of an inch wide. The abrasions appeared consistent with ligature marks, possibly the result of Sherri's wrists having been bound with a rope or cord. Both of her wrists were also smeared with blood.

Selser made note of several cuts and abrasions on Sherri's hands. On the back of her left hand, along the base of her thumb, Selser observed a cluster of small red dots. Selser suspected it could be stippling, another forensic hallmark of close-range gunshot wounds. When a gun is fired, particles of gunpowder are propelled at high velocity from the muzzle. If the gun is fired close to the victim, with nothing between the muzzle and the victim's skin, the gunpowder particles can impact with enough force to draw blood. These pinpoint abrasions appear on the skin as red dots. Stippling can occur around the gunshot entry wound or any body part that is exposed and within range of the gunpowder effect. Stippling on a victim's hand can indicate the hand was outstretched toward the muzzle when the gun was fired.

Selser documented fifteen distinct injuries to Sherri's head, the majority of which were on the right side of her face. The most severe were around her right eye, which was bruised and swollen shut. Before Sherri's body was washed during the autopsy, dried blood had been caked around her eye and smeared across her face and forehead. Cleaning off the blood allowed Selser to see her injuries more clearly.

Selser observed near Sherri's right eye an oddly shaped wound that was partly straight and partly circular. The straight part was half an inch long and bisected the circle. The skin at the center of the circle, however, appeared undamaged compared with the perimeter, which was darkly bruised. Selser thought the injury pattern might be an identifiable toolmark. As the name suggests, a toolmark was a mark imprinted on the body by whatever tool or object caused the blunt force trauma. To document the possible toolmark, Celaya took close-up photos.

Although the injury near Sherri's eye was well documented during her autopsy, no analysis of the toolmark occurred in the months after her murder. Not until 2009, more than twenty years later, was the tool-

.38 Smith & Wesson model 49 revolver (exemplar gun, side and muzzle views)

mark pictured in the autopsy photos compared to the muzzle of a specific make of gun, a .38 Smith & Wesson model 49 revolver. The model 49 was a small revolver with a two-inch barrel. Its compactness made it

Left to right: cast of muzzle, muzzle view, silicone mold (2009 images)

a popular choice as a backup weapon among LAPD officers in the 1980s.

Because the murder weapon used to kill Sherri has never been recovered, an exemplar Smith & Wesson model 49 was used to produce a cast model of its muzzle. The replica cast of the muzzle tip included the gun sight, a steel prong nearly flush with the tip of the barrel, just above the muzzle hole.

Without the actual murder weapon, it is impossible to say definitively that the muzzle of a Smith & Wesson model 49 revolver caused the toolmark injury near Sherri's eye. Nor was it possible to tell from the autopsy photographs how the toolmark was imprinted. Was Sherri pistol-whipped with the muzzle of the gun? Or was the muzzle pressed to the corner of her eye so hard that it bruised and broke the skin? Based on the autopsy photographs, either scenario was possible.

When an image of the muzzle cast was overlaid on the photo of Sherri's eye injury, the concordance between them was striking. The straight laceration was consistent with the gun sight above the muzzle, and the circular abrasion with the muzzle itself. The lack of bruising at the center of the circular abrasion lined up with the muzzle hole. Unlike the steel gun parts, the muzzle hole was a void, which left the skin under it relatively undamaged.

A second toolmark just below Sherri's eye was fainter but also consistent with the gun muzzle. The other injuries to her face and head were too generalized to determine forensically whether they also were caused by the gun, or a different hard object.

Selser also noted an injury inside Sherri's mouth, a half-inch laceration of the upper frenulum, the small flap of skin between the upper gum and lip. A torn frenulum was consistent with a hand held over Sherri's mouth during the fatal struggle. Merely placing a hand over someone's mouth was unlikely to tear the frenulum. Significant force had to have been applied to stretch the skin and cause it to tear.

Selser found no injuries during the autopsy to suggest that Sherri was

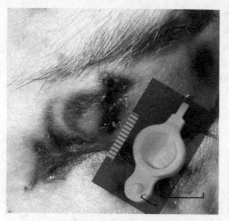 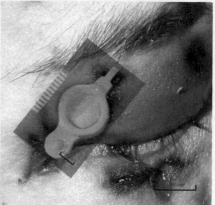

Muzzle cast overlay on Sherri's autopsy photo (2009 images)

sexually assaulted. Selser was unable to determine the time of death, which was later recorded on Sherri's death certificate as "unknown."

At the end of the autopsy, Selser collected a blood sample from Sherri. It was standard practice in homicide cases for the coroner to preserve a sample of the victim's blood. Although DNA analysis did not yet exist in 1986, ABO blood typing had long been used to interpret blood evidence at crime scenes. If investigators knew the victim's blood type and discovered blood of a different type at the location, that information could help detectives to identify or exclude potential suspects.

Sherri's blood sample was stored initially in a vial. Later that day, a coroner's evidence custodian, Joe Murillo, picked up the vial from the autopsy room and took it to the evidence room in the basement of the building. There, Murillo filled out a blood swatch card, a three-by-five-inch card with a square of cloth affixed. He poured Sherri's blood from the vial onto the cloth square, then signed his name and noted the date and time on the coroner's evidence log. The swatch card remained on the counter in the evidence room overnight to dry. When Murillo came into work the next morning, he placed Sherri's blood swatch card in one of the coroner's freezers, filed numerically by case number, to be stored indefinitely.

Murillo was also responsible for preserving the clothing Sherri wore when she was killed. The day after the autopsy, he retrieved her bathrobe, tank top, and panties from the coroner's drying room. He packaged each item separately in a brown paper bag, then wrapped the three bags in brown paper to form a single bundle, which he tied off with string. Murillo stored the bundle of Sherri's clothes on a shelf in the evidence room, alongside bundles of clothes from countless other cases.

On the day Sherri's autopsy was performed, the major news stories were political turmoil in the Philippines and growing recriminations at NASA over the month-old *Challenger* disaster.

In that day's *Los Angeles Times*, Sherri's unsolved murder merited only a paragraph under "Local News in Brief." The *Times* report identified Sherri by name, but John only as "her husband." The *Times* also misstated how many times she was shot. Under the headline WOMAN FOUND SLAIN IN APARTMENT IDENTIFIED, the paper reported:

> *Police on Tuesday identified a woman found shot to death in her ransacked Van Nuys apartment Monday as Sherri Rae Rasmussen, 29. Homicide detectives believe Rasmussen was killed when she surprised one or more intruders who stole her automobile after beating her and shooting her once in the upper body. Investigators were searching for the car, a silver two-door, 1985 Model 318i BMW with the license plate 1MJK850. Rasmussen had stayed home from work on Monday because she was ill, police said. Her body was discovered on the living room floor when her husband returned from work about 6 p.m.*

The *Los Angeles Daily News* also ran a story on Wednesday, headlined SLAYING VICTIM IDENTIFIED. As in the *Times*, Sherri was named but John was not. The *Daily News* story included a quote from Van Nuys homicide coordinator Roger Pida. Pida's statement seemed to exonerate John completely. The *Daily News* reported:

> *A woman found dead in her Van Nuys home was identified by police Tuesday as Sherri Rae Rasmussen, nursing director of the 151-bed critical-care and surgical units at Glendale Adventist Medical Center.*
>
> *Los Angeles police theorize Rasmussen, 29, was bludgeoned and shot to death Monday by a burglar she surprised in her condominium on Balboa Boulevard in Van Nuys.*
>
> *There were no signs of forced entry, Van Nuys Detective Roger Pida said.*
>
> *Althea Kennedy, vice president of nursing at the hospital, said Rasmussen called in sick Monday, apparently because she strained her back during an aerobic workout.*

Rasmussen's husband found her body on the living-room floor when he returned from work at 6 p.m. Monday, Pida said.

"Her husband is not being considered a suspect in this at all," Pida said.

The condominium was ransacked and the newly married couple's silver 1985 BMW was missing from the garage in the complex. Police issued an all-points bulletin for the vehicle with license-plate number 1MJK850 and its occupants.

Investigators do not have any suspects in custody.

Although the *Daily News* reported that Sherri had stayed home from work because she hurt her back doing aerobics, and attributed that information to her boss, Althea, the provenance of this story is murky. According to what John told Mayer on the night of the murder, Sherri decided to stay home because she was dreading having to teach a class that day at the hospital. John did not mention aerobics or any back injury to Mayer. John said Sherri told him she called the hospital and "talked to somebody," but John did not hear the actual phone call. When John was interviewed by the LAPD in 2009, John repeated his belief that Sherri had stayed home not because she was sick, but because she did not feel like teaching the class. John also said in 2009 that Sherri did not go to aerobics. It is unknown whom Sherri spoke with at the hospital the morning of her murder, and what reason she gave them for not going into work.

A third news article that day about Sherri's case ran in the *Foothill Leader*, a local paper that covered the San Gabriel Valley and nearby Glendale, where Sherri worked. The story, headlined NO LEADS IN NURSE'S MURDER, referred to John but did not name him. The *Foothill Leader* reported:

Police do not have any suspects yet in the murder of a nursing director at Glendale Adventist Medical Center who was found dead at her Van Nuys apartment Monday.

Sherri Rasmussen, 29, was discovered beaten and shot to death about 6 p.m. at her 7100 Balboa Blvd. apartment, authorities said.

She had been the nursing director in charge of the Critical Care and Surgical Unit at Glendale Adventist Medical Center, Wilson Terrace Campus, a hospital official said.

No details were immediately available regarding Rasmussen's death, but police reports indicate that her car was stolen at the same time.

She apparently had been home, sick from work, when the incident

happened, and her husband came home to find her shot and the house
burglarized.

Upon hearing the news of her death Tuesday, hospital co-workers
were "deeply shocked and saddened," said Ken Rozell, the hospital's public
information coordinator.

"She was very well liked—a big part of the nursing team," Rozell said.

At the hospital, Sherri's colleagues Althea and Romelda spent Wednesday morning planning her memorial service. They decided with the Rasmussens that the service would be held in two days' time, on Friday, at the Vallejo Drive Seventh-Day Adventist Church across the street from the hospital. Althea wanted the service to be held close by, so as many of Sherri's colleagues who wished to attend could do so. Romelda volunteered to take the lead in organizing the service.

Planning Sherri's funeral and burial fell to the Rasmussens. Nels recalls he asked John, in a conversation at their motel, whether John wanted to be part of the planning for the funeral. According to Nels, John had nothing to offer. Nels suggested he and Loretta could purchase a family plot in Tucson. John replied he thought it was a good idea for Sherri to be buried in Tucson and for the Rasmussens to make the arrangements. John's apparent ambivalence about Sherri's burial arrangements made Nels feel that John had no interest in Sherri anymore. It made him feel sad for Sherri, even though he knew that she would never know.

According to the Rasmussens, Mayer warned them that the injuries to Sherri's face were so severe they might not want to see her body. Mayer said they might never be able to forget the sight. Nels decided he would rather remember Sherri the way he last saw her, with a smile. The Rasmussens never viewed Sherri's body, either in Los Angeles or in Tucson, before her burial.

During the day on Wednesday, Nels, Loretta, and Connie went to Forest Lawn mortuary to purchase a casket. Connie knew Sherri had always had a phobia about what happened after a person died and was buried. Sherri once told her sister, when they were younger, that the thought of worms and bugs getting into her body creeped her out. It was important to Connie that Sherri's casket was a completely airtight, top-of-the-line model.

Connie also arranged for Sherri to be buried with a lime-green orchid corsage. Lime-green was Sherri's favorite color. When Connie and Sherri were in high school together in Arizona, their school held occasional socials where boys asked girls out and everyone got dressed up for the night. Connie recalled one social for which Sherri had no date. Connie bought Sherri a lime-green orchid corsage so she would not feel inferior to the girls whose dates had given them corsages to wear.

The Rasmussens had to decide on short notice what clothes to bury Sherri in. Just a few weeks earlier, Nels and Loretta had given Sherri a few dresses for her birthday. Loretta had bought the dresses at Casual Corner, a women's clothing chain.

Nels and Loretta recall they asked Mayer on Wednesday afternoon for access to the condo so they could retrieve one of Sherri's birthday dresses. According to the Rasmussens, Mayer told them, "You won't be getting back in there for at least several days. There's an investigation in progress."

From the Rasmussens' perspective, being denied access to the condo by the LAPD seemed at the very least unfair. Nels knew John and his parents had been permitted inside since the murder, accompanied by a police officer, to get things John needed. According to the Rasmussens, however, Mayer never let them into the condo in the days after Sherri's murder, even with a police escort. In the end, Loretta and Connie went back to Casual Corner and repurchased one of the dresses they had given Sherri for her birthday. Not being allowed to see the crime scene also fueled Nels's growing impression that important information about Sherri's murder was being withheld from him and Loretta.

Connie shared her father's frustration with how little information the LAPD seemed willing to share with her family. Connie's impression of the detectives was that they were very secretive and wouldn't tell or show them anything. Connie wanted to see the crime scene to know what had really happened. Perhaps because she considered herself a visual person, Connie felt she needed tangible evidence to accept that what the police had told them was true. It made no sense to her that burglars would take the risk of breaking into a home and then kill someone but leave basically empty-handed.

Her parents followed Mayer's lead and did not insist on seeing the condo or Sherri's body. Although it complicated Connie's own acceptance of her sister's death, she honored her parents' wishes. Had she been given the choice, she would have wanted to see Sherri one more time. As terrible as it would have been, Connie wanted to be able to hold her sister and say goodbye. Connie felt that when you touch something, you know it, versus when someone just tells you. The way the detectives spoke to her family made her feel they were hiding something. For Connie, the LAPD's secrecy created a void her imagination rushed to fill. Connie knew her mind was playing tricks on her, but still she thought, "Maybe Sherri's not dead. Maybe something happened and she had to join the witness protection program." Connie struggled to accept the reality.

One legitimate reason the LAPD could have offered the Rasmussens for denying them access to the crime scene was the presence of ninhydrin, the toxic chemical used to enhance latent fingerprints. On Tuesday, the same day the Rasmussens arrived in Los Angeles, an LAPD fingerprint analyst sprayed ninhydrin on the walls in the condo's front entryway. Because the chemical reaction can take up to seventy-two hours to develop, it would not have been unreasonable for the police to seal the location for that long.

In Sherri's case, seventy-two hours from Tuesday was Friday, the day the Rasmussens left Los Angeles and returned to Tucson for Sherri's burial. According to Nels and Loretta, however, Mayer never cited ninhydrin as an explanation for why they could not retrieve a dress to bury Sherri in. The Rasmussens did not get into the condo until they returned to Los Angeles a few weeks later. By then, the condo had been completely cleaned up, with the living room carpet replaced, other cosmetic repairs made, and all evidence of the murder removed.

Mayer did mention ninhydrin to John during his interview on Monday night, a few hours after John discovered Sherri's body. Mayer told John they would do a walk-through of the condo the next morning. Mayer assured John, "I'll be right with you and everything will be taken care of, and you can get out whatever you need for a day or so, all right? Because you won't be able to go back into your apartment for about three days, because we're going to have to do some things on the walls to lift some fingerprints off the walls. It's called the ninhydrin process, and it's a little caustic chemical activity, so you won't be able to go in for a couple of days after that. I'll allow you to get some clothes out and everything, so everything will be all set."

John and his mother, Margaret, met with the detectives in the condo on Tuesday morning. John may have taken that opportunity to retrieve a few days' worth of clothing, as Mayer suggested he could. Soon after the walk-through ended, the LAPD's fingerprint analyst sprayed the ninhydrin solution, and the condo was sealed.

Mayer denied in his 2014 interview that he ever barred the Rasmussens from entering the condo after the murder. "That's not true," Mayer said of the Rasmussens' account. Asked whether the ninhydrin prevented him from granting Nels and Loretta access to the crime scene, Mayer replied, "Not really. We would have let them get in if they wanted to. We would have let them get whatever they want. They never asked to do that. What reason would I have for not giving her some kind of clothing out of that house? Are you kidding me? I mean, come on. What would that do, or detract, or add to that case? Nothing. To put some particular dress on your daughter when you're going to bury her, or something like that? There is no way. Common sense even figures that out." Mayer insisted, "There is absolutely, professionally no way that I wouldn't allow a parent to go obtain anything of his deceased daughter's to make him pleased, or to make him feel a little bit better. There isn't a homicide detective around that wouldn't allow that to occur. That's bitterness talking."

Only two entries were recorded in the typed version of the LAPD's chrono for the afternoon of Wednesday, February 26, the second full day of the investigation.

The first entry read: *"1500—Booked purse rec. from loc."* Sherri's purse had been in the LAPD's hands for two days, since Monday evening. Earlier that day, it had been brought to a neighbor's door by two Latino men, who apparently found it nearby and wanted to return it. Later that night, the neighbor gave the purse to the police.

Although Sherri's BMW and her brown leather purse were the only two items stolen in the supposed burglary, no inventory of the recovered purse's contents was recorded in the typed chrono. The LAPD's follow-up report only noted, in reference to the detectives' walk-though with John the morning after Sherri's murder, *"John was unable to ascertain if anything was missing from the residence other than Sherri's purse and its contents."* The follow-up report did not specify what was in the purse, either before it was stolen or after the neighbor turned it over to the LAPD.

According to the Rasmussens, they never saw Sherri's purse after it was recovered.

When Loretta learned that Sherri's purse had been found, she thought of Sherri and John's marriage certificate, and a conversation she had with Sherri a month or so before her death. The conversation took place in the wake of an argument between Sherri and John over their finances. Sherri planned to open separate savings accounts for herself and John, in addition to a joint checking account. Sherri was still using her maiden name professionally but was transitioning to Sherri Ruetten in her personal life. Loretta suggested she keep the marriage certificate in her purse, in case she needed to prove her identity at the bank. Loretta believed Sherri had kept the marriage certificate in her purse since that conversation. More recently, Loretta had sent her a check, made out to Sherri Rasmussen, for her and John's wedding photographs. Loretta thought Sherri might have needed the marriage certificate to cash the check.

According to the Rasmussens, Loretta informed Mayer that she believed Sherri kept the marriage certificate in her purse, and asked him whether it was still in the purse when it was found. Mayer told them it wasn't, the Rasmussens recall. The Rasmussens also asked John about the marriage certificate, in the days after Sherri's murder, but John said he didn't know anything about it. According to the Rasmussens, Mayer never picked up on the symbolism and potential significance of the missing marriage certificate, or raised it with them again.

In the absence of any definitive information about what happened to the marriage certificate, Nels developed two theories. The first involved John's ex-girlfriend. Despite what the detectives had told him, Nels still considered her the prime suspect in Sherri's murder. Because nothing else of value was apparently stolen from the purse, Nels thought maybe the ex-girlfriend took the marriage certificate as some kind of twisted trophy. Nels believed it was a strong possibility.

Nels's other theory reflected how much his trust in John had eroded. Although Nels had no proof, he also thought it was possible that John had kept the marriage certificate. Nels presumed that John knew about the separate accounts that Sherri had set up at the bank. Nels wondered if possession of the marriage certificate enabled John to access Sherri's other accounts and clean them out. According to Nels, he asked John about the accounts in the days after Sherri was killed, but John would not answer any questions at all about his and Sherri's finances.

Just a few weeks prior, when John and Sherri visited Tucson for her birthday, Nels had tried to persuade them to move there. Nels and Loretta took them to look at houses for sale. Nels offered to help with the down payment and told John he would help him find a good job. Nels thought John seemed in favor of the idea at the time, although Sherri ultimately told her parents no. It bothered Nels that in the span of a few weeks, John went from being interested to all of a sudden having no interest in talking about anything, not even Sherri's own bank accounts, after her death.

In 2009, John was asked by an LAPD detective whether his and Sherri's marriage certificate was taken in the murder. John said he did not recall what was taken and would check to see if he still had it. Later that day, John informed the LAPD that he was unable to find the marriage certificate, and that he did not recall having one returned to him during the investigation.

Nothing about Sherri and John's missing marriage certificate was documented in 1986 in the LAPD's typed chrono or the follow-up report. What happened to their marriage certificate, and whether it was intentionally stolen, may never be known.

The second Wednesday afternoon entry in the typed chrono read: *"1600—Started clue book. Sent rotator notice to Air Support and PIC."* The follow-up report recounted, *"On 2-26-86, Detective Hooks began a clue book regarding burglary suspects who may be operating in the area as well as that of West Valley which borders Balboa on the west side of the street. On 2-26-86, detectives contacted Air Support and Parking and Intersection Control with regards to the outstanding BMW taken during the crime. Rotator notice was sent to each."* The 4:00 p.m. chrono entry was the last the detectives recorded in the first forty-eight hours of the LAPD's investigation of Sherri's murder.

Stephanie spent Wednesday, February 26, on patrol at the nearby Devonshire Division. Her partner that day was Officer William Orndorff. Stephanie wrote in her diary, *"I drove today. Bill was a nice guy. We stopped for coffee at Winchell's. The day wasn't too exciting. We got a Code 30 up in the hills off Balboa. We checked out the house. It was fine. Then we saw this Mexican sitting in a old beat up veh. We talked to him. He said his friend lived down the street and he was waiting for him. Well his friend showed up. I wrote the guy a ticket for expired tabs. Then this black guy walked by, he had been handing out pamphlets. We ran him and he had a warrant. So we took him in. This guy was a bum from downtown and boy did he smell. We had Chinese food from Roscoe & De Soto. It was completely free. That was about it for the day."*

Orndorff was interviewed by LAPD detectives in 2009, a year after he retired from the LAPD. Orndorff remembered Stephanie as "hyper," but said he had no recollection of working with her on a regular basis or on February 26, 1986, specifically.

Stephanie noted in her datebook a single appointment on that Wednesday: *"Photo Class."* Stephanie did not indicate what time the class took place, and it is unknown whether she attended.

On Wednesday evening, Sherri's friend Jayne visited the motel in Van Nuys where the Rasmussen and Ruetten families were staying. The Rasmussens had called Jayne and asked if she could take Sherri and John's cat, Bozo. Nels and Loretta had kept Bozo in their motel room for a day and a half, since they arrived in town, but the Travelodge had a no-pets policy. Jayne and her fiancé Mike Goldberg drove out to the motel.

In the three years that Jayne and Sherri lived together, Jayne had grown close with the Rasmussen family, particularly Nels. Mike also already knew Nels and Loretta. Jayne and Mike had last seen Sherri and John ten days before the murder, when they visited them to announce their own engagement.

When Jayne and Mike pulled up to the motel, she saw the Rasmussens standing outside in the courtyard. Jayne jumped out of the car and rushed over to Nels. According to Jayne, the first thing she asked him was, "Did John tell them about the ex-girlfriend? Do the police know about the ex-girlfriend?" At the time, Jayne, like Nels, did not know John's ex-girlfriend's name.

Jayne recalls that Nels told her, in reference to John and the detectives, "Yes, he told me he told them. He was forthcoming."

Nels remembers the conversation slightly differently. Nels also recalls that Jayne immediately brought up the ex-girlfriend, but he remembers her asking him a different question: "What have the police told you?" According to Nels, he told Jayne that he asked the police whether John's ex-girlfriend had been interviewed.

The Rasmussens seemed to Jayne to be in shock. Jayne hardly saw John, except wandering around the courtyard looking ashen. Jayne recalls Loretta told her that day about not being allowed inside the condo to retrieve a dress for Sherri and having to go back to Casual Corner to buy one for her burial. While Jayne and Mike talked with the Rasmussens, someone shared a memory of Sherri that made everyone laugh. Jayne recalls that Nels said, "Boy, I never thought I'd ever laugh again." Jayne did not sense any tension between Nels and John while she was at the motel. As far as Jayne could tell, everyone seemed to be on the same wavelength.

Part of the reason Jayne agreed to take Bozo was because John said he was planning to stay at his parents' house and that his mother wouldn't let him have the cat there, either because she didn't like cats or was allergic to them. Jayne thought, "There's no way this cat is going with you, then, because your mother will have it put down. Sherri loved this cat." Jayne wasn't about to let anybody do anything to Bozo. She told John, "I'll keep the cat."

Jayne and Mike adopted Bozo and kept him as a pet for nine years, until Bozo's death in 1995 at age sixteen, old for a cat. For those nine years, Bozo was Jayne's connection to Sherri incarnate. Because Bozo was at home when Sherri was murdered, he was the only eyewitness to what happened. Bozo presumably saw who did it, and who knows what else. As the years passed without answers, Jayne sometimes looked at Bozo and wished that cats could talk.

The next day, Thursday, February 27, the *Los Angeles Times* ran a follow-up story on Sherri's murder, which again misstated the number of times she was shot. The *Times* reported, *"Los Angeles homicide detectives on Wednesday were searching for suspects in the Monday morning death of Sherri Rae Rasmussen, 29. Police said they believe Rasmussen was killed when she surprised one or more intruders who beat her and shot her once before stealing her car."*

The *Times* also repeated the notion, later denied by John, that Sherri had stayed home on Monday because she had hurt herself doing aerobics. The *Times* reported, *"Hospital spokesman Ken Rozell said Rasmussen had taken a day off work because she had injured her back while doing aerobic exercises."* The *Times* story ended with a quote from Althea: "I can't imagine not working with her. She was such an important part of the team."

Stephanie reported for duty as usual on Thursday morning. Her patrol partner on February 27 was Mike Alexander, whom she had just worked with on February 25, the day after Sherri's murder. In 2012, more than twenty-five years later, Alexander testified in court that he had no independent memory of working with Stephanie that week and could not recall whether she had any visible scratches or injuries.

Stephanie's friend Jayme Weaver also worked day watch at Devonshire on Thursday. Weaver was assigned to an L car, with no patrol partner. Stephanie and Weaver likely saw each other during roll call, however. According to Stephanie and Alexander's joint DFAR log of all their activities on patrol, roll call lasted forty-five minutes, from 7:30 to 8:15 a.m. Weaver testified in 2012 that she had no specific recollection of seeing or talking with Stephanie that day.

According to their log, Stephanie and Alexander's first call Thursday morning was a Code 30, a burglar alarm call, at a house on a quiet cul-de-sac. They determined the resident was at home and left after twenty minutes, at 8:50 a.m., their log indicated.

The second radio call they recorded on their patrol log was in a different residential neighborhood, about five miles away. According to their log, they drove the five miles in five minutes and arrived at 8:55 a.m., remarkable time even if it were not the morning rush hour. Their log indicated they spent forty-five minutes at the second call, a report of a vagrant in a vehicle, and left that location at 9:40.

The next call logged by Stephanie and Alexander, a truck on fire on the 405 freeway, occupied them from 10:25 to 11:10 a.m. Ten minutes after they left the truck fire, Stephanie wrote a traffic citation to a driver. From 11:30 to noon, they handled another residential alarm call. Stephanie noted on their log, "*OFCRS ✔ RESID NO EVID OF 459 ACTIVITY*"; 459 is the California penal code section for burglary.

Stephanie and Alexander's log stated they took Code 7, LAPD shorthand for their meal break, from noon to 12:45 p.m. After lunch, the only afternoon activity they recorded was a 211 call, a robbery report that proved unfounded, from 1:10 to 1:40 p.m. At the end of their watch, Stephanie and Alexander submitted their patrol log to their sergeant, who approved the form by initialing it at the bottom.

In her diary entry for Thursday, Stephanie made reference to some of the same incidents she and Alexander documented on their log. Stephanie's diary also revealed she and Alexander ran some personal errands on duty, which they neglected to include in their official log. Stephanie wrote:

A49
ALEXANDER
0730—1615
DEV
2-27-86

I drove today. The day was very slow. There was almost no calls and nothing was happening.

I wrote 1 ticket.

We picked up our pay stubs and Mike had to go to the bank. Then a call came out. Sgt. Flores needed help on the San Diego FWY N/ of Nordhoff. A big truck had overturned and was on fire. We took the call and then it got upgraded to Code 3. So I got to drive w/ lights and Siren on. The truck was still on fire and traffic was backed up. We stood by for the fire department and then directed traffic.

We ate at La Fiesta for free. While we were eating a unit showed up. I thought they were going to join us for lunch but Mike's Emergency Rover went off and a few other units and the helicopter showed up. It was pretty funny.

I just drove around trying to stay awake. We did have a call for some kids who were creating a problem on the bus at Montgomery & Dev. There were kids packed on the bus. So RTD security came and threw them off.

Nels recalls that by Thursday morning, the coroner's office had notified John he could collect Sherri's personal effects, which consisted of the jewelry she was wearing when she was killed: her wedding band, a thin gold necklace, and diamond earrings that were a gift from John.

Because the Rasmussen and Ruetten families were staying at the same motel, and their rooms were just a few doors apart, it was hard for John to come or go without Nels being aware of it. Nels had been after John to get a copy of Sherri's autopsy report. Thursday morning, John told Nels he was going to the coroner's office to pick up Sherri's jewelry. John asked Nels if he wanted to come with him. Nels agreed.

According to Nels, there was very little conversation between him and John during their drive downtown, but also not much tension. Nels believed they were both very upset. Nels still felt he was trying to analyze the situation and understand what he was dealing with.

Later, in hindsight, Nels regretted that he did not ask John more questions during their drive to the coroner's. Nels did not know it then, but the drive turned out to be the only time he and John were alone together in the week after Sherri's murder. According to Nels, whenever else he was around John that week, whether at the motel or elsewhere, John's father was always right there. At least one of John's siblings and his brother-in-law were attorneys. Nels got the feeling that John had lawyered up. According to Nels, whenever he asked John a question, John wouldn't answer him unless he cleared it with his family. His sense that he could not talk with John without another Ruetten family member present became one of the things that bothered Nels the most that week. But on Thursday morning, during their drive to the coroner's, neither Nels nor John knew what the days ahead held, or that their relationship would continue to deteriorate.

Nels recalls that when they got to the coroner's, John had to show identification and sign a log before Sherri's jewelry was released to him. While Nels waited, he saw a clerk on duty at a desk, which gave him an idea. Nels went over to the desk and said, "I'd like to get a copy of the autopsy."

"Who are you?" the clerk asked, Nels recalls.

"I'm Sherri's father."

"Fine, just a minute."

The clerk went away and came back minutes later with a photocopy of Sherri's autopsy report. Nels had to pay for the copies, show his ID, and sign for the report before the clerk let him have it. Nels recalls that John was given Sherri's effects in a clasp envelope. John looked inside the envelope to ensure everything was there. Nels and John then drove back to the motel.

Nels promptly read his copy of the autopsy report. Because Nels was a dentist, he was not intimidated by the medical jargon used to describe Sherri's injuries. Two things Nels read in the autopsy report jumped out at him. The first was the bite mark on Sherri's left forearm. Nels was a practicing dentist with patients, not a forensic dentist, but he knew it was common practice at that time for law enforcement to use bite mark comparisons to identify suspects and convict criminals.

The other thing in the report that caught Nels's attention was the description of the two spent bullets recovered during Sherri's autopsy. One of the slugs was described as *"a 9 mm. silvery flattened-nose, gold based missile."* Nels was a gun owner and familiar with different types of ammunition. Nels knew that nine-millimeter bullets were almost identical in size to .38 caliber bullets. Among Nels's dental patients were several Tucson police officers, who, when they came in for treatment, were usually in uniform and armed. Before an officer sat in the dental chair, he removed his gun belt and placed it on the counter out of the way. Because Nels had an interest, he sometimes talked guns with them. Nels knew from these conversations that .38-caliber ammunition was standard issue for police officers.

Nels's relationship with Mayer, like his relationship with John, was not static but evolved with each interaction they had in the days after Sherri's murder. According to Nels, the amount of time he met with Mayer was probably not more than a third of the total time he and Loretta spent at the Van Nuys station. Nels recalls that Mayer would talk with him and then meet with other people. When Nels wasn't with Mayer, he and Loretta sat in a small waiting area.

Nels and Loretta recall that between Tuesday and Friday, when they returned to Tucson, they met with Mayer at the station daily, and sometimes twice a day. Nearly all of their discussions with the LAPD about the investigation of Sherri's murder were between Nels and Mayer alone. Nels recalls only two meetings where another detective was present in the room. Even during those meetings, everything went through Mayer, according to the Rasmussens.

One was with Mayer and Hooks. Nels recalls the meeting took place at the station on either Wednesday or Thursday. In a tape-recorded interview with LAPD detectives in 2009, Nels recounted, "I told Lyle, being a dentist I had a little bit of knowledge about how they handle bite marks. I asked him, 'Did you have a dental expert look at it? Were any impressions taken? Did they have photographs taken that they could take measurements with?' He said that the area was such that it didn't leave a complete bite. I guess it was almost to the bone, but it didn't leave a complete bite. I don't know what he meant by 'didn't leave a complete bite.' I said, 'Well, that is one area—a bite mark is as good as a fingerprint.'"

According to Nels, during the discussion of the bite mark, Hooks brought up that it could have been a female who killed Sherri because, Hooks said, "Women bite." Hooks's statement appeared to upset Mayer, who shot a look at Hooks that Nels interpreted to mean Hooks should keep his thoughts to himself.

During the same meeting, Mayer talked about the details of the fight that led up to Sherri's murder. Mayer said the fight covered quite an area, from the second floor down to the first-floor living room. Mayer also said Sherri left a fingernail within inches of the alarm panel on the wall near the front door. Nels thought that if Sherri was expecting anyone, she would have kept her handheld panic alarm in her pocket and wouldn't have needed to go for the wall panel. According to the Rasmussens, the detectives never told them whether the handheld panic button was found in the condo, and if so, where in relation to Sherri's body.

In Nels's 2009 interview with the LAPD, he recounted Mayer's description of the fight, which struck Nels as far-fetched from the moment he heard it. Nels recalled, "Lyle said it easily went on for forty-five minutes to an hour and a half. I again asked Lyle if he'd talked with the lady police officer. As I said, if a fight went on that long, I doubt it's a man. Then Lyle ignored my statement entirely and said it well could be that I'm responsible for her death, because she fought. I told him that it certainly required checking into, and he informed me that I had been watching too much TV."

Mayer's statement about the duration of the fight only reinforced his belief that John's ex-girlfriend could have killed Sherri and should be investigated. Nels thought there was no way on God's green earth that a woman could fight off a man for forty-five minutes. He told Mayer, "Besides, Sherri was bit." According to Nels, if looks killed, Hooks would have died, because Mayer appeared furious with him. Mayer only allowed Hooks in the room that one time, Nels recalls.

Nels had another meeting with Mayer at the station on Thursday, after he and John returned from the coroner's office. According to Nels, Mayer was asking him questions, when Nels mentioned, "By the way, I got my own copy of the autopsy." Mayer looked as if Nels had pulled the chair out from under him.

Mayer asked him where he got it. Mayer was looking around for something as they talked, and had a book in his hand. Nels explained how he went to the coroner's with John to get Sherri's jewelry and paid for a copy of the autopsy report. According to Nels, when he told Mayer how he had obtained it, Mayer slammed the book down. In the moment, Nels didn't understand why Mayer was so upset. It was only later, as the investigation went on and Nels revisited the memory, that he realized it was the fact that he had obtained Sherri's autopsy report on his own, without Mayer's clearance, that likely ticked Mayer off.

Nels also discussed with Mayer the two bullets recovered during Sherri's autopsy. In his 2009 LAPD interview, Nels recounted, "I mentioned to Lyle the fact that they were similar, if not the same, as what police are issued." According to Nels, Mayer never acknowledged what Nels said about the bullets. "He never acknowledged. He wouldn't deny it. He wouldn't say, 'Okay,' or whatever. He would just go on with whatever he wanted to talk about," Nels informed the LAPD in 2009.

As things went along with Mayer, day by day that week, Nels became ever more insistent and emotional about bringing up the subject that seemed to irritate Mayer the most: John's ex-girlfriend, the female cop. Nels felt Mayer was on his case from Wednesday on. After a certain point, according to Nels, whenever he met with Mayer, Mayer got loud with him. Mayer was not afraid to let Nels know he didn't want his input and often punctuated their conversations with petulant gestures like slamming a book down, throwing papers, or handing something to Nels and then grabbing it back from him. Nels resolved not to let it bother him. At the same time, Nels sized Mayer up and thought to himself, "You know, if push comes to shove, I think you might get shoved a little harder than you can shove." Nels wasn't stupid enough to raise his hand against Mayer. Nels knew that if he dared, he stood to lose a heck of a lot more than he gained.

According to Nels, he refused to let go of the subject and kept badgering Mayer. Things with Mayer came to a head during a meeting between them on Thursday. He had mentioned the ex-girlfriend to Mayer so many times by then that Mayer got tired of listening to him and lost his cool. Mayer slammed a book down and told him, "You know, you've been watching too much television. There's no need to go there. There's nothing there."

The tacit message Nels took from Mayer at the time was, "I'm getting disgusted with you. You're not helping." Nels thought that Mayer didn't want any help. Nels felt that what Mayer wanted was to convince him that burglars had killed Sherri. Nels believed burglars who killed but did not steal any valuables were as rare as hen's teeth.

Nels sensed Mayer was trying to bulldoze him, but he was determined not to bulldoze easily. Mayer's bluster had the opposite effect of what he believed Mayer intended. The angrier Mayer got with him, the more Nels felt convinced that he was getting closer to the truth.

According to Nels, Mayer never let on that he heard anything he said about John's ex-girlfriend. In Nels's 2009 interview with the LAPD, he recounted of Mayer, "He just ignored it. He never once, never once, answered my questions or answered any statement that I gave him referring to this police officer. He went right on with his story, or went on to another subject. He would ignore it completely. The only time that he addressed it was when he informed me I'd been watching too much TV."

Nels recalls that after one of his meetings with Mayer late in the week, most likely on Thursday, he and Mayer came out of the interview room and saw John and his father, Richard, in the hallway, talking with another man, an LAPD polygraph examiner. When he and Mayer came up on them, they were discussing the polygraph that John had been unable to complete. Within earshot of Nels, John, and Richard, Mayer and the polygraph examiner talked about what the results meant, and what to do next, Nels recalls. According to Nels, Mayer described John's polygraph results as "inconclusive" because John was "too stressed" and "too emotionally involved." Mayer told the polygraph examiner, "We're going to give him a day or two to calm down and we're going to give him another one."

When Richard heard Mayer suggest that John take a second polygraph exam, he became irate. Nels recalls that Richard raised holy hell, hollering at Mayer like Nels couldn't believe. Richard said John wasn't going to be pushed around. Richard also said his daughter and son-in-law were attorneys, and that they would make California shake before John submitted to another polygraph exam. Nels recalls Mayer gave Richard his full attention and tried to calm him. Mayer told him, "We're not going to do it. It's not worth it. They won't recognize it anyway"—a reference to polygraph results being inadmissible in court. Richard calmed down after that, Nels recalls. According to Nels, the polygraph examiner told Nels before they parted in the hallway that John had actually failed his polygraph exam.

Mayer, interviewed in 2014, said he had no recollection of John's father objecting in 1986 to John being given a second polygraph exam. Mayer also denied that Richard or Nels played any role in his decision making about John's polygraph. According to Mayer, "John's dad wouldn't have anything to do with it whatsoever, anyhow. Nels didn't have anything to do with the polygraph. He never said anything like that to me, ever, never ever. First of all, why would you give him the opportunity to do this? The parents don't run the investigation. I mean, come on."

According to Nels and Loretta, their only other meeting with Mayer when another detective was present was on Thursday afternoon. Nels and Loretta recall it was their last meeting with Mayer before they returned to Tucson on Friday to prepare for Sherri's burial. Apart from their initial meeting with Mayer on Tuesday, it was the only meeting Loretta attended with Nels.

When the Thursday afternoon meeting began, it was just Nels, Loretta, and Mayer, recall the Rasmussens. The interview room had a round table, at which Loretta sat down first. When Nels sat down, he turned his chair around and sat in it backward, so the back of the chair was in front of him. Nels felt nervous and full of adrenaline. Since Monday night, when he had received belated notification of Sherri's murder from John's father, his doubts about what John knew had steadily mounted. Nels never believed that John had anything to do with the crime itself. At the same time, Nels felt that John wasn't reacting the way Nels thought he should, after having just lost his new wife, whom he supposedly cared about.

Nels recalls he told Mayer he thought John was acting strange. According to Nels, he urged Mayer, "We need to get John. We need to get him cornered, and go up one side and down the other, and interrogate him to no end, because we've got to break him. He knows more than he's saying, because he won't be around me, number one. Number two, his dad is unbelievably protective."

Nels recalls that Mayer replied, "What do you want us to do? Beat the hell out of him to find out?"

"It might be a start," Nels recalls he told Mayer. Nels knew it was a stupid idea. Even so, he figured it wouldn't hurt for John to at least face the threat of harm.

According to the Rasmussens, Mayer told Nels, "Just a minute." Mayer left the interview room briefly and came back with a second detective whom Nels and Loretta had not seen or spoken with previously. Nels recalls the second detective was short and much lighter built than Mayer, a description that matches Roger Pida, Mayer's supervisor. Mayer and the other detective sat down at the table.

"Now, tell him what you told me," Mayer instructed Nels.

Nels repeated to both detectives what he had just told Mayer about John acting strange and hanging close to his father. Nels gripped the chair back as he talked and vented his frustrations with John, and with his parents for keeping him away from him. Nels told the detectives that John's parents needed to get at him, and get at him good, so John would talk and reveal what he knew.

According to the Rasmussens, when Nels finished, Mayer and the other detective looked at each other. The other detective smiled, then stood up from the table. Mayer said to the other detective, "You know, we don't know. We're not sure who we need to protect in this situation, are we?"

Nels took Mayer's statement as a warning that the detectives were going to put somebody on him to watch his behavior. Nels recalls he told Mayer, "You guys are unbelievable, if you think that I'm stupid enough that I'm going to take and raise my hand against somebody. Because I know that would be putting myself in reverse, and not letting myself go forward." As for the implication they might need to put John under police protection, Nels recalls that he said, "No one's going to hurt your little John."

According to Nels, Mayer threatened him and suggested he would get in trouble if he didn't lay off John. Nels recalls Mayer told him, "You better be careful, or you may end up facing a situation that you may not find comfortable."

Nels and Loretta never again saw or met with the other detective Mayer brought into the interview room that day.

In 2009, Pida was interviewed by LAPD detectives about his recollections of the Rasmussen crime scene, his involvement in the subsequent investigation, and the burglary theory. Pida said that he had vacated the Van Nuys homicide coordinator's position in June or July 1986, a few months after the murder. Pida also said he was never told and never heard in 1986 about the victim having problems with anyone.

None of the Rasmussens' face-to-face meetings with the detectives in the three days after Sherri's murder were tape-recorded, summarized, or otherwise documented in the LAPD's murder book for Sherri's case. Nor were any meetings that week with the Rasmussens memorialized in the typed chrono or the follow-up report, neither of which was prepared until May 1986, three months later.

According to the LAPD's official records, the Rasmussens contributed no leads or information whatsoever on any potential suspects, including John's ex-girlfriend, the female police officer Nels recalls he hounded Mayer about all week. Nor is there any record that Nels ever alerted the detectives to any possible motive for Sherri's murder other than the burglary theory pursued by the detectives from the first forty-eight hours of the investigation on. Looking at the LAPD's case file, on its face, it is as if none of the meetings and conflicts recalled by the Rasmussens ever happened. For all intents and purposes, Nels, Loretta, the concerns they insist they expressed, and the information they provided were rendered invisible to any detectives who might later inherit the case.

As far as Nels knew at the time, despite all his pleas to Mayer, the detectives never checked out John's ex-girlfriend to eliminate her as a person of interest in Sherri's murder. Nels believed that the detectives had their minds set on it being a burglary and never wavered.

Indeed, there is no indication anywhere in the LAPD's typed chrono or the follow-up report that the detectives ever investigated, interviewed, or even contacted Stephanie Lazarus, whose name the Rasmussens did not know at the time.

Mayer, interviewed in 2014, insisted that during the week after Sherri's murder, the Rasmussens never told him, even one time, about any police officer ex-girlfriend of John's. Mayer adamantly denied that he protected a fellow officer, or that he would hesitate to go after a cop suspected of murder. Mayer said of Stephanie, "Here is Mr. and Mrs. Rasmussen saying, 'Oh, we had been covering up for her.' I couldn't tell you who she is when she walks in the door. I had never seen her . . . It was a professional insult to me. They're just running everything in the whole wide world out at that point, saying that we were incompetent idiots, or we were hiding something then. What would we do that for? Why would we not? Of course we would arrest a policeman if they were involved in anything like this."

Mayer was also interviewed in 2011 by a defense investigator, a retired LAPD detective, about his work on the Rasmussen case in 1986. Mayer's 2011 interview was not tape-recorded. Mayer's statements were instead memorialized in a twenty-six-page interview summary, which was later entered into evidence in court.

According to the summary of Mayer's 2011 interview, *"Lyle said we never got information that Stephanie Lazarus was involved. Lyle was asked about the family of Sherri stating that they had notified him about Stephanie Lazarus' possible involvement and that even John Ruetten notified him. Lyle said No, that's not true. And if it was true, he would have absolutely followed up on it."*

Midway through Mayer's 2011 interview, he instructed the defense investigator to write down the following statement: *"I have never met Stephanie Lazarus professionally, or personally . . . I have absolutely no indication who this person was whatsoever. What reason would I have to try and defend her? None. As a matter of fact, I'd only be hurting my own professional credibility if I did that. Believe me . . . I don't know this gal. I could care less about this gal (referring to Stephanie Lazarus)."*

Mayer also recounted in his 2011 interview what John told him about Stephanie in 1986: *"To the best of Lyle's recollection, he (referring to John Ruetten) never ever gave us her name at the time of the murder . . . When we talked to him, naturally, we said, Look, is there a former girlfriend, is there a girlfriend, is there whatever. Lyle said John stated that there was a casual acquaintance. That was it. No girlfriend. No ongoing affair, no nothing. Lyle said we checked every way that we possibly could with regards to that and with everybody that we talked to and it was no indication that there was somebody else. Lyle said when we pressed harder and harder, and harder, and harder later on, he came up with Stephanie Lazarus and he said she was a casual acquaintance that they went to college together. That it was, it was a police officer. That was the totality of his information."*

Later in his 2011 interview, Mayer was asked *"what his protocol would be if Stephanie Lazarus's information came to him and he knew that she was a police officer. Lyle said that's a complicated question; he said let me give you two things that would have occurred. First, anytime that you find out or you know that a policeman is involved in some specific crime, you would have had to go to a supervisor, and then he would have had to initiate either a personnel complaint or a personnel investigation, and more than likely a personnel complaint."*

Mayer asserted in his 2011 interview that any investigation of Stephanie in 1986 likely would have been futile: *"Lyle stated that if Stephanie Lazarus specifically would have been a suspect, there would have been a personnel complaint initiated against her. And hypothetically, at that particular time, what would we have done? We would have advised her of her Constitutional rights, and she would have done what? She would have said, I'm going to talk to my lawyer. Lyle said you could not force her to take a polygraph. You could do nothing else but type the blood. That's all that we could do then. That's it . . . You would have been dead, done in the water."*

Mayer also defended the 1986 investigation he led. According to his 2011 interview summary, Mayer said, *"It was a tragedy to the family, but if you examine all of this stuff . . . It's not like we said, No, we weren't going to try and find anybody who killed this person. He said they arrested probably, he didn't recall, in the course of years, 20 people. Lyle said every burglar that got arrested, we ran his fingerprints through whatever we had there. He said we tried to find every car that it was associated with. So professionally, Lyle says it's very disappointing that persons have hinted that we did nothing because this person turned out to be a police person. That's so obscenely absurd, it's unreal. Who cares, if it's a policeman, put his ass in jail. Lyle says we're no different than anybody else. Put him in jail. If we would have known that, come on. There are good guys, there's bad guys. There's bad policemen."*

Mayer insisted in his 2011 interview that he had nothing to hide, and no reason to cover up for another officer: *"Lyle stated what would I possibly gain for this? Lyle then wanted to make sure I wrote the following down: Remember this, I was not the only detective involved in this case. I was the primary detective and Hooks was my initial partner. Now, it's important that you write this down. Lyle says every primary investigator has to submit in his conclusions and his theory to his immediate supervisor, which is the*

Detective III, who has to give it to the Lieutenant II, who runs the detective
unit, who has to give it to the Captain, who ultimately has to commit it to
Robbery-Homicide to review the case. Lyle stated the primary detective can't
formulate an opinion and be the only person involved in that opinion. He
said they were all fooled." Mayer said, "We were trying to go do a good job
here. It's not like we were hiding something. We did everything proper."

Stephanie made no reference in her voluminous diaries, at least in the
five months after Sherri's murder, to ever being contacted by any detective
investigating her homicide. Nowhere in Stephanie's diary did she betray
any apparent anxiety over the LAPD's investigation of Sherri's murder,
express any interest in the status and direction of the investigation, or even
acknowledge that John's wife had been killed. Nor did Stephanie write in
her diary about reaching out to anyone after the murder, including John, her
closest friend for several years before John met Sherri. Looking at Stephanie's
diary, on its face, it is as if Sherri's murder never happened.

In 2009, two LAPD homicide detectives sat down with Stephanie and
interviewed her about Sherri's murder, twenty-three years earlier. Stephanie was unaware how much the detectives already knew about her and the
case. Stephanie was also unaware that the interview was being recorded,
via a tiny video camera hidden inside a three-ring binder the detectives
placed on the table between them.

What Stephanie herself knew of the LAPD's investigation into Sherri's
murder, prior to her interview with detectives in 2009, is unknown. Since
her 2009 LAPD interview, Stephanie has not answered any additional questions or made any public statements about her involvement in Sherri's
murder. Nor has Stephanie ever revealed what she knew about the LAPD's
investigation, and when she knew it, during the more than two decades that
Sherri's homicide went unsolved.

For several years in the 1990s, Stephanie worked as a detective at
Van Nuys, where Sherri's case remained open and unsolved. During her
years at Van Nuys, Stephanie was known to volunteer for morning watch,
the overnight hours, when the station was mostly deserted. Stephanie
worked as a detective on at least one Van Nuys homicide case, and she
enjoyed unfettered access to the Rasmussen murder book while she was
assigned there. Whether she availed herself of the opportunity to peruse
the murder book, and tamper with it, may never be known. Nothing but
her sense of propriety stood in the way of her doing, and reading, whatever she pleased.

The total absence of documentation in the LAPD's typed chrono and follow-up report that Stephanie was ever contacted or interviewed in 1986, along with her silence on the subject in her diary, suggest that she was off the radar of the detectives who initially investigated Sherri's murder. If she was on their radar, and the detectives took any steps to check her out, there is no record of it in the murder book for Sherri's case.

In her 2009 LAPD interview, however, Stephanie admitted under questioning that she did in fact speak with an LAPD detective about the murder of Sherri Rasmussen. Stephanie did not say how long after the murder the conversation took place, nor did she identify the detective she spoke with.

For the first ten minutes of her 2009 LAPD interview, Stephanie answered several questions about her relationship with John, from the time they met at UCLA. Stephanie finally protested, "I don't understand why you're talking about some guy I dated a million years ago."

"Well, do you know what happened to his wife?" one of the detectives asked.

"Yeah, I know she got killed."

"What did you hear about that?"

"I saw a poster at work. I'm sure I spoke to him about it," Stephanie said, referring to John. "I think I spoke to another friend of his about it."

"And how did—how did you first learn about that?"

"Geez, someone could've called. I could've heard it at work. I think at one point there may have been a flyer or something. I know a good friend of his—"

"Were you on the job back then, when that happened?"

"Yeah, I think so. Yeah, I'm sure I was on the job. That's why I would've heard about it with a flyer."

Later in her 2009 LAPD interview, one of the detectives asked her, "When you heard about John's wife being killed, I mean, what was your reaction? You thought you heard about it, what, through a friend or in a bulletin or something?"

"Either a friend or a bulletin. I obviously—I mean, I called. I called the family. I called maybe some of his friends that I knew. I mean, obviously, it's a shock. If you're—if I heard it at work, you know, which I may have—I faintly remember a bulletin going around. Either that or somebody called me. I also don't remember . . . And then I called—probably called his family, called—I don't know initially—I can't say if I initially spoke to him or not.

I honestly don't remember. I may have said to somebody, hey, have him call me if he wants to talk, and then he may have done that," she said, referring to John.

"Do know what the circumstances were regarding her death?"

"Geez, let me think back. Geez, I don't know if it was—you know, if it was a burglary or something. Yeah, it's—I mean, it's been so many years. I—I mean, I can faintly think that I may have saw a flyer . . . It may have had her picture on it. You know, I may—that's why I say if somebody had called me, I may not have known what her last name was. I may have. I mean, maybe if you told me, I would remember it, you know?"

"Do you remember her first name?"

"Shelly, Sherri. I don't know. Something. You know, like I said, it's been so many years."

Several minutes later, Stephanie was asked, "Did detectives ever reach out to you ever? Anybody ever—"

"No, no one's ever talked to me. I don't think anybody ever talked to me about—about him," she said, meaning John.

"'Cause it seems like back then you would've been—"

"You know—well, I take—I'm thinking that I did talk to a detective. God, but what division was it?" she asked.

"In Van Nuys."

"And where was I working?"

"1986."

"I would have been working Devonshire."

"Uh-huh."

"You know, I'm thinking that I did speak to somebody."

"Oh, really? Okay."

"I couldn't tell you who it was. It was probably on the phone."

"Would it have been somebody in regards to this or just—"

"Yeah," Stephanie replied.

"Uh-huh."

"Yeah. I don't even know if you said a name, if I would remember it, because I worked Van Nuys for a while," she said.

The detectives pressed the subject again later in the interview. In reference to the unnamed detective she spoke with after Sherri's murder, Stephanie was asked, "Do you remember—would you remember any of the conversation as far as what they were looking for or—?"

"Couldn't say. I mean, they may have told me. I said, Hey, you know, I went to school with him. I either—they either—somebody called me or I saw the fly—I—I may have seen the flyer at that point, and I called up. If—if someone's name was on the flyer, I may have called to speak to them. I said, hey, if there's anything I can do, you know, call me. This is where I work. You know, I went to, you know, school with him."

"Uh-huh."

"I couldn't say. I couldn't tell you who it was."

"But you do remember that, that someone you think reached out to you?"

"You mean the detective?" Stephanie asked.

"Yeah, called you up and talked to you."

"Or I called them, one of the two, but, yeah, you know, I remember talking to somebody, but—I'm thinking it was a man. I'm sure there were probably more men back then . . . So, again, that's—I mean, that's really all I can remember about that," Stephanie said, the last time the subject came up during her 2009 LAPD interview.

In the early 1990s, Stephanie also told at least one fellow LAPD officer that detectives had once interviewed her regarding a murder. In 1992, two years before she made detective and three years before she transferred to Van Nuys, Stephanie was assigned to the Background Section of the LAPD's Personnel Division. For more than a year, she worked as an LAPD background investigator, vetting civilians who aspired to become police officers to ensure they had no skeletons in their closets.

An LAPD officer also assigned to the Background Section in the early 1990s, Lydia Leos, once overheard Stephanie talk about being interviewed by detectives on a homicide case. Leos recalled Stephanie said the interview concerned an ex-boyfriend's girlfriend who had gone missing and was possibly shot.

John Ruetten, during an interview with LAPD detectives in 2009, said he had no recollection of any interactions with Stephanie in the immediate aftermath of Sherri's murder. John was asked, "So there was no contact after the February twenty-four incident? She never reaches out to you? You don't reach out to her like, 'Oh my God. What has happened?' She doesn't contact you?"

"No. Nothing in the consoling sort of sense. Exactly. You said it exactly right. None of that was going on," said John.

"I know this is a strange question, but do you know if she showed up at any of Sherri's services?"

"I don't think so."

"There wasn't correspondence at all? She didn't write you a letter or card?"

"No. Nothing. Nothing that I can recall. But I would recall it, I think, if there would have been," John said.

"I guess our position would be, if she is a very close friend, almost an eight, nine, ten year close friendship—"

"Right. She was a close friend. But it was different. That's the point. We already know that. She was left behind," John said of Stephanie.

"I would have thought that at least she may have said, 'Are you okay?' What we are having a hard time grasping is that she would have at least made contact with you and said, 'Are you going to be okay?' As close as you two were."

"I know," said John.

"It's very easy for us to Monday morning quarterback this, our investigators and the relationship and everything."

"Yeah, I don't recall anything of that nature happening," John said.

In 2012, three years after his interview with the LAPD, John testified in court that Stephanie never contacted him after Sherri's death to offer him her condolences. John also testified that Stephanie never reached out and offered to help him navigate the LAPD's bureaucracy, or to assist in any way with the investigation of his wife's murder, although Stephanie was the only LAPD officer that John knew.

The first investigative activity documented by the Van Nuys detectives on Thursday, February 27, was at noon, roughly the same hour that an LAPD helicopter was hovering over Stephanie's location, thanks to her partner's balky emergency rover, according to her diary.

According to the typed chrono, the detectives called a cartographer at SID, Howard Huckman, and requested he make a drawing of the crime scene. Huckman agreed to come to Van Nuys the following week.

The detectives arranged to meet at the condo sooner, at 8:30 Friday morning, with a ballistics expert from SID. Sherri had suffered three gunshot wounds, but only two bullets were recovered at her autopsy. The detectives had found no bullets at the crime scene, during their walkthroughs of the condo earlier that week. The detectives wanted SID to perform a trajectory analysis and hopefully locate the missing third bullet.

Mayer also requested that SID Firearms pick up the two bullets at the coroner's and analyze them for type and caliber.

Thursday afternoon, the typed chrono indicated, "*Called John Ruetter to try to get him to I.D. the statue she was hit with.*" It was in fact a heavy ceramic vase, not a statue, that Sherri was struck with. Mayer also fielded a call from a Detective Graham in the Wilshire Division homicide unit. Graham informed Mayer that he had read his teletype on the murder. Graham said he had a similar case, also a shooting, that he thought might be related. At Mayer's request, SID later performed a microscopic comparison of the bullets from Sherri's autopsy with those recovered in Graham's case and determined they did not match.

At 3:00 p.m. on Thursday, Mayer called the UCLA Police Department and spoke to a Detective Shain. The follow-up report recounted, "*Detective Mayer knew from John Ruetten that Sherri taught on the campus at times. Mayer questioned if there were any type of reports of incidents where Sherri Rasmussen might have been a victim. Detective Shain checked all records. Negative results.*"

Later Thursday, according to the typed chrono, the Van Nuys detectives spoke with a Detective Burris at the LAPD's West Valley Division, which bordered Van Nuys: "*1515 | Contacted Det. Burris W. Valley Homicide re: A burg / 459. Burris stated his victim was strangled, probably unrelated.*"

The next entry in the typed chrono stated, "*1530 | Contacted Gracie Aid, ordered batch run on RD's 941 & 1039, also pacmis run on 7100 Balboa.*"

"Gracie Aid" was not a proper name but shorthand for Gracie, a clerk assigned to AID, the Automated Information Division, the arm of the LAPD responsible for gathering crime and arrest data. The LAPD split the more than four hundred square miles of Los Angeles it was responsible for policing into geographic divisions, of which Van Nuys and Devonshire were two. Each LAPD division was comprised of several Basic Car Areas, the boundaries of which guided the deployment of patrol cars. Each Basic Car Area was further broken down into smaller, numbered Reporting Districts. The system allowed AID to compile crime and arrest data by location, which was useful for statistical reporting as well as for investigative purposes.

Although the computer databases employed by the LAPD during the 1980s seem primitive in hindsight, they were close to cutting-edge at the time. The primary database maintained by AID was the Police Arrest and

Crime Management Information System, PACMIS. Crime, arrest, and other police reports from across the city flowed to a room full of analysts at AID. Each individual report was read and assigned codes according to the type of incident, location, and other details. The coded information was then inputted manually into the PACMIS database.

Because the PACMIS data was stored on large spools of magnetic tape, and there was no front-end user interface, LAPD detectives in the 1980s were unable to access the database directly. When specific information was needed from the database, AID analysts had to write program code, line by line, to define the requested search parameters. Despite the labor-intensive coding process, PACMIS accommodated a broad range of search criteria, which could be combined in myriad ways per the detective's wishes. PACMIS searches could be very narrowly tailored—for example, all white males younger than twenty-five and less than six feet tall arrested for burglary during a certain week within a single Reporting District. Alternatively, a detective could cast a much wider net, using more expansive search criteria, such as all crimes and arrests in multiple RDs over a period of months or even years.

A "batch run" referred to how AID's ad hoc database searches were performed, once the code was written and ready to run. The computers and bulky spools of magnetic tape that comprised PACMIS were not handled by AID and the LAPD, but by another city department, the Los Angeles Information Technology Agency, ITA. ITA and the PACMIS tape spools were physically located four stories below City Hall East, on the same underground floor as the city's emergency dispatch and command centers. Programs written by AID analysts were placed in queues at ITA according to which magnetic tape spools needed to be searched. Running the programs in batches was more efficient than having to mount and unmount tapes each time an individual search request came in. Once the proper tape spool was mounted, all the programs in the queue were run and the search results sent to AID. The turnaround time for a typical database search ranged from less than an hour to more than twenty-four hours.

The Van Nuys detectives did not specify in the typed chrono what additional search parameters they requested of Gracie at AID, beyond *"ordered batch run on RD's 941 & 1039, also pacmis run on 7100 Balboa."* The murder location, Sherri and John's condo at 7100 Balboa Boulevard, was in Reporting District 941. The detectives did not explain in the typed chrono the possible significance of Reporting District 1039 to Sherri's murder. Nor did the detectives indicate whether they were interested in reports of crimes, arrests, or both in the requested RDs, and over what period of time.

The PACMIS search was not referenced again in the typed chrono until April 2, more than a month later. The April 2 entry read in full, *"Rec'd Pacmis work-up on 7100 Balboa."* The search parameters and the contents of the "work-up" were not further described in the typed chrono. In the follow-up report, neither the RD and PACMIS runs ordered on February 27, nor the "work-up" received on April 2, were mentioned.

The last investigative activity the detectives documented Thursday in the typed chrono referenced the motel where the Rasmussen and Ruetten families stayed that week: *"1630 | Travel Lodge received info on broken statue."* The typed chrono did not specify whether the information came from John or the Rasmussens. Nor was the actual information obtained recorded in the typed chrono, beyond the fact that information was received.

According to the LAPD's follow-up report, Hooks on Thursday reinterviewed Anastasia Volanitis, the neighbor who was given Sherri's purse by two men who came to her door early Monday afternoon, hours before the murder was discovered. The follow-up report indicated, *"On 2-27-86 Detective Hooks reinterviewed Anastasia. She stated she knows her complex gardeners on sight as they have been there for some time. She stated the two male Latins who found the purse and attempted to return it are not the same as the regular gardeners."* The typed chrono made no reference on February 27 to Hooks's reinterview of Anastasia.

According to her diary, Stephanie finished her patrol rounds at Devonshire and went off duty at 4:15 p.m. that Thursday. Her datebook for February 27 listed two events: *"School"* and *"B-ball finals."* It is unknown whether the basketball final was an LAPD women's team game or some other one in which Stephanie played.

Sherri's friends and hospital colleagues, meanwhile, continued to reel from the emotional shock and senselessness of her death. In terms of their knowledge of what happened to Sherri, and the status of the LAPD's investigation of her murder, Sherri's friends were even less informed than the Rasmussens.

When Jayne and her fiancé, Mike, visited the Rasmussens at their motel on Wednesday evening, Jayne did not worry about whether she was imposing on Nels and Loretta, or invading their privacy, because she had known them for years.

Peggy Daly, Sherri's closest friend at work, barely knew the Rasmussens. Peggy had met Nels and Loretta only once, several months prior, when Sherri brought her parents to the hospital during one of their visits to Los Angeles. Unlike Jayne, Peggy did not see the Rasmussens until Friday, at the hospital's memorial service for Sherri. Peggy heard at work that Sherri's burial was to take place in Tucson on Sunday, but also that the funeral was for family only. Peggy did not have the nerve to ask Nels and Loretta if she could attend anyway. She thought it would be inappropriate to ask, since she didn't know the family well.

Peggy's emotional isolation relative to Sherri's friends who were closer with the Rasmussens was compounded by how she coped with tragedy in her own life. When Peggy was eleven years old, she lost her brother, and two years after that, her father. She emerged from adolescence with a preternatural ability to compartmentalize grief. Peggy's default response to painful memories and feelings was to relegate them to the back of her mind as best as she could, and not look back.

The person most attuned to Peggy's well-being in the days after Sherri's death was someone whom, ironically, she did not know very well. Glenn Crabtree, the hospital's director of design construction, was in a meeting with Peggy on Tuesday morning when she learned that Sherri was murdered. Glenn witnessed firsthand Peggy's devastation. Glenn, Peggy, and Sherri were about the same age, much younger than most of their colleagues at the hospital. Glenn knew that Peggy and Sherri were very close. Until Sherri's death, he thought of her and Peggy as inseparable. Suddenly, sorrowfully, it was no longer so.

All week, Glenn wanted to tell Peggy that he was thinking of her, and how terribly sorry he was, but he wasn't sure how to say it. Glenn didn't want her to feel pressured or to misinterpret his intentions. Glenn did not know Peggy well enough to know whether she was single or in a relationship. He had moved to Los Angeles to start his life over, after a brief failed marriage. He considered the marriage a disaster and had decided he was never going to get married again. He was just looking for friends, and to be a friend, if Peggy wanted him to be.

On Thursday, the day before Sherri's Glendale Adventist memorial service, Glenn decided to write Peggy a letter and share with her a poem he had written to console himself, earlier in his life. On a blank sheet of hospital letterhead suitable for business correspondence, Glenn handwrote:

27th Feb.—86.

Dear Peggy,

Some time ago I penned a few lines in a note book of mine, created out of a need to express feelings and thoughts that were personal to me. Only my close friends knew <u>some</u> of my feelings. No one ever fully understands but those that try become more meaningful. I just want to let you know that I care.

> *By chance I saw two sparrows*
> *While working on a farm*
> *And it was evident that one of them*
> *Had come to a grievous harm*
>
> *Though on approach, surprisingly*
> *Its friend would not let go*
> *In spite of danger, stayed and sang*
> *Putting on a grand old show.*
>
> *The injured bird on the ground*
> *Joined in the tuneful song*
> *As if to tell the whole wide world*
> *That there was nothing wrong.*
>
> *So I moved back and all the while*
> *They sang their duet sweet*
> *And all the people passing by*
> *Never saw the broken wings and feet.*

Caring for you,
Glenn

18

"God Holds the Key"

(February 28 to March 2, 1986)

By Friday, February 28, four days after Sherri was killed, her case no longer commanded any attention from the local news media. On Tuesday, a KABC television news crew had gone to Glendale Adventist and taped interviews with a few of Sherri's colleagues, but for unknown reasons, the report never aired. The Rasmussens recall no other TV news coverage of Sherri's case that week while they were in Los Angeles. On Friday, unlike the previous three days, no stories about Sherri's case ran in any of the local papers. The next newspaper story on the status of the LAPD's investigation was not until October, nearly eight months later.

The Van Nuys detectives' follow-up report recounted of Friday morning, "*Detectives returned to the crime scene for further investigation. Trajectory drawings were completed. An attempt to locate spent bullets were [sic] made. Blood samples were taken. SID Print Expert Aames [sic] obtained additional fingerprint lifts.*"

No one had entered the condo since Tuesday, when Ames, the fingerprint analyst, sprayed ninhydrin on the walls in the front entryway. According to the typed chrono, several other LAPD personnel met Mayer and Hooks there at 8:45 Friday morning.

At 8:55, the typed chrono indicated, "*Contacted SID for criminalist to recover blood from garage stairway wall.*"

Among the personnel already at the location were two officers from the SID firearms and explosives unit, George Luczy and Herbie Williams, who were there to perform a bullet trajectory analysis. The goal of the trajectory analysis was to determine where in the condo the gunshots were fired, to help the detectives reconstruct how the murder unfolded. Luczy and Williams were also on the lookout for any slugs or other ballistics evidence that might identify the murder weapon.

In order to trace the path a bullet traveled, it must have struck at least two objects some distance apart. By attaching a length of string to the farthest bullet strike, and running the string back through the other bullet holes to the point of origin, it was possible to reconstruct the bullet's trajectory, and the approximate location of the gun when it was fired. The technique was known as "stringing" a crime scene.

On the second floor, Luczy and Williams observed two holes in the floor-length drape on the sliding glass door to the balcony. Williams drew a diagram to document the location of the holes. One was in the upper left quadrant of the drape, about six feet off the floor. The other hole was closer to the center of the drape and lower, about two and a half feet off the floor. Behind the drape, most of the glass in the doorframe was gone. The glass that remained in the pane was bowed slightly outward, which suggested the bullets were fired from somewhere inside the condo. The broken glass strewn on the balcony and driveway below bolstered that conclusion.

Luczy and Williams went outside to investigate where the two bullets that pierced the drape had landed. They were able to locate only one bullet strike, on a drainpipe across the driveway. Luczy and Williams searched the area around the downspout but were unable to find either of the two expended bullets.

Luczy and Williams next considered which of the two holes in the drape was more likely to correspond with the hole in the drainpipe outside. By threading the string through the upper hole, they were able to rule out that it was caused by the same bullet that struck the drainpipe. The slope of the bullet trajectory from inside the condo to the drainpipe, as illustrated by the string, was slightly downward. For a bullet to pass through the upper hole, six feet off the floor, and hit the drainpipe outside, the gun would have to have been held even higher, overhead or while standing on something, and fired sharply downward. Luczy and Williams judged it an unnatural, improbable firing position. It seemed more likely the bullet that produced the upper hole exited the condo on an upward trajectory, not downward.

When the string was pulled taut through the lower hole, it aligned with the bullet hole in the drainpipe outside. Luczy extended the string across the breakfast room until he hit a wall, near the open doorway to the dining room. The distance from the wall to the drape was about ten feet. Based on their analysis, for the bullet to have created the lower hole and struck the drainpipe across the driveway, the gun could have been held at any point along this path when it was fired.

Downstairs, on the first floor, Luczy observed a bloodstain and an apparent bullet impact in the living room carpet, thirty inches in front of the fireplace. The location corresponded to where Sherri's body was found. Luczy thought the slug that impacted the carpet might be embedded underneath it.

Among the tools Luczy carried with him on his rounds was a sharp knife. He cut into the carpet and the rubber padding beneath. Using the bullet hole as his starting point, he sliced the carpet a good distance out in four directions, then peeled back the carpet and padding. The floor underneath was concrete. Despite a thorough search, Luczy was unable to find the expended bullet.

There are several plausible explanations for why the bullet that struck the carpet could not be found. One possibility was that it had already been collected. Two bullets were recovered during Sherri's autopsy on Tuesday. One fell from the folds of Sherri's robe when her clothes were removed. The medical examiner found a second bullet lodged in Sherri's back, just under her skin. Either one could have been fired while she was lying on her back in the living room. Two of the three gunshot wounds to her chest were through-and-through, meaning the bullets completely exited her body. The absence of a bullet in the living room also opened the possibility that Sherri suffered at least one of her through-and-through wounds upstairs, by one of the two bullets that passed through the drapes, before the fight moved downstairs.

The lack of shell casings suggested the murder weapon may have been a revolver rather than a semiautomatic. When a semiautomatic is fired, the casing is ejected. When a revolver is fired, the casing remains in the gun's cylinder. If the murder weapon was a semiautomatic, Sherri's killer would have had to collect any bullet casings before fleeing the crime scene.

While Luczy and Williams moved around the condo looking for ballistics evidence, fingerprint analyst Mike Ames inspected the areas he had sprayed with ninhydrin three days earlier. Ames identified one bloody handprint that was enhanced by the chemical reaction. The print was low on the wall beside the door to the garage stairs. Ames sketched a diagram

Bloody handprint later identified as Sherri's (February 28, 1986 LAPD photo)

to document its location, thirteen inches off the floor, the same height as a nearby electrical socket.

Ames observed that the palm of the handprint was closer to the floor than the fingers. Ames drew an arrow on the diagram to indicate the orientation of the handprint. Ames also had black-and-white photographs of the handprint taken, so comparisons could be made at the crime lab. Black-and-white was standard when photographing latent prints because it rendered ridge structure in better contrast and detail than color. Ames designated the newest print as print package C, to distinguish it from the two sets of lifts previously collected at the condo.

A week later, based on the photograph, another SID fingerprint analyst matched the bloody handprint on the wall to Sherri's left hand.

For unknown reasons, no black-and-white close-up photographs were taken of the single fingerprint most likely to have been left at the crime scene by the suspect rather than Sherri herself. During the detectives' initial walk-through of the condo on Monday night, hours after Sherri's body was found, perhaps the most prominent and suggestive clue they were confronted with were the two video components left stacked in the front entryway, at the base of the stairs to the second floor. The component on top was a Sony digital disc player. In his walk-through notes on Monday night, Hooks wrote, *"A bloody fingerprint appears on top of the disc player."*

A bloody print that was still wet was typically photographed, rather than dusted and lifted with tape. Attempting to lift a wet print risked

View downstairs to video components in entryway (LAPD crime scene photo #50)

destroying the all-important ridge structure, instead of preserving it as evidence. If the bloody print was on something that could be transported easily, the fingerprint analyst could request the item be taken to the crime lab, where it could be examined and photographed under better-lit conditions than in the field. However, depending on the location and circumstances of the case, the fingerprint analyst also had the discretion to have the item and the print photographed in situ, at the crime scene.

With respect to the bloody fingerprint on the Sony disc player, neither happened. Although the stacked video components are visible in at least four separate crime scene photographs taken in the first hours of the LAPD's investigation, none captured the bloody print with sufficient clarity and detail to allow for later print comparisons. Nor was either component ever booked into property by the LAPD and retained as evidence. Apart from the passing reference in Hooks's walk-through notes, no additional information about the fingerprint on the disc player was documented in the typed chrono or the follow-up report.

At 9:50 a.m., according to the typed chrono, SID criminalist Doreen Music took a sample from the bloodstain on the garage wall with a small cloth square, which became item 13 on the LAPD's property list. The entry regarding Music was the last investigative activity the detectives logged on Friday morning.

Mayer, in an interview in 2014, recounted that their theory of what happened to Sherri evolved with their improved understanding of the crime scene. According to Mayer, he and Hooks repeated their walk-through of the condo several times. Mayer recalled that he directed Hooks to stand in different places around the condo, to test whether Mayer could see him from where he stood and thus establish sight lines for what Sherri may have seen in the moments leading up to the fatal confrontation.

Based on the information that Sherri had called in sick to work, Mayer assumed she was in bed on the third floor of the condo when she heard noises downstairs. Mayer pictured Sherri putting her robe on and walking down to the second floor. Mayer believed Sherri turned and discovered an intruder armed with a gun. Mayer theorized this led to a tremendous struggle near the kitchen. The bullet trajectory strings showed where the first shots were fired. In Mayer's mind, the string lines proved their working theory exactly.

According to Mayer, he and Hooks also investigated where inside the condo it was possible to hear someone at the front door. Mayer had Hooks go up to the master bedroom on the third floor and lie down on the bed with the covers over him, while Mayer rang the doorbell downstairs. According to Mayer, the doorbell could not be heard from the bedroom. Mayer recalled that he also had someone go down to the garage to see what could be heard from there. Mayer concluded that if Sherri was asleep in bed, she would not have heard someone at the front door, even if the doorbell was rung repeatedly.

Mayer thought that if Sherri had been able to hear the doorbell, she would have put more clothing on before going downstairs. Mayer also believed if Sherri had heard someone at the front door and gone to investigate, the confrontation would have begun in the entryway rather than on the second floor, as the crime scene evidence indicated it did. How Sherri was dressed, and where the fight started, suggested to the detectives that her killer was already inside before she discovered their presence.

Mayer said that all the detectives in the Van Nuys homicide unit talked about what they believed had happened. According to Mayer, they agreed that an interrupted burglary was more than likely what had occurred. Mayer described their burglary scenario as the best formulated investigative theory they could come up with, given the limited information they had at that time.

According to Jayne, who lived there with Sherri before John moved in,

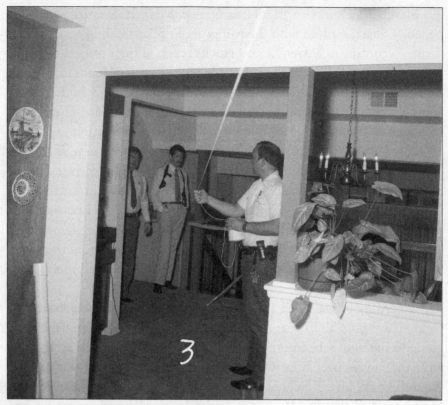

Left to right: Mayer, Hooks, and Luczy on second-floor landing
(February 28, 1986)

the doorbell was indeed audible from both bedrooms on the top floor. Jayne's bedroom was farthest from the front door, and up a short staircase from Sherri's bedroom, which was directly above the living room. During the time Jayne lived there, the head of Sherri's bed was against her bedroom wall closest to the front of the condo, basically above the condo's front entryway. In Jayne's opinion, if Sherri had been in bed, she would have heard the doorbell, or even a knock at the front door. Jayne recalled she could hear the doorbell from her own bedroom at the very back of the condo, although probably not a door knock, unless it was very loud or persistent.

Although Jayne was one of Sherri's closest friends, and was intimately familiar with her habits and the layout of the crime scene, she was never contacted or interviewed by the LAPD in 1986. There is no record in the murder book that the detectives ever questioned John about whether the doorbell could be heard from the bedroom, either.

———

About the same time on Friday that Mayer, Hooks, and the SID forensics personnel wrapped up their work at the condo, Sherri's colleagues at Glendale Adventist Medical Center gathered for a memorial service in her honor.

The service was held at the Vallejo Drive Church, across the street from the hospital. Sherri's colleague Romelda Anderson organized the program. Charles Cook, the pastor of the Rasmussens' church in Tucson, co-officiated with Barry Crabtree, the pastor of the Vallejo Drive Church, who was Glenn's father. Peggy planned all the music for the service. Before the service, Cook tried to persuade Peggy to speak about Sherri, but she was too distraught and told Cook there was no way she could do it.

When Jayne and Mike arrived for the memorial service, they saw John in the church lobby and spoke briefly with him. Jayne recalls John looked like a wreck. His skin was ashen, and he couldn't stop trembling. The way John paced back and forth made Jayne fear he was about to either throw up or keel over. He reminded her of nursing patients she had seen get very pale and restless just before they went into cardiac arrest. In her experience, people who looked as stricken as John did that morning soon had to be resuscitated. Jayne tried to reassure him, "We'll get through this. We have to."

Although it was the middle of a workday, Sherri's colleagues filled the church. The turnout reflected how respected and beloved Sherri was at the hospital. The Rasmussen family and John's parents also attended, along with many of Sherri's and John's friends. There were classmates of Sherri's from Loma Linda, where she earned her nursing degree, and colleagues from UCLA Medical Center, where she started her meteoric career. Because Sherri was to be buried in Tucson, and the Rasmussens had requested a family-only funeral, her memorial service in Glendale was the last opportunity for most everyone else in her life to pay their respects and say goodbye.

The memorial service, which was videotaped, began with hymns and a prayer. Romelda was the first speaker. On Tuesday night, after everyone at the hospital learned of the murder, Romelda had gone home and written down her thoughts about Sherri. She was not thinking at the time about any memorial service but wrote purely to get her feelings out. Sherri's murder was so shocking that she was at a loss for how else to ground herself. Much of what Romelda said at the service was verbatim what she had written on Tuesday. Before she approached the lectern, she told the hospital's chaplain that if she couldn't make it through, he would have to read her remarks.

Romelda said, "I stand here on behalf of friends and colleagues, with the hope that we can share our Sherri with those of you who may not have had the privilege of knowing her." Romelda recounted several stories about Sherri, and closed her remarks, "She was a joy to be with. Just as much as she was respected and admired, appreciated and loved, she is now missed, with a feeling of loss too deep to put into words." Romelda paused to compose herself. "Sherri. She gave, she shared, she taught, she cared, that we might be better nurses, better professionals, better persons, and better friends, and we are, thanks to a special person who came and touched our lives in such an exceptional way. We have been blessed with a legacy that we can cherish, and also share with each other. We say goodbye to our dear friend for now, but we look forward to that time and land where there will be no sorrow, no pain, no tears."

Pastor Cook acknowledged how many of Sherri's colleagues were present. "I look here at this attendance, and I think it's marvelous to have the kind of voice that's stated by your presence, of your concern for a fellow worker. John and Nels, Loretta, and Connie and Teresa, I don't know of any human emotion that could be encouraged more, than when you look about and see this kind of support," Cook said. The video camera panned to the assembled mourners. Every pew was full. At the very back, several more people stood, silhouetted by the church's sunlit stained-glass windows.

Cook recited a few lines from scripture, then said, "But while we remember these things, we are not without trouble. We have lots of trouble. We can cry out at times like this, 'It isn't fair.' And that's right, it surely isn't. But whoever said that life was fair? Not since the enemy entered into the hearts of created beings, so many, many years ago in heaven, life hasn't been fair. There will be a fairness ultimately, in all the judgment, but don't look for equality nor fairness in this life."

Cook said, "I remember the Rasmussen family as a close-knit, loving family. They supported one another in their family. They come from strong stock. Sherri's sisters, Connie and Teresa, were just little girls back in 1962 when I met this family . . . And then there was that little round-faced, bright, warm, smiling Sherri. She was the thoughtful one of all the children in the school . . . Sherri was the calm one. Sherri was the one who brought tranquillity and coordination, with her emotional and her mental stability, cooperating any place you asked her to cooperate. Serious about life, this young girl, as I saw her growing up from the age of four. Serious about life, but not heavy. Hopeful about the future, but not austere. As she proceeded in life, those characteristics that were so obvious in her early life, those caused her to set her objectives in life, and she worked toward them, and she was resolute until she had accomplished them. Peggy Daly, the director of nurses, shared with me this morning the progressive contribution that Sherri was making toward excellence in nursing. It's just like her, it didn't surprise me a bit, when I learned about her professional accomplishments, because that's the way she is, the way she was.

"But after having these memories and thinking about so many things that we could elaborate on, one cannot help but wonder: Why was she cut down, when the future seemed to hold so much promise, and she had so much to offer our society, when there are those in our society walking the streets who are malignant to society, who perform the position of a leech and contribute little or nothing, only the negative?" he asked. The question Cook posed had no answer. Cook said, "But she's gone. We remember her well, and our lives are richer as a result of being with her for these twenty-eight years, twenty-nine years."

Cook then invited anyone who wanted to say some words about Sherri to come up to the front of the church, where there was a handheld microphone ready.

Althea Kennedy, Sherri's boss, was first. "I would just like to say that it was a joy and a privilege to work with Sherri. I think Romelda has expressed how all of us felt about her. But in working with Sherri, it was truly a joy, and I think there's nothing better than enjoying it when you work. She won't be forgotten. Her plans, her projects that she was working with the group on will continue, and our memory of Sherri will always be there. And we know the things she was interested in, the things that she felt very strongly about, and we want to continue to work toward those goals in her memory," said Althea.

After another of Sherri's former colleagues, John was next to speak. He wore a taupe suit and a dark tie. In front of everyone gathered to honor Sherri, he began his remarks, "There's only one person here who knows what Sherri was as a wife. And it's my responsibility to speak for the family, too."

John sighed into the microphone. His body language was noticeably different from the speakers who preceded him, all of whom had maintained eye contact while they paid tribute to Sherri. John spoke mostly with his eyes downcast at his feet. John's tone of voice was wounded, as if the pain he felt made it hard for him to see beyond himself.

"Sherri, um, was, um . . . I just started a new job, and, um, talk about support," John said. John turned and glanced behind him at the hospital staff seated on the dais. "It . . . You know, we've heard a lot about what Sherri put into her profession. It took a lot out of her, too. And she had a lot left for her family and for me.

"It's, um . . . I mean . . . Sherri at work was such a professional, but at home, she was such a kid, and there is no way to describe that." John looked up, and for the first time during his remarks, did not avert his eyes from his audience. "There's no way for people who didn't know that part of her to understand that. I want everybody here to know that," he said.

John returned his gaze to the carpet and went on, "Her family, from the first day we met, we knew that everything was right. My parents loved Sherri as much as they love any one of their kids. I just want to thank you all for coming, and I want you to know that Sherri was the best professional in the world, she was the best wife that anybody could ever have, and she was the best sister, daughter. She wanted to make everybody happy, and it always frustrated her that she couldn't, in work, at home . . ." John sighed, then said, "It's just . . ." but trailed off without completing the thought. He waved his hands to signal that he was too emotional to say any more. John turned away and handed the microphone off.

At least one of Sherri's colleagues at the service, Peggy, was offended by how John eulogized Sherri. Peggy felt insulted that John would stand before an audience of Sherri's colleagues and, the way she saw it, basically tell everyone, "You guys didn't really know Sherri like I knew Sherri. You knew her only in a professional way."

Peggy was terribly hurt and saddened by the situation already. She felt angry at what she perceived as John's major pity party, and his implication that the assembled were just professional acquaintances to Sherri. Peggy thought of Sherri as her best friend. As angry as she felt at John for what he said, she could see he was a mess. She knew he did not intend to discount how she and others at the hospital felt. But that was how Peggy took it at the time.

Not all of Sherri's colleagues shared Peggy's negative reaction to John's eulogy. Glenn Crabtree interpreted John to mean, "You've all known Sherri professionally or as a friend, but I knew her as a lover." Glenn was not offended and did not think John's remarks discounted anyone else's feelings. But Glenn was not as close to Sherri as Peggy was. Neither of them knew John particularly well.

The last testimonial, after John's, was delivered by an older male physician dressed in blue surgical scrubs. Among the units Sherri oversaw as the director of critical care nursing was the surgical intensive care unit. The physician's attire suggested he had stepped away from the operating room to attend Sherri's service. "I just wanted to thank Sherri for being a member of the Ethics Committee, where her intelligence, thoughtfulness, sensitivity, and willingness to make decisions, which are not always easy, were very much respected," the surgeon said.

Jayne had never before attended a memorial or funeral at which people were invited to come up and speak publicly about the deceased. That wasn't the custom in Canada, where she grew up. Until Sherri's murder, Jayne had never experienced the loss of a loved one, let alone a death as sudden and shocking as Sherri's. She wanted to get up and say something, but she was such an emotional wreck that she didn't think she could. Jayne always regretted that she didn't.

Pastor Cook said, "I last spoke to Sherri last fall, just before you were married, John. And she was so happy and so hopeful, and she sort of brought me up to date a little bit about her life. So, friends, where do we go from here?" Cook recited some scripture, then asked, "What would Sherri say to us? She would say, 'Live on. Hope on. Believe on. And serve on.' Wouldn't she? That's how she'd say it. And so that is a terrific legacy to be left." Cook concluded his remarks by quoting a poem:

> Life is a story, volumes three—
> The past, the present, and the yet to be.
> The first is finished and laid away,
> And the second we're living day by day.
> The third, the last of volumes three,
> Is hid from sight. God holds the key.

When the service ended, Peggy went over to Nels and Loretta to offer them her condolences. Loretta mentioned to Peggy that the detectives had not let them into the condo to retrieve a dress to bury Sherri in. Loretta told Peggy that she and Connie had gone and bought a new dress.

Jayne did not find out that she might not be welcome at Sherri's funeral until the memorial service. She happened to ask her friend Nancy, who had worked with her and Sherri at UCLA, "Are you going to go to Tucson? Do you want to go together?"

"Oh, I'm not going to Tucson. It's only for family," Nancy told Jayne.

Jayne knew there was no way that she could say goodbye to Sherri at the memorial service, right then and there. Afterward, she went up to Loretta and said, "I want to come to the funeral, but they said it's only for family."

"Well, you're family. See you on Sunday," Loretta replied.

Several of John's college friends also attended Sherri's memorial service. Matt and Anita Gorder were there. So was David Neuman, John's college roommate, who had also been Stephanie's friend.

In the years after graduation, John and David remained friends and saw each other regularly. David attended John and Sherri's wedding, and in the three months since had socialized with them once or twice. He thought John and Sherri seemed extremely happy together. They struck David as almost the stereotype of newlyweds, delighted with each other and to be married.

David learned of Sherri's murder the day after it happened, through a phone call from another UCLA friend, Mike Boldrick. As David processed the news, he recalled his conversation with Stephanie, more than five years earlier, when she had confided to him about her feelings for John. David had seen Stephanie a few times since college, including once at a friend's wedding that John also attended. After Sherri's murder, the thought crossed David's mind, "Could Stephanie be involved?" Then he thought, "What a terrible person I am, to think that my college friend Stephanie is capable of murder."

When David saw John at Sherri's memorial service, John seemed devastated, as shattered as David had ever seen another person. In David's experience, when friends of his were dealing with a tragedy, he tried to take his cues from them. If the friend wanted to talk about what had happened, then they talked. If he sensed that they didn't want to talk about it, he didn't force them, but just tried to be present and offer his unconditional support. The sense that he got from John, when he saw him at Sherri's service, was that John was so deep in grief that he did not want to talk about the murder. David never mentioned his fleeting suspicion of Stephanie to John.

John, in his 2009 LAPD interview, was unable to recall much about Sherri's memorial service. John told the detectives, "We had one in the . . . Well, there was one, obviously, in Tucson, you know, with the burial and so forth. There was one in L.A. It was big. I just can't . . . I'm trying to remember the location. It was somewhere. I just don't remember the location, exactly."

Nels and Loretta flew back to Tucson on Friday afternoon, following Sherri's memorial service. Teresa, who was five months pregnant, took a separate flight the same day with her husband, Brian. Teresa cried the whole flight. She could tell from how the poor stewardesses looked at her that they thought she was going to fall apart. Teresa put on the free headphones she was given when they boarded, plugged them into her armrest, and tuned to the in-flight radio station. As their flight landed, she listened to a new song, "Take Me Home," that had just been released by Phil Collins. Teresa could think only of her sister, and that Sherri was going home. From then on, whenever Teresa heard that song, or even thought about it, she was moved to tears.

———

The Van Nuys detectives, having completed their forensic work at the condo earlier Friday, visited Sherri's workplace that afternoon. The typed chrono indicated, *"1400 | Glendale Adventist Hospital, rec'd threat phone—info from security director Ulack."* The hospital's security director at the time was actually Jim Feldman. Bob Vlack was the assistant security director.

Vlack's name was spelled correctly in the follow-up report, which recounted: *"On 2-28-86 at 1400 hrs., Detectives Mayer and Hooks went to Glendale Adventist Hospital and spoke to the Director of Security Mr. Vlack. Detectives were informed that Sherri Rasmussen did receive an annoying phone call while she was working at the hospital. The annoying call was in relation to a hiring problem within a nursing capacity. They had done an investigation into the matter. A copy of their report was given to detectives. After close examination of the report and the cause of the call, detectives realized that there was no apparent connection to [sic] the annoying call and the crime that detectives are investigating. The call information is contained in the murder book."*

The LAPD has never made public the Glendale Adventist security report about Sherri. For that reason, several important aspects of the report remain shrouded in secrecy. It is uncertain who wrote the report, how many pages it is, and when it was written. Was the author the same person who "had done an investigation into the matter," as the detectives wrote, or someone else in the hospital's administration? How extensive was the hospital's investigation? Who was interviewed? What did Sherri say? Without the report, it is impossible to answer these questions or to know how thorough an investigation the hospital conducted.

The detectives' allusion to a "hiring problem within a nursing capacity" is consistent with a conflict Sherri had with a nurse whom she had denied a promotion. Apparently, the Glendale Adventist security report made no reference to Stephanie Lazarus, John Ruetten, or the incident during John and Sherri's engagement when Stephanie went to the hospital and confronted Sherri in her office.

It is unknown whether the assistant security director interviewed by the detectives, Bob Vlack, was aware of the confrontation in Sherri's office between her and Stephanie. Nor is it known whether Sherri reported the incident to Feldman, Vlack, or anyone else at the hospital in 1985, either formally or informally. Feldman and Vlack are both deceased.

Peggy knew that she felt harassed by an ex-girlfriend of John's, a police officer named Stephanie, but not about the incident in Sherri's office. Peggy was never contacted or interviewed by the LAPD in 1986.

Althea Kennedy recalls she met briefly with an LAPD detective at the hospital and asked him, "What have you found? Any ideas about who may have done it?" According to Althea, the detective said they were still investigating, but they believed Sherri was killed in a botched burglary. The detective mentioned to Althea the video equipment left by the door, as the reason they thought Sherri had interrupted a burglary.

The lone eyewitness to the confrontation at the hospital between Sherri and Stephanie was Sherri's secretary, Sylvia Nielsen. Sherri had told Sylvia that the angry woman was John's ex-girlfriend, and that she had threatened her. Sylvia did not report the incident to the hospital or mention it to anyone else at that time.

After Sherri's murder, Sylvia recalled the incident and what Sherri had said. The possibility that John's ex-girlfriend might have killed Sherri weighed heavily on Sylvia's conscience, but she was apparently too afraid to contact the police on her own initiative and tell them what she knew. Instead, for several weeks following Sherri's murder, Sylvia kept her knowledge of the confrontation that she had witnessed entirely to herself. Sylvia was never interviewed by the LAPD, either in person on February 28 when detectives were at the hospital, or subsequently.

Mayer, in an interview in 2014, said that he did not go with Hooks to the hospital on February 28, as was indicated in the follow-up report he wrote in 1986, but that Hooks had gone alone. Mayer recalled, "Hooks had went to her work, interviewed the persons there. Because I was at the house doing the shooting tie-lines. In his opinion, when he came back, there's nothing at the hospital."

According to Mayer, he and Hooks were aware of the conflict Sherri had with the nurse and her doctor boyfriend at the hospital, and they weighed it as a potential motive for her murder. "We went through that," Mayer said. Asked whether the nurse was interviewed, Mayer replied, "That was Hooks that day, and Hooks was very confident that, 'Nah, this isn't what's happened here.'" Mayer also said that the interviews Hooks conducted at Glendale Adventist were tape-recorded.

If the detectives formally interviewed anyone at Glendale Adventist besides the assistant security director, Vlack, there is no record of it in the typed chrono or follow-up report. In LAPD homicide investigations in the 1980s, it was standard practice for recorded interviews to be assigned a tape number. The number was customarily noted in the chrono, the follow-up report, or both. The follow-up report noted, for instance, of John's initial interview, "On 2-24-86 at 2150 hrs., Detective Mayer interviewed John Ruetten at Van Nuys Station. The conversation was tape recorded on tape #104595." There is no similar indication that Hooks's interview with Vlack was tape-recorded, nor any reference to a tape number. No interview notes with anyone at Glendale Adventist were preserved in the murder book, beyond the hospital's security report. The lack of documentation suggests Mayer and Hooks did not independently verify any of the information contained in the security report.

The detectives' final entry in the typed chrono for Friday afternoon stated in full, "1440 | Checked on prints for A.L.P.S. comparison."

ALPS was the Automated Latent Print System, a statewide database of fingerprints maintained by the California Department of Justice. In the 1980s, the procedure for requesting an ALPS comparison involved mailing a one-to-one scale photograph of the print to the state lab in Sacramento. Before a case could be submitted to ALPS, the local agency first had to eliminate crime scene prints that lacked sufficient detail for comparison, as well as any identified as belonging to the victim or others not considered suspects. Rather than producing a single match between an unidentified print and a specific suspect, ALPS generated a list of possible matches in the database. The requesting agency was mailed a printout of the names, ranked in order of probability. For a print to be identified definitively, a fingerprint analyst had to obtain the candidate's print records and make a visual comparison.

The typed chrono did not indicate which detective checked on the prints or whom they spoke with, presumably at SID. Nor was it noted what information the check produced, in terms of whether any prints from the Rasmussen crime scene were suitable for ALPS comparison. In the follow-up report, the only fingerprint activity documented for February 28 was the ninhydrin-enhanced handprint Ames photographed in the condo that morning. The typed chrono entry about ALPS was the last investigative activity the detectives documented the week of Sherri's murder.

Stephanie spent the day of Sherri's memorial service on patrol in Devonshire. She and her friend Jayme Weaver were assigned to the same patrol car.

Stephanie had last partnered with Weaver nine days earlier, on February 19, five days before Sherri's murder. Stephanie concluded her diary entry on Friday, February 28, "*We went by my house for my bathing suit. So we could go to the tanning booth after work. Note: I got Sgt. Rendon to change the board so Jayme and I could work tomorrow together. My last day on day watch for a while anyway.*"

Weaver had been friends with Stephanie for almost three years. In the eleven months they had both been assigned to Devonshire, they had worked as partners more than two dozen times. Each watch was eight hours long, seated side by side. Just counting their time on patrol together, Stephanie and Weaver had spent at least two hundred hours together in the year leading up to Sherri's murder.

That Friday and Saturday, Stephanie and Weaver's time together was not limited to the hours they spent in their patrol car. On Friday, according to her diary, they also had a sit-down meal at a House of Pancakes, visited with Weaver's friends, and after work, they apparently went to a tanning salon together. On Saturday, they went to Stephanie's place to have lunch and watch *Hill Street Blues* together.

Weaver knew Stephanie's personality perhaps as well as anyone on the

LAPD. If Stephanie's demeanor or behavior changed around the end of February 1986, when Sherri was murdered, Weaver did not pick up on it at the time, or if she did, it did not register in her long-term memory. In 2012, Weaver testified in court that she had no specific recollection of working with Stephanie on February 28 or March 1, 1986, and could not remember whether Stephanie had any visible injuries at that time.

In Tucson, the Rasmussens spent Saturday preparing for Sherri's funeral the next day. Nels and Loretta did not own a family cemetery plot, so they had to purchase one before the burial.

Jayne flew in from Los Angeles on Saturday. She carried with her on the plane an ivy cutting. Three months earlier, at John and Sherri's wedding reception, Jayne's friend Nancy had caught Sherri's bouquet. Jayne asked Nancy for a sprig of ivy from the bouquet, took it home from the wedding, and planted it in a pot. As Jayne packed for her flight to Tucson, she decided to take a cutting from the ivy plant to place in Sherri's casket, because she wanted Sherri to have something forever from her wedding day.

Peggy, who did not go to Tucson, went to Saturday morning services at the Vallejo Drive Church, where Sherri's memorial service had been held a day earlier. Glenn Crabtree also attended services that morning. Glenn's father, the pastor of the church, had planned an afternoon sightseeing trip, with friends visiting from out of town, to the botanical gardens at the Arboretum. Glenn invited Peggy to come along.

At the Arboretum, out of earshot of Peggy, Glenn's father and friends asked him who Peggy was. Glenn described Peggy as a great person he worked with at the hospital. "She's just lost her closest friend, who was murdered. She needs friends," he told them.

Peggy and Glenn had never spent time together away from work before that Saturday afternoon at the Arboretum. Glenn did not bring up the condolence letter and poem he wrote for Peggy the day before. Peggy did not mention it either.

The following day, Sunday, March 2, was Stephanie's first off duty in almost a week, since Monday, February 24, the day Sherri was murdered. Because Stephanie kept a diary only on workdays, the sole evidence of how she spent her day off was her datebook. For March 2, she wrote her off-duty status and two names of unknown significance, Pierce and Diane. The only appointment she noted for Sunday was a 3:00 p.m. *"Sun Tan."*

Sunday in Tucson, Sherri's family gathered for her body to be laid to rest. Sherri's extended family at the funeral included her grandparents, aunts, uncles, and cousins. John and his parents, Richard and Margaret, were also there, but not John's siblings. Of her closest girlfriends, only Jayne and Donna Robison attended.

When Jayne arrived at the funeral home on Sunday morning, she saw John and told him about the ivy she had grown from Sherri's wedding bouquet. John went to get the funeral director.

Jayne knew the Rasmussens had decided on a closed casket funeral. Nels and Loretta had made the decision without seeing Sherri's body, after Mayer told them her facial injuries were severe and warned them they might never forget the sight. Connie and Teresa followed their parents' lead, although both later regretted not getting a final moment with their sister to say goodbye. Among Sherri's loved ones, only John bore the burden of having seen Sherri's injuries firsthand.

When Jayne showed the ivy cutting to the funeral director, he surprised her by asking if she wanted to place it in the casket herself. She had not contemplated that possibility. Jayne felt taken aback and didn't know what to do. She was concerned that the Rasmussens wouldn't want her to see Sherri. She also wasn't certain she was prepared to see the body. Jayne looked at John and the funeral director for guidance, but they offered none. She felt she had no time to think. "No, I don't believe so," she told the funeral director. Later, Jayne wondered if she should have said yes. Like Sherri's sisters, Jayne always regretted not getting a final moment alone with her.

The funeral home's small chapel was filled to capacity for Sherri's service. Prayers were led by Pastor Carl Groom, who had married Sherri and John just three months earlier. Groom had also been Sherri's teacher when she was a schoolgirl. He had performed funerals for other former students in his long career as a pastor, but after Sherri's, Groom told Nels that hers was the hardest he had ever done.

Following the chapel service, everyone filed out past the closed casket, which was draped with pink velvet. On top of the casket was a framed photograph of Sherri. Loretta gave the photo to Donna to keep. Jayne stood outside the funeral chapel and watched as Sherri's casket was placed in the hearse. One of Sherri's cousins saw her crying and gave her a lace handkerchief. Jayne was touched by the gesture of kindness. As Jayne stood there, she could hear a song by Heart, "These Dreams," playing from somewhere inside the funeral home. The song made her picture Sherri hovering between this world and the next. Jayne believed it was a message from Sherri.

Jayne did not sense any tension between Nels and John, or between Nels and John's parents, while she was in Tucson. John's emotional state seemed to her not much better on Sunday than on Friday, when she had seen him at the memorial service.

Nels recalls that his frustration with John simmered throughout the weekend of Sherri's funeral. Nels could not understand why John was so reluctant to answer his questions or even to talk with him one-on-one. Nels believed John's parents were protecting him by keeping him away from Nels, because they knew if they didn't, he would corner John and keep badgering him. He had no intention of letting up on John until he got the truth from him. Nels looked for opportunities to press John while he was in Tucson. But, as in Los Angeles, he made little headway, he recalls.

Nels and Loretta invited everyone to a reception at their home following Sherri's burial. According to Nels, moments after the service at the cemetery ended, John's mother, Margaret, came up to him where he stood, not ten feet from Sherri's grave, and said, "Nels, you have to get off John's back and let him get on with life."

Nels was baffled by Margaret's sentiments. Sherri's casket was not yet in the ground. He did not understand how you could be married to someone and then, the minute they were gone, wash your hands of them. Nels felt it was almost soulless.

According to the Rasmussens, John's parents also informed them at the cemetery that they and John could not attend the reception at their home because they needed to get to the airport to catch their flight back to San Diego. Loretta thanked the Ruettens for coming to the funeral.

Jayne did go to the Rasmussens' for the reception. Jayne sat in a chair in the living room and did not move for hours, still in shock that Sherri was dead. Nels's mother, Matilda, was also seated in the living room. Sherri's grandmother struck Jayne as a tough old woman who had worked hard all her life. Matilda was very religious and sure of her beliefs. At one point, when the mood was particularly somber, Matilda looked around the living room, and said, "Why is everyone so sad? Sherri is in a better place."

It did not feel that way to Jayne at the time. Sherri may have been in a better place, but it wasn't where Jayne was.

Some of the family who attended Sherri's funeral had flown in from out of state. Several hours into the reception, Nels had to drive someone to the airport for their flight home.

At the time, Tucson's airport was not very big. The terminal had only a few gates for boarding. When Nels dropped off his relative inside, he was surprised to see John and his parents still there, waiting for their flight.

In those days, there was minimal security between the check-in counters and the boarding gates, and people could move freely between them. According to Nels, when the Ruettens saw him walking toward them, they looked shaken to see him. John and his parents did not know that it was a chance encounter, and that he had not come to the airport specifically to see them. Nels sensed the Ruettens thought he was up to no good.

Nels asked the Ruettens what happened to their flight. John's father offered some explanation for the delay that sounded implausible to Nels, given the number of hours that had passed since their parting conversation at the cemetery.

Nels did not challenge the Ruettens' explanation because he didn't see the point of doing so. But he took it as proof that John and his parents simply had not wanted to come to the reception. Nels believed the Ruettens just wanted to leave and get away the first moment they could. Nels never saw John's father, Richard, again.

19

"A Well-Reasoned, Carefully-Documented and Insightful Investigation"

(March 3 to April 8, 1986)

Stephanie was off duty at Devonshire on Monday, March 3, her second day off in a row. One week had passed since Sherri's murder.

The Van Nuys detectives did not document any investigative work on Sherri's case over the weekend. According to the LAPD's typed chrono and follow-up report, their investigation resumed at the crime scene on Monday morning. Hooks recanvassed the condo complex for witnesses who might have seen a suspect or heard anything around the time of the murder. Hooks was unable to locate anyone.

Mayer meanwhile hand-delivered to SID a chilling item of evidence from the crime scene, a quilted blanket found near Sherri's body. The blanket, handmade by her grandmother, was riddled with bullet holes. The fabric around some holes appeared singed and dark with gunshot residue. The next four entries recorded in the typed chrono pertained to the blanket:

3-3-86	1000	SID crime lab—blood 2nd sample taken. This was off the blanket.
	1030	Raffel #C9982 took GSR from entry into the blanket.
	1130	Booked blanket into property.
	1200	SID firearms—took blanket from prop and went to firearms
		They will attempt to show that the blanket was used to muffle the sound of the shots. In addition, they will photograph the contact wound to the blanket. They will also re-construct the blanket and show entry and exit wounds.

Monday afternoon, the typed chrono indicated, *"1305 | Called Tom Ruetter . . . no answer left message."* Tom was John's brother.

Ten minutes later, Mayer called SID latent fingerprint analyst George Herrera. Herrera's name was misspelled as "Heuera" in the typed chrono. According to the follow-up report, Herrera informed Mayer that one lift obtained from the banister would be photographed and submitted to the Cal-ID database for comparison.

Tom Ruetten called the detectives back at 2:00 p.m., the typed chrono indicated. The detectives wanted to know the name of John's friend who had visited John and Sherri the day before her murder. Tom identified the friend as Mike Boldrick. Tom said he would have Mike call Mayer as soon as possible. Mike called the detectives half an hour later. He agreed to come in for an interview and fingerprints the next day.

The detectives' main focus the rest of Monday was locating Sherri's stolen BMW. At 2:15 p.m., Mayer called the Valley Traffic Division and requested a grid search. The follow-up report recounted, *"Mayer attended the VTD Motor roll call and gave information regarding the crime. The search was conducted by the motor units with negative results."* The detectives also alerted Air Support to the vehicle's description, so the LAPD's fleet of helicopters could keep an eye out for it from above.

The last investigative activity the detectives recorded on Monday, at 3:00 p.m., was that Hooks spoke with the supervisor of the Valley Parole Unit and provided him with information about the crime and stolen vehicle. The typed chrono indicated that the information was read to officers at PM watch roll call.

Late Monday night, Stephanie reported for duty at Devonshire, part of the Valley Bureau. It is unknown whether the description of Sherri's stolen BMW was also read to officers at Devonshire morning watch, the shift after PM watch. If it was, Stephanie made no mention of it in her diary. She wrote, *"It was work out day tonight. My first night on mornings . . . First thing we did was go to the Donut Shop, Reseda—Fosters. Kirk and Rost met us. We stayed there until 0100"*—an hour and a half into their watch. Later, Stephanie and her partner pulled over a drunk driver and delivered his blood sample to the Van Nuys station, a short drive away. *"The first night wasn't that bad, but I was falling asleep in the car easily,"* she wrote.

Although Stephanie's days were free, since she was back to working nights, the only plans she noted in her datebook the next day, March 4, were *"0900—Tan appt."*

Coincidentally, the Van Nuys detectives resumed their investigation Tuesday morning at the same time as Stephanie's tanning appointment. At 9:00 a.m., according to the typed chrono and follow-up report, Mayer interviewed Mike Boldrick, John's friend who had visited the day before the murder. Mike recounted that he got there Sunday around 12:30 to 1:00 p.m. and stayed until about 4:30. Mike said he and John went in and out the front door twice, when they went for a run in Balboa Park. Mike told Mayer he was not aware of any marital problems between John and Sherri, according to the follow-up report. There is no indication in the typed chrono or follow-up report that Mayer's interview with Mike was tape-recorded.

Tuesday at 9:15 a.m., the detectives attended another roll call, for Valley motor officers on day watch, the shift after morning watch. Stephanie had just gone off duty and was not present for the Van Nuys detectives' briefing.

Tuesday afternoon, Mayer visited John's workplace and interviewed one of his colleagues. In the typed chrono, the name of John's employer, Micropolis, was misspelled, and the name of the street the company was located on was omitted. The typed chrono recounted in full, *"1300 | Went to 21329 Microplois Industry to interview Paul Marsh. He pretty much gives John Ruetter an alibi about work and the time of death."* According to the follow-up report, Marsh told Mayer, *"The best I remember is that John Ruetten was at work on 2-24-86. He was not gone from the office that I remember . . . We do not have to punch in or out on a time clock . . . John never appeared scratched up when I saw him at work on that day. He never appeared nervous to me."*

By 2:30 that afternoon, the detectives had obtained a photo of a 1985 BMW 318i, the model of Sherri's stolen car. *"Will have the photo reproduced with the license number,"* the typed chrono indicated, the last investigative activity recorded Tuesday.

The same day at the LAPD crime lab, officer George Luczy of the SID Firearms and Explosives Unit completed his report on the pair of bullets recovered during Sherri's autopsy. Luczy, who had performed the string line trajectory analysis at the condo a few days earlier, examined the bullets with an eye to answering two questions: What make and type of ammunition were they, and what make of gun may have fired them?

Luczy reported that both bullets were *"consistent with .38/.357"* caliber ammunition. Bullet weights are measured in units called grains, seven thousand of which equal one pound. The first bullet weighed 119.2 grains, and the second 124.7 grains, he noted. Luczy described both bullets as *"of semi-jacketed soft point construction with a single cannelure."* "Semi-jacketed soft point" meant the bullet's copper jacket stopped short of an exposed lead tip. A "cannelure" was a distinct pattern of grooves imprinted around the bullet's cylinder during manufacturing.

Different makes of ammunition have telltale characteristics that ballistics examiners rely on to try to identify the bullet's manufacturer. Luczy's report did not address which brands of ammunition were consistent with the caliber, weight, and other qualities of the two bullets fired into Sherri's chest. Although Luczy did not note it in his report, both bullets were perfectly consistent with a make of ammunition that was undoubtedly familiar to any LAPD officer in 1986: Federal brand .38 special +P.

From 1981 to 1988, Federal .38 special +P was the only type of ammunition that rank-and-file LAPD officers were authorized to carry and use. Like the two bullets Luczy examined, the LAPD's standard ammunition had a copper semi-jacket, a soft point exposed lead tip, and a single cannelure. The weight of an unfired cartridge was 125 grains, nominally more than the slugs recovered during Sherri's autopsy.

With respect to the murder weapon, Luczy reported, *"Both bullets bare [sic] rifling impressions of five lands and grooves with a right hand twist and were possibly fired from a Smith and Wesson, I.N.A., Llama, Ruger, Iris Orbea, Gabilan or any other unlisted firearm with similar specifications."*

Near midnight on the day the ballistics report was completed, Stephanie reported for duty at Devonshire station. *"I was much more awake tonight or at least I felt a little better,"* she wrote in her diary. For the second straight night, she and her partner arrested a drunk driver and later delivered their evidence sample to the Van Nuys station. *"I wrote the report at the desk after falling asleep a few times. We took the urine to Van Nuys. We stopped for bagels on the way home, went to the cleaners, and that was EOW,"* she recounted. Stephanie went off duty at 8:15 Wednesday morning.

The Van Nuys detectives resumed their investigation less than an hour later, at 9:00 a.m. on March 5, when their typed chrono noted the comple-

---

```
Ammunition
1.    All duty and off-duty ammunition shall be 125 gr,
      semi-jacketed soft point, .38 spl+p, muzzel velocity of
      1000 feet per second out of the barrel maximum.
2.    The issue ammunition is Federal.
```

LAPD Manual regulations on allowed ammunition (1986)

tion of a *"condo sketch and re-canvas [sic] report."* Later Wednesday morning, Mayer attended roll call for Metro Task Force officers and briefed them on the crime and missing vehicle. The last investigative activity the detectives recorded Wednesday, at 11:15 a.m., was that Ham Watch, a volunteer group of civilian ham radio operators, *"will conduct a 1 mile grid search around the location . . . This will take place on 3-7-86,"* the typed chrono stated.

At the crime lab on March 5, SID fingerprint specialist George Herrera completed his analysis of all thirty-four latent prints collected at the crime scene.

Herrera's initial task was to evaluate each print and classify it as either "identifiable" or "non-identifiable." Identifiable prints had sufficient detail to compare to a known exemplar, for instance the prints of the victim or a suspect. Non-identifiable prints lacked the minimum characteristics to determine whose prints they were. The LAPD's print specialists who worked in the field were trained to lift any print that might have value. How much information a print had was judged later, in the lab, under magnification and better lighting conditions than existed in the field.

Herrera examined each print through a loupe magnifier, to better discern the fragments of ridges, whorls, and loops that might lead to an identification. Of the thirty-four prints lifted at the crime scene, Herrera classified twenty-three as identifiable. Prints deemed non-identifiable were not discarded but retained for possible reexamination later.

Herrera's next step was to compare the identifiable prints to the prints of the victim and anyone else with legitimate access to the location, such as a spouse. Prints matched to the victim and others whose presence was easily explained were dubbed "elimination" identifications. Elimination identifications enabled Herrera to focus more intently on the remaining identifiable prints, those most likely to have been left at the crime scene by unknown persons of interest.

The only sets of exemplar prints that Herrera was directed in 1986 to compare to the crime scene prints were Sherri's, John's, and his friend Mike Boldrick's. No print comparisons were requested for Stephanie Lazarus, despite the fact that as a police officer, her prints were already on file with the LAPD at the time. Not until 2009 were the crime scene prints belatedly compared to Stephanie's. No matches were made.

Of the twenty-three identifiable prints collected at the crime scene, Herrera in 1986 identified five as Sherri's, ten as John's, and one as his friend Mike Boldrick's. Four other identifiable prints were later matched to Steve Hooks, the Van Nuys homicide detective who was among the first responders after the murder. Who left the remaining identifiable prints has never been determined.

Also on March 5 at SID, in the Firearms and Explosives Unit, Luczy examined the bullet-riddled blanket found at the crime scene near Sherri's body.

In 1986, it was not yet standard practice at the crime lab to document physical evidence by photographing it. Luczy instead drew a sketch of the blanket, on which he noted the locations of the bullet holes and other possible evidence. The handmade blanket's outer fabric was a quilted patchwork of patterns and pastel colors. Inside was a thick layer of lightweight polyester batting.

Because the blanket was one of a kind, and evidence in a homicide case, Luczy could not wrap it around a gun and test-fire a shot to see how significantly it muffled the report. Based on the blanket's thickness, however, he believed it would have effectively suppressed the sound of gunshots.

Luczy inspected the blanket for evidence to support the theory that it was used as a makeshift silencer. Luczy was also looking for clues about the murder weapon, and what type of gun it was. He noted three groups of bullet holes in the blanket, which he labeled A, B, and C. The letters were arbitrary, since it was impossible to reconstruct the sequence of shots from the condition of the blanket alone.

Group C consisted of two bullet holes just below the center of the blanket. Around one hole, Luczy noticed dark marks on the fabric, which he suspected were soot and gunpowder residue deposits. One deposit in particular, to the right of the bullet hole, had a distinctly linear shape. Luczy recognized it as barrel cylinder gap discharge, a phenomenon unique to revolvers. Its presence on the blanket confirmed that the murder weapon was a revolver, as opposed to a semiautomatic handgun.

Unlike guns that do not have a cylinder, for a revolver to function properly, there must be a paper-thin gap between the cylinder that holds the bullets and the entrance to the gun barrel. Without some space between the two, the cylinder could not open and close, or spin within the frame of the gun.

When a revolver is fired, burning gunpowder produces a dramatic increase of air pressure inside the gun, which propels the bullet down the barrel. In the split seconds before the bullet has fully exited the barrel, it briefly obstructs the gaseous high-pressure mix of hot air, smoke, and soot from escaping down the barrel. As a result of the blockage, some trapped gases blow out of the sides of the revolver, through the barrel cylinder gap.

If a revolver is wrapped in fabric and fired, the gunshot residue that escapes through the barrel cylinder gap is deposited on the material in contact with that part of the gun. Because the barrel cylinder gap is straight and narrow, the mark imprinted on the fabric has the same shape.

No direct comparisons were made in 1986 between the blanket evidence and any particular makes and models of revolvers. In Luczy's written report on the bullets recovered during Sherri's autopsy, he listed several gunmakers as possibilities for the murder weapon. The first gunmaker Luczy named in his report was Smith & Wesson.

It was not until 2009, more than twenty years later, that the blanket evidence was compared to an exemplar of a specific revolver, the Smith & Wesson model 49, a .38 special revolver with a two-inch barrel. The gun's compact size made it a common choice of backup weapon among LAPD officers in the 1980s.

The Smith & Wesson model 49 was the backup weapon that Stephanie had carried ever since she became a cop. Stephanie purchased hers from the gun shop at the LAPD academy on February 29, 1984. The following day, March 1, she presented the gun to the LAPD armorer for inspection and registration, as she was required to do before she was authorized to

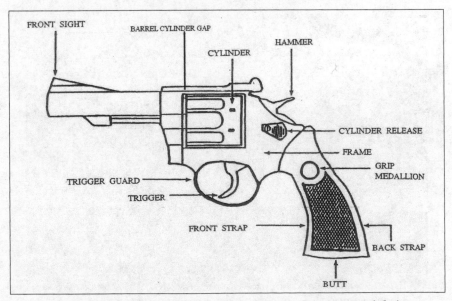

Diagram of a conventional double-action revolver (court exhibit)

carry it on duty. The armorer's approval was recorded on Stephanie's LAPD firearms inspection record, also known as her gun card, which listed the make, model, barrel length, and serial number of all the firearms an officer was authorized to use. On March 2, the day after Stephanie registered her new backup weapon with the department, she graduated from the LAPD academy.

The murder weapon that was used to kill Sherri Rasmussen has never been recovered. In 2009, the LAPD reexamined the bullet-riddled blanket from Sherri's case. The distance between the barrel cylinder gap discharge mark and the closest bullet hole was exactly two inches—the length of the barrel on Stephanie's backup gun.

When an exemplar of a Smith & Wesson model 49 revolver was placed atop the blanket, the gun's barrel cylinder gap lined up perfectly with the linear deposit, and the muzzle with the bullet hole.

Stephanie reported for duty at Devonshire late on March 5, the same day Luczy completed his examination of the blanket. It is unknown whether, little more than a week after Sherri's murder, Stephanie still carried her backup weapon, the Smith & Wesson model 49 revolver with a two-inch barrel, when she went out on patrol.

On Thursday, March 6, the Van Nuys detectives documented no activity on Sherri's case until late that afternoon. At 3:30 p.m., according to the typed

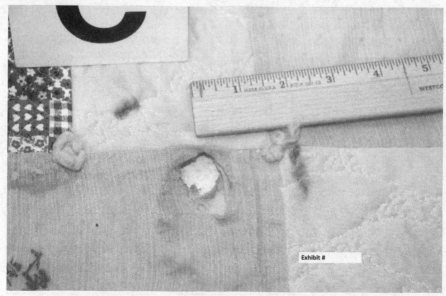

2009 LAPD photo of bullet hole and gunshot residue on blanket

2009 LAPD photo of bullet hole with Smith & Wesson model 49 revolver

chrono, Mayer and Hooks interviewed an unnamed informant about burglaries in the area. The identity of the informant, and what they had to say, was not documented in the murder book. At 4:30 p.m., the detectives spoke to a resident on the street that ran along the east side of the Balboa Townhomes complex, McLennan Avenue. *"They were of the opinion that one of his gardner's [sic] may have found the purse taken and attempted to return it,"* the follow-up report recounted. The name of the street the resident lived on was misspelled in both the typed chrono and the follow-up report as "McLean." The name of the resident the detectives spoke with was not documented.

Also on March 6, Greg Matheson, a criminalist at SID, obtained from the LAPD's property division several items of evidence in Sherri's case. Matheson worked in SID's serology section, which analyzed biological evidence collected at crime scenes. The evidence Matheson analyzed in 1986 included LAPD property items 1 through 6, the blood swatches taken at the condo; item 7, the bloodstained dish towel that John used to shroud Sherri's face; and item 8, the bloodstained length of white rope found in the front entryway. It would take Matheson three weeks to complete the blood work.

The only appointment Stephanie noted in her datebook for March 6 was for a facial at 4:30 that afternoon.

Hours later, close to midnight, Stephanie reported for duty at Devonshire. Her patrol partner that night was Betty Kleffman. Stephanie recounted in her diary, *"Kleffman drove tonight thank god. I didn't sleep very much today. I was very tired. In fact all I did all night was to sleep. I couldn't keep awake if you paid me. So we just drove around . . . I was really so tired I didn't really care."*

Stephanie had scheduled days off on Saturday, March 8, and Sunday, March 9. Because she was assigned to morning watch, her weekend began at 8:15 Friday morning. The only plans she noted in her datebook for March 7 was a tanning appointment at 9:00 a.m.

Once again, as it happened, the Van Nuys detectives resumed their investigation Friday at the same time as Stephanie's tanning appointment. The typed chrono indicated the detectives called Isaac's Landscape and left a message. The resident on McLennan Avenue had told the detectives the gardeners who found Sherri's purse and tried to return it may have worked for Isaac's. The 9:00 a.m. phone call was the only investigative activity the detectives recorded in the typed chrono during the day on Friday, March 7.

According to the follow-up report, Mayer was informed at 4:10 p.m. Friday that the *"volunteer Ham Watch Unit would do a two square mile grid search of 7100 Balboa looking for the stolen vehicle taken in this crime."* The dearth of additional documentation in the murder book about the volunteer grid search suggests that it was unsuccessful, if it took place at all.

Friday evening was foggy and chilly. At 8:10 p.m., an LAPD Valley Traffic Division officer, Leona Thomas, was on patrol in Van Nuys when she noticed a silver BMW 318i parked on the street at the corner of Zombar Avenue and Cohasset Street. Zombar and Cohasset was a quiet intersection just east of the 405 freeway, in a nondescript residential neighborhood. Apart from a nursing home on one corner, the block was lined with modest single family homes and low-rise apartment buildings.

The BMW was found unlocked, with its keys in the ignition. No damage was evident to the vehicle. Thomas confirmed the license plate matched the BMW reported stolen in connection with a homicide, then notified the Van Nuys watch commander. The watch commander in turn called Mayer, who came out to the location. Mayer supervised the transportation of the BMW to Valley Property, where it would be protected from the elements. The forecast called for light rain overnight. According to the typed chrono, officers conducted a *"foot-to-foot"* search for the murder weapon in a *"vacant lot at Zambora [sic] & Cohasset,"* with negative results.

The whereabouts of Sherri's BMW in the eleven days between February 24, when it was stolen, and March 7, when it was found, remains a mystery to this day. Nor is it known why the BMW was abandoned at that location. Zombar and Cohasset was about two miles east of John and Sherri's condo and a mile south of Roscoe Boulevard, the boundary between the LAPD's Van Nuys and Devonshire Divisions. One possible motive for leaving the BMW at that location was its proximity to a nearby school for adolescents with emotional and behavioral problems. The school was located on Saticoy Street, two short blocks from Zombar and Cohasset. The intersection where the BMW was abandoned was also less than a mile drive from the nearest on-ramp to the 405 freeway, at Sherman Way.

It is unknown how many days or hours the stolen BMW sat on the street, unlocked and with its keys in the ignition, before Thomas found it Friday, two hours after nightfall. Was the BMW abandoned there as bait for any troubled schoolkid who happened to walk past it? Any teenager tempted to take the BMW for an innocent joy ride could have become, easily and unwittingly, a prime suspect in Sherri's murder.

Mayer, in an interview in 2014, recalled that he was thrilled when Sherri's BMW was recovered. According to Mayer, the location where the car was found was "absolutely an area that burglars lived, and burglars fenced property, and burglars used to conduct their activities from." Mayer also described the neighborhood as a "very, very, very bad ol' area," a "big burglary area," and "just a little trashed out, low-life" stomping ground for burglars and dope dealers.

Mayer recounted that when the BMW was found, he thought, "The burglar is cruising around in this neighborhood, drove it around there, dropped it off, and got out of Dodge." The fact that the car was not stripped of its radio or other parts Mayer construed as additional evidence that "It was just used to get out of town. But it was legally parked in an area that cars of that nature were not unreal, but it also didn't fit that particular area. There's bad dope dealers that drive BMWs all the time. There's burglars that are driving BMWs. But the fact that it was that area led us to believe that, 'Okay, the guy committed the crime, jumped in the car, drove the car and got out of Dodge, and got over to an area where he was safe in, or lived in, or whatever.'"

According to Mayer, the other detectives in the Van Nuys homicide unit, including his partner Hooks, their supervisor, Pida, and Pida's supervisor, Durrer, all agreed that where the BMW was abandoned strengthened their theory that Sherri was killed in a burglary. Mayer said, "So that was something else that all of us, again, felt like, 'Yes, this is another little thread of information that leads to our theory.'"

According to the typed chrono, the detectives were back at work early on the morning after Sherri's BMW was recovered, although it was a Saturday. At 8:30 a.m., Hooks spoke with the owner of Isaac's Landscaping, who told him that none of his gardeners had found Sherri's purse or attempted to return it.

Mayer meanwhile met SID criminalist William Moore and Mike Ames, the latent print specialist, at Valley Property at 9:00 a.m. to examine the BMW. Evidence photos of the recovered BMW were also taken the same morning.

Ames dusted the interior and exterior of the BMW with fingerprint powder, focusing on surfaces he thought a suspect might have touched, including the door handles, windows, and rearview mirror. He lifted a total of five latent prints: one on the driver's side seat-belt connector, three from the inside of the driver's window, and one from the inside of the passenger's window.

Later, in the crime lab, the three prints on the driver's window were identified as John Ruetten's. The print on the passenger window was eventually matched to Brian Lane, Sherri's brother-in-law, who drove the BMW the day before her murder. The last latent print, on the driver's seat-belt connector, was deemed not identifiable.

Moore's assignment was to search the car's interior for any physical evidence related to the homicide. He started his examination with the keys, which were still in the ignition. On both sides of the BMW's key, Moore observed residue he suspected could be blood. He swabbed the key with a sterile cotton swatch, which was later booked as item 20 on the LAPD's property list for Sherri's case. He also saw possible bloodstains on the driver's armrest and the upper edge of the driver's side door, and took separate evidence samples from each. In a tray between the front seats, he noticed a brown fiber that resembled a human hair. Moore collected the fiber and placed it in an evidence envelope, booked later as property item 23.

Ames and Moore were finished with the BMW within a few hours. At 11:30 a.m. Saturday, Mayer and Hooks drove it to the condo and released it to John Ruetten. The detectives documented no other investigative activity the rest of the weekend.

Stephanie was off duty on Sunday, March 9. Shortly after 2:00 p.m., she walked into the Santa Monica Police Department headquarters, a few blocks from the beach. Stephanie identified herself as an LAPD officer and said she wanted to report a crime.

Although Santa Monica was within Los Angeles County, it had its own city government and police force that operated independently of the metropolis around it. Stephanie, as an LAPD officer and lifelong Angeleno, undoubtedly knew that Santa Monica was a separate police jurisdiction from Los Angeles.

Elaine Sena-Brown, a community service officer for the Santa Monica police, was at the desk when Stephanie came in, and took her report. Stephanie told Sena-Brown that her car, a 1981 Toyota Tercel, had been broken into while parked on the street in Santa Monica, and several items stolen from it. Among the property she reported stolen was a gun that she claimed was in her car's glove box. Sena-Brown wrote in the narrative section of the crime report, based on what Stephanie told her:

> *I was dispatched to HQ regarding a grand theft report. I spoke to Lazarus who said she locked her car on 3-9-86 1300 hrs.*
>
> *She returned to her car approx. 50 minutes later and discovered the lock had been punched on the driver's side door. A gym bag which was on the front seat was gone, cassettes, money and a gun were taken from the glove box.*
>
> *On 3-9-86 1300–1350 hrs., unknown persons punched the lock on Lazarus' car. Once inside the suspect took a gym bag that was on the front seat, cash, cassettes and gun from the glove box. The suspect fled unseen.*

Stephanie, as the reported victim of the crime, had to provide her personal information, including her full name, birth date, and occupation, *"police officer."* She gave the address and phone number for the LAPD's Devonshire station as her work contact information. She listed a PO box for her home address and did not volunteer her home number. The crime report form also had space to list any witnesses and suspects. Per Stephanie's description of the crime, Sena-Brown left those sections blank. Stephanie itemized the stolen property, and its monetary value, as follows:

ITEM NO.	LOSS	VALUE
1	SMITH/WESSON MODEL 49 2 INCH, BLUE STEEL, 5 SHOT .38 CAL REVOLVER-SERIAL ACM6890	220.00
2	GYM BAG—BLUE CONTAINING MISC. CLOTHES	25.00 20.00
3	(6) MUSIC CASSETTES—10 EA	60.00
4	U.S. CURRENCY (1)'s AND COIN	5.00
	TOTAL VALUE	330.00

At the end of the narrative section of the crime report, Sena-Brown handwrote, *"I.D. Tech Requested."* The note was a reference to a technician from the Santa Monica police forensics unit. Sena-Brown typically requested an I.D. tech by walking across the hallway to the Identification Bureau. If no I.D. techs were in, Sena-Brown called dispatch and asked them to send one to meet the person who filed the report.

Burglaries from motor vehicles were relatively commonplace in Santa Monica in the 1980s. Santa Monica was divided for crime reporting purposes into several beats. The address where Stephanie said her car was parked when it was broken into, 1235 Second Street, was in beat 3. According to police records, fifty-four burglaries from motor vehicles were reported in beat 3 between February and April 1986. Stephanie's was the only one reported there on March 9.

Sena-Brown, when she took walk-in reports similar to Stephanie's, sometimes left the desk and went to see the vehicle reported broken into. Other times, she requested that an I.D. tech examine it for fingerprints and other possible forensic evidence. In order to distinguish between innocuous fingerprints and a possible suspect's, it would have been necessary for the I.D. tech to obtain a set of exemplar prints from the person who reported the crime.

In 2012, more than twenty-five years after she took Stephanie's report, Sena-Brown testified in court that she could not recall whether she went out to Stephanie's car to verify that the driver's door lock had been "punched," as Stephanie had described. Nor could Sena-Brown recall whether an I.D. tech responded and met Stephanie, either at the station or her car. Other than the note that an I.D. tech was requested, there is no record that the Santa Monica police ever conducted a forensic examination of Stephanie's car, or even saw it, before she left the station.

Any police department in California that receives a report of a stolen gun is required to enter that information into the Automated Firearms System, a database of individual gun histories maintained by the state Department of Justice. A firearm's history included its make, model, caliber and serial number; the name and birth date of its owner; when it was purchased; and if it has ever been reported lost or stolen. Law enforcement agencies statewide can query the database using different combinations of search criteria to, for instance, use a gun's serial number to identify its owner, or trace the ownership of a particular gun over time.

According to the AFS history for Stephanie's backup revolver, the Santa

Monica police designated her gun as stolen the same day she filed her report. Because there was no database field in AFS for the gun owner's occupation or employer, the entry for her stolen gun did not indicate that she was an LAPD officer.

Stephanie had received extensive firearms training from the LAPD. As a police officer, she had better than average knowledge of how gun-related crimes were investigated and the role ballistics evidence played in solving them. She undoubtedly knew that bullets recovered at crime scenes could be analyzed to determine what type of gun fired them. It was also common knowledge for a cop that without the actual gun, and the ability to test-fire a bullet to compare to the crime scene slugs, a definitive match to a specific gun is impossible to prove in court.

Given her police training and experience, Stephanie was likely also familiar with how the AFS database worked. The database was not set up to automatically notify a police department when one of its officers reported a gun stolen. If the officer failed to notify their own department of the theft, the only way for the department to find out was to proactively search AFS for their firearms history. Still, once the Santa Monica police updated the status of Stephanie's revolver in the AFS database, a simple database search by any LAPD detective would have revealed instantly that she had reported the gun stolen on March 9, thirteen days after Sherri's murder.

LAPD policy in 1986 required officers to promptly report any gun theft to the department. An officer's obligation to notify their own department that their gun was stolen was not just a matter of policy. It was also common sense, and strongly in the officer's interest, to report the theft. By definition, a stolen firearm is no longer in the possession and control of its registered owner. The owner has no idea where the stolen gun is, nor whose hands it may later fall into. If the stolen gun were ever used in a crime, the officer presumably would want their own department to know in advance that the gun was not in their possession.

Despite these incentives, and the risks inherent in defying the department's firearms policy, Stephanie never notified the LAPD that her revolver was stolen.

Stephanie had at least one conversation about the gun in the days after she reported it stolen, with her fellow cop and former roommate Mike Hargreaves. Hargreaves had moved out less than a month earlier, on February 14, ten days before Sherri's murder. In 2012, Hargreaves testified in court that he had a face-to-face conversation with Stephanie in 1986, soon after he moved out, during which she said that she had lost her backup weapon in Santa Monica. Hargreaves knew that Stephanie's backup was a .38 caliber revolver with a two-inch barrel. His impression at the time was that she had lost the gun a day or so earlier. As best as Hargreaves could recall on the witness stand, so many years later, their conversation was about how Stephanie could report the gun lost, and to whom she should report it.

According to Hargreaves, Stephanie never mentioned to him in 1986 that her car was broken into, or that the gun was stolen from the glove box, as she had reported to the Santa Monica police. Stephanie told Hargreaves that she had her backup gun in a fanny pack and had lost the fanny pack while in Santa Monica.

After Hargreaves moved out, he sometimes rode with Stephanie in her car, the 1981 Toyota Tercel. Hargreaves never observed any damage to the car, including to the lock on the driver's side door. Nor did she ever tell Hargreaves that her car had been damaged in a burglary. When Hargreaves testified in 2012, he was unable to remember whether Stephanie had any visible injuries, or complained to him of any injuries, when they discussed her backup gun in 1986.

The FBI maintains a database similar to AFS called the National Criminal Information Center, which serves as a clearinghouse for firearms data from all fifty states. Anytime a police department anywhere in America recovers a stolen gun, an entry is made in the NCIC system. According to the AFS and NCIC databases, the gun that Stephanie reported stolen in Santa Monica in 1986 has never been recovered.

In her datebook for Sunday, March 9, Stephanie made no reference to going to Santa Monica, nor anything about her car being broken into, her gun being stolen, or emergency repairs for her driver's side door lock. The only appointment Stephanie noted for Sunday was for another "*tan*" at 5:30 p.m., about three hours after she reported her gun stolen in Santa Monica.

Stephanie reported for duty at Devonshire at 11:30 that night. She wrote in her diary, "*I was the report car tonight. I took the next 2 nights off with T/O Time. The weather was very bad tonight. It poured all night . . . I went to my house, packed up to go to Lake Arrowhead. I cleaned up my place a little. Then I went back and worked the desk . . . I took a few reports at the desk and got to leave about 0745. I was glad I didn't have to work the next three nights.*"

The Van Nuys detectives resumed their investigation Monday morning at 8:00 a.m., shortly after Stephanie got off work and left town for Lake Arrowhead, two hours east of Los Angeles. The first two entries in the typed chrono on March 10 stated in full, *"0800 | Called Nels Rasmussen and gave up date [sic] on case"* and *"0900 | John Ruetter called—gave him up date."* No additional details of the phone conversations with Nels or John were documented in the murder book.

Later Monday, the detectives received a call from George Herrera, the SID fingerprint analyst. The typed chrono indicated, *"1300 | Call from Heruera [sic] about prints. He says that there are 3 lifts obtained from inside the car. They have been eliminated from victim and husband."* The follow-up report recounted the same information, that three good lifts were obtained from the BMW, and that Herrera had eliminated John and Sherri as their source.

Herrera's written report on the five fingerprints taken from the BMW actually stated that four were identifiable, not three, as the detectives wrote. Also contrary to the information in the typed chrono and follow-up report, Herrera in fact identified one of the prints from the BMW as John Ruetten's. Two other prints from the BMW were also later identified as John's. The reason for the discrepancy between the information recorded in the typed chrono and follow-up report and the actual latent print results is unknown.

An hour after the call from Herrera, the typed chrono stated, *"1400 | John Ruetter came in. Gave him run down on case. Asked him to take poly. Yes! Set poly for 3-12-86 at 0900."* The follow-up report recounted a similar conversation, although it did not mention that John came to the station. According to the follow-up report, *"On 3-10-86 Detective Mayer contacted John Ruetten. Mayer requested Ruetten take a polygraph examination to eliminate him as a suspect in this crime. Ruetten agreed."*

No explanation was documented in the typed chrono or follow-up report as to why, if the detectives believed Sherri was killed in an attempted burglary, and they had already verified John's alibi, Mayer requested John to take a polygraph exam two weeks after the murder. Nor is it apparent, if burglars killed Sherri, why John would be at all reluctant to take a polygraph exam, and why his assent was noted in the typed chrono with the exuberant or surprised exclamation, "Yes!"

According to the typed chrono, the first thing the detectives did the next day, Tuesday, March 11, was call John's father: *"0800 | Called and spoke with Richard Ruetter, the parents [sic] of John."* No details of the conversation were documented in the murder book, so it is unknown whether they discussed the polygraph exam that John had agreed to take a day earlier, per the typed chrono and follow-up report.

Following their call with Richard Ruetten, the next activity noted in the typed chrono was Tuesday afternoon, when Hooks met with an informant. The typed chrono stated, *"1250 | Hooks met with 'Angel' gave him $20.00 Secret Service at Bassett and Gloria. Gave info regarding 'Alex' M/M Burglar who has been hitting Balboa."* "M/M" was shorthand for "Male/Mexican." At that time, "Mexican" was the LAPD's catchall description for anyone Hispanic. The intersection of Bassett Street and Gloria Avenue was a residential street corner about a mile southwest of where Sherri's BMW was abandoned. No additional information was documented in the murder book about the identities of Angel and Alex.

The last typed chrono entry on Tuesday referenced John's polygraph exam the next day: *"1600 | Spoke with John Ruetter. He will take poly on 3/12. He also believes the victims check book may have been taken."*

The only entry recorded in the typed chrono for Wednesday, March 12, stated in full, *"0900 | Poly of John Ruetter by Blair Eckert. Denies poly."* The follow-up report recounted, *"On 3-12-86 a polygraph examination was given to John Ruetten by senior polygraph examiner Blair Eckert, SID LAPD. The results of the examination were inconclusive due to the fact that John Ruetten was too emotional to give an accurate reading. There were major discrepancies in the results of the answers. The test may be repeated at a later date after the shock of the events have settled in John's mind."*

The "major discrepancies in the results of the answers" that John gave during his polygraph exam were nowhere delineated in the murder book. Nor were the questions John was asked, or the SID tape number, noted anywhere in the typed chrono or follow-up report. No other contemporaneous documentation from John's polygraph was retained in the murder book. Eckert, the LAPD polygraph examiner, died in 1995.

Eckert's written report on John's polygraph exam, dated March 12, 1986, described the purpose of the examination as *"to determine whether Mr. RUETTEN is truthful when he denies striking his wife on the head, biting her on the arm, and shooting her inside their townhouse (apartment) at 7100 Balboa #205 on 2-24-86."*

Eckert's summary of the examination results read, *"Mr. RUETTEN's physiological response to relevant questions reflect apparent deception. Those responses may have been caused by emotions other than 'fear of detection of deception,' for example embarrassment, anger, grief, etc. NOTE: Det. Mayer was cautioned prior to this examination of the strong possibility of contamination of the results due to emotionality of the examinee."*

Customarily, the "relevant" questions a polygraph subject was asked were devised and agreed upon, before the interview, by the examiner and the detective. According to Eckert's documentation, the relevant questions John was asked during his polygraph examination on March 12 were: Were you inside your apartment when Sherri got killed? Did you shoot Sherri? Before last year, did you ever think about killing anyone? Before last year, have you ever committed any crime that, if it became known, you could have gone to jail for it? Did you strike Sherri on the head the day she was killed? Do you know where the gun was disposed of that was used to kill Sherri? Before last year, have you ever hurt someone you didn't have to?

There is no indication in Eckert's documentation that John was asked any questions during his polygraph exam about Stephanie Lazarus, his relationship with her, or her possible involvement in Sherri's murder.

Stephanie returned from Lake Arrowhead late Thursday night, March 13, in time for morning watch on Friday. In her diary, she wrote: "*Tonight was my first night after 3 off . . . It was nice. I drove. First I stripped [sic] searched a female Hype for the task force. We went to Fosters for donuts. I had a bagel and donut. We didn't do much tonight. I was surprised I didn't get really tired.*" Later that watch, she recounted, "*A unit was following a poss. veh with kids shooting . . . We saw Sgt. Abrams he was also lost. Next thing you heard on the radio was 'T/A at Reseda/Citronia I'm involved.' Sgt. Abrams crashed into a fire hydrant. Water was gushing everywhere. It was funny to see.*" She ended up taking Code 7, her meal break, with Abrams: "*I went w/ Sgt. Abrams. He drove. He said it would be too embarrassing if I drove since he crashed.*"

The Van Nuys detectives documented no investigative activity in Sherri's case on Friday, March 14, or over the weekend.

A few weeks after Sherri's murder, once the LAPD was done collecting evidence in the condo and the place had been cleaned up, John moved back in and tried to make a go of living there. Because John was afraid to stay in the condo by himself, his mother, Margaret, spent some nights there with him.

Around the same time, after Sherri's BMW was recovered by the LAPD and returned to John, Jayne heard that John was looking to sell his own car, a Mazda RX-7. John had bought the Mazda, a maroon two-seater, soon after he and Sherri married. Little more than three months later, he was stuck with two cars and responsibility for two sets of car payments. Jayne believed John did not want to give up Sherri's car because of his sentimental attachment to it.

A nurse Jayne worked with, Joyce, said she might be interested in buying John's car. Jayne and Joyce drove out to Van Nuys so she could take the Mazda for a test-drive. Jayne recalls John and his mother were both at the condo. Jayne had not been there, where she had lived for three years as Sherri's roommate, since before the murder. It appeared to Jayne that everything inside had been restored to the way it was.

Jayne and Margaret stayed behind while John and Joyce went to look at the Mazda. Jayne felt uncomfortable around John's mother. She wanted to walk around the condo and think about Sherri but did not feel free to do so with John's mother there, so she just sat in the living room. Margaret remained upstairs in the kitchen area while they waited for John and Joyce to return.

Jayne saw some VHS tapes on a shelf in the living room. Less than two years earlier, when she and Sherri were still roommates, they had taped several TV broadcasts of the Summer Olympics. Jayne and Mike and Sherri and John were brand-new couples back then. She and Sherri had sat on the couch and watched the opening and closing ceremonies together. Jayne also noticed a videotape from her and Sherri's vacation to Club Med in Mexico, just before the Olympics. She thought about asking Margaret if she could have the tapes but couldn't muster the nerve.

When John and Joyce came back, Jayne asked him for the Club Med tape. Jayne felt she had a right to it as a keepsake, since it was her and Sherri's vacation, which they had paid for together, including the commemorative video. She sensed that for John, it was very hard to let anything of Sherri's go. Jayne told him that the trip meant a lot to her. John let her take it. She was so happy she decided not to push her luck by asking for the Olympics tapes too. John eventually sold his Mazda to Joyce. Jayne's impression at the time was that John intended to stay in the condo.

Sherri's family and friends each grieved in their own way, a process that felt at times as inexplicable as Sherri's death.

Jayne did not know what to do with her grief in the days following Sherri's murder. Her boss at UCLA told her, "I think you should keep working. I think that would be good for you." She followed her boss's advice. Later, in hindsight, Jayne came to feel that what she should have done was stayed home and bawled her eyes out for days. Jayne understood better why people say "I've lost someone" when they talk about the death of a loved one. For weeks after the murder, she felt as if she was searching for Sherri. Once while Jayne was driving home on the 405 freeway, a car passed her, and she thought she saw Sherri in it. She wanted to believe that Sherri wasn't really dead, but was in the witness protection program, living someplace safe where her friends and family could not contact her.

Jayne felt preoccupied by concerns that she knew made no sense. She worried about whether anyone had picked up Sherri's dry cleaning after she was killed. Back when they were roommates, Jayne did their laundry and dry cleaning in exchange for Sherri typing some of her papers for school. Jayne wondered if John had remembered to pick up Sherri's dry cleaning, or if her clothes were still waiting to be collected. Jayne felt she should tell somebody, "Hey, there might be some dry cleaning that was left." She knew it was a crazy thing to worry about, yet it weighed on her, as if abandoning Sherri's clothes was somehow akin to abandoning her friend.

Others of Sherri's family and friends changed their daily habits, sometimes permanently, to cope with their grief. Loretta found that she could no longer bear to listen to music on the car radio, because Sherri always used to play music in the car.

Nels and Loretta returned to Los Angeles one weekend in mid-March and saw John and his mother at the condo. The purpose of the Rasmussens' trip was to pick up some of Sherri's personal effects, mostly clothes and books John did not wish to keep.

According to Nels and Loretta, they spent five or six hours at the condo packing up Sherri's things. Sherri had lived there for more than five years, much longer than John, who had moved in less than a year earlier. The Rasmussens did not discuss with John whether he planned to remain in the condo, or if he had yet to decide.

Nels did not know if and when he would get another chance to be inside the condo. He was still working out in his head how Sherri's murder might have unfolded. To check possible bullet trajectories, Nels brought with him some fishing line. He handed Loretta one end of the fishing line and asked her to stand on the second floor, near where Sherri usually kept her purse. In Nels's mind, that was where the confrontation likely started. Just as the LAPD's ballistics experts had done weeks earlier during their own bullet trajectory analysis, Nels ran the fishing line from where Loretta stood, through the breakfast room, to the sliding glass balcony doors. The angle seemed to Nels dead-on. He believed it proved where the initial gunshots were fired, and in what direction.

According to the Rasmussens, Nels's experiment with the fishing line made John very emotional. Nels recalls that John told him, "What are you doing that for? That's left up to the police." Nels explained that he wanted to get the angles and locations of the shots that were fired. John was uneasy about it, Nels recalls.

At one point, while Nels and Loretta were packing, they ran out of boxes, and John offered to take Nels to the store to buy more. They took Sherri's BMW because his Mazda, which he still had at the time, was too small for hauling boxes. John lamented to Nels about having to sell his own car. Nels felt John spoke as if he was supposed to feel sorry for him for having to sell his sportster and keep Sherri's BMW.

As they drove to get the boxes, Nels noticed that John checked the rearview mirror constantly, more than he kept his eyes on the road. Nels thought John seemed afraid that someone could be following them. Nels's more immediate concern was that John was going to drive into traffic. Nels did not notice anyone tailing them, although he spent more of the drive watching John than behind them.

About a month before her murder, Sherri had told Nels she felt someone was watching and following her in public. Sherri did not say who she thought it was, but she described the person as "dressed like a boy," with "eyes that looked like they could see right through you." Nels believed at the time that Sherri was talking about John's ex-girlfriend. After the murder, Nels had tried several times to inform Mayer of what Sherri told him. He had also asked John, in the days after the murder, what he knew about Sherri being followed. John claimed to be unaware that Sherri was ever followed, Nels recalls.

The very possibility that John seemed to think he was being followed immediately reminded Nels of what Sherri had told him. The way John drove and acted reinforced Nels's conviction that John knew more than he said or was prepared to admit.

At the condo, out of earshot of John, Margaret told Loretta that she was concerned about him. Margaret said that John seemed unable to concentrate since Sherri's murder. She also told Loretta that a few days earlier, while she and John were in the condo, a bird flew into the skylight and made a loud noise. She said John was so startled that he jumped into a closet, and he'd stayed there for an hour. Loretta recalls Margaret told her, "I couldn't console him, and I couldn't get him to come out."

The same weekend that Nels and Loretta picked up Sherri's things in

Van Nuys, they also visited with Jayne and Mike at their place in Venice. Jayne had not seen the Rasmussens since Sherri's burial in Tucson a couple of weeks earlier. She thought Nels and Loretta were still in shock. They seemed to have a difficult time talking, as if they weren't sure what they wanted to talk about, or whether they could talk about it. Jayne had so many questions she wanted to ask about the LAPD's investigation, and what the Rasmussens might know that she didn't, but they seemed too upset to her to push the subject. Her impression was that Nels was deeply frustrated with the LAPD and the progress of the investigation to that point. Jayne knew Nels felt that the detectives handling Sherri's case had rebuffed his efforts to help them.

One of the hardest things for Jayne to accept was that Sherri would not be part of her wedding. The last time she saw Sherri, ten days before her murder, Jayne had shared the news of her and Mike's engagement. Sherri gave her some bridal magazines that she had saved for her, and told her that her wedding day was the happiest day of her life. Jayne had looked forward to going shopping with Sherri for her dress, and getting her opinion on every aspect of the wedding plans.

Jayne and Mike had not yet set a wedding date when Sherri was killed. When Nels and Loretta visited in mid-March, the wedding plans were still up in the air. Loretta encouraged her to find a dress. She told Jayne, "You need to go ahead. Sherri would have wanted you to do this." Jayne had waited years to try on wedding dresses, get married, and be happy. She was instead so grief-stricken that when she went to look at wedding dresses, she wore all black and couldn't stop crying. Once, when Anita accompanied her to the bridal shop, the saleswoman asked Jayne, "Are you sure you want to get married?"

"She's fine," Anita replied. "Let's keep trying on dresses. She'll be okay."

Life also moved on without Sherri at Glendale Adventist Medical Center, though for some of Sherri's colleagues, things were never the same. Sylvia was so traumatized by her murder that she couldn't go back into their office. The hospital had to move Sylvia to a different desk. The task of packing up Sherri's office fell to Peggy.

It seemed strange to Peggy, at the time, that the detectives investigating Sherri's murder did not contact her for an interview. On the day Sherri was killed, Peggy had called her at home to check on her and left a message on the answering machine. Peggy assumed the police had the tape, and that it was just a matter of time before she would hear from them.

In the weeks after the murder, the only theory of the crime that Peggy heard discussed at the hospital was the police's theory, that Sherri was killed in an attempted burglary. The story Peggy heard was that John and Sherri had entertained the day before and inadvertently left their front door unlocked. Peggy had been to the condo and knew that Sherri and John usually came and went through the garage, rather than the front door. Peggy heard that the burglars came to the front door and rang the doorbell, which was apparently broken. When no one answered, they tried the door, found it open, and went inside, unaware that Sherri was home upstairs.

Peggy's upbringing had trained her to trust the police. Several of her uncles, and their wives, were in law enforcement. She had no reason to think that anything the LAPD said about Sherri's murder was not the gospel truth. At that point in her life, she believed that if the police said it, it must be true.

Still, as time passed without news of an arrest, she sometimes thought of what Sherri had told her, about feeling harassed by John's ex-girlfriend. Peggy felt in her gut that John's ex-girlfriend had something to do with Sherri's death, but she did not broach the subject with anyone at the hospital. Peggy waited in vain for the detectives to contact her.

Romelda Anderson, another of Sherri's colleagues, heard a theory that Sherri was killed by gardeners who had committed a similar crime elsewhere. She considered it speculation. Romelda was more focused on carrying on the work that Sherri had been doing up until her murder. Along with Sherri's management responsibilities, she had served on many hospital committees. Before she was killed, she had been leading the hospital's planning for Nurses Day, an annual event in May. Romelda tried to honor Sherri by picking up her mantle.

Sylvia remained troubled by the murder even after she changed desks. Besides Sherri, Sylvia's closest acquaintance at the hospital was Althea's secretary, Vera. Vera had worked at Glendale Adventist for fourteen years, since 1972. By virtue of Althea's position and Vera's seniority, Sylvia and the other secretaries in the nursing division informally reported to Vera. During the years she and Sylvia worked together, Sylvia often came by her desk to chitchat.

According to Vera, sometime in mid-March, about three weeks after the murder, Sylvia came to her and said, "I have something very bad to tell you, but I don't want you to mention it to a soul." Vera felt she had to give

Sylvia her confidence. She promised her that she would keep the secret, whatever it was.

Sylvia proceeded to tell Vera a disturbing story from before Sherri was killed. Sylvia recounted that one day at lunchtime, a woman came in and asked to see Sherri. Sylvia said that the woman seemed very angry and agitated. When Sherri returned from lunch, she and the woman went into her office and closed the door. After a while, the woman came out, followed by Sherri, who was in tears. Sylvia said that the next morning, Sherri told her that the woman was John's ex-girlfriend and also said, "She threatened me, Sylvia."

Vera was very surprised by Sylvia's story. It was not unusual for Sylvia to come tell her her problems, but this was a big one. Although Vera was aware that Sherri and John were recently married, she knew nothing of John's past romances. Sylvia had not mentioned the confrontation to anyone when it happened but evidently had dwelled on the incident, and what to do about it, since Sherri's murder. She told Vera, "I don't know what we can think about this, but that's what happened."

Sylvia did not say, and Vera did not ask her, why she waited weeks to tell someone, and why the person she finally decided to unburden herself to was Vera. Nor did she say what she expected Vera to do with the information, except to tell no one, which Vera had promised before she knew the nature of the secret. Vera's impression of Sylvia was that she was too shy ever to go to the police on her own and report what she knew. Vera thought Sylvia did not want to get involved.

Vera did not know if Sylvia believed that she would tell Althea, or call the police and report what Sylvia said, despite what she had promised. She wondered if Sylvia thought, "Vera will do it. Vera will call."

But Sylvia had sworn her to secrecy. Vera felt she could not go back on her word.

Sylvia and Vera never again discussed the story she told her that day. Within a few months, Sylvia left Glendale Adventist for a job at another hospital.

Nels and Loretta received a Christmas card from Sylvia later that year. Sylvia wrote inside, *"Dear Dr. & Mrs. Rasmussen . . . I know Christmas will be sad for you this year, but I pray that the Lord will give you strength to get through. I did receive the memorial card and thank you so much. It was a beautiful tribute to Sherri. I will close for now and do take care. Love,*

Sylvia." Sylvia made no mention of the information that she had confided to Vera.

Vera kept Sylvia's secret for years, long after the two women fell out of touch. Despite the passage of time, Vera never forgot Sylvia's story. The possibility that the police might be unaware that John's ex-girlfriend had come to the hospital and threatened Sherri sometimes weighed on Vera's conscience.

In 1997, eleven years after Sherri's murder, Vera was in the office by herself one day when she thought, "I've got to tell somebody. I'm going to call the police." She dialed the LAPD and asked to speak with the detective who handled Sherri Rasmussen's case.

Vera was unaware that by 1997, the ranks of the Van Nuys homicide unit no longer included the two detectives who in 1986 had led the initial investigation of Sherri's murder. Mayer retired from the LAPD in 1991, five years after Sherri's murder. Hooks was reassigned from the homicide unit in the mid-1990s. In addition, Mayer and Hooks's supervisor in 1986, Roger Pida, had retired from the LAPD in 1989.

In the years between 1986 and 1997, several other detectives had cycled through the Van Nuys homicide unit to replace those lost to retirement or reassignment. Among the detectives who worked Van Nuys homicide in 1996, the year before Vera called, was Stephanie Lazarus. LAPD records indicate that Stephanie was assigned to the Van Nuys homicide unit from January 21 to March 16, 1996, during which time she worked at least one homicide case. At the conclusion of her stint with Van Nuys homicide, the LAPD promoted Stephanie to Detective II and reassigned her to Internal Affairs. On August 31, 1997, after more than a year as an Internal Affairs detective, Stephanie returned to Van Nuys as a higher-ranked detective. Stephanie's second assignment at Van Nuys lasted until January 17, 1999.

On the day in 1997 that Vera called Van Nuys homicide, the detective who came to the phone identified himself to her by his first name only, Dan. She told the detective that she had information about the murder of Sherri Rasmussen in 1986 and started to recount what Sylvia had told her eleven years earlier. Vera described her information as hearsay and admitted that she had not witnessed the actual confrontation between Sherri and the ex-girlfriend. She explained that the only eyewitness to what happened was Sherri's secretary, Sylvia Nielsen.

Vera wanted the police to know the full story. She was about halfway through it when she sensed the detective was not listening to her. She had assumed that the police would be interested in the information she wanted to report. She had agonized for years over whether she should break her promise to Sylvia. When her conscience got the better of her, and she finally called, the impression she got from the detective, Dan, was that he couldn't have cared less about hearing about Sherri Rasmussen and what Vera had to say.

Vera expected the LAPD would take her tip and do some follow-up investigation to determine if the ex-girlfriend had any connection to Sherri's murder. She gave Dan her name and contact information, in case he needed to reach her, and he thanked her for calling. Still, by the time she hung up the phone, she felt certain that the detective's notes on their conversation, if indeed he had taken any, were headed for the round file. Vera never heard back from Dan or any other detective in the Van Nuys homicide unit.

No record of Vera's phone call or what she reported was made in the chrono for Sherri's case. But Vera, given her long experience as a secretary, was accustomed to documenting her important phone calls. During her conversation with the detective Dan in 1997, she jotted notes on a scrap of paper. Vera wrote down the LAPD phone numbers that she called and *"Dan/Detective. Talk to detective, report to him info that was given to me by Sylvia Nielsen, secretary of Sherri's."* Vera kept the scrap of paper, first at the hospital and later at home, and never threw it away.

Sylvia Nielsen died in 2000, three years after Vera called the LAPD and provided Sylvia's name. Sylvia was never contacted or interviewed by the LAPD about the confrontation she witnessed between Sherri and John's ex-girlfriend. Nor did detectives ever show Sylvia a photograph of Stephanie Lazarus to see if she could identify her as the woman who Sherri said had threatened her.

Back in 1986, in the weeks after Sherri's murder, Vera and Sylvia were not alone in privately questioning the LAPD's theory of what happened to Sherri. Sherri's sister Connie could not understand why burglars would steal her BMW only to leave it on the street less than two weeks later. Why wouldn't the burglars have taken the BMW to a chop shop, or driven it down to Tijuana? Connie figured they could have gotten rid of it within hours, possibly even before the car was discovered missing. Why would burglars break in, steal nothing except Sherri's purse and car, and then neither keep nor fence what they stole? It did not fit with what Connie knew, or thought she knew, about how burglars operated.

Jayne's skepticism of the botched-burglary theory stemmed from her familiarity with the condo. She heard that the police thought the fight had started outside the kitchen on the second floor and ended in the living room downstairs. Jayne knew the layout of the condo, and the sight lines between the first and second floors. She tried to imagine how a burglary could have escalated to murder. Why had the burglars not fled when they realized someone was home upstairs? How had things turned violent instead?

Jayne also knew Sherri's personal habits, including her morning routine of going to the kitchen to feed Bozo, her cat. If Sherri slept in, and Bozo was hungry, he would go to her in bed and wake her. Jayne pictured Bozo waking Sherri, and Sherri coming downstairs from her bedroom, unaware that she was not alone in the house.

In Jayne's opinion, if the burglars were down in the living room or near the front door, they would have seen Sherri as she walked to the kitchen. It seemed possible that Sherri would not have seen the burglars, unless she happened to look in that direction. Jayne believed that if Sherri had seen someone, she would have gone to them, and the confrontation would have started downstairs rather than near the kitchen.

Jayne knew that once Sherri reached the kitchen, she could not see anyone on the first floor from there, or vice versa. Jayne thought that at that point, the burglars could have simply walked out the front door unseen. It didn't make sense to Jayne that rather than make a clean getaway, the burglars would instead go upstairs and confront Sherri as she came out of the kitchen. In Jayne's mind, burglars want to get in and out. They could have walked away, so why didn't they? It wasn't like Sherri had diamond chandeliers, or anything worth killing someone over. Jayne thought Sherri's murder seemed too personal to have been committed by a panicked burglar.

Knowing Sherri as well as she did, Jayne could think of only one person who would want to hurt her. Sherri had talked with Jayne on several occasions about John's ex-girlfriend. Sherri told her that the ex-girlfriend had come to the hospital and threatened her. She also knew that John's ex-girlfriend was a police officer.

Jayne assumed that the detectives on Sherri's case had taken a hard look at the ex-girlfriend as a suspect. She figured there must have been fingerprints recovered after the murder, and that the LAPD fingerprinted its cops. Jayne presumed the detectives had checked the crime scene fingerprints against the ex-girlfriend's and must have cleared her of involvement.

Even so, she was convinced that it had to be the ex-girlfriend. Nothing else made sense.

By the time Jayne realized that the detectives were not going to come talk to her, she had already heard a lot from Nels about how the detectives had snubbed him. Jayne knew Nels was not an easy guy to snub. Jayne thought, if the detectives were going to push Sherri's parents away, how would they treat her if she went to them? She believed they would look at her and say, "Who are you? Why would we want to talk to you?"

Not at the time, but years later, Jayne came to believe that the reason the detectives never contacted her in 1986 was because of the possibility that she would mention John's ex-girlfriend, the LAPD officer. Jayne thought the detectives did not want the ex-girlfriend's name to come up again, because if it did, especially repeatedly, they would have had to document her in the case file as a potential suspect. In Jayne's opinion, if the detectives had interviewed Sherri's closest friends after her murder, instead of only John, the detectives would have heard about Sherri's history with the ex-girlfriend from at least three or four people. Jayne believed the detectives would have been compelled to investigate the ex-girlfriend rather than just pursue their preferred theory that Sherri was killed during a botched burglary.

None of Sherri's friends or colleagues who knew about John's ex-girlfriend were ever contacted or interviewed by the LAPD in 1986. Among those who knew Sherri best, only John was formally interviewed, and during that interview, conducted by Mayer on the night of Sherri's murder, John did not mention Stephanie.

In 2009, more than twenty years later, John was reinterviewed by the LAPD and asked to recount what he told Mayer and Hooks about Stephanie in 1986. John recalled that he first brought Stephanie to the attention of Mayer and Hooks the morning after Sherri's murder, during the detectives' walk-through of the condo with him and his mother. According to John, he told the detectives Stephanie's full name and that she was a police officer. John also claimed that he informed Mayer and Hooks during the conversation that Stephanie went to see Sherri at the hospital. But nothing that John told the detectives about Stephanie the day after Sherri's murder was recorded in the typed chrono or follow-up report. John recounted in 2009 that Mayer and Hooks never brought up Stephanie to him again.

Later during his 2009 LAPD interview, John claimed that he also followed up with the detectives about Stephanie subsequently, although he did not specify when. John said, "I probed them later and said, 'What about this thing with Stephanie?' And that's when I got the answer, 'This is a dead end. It's not going anywhere.' Those are the types of words I remember. They may have actually explained to me that, you know, something about them knowing that she couldn't have been there or something, but I don't recall that. I'm very much speculating there. What I do remember is that I asked them, and they said, 'This is not going anywhere. It's not what happened.'"

"You made contact with them to find out whether they looked at this angle you'd given them?" John was asked.

"Yeah, there was a lot of contact. I mean, this wasn't one or two times that I remember. I was meeting with the detectives many times over a period. I don't know exactly when that was. I don't remember all of them, but at one point, I just remember asking, 'Where is it at?' and that's the answer I got." John said the detectives never said anything to him about having been told by Nels or anyone else "that Stephanie was, you know, in any way or shape threatening" Sherri. John said, "There was nothing. That's about what I can remember. And I think that's what it was. I mean, these are the things I probably am a little more clear on, I think."

Later in the interview, John was asked about Stephanie, "Did the police ever tell you that she had been cleared? Did the cops investigating this Stephanie angle, did they ever get back to you on this? As far as, 'This is what we've done. This is what we've checked. This is a possibility.'"

"No. That's why I'm a little upset with myself for not probing that further. What I recall is, I asked them about Stephanie, and they said, 'We've eliminated that possibility.' Something to that effect. They didn't say, 'We did this.' I don't recall them saying, 'We did this, this, or that.' But that's what I recall."

John was also asked, "Do you remember which detective explained to you that this was a dead end?"

John answered, "I think it wasn't Hooks. Because the lead guy, I think, was the other guy. Wasn't he Lyle?"

"Lyle Mayer. He was the lead IO"—LAPD shorthand for Investigating Officer.

"Yeah. I think it was Lyle. I think that would be the one I would have asked it to, because of that. That's what I recall," John said in 2009.

Back in 1986, Friday, March 14, marked one week since Sherri's stolen BMW was recovered by the LAPD. A full workweek had passed uneventfully since Stephanie had reported her gun stolen in Santa Monica. Stephanie betrayed no guilt or anxiety in her diary or lifestyle. In her datebook for March 14, she noted a tanning appointment at 8:30 p.m., a few hours before she went into work that night.

Stephanie's characteristic lack of empathy remained on vivid display in her diary. Her patrol partner for morning watch on March 15 was Dave Schmid. Stephanie wrote in her diary, *"Schmid drove. Not much was going on tonight . . . We didn't do much until 0800 when Dave drove up near the nursery on Balboa/Woodley. We saw this car parked way off the dirt lot. So we checked it out. The man was sleeping in his car and lived right down the street. Seemed kinda weird. So I ran him and he had a poss. warrant. I asked him and he got defensive. Very bad attitude. So we were going to take him to the Station to check him out. But he was screaming that he was just arrested and he had the receipt in the car. We checked his car and couldn't find the receipt. Then he started freaking out and kicked the front Driver's seat and bent it a 45° angle. So we hogged [sic] tied him in the back and asked for a Sgt. which was horrible because it was so late. So we got him to the Station. He was crazy in the car and gave this glare that really scared me. All he did was cry like a baby. At the Station in the cage he was a real baby."*

A few nights later, for morning watch on March 17, Stephanie recounted in her diary, *"At 0100 we had to go to the Station. I had to conduct a Rape Investigation. At first this Rape seemed legitimate. But as the story went on this blk female who lived at 91st and Vermont downtown got picked up by a blk male at 2300, went home with him to Merridy/Zelzah where he raped her and took her $21.00. It was rather the usual story for a prostitute. She doesn't get paid so she claims rape. We went by the apt and he wasn't there. We took her to West Park for medical treatment. Then we went back to the Station to finish reports and see what we were going to do w/ her. We had to go to Parker Center to book the rape kit so we took her w/ us. She called her mom. There is always so much paper work for such a unnecessary report. We stopped by Western Bagels on the way home, got some bagels."*

The Van Nuys detectives, after three days with no documented activity in Sherri's case, recorded two entries in the typed chrono on Monday, March 17. The first stated in full, *"0900 | Spoke with Mr. Rasmussen about investigation."* The second indicated, *"0915 | Spoke with John Ruetter at home. He says that he is taking a leave of abscence [sic] and will be staying at parents home in San Diego."* No additional details of the conversations with Nels and John were preserved in the murder book.

The following day, March 18, the typed chrono noted, in reference to

3-18-86	1300	Skoke with Musick at SID on blood and fibers.
	1400	Spoke with Matheson about blood activity. He is of the
		opinion at this time victim is type A - Suspect type O.

LAPD typed chrono excerpt for March 18, 1986

ON 3-18-86 DETECTIVE MAYER CONTACTED SID SEROLOGY UNIT AND SPOKE WITH
G. MATHESON. #B8927. MATHESON COMPLETED A LOS ANGELES POLICE
DEPARTMENT ANALYZED EVIDENCE REPORT DR # 86 09 10480 DATED 3-4-86. TH
REPORT HAS TO DO WITH BLOOD. ATTATCHED AS ADDENDUM #6 ARE THE
RESULTS OF THE REPORT. MATHESON FURTHER INFORMED MAYER OF THE
FOLLOWING INFORMATION. VICTIM'S BLOOD TYPE IS O. SUSPECT'S TYPE IS
A. ATTACHED AS ADDENDUM #6 IS A BREAK DOWN OF THE IMPORTANT ITEMS
TESTED.

LAPD follow-up report excerpt re: March 18, 1986 (May 21, 1986)

Greg Matheson, a criminalist in the serology unit at SID, *"1400 | Spoke with Matheson about blood activity. He is of the opinion at this time victim is type A—Suspect type O."*

The follow-up report for Sherri's case also recounted a conversation between Mayer and Matheson on March 18, but reversed the victim's and suspect's blood types: *"On 3-18-86 Detective Mayer contacted SID Serology Unit and spoke with G. Matheson #B8927. Matheson completed a Los Angeles Police Department Analyzed Evidence Report DR # 86 09 10480 dated 3-4-86. The report has to do with blood. Attached as Addendum #6 are the results of the report. Matheson further informed Mayer of the following information. Victim's blood type is O. Suspect's type is A. Attached as Addendum #6 is a break down of the important items tested."*

Matheson's analyzed evidence report and the "break down of the important items tested" both stated that Sherri's blood type was in fact O, not A, as the typed chrono indicated, apparently mistakenly.

Prior to DNA analysis, the principal forensic method to identify the source of blood at a crime scene was ABO blood typing. In the United States, about 99 percent of the population has one of four blood types: O, A, B, or AB. The most common blood type for Americans is type O, followed closely by type A. Blood type B is significantly rarer, and AB rarer still.

Although ABO blood typing is much less precise than DNA analysis, it allowed investigators to distinguish between blood from different people, as long as they did not have the same blood type. In homicide cases, it was standard practice during the victim's autopsy for the medical examiner to obtain a blood sample. If the victim was blood type O, for instance, and other blood found at the crime scene was type AB, investigators could presume the suspect had that relatively uncommon blood type. Even in that best-case scenario, ABO blood typing was far from a smoking gun, but investigators could use the information to exclude potential suspects.

According to Matheson's Analyzed Evidence Report, he tested thirteen individual items of evidence, plus Sherri's blood sample taken during her autopsy. Six of the thirteen items were type A, the results indicated. Two items were type O, the same as Sherri's reference sample. Three items were a mixture of types A and O. Matheson was unable to identify the blood type for two items. Based on the presence of type A blood that it seemed could not be from Sherri, Matheson's opinion was that the suspect was blood type A.

What Matheson did not know, and could not have known at the time, given the limits of forensic science in 1986, was that Sherri was among the one percent of Americans with a blood type variant. Sherri's blood group was a rare subtype of O that, when analyzed for ABO blood type, sometimes appeared to be O, sometimes A, and sometimes a mixture of A and O.

In 2009, DNA analysis was performed on several evidence items that Matheson had ABO blood-typed in 1986. The DNA results proved that what originally seemed to be blood from two different people, Sherri with type O blood and a suspect with type A blood, was actually from a single source, Sherri. Stephanie Lazarus's DNA profile was not compared to the blood evidence collected from the crime scene until 2009. Her DNA did not match any of the blood evidence. All the blood evidence that was DNA tested in 2009 proved to be Sherri's.

Because Sherri's blood type variance was undetectable with ABO testing, and the science to identify her subtype did not exist in 1986, there was no way for Matheson or the detectives to know, or even suspect, that the blood type information reflected in the 1986 lab results was wrong.

Stephanie was off duty on Wednesday, March 19. On her day off, she visited the gun shop at the LAPD academy, where, two years earlier, she had purchased the Smith & Wesson model 49 .38 revolver that she reported stolen in Santa Monica.

Stephanie picked out a new backup weapon, a Smith & Wesson model 649 .38 revolver, and paid for it. The gun shop clerk had her fill out and sign a 4473 form, the firearms transaction record required by federal law. The form recorded the make, model, caliber, and serial number of her new gun, along with her driver's license number and LAPD serial number. Stephanie handwrote on the form her name, height and weight, birth date, and other personal information. The form also posed a series of yes-or-no questions that she was required to answer in writing. The form warned that any false statement was a crime punishable as a felony. One question was *"Are you a fugitive from justice?"* Stephanie wrote "NO."

Later that day, Stephanie presented her new gun to the LAPD armorer for inspection and registration. Once the armorer verified that the gun met the department's specifications, it was added to the officer's Firearms Inspection Record, or gun card, which listed all the firearms the LAPD had approved that particular officer to use. LAPD policy also required officers to notify the armorer by phone or in person if one of their previously approved guns was "transferred to another owner," which would seem to include if a registered gun was lost or stolen.

Stephanie had the opportunity to notify the armorer in person on March 19, when she presented her new revolver for approval. Only ten days had passed since she had reported her original backup weapon stolen in Santa Monica. In order to register her new revolver, the armorer pulled

Stephanie's LAPD Firearm Inspection Record

Stephanie's gun card, which at the time listed only two firearms: her department-issued duty gun, and the Smith & Wesson model 49 revolver that she had reported stolen. Had she told the armorer what she told the Santa Monica police on March 9, the armorer would have marked the Smith & Wesson model 49 as stolen on her gun card. There is no indication on Stephanie's LAPD gun card that she informed the armorer about her stolen revolver on March 19, or anytime thereafter.

The next day, March 20, the Van Nuys detectives noted in the typed chrono, "*1400 | Spoke to John Ruetters Mother. John in San Diego—He will sell his condo.*"

In her diary for morning watch on March 20, Stephanie wrote, "*I found out that I was going back to day watch. I had put my name on the wish list more as a joke and because a few guys came back from vacation. I got days and I think some of the guys at work weren't too happy. But they didn't put their name on the list.*"

Monday, March 24, marked one month since Sherri's murder. The Van Nuys detectives documented no investigative activity on the case between Thursday, March 20, and Wednesday, April 2.

While on patrol on March 25, her second to last shift on morning watch, Stephanie had an opportunity to demonstrate her familiarity with fingerprint evidence. The incident shows she knew how latent prints were collected and was cognizant of their power to solve crimes. Her police training and experience may explain why none of Stephanie's fingerprints were found at the condo or in Sherri's stolen BMW. She wrote in her diary: "*We got a window smash call at Thrifty's on Reseda. The window was smashed and they took cigarettes. The manager came about 1/2 hour later . . . I took a print off a plastic corner of the cigarette compartment.*"

Stephanie's rank at that time, after two years on the job, was Police Officer II. LAPD officers referred to rank informally by letter and number. A Police Officer III was a P-3. A Detective II was a D-2. A P-2 who wished to be promoted to P-3 had to pass a written exam administered annually. Attaining the rank of P-3 was a stepping-stone to becoming a sergeant or detective. Stephanie had taken the P-3 exam once already, a year earlier, in March 1985. "*I got a 43 and one needed a 48. Oh well next year,*" she wrote in her diary then.

True to her word, Stephanie again sat for the P-3 exam on Thursday, March 27, the 1986 test date. Because she was on morning watch, she had to take the exam right after she went off duty. In her diary, she recounted,

"Work out tonight . . . I was going to work with Schmid, because we were going to get off early to take the P-III exam. Then someone didn't show up so I ended up working by myself. Sgt. Ryan said don't make any traffic stops which I wasn't going to anyway, working by myself at night. The weather was bad, raining. So I talked to Izzo at the desk until about 0100. Then I went to go get Sgt. Wonders a bran muffin. Nothing was open due to Easter . . . The P-III exam was very hard. I'm sure I didn't pass. This was my last night on morning watch. I was happy."

The Van Nuys detectives resumed their investigation of Sherri's murder on Wednesday morning, April 2, according to the typed chrono. Thirteen days had passed since the detectives had last recorded any investigative activity in the case.

The lone typed chrono entry on April 2 stated, *"0800 | Rec'd Pacmis work-up on 7100 Balboa."* Detectives could not query the PACMIS database themselves but had to submit search parameters to AID, the LAPD's Automated Information Division. According to the typed chrono, the detectives first requested a *"pacmis run on 7100 Balboa"* on February 27, three days after the murder. On March 18, the typed chrono stated, *"Spoke to Dante Devera AID at XT (5) 2518 he is going to do the run at 7100 Balboa for 459's and any crimes"* (459 is the California penal code section for burglary). Why it took another two weeks for AID to complete the PACMIS run is unknown. By the time the detectives received the "work-up" on April 2, more than a month had passed since their original request. No additional details about the PACMIS work-up, and what it showed, were recorded in the typed chrono or follow-up report.

The Van Nuys detectives documented no additional investigative activity in Sherri's case until April 8, the following week.

Stephanie's first day back on day watch at Devonshire was Thursday, April 3. In her diary, she recounted running several errands while on duty and also noted, *"I got a rating from Sgt. Florez. The rating was good."*

Two days later, for her patrol watch on April 5, Stephanie wrote, *"The day was slow. We had only 4 radio calls probably because it rained in the afternoon . . . I had ridden by bike to work today. But Mom had come by the Station and I got a ride home from Mom. The next day when I picked up my bike, some jerk had let the air out of the front tire and moved my bag around. Someone doesn't like me."*

The next day, Sunday, April 6, Stephanie butted heads with her patrol partner, Sally Barnes. Stephanie recounted in her diary, *"I got the equip-*

ment so I decided I would drive. Sally had to fix her hair. I got the car ready. Sally said, Oh you driving? I said, Is that OK? And she kinda said, I'm not real thrilled. I wasn't going to let her intimidate me . . . Sally is very bossy, always telling me where to turn, how to do something. I can see why people don't like working with her."

The Van Nuys detectives resumed their investigation of Sherri's murder on Tuesday, April 8, six days after their last activity on the case, per the typed chrono.

The first typed chrono entry on April 8 stated in full, *"0930 | Spoke with Nels Rasmussen RE: 187 PC advised"* (187 is the California penal code section for murder). The call with Nels was not tape-recorded, and no additional information about what he was "advised" was documented in the typed chrono. The follow-up report made no reference to a call with Nels on April 8.

Next, the typed chrono indicated, *"1255 | Contacted Rowley RE: Alps prints, no make."* According to the follow-up report, *"On 4-8-86 Detective Mayer received information from SID Latent Prints Section that there were no makes on the ALPS prints checked."* ALPS was the fingerprint database maintained by the California Department of Justice. "No makes" meant no potential matches were identified in the database for the fingerprints the LAPD had submitted.

By April 8, more than six weeks into the LAPD's investigation of Sherri's murder, the Van Nuys detectives had not arrested or even identified any suspects in the case. Nor had the detectives recovered the murder weapon, which forensic evidence suggested was a .38 revolver with a two-inch barrel.

On February 24, the night of Sherri's murder, Mayer had interviewed two witnesses at the Van Nuys station: John Ruetten and Evangelina Flores, a neighbor's housekeeper. Both interviews were tape-recorded. In the six weeks since, the Van Nuys detectives had conducted no additional interviews that were tape-recorded, and no formal interviews at all with any of Sherri's family or friends other than John's initial interview.

On April 8, despite the lack of tangible progress in the investigation to that point, LAPD Chief Daryl Gates issued a signed commendation that thanked the Van Nuys detectives for their "good work" on Sherri's case. The memo, on Gates's official letterhead, stated in full: *"The talent, attention to detail and diligence of L.A.P.D. Detectives are a continuing source of pride to me; and your Murder Book, recently audited by Inspec-*

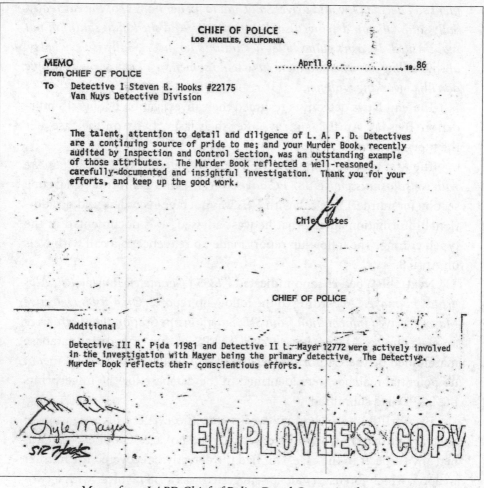

CHIEF OF POLICE
LOS ANGELES, CALIFORNIA

MEMO   ....April 8..........., 19 86
From CHIEF OF POLICE
To   Detective I Steven R. Hooks #22175
     Van Nuys Detective Division

The talent, attention to detail and diligence of L. A. P. D. Detectives
are a continuing source of pride to me; and your Murder Book, recently
audited by Inspection and Control Section, was an outstanding example
of those attributes. The Murder Book reflected a well-reasoned,
carefully-documented and insightful investigation. Thank you for your
efforts, and keep up the good work.

                                                Chief Gates

                           CHIEF OF POLICE

. Additional

Detective III R. Pida 11981 and Detective II L. Mayer 12772 were actively involved
in the investigation with Mayer being the primary detective. The Detective.
Murder Book reflects their conscientious efforts.

EMPLOYEE'S COPY

Memo from LAPD Chief of Police Daryl Gates, April 8, 1986

tion and Control Section, was an outstanding example of those attributes. *The Murder Book reflected a well-reasoned, carefully-documented and insightful investigation. Thank you for your efforts, and keep up the good work.*"

For unknown reasons, Gates's commendation was addressed to Hooks, the lowest-ranked detective assigned to Sherri's case, rather than Mayer, the lead investigator, or Pida, their supervisor. A postscript at the end of the memo stated, "*Detective III R. Pida 11981 and Detective II L. Mayer 12772 were actively involved in the investigation with Mayer being the primary detective. The Detective Murder Book reflects their conscientious efforts.*"

The commendation from Gates bore his signature and, at the bottom of the page, those of Pida and Hooks. A third signature, between Pida's and Hooks's, read *"Lyle Mayer,"* although Mayer himself had not signed it. In an interview in 2014, Mayer identified the signature as that of a secretary who had signed his name for him. Mayer said that he "never even saw" the memo from Gates in 1986. Asked why Gates had addressed the commendation to Hooks rather than to him, the lead detective, Mayer said, "They just picked up whatever detective was on the case."

Gates did not indicate in his memo how Sherri's case came to his rarefied attention, at the very apex of the LAPD. On paper, viewed strictly through the prism of the murder book compiled by the Van Nuys detectives, the circumstances of Sherri's homicide were utterly unremarkable: a badly botched but garden-variety burglary, one of hundreds attempted across Los Angeles in 1986.

Nor did Gates's memo account for how the Rasmussen murder book came to be audited by the LAPD's Inspection and Control Section. Random audits of murder books were infrequent, but not unheard of, under the department's practices in the 1980s. The Inspection and Control Section was also empowered to perform a directed audit, if there was some controversy or potential controversy attached to a particular case. It is unknown whether the audit of the Rasmussen murder book was random or directed, and if the latter, who ordered it.

Among veteran LAPD homicide detectives, audits by the Inspection and Control Section were widely considered a joke. Many of the auditors had never worked homicide or even had any level of detective experience. For that reason, many murder book audits amounted to little more than a check that administrative procedures had been followed and due dates met. Gates did not disclose in his memo the names of the auditors at the Inspection and Control Section who reviewed the Rasmussen murder book. Nor is it apparent from Gates's memo when Sherri's case was referred to the Inspection and Control Section, and on what date the murder book was examined, prior to April 8.

Nowhere in Gates's commendation did he acknowledge that the Van Nuys detectives, six weeks into their investigation of Sherri's murder, had not identified any suspects or made an arrest in the case. Whether it was Gates's regular practice as chief of police to commend detectives for unsolved homicide cases is unknown. What is evident from the commendation is that by April 8, 1986, Gates was both aware of Sherri's case and expressly approved of the focus and direction of the detectives' investigation.

Gates died in 2010. In July 2009, the journalist Jan Golab of *LA Weekly* interviewed Gates about Sherri's case. Gates denied that the LAPD was unwilling in 1986 to pursue a murder case against Stephanie. Gates admitted to "just a vague recollection of the murder itself, and then only because it was a fairly brutal murder."

Of all the unanswered questions raised by Gates's April 8 commendation to the Van Nuys detectives, perhaps the most vexing is what records the LAPD's Inspection and Control Section actually reviewed from the murder book in Sherri's case.

Far and away the most important document in any LAPD murder book is the chrono, the detectives' day-by-day log of all investigative work undertaken since the first hours of the case.

April 8, the date of Gates's memo, was only six weeks after Sherri's murder, and more than two weeks before the detectives' "sixty-day" follow-up report was due on April 25. For unknown reasons, the Van Nuys detectives did not complete the follow-up report for Sherri's case until May 21, eighty-six days after her murder.

Like the follow-up report, the typed chrono did not yet exist when the Inspection and Control Section audited the murder book in Sherri's case and Gates commended the detectives. The typed chrono was not created until mid-May, as an addendum to the follow-up report.

The only version of the chrono that existed in April 1986 was the original handwritten chrono, which later disappeared from the murder book. Although the handwritten and typed versions of the chrono are supposed to be verbatim, the missing handwritten pages preclude a direct comparison in Sherri's case. As a result, it may never be known whether the typed chrono is a true version of the original.

While the most authoritative record of the first three months of the LAPD's investigation into Sherri's murder was not preserved for posterity, Chief Gates's April 8 memo commending the detectives for their "well-reasoned, carefully-documented and insightful investigation" was retained in the murder book, where any detectives who happened to pick up Sherri's case in the future would be unlikely to miss it.

20

The Burglary Suspects

(April 10 to May 21, 1986)

Early Thursday afternoon, April 10, a resident of the condo complex at 6840 Balboa Boulevard, just a quarter mile south of where Sherri was killed, came home and discovered her front door ajar. Inside were two male burglars. The resident, a woman in her late twenties named Lisa Rivalli, shouted at the men to get out. One of the burglars was armed with a revolver, which he pointed at Rivalli before she fled to a neighbor's and called the police.

A Van Nuys patrol officer, David Moye, responded to the burglary call. Moye interviewed Rivalli and wrote out a preliminary investigation report, a fill-in-the-blank-style LAPD form.

Moye designated the suspect who pointed the gun at Rivalli S-1, and the second suspect S-2. The gun that S-1 brandished was described as a blue steel revolver with a four-inch barrel. Both suspects were listed as M/M, LAPD shorthand for Male/Mexican. S-1 was described as forty years old, five feet four and 160 pounds, with black hair, brown eyes, and a *"pot belly."* S-2 was described as between twenty and twenty-four years old, five feet six and 130 pounds, with black hair, brown eyes, and *"thin, shoulder length hair."* The suspects' car was listed as a blue Ford station wagon.

Moye recorded the time of the incident as 1:00 p.m. In the narrative section of the report, Moye wrote, *"Vict opened her front door and she obs S-2 picking up her stereo from the floor. Vict stated 'Get out of my house.' S-2 then fled via front door. Vict obs S-1 as he approached vict via the stairs*

to vict's bedroom. S-1 pointed a B/S 4" revolver at vict and vict fled . . . No
statements were made by susps during crime."

Mayer and Hooks heard about the burglary report the next day, on
Friday morning. The detectives' follow-up report for Sherri's case recounted:
"On 4-11-86 at 0845 hrs., Detectives Mayer and Hooks received information
that a residential burglary took place at 6840 Balboa Blvd unit #502 . . .
Detectives Mayer and Hooks interviewed victim Liisa [sic] Rivalli at length.
Mayer and Hooks went to the location with Rivalli and were show [sic] the
condo. Detectives noted that the location was almost an exact replica of the
7100 Balboa location. Both are condo's [sic] with security gates. Both have
security lock type entrances. Both have subterranean garages that have stairs
leading up to the condo from inside of the garage. In this burglary the sus-
pects, once inside, immediately stacked stereo equipment by the garage stairs
door. . . . Both burglaries were daytime, same times of occurrence . . .
Detectives Mayer and Hooks were of the opinion that the suspects who bur-
glarized Rivalli's residence very well could be the same suspects that com-
mitted the burglary/murder at 7100 Balboa."

In 2012, LAPD detectives reinterviewed Rivalli about the long-ago burglary, which was never solved. Rivalli recalled that the "lead detective" on
the case in 1986 told her that she was lucky, because a woman down the
street had surprised the same burglars and was shot to death.

Rivalli recounted in 2012 that on the day of the burglary, she left her
condo to walk to a McDonald's down the block. Rivalli noticed a blue station wagon, with a Hispanic man seated inside, parked in the alley that ran
behind her condo complex.

When Rivalli returned from lunch, the station wagon was still parked
there, but the man was no longer in it. She then discovered that the security gate for the complex had been stuffed with tissues to prop it open. As
Rivalli went to put her key in her front door, it swung open. She saw the
man from the station wagon standing next to her entertainment center,
stacking stereo equipment in a yellow bag. When she shouted at him to get
out, a second man came downstairs and pointed a gun at her.

Rivalli recalled in 2012 that the burglars pried open her jewelry box and
stole ten to fifteen pieces. Her car was in her garage the entire time and was
not touched or taken. The only property the police ever recovered was the
yellow bag, with one stereo component still inside. Rivalli recalled that the
police fingerprinted her residence after the burglary, but she did not know
whether they obtained any prints.

The Van Nuys detectives documented no investigative activity in Sherri's case between April 11, when they learned of the nearby burglary, and April 18, when LAPD composite sketches of the suspects were completed. According to the follow-up report, *"On 4-18-86 at 0900 hrs., Rivalli completed a composite drawing of both the suspects in her burglary, with the aid of SID composite artist Ponce. Rivalli stated that the drawings closely resemble the persons who committed the burglary at her residence. In addition, Rivalli gave Detective Mayer information regarding a United Parcel delivery man by the name of Bob Holten who may have been a witness to the burglary. Detective Mayer had the composite drawings photographed and distributed them to patrol officers and detectives in the Van Nuys and West Valley Divisions."*

Mayer interviewed Holten, the UPS deliveryman, the following day, Saturday, April 19. The address of the Rivalli burglary, 6840 Balboa Boulevard, was misstated in the typed chrono, which recounted, *"Interviewed Bob Holten. Obtained statement concerning his involvement as a wit at 6040 Balboa on 4-10-86. Showed him composite of susp #1. He feels that the susp looks very good!"*

The next typed chrono entry, the last activity the detectives recorded on Saturday, indicated, *"2000 | Took Sgt. Haponsol to 6740 Havenhurst [sic]. That is the location that Bob Holten claims he saw a susp that looks like susp # [sic]."* The address, 6740 Hayvenhurst Avenue, was a small apartment building just southeast of the stretch of Balboa Boulevard where Rivalli lived and Sherri was killed.

The follow-up report, meanwhile, recounted, *"On 4-19-86 Detective Mayer made numerous follow up investigations that led to the identity of Robert C. Holten as being the United Parcel delivery person who was a witness to the burglary of Rivalli's home. Mayer obtained a statement from Holten regarding what he saw at the location. All his information substantiated what Rivalli had told Mayer and Hooks. Detective Mayer's opinion that Rivalli's burglars being the same as the ones who burglarized 7100 Balboa was even more so firmed by Holten's observations. Holten provided Detective Mayer with additional information. Holten was of the opinion that he had observed one of the suspects again. Holten was of the opinion that he had observed suspect #2 in the composite drawings, at 6740 Havenhurst [sic] standing outside the apartment complex."*

The reason for the discrepancy between the typed chrono, which indicated that Holten recognized suspect #1, and the follow-up report, which

1600	Went to 28833 Flower Park Lane, Canyon Country. Interviewe
	Bob Holten. Obtained statement concerning his involvement
	as a wit at 6040 Balboa on 4-10-86. Showed him composite o
	susp #1. He feels that the susp looks very good!
2000	Took Sgt. Haponsol to 6740 Havenhurst. That is the locatio
	that Bob Holten claims he saw a susp that looks like susp #
2100	EOW.

LAPD typed chrono excerpt for April 19, 1986

MAYER OBTAINED A STATEMENT FROM HOLTEN REGARDING WHAT HE SAW AT THE
LOCATION. ALL HIS INFORMATION SUBSTANTIATED WHAT RIVALLI HAD TOLD
MAYER AND HOOKS. DETECTIVE MAYER'S OPINION THAT RIVALLI'S BURGLARS
BEING THE SAME AS THE ONES WHO BURGLARIZED 7100 BALBOA WAS EVEN MORE
SO FIRMED BY HOLTEN'S OBSERVATIONS. HOLTEN PROVIDED DETECTIVE MAYER
WITH ADDITIONAL INFORMATION. HOLTEN WAS OF THE OPINION THAT HE HAD
OBSERVED ONE OF THE SUSPECTS AGAIN. HOLTEN WAS OF THE OPINION THAT H
HAD OBSERVED SUSPECT #2 IN THE COMPOSITE DRAWINGS, AT 6740 HAVENHURST
STANDING OUTSIDE THE APARTMENT COMPLEX. ATTACHED AS ADDENDUM #20 IS
ROTATOR NOTICE WITH TWO COMPOSITE DRAWINGS MADE BY VICTIM RIVALLI ON
DR# 86 09 17448.

LAPD follow-up report excerpt re: April 19, 1986 (May 21, 1986)

indicated he observed suspect #2, is unknown. Also unknown is which of
the two suspects Holten actually saw.

The follow-up report, written by Mayer himself in May 1986, stated that
it was *"Detective Mayer's opinion"* that the Rivalli burglary suspects were
"the same as the ones who burglarized 7100 Balboa." In an interview in 2014,
however, Mayer insisted his belief that the crimes were connected was not
his alone. Mayer said, "This wasn't just Lyle Mayer's theory. We're working
as a team. We're working as a unit. I mean all of us. Believe me, there were
many detectives that I showed this crime scene to, great investigators that
I knew from around everywhere, that said, 'Yeah, I mean that looks plausible to me.'"

Along with Mayer, and his supervisor, Roger Pida, another of the most experienced investigators then assigned to the Van Nuys homicide unit was Mel Arnold. Arnold was a Detective III, the same rank as Pida. Mayer, Pida, and Arnold had worked homicide together in Van Nuys for five years, since 1981. Pida and Arnold were particularly close, a bond forged during their nine-plus years as partners investigating burglaries, and later homicides, in Van Nuys. Pida and Arnold were such good friends that, a year earlier, the *Los Angeles Daily News* had profiled them in an article about exemplary male friendships. The article recounted their willingness to take a bullet for each other, the camaraderie they shared on the job and off duty at "their favorite watering hole," and their intertwined family lives. Arnold succeeded Pida as the Van Nuys homicide coordinator in mid-1986, just a few months into the LAPD's investigation of Sherri's murder. Arnold ran the Van Nuys homicide unit from mid-1986 until 1991.

Arnold first entered the Rasmussen investigation on Sunday, April 20. The lone typed chrono entry that day stated, "*0600 | Checked location with Det. III Mel Arnold to verify surveillance to be conducted 4-21-86.*"

The following morning, Monday, April 21, the detectives met at the Van Nuys station to set up surveillance on 6740 Hayvenhurst Avenue. Mayer also enlisted two specialized LAPD units, CRASH and COBRA, to search for the burglary suspects. CRASH, an acronym for Community Resources Against Street Hoodlums, was an antigang unit. COBRA, short for Covert Operations to Battle Recidivist Activities, was a plainclothes unit that shadowed recent parolees.

Later Monday morning, a CRASH detective gave Mayer the name of a man, Gustavo Bonilla, who apparently closely resembled the suspect in composite sketch #1. Mayer went to the LAPD's Records and Identification Division and obtained a booking photo of Bonilla. Their focus on Bonilla intensified throughout the day. The follow-up report stated, "*Mayer prepared a photo line up consisting of 5 photographs and one of Bonilla. Victim Rivalli was shown the photo line-up. She was of the opinion that the photo of Bonilla closely matched the suspect #1 in her composite drawings. She was not positive that Bonilla was one of the suspects.*" Rivalli's statement was characterized in the follow-up report as a "*partial ID.*"

Mayer contacted COBRA and requested surveillance on Bonilla. The follow-up report recounted, "*The surveillance revealed that Bonilla did have a station wagon, but the color of the vehicle was green. Detective Mayer checked further and found that Bonilla was on parole for receiving stolen property.*" Mayer called the parole officer and informed him that Bonilla was a possible suspect in an unsolved burglary-homicide.

The next day, April 22, COBRA officers in search of Bonilla staked out an address in Downey, twenty-five miles southeast of Van Nuys, starting at 6:00 a.m. That afternoon, other COBRA officers tailed and arrested Bonilla's twenty-two-year-old son, who had a criminal record and was in possession of heroin. *"Officers brought susp into the station who closely resembles the suspect. Prepared photo line up and showed to victim Rivalli—Negative . . . she says similar but no mustache,"* the typed chrono stated.

Stephanie spent day watch on Tuesday, April 22, on loan to Devonshire detectives, according to her diary. Her partner was a detective named Dick Ward. Stephanie seemed to enjoy the opportunity to play detective for a day. In her diary, she wrote, *"I got to go on a ride along with Auto Det Ward. We went to Ross Baker Tow and he showed me a lot about VINs on Veh. Then we went to a few car Dealers so Ward could show a photo of a susp who used to work for the car dealers and was now stealing the cars . . . It was a very interesting day and I really learned a lot."*

On April 23, a Van Nuys patrol officer informed Mayer that he had *"stopped a suspect who matched the composite,"* the follow-up report recounted. The officer had obtained a booking photo of the man, Francisco Robles, and gave it to Mayer, who in turn shared it with Rivalli. The report noted, *"Robles has a relative with a station wagon which matches the description of the one used in the crime . . . Mayer showed the photograph of Robles to Rivalli. She informed Mayer that the hair style was similar but it did not appear to be the same person."*

Mayer and other LAPD officers again staked out Bonilla's home in Downey on Thursday morning, April 24. As soon as the senior Bonilla stepped outside, he was taken into custody. According to the follow-up report, *"A search of his vehicle disclosed numerous items of what detectives thought to be stolen property. Herion [sic] was found in the ashtray of the vehicle . . . Unfortunately Bonilla has not been identified as a suspect in the Rivalli or Rasmussen crimes. Bonilla's prints were compared to the crimes with negative results. Just a coincidence of a look a like [sic] bad guy at this time."* A felony drug charge was later filed against Bonilla, the typed chrono noted.

Although by April 25, it had been sixty days since Sherri's murder, the standard due date for the follow-up report on an unsolved homicide, the Van Nuys detectives did not complete the follow-up report in her case until

May 21. Why the follow-up report was produced late was not documented in the murder book.

The Van Nuys detectives recorded no investigative activity in Sherri's case between April 24 and 28. When they resumed their investigation, their focus remained squarely on burglary suspects. On Monday morning, April 28, Mayer contacted a Sgt. Primmer, whom the follow-up report described as a liaison to *"all Valley burglary units. Mayer provided Primmer with information regarding the two burglaries,"* a reference to Rivalli's burglary and Sherri's homicide. Later Monday, Mayer received a tip from a patrol officer about another possible suspect who resembled the composite sketch. *"The suspect does not appear to be the same as the one described by victim Rivalli at this time. Investigation is continuing into him,"* the follow-up report stated.

The only activity the detectives documented on April 29 pertained to the intersection where Sherri's stolen BMW was abandoned, almost two months earlier. According to the follow-up report, *"On 4-29-86, Detective Mayer made a recovered vehicle check via Automated Systems. This check was done to ascertain whether or not the area around Zombar Street [sic] and Cohasset Street is a drop area for stolen vehicles. In addition, Mayer was attempting to see if any arrests had been made in the area with regards to this information . . . There does not appear to be any connection."* The typed chrono stated more succinctly, *"Nothing indicates that it is a drop spot."*

The Van Nuys detectives recorded no investigative activity on Sherri's case between April 29 and May 10.

During morning watch on May 10, Stephanie and her patrol partner answered a call on Roscoe Boulevard. She noted in her diary that the location was close to John Ruetten's old apartment, where he lived before he moved in with Sherri. It was at the Roscoe apartment that she had called John in tears after she learned of his engagement. Although less than a year had passed since then, she betrayed no heartache, anger, regret, nor any emotion at all, when she mentioned John in her diary. Stephanie wrote, *"We got a few calls on Roscoe. 1 for a 415 behind John's old apt. Then we got a DUI. The guy was really nice & was one of the most polite DUI's I've ever arrested . . . We didn't do much the rest of the night . . . I put in for 15 min OT and Lt. Aggas got really mad. Like it was his money."*

The LAPD's Memorial Relay Race, an annual event championed by Chief Gates to honor officers killed in the line of duty, was held later that day, Saturday, May 10, at Chatsworth Park, within the Devonshire Division. All LAPD officers were encouraged to run, but participation was voluntary. Stephanie, despite having been on duty all night, ran on a team in the "mixed division," comprised of both male and female officers. Also on Stephanie's team was her old friend from the Hollywood Division and the LAPD women's basketball team, Nina Greteman.

The *Los Angeles Times* covered the event and reported that more than a thousand runners participated. The *Times* quoted Gates, "*We do this to try to encourage the concept of the LAPD as one big family.*"

According to Greteman, Stephanie seemed fine and in good spirits that day. Nothing about Stephanie's demeanor at the time made Greteman suspect anything was going on with her beneath the surface. Their relay team finished first in the mixed division. After the race, there was an awards ceremony in which the winners were called up and presented with medals by Gates himself.

Greteman had been an LAPD officer for almost three years, but before that day, she had never met Gates. She considered Gates larger than life, in a way that inspired awe from rank-and-file officers. For Greteman, and she believed for anybody who worked in the department at the time, it was a big deal to meet Gates in person, let alone to be congratulated and handed a medal by him.

Greteman knew that Gates loved LAPD athletics, and running in particular. Greteman and Stephanie must have seemed like exemplary young female officers to Gates, precisely the type the department was eager to have in its ranks: college educated, extremely physically fit, and enthusiastic about department traditions like the Memorial Relay Race.

Greteman recalls Stephanie seemed to share her excitement when they realized, after the race, that they would get to meet Gates face-to-face. Whether the awards ceremony was also Stephanie's first time meeting Gates is unknown. Nor is it clear what Gates knew about Stephanie when they met and were photographed together that day.

More than thirty years later, Greteman cannot recall what Stephanie said to Gates, and vice versa, when they went up to receive their medals that day in May 1986. However, a candid snapshot taken during the encounter shows Stephanie with a broad smile on her face. Nothing in the photograph suggested that Stephanie felt anxious in the presence of Gates, or worried in any way about her future, let alone her past. To the contrary, Stephanie appeared remarkably untroubled.

Left to right: Nina Greteman, LAPD Chief Daryl Gates, Stephanie Lazarus
(May 10, 1986)

Stephanie made no mention in her diary of her encounter with Chief Gates, although she kept for posterity a copy of their photograph together.

The Van Nuys detectives, following ten days with no documented activity in Sherri's case, resumed their investigation on May 10, the same day as the Memorial Relay. Mayer received a copy of a crime report for a new burglary at 7100 Balboa Boulevard, the condo complex where Sherri lived and was killed. The follow-up report indicated, *"It appears from the investigation . . . that this is merely a non-connected report. No prints were taken in the crime. Nothing of value was taken. Most probably just vandalism or a bum entering a location for some place to stay while the victim was gone."* After the reference on May 10 to the unconnected burglary, the detectives recorded no investigative activity until May 18.

On Monday, May 12, Stephanie spent most of her watch preparing for her upcoming job interview at the LAPD academy. A few days earlier, during a Devonshire Division training day, she had heard about an opening for a female physical training instructor and decided to apply. Stephanie wrote in her diary, *"I worked the desk tonight. Which wasn't too bad. I took*

2 reports all night. But I got a lot of personal business done. I shined my badge, buttons, and got my uniform ready for my interview at the academy."

Stephanie's patrol partner for morning watch on May 15 was Sally Barnes. Midway through their watch, while they were on duty and ostensibly out on patrol, they drove to a secluded area to sleep. Stephanie recounted, *"We surely didn't do much . . . We drove around a bit. Then at about 0300 Sally went up to Tampa north of Rinaldi. There are trails up there. So she parked & we slept for 1 1/2 hours. I really didn't like doing it and wouldn't want to do it all the time. We were pretty well hidden but I think the house to the West could poss see. We then went and ate and didn't do really anything else."*

On Sunday morning, May 18, according to the detectives' follow-up report, *"A neighborhood watch meeting was conducted at 7100 Balboa at the home of Carolyn Gregory . . . There were 30 persons in attendance. The officers conducting the meeting gave information on condo security measures and personal safety measures. Both burglaries at 7100 Balboa and 6840 Balboa were discussed. No new leads or investigative clues were obtained by the officers. This investigation is still ongoing."*

The last investigative activity documented in the typed chrono was on May 19, two days before the date of the follow-up report in Sherri's case. The first entry on May 19 listed by name two new possible suspects, both described in the typed chrono as *"Burglar—Hypes."* The final typed chrono entry noted, *"Sent Van Nuys Area top ten burglars names to Herrera on 187 PC prints."*

Stephanie's patrol partner for morning watch on May 20 was Bill Walker. In her diary, she wrote, *"It was work out night tonight. I'm about the only one that works out . . . First thing we did was take blood to Van Nuys. Then we had a Tommy Burger . . . We just joked and laughed all night. We didn't get 1 radio call."* She ended her diary entry, *"NOTE The probationer Griffin resigned. I guess she realized her situation. I still don't know about the job. Just hoping I get it."* Almost three months after the murder of Sherri Rasmussen, Stephanie betrayed no concern about her own fitness and prospects for advancement in the LAPD.

The follow-up report the Van Nuys detectives completed for Sherri's case was fifty pages long. Although the report named *"Det. II L.O. Mayer"* and *"Det. I S.R. Hooks"* as the two detectives assigned to the case, there is no indication within it which one of them authored it. On the front page, the follow-up report's Fact Sheet, Sherri's cause of death was listed as *"Gunshot Wounds,"* and the motive as *"Residential Burglary."*

```
                    UNSOLVED MURDER INVESTIGATION

                         PROGRESS REPORT

                         FACT SHEET


    VICTIM:                        RASMUSSEN, SHERRI RAE
                                   DR # 86 09 10480
                                   CORONER CASE # 86 2676


    DATE/TIME OCCURRED:            2-24-86, BETWEEN 0730 AND 1100HRS.
                                   MONDAY

    LOCATION OF OCCURRANCE:        7100 BALBOA BOULEVARD, UNIT #205
                                   VAN NUYS, CALIFORNIA

    CAUSE OF DEATH:                GUNSHOT WOUNDS

    MOTIVE:                        RESIDENTAL BURGLARY

    AREA OF OCCURANCE:             VAN NUYS AREA

    DETECTIVES ASSIGNED:           DET.II  L.O. MAYER  12772
                                   DET.I   S.R. HOOKS  22175

    DATE OF THIS REPORT:           MAY 21, 1986



                         ADDENDA

    SUBJECT         ADDENDUM NO.   SUBJECT              ADDENDUM NO

    CHRONOLOGICAL RECORD     1     VEHICLE REPORTS           7
    FORM 3.11.6
                                   ARREST REPORT             8
    CRIME SCENE LOG          2
    FORM 3.11.4                    RELATED CRIME REPORTS     9

    CRIME REPORT             3     WITNESS LIST AND STATEMENTS   14
                                   FORM LAPD 03.11.7
    DEATH REPORT             4
                                   CORONERS REPORT          19
    PROPERTY REPORTS         5
                                   COMMUNICATIONS           20
    SID REPORTS              6


                         PAGE (1)
```

LAPD follow-up report, page 1 (May 21, 1986)

Hooks testified in court in 2012 that it was Mayer who wrote the May 1986 follow-up report for Sherri's case. Hooks also testified that the investigative conclusions contained in the follow-up report were "not completely" his own conclusions at the time.

Despite Hooks's belated acknowledgement, under oath, that he considered the follow-up report's conclusions incomplete, he nevertheless signed it in May 1986. On the witness stand in 2012, Hooks said he did not recall whether he ever expressed to anyone in 1986 that he did not completely agree with the conclusions in the follow-up report.

Mayer, during an interview with a defense investigator in 2011, was adamant that the investigative conclusions in the follow-up report were not his opinion alone, but also that of Hooks, their supervisor Pida, and their commanding officer, Durrer, all of whom were consulted and concurred with him. According to Mayer, everyone in the Van Nuys homicide unit was of the opinion that burglary was the primary motive for Sherri's death.

The first section of the follow-up report, Synopsis, was an extraordinarily detailed yet largely fantastical narrative of Sherri's murder. Much of the account was pure conjecture, rather than based on hard evidence, even as it was framed as fact:

> On February 24, 1986 at 0730 hrs. Sherri Rasmussen was home alone. This day was to be a normal working day for her but she did not go to work because of being sick. Her husband, John, had left the residence at 0730 to go to work.
>
> Between 0730 hrs and 1000 hrs. unknown suspect or suspects entered the victim's residence via an unlocked front door. Once inside the location the suspect or suspects began burglarizing the premises. The burglarizing of the premises caused noise. The victim, who apparently was in the upstairs master bedroom at the time, heard noises caused by the burglar or burglars. The victim, who had been lying in bed, got up and exited the master bedroom. She walked down the stairs from the second floor. Upon the victims [sic] arrival on first floor, she was walking in the portion of the condo that is described as the bar / dining room area. When she turned the corner from the stairs area to the bar / dining room area she confronted a suspect. This suspect was armed with a handgun. The victim observed that the suspect was holding a handgun. The victim grabbed for the handgun and a struggle ensued. During this struggle two shots were fired. The shots did not strike the victim. The shots did go through the kitchen sliding glass door window, in a northerly direction.
>
> After the struggle that took place at the bar/dining room area, the victim either was forced towards the living room area of the condo or she ran from the suspect and attempted to activate the help button of the residential alarm. This alarm is physically located on the wall of the entry hallway approximately 30 feet from the bar / dining room area. In the entry hallway of the condo a second struggle between the suspect and the victim

took place. This fight, from the crime scene observations, was extensive. The victim attempted to activate the alarm button. The suspect was restraining the victim from doing so. The fight was very physical. The victim was possibly winning this portion of the fight. The suspect bit the victim on the inner left forearm. The bite was so severe that it is good for comparison after being photographed and casted.

This second fight progressed from the entry hallway to the living room proper. In the center of the living room, the fight continued. The victim was standing in the middle of the living room. The suspect obtained a porcelain statue from a stereo wall unit. The suspect struck the victim on the head with the porcelain statue at least twice. The victim fell to the floor, lying on her back, face up. The suspect obtained a quilted robe, wrapped the handgun in the blanket and shot the victim three times. Two of the shots were almost contact wounds. The third shot was a full contact wound. All the shots were fired into the victim's chest.

The suspect then went back to the bar / dining room area and removed the victim's purse from the bar. The suspect then removed the victim's keys from her purse. The suspect then exited the condo via the garage door leading to the underground garage. Once inside the garage proper, the suspect activated the garage door opener button on the wall. The suspect then entered the victim's vehicle and drove out of the garage.

The first half of the Crime Scene Investigation section of the follow-up report was a verbatim transcript of Hooks's handwritten notes from their initial walk-through the night of the murder. The rest of the section was a rundown of physical evidence collected from the crime scene and all the SID forensic analysis performed to date. Among the evidence listed in the follow-up report, but untested in 1986, was the *"swab of bitemark on left arm"* taken the night of Sherri's murder.

Almost half of the report, twenty-four pages, consisted of a chronological narrative of all the investigative activity conducted by the detectives since the start of the case. The information tracked the dates, times, and actions recounted in the typed chrono, but it was presented in standard prose rather than the clipped shorthand used in the typed chrono.

The Evidence section of the follow-up report indicated that twenty-eight items had been booked to that point in the investigation and noted that a property report was attached. The bite mark swab was nowhere listed on the LAPD's property report, since it was collected by the coroner's office, not SID. Also noted in the follow-up report were the results of three SID analyzed evidence reports. Sherri's sexual assault kit indicated that she was not sexually assaulted. The bullet-riddled quilted blanket tested positive for gunshot residue. The vase (not statue) that Sherri was bludgeoned with was dusted for fingerprints, but no identifiable prints were obtained.

The Victim's Information section of the follow-up report stated in full:

The victim was a female Caucasian, 29 years of age. She was 5 feet 11 inches tall and weighed approximately 140 pounds. She was described as being an athletic person in excellent shape. Her date of birth was 2-7-57. She was employed as the Director of Critical Care nursing at Glendale Adventist Hospital in Glendale. She had a master's degree in nursing administration. She was well liked at work and in the community. She taught at the hospital as well as at UCLA. She did community service in the West Los Angeles area. She was married to John A. Ruetten in November, 1985. They were happily married and there does [sic] not appear to be any problems between the two. She did not have children. This was her first marriage. It was John's first marriage. Sherri comes from a well-to-do family. The father is a dentist in Arizona. Sherri and John did not have money problems. Both had jobs where they were well paid. Sherri can best be described as a pillar to the community.

Sherri did have a plan for emergency. She was not going to be taken away and harmed if danger arose. She had a plan at her residence that she would attempt to activate the alarm, if possible. If not, she was going to run to her bedroom, close the door and jump out the bedroom window. This information came from her father, Nels Rasmussen, who always taught Sherri to be a fighter and not give in. Apparently this plan may have been a contributing factor in her death.

This reference to Nels, which cast blame on him for his daughter's murder, was the only time he was mentioned in the follow-up report. According to Nels, he had never given any such advice to Sherri, about what she should do in an emergency, nor did he ever tell Mayer that he had.

The Suspect Information section of the follow-up report stated in full, *"At this point in the investigation there are no clear cut suspects. This matter will be covered in the Investigative Conclusion portion of this report."*

That section, the last in the follow-up report, shared the same cinematic,

```
SHERRI DID HAVE A PLAN FOR EMERGENCY.  SHE WAS NOT GOING TO BE TAKEN
AWAY AND HARMED IF DANGER AROSE.  SHE HAD A PLAN AT HER RESIDENCE THA
SHE WOULD ATTEMPT TO ACTIVATE THE ALARM, IF POSSIBLE.  IF NOT, SHE WA
GOING TO RUN TO HER BEDROOM, CLOSE THE DOOR AND JUMP OUT THE BEDROOM
WINDOW.  THIS INFORMATION CAME FROM HER FATHER, NELS RASSMUSSEN, WHO
HAD ALWAYS TAUGHT SHERRI TO BE A FIGHTER AND NOT TO GIVE IN.
APPARENTLY THIS PLAN MAY HAVE BEEN A CONTRIBUTING FACTOR IN HER DEATH
                          PAGE 42
```

LAPD follow-up report, page 42 (May 21, 1986)

speculative quality of the Synopsis, with numerous assertions ungrounded in evidence. The Investigative Conclusion section stated:

> *This case stems from a residential burglary. One of the suspect [sic] who committed this burglary was armed. During the commission of the burglary the victim was home. The victim surprised the suspects. A suspect pulled the gun and a struggle over the gun took place. The victim had hold of the suspect's gun while he was holding the weapon. Shots were fired during the first struggle. The suspect was able to get away from the victim's grasp. The victim realizing the possibility of great bodily harm, ran from the suspect and attempted to activate the residential alarm panic button. The suspect regained a form of control over the victim. A second struggle took place where the victim was severly [sic] bitten on the arm. The victim was winning this second struggle. The suspect broke free and forced the victim into the living room of the condo. A third struggle took place. The victim was struck on the head and face with a poreclin [sic] vase. The victim fell to the floor. The suspect wrapped the gun in the victim's quilted bathrobe which had been lying on the chair next to the fireplace. The suspect wrapped the gun in order to muffle the sound of the gunshots while he executed the victim who was knocked out at the time. The suspect then returned to the bar area of the dining room and stole the victim's purse. The suspect exited the garage stair's [sic] door and entered the garage. In the garage he activated the garage door opener button. He then entered the victim's 1985 BMW and drove out of the garage and away from the scene. The suspect drove the vehicle to Zombar and Cohasset, approximately two miles away to the north, and parked the vehicle, leaving it unlocked with the keys inside.*

It is this detective's opinion that there were two suspects. This is based on the following information. The suspects knocked on the victim's door for some time. There was no answer. They rang the door bell which unknown to them was not operating. They tried the door and found it to be unlocked. Once inside, one suspect began to remove the stereo equipment from the wall unit in the living room. While doing so, the suspect did not realize that the speaker wires were attached to the component that he was removing. This caused the falling of some items to the top of the TV. The suspect stacked those items on the entry floor near the stairs. At this time the victim, who was upstairs, heard the noise caused by the burglars. She left the bedroom and came downstairs. She may have been of the opinion that the family cat had caused problems. Once downstairs, the victim turned towards the bar / dining room area. The victim surprised the second burglar who was looking through the victim's purse which was lying on the bar counter. A struggle took place. Two shots were fired. The suspect who was stacking the stereo equipment fled the condo, leaving the other burglar to fight the victim. There is no doubt that the victim was executed by the armed burglar. Although during some portions of the struggles, the victim was at one point winning. She may have been executed because of this very fact.

The method of operation of the burglars at victim Rivalli's burglary indicated to detectives that their method of operation is so very similar to the method used in the Rasmussen burglary/murder. All their acts indicate that they very well could be the same suspects. The vehicle used by the suspects on the Rivalli burglary could very well be the one used by the suspects in the Rasmussen crime.

Detectives are of the opinion that in the Rasmussen crime the suspect who left his partner at the scene took the getaway car. This forced the other suspect to steal Rasmussen's vehicle. The fact that these burglars are armed during the burglary also leads detectives to believe that they are the same suspects. In addition, the property they immediately attack is stereo equipment. They stack the stereo equipment by the entryway. Burglars who do these things do not usually walk to a location, commit a burglary and walk away. The locations of both burglaries are just down the street from one another.

There is no doubt the suspect knew he killed Rasmussen. This is why he was armed when he committed the Rivalli burglary . . . This homicide case will be most likely solved through the comparison of fingerprints related to the crime. Detective Mayer has submitted the Van Nuys prints of the "Van Nuys Top Ten Burglary Suspects" to prints for comparison.

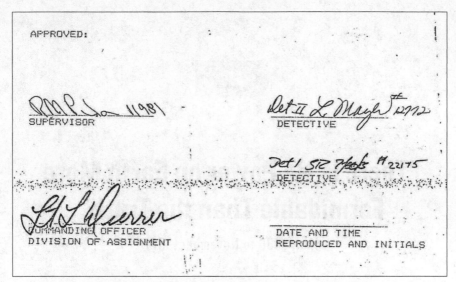

LAPD follow-up report signature page (May 21, 1986)

The detectives' report also noted, *"As of 6-1-86, no second polygraph of John Ruetten, the husband, has been scheduled. This is due to his emotional state and the fact that he was present at the crime scene. It is felt he will never be a suitable candidate for a second menaingful [sic] polygraph."*

The last page of the follow-up report, page 50, was the signature page. It was signed "Approved" by Mayer and Hooks; Pida, their supervisor; and Durrer, their lieutenant and the commanding officer of Van Nuys homicide.

No mention was made in the follow-up report of Stephanie Lazarus, nor any possibility of an alternative motive for what happened to Sherri, other than the detectives' theory that she was killed by the same men who burglarized Rivalli, more than six weeks after Sherri was killed. By the time the follow-up report was completed, the Rivalli burglary was itself six weeks old. The suspects remained unidentified and at large.

21

"There Is No Power on Earth More Formidable Than the Truth"

(May 1986 to November 1987)

Stephanie in late May appeared focused on the future, and in particular, taking the next step in her LAPD career. She had been assigned to Devonshire for more than a year. Despite the light workload and cushy conditions at "Club Dev," Stephanie seemed eager to move on, and to move up within the department.

In late March, about a month after Sherri Rasmussen's murder, Stephanie had taken the LAPD's written exam for Police Officer III. Two months later, she was still waiting to hear whether she passed. In early May, while at the LAPD academy for a training day, she heard about a job opening there for a physical training instructor. She applied for the position but had not yet been called in for a formal interview.

Even as she aspired to promotion to P-3, a supervisory rank, she routinely disparaged in her diary various officers she worked with for their incompetence, moodiness, and other perceived faults. She seemed to judge other female officers particularly harshly. Her partner for morning watch on May 22 was Betty Kleffman. Stephanie recounted, *"Betty drove since I drove the night before. She was really starting to get on my nerves. I don't recall what we did up until we went on a call with a man w/ a gun. Betty had her rover turned up and Taylor yelled at her. Betty really had no clue."*

Very rarely did Stephanie express any empathy for the people and situations that she encountered while on patrol. An exception was later that night, when she and Kleffman answered an overdose call in Granada Hills, where Stephanie lived at the time. In her diary, she wrote, *"It turned out that a 15 year old girl took 200 Tylenol w/ Codeine and some Actifed and sleeping [sic] around 0200 am. Her father found her at 0600 hours took her to the hosp and she died at about 0905. I wrote the injury report, booked the suicide note, and had picked up a copy of the victim's handwriting from her house. It was really sad to see the girl. She was shaking and they pumped her stomach. Really sad. I assisted detective Lyons with the report."*

Stephanie noted in her diary on May 26, *"Lt. Aggas wasn't too bad to work w/ tonight. I think he has his different moods. I still haven't heard about the job interview yet at the Academy."*

Stephanie's job interview took place on Friday afternoon, May 30. Two days later, the next day she worked, she wrote in her diary, *"On 5-30-86 (1430) I had my interview at the Academy. Lt. Frelen & Sgt. Dossey interviewed me. I think the interview went pretty well. I should find out by Wed. at the latest. I found out on 5-31-86 in the mail I didn't pass the P-III exam. I didn't expect to. Maybe if I studied harder."*

On Wednesday, June 4, Stephanie reported in her diary, *"I found out from Mike Hargreaves that I didn't get the job at the Academy. They gave it to a guy. Apparently only 2 guys interviewed and the one had a lot of experience."* On the bright side, she wrote, *"I will be going back to day watch thank God."*

According to the chrono for Sherri's case, the Van Nuys detectives resumed their investigation on Friday, June 6. More than two weeks had passed since the final entry in the typed chrono, on May 19. Following the completion of the follow-up report on May 21, the chrono reverted to handwritten entries, in contrast to the preceding thirteen typed pages, the only record of the first three months of the investigation that were retained permanently in the murder book.

The chrono stated, *"6/6/86 | 500 | Recd info from No. Hwd that a suspect by the name of Stephen Vulpis . . . was in custody. He may be a suspect in their murder. He is a burglar who works with a partner. Ran his prints against the crime."*

It is unknown which Van Nuys homicide detective wrote the June 6 chrono entry. Mayer, in an interview in 2014, recalled that detectives customarily put their name or initials at the end of any chrono entry they made, to indicate who wrote it. This practice enabled other detectives to pick up the chrono for a case and identify who had worked on it previously, and what they had contributed to the investigation.

Unlike nearly all other crimes, there is no statute of limitations for murder. Unsolved homicide cases often outlast individual detectives' careers. Given the sheer number of LAPD detectives, and the reality that turnover within homicide units was both common and inevitable, detectives could not rely over the long term on the distinctiveness of their penmanship to identify who had done what in a case, and when.

Mayer also recounted in 2014 that many other detectives besides himself worked on Sherri's case in the months and years after her murder. Mayer said, "There were probably at least twenty different guys that worked on that case, along with me. There was twenty different pairs of eyes and minds that were reviewing all of this information, and going, 'No, we still believe that's the primary emphasis of the case,' and, 'No, we still believe what the initial detectives thought is the premise.' That's what we're continuing to focus on, and working on. Each of these guys would review that. It wasn't like I was the only guy in the world that said, 'No, this is absolutely what happened, and there couldn't be any other reason.' So now you understand how many different sets of eyes, and minds, were on that case."

Despite Mayer's recollection of the Van Nuys homicide unit's notekeeping practices at the time, in the chrono for Sherri's case, the first handwritten entry on June 6 and virtually all that followed contained no indication whatsoever of who wrote it, such as the detective's name, initials, or LAPD serial number.

The Van Nuys Division held a picnic for officers and their families on Saturday, June 7. As was customary on the day of a division's picnic, officers from nearby divisions were reassigned to cover patrol duties. Among the officers loaned to Van Nuys for morning watch on Sunday, June 8, was Stephanie Lazarus.

On Wednesday morning, June 11, an unidentified detective handwrote two entries in the chrono for Sherri's case. The first was a call from SID notifying Homicide that the fingerprints of the burglary suspect in custody in North Hollywood, Vulpis, did not match the prints in Sherri's case. The second chrono entry, at 10:00 a.m., stated, *"Rec'd phone call from Mr. Bell, Hartford Insurance Co. regarding the life insurance of Sherri—the Beneficiary of the policy is the mother, Loretta."*

The life insurance policy referenced in the chrono was provided to Sherri by Glendale Adventist as part of her employee benefits. Sherri had completed the paperwork when she was hired in early 1984, a few months before she met John.

Loretta did not learn that Sherri had a life insurance policy, and that she was the beneficiary, until she received a phone call from Althea Kennedy, Sherri's boss, several weeks after the murder.

Among the documents Althea had to provide to the insurance company before it would pay out the policy was Sherri's autopsy report. Althea called the Van Nuys detectives and requested they send her a copy.

Althea recalls she spoke with the detectives only a few times in the months following Sherri's murder. Whenever she did, she inquired about the status of Sherri's case. The detectives consistently replied that their investigation was ongoing, but they still believed that Sherri was killed during a botched burglary. The detectives also told Althea that another condo near Sherri's was burglarized, which they said was probably related. The detectives were polite in their interactions with her. Althea did not doubt what the police told her.

Althea read Sherri's autopsy report when it arrived from the LAPD. Although she was a vice president at Glendale Adventist, she had worked as a hospital nurse for many years earlier in her career, before her promotion to management. Althea readily understood the medical terminology used to describe Sherri's injuries, which were far more extensive than she had imagined.

It was obvious to Althea, based solely on her review of the autopsy report, that Sherri had fought hard for her life. Althea knew Sherri was tall and very athletic. As she read the litany of injuries, including the many cuts and bruises on Sherri's face and the bite mark on her arm, she thought, "My goodness, she must have been getting the better of somebody, and they decided to shoot her instead." Althea could not understand why Sherri would take on two men with a gun rather than try to get away. Althea never spoke to the detectives, the Rasmussens, or anyone at the hospital about her impressions of Sherri's autopsy report.

John was apparently unaware when Sherri was killed that she had a life insurance policy through Glendale Adventist. During John's initial, tape-recorded interview with Mayer on the night of the murder, Mayer asked him point-blank whether he and Sherri had life insurance. John said that he thought he had a $50,000 policy through his work, but that as far as he knew, Sherri had none.

At some point in the months after Sherri's death, however, John and his parents learned that she did in fact have life insurance, but John was not the beneficiary. The Ruettens felt John should be the beneficiary of Sherri's policy, since they were married.

Vera, Althea's secretary, recalls that John's mother called Althea about Sherri's life insurance policy. John's mother wanted to know if John could have the insurance proceeds, because he needed the money, she told Althea. Althea explained that the designation Sherri made was legally binding, and nothing could be done to make John the beneficiary. According to Vera, John's mother tried very hard to pressure Althea into redirecting the money to John, but Althea held firm that it was out of her hands.

When the insurance check arrived at the hospital, Althea wrote two letters that she asked Vera to type for her, Vera recalls. The first was a cover letter to Loretta that noted the check from Sherri's life insurance was enclosed. The second letter, to John's mother, reiterated that Althea had no control over who was the beneficiary of Sherri's policy. Althea did not inform the Rasmussens that John's mother had pushed for the money from Sherri's life insurance to go to John instead of Loretta.

The title to John and Sherri's condo passed automatically to John upon Sherri's death, along with responsibility for the mortgage. Nels recalls that after Sherri's murder, he spoke with John only once about his plans for the condo. He didn't raise the subject when he and Loretta went there in March to box up Sherri's belongings. At the time, John was staying in the condo with his mother. Nels and Loretta thought John had not yet made up his mind about whether he could live there by himself.

According to Nels, soon after they returned home from that trip, John called him and said he needed $10,000 for mortgage payments. John wanted Nels to come up with the money so he could keep the condo.

Nels knew that when Sherri and John refinanced the condo in 1985, its value had appreciated about $30,000 from what he had paid for it in 1980. Nels offered to buy the condo back from John at the price it was appraised for in 1985. According to Nels, John hung up on him and didn't call back.

John's resolve to stay in the condo where Sherri was killed proved short-lived. Less than a month after the murder, he decided he could not continue to live there. He took a leave of absence from his job at Micropolis, to which he never returned. John moved in with his parents in San Diego and lived with them for the next nine months.

Sherri's colleagues at Glendale Adventist heard that John had moved away soon after her murder. As months passed without news of an arrest, or any update on the status of the investigation, at least some of her former colleagues began to wonder where John was in all of this, and why he was not more visible and vocal in demanding answers about who killed his wife.

People expected him, as the husband, to lead the charge for justice on Sherri's behalf. Rather than step up and assume that mantle—for instance, by appealing to the public for information—John seemed to disappear instead.

John's silence was conspicuous enough that, according to Althea, people even asked her, "Why haven't we heard anything from him? Do you think he's involved?" Althea responded that she didn't think John had anything to do with Sherri's death. Still, Althea didn't really know John, and she could not explain his behavior in the wake of his wife's murder, even as her case remained unsolved and her killer at large.

Notwithstanding the questions prompted by John's low profile, word also circulated at the hospital that he had a rock-solid alibi. In the end, Sherri's colleagues deferred to the police investigation and accepted as true the theory that she was killed by two Mexican burglars. Vera recalls that Sherri's death was discussed at the hospital for a few months, but as time went on, people talked about her less, and no longer dwelled on who may have killed her. In Vera's opinion, people just forgot about Sherri and got on with their own lives.

At least one of Sherri's colleagues heard from John in the months after her murder. Peggy received in the mail a memorial booklet that the Rasmussens produced as a keepsake for Sherri's family and friends. One of Nels's patients owned a print shop in Tucson and printed them free of charge. Peggy's booklet came inscribed with handwritten notes from both Loretta and John.

The twelve-page booklet was printed on heavyweight paper, with a cardstock cover that simply read SHERRI. Two color photographs, one a portrait of Sherri and the other of Sherri and John hugging and smiling on their wedding day, were affixed inside the front and back covers, respectively. The text included Sherri's colleagues' remarks at her memorial service, selected passages from scripture, and a collection of quotes *"that brought a lot of happiness and understanding to Sherri."* One quote, attributed to the novelist Margaret Runbeck, read *"There is no power on earth more formidable than the truth."*

In addition to Peggy and other family and friends, Loretta also sent copies of the memorial booklet to Matt and Anita Gorder, and to Matt's parents in San Diego.

Over the course of John and Matt's years-long friendship, the Ruetten and Gorder families also grew close, in particular John's mother, Margaret, and Matt's mother, Bonnie, who were best friends. Because John and

Matt were classmates throughout high school and college, they had many friends in common. Margaret knew of many people in Matt's life, and Bonnie of many people in John's.

Among them was Stephanie Lazarus, whom Bonnie thought of as John's ex-girlfriend. Bonnie had mentioned Stephanie to Matt once or twice. Matt presumed that his mother heard about Stephanie via Margaret Ruetten.

Loretta met Bonnie Gorder only once in person, at Sherri and John's wedding. Matt's parents may also have attended the Glendale Adventist memorial service, little more than three months later, although Loretta cannot recall for certain. Both times, for very different reasons, there were so many friends and family present that Loretta had little opportunity to chat with anyone for very long. Loretta has no recollection of speaking with Matt's mother on either occasion.

A few months after Sherri was killed, Loretta received a phone call one day at home, out of the blue, from Bonnie Gorder. According to Loretta, Bonnie informed her on the phone that John's ex-girlfriend was capable of murder. Loretta did not know what to say, partly out of shock, and partly because she hardly knew Matt's mother. Bonnie did not tell Loretta the name of John's ex-girlfriend, but described her as a "very volatile" person, Loretta recalls. Bonnie also said the ex-girlfriend had the sort of disposition that when she played a game, she played to win, and if she lost, she was prone to go berserk.

Bonnie did not tell Loretta why she decided to call her, or what she expected her to do with the information about John's ex-girlfriend. Nor did Bonnie say whether she had told anyone else—for instance, the police— that she suspected John's ex-girlfriend could have murdered Sherri. Whether Bonnie discussed her suspicions with Margaret Ruetten, her best friend, who had known Stephanie well for years, is unknown. If Bonnie ever reported her suspicions to the police, there is no record of it in the murder book for Sherri's case. Bonnie Gorder died in 1995.

Mayer, in an interview in 2014, described John in the months after Sherri's murder as "noncommunicative." According to Mayer, throughout the entire time he worked on Sherri's case, John never once contacted the detectives. Mayer recalled that John's attitude was "I don't want to know. That part of my life is over."

Stephanie, meanwhile, moved on with her life as well. On June 12, she received a commendation from the LAPD for her conduct on patrol, specifically *"good, clear"* radio broadcasts and *"fine FI's"* (field interviews). It was the first official commendation Stephanie had received in over a year, since May 1985, when the LAPD had commended her for her *"enthusiasm and positive attitude."*

On June 17, Stephanie wrote in her diary, *"I'm going to day watch and I'm assigned to the desk. I won't have to work w/ different weirdos for 1 month. I still like the job, but I'm getting a little tired of the soap opera atmosphere and working w/ some people you just don't want to work w/. But I guess that's probably true at any job except when you have to sit in the car for 8 hours w/ someone."*

Five days later, on June 22, Stephanie wrote, *"Today was my first day watch . . . I felt great. To get off morning watch was a relief. I'm assigned the desk all month which is okay since we get off at 1530 . . . I can't tell you how relaxed I was working the day watch desk."*

Stephanie was off duty from June 24 to 26, while she represented the LAPD at the 1986 California Police Olympics. She competed on the LAPD women's basketball team, which won the gold medal for the second year in a row.

On July 10, according to her diary, Stephanie went on a long lunch date with a guy she had met at the Police Olympics, a DA investigator named Alfred Winfield. *"We had lunch from about 1145 to about 1430 . . . I was going to deduct over the 45 min, but everyone else takes 1–2 hour lunches sometimes and there are times when we don't get any. Then I only had 1 hour left before EOW. Easy day,"* she wrote in her diary.

Stephanie also spent most of her patrol watch on July 15 visiting other apparent crushes of hers. She recounted in her diary, *"I worked by myself . . . It was work out day today so I lifted weights. I got finished about 0830. First thing I did was go visit Gene at work. I don't know why. We planned to have lunch together. Then I went to my P.O. Box, got my mail, and dropped it off at my house . . . I had lunch with Gene. I then went to visit Mark and Greg. Mark wanted me to go and play a joke on a friend of his who was working on his boat . . . I played the joke real quick and then Mark came by. I don't think the owner thought it was real funny . . . I didn't do a thing all day."*

On July 18, Stephanie went to the academy shooting range to qualify with the shotgun, a periodic requirement for all officers. While she was there, she also shot the "bonus course" with her duty revolver. The bonus course required officers to fire forty rounds at targets from 7 to 25 yards away. Each bull's-eye was ten points, so a perfect score was 400. The minimum passing score was 280. Officers who scored above 300 were awarded a medal and bonus pay from the department. Stephanie shot 326.

To the degree that Stephanie distinguished herself on the job, it was not through acts of bravery or service to the public, but rather her devotion to the department and its culture. On Saturday, July 26, the Devonshire Division held a picnic for officers and their families. Stephanie volunteered to organize games. *I got to judge the bake off with Lyle Alzado (ex-Raider), his girlfriend and Judge Luros . . . Everyone seemed to have a good time. The picnic was fun, seeing everyone's wife and kids,* she recounted.

Stephanie's willingness to volunteer for events like the Devonshire picnic was noted by other officers and her superiors at Devonshire. In her diary on July 28, she noted, *Everyone thanked me for the neat games we played at the picnic.*

August 3 was the date chosen by Jayne and Mike for their Los Angeles wedding. For months after Sherri was killed, Jayne experienced survivor's guilt, although she did not have a name for it at the time. She felt certain something horrible was going to happen to her, out of the blue, like had happened to Sherri. For as long as they had been friends, Jayne had always thought of Sherri as leading a charmed life. She thought, "If this can happen to Sherri, what does that mean for the rest of us less charmed people?" Jayne feared it was just a matter of time until the other shoe dropped on her or Mike.

Jayne and Mike lived together in Venice during their engagement. She took to warning him to be careful whenever he left the house, even for something as innocuous as going to get the newspaper.

Mike finally asked her, "What do you think's going to happen? I'm going to get hit by a car?"

"Oh, nothing that benign. I think a lightning bolt is going to come out of the sky and kill you. I don't know what might happen to you. But nothing good."

In mid-July, Jayne and Mike had a wedding ceremony in Windsor, Ontario, where she grew up. Jayne had six siblings, all brothers. The day before their wedding in Windsor, she went out to get her nails done. Her brothers decided to keep Mike occupied by taking him canoeing. By the time Jayne got home, the canoe trip was already over. Still, she was hysterical when she found out.

"Are you crazy? You could have drowned. What were you thinking?" she demanded of Mike.

"Jayne, the water was three feet deep. They would have had to hold my head underwater."

Their wedding in Los Angeles, two weeks later, was held at a friend's home in Westwood. Both the Rasmussens and John Ruetten attended. Sherri's sister Teresa also went with her husband, Brian, and their infant son. Loretta recalls that it was a tough wedding emotionally for her and Nels to attend, but they made the trip from Tucson to be there for Jayne. John made the effort to come up from San Diego as well. Jayne's matron of honor was Anita Gorder, Matt's wife.

Jayne did not get to spend much time on her wedding day with individual guests, so she cannot recall whether there was any tension between Nels and John. Jayne felt everyone there was still connected by a sense of grief and shock at Sherri's murder. She especially felt for Teresa, who was coping with her firstborn child and the death of her sister at the same time. Jayne was grateful that the Rasmussens and John came at all. Later, when Jayne got her wedding photos, she felt she could see a blank space in them where Sherri should have been.

On Saturday, August 9, Stephanie worked the desk with her friend Jayme Weaver. She and Weaver had both been assigned to Devonshire since March 1985. Over the next sixteen months, they worked as patrol partners at least forty times. Stephanie was assigned to Devonshire until May 1988, when the LAPD promoted her to Police Officer III. Weaver worked at Devonshire until 1990.

In 2012, Weaver testified in court that at some point while they were assigned to Devonshire, Stephanie mentioned that her ex-boyfriend's wife had been killed. Weaver was unable to recall more precisely when the conversation took place, although based on when Sherri was murdered, and the dates Stephanie worked at Devonshire, it must have been between February 1986 and May 1988.

Stephanie's diary abruptly ended on August 10, 1986. For nearly two years, ever since she was a probationary officer at Hollywood, she had chronicled every shift she worked as a police officer. Nothing Stephanie wrote in her August 10 diary entry hinted that it would be her last, or that she intended to stop keeping a diary.

One possible explanation is that Stephanie simply decided to stop. It is also possible, however, and perhaps likely, given her history as a dedicated diarist, that she never abandoned the practice. Whether the LAPD is in possession of any additional diaries that Stephanie wrote later in her career is unknown.

Stephanie never addressed in her diary what motivated her to commit her experiences to paper as a young officer at Hollywood and Devonshire. LAPD officers were not required to keep a personal record of what they did on duty. Nor is it apparent on the face of her diary whether she wrote it purely for herself, to read sometime in the future, or anticipated that others might read it one day.

If Stephanie had not been so meticulous in documenting her activities early in her career, little would be known about her state of mind in the sixteen months leading up to Sherri's murder, and in the six months after. Much less also would be known about Stephanie's character and ethics, both as a person and as a police officer. If Stephanie did keep a diary through the late 1980s and into the 1990s, what she wrote would be of significant public interest, especially in light of the assignments she worked as she steadily climbed the ranks through her long LAPD career.

In March 1988, two months before her promotion to Police Officer III, Stephanie completed an eighty-hour LAPD training course, Drug Abuse Resistance Education, better known by its acronym, DARE. The DARE program sent uniformed officers into schools to warn children about the dangers of illegal drugs.

DARE was the brainchild and a signature initiative of LAPD Chief Daryl Gates. Gates introduced DARE in Los Angeles public schools in 1983, the same year that Stephanie joined the LAPD. DARE's message dovetailed with the "Just Say No" campaign led by First Lady Nancy Reagan, and Chief Gates's pet program quickly went national. Gates's association with DARE, and his outspokenness about the threat he believed casual drug use posed to society, made him a leading figure in the "War on Drugs" declared by public officials in the mid-1980s.

By the time Stephanie took the LAPD's DARE training in 1988, the program was well established. The LAPD maintained a unit of several DARE officers within its Bureau of Special Investigations. Schools that participated in the DARE program typically received a weekly visit from officers for a few months. Kid-friendly anthropomorphic mascots like McGruff the Crime Dog sometimes accompanied DARE officers on their rounds.

In May 1988, upon her promotion to Police Officer III, Stephanie was reassigned from Devonshire to the Bureau of Special Investigations. Public recognition of the DARE program was peaking. A few months later, in September 1988, President Ronald Reagan proclaimed the first national DARE Day.

In lieu of any diaries from later in Stephanie's career, her midcareer commendations from the LAPD shed some light on how she distinguished herself within the department and eventually earned promotion to detective.

Stephanie's first commendation at her new assignment came in November 1988, six months after she arrived from Devonshire. The commendation read in full, *"Thanks for hard work and selflessness at DARE Dinner."*

How much personal contact Stephanie had with Chief Gates while she worked at DARE is unknown. Stephanie's assignment with DARE lasted for more than four years, until August 1992, little more than a month after Gates resigned as LAPD chief.

Stephanie had at least some contact with Gates. In February 1989, just shy of three years after Sherri's murder, Gates and Stephanie were photographed together at a DARE event at a school in the San Fernando Valley.

Stephanie received two commendations in 1989. The first, in February, noted a letter of appreciation from an elementary school for her performance in the DARE program. The second, in May, commended her for *"outstanding conduct in welcoming the public at the 19th Annual Police-Celebrity Golf Tournament,"* more evidence of Stephanie's career-long pattern of dedication and service at LAPD social events.

A few weeks after Stephanie earned official plaudits for her presence at the department's celebrity golf tournament, she completed a forty-hour LAPD training course called DARE—Training of Trainers. Chief Gates's antidrug program, by then in its sixth year, continued to attract interest from police departments across the country, and even internationally, that wished to introduce it in their own communities. Other agencies routinely looked to the LAPD for DARE training and guidance on best practices. Stephanie soon assumed a role as a DARE instructor.

Relatively little is known

Back row, left to right: Stephanie Lazarus, LAPD Chief Daryl Gates, Yogi the Bear, Councilman Hal Bernson, February 1989

about Stephanie's social life in the late 1980s and early 1990s. In her interview with LAPD detectives in 2009, she recounted that she casually dated a few guys after John but did not describe any of the relationships as serious, or any of the men as a boyfriend.

Among the officers Stephanie worked with at DARE in 1988 and 1989 was Mike Hargreaves, her former roommate who moved out on Valentine's Day 1986, ten days before Sherri's murder. Hargreaves had remained friends with Stephanie after he moved out. In 2012, Hargreaves testified in court that he never knew Stephanie to have a boyfriend in the years between when her relationship with John ended and when they worked at DARE, a period of several years.

Hargreaves testified about one conversation, while at DARE, in which he and another officer chatted with Stephanie about why she was not dating anyone. Hargreaves described the conversation as lighthearted. Stephanie told him and the other officer that she was very picky and would not date anyone who fell short of her requirements. More specifically, Stephanie said that for her to date someone, he had to be tall, athletic, and handsome, "like John." Hargreaves took her to mean her ex-boyfriend John, whom he had never met. From then on, Hargreaves sometimes joked with Stephanie about what he called her "John standard" for prospective boyfriends.

John, in an interview with LAPD detectives in 2009, recounted that he had had no contact with Stephanie for two to three years after Sherri's murder, until sometime in 1988 or 1989. According to John, his belief that Stephanie was not involved in Sherri's murder was based on what the original detectives told him in 1986. John, however, never told the original detectives about the full extent of his relationship with Stephanie. John instead told them half-truths that minimized his romantic history with Stephanie, and by omission, glossed over his responsibility for the problems between Stephanie and Sherri. For instance, although John insisted he informed the LAPD after the murder that Stephanie had visited Sherri's office, he neglected to mention his role in precipitating that confrontation by having sex with Stephanie while he was engaged to Sherri.

John said in his 2009 LAPD interview that after Sherri was killed, he decided he had to leave Los Angeles for a while. He never returned to his old job. John lived with his parents in San Diego through the end of 1986.

In May 1986, three months after Sherri's murder, John found a new job in San Diego through a friend of a friend. His new employer was primarily a military contractor. John worked there for almost a year. The work wasn't what he would have liked, and he considered it a really bad job, John told detectives in 2009.

In early 1987, John moved out of his parents' house and into his own condo in Tierrasanta, a San Diego suburb. A few months later, John called his former boss at Rohr Industries, an aircraft parts manufacturer in Chula Vista, where he had once worked for a summer. John recounted in his 2009 LAPD interview, "I never thought I would ever be back at Rohr. But I called him up and said, 'Hey, I could use a different job.' He said, 'When can you come?' They loved me when I was a summer engineer there." John worked at Rohr and lived in his Tierrasanta condo from 1987 until 1991.

Later in John's 2009 LAPD interview, the detectives asked him to recount his interactions with Stephanie following Sherri's murder. "After February 24, 1986, how many contacts were there, either Stephanie Lazarus contacting you, or you contacting Stephanie Lazarus?" John was asked.

"This is tough to get at. But in that, I would say, eighty-eight, eighty-nine, ninety, I don't know the exact dates but it was well afterwards"—referring to Sherri's murder—"there were a couple of contacts. Stephanie wasn't pursuing me. I'll just be very clear about that. I think I may have gone up to L.A. for something, to do something, and on some—now I'm thinking, 'Why did I do this?'—on a whim I contacted her. She just seemed like the normal Stephanie. So you're talking about a situation. I feel a little stupid for having contact with her after all this. But she was my best friend. They said she was cleared. It was a robbery situation. I still felt, 'Why am I doing this?' I'll be frank. But, same old person . . . Nothing I ever saw in her suggested anything other than the normal Stephanie. That's the truth."

"Did you guys discuss the murder itself?"

"Well, she obviously knew about it. I don't remember me . . . I always assumed she knew about it, because we had mutual friends and so forth. The only thing that I ever recall is that I did say to her at one point, 'You should know that I told the police that you went and visited Sherri at work.' That didn't seem to faze her. I mean, I didn't challenge her. I always assumed that was true. It was just a statement of fact. It did not seem to . . . I don't even remember any real reaction. I do remember making that statement to her," John said. As with the original detectives in 1986, John did not volunteer to LAPD detectives in 2009 what Stephanie had told Sherri at the hospital. As far as John was aware at the time of his 2009 interview, only three people knew that he and Stephanie had sex in 1985 during his engagement to Sherri, and one of them was dead.

Absent that critical piece of information from John, the detectives in 2009 proceeded blindly with their next question. "So you contacted her. The best that we can recall, it was in the late eighties, early nineties. You placed a telephone call to her. You went to see her in person in the Los Angeles—"

John said, "Yeah, I think that was the first contact. But I don't remember. It was like four or five totally spaced out contacts over maybe two years. I think that was in L.A., the first one, because I found out sometime later—and I don't even remember how I found this out, I'll be frank with you—that she was going to be in Hawaii at the same time I was going to be visiting some friends over in Pearl City. So I went over. She was in Kauai. She was actually in a time share over there with some guy, who I don't think was her boyfriend per se. But they were over there, and I hung out with them for a couple days. We played some tennis, paddled up and down the river. So I'll just say, I did have . . . We had contacts. But there was nothing strange in that. Stephanie was not pursuing any kind of a relationship, long-term."

"Did she ever contact you in any way, or were you initiating the contacts with her?"

"I certainly was the first initiator. That's what I recall. But whether she did or not after that, she was not calling me. She was not trying to get dates with me. There was no pursuit. Did she call me once? She might have."

"So there were about four or five contacts, over about a two-to-three-year period there, that we're looking at, eighty-eight to ninety-one, somewhere in there? Eighty-nine, ninety? Somewhere in there?"

"Yeah, somewhere in there. So that's the range that I recall. That was it. That's it. That's what I know," John said in 2009.

LAPD detectives later determined, based on a visitor's book kept by John's friends in Hawaii, that he had visited them on July 24, 1989, after which he flew to Kauai to meet up with Stephanie.

In truth, John had more contact with Stephanie in the years after Sherri's murder, and a more intimate relationship, than he admitted to detectives in his initial 2009 LAPD interview.

In 2012, John testified in court that he reinitiated contact with Stephanie in 1989, about three years after the murder. John said on the witness stand, "I had learned that she and a friend of hers were going to be in Hawaii. I was planning to visit some friends in Hawaii. And so I think that was the first time." John testified that he had no recollection of how he found out about Stephanie's plans to travel to Hawaii.

Asked to recount his conversation with Stephanie in Hawaii about Sherri's murder, John testified, "I told her that I had told the police that she was upset over, you know, me—upset and had visited, you know—that she had visited—Stephanie visited Sherri at her workplace." Stephanie did not deny to him that she had gone to the hospital to see Sherri, he testified. John thought Stephanie seemed unfazed when he told her that he had given her name to the detectives on Sherri's case. John also testified that he and Stephanie did not have sex while they were in Hawaii.

After their meeting in Hawaii in 1989, John saw Stephanie again in California, "I think on maybe two or three other occasions," he testified in 2012. Asked over what period of time, John replied, "My sense is it was very spread out. Maybe even a year or—it's hard to say on that."

"So beginning in eighty-nine, for maybe a year after?"

"Year and a half, yeah, something like that."

"You saw her two or three times?"

"That's my recollection."

"And did you have sex with her during any of those times that you saw her?"

"I can remember twice," John testified.

John testified in 2012 that he could not recall whether Stephanie ever called him, or if he always called her, after they returned from Hawaii in 1989. Although Stephanie was an LAPD officer, the agency responsible for Sherri's unsolved murder, she never offered any help with respect to the investigation, John testified. John did not say whether it ever occurred to him to ask Stephanie for her help. John testified that he could not recall Stephanie ever asking him about Sherri's death, or of ever discussing the murder with her, other than their one conversation in Hawaii in 1989.

LAPD detectives also interviewed Stephanie in 2009, a few weeks after John's interview. Stephanie was asked whether she and John had problems after their relationship ended. "Was it friendly? Not friendly?" the detective asked her.

Stephanie replied, "No, I don't think it was not friendly. I mean, we were friendly. I know that we went to Hawaii at one point."

Later in the interview, she was asked, "After John's wife died and you said you may have been talking to him, did your relationship start up again?"

"I would say, no. Again, can you give me a year? I mean, this is, like, 2009."

The detectives informed Stephanie that John's wife died in 1986.

"Okay. Like I said, I'm—I'm faintly remembering that I went to Hawaii with my friend Greg. Greg and I got certified for scuba diving. And I'm thinking that John met us there, meaning Greg and I." Stephanie said she would have to look at her vacation photos to know what year she met John in Hawaii. "Other than that, I can't even say—he may have called me, you know, at my home. I may have called him," she said.

The detectives returned to the subject again later in the interview. "As far as you recall after John's wife died, did you start a relationship again with John, or dating casually, or anything like that?" Stephanie was asked.

"Like I said, he met Greg and I in Hawaii. Okay?"

"That was something you guys kind of planned to go, like, go as a group, or you ran into him, or—"

"No, I—I think that—obviously, I must've talked to him. And I said, hey, I'm going to Hawaii with my buddy, Greg. We're—we're scuba—we just got certified scuba diving. We're going to be in Hawaii. Hey, if you want to come join us, come join us. And I think that's what it was. I may have asked some other people as well. You know, what island did we go to? I think the Big Island and Kauai. He either met us on the Big Island or Kauai. I'm thinking Greg and I might've scuba dived a lot on the Big Island as well as Kauai. I—I don't remember which island again. I'd have to look at my pictures. I traveled a lot on my vacations. I mean, I was always gone for at least a month. And I would go places, and I would either run into people or, you know—you know, meet people," Stephanie told the detectives.

Stephanie did not volunteer to the detectives that she saw John subsequently in California, after they returned from Hawaii. Nor did she inform the detectives that she and John resumed their sexual relationship around 1989 or 1990, as he later testified.

Stephanie's LAPD career continued apace into the 1990s. Three of the four commendations Stephanie received in 1990 pertained to DARE. The Florida Department of Law Enforcement and the New York Division of Criminal Justice Services each sent letters of appreciation to Stephanie for DARE training. The municipality of Kingston, Jamaica, also sent her a letter of appreciation, *"for courtesies extended to them on visit to L.A. to learn about D.A.R.E."* The fourth commendation she received in 1990 was for *"professionalism and dedication to duty for participation in the LAPD Venice Beach recruitment drive."*

In September 1990, midway through Stephanie's four-year DARE assignment, Chief Gates traveled to Washington, D.C., to testify before Congress about the ongoing "War on Drugs." Gates famously testified to Congress that casual drug users "ought to be taken out and shot."

Days later, at an LAPD Medal of Valor ceremony in Los Angeles, Gates defended the remark and insisted he meant it. As he saw it, recreational drug use was tantamount to treason. "There are people dying all over this country, and we've still got people who just want to party. I think they're hypocrites. I think if we want to prosecute a war on drugs, we've got to get serious about our disdain for those who continue to sustain this war and aid the enemy. And that's what casual drug users do. I want casual drug users to recognize exactly how treasonous I think their acts are . . . They're aiding and abetting the enemy. They're supporting the enemy. They're giving money to the enemy," Gates said at the ceremony, the *Los Angeles Times* reported.

The next year, 1991, Stephanie received five commendations, three for her work with DARE. In July, the LAPD commended her *"attention to duty, commitment to D.A.R.E. and demonstration of esprit de corps for participation in D.A.R.E. To Read Luncheon."* The next month, she was commended for *"loyalty, attention to duty and unselfish work ethics which made the D.A.R.E. Latin America training seminars a success."* In November, the LAPD commended her *"participation in the annual National D.A.R.E. Celebration which through dedication and professionalism has made D.A.R.E. a premier drug prevention program."*

The LAPD also commended Stephanie in 1991 for her *"willingness to work overtime, and attention to duty in tedious task of manual counting of numerous cases from books."* The fifth commendation Stephanie received that year was a letter of appreciation from the William H. Parker Police Foundation, *"for participation in the 1st Annual Police Striped Bass Tournament."* Parker had been LAPD chief of police from 1950 to 1966, and a mentor to future chief of police Daryl Gates, who as a young officer was Chief Parker's driver.

Stephanie received eight commendations in 1992, four of them for DARE. These included letters of appreciation from a Los Angeles elementary school for her *"dedication and hard work on the D.A.R.E. program,"* from the City of San Diego for DARE training, and from the Bandon, Oregon, Police Department *"for D.A.R.E. training at the Oregon Police Academy."*

It was while teaching DARE in Oregon in April 1992 that Stephanie met her future husband, Scott Young. Scott was an Oregon police officer and twenty-seven years old at the time, four years younger than Stephanie, who was his DARE instructor. Although Scott did not bear a close resemblance to John, he evidently met Stephanie's standards for a potential boyfriend in that he was tall, athletic, and handsome.

Coincidentally, John met his second wife, Kim, the same year that Stephanie met Scott. In 1991, John moved back to the Los Angeles area from San Diego to take a job with Entech Instruments, a laboratory equipment manufacturer. John found a place to live in Thousand Oaks, close to Entech's offices in Simi Valley. Sometime the following year, John met Kim on a blind date arranged by his cousin Laura. John and Kim were both in their early thirties when they met. In 1993, a year after they began dating, John and Kim married, and soon after started a family.

The other commendations Stephanie received in 1992 suggest that she performed at least some casework that year, in addition to teaching DARE. In January, the LAPD commended her *"dedication to duty, attention to detail and willingness to assist in the reduction of backlog cases."* No details were noted in her personnel report about the nature of the backlogged cases or how she specifically assisted. Similarly, in July, the month before Stephanie's assignment to DARE ended, she received a letter of appreciation from the Los Angeles County District Attorney's Office for *"enthusiastic attitude and hard work that caused a case to reach a successful conclusion."*

In August 1992, a few months after Stephanie met Scott, the LAPD reassigned her to the Personnel Division, which served as the department's human resources arm. The summer of 1992 was a time of crisis and upheaval for the LAPD, following the L.A. riots in April and the forced resignation of Chief Gates in June of that year.

Stephanie's new assignment was as a background investigator of prospective LAPD officers. All civilian recruits had to submit to and pass a comprehensive background check, which included fingerprints, a review of employment and financial records, a face-to-face interview, and interviews with their family and friends.

From the get-go at her new assignment, Stephanie demonstrated the same enthusiastic team spirit that distinguished her at DARE, and before that, at Devonshire. In September 1992, just a month after her transfer, the LAPD commended her for *"hard work and unselfish dedication in the Personnel Division fundraiser."*

Stephanie worked for more than a year as an LAPD background investigator. How many recruits she investigated, and what percentage she rejected as unfit for police work, is unknown.

One LAPD recruit who passed muster with Stephanie nevertheless remembered the experience as unexpectedly harrowing. The recruit, who later became a detective, was a woman who had attended UCLA with Stephanie and considered her a friend during college. When Stephanie's friend applied to the LAPD, and learned that Stephanie had been assigned as her background investigator, she thought it was a lucky break.

Her friend's expectation that Stephanie would go easy on her was promptly dispelled at the interview. The friend was shocked at how tough Stephanie was on her during questioning. She felt so intimidated and caught off guard that she nearly confessed to crimes she had never committed.

We know that Stephanie rejected at least one aspiring LAPD officer during her stint as a background investigator. In July 1993, the LAPD officially commended Stephanie for her *"hard work, outstanding investigative skills and dedication to duty that allowed an unqualified candidate to be disqualified for hire."*

Among Stephanie's supervisors in the Background Section was a Sgt. Patrick Findley. Findley was interviewed by LAPD detectives in 2009. The interview was not tape-recorded but one detective took handwritten notes. According to these notes, Findley said that he brought Stephanie into the unit, and described her as a "bulldog" who always completed her assigned tasks.

At least one officer whom Stephanie worked with in the Background Section, Lydia Leos, overheard her talk at that time about once being interviewed by detectives on a homicide case. According to Leos, Stephanie said the case involved an ex-boyfriend's girlfriend who went missing and was possibly shot. Findley, however, told detectives in 2009 that he never heard any comments or statements indicating that Stephanie was interviewed or the subject of any investigation, during the time he supervised her work as an LAPD background investigator.

Findley did recall meeting at a Christmas party Stephanie's boyfriend at the time, Scott. Findley knew that Scott was testing to come on the job at the LAPD.

In 1993, a year after Stephanie and Scott met, he left Oregon and moved in with her at her condo in Granada Hills. That December, Scott became an LAPD officer.

In January 1994, Stephanie's condo was destroyed in the Northridge earthquake, the epicenter of which was only five miles away. Several of Stephanie and Scott's fellow LAPD officers volunteered to help move their intact belongings to a new place in Simi Valley, where Stephanie had once lived as an adolescent.

Two months later, in March 1994, little more than eight years after Sherri's murder, the LAPD promoted Stephanie from Police Officer III to Detective I.

Stephanie's first assignment as a detective was with the LAPD's Investigative Analysis Section. Although IAS was part of the Detective Bureau, IAS detectives were unlike most working detectives in that their primary responsibility was not investigating criminal cases. The mission of IAS was to coordinate training for all LAPD detectives, establish standard investigative procedures, and promote best practices. IAS maintained the department's manuals for detective operations, including its Homicide Manual and various guides to investigative resources available to LAPD detectives.

In addition to the veritable library of training material she had easy access to at IAS, Stephanie in 1994 also completed the LAPD's eighty-hour basic detective course, and a separate eight-hour course called Interrogation Secrets.

In March 1995, following a year at IAS, Stephanie was reassigned by the LAPD to Van Nuys, where Sherri's case remained open and unsolved.

During the spring of 1995, when Stephanie began her assignment at Van Nuys, America's collective attention was trained on a courtroom in downtown Los Angeles, where the murder trial of O. J. Simpson was under way. Simpson stood accused of killing his ex-wife, Nicole Brown, and a second victim, Ronald Goldman, in June 1994. From the start of Simpson's trial in January 1995 through the not guilty verdict in October, all the court proceedings were televised live across the country. On a nightly basis, video from the courtroom was rebroadcast as fodder for a Greek chorus of legal experts who weighed in on that day's witnesses, evidence, and attorney theatrics. Thanks to the blanket media coverage, interest in the Simpson trial was intense nationwide, but especially in Los Angeles, where it was a local story, and within the LAPD, which had investigated the murders.

The most damning evidence against Simpson, as proclaimed by both the prosecution and the media, was the presence of his blood at the crime scene. Blood from both victims was also found on a glove and socks recovered at Simpson's home, as well as inside his Ford Bronco. To prove whom the blood came from, the prosecutors used DNA analysis, which prior to the Simpson trial was relatively unfamiliar to the public. Prosecutors in Los Angeles had introduced DNA evidence in several criminal cases since 1989, but never in a trial as high profile as Simpson's. The importance of the DNA evidence in Simpson's case was heightened by the fact that there were no eyewitnesses, and no murder weapon was recovered by the LAPD.

Because the DNA evidence against Simpson appeared so incriminating, his defense team was expected to fiercely challenge the admissibility of the lab results. Under California law, a court could admit only evidence it deemed reliable and "generally accepted" by scientists. In other criminal cases and courtrooms around the country, defense lawyers had convinced some judges that DNA analysis was too new, and the underlying science too unsettled, for DNA results to be admitted as evidence. Simpson's lawyers filed a pretrial motion to exclude the DNA results, but on the eve of trial, they withdrew it. The dramatic change of strategy effectively conceded that DNA analysis was a scientifically valid method of forensic identification.

During Simpson's trial, the prosecutors laid out the DNA evidence against him in painstaking detail. Over several days of highly technical testimony, half a dozen LAPD criminalists and other expert witnesses explained how DNA analysis worked, and how minuscule the odds were that the blood recovered at the murder scene could have come from anyone but Simpson—one in 170 million, according to the prosecution's case. Simpson's defense team responded not by attacking the science of DNA analysis, but by highlighting apparent errors in how the LAPD had collected and handled the blood evidence before it was DNA tested. Astonishingly, Simpson's team successfully recast the DNA results as evidence not of Simpson's guilt, but of a racially motivated plot by the LAPD to frame him for murder.

According to the transcript of Simpson's trial, which ran more than fifty thousand pages, the term "DNA" was spoken more than ten thousand times in court, and countless more on television. Notwithstanding Simpson's acquittal, millions of Americans learned of the existence of DNA analysis, and its science-fiction-like potential to revolutionize how the police investigated murders. The verdict was also an enormous embarrassment for the LAPD. On the biggest stage imaginable, Simpson's defense team exposed the LAPD's evidence handling and crime lab practices as sloppy and outdated. The negative attention spurred the LAPD to improve policies and procedures at its crime lab, in expectation of many more DNA cases in the future.

Although it is unknown how closely Stephanie followed the Simpson trial, there is no doubt that by 1995, when she began her assignment at Van Nuys, she had heard of DNA. Given her training and status as an LAPD detective, Stephanie surely also knew that the department had started to utilize DNA analysis to solve murder cases.

If Stephanie felt at all uneasy about the advent of DNA analysis, and its rising prominence around the time she arrived in Van Nuys, she did not show it. She instead continued to burnish her image within the department as enthusiastic, helpful, and above all, dedicated to the LAPD.

Stephanie received her first official commendation at Van Nuys in May 1995, two months into her assignment there. The commendation was for *"working the 24th Annual LAPD Celebrity Golf Tournament— outstanding job, provided security and worked as a team."* Among the celebrities who participated that year were the actor Jack Nicholson and the boxer Sugar Ray Leonard.

The same month that Stephanie was commended for working the LAPD's celebrity golf tournament, she appeared, in uniform, as a contestant on the TV game show *Family Feud*. The show typically featured two families that competed to match responses to survey questions. The episode Stephanie was in, that season's finale, pitted four LAPD officers against four LAFD firefighters.

Stephanie on the season finale of Family Feud, *May 1995*

Stephanie's episode of *Family Feud* turned out to be the last ever hosted by Richard Dawson, the gregarious longtime star of the show. Ratings for the show were down, in part due to competition for viewers with the ongoing O.J. trial. Dawson told the studio audience, which included Stephanie's boyfriend, Scott, and her mother, "I just wanted to say that if this has to be the last show that I tape, I couldn't be in classier company."

Stephanie's LAPD team prevailed by more than $10,000. At the end of the show, Dawson invited all the contestants and their families up on stage. Stephanie stood front and center, right behind Dawson. As Dawson bade farewell, she proudly beamed and held a placard emblazoned with how much money the LAPD had won. Stephanie's mother and Scott stood behind her and clapped.

The only other commendation that Stephanie received at Van Nuys, in December 1995, was a *"letter of appreciation from Visiting Nurse Association for assistance provided when a doctor was threatened."*

What types of crimes Stephanie investigated as a detective at Van Nuys is for the most part unknown. Stephanie worked at least one case with the Van Nuys homicide unit, the murder of a fifty-seven-year-old man, Nubar Chilian, who was stabbed to death in January 1996. LAPD time books indicate Stephanie was assigned to Van Nuys homicide for almost two months, from January 21 to March 16, a period that included the tenth anniversary of Sherri Rasmussen's murder.

Stephanie's assignment to the Van Nuys homicide unit gave her unfettered access to the Rasmussen murder book, including all of the LAPD's

LAPD Van Nuys Homicide Unit time book, January 21 to February 17, 1996

DEPLOYMENT PERIOD 2/96 WATCH _____
PERIOD DATES: FROM 2/18/96 TO 3/16/96
AUDITED BY: _____

TIME BOOK CODES:
AW-ABSENT WITHOUT PAY
BL-BEREAVEMENT LEAVE
FI-FAMILY ILLNESS
HW-HOURS WORKED
IO-INJURED ON DUTY TIME
JO-JURY DUTY(PAY-CIV. ONLY)

LP-LEAVE WITH PAY
LW-LEAVE WITHOUT PAY
ML-MILITARY LEAVE WITHOUT PAY
MP-MILITARY LEAVE WITH PAY
PM-PREVENTIVE MEDICINE
RF-RELIEVED FROM DUTY
*-PENALTY DAY

ST-SICKTIME
SP-SUSPENSION
TO-OVERTIME OFFICHE AND ONE-HALF TIME)
TS-OVERTIME OFFSTRAIGHT T TI
VC-VACATION
WC-WORKERS' COMPENSATION

NAMES	ASSIGN-MENT	DATE			Bal. Fwd. accrued overtime	NOTES
FISK, S.	D-3	9W1				
DEJARNETTE, D.	D-2	9W2				
MOSELEY, P.	D-2	9W3				
LOPEZ, A.	D-1	9W4				
LAZARUS, S.	D-1	9W5				
KRAUSS, S.	P-3	9W6				
ENRIQUEZ, D.	P-3	9W7				

LAPD Van Nuys Homicide Unit time book, February 18 to March 16, 1996

investigative reports produced to that point in the case. Whether Stephanie availed herself of the opportunity to pull the murder book, either to read up on the investigation, to try to tamper with the case file, or both, is unknown. Did Stephanie work with any detectives who were involved in or responsible for the investigation of Sherri's unsolved murder? Did she ever discuss the case with them, or with anyone else in the homicide unit? These questions may never be answered satisfactorily. Stephanie's assignment to Van Nuys lasted a year.

In March 1996, the LAPD promoted Stephanie to Detective II and reassigned her from Van Nuys homicide to Internal Affairs.

Six months later, in September, Scott and Stephanie married. Stephanie was thirty-six at the time, and Scott thirty-one.

Stephanie worked for a year and a half as an Internal Affairs detective, investigating allegations of wrongdoing by other LAPD officers. Her commanding officers gave her a glowing performance evaluation for the rating period from November 1996 to August 1997, the last ten months of her Internal Affairs assignment.

The supervisor who reviewed Stephanie's performance in 1997 was a Lieutenant II at Internal Affairs, Joseph Ramm. The "narrative evaluation" portion of the rating report had a valedictory tone, since she had already secured her next assignment after Internal Affairs. Lt. Ramm wrote:

Detective Stephanie Lazarus began this rating period at the Special Operations Section of Internal Affairs Group. A seasoned detective with a well rounded background, she was a valuable member of the SOS team.

SOS is a prestigious assignment within IAG because SOS handles the most sensitive, confidential and complex investigations. These investigations require a great deal of job knowledge, dedication and stamina. She willingly accepted this responsibility and energetically conducted thorough investigations with the intent of determining the "Truth of the Matter" . . .

Due to Detective Lazarus' curious nature and boundless energy her cases usually mushroomed into much more involved investigations than were originally perceived. Her willingness to put in countless hours gave the reviewer a much better picture than would have otherwise been expected. She understood what the issues were in cases and left no stone unturned. Her knowledge of computers and computer systems was exceptional. In any of her investigations that dealt with computer issues she showed a heightened level of intensity . . .

At SOS there is a breakfast meeting once a week where cases and new information are discussed. Detective Lazarus is always a contributor during the meetings and makes insightful additions to the discussions . . . The working environment at SOS was better because of Detective Lazarus. She has an excellent sense of humor and participates in the office banter. Also, she has taken her turn in being involved in setting up morale building events for the office . . . Detective Lazarus was one of the reasons SOS was a good place to work.

All who work IAG know that they are in limited term positions and must eventually find a position. Detective Lazarus protected herself for that eventuality by accepting a position at Van Nuys detectives. IAG's loss has been Van Nuys' gain. Detective Lazarus has demonstrated that she is capable of and desirous of increased responsibility.

Steph, thank you for all your hard work!!

The commanding officer of the Internal Affairs Group, Captain III George Ibarra, approved Stephanie's rating report and jotted a personal note to her: *"Stef: Thanks for your hard work while at IAG. Good luck in your new assignment. George."*

Stephanie's second stint at Van Nuys began in August 1997 and lasted more than a year. In January 1998, she completed the LAPD's eighty-hour detective supervisor course, although she was never promoted to Detective III.

Some of Stephanie's colleagues during her second assignment to Van Nuys recall that she often volunteered to work morning watch. Most officers dreaded the graveyard shift. Stephanie's eagerness to work morning watch may well have been connected to how deserted the station became late at night, when virtually all the division brass and other detectives were at home asleep. As a Detective II, Stephanie outranked most officers on morning watch, which empowered her to work without much direct supervision. She already knew her way around the station, including where the murder books for unsolved cases were stored, from her assignment to the Van Nuys homicide unit a few years earlier.

In January 1999, after almost a year and a half at Van Nuys detectives, Stephanie was reassigned to Devonshire, the same division she had worked as a patrol officer in the 1980s, at the time of Sherri's murder.

Only Stephanie knows for certain what motivated her career trajectory, and how she secured the series of assignments she worked after she left Devonshire in 1988. Nor is it clear what support she may have had within the LAPD, for instance from any mentor or mentors among the brass, as she ascended the ranks from newly promoted Police Officer III to veteran Detective II.

Stephanie's LAPD career path appears in hindsight extraordinarily brazen. Nearly every one of Stephanie's midcareer assignments either shadowed Sherri's unsolved case or served to insulate her politically from potential scrutiny and investigation for murder.

The LAPD at that time consisted of eighteen geographic divisions, of which Van Nuys was just one. The odds are slim that Stephanie was assigned randomly to Van Nuys in 1995 for her first stint there as a detective. Her second assignment to Van Nuys was neither a coincidence nor the luck of the draw. Stephanie's final rating report from Internal Affairs strongly suggests that she orchestrated her return to Van Nuys in 1997.

Stephanie's other assignments, starting with DARE, afforded her proximity to the department's top brass, a key catalyst in countless police careers. Within an organization as vast and hierarchical as the LAPD, familiarity with the brass conferred status and legitimacy. The fact that Chief Gates was DARE's most prominent booster was well known even outside the LAPD, and presumably not lost on Stephanie. The wholesome reputation of the DARE program may also have helped her project an image as a trustworthy officer whose values and priorities were aligned with the department's. Stephanie's readiness to volunteer for LAPD morale building and fundraising events projected the same qualities. So did her consistent participation in law enforcement athletic competitions like the California Police Olympics. No one was more supportive of the LAPD's athletic programs than Chief Gates.

Later in Stephanie's career, as an LAPD background investigator and an Internal Affairs detective, she deftly and sanctimoniously insinuated herself into the department's mechanisms for weeding out miscreant officers. Via these assignments, she not only learned the ins and outs of how the LAPD conducted investigations of officers suspected of serious crimes, she also bolstered her own reputation as an officer who was devoted to protecting the integrity of the department from those who might tarnish the badge. Many officers could not stomach the discomfiting task of investigating fellow cops. Stephanie evidently had no such compunctions.

However prestigious Stephanie's midcareer assignments were perceived to be within the LAPD, only her two stints in Van Nuys embodied the sort of traditional, in-the-trenches police work performed daily by most detectives. In hindsight, Stephanie's assignments were either self-serving, as at Van Nuys, or benefited the department more directly than the public she was sworn to protect and serve. Stephanie's work with DARE, as a background investigator, and at Internal Affairs was not the sort of noble police work that measurably lowered the city's crime rate, or that delivered justice to victims of violent crime. Over the course of her entire twenty-three-year LAPD career, Stephanie received zero commendations for any acts of heroism or valor, such as putting herself at risk to rescue a civilian or to take a violent criminal off the streets.

Only Stephanie knows how calculated her career path was, or whether she improvised her way from assignment to assignment. She never articulated in her diaries, at least through August 1986, what kind of career she expected to have, nor what she hoped to accomplish as a police officer. Stephanie's diaries consistently betrayed no worries about her future, and little concern for her past, beyond the events of that particular day's patrol watch.

In Stephanie's last known diary entry, on August 10, 1986, she wrote:

XL41
DEV
0730—1615
8-10-86

Today I really didn't do much. It was very hot outside. My first call was a screaming woman at 17171 Roscoe. A neighbor called. We found the woman who had been in a boyfriend's apt. She was hysterical. She kept screaming at the top of her lungs. We took her outside after calling her parents to pick her up. The woman was 25 years old and definitely a looney tune. She was under the influence of something, but Becker didn't want to mess with her.

Prior to the call I delivered Baseball Cards to Brian and Cary Ross's son. Everyone was sleeping so I just left them.

I went by my mailbox and house.

I made Golf reservations at Knollwood.

I visited with the Paramedics on Balboa.

I got a 415 man call with Burr. The man was retarded and had been drinking. His mother drove by so we took him home.

We went to Granada Hills and washed our hands. The man was really disgusting. Then I took a call, Runaway Juvenile. I went to 8400 Amigo #8. The man said he didn't call. So I was waiting for a call back and he came out and said he called. He didn't want the girl to know he had called.

I went inside the house.

The girl had run away from her mom in West Valley. I took her to the Station, got ahold of her mom at work. The mom was going to pick her up. I left her at the Station. What was interesting was that her mom wanted to handcuff her and take her to a hospital in Pasadena.

I really did nothing today. I filled in the log w/ extra patrols.

The Van Nuys detectives resumed their investigation of Sherri's murder on August 19, nearly eight weeks after their last documented activity on the case. An unidentified detective handwrote in the chrono, regarding a murder suspect in a different case, *"8/19/86 | Ran Robert P. Meyer LA# 16891764M (187 PC West Valley). Killed two ladies."*

According to Nels and Loretta, in the months after Sherri's murder, they called the Van Nuys detectives regularly to inquire about the status of the investigation. In spite of what the detectives had told him, Nels remained convinced that Sherri was not killed in an attempted burglary.

He still wanted to know what the detectives had done to clear John's ex-girlfriend as a suspect.

According to Nels, whenever he called, he started off the conversation by asking if they had done or found anything on the female police officer. The detectives never gave him an answer, but just blew the question off, as though he hadn't said anything, Nels recalls. Though the detectives assured him they were still working Sherri's case and looking at this or that lead, everything they told him pertained to burglary suspects. Nels felt certain the detectives weren't really investigating. Nels thought competent investigators don't keep their eyes on only one goal and close them to everything else.

Most days, Nels was too busy seeing patients at his dental practice to make or receive any phone calls. Loretta managed Nels's practice full time and was also busy, but it was easier for to her to place calls during business hours.

According to Loretta, she called the Van Nuys detectives regularly, for years, to ask about any progress in the investigation. Loretta would tell whoever answered the phone that she was Sherri's mother and ask to speak with the detective handling the case. Sometimes Mayer or another detective took the call. Other times, she was asked to hold. Loretta recalls it was not unusual for her to be left on hold for as long as twenty or thirty minutes. Loretta wondered at times whether the detectives made her wait because they wanted her to hang up and stop calling them for updates on Sherri's case.

Sherri's sister Teresa called the detectives several times following the murder as well. Teresa recalls her phone conversations with the detectives were always very short and concerned what they were doing to find the burglars who killed Sherri. The detectives never asked Teresa about her relationship with Sherri, or about Sherri's relationship with John. They just told her, "Yes, we're working on it. I'll let you know."

The LAPD's chrono for Sherri's case contains no record of regular phone calls from the Rasmussens.

Mayer, in an interview in 2014, recalled that it was Nels who called him for updates on Sherri's case, and that Loretta never called. Mayer said of Nels's calls, "In those times, and in those instances, you're just letting the parents vent. 'What have you done?' Then you explain, 'Well, we arrested these guys and these guys. We've eliminated them.'" Mayer said he could tell that Nels was frustrated but never felt that Nels really got angry at him. Mayer said, "This is a distraught parent. I totally feel for them. I have affection for them. I would like nothing more than to solve this for them."

Mayer also said he did not necessarily speak with Nels every time he called. Mayer said, "You have to remember, in that time frame and during that time period, I wasn't always the one that would take his telephone call. There could be anyone in the office. I'm not sitting there twenty-four-seven, eight to four, sitting there waiting for his telephone call. I'm working on a myriad of other cases. Some other guy in the unit could pick up the call. 'Hello, Mr. Rasmussen. Yeah, no, I do know that no one has been arrested, or blah blah blah.' Many times he would call. He would speak to someone else other than me. He would speak to Pida"—Mayer's supervisor, the Van Nuys homicide coordinator.

According to Mayer, the Van Nuys unit's custom at that time was not to document every phone call they received on a case, particularly if it was just a request for an update. Mayer said, "You wouldn't log every single one of them, because sometimes it would be, 'What's new? Is there anything new?' You go, 'You know, Nels, no, there really isn't, I'm sorry. We've done this and that.' That you wouldn't necessarily write in your chronological log, because it's just an insignificant telephone communication about something, to find out what's going on. It's like, 'Hey, is my tire fixed on my car?' You don't write that down, every second. If there was some specific, absolute significant thing that was involved, you'd certainly record that."

The Van Nuys detectives logged four chrono entries on Monday, September 8, their first documented activity on Sherri's case since August 19, almost three weeks earlier. Unlike all prior chrono entries to that point in the case, the unidentified detective who handwrote the entries on September 8 noted the month and day, but not the year, 1986. Over two pages, the chrono stated:

9/8	1100	Verified with Leo—SID—This case will be resubmitted to Alps—this week (9-8—9-12)
9-8	1100	Rec'd phone # of Rene Elliott psych. 662-9052. She may assist?
9-8	0900	Called and made apt for 9-10-86 6pm with psychic.
		662-9052—203 Dracena #309 Hollywood.
9-8	0900	Spoke with Relatives. Verified they will be here 9-19-86
		Friday 9 AM meeting

ALPS was the Automated Latent Print System, the statewide fingerprint database.

Rene Elliott, as the chrono indicated, was a psychic who lived in Holly-wood. Mayer recounted in his 2014 interview what led him, six months into the LAPD's investigation of Sherri's murder, to seek the assistance of a psychic. One of the reasons Mayer cited was John's inconclusive polygraph.

Mayer explained, "We were looking for any clues that we possibly could. We probably, throughout the period of those times, we probably arrested twenty-five burglars. Every time somebody was arrested for burglary, resi-dential burglary, or residential burglary with a gun involved, we got the guy's name. We ran his fingerprints against our crime scene information. Nothing. We'd shoot photographs. We'd do anything. Nothing. We had nothing. We had the next-door woman that heard noises at eight o'clock in the morning. Other than that, we had zero. Zero. We'd do anything. I utilized the services of a psychic to come out with me, go through the crime scene, go through whatever. I did things that were so out there, trying to do anything to get a little bit of a lead. Again, one of the reasons I did that specifically was because of the inconclusive activity of John on the poly-graph, so I said, 'Okay, lady psychic, blah blah blah.' I was scraping the wall for any possible activity."

According to the chrono, the consultation with Elliott took place on Wednesday evening, September 10. No other investigative activity was doc-umented in Sherri's case that day, or the day before. Like the preceding chrono entries on September 8, only the month and day, but not the year, was recorded. The entry, handwritten by an unidentified detective, stated in full, "9-10 | 1800 | Met with psych. rec'd info." The actual information received from the psychic was not documented in the chrono.

One need not be psychic to foresee the risk in failing to note what year a specific entry was made, in a chronological log that spanned multiple years and pages. If the year were omitted only in sporadic chrono entries, and indicated clearly in other entries on the same page, the lapse would be inconsequential. But neglecting to record the year in successive chrono entries, over several pages, could sow confusion later about how the inves-tigation unfolded.

In Sherri's case, the Van Nuys detectives handwrote a total of twenty-three chrono entries between September 1986 and the end of 1987. This stretch of the investigation was chronicled in five chrono pages, ostensibly pages 15 to 19, although the pages were not numbered to indicate their cor-rect order. In twenty-one of the twenty-three entries, only the month and day, but not the year, was recorded. The two entries in which the year was properly noted were on the same page. The other four pages of entries could be interpreted, at a glance, as dating from either 1986 or 1987.

Sometime between 1987 and 2008, the order of these five chrono pages was shuffled in the murder book for Sherri's case. Page 16, which recounted the investigation from October 1986 ("10/23") through May 1987 ("5/18/87"), ended up as page 19. The actual pages 17, 18, and 19 became pages 16, 17, and 18. As a result, all the entries on those three pages, dated from "11-16" to "11/23," incorrectly appeared to be from November 1986, when in fact they were made a full year later.

One of these entries, dated "11-19," contained the only mention of Stephanie Lazarus in the chrono prior to 2009. Confusion about what year Stephanie's name entered the murder book, 1986 or 1987, persisted within the LAPD through at least 2009. Although a close reading of other entries on the same page indicated that the entry about Stephanie was made in November 1987, LAPD detectives in 2009 described it in the chrono, mistakenly, as *the 11/19/86 entry in the chronological record."*

Following the consultation with the psychic on September 10, 1986, the next activity recorded in the chrono was nine days later, when the detectives met with Nels and Loretta at the Van Nuys station. The purpose of the meeting was to discuss a reward for information that might lead to an arrest in Sherri's case.

According to the Rasmussens, they first considered offering a reward in early March. The week after Sherri's burial, Nels called an attorney, a friend of his daughter Connie. Nels and the attorney discussed whether to offer a reward, but he did not pursue the idea at the time.

By September, more than six months had passed since Sherri's murder. No arrests had been made by the LAPD, and none seemed imminent to the Rasmussens. To the contrary, it appeared to Nels that as time went on, the detectives' activity on the case was dying out. Nels and Loretta revisited the reward idea as a way to try to get something going in the investigation, they recall. According to the Rasmussens, they scheduled a meeting with the detectives in Van Nuys for the specific purpose of discussing the reward offer with them in person. Nels and Loretta recall that Mayer and Hooks were at the meeting. According to Nels, when they raised the idea of a reward for information, Mayer was all for it.

According to the Rasmussens, they asked the detectives during the same meeting what had been done to eliminate John's ex-girlfriend as a suspect. More specifically, the Rasmussens recall they told the detectives about the phone call Loretta had received from Bonnie Gorder, the mother of John's good friend Matt. In the call, Bonnie told Loretta that John's ex-girlfriend was capable of murder. According to the Rasmussens, Mayer brushed that information off as though there was still nothing there to investigate. They also recall Mayer mentioning that he was considering consulting with a psychic on Sherri's case, although he did not say then whether he had or hadn't already.

Mayer in his 2014 interview had a different recollection than the Rasmussens about whose idea it was to offer a reward in Sherri's case. According to Mayer, he suggested the reward idea to the Rasmussens, not the other way around.

The chrono did not indicate whose idea the reward offer was. Had the meeting with the Rasmussens been tape-recorded, which the detectives were equipped to do, there would be no ambiguity about what questions the Rasmussens asked the detectives during the meeting and what other information was exchanged. There is no indication in the chrono, such as a tape number, that the meeting was recorded.

The names of the detectives who attended the meeting were not documented in the chrono either. The only official record of what was discussed was a chrono entry, handwritten by an unidentified detective, which stated in full, *"9-19 | 0900 | Met with Parents discussed case. Got steps set up for reward fund thru Judge Bernie Kamins."* Kamins was a Los Angeles Superior Court judge.

Following the meeting with the Rasmussens on September 19, the Van Nuys detectives documented no investigative activity in Sherri's case until October 21, two days before they had scheduled a press conference to announce the reward offer.

Stephanie, meanwhile, continued to report for duty as usual at Devonshire. On September 26, a week after the Rasmussens met with the Van Nuys detectives, the LAPD commended her *"search techniques and attention to duty in correlating two events which resulted in the arrest of two GTA suspects,"* short for Grand Theft Auto.

The amount of the reward offered in Sherri's case was $10,000, of which the Rasmussens put up $8,000, they recall, while John's parents and Matt Gorder's parents also each contributed $1,000. Nels and Loretta did not ask the Ruettens and Gorders for any money for the reward, but both families offered, the Rasmussens recall. Nels and

Loretta assumed the Ruettens and Gorders heard about the reward idea through John.

Bonnie sent the Rasmussens a note about her family's contribution. Her note read:

> Dear Nels & Loretta,
> Hope this helps to prevent some other lovely person from Sherri's fate and grief from all families and friends.
>   Sherri had so much to offer the world and we don't want her killer to continue to take the lives of innocent people. How dare they!
>   Best wishes to you in living with the thoughts that you must have. I keep Sherri's memorial folder on my coffee table and think of her, you two, John, and the Ruettens often.
>
> > God Bless You,
> > Bonnie Gorder

Bonnie made no reference to the call that she had placed to Loretta, some months earlier, about John's ex-girlfriend.

Matt Gorder, Bonnie's son, was interviewed by LAPD detectives in May 2009. According to the LAPD's written summary of his interview, Matt recounted his impressions of John and Stephanie's relationship while at UCLA and after they graduated. Matt described John and Stephanie as "very close" but said he viewed their relationship as platonic. Matt believed that Stephanie was romantically interested in John, but he was not physically attracted to her. Matt's interview summary indicates he also told detectives that "*Lazarus became close with Ruetten's family . . . Lazarus was well liked by the Ruetten family and made several visits with Ruetten to San Diego to visit.*"

Matt said that after Sherri's murder, the details he heard "*were that Rasmussen had been home instead of work, her place had been burglarized, Rasmussen had been killed and her car had been taken.*" Matt apparently learned these details independent of John. In a subsequent LAPD interview, in June 2009, Matt recounted that he and John never discussed Sherri's murder or the LAPD's investigation of it, and that John never mentioned Stephanie to him, after Sherri was killed.

According to Matt's May 2009 LAPD interview summary, however, his mother was not the only person in John's circle of friends who suspected that Stephanie may have had something to do with Sherri's murder. Matt's interview summary recounted:

Among close friends in the nursing community, there had been a problem in the months before the murder that Rasmussen and Lazarus had a verbal confrontation at Rasmussen's place of employment. Gorder was under the impression that the police investigation may have taken a look at an existing problem between Rasmussen and Lazarus.

There were several people close to Ruetten and Rasmussen that believed Lazarus may have been involved in the Rasmussen murder. It was believed that such information was known to the investigation. The Rasmussen family also hired a Private Investigator to examine the Lazarus angle of the investigation.

Information had developed among those close to Rasmussen and Ruetten that Lazarus was stalking Rasmussen. Lazarus had shown up dressed inappropriately at Rasmussen's work and Gorder considered such an act unprofessional for an LAPD Officer.

[Gorder] and his wife were not contacted as part of the initial investigation. It was unclear to Gorder if Lazarus was eliminated or identified as a suspect.

How Anita learned of the confrontation between Sherri and Stephanie at Glendale Adventist is unknown. According to the Rasmussens, they never hired a private investigator to "examine the Lazarus angle" after Sherri was killed, in part because at the time, unlike the Ruettens and Gorders, they did not know John's ex-girlfriend's name.

In October, Nels and Loretta once again traveled from Tucson to Los Angeles, in order to be present for the LAPD's press conference about the reward offer in Sherri's case. Nels recalls that while they were in town, he contacted Glendale Adventist to seek their help in advancing the investigation. Nels thought there might be something in Sherri's employee records about the problems that she had experienced at work, and mentioned to her parents, in the year before her murder. Nels and Loretta knew that she had received a series of obscene phone calls, which Sherri attributed to a disgruntled nurse and her doctor boyfriend. Sherri had also told her parents about the confrontation in her office with John's ex-girlfriend.

According to Nels, the hospital would not allow him to see any part of Sherri's personnel records and would not share with him any reports it had on the incidents. He sensed that Glendale Adventist's main priority was to protect its reputation. Nels believed the hospital was paranoid that any information they released could somehow come back to bite it and make Glendale Adventist look bad.

Nels and Loretta recall they met with Mayer and Hooks at the Van Nuys station in advance of the press conference. Mayer showed them composite sketches of the two Mexican burglary suspects during the meeting. It was apparent to Nels that Mayer intended to stress the burglary theory at the press conference. Mayer was in charge of the press conference because he was the lead investigator on Sherri's case. According to the Rasmussens, Mayer also told them that he didn't want Nels to talk at the press conference. Mayer said that he would do the talking.

Nels felt the suspects should be described more broadly than as burglars. Nels recalls he told Mayer, "We shouldn't stick to that because we don't know. We should say we want more information, and we're willing to accept any information."

Nels recalls that Hooks agreed with him and said to Mayer, "We shouldn't tell them what kind of information we want. We should let them say what they think, or what they've seen, or what they've heard."

According to the Rasmussens, Mayer dismissed Hooks's suggestion and made it clear that he did not want to hear anything about anybody but the two Mexican burglary suspects. Nels recalls Mayer said, "Just keep your thoughts to yourself and things will be okay."

Nels's impression of Hooks was that he had a heart and was an honest man. Nels believed that Hooks knew the truth, and wanted to do something, but lacked the nerve to go against Mayer. According to the Rasmussens, after Mayer throttled Hooks's opinion during the meeting, Hooks held back and seemed afraid to say or do anything. Hooks's involvement in Sherri's case seemed to end soon after the press conference, the Rasmussens recall.

In the chrono for Sherri's case, there is no record of any meeting between the Rasmussens and the detectives prior to the press conference. No notes taken by Mayer or Hooks during the meeting were retained in the murder book.

According to the chrono, the detectives held two press conferences on Thursday, October 23, one at 10:00 a.m. and a second at 4:00 p.m. No additional details about the press conferences were recorded in the chrono, including which news outlets dispatched reporters and who else attended. Nels and Loretta recall that John did not attend.

According to the Rasmussens, among the media present was a local radio station. After one of the press conferences, Nels saw the station's news van parked outside and a reporter milling nearby. Nels walked over, introduced himself as Sherri's father, and struck up a conversation. Nels gave the reporter his phone number, in case the station received any calls in response to the reward offer.

Nels recalls that Mayer overheard him talking with the reporter and came over to them. In front of Nels, Mayer said all tips and information had to go through the LAPD and instructed the reporter not to relay any calls to anyone except the LAPD.

Nels had expected that since he and Loretta put up the bulk of the reward money, they would be notified of any information the LAPD received about Sherri's case. Before he and Loretta left, Nels talked with Mayer and said, "I'd like to see some of the things they're calling in, to give me an idea of where we're at." According to Nels, Mayer told him that it was against the law for the police department to share any information whatsoever about any tips the LAPD might receive. In reality, there was no such legal prohibition. "You can't see any of that, no matter what," Nels recalls Mayer informed him. Nels asked Mayer, "How's that going to work? You can shut out the ones you don't want." Mayer was unmoved, Nels recalls.

According to Nels, he also asked Mayer why he had not contacted or interviewed any of Sherri's family or friends as part of the ongoing investigation. Mayer replied, "They're available if I need them." Nels felt it was obvious that Mayer wasn't looking for anyone except the two burglars.

Nels couldn't understand why the LAPD would shut him out, since they both had the same goal: to solve Sherri's murder. Nels wanted to work with the LAPD but he felt that Mayer did not want to work with him. According to Nels, Mayer did not miss any opportunity to remind him who was in control of the investigation. Nels believed that every chance Mayer got, he tried to drive him a little deeper into the sand.

The *Los Angeles Times* sent a reporter to cover the press conference. On October 23, the *Times* ran a story accompanied by a photo of Sherri and the composites of the two burglary suspects. The story made no mention of John Ruetten. The *Times* reported:

> A $10,000 reward is being offered for information leading to the arrest and conviction of the killers of a prominent hospital nurse shot to death in her Van Nuys condominium earlier this year, police said.
>
> The parents of Sherri Rae Rasmussen, 29, director of critical care nursing at Glendale Adventist Medical Center, are offering the reward to help police,

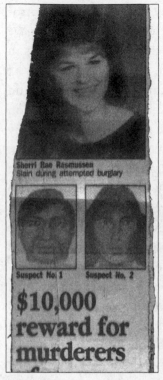

Sherri Rae Rasmussen
Slain during attempted burglary

Suspect No. 1   Suspect No. 2

$10,000 reward for murderers

Los Angeles Times,
October 1986

who have been unable to locate the two men they believe killed Rasmussen during a daylight burglary Feb. 24.

Police Detective Lyle O. Mayer said investigators believe the intruders may have been the same men who came precariously close to killing another woman in a botched burglary two months later and three blocks from Rasmussen's home.

The victim of the second break-in walked into her apartment and confronted two men stacking stereo equipment by the front door, Mayer said. The woman ran off when one of the men pointed a gun at her, he said, and the intruders left without taking anything.

The men were described as Latino, between 5 feet, 4 inches and 5 feet, 6 inches tall, with dark skin and hair, Mayer said. They were seen leaving the second burglary in a royal blue 1975 or 1979 Ford station wagon.

Mayer said persons with information should contact homicide detectives at the Los Angeles Police Department's Van Nuys Division. He said the identity of informants will remain confidential.

On Friday, October 24, the day after the press conferences, the Van Nuys detectives recorded a single entry in the chrono for Sherri's case. The subject was Lisa Rivalli, the victim of the April 10 burglary attempt near Sherri and John's condo. The entry, which misspelled her last name, indicated that she had left Los Angeles. An unidentified detective handwrote *"10/24—Was contacted by Lisa Rivailli"* and her new phone number and home address.

Nels and Loretta returned home to Tucson with the hope the reward would lead to a break in Sherri's case. Their initiative and involvement in setting up the reward helped them feel better about the case, because it felt as if they were doing something proactive, rather than accepting that her murder might never be solved. Their late realization that any information generated by the reward offer would go through Mayer and would not be shared with them dashed their hopes. The weeks and months following the reward announcement were very discouraging, the Rasmussens recall. According to Nels and Loretta, they heard nothing from the detectives about whether any tips were received from the public, nor any other updates on the progress of the investigation.

If the LAPD received any tips about Sherri's case in response to the reward offer, none were recorded in the chrono. Following the October 24 entry about Rivalli's change of address, the detectives documented no investigative activity in the chrono for Sherri's case until May 1987, more than six months later.

Nothing was recorded in the chrono on December 9, 1986. On that date, according to a witness statement handwritten by Mayer, he received a call from Nels's father, Nels Rasmussen Sr. The December 9 statement appears to describe a call that Nels Sr. had received about six weeks earlier, on October 24, the day after the reward announcement. Mayer wrote, *"On or about Oct. 24—86—Sr. Rass—said name—girl—knew Sherri (poss. calling from LA). $. She knew Sherri—went H.S. (Private School in Scottsdale. Thunderbird Academy). Caller had to get in touch with Jr. that day. Sherri death involves conspiracy . . . John dark haired women and two other men."*

The statement does not name the person who called Nels Sr., but Mayer's notes suggest that it was a female high school classmate of Sherri's. Along with the caller's identity, it is a mystery why she called Nels Sr. rather than Sherri's parents, and why Nels Sr. waited six weeks to relay the message to the LAPD. Both the timing of her call and the dollar sign Mayer jotted in his notes suggest that she placed the call in response to the reward announcement. But if she wished to collect the reward, why did she not call the LAPD directly to report what she knew? Was it her or Nels Sr. who stated that Sherri's murder involved a conspiracy? Mayer's notes do not indicate. Was *"dark haired women"* a reference to Stephanie Lazarus or some other brunette connected to John? Who were the *"two other men,"* and what was their role in the purported conspiracy?

Unfortunately, these questions are likely to remain unanswered. Nels Sr. died in 1995. Nels and Loretta have no recollection of his father telling them in 1986 about any call he had received from a high school classmate of Sherri's. According to Nels and Loretta, Mayer never mentioned to them the call he had received from Nels's father.

In June 2009, Mayer was interviewed by LAPD detectives and asked about the witness statement he wrote in December 1986. The chrono recounted, *"The detectives showed Nels Rasmussen's 12/9/86 statement to Mr. Mayer, but it did not refresh his memory and he could not interpret the contents of the notes, which he hand wrote."* The 2009 chrono entry did not clarify why Mayer was unable to interpret his own notes, nor did it indicate whether the detectives asked him any follow-up questions.

There is no record in the murder book that Mayer did any follow-up investigation of the tip he evidently received in December 1986 that Sherri's murder involved a conspiracy related to John, rather than resulted from a botched burglary.

Loretta tried to keep up a relationship with John, following Sherri's death. The Rasmussens still had their sailboat in San Diego, where John had moved soon after Sherri was killed. Nels and Loretta went sailing for Christmas 1986, their first holiday season without Sherri. Loretta recalls that while they were in San Diego, she went to see John and gave him a Christmas present, a microwave oven for his new place.

At midnight on December 31, the LAPD closed the books on its 1986 crime statistics. Every murder victim, irrespective of their life story and the circumstances of their death, is also fated to become a statistic. Robert F. Kennedy's assassination at the Ambassador Hotel in June 1968 was both a singular event in American history and one of 349 homicides recorded in Los Angeles that year. In 1986, Los Angeles registered 831 homicides, of which Sherri's was just one.

At the end of every calendar year, for crime reporting purposes, all homicides are classified as either "cleared" or "unsolved." Cleared cases include those cleared by arrest and a second category, "cleared other." Cases can be designated as "cleared other" when the police have identified the suspect but an arrest is impracticable, for instance if the suspect is dead.

The job performance of homicide detectives, and homicide units, is measured primarily by their clearance rate, the percentage of total murders solved. In 1986, LAPD homicide detectives citywide cleared 538 murders, a clearance rate of 65 percent.

Twenty-eight homicides, including Sherri's, were recorded in Van Nuys in 1986. By year's end, the Van Nuys homicide unit had cleared twenty-three, a clearance rate of 82 percent. Mayer was the lead investigator on eight homicide cases in 1986, according to LAPD records. Mayer solved six of the eight cases before the end of the year, a clearance rate of 75 percent.

Sherri's was among the five Van Nuys murders in 1986 that remained unsolved when the calendar flipped to 1987. The Van Nuys homicide unit retained responsibility for the unsolved cases from 1986 and all prior years, in addition to whatever fresh homicide cases the new year inevitably brought.

Peggy organized a Nursing Education Day at Glendale Adventist in February 1987, to mark the first anniversary of Sherri's death. Peggy knew how committed Sherri was to education, so it seemed an appropriate way to honor her memory. The program consisted of a series of lectures on critical care nursing. All the nurses who attended received continuing education credits. Nels and Loretta traveled from Tucson to be there. Peggy took all the photos she had of Sherri and pasted them on a poster board that she put on display. At the end of the day, when Peggy went to retrieve the poster board, it was gone. Peggy lost all her photographs of Sherri, including every one she had of her and Sherri together.

Like Jayne, Peggy always regretted that Sherri did not live to see her get married, especially since Sherri had known Peggy's future husband. One bittersweet consequence of Sherri's death was that it brought Peggy together with Glenn Crabtree. Peggy was in a meeting with Glenn when she learned that Sherri had been murdered. Days later, Glenn sent Peggy a letter and poem he wrote, which he thought might lift her spirits. Not long after that, they started dating. Peggy and Glenn married that December, on New Year's Eve, and eventually had three children. When their daughter was born, they named her Taryl Rae. Rae was Sherri's middle name.

In March 1987, Loretta and Teresa traveled to San Diego, where John had leased a new condo, to pick up some of Sherri's furniture that John did not want. Nearly all the furniture John inherited from the Van Nuys condo was originally Sherri's, since she had lived there for several years prior to his moving in. Nels stayed behind in Tucson because he wasn't talking to John and did not wish to see him. Loretta and Teresa drove to San Diego on March 16, Loretta's birthday. Loretta recalls it snowed as they drove over the mountains.

John's new place was on the second floor of a two-story building. His front door was up an open-air staircase, at the top of which was a landing shared by John and a neighboring unit. Loretta recalls that when she and Teresa reached the landing, they noticed that John's neighbor's door was ajar. Loretta thought nothing of it, and went ahead and knocked on John's door.

When John came to the door and saw his neighbor's door open, he became very worried, Loretta recalls. In her experience, people sometimes left their doors open, and it wasn't necessarily a cause for concern. John seemed scared to death that something was wrong. He wanted to have the police come check it out, but at the same time he seemed afraid to call the police. Loretta was intent on picking up Sherri's things and starting the drive back to Tucson. Someone eventually came and closed the door, after which John seemed better, Loretta recalls.

On April 7, Mayer completed a "one year progress report" on the status of Sherri's unsolved murder. Mayer's official report stated in full, *"No additional leads have developed in this case."* Mayer's report was signed and approved by his supervisor, Detective III Mel Arnold, the Van Nuys homicide coordinator. At the time, Arnold had supervised the unit for almost a year, since mid-1986, when he assumed the role from his good friend and fellow Detective III, Roger Pida. Mayer, Pida, and Arnold had worked together in the Van Nuys homicide unit for several years. Arnold remained Van Nuys homicide coordinator until 1991, the same year Mayer retired from the LAPD.

According to the chrono for Sherri's case, the Van Nuys detectives resumed their investigation of her murder on May 18. The May 18 chrono entries, unlike the several prior ones, noted the full date, including the year, as well as the name of the detective who apparently wrote them, Arnold. Both entries on May 18 referenced Wendell Clements, an SID fingerprint analyst. The two entries stated *"Det. III M. Arnold. Contacted Wendell Clements about putting prints thru computer. He claims that he will send it through the computer, LAPD computer"* and *"This print will be auto-sent through our computer—then if no hit it will go auto to ALPS—as per Clements."*

Following the May 18 entries about the fingerprints, no investigative activity was documented in Sherri's case for the next six months, until November 1987.

In June, Stephanie participated in the 1987 California Police Olympics, held that year in Stockton. Stephanie won four medals for the LAPD, two gold and two silver.

August marked the first wedding anniversary of Jayne and Mike Goldberg. Although more than a year had passed since Sherri's murder, Jayne's grief had hardly abated. The night before her anniversary, she went to see a psychologist. Jayne recalls the psychologist asked her, "Isn't it interesting that you're here, the day before your first wedding anniversary?"

"Well, I feel guilty about being happily married, because Sherri didn't get a chance to be married for a year," Jayne replied. Jayne still felt that something terrible was bound to happen to her or Mike at any moment.

Later, as Jayne left the psychologist's office, it dawned on her that the bad thing she kept waiting to happen had already happened, when Sherri was killed. It felt like a eureka moment to Jayne, to finally understand why she had been unable to shake her sense of a looming catastrophe.

Jayne and Mike went on to have two children, including a daughter whom they named Mollie Rae. Jayne was unaware at the time that Peggy had also given her daughter the middle name Rae, after Sherri's. Jayne and Peggy did not learn of the concurrence until many years later, when their daughters were of college age.

On November 5, Stephanie was commended by the LAPD *"for [the] outstanding manner in which [she] resolved a complicated dispute while leaving parties with a good impression of LAPD."* The circumstances of the dispute, and what exactly Stephanie did to burnish the LAPD's image, were not documented in her personnel file.

By that November, Sherri's murder was more than eighteen months in the past. A full year had passed since the LAPD's announcement of a $10,000 reward for information. Yet it seemed to the Rasmussens that the LAPD was no closer to solving Sherri's case than on day one of the investigation.

Nels and Loretta could not accept that Sherri's murder might never be solved. In an effort to reinvigorate the investigation, they decided to renew the reward offer. According to the Rasmussens, they contacted Mayer and he agreed to the idea. A new press conference was scheduled for November 23, which would have been Sherri and John's second wedding anniversary.

Nels also recalls that in advance of the press conference, he called Mayer about the bite mark on Sherri's arm. As a dentist, Nels knew that the police considered bite marks identifiable, like a fingerprint. A dental cast of the bite mark had been made by the coroner's office as part of her autopsy. Nels requested Mayer send him photos of the dental cast.

According to the chrono, the Van Nuys detectives resumed their investigation of Sherri's murder on Monday, November 16. At the top of chrono page 17, an unidentified detective handwrote *"Weekly Calls to Victim's Parents."*

However, according to Nels and Loretta, at no point during the LAPD's entire investigation of Sherri's murder, and for certain never in 1986 and

LAPD 03.11.6 (1/82)		CHRONOLOGICAL RECORD		
INSTRUCTIONS: This form is used to document any past or future investigative events deemed necessary to control or develop this case.				DR
DATE	TIME	INVESTIGATION		
		Weekly Calls to Victim's Parents —		
11-16	1600	*Called Dr. Vail. Consultant LA County Coroner. ph# 213- 226 5052 ✓ 213 226 8087 LA C. #*		
		he will recheck Casts for any info he can give. will get us photos for Ras.		

LAPD chrono entries on November 16, 1987 (top of chrono page 17)

1987, did they ever receive weekly calls from Mayer, Hooks, or any other Van Nuys homicide detective. No other information was documented in the murder book about the purported weekly calls to the Rasmussens—for instance, when the calls were placed, and what information was exchanged. Who wrote the puzzling chrono entry, and why a detective would write *"Weekly Calls to Victim's Parents"* in the official log for a homicide case when no such calls were ever made has never been explained or accounted for by the LAPD.

Below *"Weekly Calls to Victim's Parents,"* the same detective wrote *"11-16 | 1600 | Called Dr. Vail [sic]. Consultant LA County Coroner."* Dr. Gerald Vale was the coroner's chief forensic dentist. The day after the murder, Vale had told Mayer and Hooks that the bite marks on Sherri's arm were so severe and distinctive that they were good for comparison, if a suspect were apprehended. The rest of the November 16 chrono entry indicated of Vale had *"He will recheck casts for any info he can give. Will get us photos for Ras"*—apparent shorthand for Nels Rasmussen.

A second chrono entry Monday afternoon recounted, *"11-16 | 1615 | Called Press Room—to set up Times story."*

The detectives recorded two chrono entries on Wednesday, November 18, both in anticipation of the upcoming press conference. The first entry, at the bottom of chrono page 17, stated, *"11-18 | 1500 | Press Confer-*

LAPD chrono entry on November 19, 1987 (bottom of chrono page 18)

ence Set Up," along with the names and phone numbers of two newspaper reporters. The second entry on November 18, at the top of chrono page 18, detailed the Rasmussens' travel plans to Los Angeles for the press conference: "11/18 | 1530 | Nels & Loretta notified—they are coming in on A/W flight 474—7:25 on 11/23/87."

Among the entries the detectives recorded in the chrono on November 19, nearly two years into the LAPD's investigation of Sherri's case, was the first mention in the murder book of Stephanie Lazarus.

The reference to Stephanie, handwritten by an unidentified detective, was sandwiched between several other chrono entries about the press conference. The chrono entry about Stephanie read: "11-19 | 1500 | John Ruetten called—verified Stephanie Lazarus—P/O was former girlfriend."

Nothing more about Stephanie was documented in the chrono or murder book in November 1987, nor for the next twenty years. No indication was made in the chrono that P/O stood for Police Officer, or that the police department Stephanie worked for was the LAPD. No additional details were recorded about John and Stephanie's relationship, including what possible relevance it had to Sherri's murder. Only John knows what prompted him, almost two years into the investigation, to call the detectives and verify that Stephanie Lazarus was his ex-girlfriend.

Nels and Loretta woke before dawn on Monday in Tucson and took an early morning flight to LAX in order to get to Van Nuys in time for the 9:00 a.m. press conference. Sherri's sister Teresa, five months pregnant when Sherri was killed, attended with her son, who was by then a toddler. John also came up from San Diego for the press conference, unlike in October 1986, when the reward offer was first announced.

Nels recalls he did not talk with John at the press conference. Nels felt that John had made it plain he wasn't going to help him push for answers about who had killed Sherri. Nels felt humiliated at the thought of even acknowledging John, so he just ignored him. When it came time to address the media, Loretta sat between John and Nels. Teresa sat on her father's other side, with her son on her lap.

At the time, Nels had no knowledge of what John had told the LAPD about his police officer ex-girlfriend, following Sherri's murder. Nels also had no idea that four days earlier, on November 19, John had called the Van Nuys detectives and verified Stephanie's name for them.

Not until more than twenty years later did Nels learn that the only reference to John's ex-girlfriend in the murder book prior to 2009 resulted from a call John placed to detectives in November 1987. Although he had no proof of a connection, Nels suspected in hindsight that the timing of John's call, just days before the reward offer was renewed, was not a coincidence. No one knew at the time when the LAPD might make an arrest in Sherri's case. Nels speculated that John may have reported Stephanie's name to detectives on the chance that, if she did kill Sherri, and the LAPD arrested her, John would have a claim on the reward money.

Among the media that covered the press conference was the *Los Angeles Times*. Under the headline PARENTS OF SLAIN NURSE SEEK HELP IN FINDING KILLER, the *Times* reported,

> *Nels and Loretta Rasmussen came from Tucson, Ariz., to the Van Nuys police station to renew their offer of a $10,000 reward for information leading to the arrest and conviction of the killers. Sherri Rasmussen's husband, John Ruetten, an engineer in San Diego, and sister, Theresa [sic] Lane, of Loma Linda, joined them in asking anyone with knowledge of the crime to come forward. "It's been nearly two years of hell not knowing who did this to Sherri or why," Ruetten said. "You try to move on, but it's hard to do when you're always going over in your mind how it might have happened."*

The reward offer also made the evening news on local television station KNBC. KNBC reporter Laurel Erickson reported from in front of John and Sherri's condo, "A $10,000 reward is being offered tonight for the capture and conviction of two brutal burglars working the San Fernando Valley . . . As a hospital director of critical care, 29-year-old Sherri Rae Rasmussen was used to emergencies, but neighbors say she must have panicked when she surprised two burglars in her townhouse last February. Instead of pushing the newly installed security alarm button, Rasmussen tangled with a gunman. She was shot and killed . . . Then, six weeks later, just three blocks from here, another burglary. Again, the victim discovered the suspects. This time, before one of the suspects could pull the trigger, she managed to get away."

As the screen showed the LAPD composite sketches of the two burglary suspects, Erickson narrated, "Investigators believe these men killed Rasmussen, and would have killed the second woman, had she not gotten away. She and others provided a description. They said the burglars fled in a 1970s royal blue Ford station wagon."

The report cut to footage of Mayer at the press conference. Mayer said, "We have obtained fingerprints in the crimes. We are of the opinion, at this time, that the suspects may be illegal aliens." Erickson concluded her report, "Detectives asked the public to call Van Nuys police with any information that might solve this case, before the gunmen strike again."

Among the viewers who watched the KNBC report the night it aired was Sherri's friend Jayne. When Jayne heard the reporter say on television that Sherri must have panicked and fought with her attackers instead of going for the alarm, she was angry. Jayne thought, "Sherri didn't panic." She knew Sherri was always calm, even under dire circumstances. Jayne saw her in many life-and-death situations when they worked together at UCLA Medical Center. Never once had she seen Sherri panic.

Jayne had even talked once with Sherri about what to do if someone pulled a gun on you. Jayne was taking a self-defense class at the time. She told Sherri the instructor said you needed to either talk your way out of it, or run away if you could. Jayne believed that Sherri was trying to get away before she was killed and fought only because she must have had no other choice.

Jayne felt the news report made it sound as if Sherri was hysterical, as though her murder was her own fault rather than something terrible that happened to her. She wanted to call the reporter and tell her, "You didn't know her. How can you say that about her? She wouldn't have panicked. She was in a terrible situation."

Jayne also felt disappointed in John when she saw the footage of the press conference on the news. Jayne knew John as well as any of Sherri's friends did. Her perception of him, based on his body language as he sat next to the Rasmussens at the press conference, was that he did not want to be there. Jayne knew Nels was obsessed with finding out what happened to Sherri. She wanted John to be more obsessed than he appeared to be.

As time passed, and nothing seemed to result from the press conference and reward offer, Jayne gradually lost hope that she would ever learn what happened to Sherri. Then, almost a year later, in August 1988, she read an article in the *Los Angeles Times* about the growing acceptance of bite mark evidence in criminal cases.

The article profiled Dr. Gerald Vale, the coroner's chief forensic dentist. Unbeknownst to Jayne, Vale had performed the examination of the bite mark on Sherri's arm. The article described bite mark evidence as exceedingly rare in homicide cases. One veteran LAPD homicide detective told the *Times* that he had investigated nearly a thousand murders in his career but had encountered bite mark evidence in only half a dozen cases.

Vale told the *Times*, "When there is good bite mark evidence available, it is usually crucial evidence in the case. If you are able to demonstrate that a bite mark was made by the suspect, one, you have put the suspect at the scene of the crime and, two, you have established that he committed an act of violence against the victim. And that goes a long way toward convicting him."

Jayne was stunned to read, halfway through the article, an unmistakable reference to Sherri's case, although she was not named. Sherri's murder was cited as an example of a homicide that could be solved through bite mark evidence. *"'It's crucial. Sometimes that is the only evidence going for you,' said homicide detective Mel Arnold of the Los Angeles Police Department's Van Nuys Division, describing an unsolved case in which burglars beat and fatally shot a nurse in her home. If a suspect is ever found, Arnold hopes Vale can match a carefully photographed bite mark on the woman's arm to the suspect's teeth,"* the *Times* reported.

For years afterward, Jayne remembered the *Times* story and clung to the hope that the bite mark on Sherri's arm might one day confirm her killer's identity.

Few details of the November 1987 press conference were recorded in the chrono for Sherri's case. At the top of chrono page 19, an unidentified detective handwrote, *"11/23 | 0900 | Press relations conference—Parents & sister there. Notified Press."* Why John's presence at the press conference was not also documented in the chrono is a mystery.

Nels and Loretta returned home to Tucson and once again waited for news from the detectives. According to the Rasmussens, they received no word from the LAPD whether any tips were received in response to the renewed reward offer, and no other updates on the progress of the investigation. After several months, the Rasmussens' attorney advised them not to leave the reward offer open indefinitely. Nels and Loretta donated their share of the reward funds, $8,000, to Glendale Adventist Medical Center in

Sherri's name. The reward money contributed by the Ruetten and Gorder families was returned to them, the Rasmussens recall.

The LAPD's failure to identify and catch the burglars who supposedly killed Sherri only served to strengthen Nels's conviction that John's ex-girlfriend might be responsible for Sherri's murder. But after nearly two years of pushing for answers, the Rasmussens felt worn down and dispirited by the lack of progress in the investigation, and what they perceived as the LAPD's stonewalling.

Nels's trust that the LAPD was honestly investigating Sherri's murder was undermined by how jealously it guarded all information about the case. He had already learned, through his interactions with Mayer to that point, that the LAPD would not share any information with him until Sherri's case was solved. He knew that as long as Sherri's case remained open, the LAPD could claim that it was an ongoing investigation, and on that basis refuse to release any information at all.

Nels felt the LAPD wanted him to get tired of coming at the detectives, and tired of fighting for information. In his view, the LAPD's philosophy was that eventually, inevitably, you're going to get tired, and you're going to quit. Nels believed that if the detectives could delay, delay, delay, and then give him just a little bit of information, enough that he left them alone for a while, that was fine for the LAPD, because they held all the cards.

According to the chrono, the Van Nuys detectives received not a single tip about Sherri's case following the November 1987 press conference. The two burglary suspects sought by the LAPD for Sherri's murder were never identified or arrested.

Despite the rarity of bite mark evidence in homicide cases, and the coroner's careful documentation of the bite mark on Sherri's arm, the LAPD never sought to obtain a warrant for a bite mark impression from Stephanie Lazarus. Although the chrono indicated that John verified Stephanie's name for the detectives in November 1987, and there were no other named suspects for the detectives to investigate at that time, there is no record they did any follow-up investigation whatsoever into Stephanie and her possible involvement in Sherri's murder, even to clear her name.

Following the November 1987 press conference, the Van Nuys detectives documented no investigative activity in the chrono for Sherri's case until February 1992, more than four years later.

Van Nuys had sixteen murders in 1987, a dozen fewer than in 1986. The citywide homicide count in 1987 was 812, down slightly from the 831 people, including Sherri, killed in Los Angeles a year earlier. The Van Nuys unit solved eleven of its sixteen cases before the end of the year, for a clearance rate of 69 percent. The five open cases were carried over into 1988, along with all the unsolved murders from previous years.

The next year, 1988, Van Nuys recorded twenty homicides, of which the detectives solved sixteen by December 31 that year, an 80 percent clearance rate.

The years from 1989 to 1992 were the nadir of the crack epidemic, a singularly violent time in Los Angeles history. Crime and murders spiked across the city each year, from 874 people in 1989 to 1,092 in 1992. Homicide detectives throughout the LAPD struggled to keep pace with the onslaught of new cases. By 1992, the LAPD's citywide homicide clearance rate had dropped to 58 percent, from 71 percent in 1988.

Van Nuys also saw an unprecedented rise in murders: 29 in 1989, 39 in 1990, 35 in 1991, 40 in 1992. Year after year, the backlog of unsolved homicide cases grew. LAPD homicide detectives were permitted, and even encouraged, to investigate cold cases, although fresh homicides generally took precedence.

All the while, Sherri's unsolved murder receded further in time and memory. By February 1992, when, according to the chrono in Sherri's case, the LAPD's investigation resumed, Mayer and Hooks were no longer assigned to the Van Nuys homicide unit. Mayer retired from the LAPD in September 1991. Hooks did not retire until 1998, but the last Van Nuys murder he investigated, according to LAPD records, was in October 1991, a month after Mayer's retirement.

The detectives who replaced Mayer and Hooks in the Van Nuys homicide unit, and assumed responsibility for Sherri's unsolved murder, inherited what still appeared on paper to be a tragic but unremarkable case of a burglary gone awry.

PART

The Murder of Catherine Braley

THREE

Catherine Braley

(January 14, 1988)

On the morning of her murder, January 14, 1988, twenty-six-year-old Catherine Braley awoke in her teardrop trailer home. Cathy's one-room trailer was a hand-me-down from her mother, Mary Postma, who lived in her own trailer, a stone's throw away, in the Birmingham Trailer Village in Van Nuys.

The trailer park Cathy and Mary called home was less than a mile north of the Balboa Townhomes, the leafy condo complex where Sherri Rasmussen was killed almost two years earlier. But Cathy's world had little in common with Sherri's.

Unlike Sherri, Cathy did not have the benefit of a privileged, stable upbringing. Although Cathy was hardworking, and bright, she did not harbor lofty professional ambitions. What she wanted most in life, according to those who knew her best, was to meet a nice guy, to be in a loving relationship, and to one day start her own family. To love, and to be loved.

Cathy's life more closely resembled that of another Los Angeles murder victim, Elizabeth Short, who went by Betty in life but after her death was mythologized as the Black Dahlia. Coincidentally, Betty Short's body was discovered on the morning of January 15, 1947, forty-one years, almost to the hour, before Cathy's. Both were unmarried women in their twenties when they were killed. Cathy, like Betty, had an itinerant childhood and lived around the country before she settled in Los Angeles. Cathy's romantic history also echoed Betty's. Both seemed unlucky in love, with

Cathy Braley, circa mid-1980s

serial unfulfilled relationships. Cathy and Betty each had minor brushes with the law, for alcohol-related offenses. Both women, Cathy and Betty, received more attention in death, as murder victims, than the world ever paid them while they were alive.

Like the Black Dahlia case, Cathy's murder remains unsolved. Whether Cathy will ever receive justice is unknown. As with any homicide, the odds diminish with each passing day. More years have now passed since Cathy's murder than she was alive.

In stark contrast to her violent fate, Cathy had a gentle, upbeat, amiable personality. Although life was never easy for Cathy, she was not resentful and rarely seemed sad. Cathy's friends and family remember her as kind, caring, and fun-loving. She enjoyed nothing more than to party with her friends and have a good time. Late in her life, Cathy realized that she had a drinking problem, and she struggled to control it. But even when she drank too much, Cathy was never rowdy, vulgar, or mean-spirited. She was not a violent person. Nor was Cathy's personality the type that would seem likely to inspire violence. She was honest, and not a gossip or a tease. She had no known enemies. To the contrary, Mary marveled at how easily her daughter got along with people, no matter their station in life, and at her many different circles of friends.

Cathy worked full time as a cashier in the grocery department at Fedco, a discount department store in Van Nuys. At the time of her murder, Cathy had worked at Fedco for fifteen months, earning $5.20 an hour, less taxes. In the month before she was killed, Cathy averaged fifty-hour workweeks.

The Fedco where Cathy worked was located on Raymer Street, in a somewhat gritty commercial and industrial neighborhood east of Sepulveda Boulevard. Today, a Target occupies the Fedco's old footprint.

Cathy's social life revolved around a few neighborhood bars where she was a familiar presence. She liked going out to the bars after work because that's where her friends were. Many days, Cathy would wake up, go to work, work all day, go straight to the bar, unwind for a few hours, go home to her trailer to sleep, and then do it all over again the next day.

LAPD aerial photo of Raymer Street and Burnet Avenue, looking south.
The Hunter bar, on the southwest street corner, is at the center of the photo.
(January 21, 1988)

The two bars Cathy frequented most often were the Hunter and the Noble Inn, which people called the Noble. Both were walking distance from the Fedco where Cathy worked. The Hunter, on the corner of Raymer and Burnet Avenue, had a liquor license and was open later than the Noble, one block over, which served beer and wine only. Before Cathy was hired at Fedco, she sometimes worked as a bartender at the Noble to make ends meet.

Most of the patrons at the Hunter and the Noble were regulars, a mix of blue-collar and white-collar workers from the surrounding neighborhood. There was some overlap between the regulars at the two bars, given their proximity, but some people preferred one to the other. The Noble was smaller and cozier, and because it was a beer and wine bar, there tended to be less hard drinking there than at the Hunter.

It was at the Noble Inn that Cathy met one of her best friends, Bonnie, who was also a regular and a onetime bartender there. At the time, Bonnie was in her early thirties, several years older than Cathy. Bonnie was divorced and the mother of two small kids, whom she was raising alone. For eight months in 1986 and 1987, Cathy rented a spare bedroom in Bonnie's house, until Cathy moved to the trailer park where Mary, her mother, lived.

Bonnie would not have invited just anybody to live with her and her kids. Bonnie had many acquaintances but very few people she counted as friends. Bonnie did not consider someone her friend until she trusted them. Bonnie knew Cathy to be a trustworthy person, if sometimes too trusting of other people herself.

Bonnie got to know Cathy well, especially once they lived together. Bonnie's house was small, and she and Cathy shared a bathroom, so they were inevitably in each other's space. Cathy got along with Bonnie's kids, especially her young son, who loved that Cathy sometimes made him pancakes for breakfast. Cathy was neat and clean, and she respected Bonnie's few rules: no drugs, no smoking, don't bring any strange men home. Bonnie and Cathy never had any issues as housemates.

Bonnie believed Cathy's essential qualities were her natural empathy and her comforting presence. If you had a problem, she would not hesitate to put her arm around you, or give you a hug, and listen without judgment. Bonnie thought Cathy wanted to believe the best of everybody she met. Bonnie did not think Cathy was stupid, or deliberately chose to see the world through rose-colored glasses. Her innocence was just part of who she was, for better or worse.

Even when Cathy was given reason to regret her naïveté, her disposition remained good-natured, as far as Bonnie ever saw. Bonnie saw Cathy angry only a couple of times, and never at her, during their friendship. Cathy's anger always seemed short-lived. Bonnie never heard her belittle anyone. If Cathy had something negative to say, she would say it in the kindest, gentlest way she could.

Although Bonnie, like Cathy, was a regular at both the Hunter and the Noble Inn, Bonnie did not drink alcohol. Her standard bar drink was a club soda with lime, or, if she felt tired, a Coke. Bonnie liked going to the bars because she enjoyed the music and the down-to-earth atmosphere. Both bars, the Hunter and the Noble, had jukeboxes that played a mix of oldies, Top 40 songs, and rock and roll. Both bars also had a full kitchen that served food made to order, a pool table, and a dartboard. Because it was not a residential neighborhood, the owner of the Noble, Denny Kline, sometimes set up an oil drum barbecue cooker outside to draw in customers, without fear of complaints from any neighbors. After Cathy was killed, Denny was one of the pallbearers at her funeral.

Over time, there developed among the regulars, by virtue of their familiarity with one another, a sense of community almost like a family. There were potlucks for holidays, and celebrations for birthdays and other milestones. The last birthday that Cathy celebrated, in August 1987, when she turned twenty-six, a surprise party was held for her at the Hunter. Cathy was good at softball and a mainstay on the Noble's team, which competed against other bars in the Valley. Even the regulars who didn't play, like Bonnie, went to watch some of the softball games. Cathy was also on the Noble's darts team. The camaraderie felt reminiscent of the bar on *Cheers*, the sitcom set in a Boston watering hole, which was at that time one of the most popular shows on television.

Neither the Hunter nor the Noble was a dive, or dirty, or a haven for hard-core drunks. To the degree that any of the regulars were alcoholics, they were functional ones who held down jobs and had to get up for work each morning. Although the bars were not unwelcoming to strangers, it was rare for unfamiliar faces to be seen there. Since most everyone knew each other, and generally got along, fights were uncommon. Disagreements were rarely more than pissing contests, defused well before anyone came to blows. It was unheard of for anyone to get hurt, until the night Cathy was murdered.

The reliable lack of drama at the Hunter and the Noble was a big reason why Bonnie felt comfortable there as a single woman. Bonnie was attractive, and her personality was sassy and confident in a way that she thought some men took as a challenge. She was used to men in bars talking her up and trying to charm her into bed. Part of her enjoyed the attention, although Bonnie felt at the time that she had no room for a man in her life. It was still fun for her to go out, see friends, dance, flirt, and make conversation, normally without a hassle or any kind of commitment. She called it going to the bar to play. How much attention can I get this evening, just for fun? How many men can I get to buy me a drink? Bonnie thought guys got off easy with her since it was just a club soda. Bonnie considered it a level playing field and all in good fun. She believed most men understood the rules as she did. If Bonnie ever felt uneasy at the bar, or people there made her depressed, she went home to relieve the babysitter.

Bonnie found it interesting and amusing to watch people, especially when they drank. It was why she enjoyed working as a bartender. Bonnie thought she could learn more about human nature from behind the bar, or on a barstool, than she could in any psychology course. Bonnie observed that when people got drunk, they became either mean or happy. Cathy and most of the other regulars at the Hunter and the Noble had the latter disposition. Perhaps in part because Bonnie was always sober, she discovered people would drink and want to tell her their secrets, as though she was a mother confessor. Most of what people said while they were drunk Bonnie considered to be true, or just below the surface of what they wanted to say all along.

Bonnie believed she had an uncanny ability to see into other people's future, a quality she called psychic intuition. Bonnie was convinced that she could look at someone and see certain things about them, and what was going to happen. Bonnie took her ability seriously and was open about it with others. Bonnie's willingness to share her intuitive insights was another reason she was a magnet in the bars for personal revelations. People wanted to know, for instance, whether they were going to get a certain job, or what was portended in their love lives. Whatever Bonnie's intuition told her about a particular situation, whether it was hopeful or pessimistic, she lived by the credo "If I see it, I say it. If I don't, I don't." Bonnie liked it straight, gave it to you straight, and expected it straight in return.

The first time that Bonnie met Cathy, at the Noble Inn sometime in 1985, Cathy asked Bonnie to read her palm.

"I'm not a palm reader," Bonnie told her.

"I don't know what else to call it."

"I'm a psychic intuitive."

"Well, what do you do see for me?" Cathy asked. Cathy wanted to know about her future with a guy, Garth Craigie, with whom she had fallen in love.

Cathy had met Garth on the first day of summer 1985 at the Palm Tree, another beer and wine bar in the Valley. Before Cathy found full-time work at Fedco, she tended bar part time at the Palm Tree as well as the Noble Inn. Cathy made note of her and Garth's "anniversary," June 21, in her datebook.

Cathy was twenty-three when she met Garth, ten years younger than him. Garth had slate-colored eyes, and a beard and mustache that she found ruggedly handsome. Cathy was attracted to manly men, average Joes who worked with their hands and had a roughneck quality. Garth worked as an auto mechanic.

Cathy and Garth dated on and off for the next two years, the longest romantic relationship of her life. Although Cathy had dalliances with several other men during her twenties, none really qualified as a steady boyfriend, Garth included. Cathy never got to experience what it was like to be in a serious, committed relationship, the one thing she most desired in her life.

Cathy's relationship with Garth was still young when she asked Bonnie to foresee their future as a couple. Bonnie's intuition told her he wasn't the right guy for Cathy. Bonnie informed Cathy he wasn't worth it. Cathy was not dissuaded.

Garth died in 2015, at age sixty-three. The only window into his and Cathy's two-year romance is what Cathy told her mother and friends at the time, and the references to him she wrote in her datebook. When Cathy saw Garth, they usually spent time together off on their own rather than with other friends. Garth was a regular at the Palm Tree but not at the Hunter or the Noble Inn, Cathy's main hangouts. Cathy's closest girlfriends never even met Garth, let alone got to know him.

Mary, Cathy's mother, met Garth only a couple of times. Cathy once brought Garth by the trailer park where Mary lived. Mary recalls they stood and talked outside her trailer. Mary's impression of Garth that day was that he treated Cathy like a lady. Cathy and Garth acted lovey-dovey and seemed to Mary as happy as they could be. That visit turned out to be the last time Mary ever saw Garth.

Cathy did not learn until after she was already involved with Garth that he was married. Garth told Cathy that he and his wife were separated and going to get divorced. Garth suggested to Cathy on at least two occasions, in June 1986 and again in January 1987, that he wanted her to move to Arizona with him. That never happened.

By the start of 1987, Cathy was working at Fedco and living with Bonnie, who had become a close friend. Bonnie related to Cathy a bit like an older sister. Bonnie had more life experience than Cathy and felt protective of her. Cathy talked with Bonnie about Garth, and what she should do. It seemed to Bonnie that Garth was dragging his feet on leaving his wife, and stringing Cathy along in the meantime. Bonnie didn't judge, but she told Cathy, "A man rarely leaves his wife." Bonnie asked her, "Even if he does, is this really what you want? Because it's going to be back and forth. And if he did it to her, what's he going to do to you?"

"But I love him," Cathy replied.

Cathy's relationship with Garth ended in June 1987. By then, Garth was living with his parents in Frazier Park, a small mountain town an hour's drive northwest of Los Angeles. Cathy decided one night to drive up there to see him. Cathy expected to find Garth working at a service station, but he wasn't there. Cathy's futile search for Garth ended with her getting pulled over and arrested for drunk driving. Cathy's car was impounded and she was jailed for several days, until Mary bailed her out.

During their drive back to Van Nuys, Mary lectured Cathy that what she had done was stupid. Mary warned her that she could have gotten killed, driving drunk on the freeway. Mary told Cathy she should stop chasing after Garth, because it would only lead to more trouble.

Cathy never mentioned Garth in her datebook again. Following her arrest on June 15, Cathy seemed to recognize the experience as a wake-up call. Because Cathy had a prior DUI on her driving record, the new case carried the prospect of a hefty fine, or, if she could not afford to pay it, more jail time.

Cathy had no savings and was unable to pull the money together in time. On October 15, four months to the day after her arrest, Cathy wrote in her datebook, *"Turned myself in 6:00 Bakersfield County Jail."* Six days later, on October 21, Cathy wrote, *"Released at 1:30 a.m."* Between her initial arrest and the later stint, Cathy spent a total of thirteen days in jail, according to a court record of her conviction. Cathy also had to pay court fees and a fine in order to resolve her case. In her datebook on November 2, Cathy reminded herself, *"Pay fine by today so court rec. by the 4th."* Cathy did not note the amount of the fine she paid, nor was it indicated in her court records.

The financial consequences of Cathy's DUI arrest continued to mount even after her criminal case was over. As a condition of her probation, Cathy had to complete a twelve-step program at a court-referred provider. Cathy enrolled in a program in San Fernando, close to Van Nuys. For each group therapy session Cathy attended, she was billed $75, almost twice what she earned for a full day's work at Fedco. By late December, Cathy owed $672.50. Cathy received a letter informing her that if she did not pay $140 within two weeks, she would be taken to small claims court.

Although Cathy lived paycheck to paycheck and had few material possessions, she tried her best to be conscientious about money, especially when she had to borrow from friends and family. In her datebook, Cathy kept careful note of her Fedco paydays, whom she owed money to, and when she repaid each debt.

Cathy moved out of Bonnie's house, amicably, at the end of July 1987.

Bonnie's sister was moving to Los Angeles and planned to live in the spare bedroom Cathy had rented for eight months.

Cathy moved from Bonnie's place to the Birmingham Trailer Village in Van Nuys, where her mother lived. Mary had moved to the trailer park several months earlier, in April. Mary lived there with her boyfriend of two years, a plumber named Dean, who went by the nickname Crash. Crash was a biker and a member of the Sundowners Motorcycle Club, which was how he got his name. Mary and Crash had their own plumbing business that Mary ran from their trailer.

When Mary and Crash first moved to the trailer park, they lived in a teardrop trailer that was only about a dozen feet long, barely big enough for a double bed and a tiny kitchenette. Mary and Crash soon upgraded to a larger trailer with a built-in bathroom and shower, and they offered their old trailer to Cathy to live in. Cathy was responsible for paying the rent for her own space. The trailer park provided hookups for electricity and running water. Since Cathy's trailer lacked a bathroom, when she needed to bathe, or nature called, she had to use the communal facilities in the trailer park's shower house. Cathy's monthly rent was $325.

Mary liked living close to Cathy, the youngest of her four children. In daylight, Mary could see Cathy's trailer, parked just across the driveway from her own. At night, it was too dark for Mary to see, but the trailer park was quiet enough that Mary could hear if a car came or went.

Cathy's car was a white Ford Falcon station wagon. For much of the time Cathy lived at the trailer park, the six months prior to her murder, her car was too broken down to drive. Cathy could not afford the major repairs it needed. Most days that Cathy worked, Mary drove her to Fedco in the morning. After work, Cathy usually caught a ride home from friends, or, if she couldn't find one, called Mary to pick her up.

Some nights when Cathy was out partying and couldn't find a ride, or if her car was running but she didn't want to risk another DUI, she walked home. Cathy seemed to think nothing of it. Mary warned Cathy against walking home drunk after dark. Mary told her, "One of these nights, somebody's going to grab you. You gotta stop this." Mary said, "Call me and I'll come and get you." Mary wondered if the reason Cathy didn't call was because she didn't want her mother to know when she was drunk.

One night while Cathy was still living with Bonnie, Mary went to the bar where Cathy was to give her a ride home. Cathy refused to get in

Mary's car. Cathy could be stubborn, especially when she drank. Mary knew from long experience that it was impossible to talk sense into someone who was drunk. Mary's father and both of her ex-husbands were alcoholics, including Ed Postma, Cathy's father. That night outside the bar, as Mary tried to persuade Cathy to come with her, Cathy fell backward in the middle of the street. Mary told her, "Cathy, one of these nights you're gonna get like this, and somebody's gonna hurt you bad." Mary finally left Cathy at the bar. Cathy ended up walking home to Bonnie's, safely. Mary believed Cathy didn't quite appreciate how dangerous it was for her to walk the streets late at night after partying.

Bonnie, too, urged Cathy to call her whenever she needed a ride home from the bar. Bonnie did not think Cathy drank in order to get drunk, but she would drink to the point that she did what she wanted to do. Bonnie believed alcohol was how Cathy coped with her disappointment at not being able to find someone who loved and accepted her the way she was. Bonnie sensed Cathy sometimes struggled with low self-esteem because she was slightly heavyset, and self-conscious about it. Bonnie thought that was why Cathy often asked Bonnie about her future with this or that guy, whoever Cathy was romantically interested in at that moment.

Bonnie considered Cathy naturally physically affectionate, a quality her drinking sometimes amplified. Bonnie was the opposite. Bonnie did not like to be touched or hugged, unless it was by someone she was dating. Cathy was more the type to greet somebody with a hug, or to throw her arm around someone at the bar, as if they were good buddies. Bonnie believed Cathy's physical affection was more friendly than sexual, although some men may have misread it.

Cathy was involved with a few other men after June 1987, when her two-year romance with Garth ended. Later that year, a month or more before her murder, Cathy had a one-night stand with a friend, Noel Warnick. Cathy and Noel had known each other for a few years, as part of the same loose-knit group of regulars who patronized the Hunter many nights after work. Noel was black and in his early forties at the time, almost twenty years older than Cathy.

Noel died in 2012. In an interview in 2011, Noel remembered Cathy as a nice, easygoing, hardworking girl. Noel considered Cathy a friend, but he knew relatively little about her life away from the bar, other than the fact she worked at Fedco. Noel recalled he and Cathy had sex only once, after they both got drunk at the Hunter one night and wound up going to his apartment. "It was just something that happened. Things like that happen some-times," Noel recounted.

Noel was a longtime employee of ITT, a manufacturing company that had an office just across Sepulveda Boulevard, walking distance to the Hunter. Noel lived alone in a modest apartment building a few blocks far-ther north, at 8123 Sepulveda. The night they had sex was the only time Cathy ever visited his apartment, Noel recalled in 2011.

Sepulveda Boulevard, a major north-south artery through the Valley, was a busy street with near-constant car and pedestrian traffic. In the 1980s, the particular stretch of Sepulveda that Noel lived on was considered sketchy, a known location for drug peddling and street prostitution.

The apartment building where Noel lived in 1988 still stands today, thirty years later, but some neighboring properties have since been razed and redeveloped. The next lot south, at 8101 Sepulveda, no longer appears as it did in the 1980s. Back then, Noel's apartment building was adjacent to a crisis management center operated by the Los Angeles County Depart-ment of Mental Health.

The crisis management center functioned as a public emergency room for the mentally ill and also provided outpatient treatment, such as

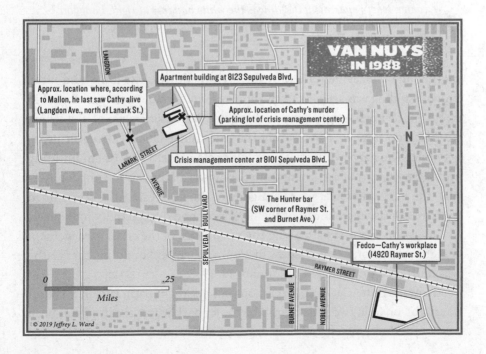

LAPD aerial photo of Sepulveda Boulevard and Lanark Street, looking west. The Crisis Management Center is the dark roofed building at center. Noel's apartment building is the white building at right. Langdon Avenue is visible by the row of trees at the top. (January 21, 1988)

methadone replacement therapy for heroin addicts. The low-slung, drab brown building was set back from Sepulveda by a small paved parking lot in front. At the north edge of the parking lot, there was a strip of dirt where the blacktop stopped a few feet short of the cinder-block wall on the property line. The narrow dirt path ran alongside Noel's apartment building and served as part of a shortcut from Sepulveda all the way to Langdon Avenue, the next side street west. Langdon, a quieter, residential street lined with trees, was where much of the neighborhood drug activity took place.

It was on this dirt path along the north edge of the crisis management center parking lot, in the shadow of Noel's apartment building, that Cathy was murdered on the night of January 14, 1988.

How and why Cathy ended up on that poorly lit path, late on a Thursday night, on foot, two miles from the trailer park where she lived, has been murky for thirty years, and may never be answered for certain.

The last person known to have seen Cathy alive, an off-duty Los Angeles County Sheriff's deputy named Bob Mallon, told LAPD detectives two days after her murder that late on the night she was killed, Cathy walked off alone from his car after they parked on Langdon Avenue, a block west of Sepulveda.

When Cathy was killed on the footpath, she may have been trying to get to the bustle and relative safety of Sepulveda Boulevard, or to Noel's apartment, where she had been once before. In 2011, a year before he died, Noel voluntarily provided the LAPD with a DNA sample. Noel's DNA profile did not match any evidence collected in 1988 from the crime scene and Cathy's body.

Also in the fall of 1987, during the few months before she was killed, Cathy befriended another man, Joey Poleno, and began a relationship with him. Joey was five feet eight and stocky, with dark hair and a mustache that belied his quiet, sensitive demeanor. Joey was thirty-four when they met, eight years older than Cathy. Cathy first mentioned Joey in her datebook on September 5, about a month after she moved to the trailer park. Cathy jotted in her datebook, *"Joey fixed plumbing for me."*

Joey worked for Preferred Plumbing. Crash, Mary's boyfriend, had also worked for Preferred until he and Mary started their own company. Joey was grateful for the job. Like Cathy in the wake of her DUI arrest, Joey was struggling at the time to get his life back on track.

Years earlier, when Joey was in his twenties, he had his own plumbing business, a wife, and two young sons. Joey's wife kept the books, as Mary did for Crash. Joey was making good money and felt successful for the first time in his life. But he also found that he didn't know how to be a good husband and father.

Joey never knew his own father. Joey's mother was an alcoholic who died when he was twelve. After that, Joey bounced between foster homes and group homes. When Joey was old enough, he joined the Marine Corps.

Joey spent three years in the Marines and got out in 1974, when he was twenty-one. The next year, he married his wife, and they started Poleno Plumbing. At the time, Joey did not realize the value of what he had. Joey loved his boys but felt he didn't know how to do things for them, perhaps because he never had a father himself. Joey had nothing growing up, and he thought he was missing out on something. Joey fell headlong into cocaine, liquor, and other women. Eight years into their marriage, Joey's wife left him and took their boys with her. Joey blamed himself.

Later, in hindsight, Joey believed he should have gotten help right then. He was still in his twenties. He still had his company. But after his wife left him, Joey discovered he didn't know how to run the business without her help. Joey was no good at bookkeeping or managing money. He found it hard to live with the choices he had made and how he had wrecked his family life. Joey used cocaine because it made him feel better about himself for a time, but the feeling never lasted. Joey suspected he had drug and emotional problems, but he was afraid to admit it. Joey felt he didn't know how to ask for help. Joey's slide continued.

After his marriage fell apart, Joey met and moved in with a woman who was divorced and had a young daughter. Joey lived with her for a few years. Joey's drug abuse worsened and landed him in jail. Joey was locked up when he learned the woman he had been living with had committed suicide. When he got out of jail, he checked himself in to the VA hospital in Long Beach. Joey asked for drug treatment but was too ashamed to reveal his emotional problems. Joey stayed at the VA for a month.

By that point, Joey had lost his company and had nothing to his name. Joey moved into a friend's house in the Valley and found work as a plumber for Preferred. Joey's boss issued him his own work truck, a green Ford pickup outfitted with pipe racks. For the first time in years, it seemed to Joey that his life was improving.

Such was the state of Joey's life in 1987 when, one night at a party, he met Cathy. Joey thought Cathy was pretty and sweet. They started talking and hit it off. Cathy went home with Joey that night, but they didn't have sex, just talked and cuddled. Joey sensed that he and Cathy were in the same boat, both trying to get their lives together.

Joey and Cathy went out on some dates, and they eventually had sex, but from the beginning, their relationship was more like a friendship than a torrid romance. Joey felt at the time that he couldn't handle being in a serious relationship, given his own problems and his guilt over his past failed relationships. Joey told Cathy it wouldn't be fair to her, that he had to make himself better first. Joey didn't want to mislead her. Joey thought Cathy understood. Joey cared about her and he believed she cared about him.

Joey and Cathy agreed they would be friends and could both see other people. He never felt any pressure from her about their relationship. Joey would have been happy for Cathy if she met someone who cared for her and could give her the type of relationship she deserved.

Not long after Joey met Cathy, he had to move out of his friend's house. Joey needed a place to stay and Cathy was behind on her bills. Cathy told Joey he could move in with her, into her trailer home, if he paid half the rent.

Joey moved into Cathy's trailer in late fall 1987. Joey already knew Mary and Crash from his job at Preferred Plumbing. Cathy told her mom, "I'm going to let him stay here, and he's going to help me pay the rent." Mary said okay, as long as Joey paid.

During the time they lived together, the last few months of Cathy's life, she and Joey slept side by side in her tiny trailer's double bed. Joey kept his boxers on and Cathy usually wore her blue gym sweats to sleep. The trailer was too small to have friends over, and Cathy and Joey both worked during the day, so they used the place as little more than a crash pad. Joey bought his own groceries and cooked for himself. Cathy almost always ate at her mom's trailer and kept her groceries there. Once in a while, on the weekend, Cathy made breakfast for Joey and herself.

Joey felt Cathy helped him out a lot, just by the way she listened to him and made him feel supported. Joey respected that Cathy was a hard worker and that she never had anything bad to say about anyone. Joey felt he could talk to Cathy about things at his job, or whatever was bothering him. Joey opened up to Cathy, a little at a time, about his emotional problems. Cathy encouraged Joey to get treatment and made sure he did. On October 22, the day after Cathy completed her DUI jail sentence, she wrote in her datebook, "*Took Joey to V.A.*" Joey thought he and Cathy were both comforted knowing someone else was there for them, that they were not alone.

Joey sometimes felt guilty that he and Cathy weren't having sex. Joey liked sex but it was difficult for him emotionally. The last time they tried, a few weeks before her murder, Joey felt too stressed to perform. Cathy didn't seem upset and just smiled at him.

Joey thought of himself and Cathy as close friends who lived together. Joey took Cathy to dinner a couple of times, to thank her. But he was wary of doing things, like going to the movies, that felt too close to what couples did. Joey thought it might send her the wrong signal. All Joey wanted from Cathy was friendship. Neither Cathy nor Joey had steady relationships with anyone else while they lived in the trailer.

Some nights, if Cathy had a date, she didn't come home. Other nights Joey didn't. They tried to respect each other's privacy. Joey did not ask Cathy where she had slept or whom she was seeing. Joey felt it would have been awkward for them to talk about, and none of his business, anyway. Nor did Cathy ever bother Joey about his personal life.

Away from the trailer, Cathy and Joey led separate lives. Joey did not hang out in the bars that Cathy frequented after work, like the Hunter and the Noble Inn. Nor did Joey spend much time, except in passing, with Cathy's other friends. Joey sometimes went out with his own friends, but less often. Most weeknights, Joey worked late, came home, showered, and crashed. Joey had nothing against Cathy going out with her friends and having a good time. In Joey's experience, girls liked to go out and have fun with their friends. Joey's attitude was, go have your fun.

When Joey first met Cathy, she was sober. They kept no liquor in the trailer, so Cathy never drank at home. It took a little while for Joey to see for himself that Cathy had a problem with alcohol. One night that Cathy had lent Joey her car, he drove to the bar where she was and found her there, wasted. Joey stayed with Cathy until the bar closed and drove her home. During the time Joey lived with Cathy, it was very unusual for her to get so drunk that she needed help getting home. Joey knew about her recent DUI arrest. Joey warned Cathy, "You've got to be careful."

Joey believed Cathy knew she had an alcohol problem. Given his own struggles with sobriety, he considered himself in no position to judge. Joey never saw Cathy use drugs, only alcohol.

Joey and Cathy were both mild-mannered and never really argued or fought while they lived together in the trailer. Cathy sometimes got annoyed with him, say, if he failed to clean up a mess, or if he came home from work tired and sweaty and lay on their bed without showering. Cathy tended to hold her feelings in when she got upset. Rather than confront Joey, she would go tell Mary and Crash and have them talk to Joey about it. Shortly before Cathy was killed, she told her mother that Joey was late with his half of the rent. Mary thought Cathy felt sorry for Joey and didn't want to have to throw him out.

Mary knew that what Cathy wanted most in life was to get married and have a family. Mary told her on more than one occasion that she was looking for love in all the wrong places, meaning in the bars. Mary thought she would have better luck finding a stable and more promising relationship if she met someone at work, or someplace else besides a bar.

Cathy did have a small circle of friends at Fedco, fellow cashiers in the grocery department with whom she often ate lunch and sometimes partied after work. When Cathy went out with her Fedco friends, they usually went to the Black Angus, a bar and restaurant on Roscoe Boulevard, not to her regular hangouts, the Hunter and the Noble.

Cathy's closest friend at work was probably Elliott Erving. Elliott was black and a few years younger than Cathy. Elliott was gay but was not out to most of his straight friends. Elliott told Cathy he was gay soon after they met. Cathy kept Elliott's confidence. Elliott considered Cathy a good friend. Elliott felt everyone at work liked and got along with Cathy.

Cathy also confided to Elliott about things in her own life. In the weeks before she was killed, Cathy mentioned to Elliott that she liked a guy, Luis Romero, who worked in the meat department at Fedco. Knowing how much Cathy wanted to meet someone, Elliott took it upon himself to let Luis know that Cathy was interested. Elliott then informed Cathy that he had talked to Luis.

The day after Cathy's murder, Mary found on the nightstand in Cathy's trailer two pages of steno pad paper, on which Cathy had handwritten what appeared to be two drafts of a letter. The first page read:

Just a few things I would like to discuss with you & get straight. I don't want you to feel like I'm putting you in a spot or anything like that.

I'll admit that I like you. I would like to go out with you. I didn't have Elliott talk to you. He seen that I was interested, he asked me and I said yes I was interested, that's all that was said. He then took it into his hands and decided to find out how you felt. I'm sorry if that made you uncomfortable. He said something about you being in an alcohol program. I would like to talk to you about that because I'm going thru the same thing, maybe not exact, but something like that.

I'd like to be able to talk to you about it. I could use a good friend & ear. I have a good ear also. I don't know how to get ahold of you, but I would at least like you to be honest with me. I don't like rejection, I'm sure you don't either.

The second draft of the letter Cathy wrote read:

I would like to talk to you sometime when we can get away from work. I'm not trying to put you in a spot. I didn't have Elliott try to get us together. He did that all on his own. But I am interested. If there is anything wrong with that I would like to know. I see that your kind of shy, but so am I. When I see you and you see me we both smile. There must be something

there as I get all excited. I have problems and I know you do too. Maybe
we can help each other. Would you please consider going out to dinner or
a movie and talking, not partying but just talk? I would like that very much.
Please respond ASAP. I need someone to share what's going on in my life.
You're not alone.

At the time Mary found the letter, she had no idea who Elliott was, other than someone Cathy must have worked with at Fedco. Nor did Mary know who the intended recipient of Cathy's letter was. Whether Cathy ever wrote a final version of her letter and gave it to Luis is unknown.

Luis Romero died in 1998 at age twenty-eight, under unusual circumstances. The *Los Angeles Times* reported that he died after he was taken into custody by the LAPD on a felony warrant for a different man with the same name. Luis was held at the Devonshire station for three hours until the case of mistaken identity was confirmed. While being released, Luis began having seizures and lapsed into unconsciousness, the *Times* reported. A hospital spokesman told the *Times* that "there were no initial signs of violence" and "no evidence of a struggle." The article also noted that the LAPD had "*ruled the incident a 'law enforcement-related death' rather than a 'death in custody' because Romero was technically a free man when he began having convulsions.*"

That Mary never met Luis Romero is not surprising. Although Cathy made friends wherever she went, her various circles of friends barely overlapped, and even then only fleetingly. Many of Cathy's good friends knew little of one another and never socialized together.

Cathy had one circle of friends from the bars, primarily the Hunter and the Noble. Cathy's closest friend in that circle was Bonnie, her onetime roommate. Bonnie was not acquainted with Cathy's circle of friends from Fedco, whom Cathy worked with full time, because they partied elsewhere. Nor did Bonnie know Joey. Cathy did not meet Joey until after she moved out of Bonnie's place. Joey never interacted with Cathy's work friends, and he was not a regular at the Hunter or the Noble Inn.

Cathy's closest girlfriend other than Bonnie was Jordan Weiner. Bonnie and Jordan knew each other, but only as mutual friends of Cathy, since Jordan did not frequent the bars. Jordan was Cathy's oldest friend, and also her best friend, from the time they met at age fourteen until the end of Cathy's life twelve years later.

Cathy and Jordan's friendship began during the summer of 1976, just before they started tenth grade together at Grant High School in Van Nuys. Jordan and Cathy lived across the driveway from each other in a small apartment complex on Burbank Boulevard. Cathy had just moved back to Los Angeles with her mother and her older brother, Joe. Jordan was living with her mom, a single mother like Mary.

Mary, Cathy, and Joe had moved there from Iowa after Mary left Ed Postma, her second husband and Cathy's father. Mary left Ed because he was an alcoholic and physically abused her. Later, when Cathy was sixteen, she went back to the Midwest and lived with her father for a few months. Cathy's stay with her father ended after Ed hit her one night for turning up the thermostat too high. Ed died in August 1988, seven months after Cathy's murder, from an alcohol-induced brain aneurysm.

Cathy and Jordan talked a lot about their childhoods and became fast friends. As teenagers, Cathy and Jordan were so inseparable that Mary joked they were joined at the hip. For fun, Cathy and Jordan did things like go shopping together on Ventura Boulevard or hitchhike to the beach. Cathy and Jordan hitchhiked all over the Valley, anywhere they needed to go. When they were old enough, Cathy and Jordan learned to drive together. Jordan's first car was a Chevy Corvair. On Wednesday nights, they took Jordan's car cruising on Van Nuys Boulevard, where they flirted with boys in souped-up cars. Neither Cathy nor Jordan had a steady boyfriend during high school.

Jordan took a photography class at school and it became her hobby. Jordan made Cathy her photography subject. One testament to the depth and longevity of Cathy and Jordan's friendship is that most of the photographs taken of Cathy while she was alive were either shot by Jordan, or Jordan is also in the photo.

Cathy left high school at the end of eleventh grade, after she passed her high school proficiency exam, an option for students in California at the time. Cathy was bored with school and eager to start working. In 1979, when she turned eighteen, she was hired by the phone company PacBell. Mary felt very proud of Cathy.

Cathy and Jordan's friendship became even closer later that same year, after Jordan's mother died. Cathy and Jordan moved into their own place, a dank little apartment in North Hollywood. Cathy and Jordan lived there together for more than a year, the first time either of them had had her own place.

Cathy worked at PacBell for two or three years, until she was fired for

Cathy as photographed by Jordan during high school, circa late 1970s

one too many times staying out late partying and not showing up on time the next morning. Mary and Jordan looked back on it as a turning point in Cathy's life, the first sign that she had a drinking problem, as well as the first time she paid a heavy price for it.

Cathy found another job, at a Thrifty's drugstore, but quit after her manager made a pass at her. By then, Cathy was twenty-one. To pay her bills, Cathy started bartending at beer and wine bars. Mary didn't like the idea, but Cathy needed to have some income. Cathy bounced between bartending and other part-time jobs until Fedco hired her.

Jordan and Cathy remained close friends and party girls well into their early twenties. Jordan was working as a secretary for a real estate agent who lived in the Hollywood Hills. Cathy and Jordan would get dolled up and go over to her boss's house for a drink, then go hang out in the little bars on the Sunset Strip. Jordan was friends with a bartender at the Coconut Teaszer, a nightclub on Sunset Boulevard popular in the 1980s. Cathy and Jordan had a lot of fun nights, out on the town, in that period of their lives.

Cathy took the only true vacation of her life with Jordan, a weeklong trip to Hawaii in 1985 to see Cathy's brother Joe, who was stationed there with the navy.

Cathy at Jordan's boss's home in the Hollywood Hills, circa 1985

In August 1987, when Cathy turned twenty-six, Jordan organized a surprise birthday party for her at the Hunter. In those days, before email and cell phones, it was hard to round up a crowd. Fewer people showed up than Jordan hoped, but she and Cathy had a good time anyway, as they always did together. It turned out to be the last birthday that Cathy celebrated.

Jordan saw less of Cathy during the last month or so of Cathy's life. Jordan was busy studying for her licensing exam to become a real estate broker. Jordan found out she passed her broker exam in late December 1987, two weeks before Cathy's murder. Cathy and Jordan went out together, like old times, to celebrate Jordan's achievement.

The final photograph taken of Cathy alive was a snapshot of her with Mary, Jordan, and Cathy's eldest brother, Danny. The four of them went out one night in early January to listen to live music. That night proved to be the last time Jordan ever saw her best friend. In the photo, everyone is smiling, blind to Cathy's fate and the tragedy that lay only days away.

On Wednesday, January 13, the day before her murder, Cathy removed from her trailer a small beige file box. The box contained Cathy's important personal papers, such as her Fedco pay stubs and life insurance policy, Red Cross blood donor card, and assorted business cards that she had

*Cathy and Jordan at the Hunter during Cathy's
twenty-sixth birthday party, August 29, 1987*

*Left to right: Mary Postma, Cathy Braley, Jordan Weiner, and
Danny Braley, January 1988*

received at one time or another. Cathy walked the box over to her mother's trailer and gave it to her. "Will you put these away somewhere they'll be safe?" Cathy asked Mary.

"What's going on?" Mary said.

"No, I just don't want them over there in that trailer," Cathy replied.

At the time, Mary assumed Cathy's request had something to do with Joey. Later, too late to ask, Mary wondered whether Cathy gave her the box for safekeeping because she sensed that something might happen to her.

Among the business cards Cathy had in the box was one that she had received from Bob Waters. Waters worked for the L.A. County Sheriff's Department, the other major local law enforcement agency in Los Angeles besides the LAPD. The LAPD's jurisdiction was the City of Los Angeles, while the sheriff's department ran the city's jails and policed areas of Los Angeles County outside the city limits. Cathy knew Waters from the Hunter bar, where they were both longtime regulars.

Mary never associated with Waters herself, but she knew of him through Cathy. Cathy was friendly enough with Waters that once, several months before her murder, he took her to a gun range to practice shooting, just for fun. Cathy brought home her bullet-riddled paper target, proud of how good a shot she was, and showed it off to her mother.

Mary assumed that the gun range Waters took Cathy to was supposed to be for police personnel only. "Oh, they just let anybody out there?" Mary asked her.

"I'm not just anybody," Cathy said.

In January 1988, when Cathy was killed, Waters was forty-one years old and had been a sheriff's deputy for nearly twenty years, almost half his life. By 1984, Waters had risen to the rank of sergeant in the sheriff's Narcotic Bureau. At the time, law enforcement's self-proclaimed "War on Drugs" was rising in intensity.

In mid-1987, after three years as a narcotics supervisor at the sheriff's East L.A. station, Waters was reassigned to a joint task force at Los Angeles International Airport. The purpose of the task force was to detect and

Sgt. Robert D. Waters's business card in Cathy Braley's file box (1988)

interdict narcotics smuggling on commercial flights into and out of LAX. The joint task force consisted of narcotics investigators and supervisors from three main law enforcement agencies: the federal Drug Enforcement Agency, the L.A. County Sheriff's Department, and the LAPD.

Waters and the small team of deputies he supervised on the LAX task force became known within the Sheriff's Department, semiofficially, as the LAX Crew. Waters and his crew worked in plain clothes and were each issued a county-owned unmarked car to drive on the job.

The joint task force operated from a single shared office at LAX. Investigators assigned to the task force worked on cases together hand in hand, and often interchangeably, irrespective of which of the three agencies employed them. This arrangement sometimes placed Waters, a sheriff's deputy, in the rare and unorthodox position of supervising LAPD detectives on the task force, in addition to the deputies under his direct command as sergeant of the LAX Crew.

On Friday, January 8, 1988, six nights before Cathy was killed, tragedy struck the L.A. County Sheriff's Department. Around seven o'clock that evening, two hours after sundown, a pair of deputies assigned to the Narcotic Bureau attempted to serve a search warrant at a suspected crack house, in the area of the city then known as South Central Los Angeles.

One of the deputies, thirty-three-year-old narcotics detective Jack Miller, was shot in the head as he entered the house, just inside the front door. In the gunfight that ensued, Miller's partner was wounded. The suspect who shot Miller, a twenty-year-old black male named Edward Walker, was found dead in the house after the raid, apparently by his own hand. Five firearms and 202 grams of crack cocaine were also recovered inside.

Miller had been a sheriff's deputy for twelve years and was married with two young daughters. Miller initially survived the shooting and was rushed to the hospital. A Sheriff's Department helicopter was dispatched to pick up Miller's family and deliver them to his bedside. Miller underwent seven hours of surgery but was declared brain-dead the following night, on Saturday, January 9. Miller's wife allowed her husband's organs, including his heart and corneas, to be donated for transplant.

Miller was beloved by his family, friends, and fellow deputies. To this day, more than thirty years after his death, new heartfelt remembrances of Miller regularly appear on his Officer Down memorial page, posted there by those who knew him in life and have never forgotten his character and sacrifice. The collective portrait of Miller that emerges from his memorial testimonials is that of a soft-spoken, kind man with a sly sense of humor, admired by many who worked with him during his twelve-year career.

Miller's funeral was planned for Thursday morning, January 14, in Granada Hills, not far from Van Nuys. That Thursday morning, Cathy woke in her trailer at about eight o'clock. Cathy showered in the trailer park's shower house and got dressed for work. Cathy wore green pants and a red blouse that day. Fedco employees wore store-issued yellow smocks at work, over their clothes. Each smock had a small embroi-

Cathy's Fedco ID badge

dered patch on the front that indicated the employee's job. The patch on Cathy's smock read REGISTER CHECKER. Cathy also wore a Fedco ID badge clipped to her smock.

As Cathy did most mornings after she got dressed, she went to her mother's trailer to blow-dry her hair and apply her makeup. Cathy had coffee with Mary until about nine thirty, when Mary drove her to Fedco. Cathy's workday started at ten. Before Cathy left the car, she gave her mother a kiss goodbye. Mary watched Cathy walk to the entrance of Fedco and go inside. It was the last time Mary saw her daughter alive.

Deputy Jack Miller's funeral was heavily attended by many of his fellow deputies in the sheriff's Narcotic Bureau. The same weekend Miller was killed, at least four other police officers across Southern California were seriously injured in unrelated violent attacks.

Among the deputies who attended Miller's funeral were Waters, the sergeant who was a regular at the Hunter, and two deputies who worked for him on the multiagency task force at LAX, Bob Mallon and Mike Turner. Mallon and Turner had been partners on the LAX Crew for about a year, leading up to January 1988.

At that time, Mallon was thirty-six years old and had been a deputy for eighteen years. He was married with two children. Mallon's assignment to the LAX task force began at the start of 1986, two years earlier. Mallon died in 2015, at age sixty-four.

Turner was thirty-nine years old and fifteen years into his career as a sheriff's deputy. Turner joined the LAX Crew in early 1987. Turner's full name, incidentally, is Michael Lewis Turner. The fact that Turner's middle name is Lewis was never documented by the LAPD in 1988, anywhere in the murder book for Cathy's case.

After Miller's funeral, a number of deputies assigned to the sheriff's Narcotic Bureau decided to go out for lunch together, to reminiscence about their fallen friend and talk about what had happened. Waters suggested they go to the Hunter because it was close by and served good sandwiches.

More than fifteen deputies, among them Waters, Mallon, and Turner, drove to the Hunter, most of them in their unmarked county-issued cars. All later reported that they considered themselves off duty. The group arrived at the Hunter around half past one that Thursday afternoon. Only Waters had been to the bar previously.

The owner of the Hunter, George Zedar, was at the bar that day. He knew Waters as a regular customer. Waters explained that they had come from the funeral of a deputy who was killed. The deputies, still dressed in the suits they wore to the funeral, sat down at a few tables and ordered lunch. Most drank beer with their lunch.

After they ate, some of the deputies in the group peeled off and left, in ones and twos, most between two and four that afternoon. Waters, Mallon, Turner, and several other deputies remained at the Hunter to continue talking and drinking. Some of the deputies started to play darts together.

Zedar, the owner, left the bar for the day at four o'clock. When Zedar left, none of the deputies appeared intoxicated to him or were creating any problems.

Cathy called and spoke to her mother twice that day, first from Fedco, around four. Earlier in the day, one of Cathy's girlfriends had called Mary and offered to pick Cathy up from work. Mary relayed the message. Cathy said she didn't want a ride from her friend but didn't say why. Cathy's friend never called Mary back, so Mary never gave her Cathy's message.

One reason Cathy may have declined a ride from her friend is that she had made plans to go out with some of her friends from Fedco later that night, after they got off work. Thursday, January 14 was a payday for Fedco employees. Cathy, Elliott, and a few of the other cashiers in the grocery department talked about meeting up at the Hunter for a few cocktails and then going out dancing in West Hollywood.

Cathy got off work at seven o'clock. Soon after, she walked by herself to the Hunter.

Elliott was delayed getting to the bar to meet Cathy. On Elliott's way out of Fedco, an assistant manager stopped him and asked him to work late. A shipment of food had just arrived and he wanted Elliot to help unpack it. Elliott knew if he didn't say yes, Fedco might cut his hours. By the time Elliott finished the extra work, it was after nine. Elliott walked to the Hunter and went into the bar. Elliott had never set foot inside the Hunter before, and he never went back again after that night.

The bar seemed crowded to Elliott, mostly with white men and not many women. Elliott didn't see Cathy, only people he didn't know sitting at the bar and around a few tables talking, drinking beer, and listening to music on the jukebox. Elliott did not consider the possibility that Cathy might be in the ladies' room. Elliott assumed Cathy and their other friends who planned to meet there had already left and he had missed them, because he was stuck working late. Elliott soon left. Cathy's other Fedco friends felt tired after work and never made it to the bar at all.

Cathy called Mary from the Hunter at about eight. Cathy did not sound drunk to Mary when she called. Cathy asked for a friend's phone number and Mary gave it to her. Mary told Cathy to call her later if she needed a ride home from the bar. Mary warned Cathy, "Don't you walk home." Cathy told her mother not to worry.

Mary was home all night, but Cathy never called again. Mary cooked dinner, spaghetti and garlic toast, for herself, Crash, and Danny, Cathy's eldest brother. Joey also came over from Cathy's trailer, at Mary's invitation, and ate dinner with them. After dinner, the four of them watched a movie, *The African Queen*, an old Katharine Hepburn film. The movie ended between eleven and eleven thirty. Joey went back to Cathy's trailer, just across the driveway, within shouting distance of Mary's trailer. That late on a Thursday night, the trailer park was quiet enough that Mary would have heard Joey's truck start if he had driven anywhere later that night. Mary did not hear Joey's truck start the rest of the night, after he went home following the movie.

At the Hunter, meanwhile, more regulars came into the bar as the evening went on. Among the regulars in the bar that night, besides Cathy and Waters, were Bonnie and Noel. Noel was there with a friend of his, Billy Clay, who was also a regular at the Hunter. Billy worked for a security company that had an office down the street from the bar. Like Noel, Billy was black and in his early forties at the time.

Bonnie arrived at the Hunter sometime between eight and nine o'clock, after she finished her shift as a bartender at another bar. Bonnie was used to seeing certain people when she walked into the Hunter. That night, Bonnie saw some familiar faces but mostly men in suits, very unusual for a Thursday night at a workaday neighborhood bar. The only person Bonnie recognized in the group was Bob Waters. Bonnie knew Waters but considered him an acquaintance, not a friend. Bonnie's long-standing impression of Waters was that he was a big-mouthed blowhard and a heavy drinker.

Bonnie went to the bar and ordered her usual drink, a club soda. The bartender on duty at the Hunter that night was an attractive blonde in her late thirties named Maruska.

Bonnie asked Maruska who the men were. Maruska told Bonnie they were policemen who had come in after a funeral. Maruska said they had been there since early afternoon. Bonnie heard one of the men say that they had "buried one of their own," and that a "nigger" had killed him. Throughout the night, Bonnie heard the same racial epithet, "nigger," thrown around repeatedly in jokes and conversations among the deputies. It appeared to Bonnie that most of the policemen were either already drunk or well on their way to it. Bonnie may have been the only person in the bar that night who remained completely sober for the entire night.

The mood in the bar felt tense and depressed to Bonnie, nothing like the fun and friendly atmosphere she expected and was accustomed to at the Hunter. Bonnie sensed from the deputies a mix of grief, anger, and fear, an emotional undercurrent that, while not as explicit as the racial tension in the air, nonetheless felt palpable to Bonnie. Early in the night, when the tension felt thickest, Bonnie thought to herself, "God, I hope it's not one of those nights."

Bonnie had been a regular at the Hunter for long enough that she had experienced Irish wakes and other sad occasions there, after friends of the bar had died, albeit of natural causes, not violently. That night felt much different to Bonnie because she did not know any of the well-dressed men, except for Waters, and there were a lot of them in the bar. Bonnie felt sympathy for the deputies, for the loss of their friend. But given the anger and volatility Bonnie sensed, her inclination was to give them their space rather than engage with them. Noel and Billy, seated at the end of the bar, seemed to be doing much the same as Bonnie, minding their own business.

Bonnie was happy to find Cathy sitting at the bar. Bonnie and Cathy had not seen each other for a few weeks, since before Christmas, so they had a lot to talk about and catch up on. Bonnie had just celebrated her birthday a week or so earlier. Cathy asked Bonnie if she wanted to go out to lunch the next day, Friday. Bonnie told Cathy she had some mail for her to pick up at her house. Cathy said she would come by between noon and one on Friday. Cathy never made it.

As the night went on, Bonnie sensed that the mood in the bar lightened up a little and became more relaxed. Bonnie attributed it to the fact that everyone, except for her, had had more to drink. Another factor may have been that the crowd started to thin out. It was a Thursday night, and many of the regulars had to get up early for work the next morning. Eventually, all the remaining deputies in the original lunch party also called it a night and went home, with the exception of three: Waters, Mallon, and Turner.

At some point, Mallon came over to where Bonnie and Cathy were sitting at the bar. Mallon asked Bonnie if she wanted a drink.

"I don't drink," Bonnie replied. Mallon sat down on the barstool next to Bonnie and continued talking her up. Mallon asked Bonnie what she did for a living. Bonnie told him, then asked Mallon the same question.

"I work for the government," Mallon said.

"That's ridiculous. What do you do?"

Mallon told Bonnie he was a police officer. Bonnie asked Mallon where he worked and he mentioned something about the airport. During Mallon and Bonnie's initial conversation at the bar, he also volunteered that he was not married, which was untrue, although Bonnie had no way to know it at the time. Bonnie was not so naive as just to take Mallon's word for it. As was her habit with men who flirted with her, Bonnie stole a glance at Mallon's left hand and saw he wasn't wearing a wedding band. Nor did Bonnie see a pale tan line on Mallon's ring finger. Bonnie always checked for the telltale tan line. As a rule, Bonnie didn't flirt with married men.

Bonnie thought Mallon looked handsome in his nice suit. She also found Mallon amusing to talk with, at first. But she had no intention of doing anything with him beyond flirting. Bonnie might have considered going out on a date with Mallon, had they met under different circumstances, and had he been sober, which he wasn't when they met. When Mallon first approached Bonnie, he seemed to her only a little drunk. But Mallon was still drinking and didn't seem to be slowing down.

Mallon, Bonnie, Cathy, and some others at the bar started playing a drinking game together, 7-11-21. Whoever lost had to buy a round of shots called a "blow job." Bonnie played along, even though she didn't drink. After Bonnie lost one game, Mallon joked to Bonnie that she owed him a blow job. Bonnie wrote "IOU" and her nickname, "Bon Bon," on the back of a business card and gave it to Mallon.

Throughout the night, Bonnie and Cathy interacted much more with Mallon than with either Waters or Turner. When Mallon first started flirting with Bonnie, he mentioned that he was there with his partner and pointed out Turner in the bar. Turner said hello to Bonnie but did not join their conversation. Turner said little to Cathy and Bonnie the rest of the night while Bonnie was there.

Bonnie prided herself on her ability to read people. She had had lots of practice, as an attractive single woman who worked as a bartender, at reading people's vibes. Bonnie's reaction to Turner, from the moment she met him, was that he was not someone she would ever want to be alone with. Bonnie considered Turner fairly handsome, but he radiated an intensity and coldness that unnerved her. Turner struck Bonnie as the type of person she needed to watch like a hawk.

Bonnie's wariness of Turner persisted throughout the night. During some of the time Mallon mingled with Bonnie and Cathy at the bar, Turner and Waters played darts and shot pool together. The rest of the time, Turner sat quietly by himself, away from the bar, at a small table near the Hunter's windows that looked out on Raymer Street. Although Bonnie saw Turner was drinking steadily, and his eyes appeared glassy, he did not get loud or obnoxious. All night, Bonnie was conscious of Turner, silent and beady eyed, as he sat and watched her, Cathy, Mallon, and others converse at the bar. The way Turner intently watched the room reminded Bonnie of a jaguar silently stalking its prey.

Up to that point in the night, Bonnie thought of Mallon as funny and entertaining. Bonnie could tell Mallon was trying hard to charm her. The more Mallon drank, the more overt and insistent his flirting with Bonnie became. At one point, Mallon told Bonnie that he owned a cabin in Parker, Arizona. Mallon said he and Turner were going to the cabin that weekend, on vacation. Mallon said Bonnie should come with them. Mallon told Bonnie she'd have a wonderful weekend with him and his partner.

Bonnie looked at Mallon like, "Yeah, right." Bonnie said, "I just met you. Why would I go with you and another guy to a cabin? Get real."

When Mallon extended the invitation to Bonnie to go to his cabin, Cathy was sitting at the bar on Bonnie's right, the opposite side from Mallon. Cathy had also been drinking steadily all night.

Cathy extended her arm to Bonnie and said, "Read my palm." It was the same favor Cathy had asked of Bonnie a few years earlier, at the start of their friendship. Bonnie considered herself a psychic intuitive, not a palm reader. Bonnie knew what she meant was, "What do you see for me?" Bonnie called the readings she did "looking."

"I don't look for people when they're drunk," Bonnie told Cathy. Bonnie said she would "look" for her the next day, when she came over to pick up her mail, if she was still interested then. Cathy said okay.

A little while later, Mallon asked Bonnie to dance. Bonnie agreed. While Bonnie and Mallon were dancing, Bonnie heard Mallon say, "Lookie, lookie." Bonnie looked down and saw that Mallon had pulled out his penis.

Bonnie was shocked and disgusted. "I'm an ex-nurse. I've seen more wieners than Oscar Mayer," Bonnie blurted. Bonnie left Mallon on the dance floor and went back to the bar, where she resumed her seat next to Cathy. Bonnie assumed Mallon did it as a joke, but she didn't think it was funny.

Ten minutes or so after Mallon exposed himself to Bonnie while they were dancing, he sat back down next to Bonnie, to her left, at the bar. Bonnie ignored him.

Waters also came over and stood between Bonnie's and Mallon's barstools, right behind them. All night, Waters had moved around the barroom, shuttling between Mallon at the bar, Turner's side table, and the pool table and dartboard.

Waters asked Bonnie, "Why are you acting like a virgin?"

"Because your friend is disgusting and whipped out his dick, and I'm not amused," Bonnie replied.

After Bonnie said that, Mallon pulled out his penis and exposed himself to Bonnie again, this time at the bar.

"Put that away," Bonnie said.

Bonnie was certain Waters saw Mallon do it the second time, at the bar, because Waters was standing right there. Bonnie didn't know who else saw Mallon expose himself, either time, but the Hunter was a small bar.

Bonnie felt it was Waters's responsibility to keep his friends, who he brought into the bar, from acting like animals. At the very least, Bonnie wanted Waters to tell Mallon to knock it off. Waters just laughed, as if Mallon was being the life of the party by pulling out his penis in the middle of a bar.

"You people are really disgusting," Bonnie said. Bonnie went back to talking to Cathy, seated to her right, and tried to ignore the deputies.

Bonnie saw Mallon signal to the barmaid, Maruska, to meet him in the kitchen. Mallon had evidently befriended Maruska sometime earlier that day. Bonnie only knew Maruska superficially, not as a friend. Mallon and Maruska went into the kitchen for a few minutes, then returned to the barroom. Bonnie did not see what Mallon and Maruska did while they were in the kitchen.

When Mallon and Maruska came back, a faster song was playing on the jukebox. Mallon and Maruska danced together, just for a song or two, after which she went back to serving drinks from behind the bar. Cathy was standing near the jukebox at the time. Mallon asked Cathy to dance with him. Cathy and Mallon danced to a couple of slow songs, for about ten minutes. Bonnie thought they were both drunk, but not slovenly so, just sort of hanging on to each other on the dance floor. Bonnie did not see Mallon and Cathy kiss or do anything salacious as they danced together.

Not long after Cathy and Mallon stopped dancing, there was tension between Mallon and Noel, who had been sitting at the far end of the bar with his friend Billy all evening. Cathy had given Noel a hug, which apparently angered Mallon.

"What is she, a fucking nigger lover?" Mallon said to Bonnie.

"No, they're friends," Bonnie said.

"What are you, a fucking nigger lover?" Mallon asked Bonnie.

Bonnie's father had been in the navy and raised her not to be racist. But at that moment, Bonnie hoped to defuse things, not throw fuel on the fire. "It's irrelevant whether I am or not," Bonnie said.

"Well, we were at a funeral for my friend who got shot by a nigger," Mallon sputtered.

"I'm out to have a good time," Bonnie said. "Let's have a good time."

Bonnie felt she needed a break and went to the ladies' room. Bonnie stayed in the bathroom for ten or fifteen minutes, playing with her makeup. When Bonnie came back, Noel was on the other side of the bar from where he had been sitting with Billy. Noel seemed very angry and was arguing with Mallon, Turner, and Waters.

"What's going on?" Bonnie asked Mallon.

"He asked me to step outside," Mallon said, referring to Noel.

Mallon went off on another tirade about nigger this, nigger that, until Noel said, "If you want to take it outside, let's take it outside."

Bonnie was between Mallon and Noel and tried to play peacemaker. "I don't know why you both don't shut up, because I'm here for a good time." Waters, who knew Noel as a regular at the Hunter, also got between them to break it up. Soon after things began to calm down, Noel and Billy left the bar. The deputies stayed. Bonnie thought Noel and Billy left because they were outnumbered and too smart to be provoked into a fistfight with a bunch of drunk cops.

Noel Warnick died in 2012, at age sixty-nine. Back in 1988, Noel was interviewed by the LAPD on January 15, the day after Cathy's murder. Noel lived in the apartment building at 8123 Sepulveda Boulevard, right next to where Cathy's body was found.

According to his 1988 typed witness statement, Noel told the LAPD:

> I was at the Hunter last night. I took a cab and I arrived about 9:00 P.M. I was with Cathy at the bar talking—I also talked to other customers—as well as sheriffs who were customers. I got into an argument with a cop I don't know because he said to Cathy, "How about a blow-job?" The cop was a male/white/5-9/160/27/34 years. I was asked to leave the bar after arguing with the sheriff.
>
> A friend of mine, "Billy," was with me. He is black, his phone number is 897-3836. He lives at 12577 Mercer. I walked home and watched the eleven o'clock news after getting food. I have lived here for about one year. I live alone.
>
> I know Cathy because we both frequent the Hunter. I remember talking to Bob Waters, in fact, he gave me his card. I thought he had a friend named Louis who was at the Hunter last night too. I thought he said Louis worked Narco Division.
>
> Cathy and I were good friends. She spent the night with me about a month ago. We had sex. We are just good friends. I don't know why Cathy was in this area.

Billy Clay died in 2016, at age seventy. Billy was not interviewed by the LAPD in 1988 until May 6, almost four months after Cathy was killed. The detective who interviewed Billy in 1988 was Steve Hooks, the same detective who had worked on the Sherri Rasmussen murder case a little less than two years earlier. Sherri's murder was still unsolved in 1988 when Cathy was killed.

Billy's 1988 LAPD typed witness statement reads in full:

> I got to the Hunter Bar around nine or nine thirty. Noel was already there. I know Cathy from the bar, but not personally. Cathy was with the sheriffs

and the conversation got pretty raunchy. Noel had words with one of the sheriff's [sic] and I grabbed him and told him to leave. We left about 11:00 p.m. and went to another bar at Roscoe and Sepulveda Pl. We stayed there until about 12:15 a.m., then went to a Mexican restaurant at Sepulveda and Roscoe. We got food and went and stood in front of Noel's apartment (8123 Sepulveda) building and ate. I finished and went to a girlfriend's in Van Nuys. I got to my girlfriend's around 1:00 a.m. I did not see anything unusual or anybody standing outside. I spoke with Noel about two weeks ago. He asked me if the police had spoken to me yet.

Once Billy and Noel left the Hunter that night, there were only a handful of people who remained in the bar, including Cathy and Bonnie; the three deputies, Waters, Mallon, and Turner; and Maruska, the Hunter's bartender. By then, it was almost eleven. Bonnie looked at the clock because she needed to get home to relieve her babysitter.

At the time, Bonnie was sitting at the bar between Cathy and Mallon. Bonnie knew Cathy had walked to the Hunter from work and didn't have her car. Bonnie told Cathy, "I've got to go. Let me take you home."

"I want to stay here," Cathy said.

Bonnie could tell by the way Cathy was looking past her at Mallon, on Bonnie's other side, that Cathy was attracted to him. Bonnie thought, "When I leave, she's probably going to go right for him."

By that point in the night, Bonnie's opinion of Mallon was that he was a drunken asshole. But Bonnie sensed no malice from Mallon toward Cathy. Nor did Bonnie suspect that any harm was likely to come to Cathy by leaving her in a bar where she was a well-known and well-liked regular, in the company of three police officers. Cathy appeared drunk to Bonnie, but not sloppy drunk. Bonnie felt Cathy still had most of her wits about her. Bonnie thought to herself, "You know what, she's going to come over tomorrow, but I wish she'd come with me now."

Bonnie pleaded with Cathy to let her give her a ride. "Are you sure? Because I don't mind," Bonnie told her.

"No, no, I don't want to leave yet," Cathy insisted. Cathy said she would be okay and would call her mother if she needed a ride.

Bonnie knew she would not be able to persuade Cathy to come with her against her will. Bonnie had kids at home and couldn't keep her babysitter waiting.

Bonnie told Cathy she would see her tomorrow when she came over to pick up her mail. When Bonnie left the Hunter, right around eleven o'clock, Cathy and Mallon were sitting at the bar, side by side, engrossed in conversation. Bonnie never saw Cathy again.

Maruska, the bartender, was interviewed by the LAPD the day after Cathy's murder. Maruska's January 15, 1988, typed LAPD witness statement reads in full:

> I am the bartender at Hunter's. I have worked here for one year. I know Cathy, she is a regular customer. I closed the bar last night at 1:00 A.M.
>
> I saw Cathy leave at midnight. I saw her outside with Bob Waters and two of his friends—one friend was named Mike—I don't know the other one. I heard some commotion outside. I looked out. I saw everyone laughing and Cathy down on the ground in a puddle of water laughing too.
>
> Mike is male/white. He was wearing a beige suit. He is 5-9/165/43/45 years.
>
> The other guy is male/white, shorter than Mike, about 5-8/180/38/40 years with a mustache, blond hair and wearing a white shirt.
>
> Cathy was a very friendly girl—she made friends with everyone. She is known to be a promiscuous party girl. Cathy was very drunk last night.

Bob Mallon died in 2015. Mallon's initial interview with the LAPD in 1988 took place on the morning of January 16, just shy of thirty-six hours after Cathy's murder. Mallon's first 1988 typed LAPD witness statement reads in full:

> I have been with LASO for about eighteen years. I am assigned to Narcotic Enforcement out of LAX. On 1/14/88, I went to a funeral in Granada Hills for a friend who was killed a few days ago. After the funeral, Sgt. Waters (Bob Waters) suggested that some of us go to a bar and have a few drinks. About twenty of us went to a bar called Hunters somewhere in the valley. I don't know exactly where it is. I'm not familiar with the valley. It was the first time I had ever been in the area.
>
> We got there between one and two (1300-1400 Hrs). While I was there, I drank, danced, played pool and had a good time. I started drinking beer and then Gin and then Whiskey. I got drunk. I mean I was drunk to the bone.
>
> While I was there, I met a lot of girls. I met a heavy set one but I don't recall her name. I don't know if I ever knew her name. She was drunk too. She lifted her shirt a couple of times in the bar and showed her tits to everyone in the bar. She did that a couple of times.

I remember there was an argument while I was in the bar. A black guy named Noel got into a little hassle with Mike (Turner, Mike). I don't know why they were arguing but it only lasted for a short while. When the argument was going on, I was sitting next to that girl. She was heavy set and had dark hair.

At about 11:30 or midnight (2330–2400 Hrs) me, Mike (Turner, Mike) and Bob (Waters, Robert) left. We all walked out together with that girl. She was drunk and couldn't even walk. She fell down at least once and maybe twice. I was just as drunk as she was. Bob and Mike left and she got into my car. We all got to the bar in our own cars. I was driving a 1985 Chevrolet Celebrity, gold, license #1NLB447. It's a county car and it's the car assigned to me.

After she got in my car, Mike checked on me to see if I was O.K. I gave him the high sign and told him I was O.K. He left in his own car. I don't know where Bob went but he left a few minutes prior to Mike. After that, the girl and I played a little kissy face. I decided to leave the area and drove for about two or three minutes. We parked on a residential street. It was well lit and I think it was west of Sepulveda. I'm not sure where I was. I was drunk and lost.

After we stopped we played kissy face for a while and she took off her clothes. I dropped my pants and tried to fuck her. We stayed in the front seat because the seats lay all the way back. I couldn't fuck her, I was too drunk. She did give me a blow job and that's all. It took about 5–10 minutes and then we got dressed.

After all that, she got mad or upset. She said she had to go. I offered her a ride and she said no. I said O.K. and she got out of the car. She walked in some direction but I don't know which. I started up the car and made a U-turn. I drove for a few blocks and hit a main street. I stopped at a gas station and got some directions to the freeway. I got on the freeway and drove home. I didn't stop to sleep, I just drove home. I hit the shoulder a few times but I made it. I got home home [sic] between 1:30 and 2:00 (0130–0200 Hrs). In fact, I think it was closer to 2:00 (0200 Hrs). When I got home everybody was asleep. Nobody got up.

The next day I called the office and called in sick. I talked to Mike twice and we only talked about the night before briefly. I don't know where she went after we got done. The last time I saw her was about 1:00 (0100 Hrs).

Mallon was interviewed a second time by the LAPD three days later, on January 19. Mallon's second typed LAPD witness statement reads in full:

On January 14, 1988, I went to a bar in the Valley called "Hunter" after a funeral. I went to that bar along with 15–20 other deputies on the suggestion of Bob Waters. I got to the bar at about 1:00 in the afternoon and started to drink. I drank the entire time I was at the bar.

While I was at the bar, I met a girl named Bonnie and a girl named Catherine. We dance [sic] and talked along with the drinking. When Bonnie and I danced, I did not expose myself. I don't recall doing that while I talked to Catherine. She did expose herself. She lifted her shirt and exposed her breast to the whole bar. Catherine was not wearing a bra.

There was a male/black named "Noel" who got into an argument with Mike (Turner) but not into a fight. Another black man got interviewed and the thing was over.

At about 1130 or midnight, Catherine, Bob, Mike and myself left the bar. We were walking towards my car when Catherine fell down. I tried to pick her up but because of her weight and my condition, I was unable to do so. Mike helped me pick Catherine up. I don't recall where Waters was at that time.

Catherine and I got into my car and then she started to give me a blow job. While she was giving me the blow job, Mike pulled his car next to mine. Mike waived [sic] at me and I waived back, and he left.

Catherine took off her clothes and I took mine off. We had sexual intercourse and I orally copulated her. While I was doing that, I saw the shadow of a male walk by. I got up and told Catherine that we had to move. We put our clothes back on and left the area. I drove away from the location and followed the directions of Cathy.

We got to Lanark and Landon [sic], and I parked the car. She unzipped me and started giving me a blow job again. I had trouble getting an erection because of my condition. Cathy stopped the blow job and said that she had to go. I told her okay. Go. She got out of my car and walked north on Langdon. I watched her for a while and noticed that she was staggering. I thought she was going to run into a tree.

I made a U-turn and left the area. I wasn't sure where the freeway was so I stopped at a Union 76 Station and got directions. I found the freeway and drove south bound on the 405 freeway. When I got to about Century

Blvd. and the freeway, I pulled over on the shoulder. I was having trouble with my driving so I turned up the radio and the air conditioner to try and get my self [sic] together.

I got home at about 1:00 and went to bed. No one was up and knew I had gotten home. The next morning, I called in sick. I talked to Turner that I wasn't coming in. I didn't say anything about what Catherine and I did. I took the day off because I was hung over.

On January 15, 1988, at about 6:45, my wife and I left our house for Parker, Arizona. We had been planning the trip to take some furniture to a place we had just bought. The trip had been planned for sometime [sic].

I can't think of anything else about the night. I haven't left anything out.

At the time, Mallon lived with his family in Lakewood, about forty miles from Van Nuys. Among the inconsistencies in Mallon's first two statements were what time he last saw Cathy and what time he arrived home. In his initial LAPD interview on January 16, which was not tape-recorded, Mallon recounted that he last saw Cathy "about 1:00" a.m. and got home between 1:30 and 2:00, but "closer to 2:00." Three days later, Mallon told LAPD detectives that he got home "at about 1:00" a.m. For Mallon to have arrived home in Lakewood by one o'clock, he would had to have left Van Nuys earlier, closer to midnight and possibly prior to the time of Cathy's murder.

Precisely what time Cathy was killed has never been established conclusively, although the most reliable accounts suggest it was between midnight and 12:30 a.m.

Although Noel Warnick apparently heard and saw nothing out of the ordinary after he got home from the Hunter that night, several other residents of 8123 Sepulveda Boulevard were earwitnesses to Cathy's murder.

One of the earwitnesses, Harold, lived alone in apartment 303. His apartment was on the south side of the building, almost directly above where Cathy was killed. Harold was black and in his early twenties at the time. Harold had no arrest record and had managed to avoid even interacting with the police to that point in his life. Harold worked full time as a retail manager for Builders Emporium, a chain of hardware stores.

Late that Thursday night, Harold was talking on the phone with his girlfriend when he heard from outside what sounded to him like a three-way argument between a woman and two men. Harold had the windows of his apartment open at the time. He also had his television on, in the background, while he and his girlfriend chatted. Harold wasn't really watching the TV, but he noticed that *The Honeymooners* had just come on when the voices started below his window. According to the TV listings in that day's *Los Angeles Times*, *The Honeymooners* aired from midnight until 12:30 a.m.

At first, Harold did not pay much attention to what was going on outside. Living on busy Sepulveda Boulevard, right next door to the crisis management center, it was not unusual for the sound of street drama to carry into Harold's apartment. Earlier that night, Harold had heard what he thought was either a gunshot or a car backfiring.

It sounded to Harold like the argument was a domestic dispute, between people who already knew each other, rather than strangers who were fighting. Harold heard one of the men say, "Come on, come on," and the woman say something that sounded like "Let me loose," or possibly "Louis." The way the woman slurred her words when she spoke led Harold to believe she was intoxicated.

Between the commotion outside and the TV playing in his apartment, Harold was having a hard time focusing on his conversation with his girlfriend. Harold shut his window to eliminate one of the distractions. "It sounds like somebody's getting killed outside," Harold said to his girlfriend. Harold meant it as a joke at the time.

Harold and his girlfriend went back to their conversation. But even with his window closed, Harold could still hear the struggle as it continued outside. It sounded to Harold as though the fight had moved away from Sepulveda toward the back of his building, alongside the crisis center parking lot. Harold could hear the sound of leaves and branches crunching under their feet, or their bodies. Harold heard the woman say "Stop it, you're hurting me," and "You bastards," and "Why are you doing this to me?" Harold thought the woman sounded genuinely in pain, like her arm was being squeezed or twisted.

Harold went to his window and looked out, but his view of the ground below was obscured by trees and darkness. Harold could not see anyone or anything that was going on down there. By this point, the fight had gone on for quite some time. Harold glanced at the TV and saw that *The Honeymooners* was going off the air.

Things seemed to Harold to quiet down for a little while. Harold heard noises that suggested to him the people who had been arguing were having sex. Harold wondered if the woman might be a prostitute.

A short time later, Harold heard the voices start up again. Harold heard the woman say, "Stop it, Louis, you're hurting me," and a man respond, "Fuck you, you bitch." The woman's voice sounded heavily slurred and raspy. Harold then heard the woman let out a loud scream. Midway through her scream, before she could let it out completely, Harold heard an even louder noise, a thud like a baseball bat hitting a tree. About the same time, Harold also heard a man say, "Come on, man, let's go, let's go." From the sound of the voice, Harold thought the man might be black, but he could not be certain. Then things got very quiet. Harold heard no voices after that.

Harold was interviewed by the LAPD multiple times in 1988, first on the morning of Friday, January 15, less than twelve hours after Cathy's murder. One of the two detectives who initially interviewed Harold was Lyle Mayer, the lead investigator on the two-year-old, still unsolved Sherri Rasmussen murder case.

Harold's typed LAPD witness statement from January 15, 1988 reads in full:

> I have lived here for some time. Many of the nights there are people fighting in apartment #104. The man that rents #104 his nickname is "Pops." There are many domestic disputes that occur in the building. On 1-14-88, around 9:45 pm, I heard a couple of gunshots. This is no big deal because I always hear shots from this area. Last night, some people in #107 had a fight. They [sic] lady, "Dorrie" got arrested. This was sometime between the Cosby Show and the eleven o'clock news.
>
> A girl was yelling around 11:30 pm. There was yelling for at least 30 to 40 minutes. The girl was cussing out the man. The man sounded like he was black. The girl yelled, "Stop, Stop." At the end of the argument I heard a crash. I think there was more than one guy down there. It sounded like a three party argument. One guy and the girl were doing most of the arguing. He was saying, "Come, come on." The girl said, "Louis, your [sic] hurting me."
>
> At the end of the argument I heard a sound like a bat hitting a tree. I don't know of anybody in this building by the name of Louis. There is a little black guy who walks up and down the street and pimps the whores. He is a male, black, 5/7, 35 years, round shaped jerri [sic] curl. He dresses in "FILA" type sports suits. Sometimes he wears a baseball cap.
>
> Sometime around 11:30, after the news, I heard a three way argument. The girl was calling, "Louis," a bastard. She said, "I can't believe you, I can't believe you." They were in the bushes below my apartment. The

voices, in the argument, started in the front area of the apartment, then
they continued to the back. They were pretty loud. The people in number
104 probably know "Louis." The girl sounded like she was drunk.

A second earwitness, a resident of the same building named Pearl
Kelly, was also interviewed by Mayer and his partner the morning after
the murder. Pearl lived in apartment 304. Pearl Kelly died in 2007, at
age eighty-seven. Pearl's typed LAPD witness statement from January 15,
1988, reads in full:

I live in my apartment alone and have lived here since 1966.

I went to bed last night at 11:00 pm and I'm a very light sleeper. My
bedroom is located so that when I look out my bedroom window I can see
the county psychiatric center roof and parking lot. Directly below my win-
dow is a walkway that extends the entire length of the apartment building.

I don't know exactly what time it was but I was awakened by voices
below my window. I believe it was in the early morning hours, it was still
dark outside. I heard a female voice say with slurred speech, "Your [sic]
hurting me, your hurting me, Louis."

I then heard the voice move along the building towards Sepulveda.
I couldn't hear his voice too well and it seemed as if he tried to keep his voice
low. I noted at one point his voice got louder but I still could not distin-
guish what was being said. I had the feeling that she was being forced along-
side the building. Just because of what I heard, "Your hurting me, Louis."

I don't know anybody by the name of Louis. I'm sure there's a drug
problem in the complex.

The girl's voice was very slurred. It sounded like she was drunk.

Pearl Kelly was interviewed again by the LAPD in May 1988, almost
four months after Cathy was killed. Steve Hooks was one of the two detectives who reinterviewed her. Pearl's May 1988 typed LAPD witness statement reads in full:

(This is a follow up to the first interview.)

I can definitely say the girl and the man who were arguing were argu-
ing [sic] were in the apartment complex. The girl was definitely white, I
can't tell what race the man was. The only thing I thought of is I may have
heard another male voice, out in the crisis management parking lot, say a

*two syllable word to the male or female. I think the time was midnight or
so, based on how light the traffic was on Sepulveda. I went to sleep at 11:15
p.m. or so.*

Four days after Hooks and his partner reinterviewed Pearl Kelly, they
interviewed a third earwitness to Cathy's murder, Charles McFadden. At
the time Cathy was killed, Charles lived in apartment 204, in the same
building on Sepulveda Boulevard as Noel, Harold, and Pearl. Charles
McFadden died in 2006, at age sixty-two. Charles's typed LAPD witness
statement from May 1988 reads in full:

*I had just finished watching Star Trek, it may have been around 0030. (Star
Trek ends at 0030). A half hour to one hour later, I heard a white girl say
"Stop it your [sic] bastards." I then heard a thud and it sounded like an
apple squashing. I heard a dissuading noise five to ten minutes after that.
By the way she was speaking, it sounded like she may have been drinking.*

Cathy's body was not discovered until shortly after 8:00 a.m. on Friday, January 15, roughly seven or eight hours after her murder.

A Los Angeles County coroner's Investigator's Report completed the
same day recounted:

*The decedent is a 26-year-old female who reportedly worked at FEDCO
store located in Van Nuys. She left the place of work about 1915 hours on
1-14-88.*

*About 0810 hours 1-15-88, she was found by Mr. Walter Lonngen (782-
1985) who works at the Crisis Management Center, department of Health,
L.A. County, whose office is located at 8101 Sepulveda boulevard [sic], Van
Nuys (scene).*

*Mr. Lonngen was about to pull out his county service car, Escort
#468183, when he discovered the decedent lying supine position on the
ground in front of his car.*

*The decedent was observed lying in a supine position with her blouse
rolled up exposing her breasts. Her pants were rolled down to her ankles
exposing her private parts. A big round piece of stepping stone probably
about 2 1/2 feet in diameter and about 30 pounds weight was noted laying
on decedent's left face. It appeared that said stone was used to crush decedent's head causing skull fracture and her brain and blood to splatter on*

the ground and wooden fence and door leading to the backyard of the building (left side of the body).

The decedent was wearing a yellow smock with writing on the right chest "Register Checker." Said smock probably belongs to the decedent's employer.

A screw driver was noted laying on the ground near the decedent's right hip (police took same as evidence). It appeared that the decedent was stabbed several times with said screw driver on [sic] the chest and probably used against her vagina (bloody).

A witness at the scene heard a woman's scream about 2300 hours on 1-14-88, saying: "Luis, Luis stop you are hurting me."

A total of $10.40 in cash was found in her pants and smock (pockets).

A bracelet was on her left wrist and a pair of earrings were on the ground. Coin purse was empty. No panties or shoes were found at the scene.

Identified by employee ID. Mother (NOK) had been notified. No other information at this time.

Cathy's autopsy was performed at the coroner's office two days later, on January 17. According to the autopsy report, Cathy died "*as a result of strangulation and blunt force head trauma.*"

Toxicological analysis, also performed by the coroner's office, determined Cathy's blood alcohol content when she died was 0.28 percent, almost three times the legal limit to drive in California at the time. No traces of any illegal drugs were found in Cathy's blood system.

According to the chronological log for the LAPD's investigation of Cathy's murder, the first detective to arrive at the crime scene was Lyle Mayer.

LAPD 03.11.6 (1/82)	CHRONOLOGICAL RECORD		1-1
INSTRUCTIONS: This form is used to document any past or future investigative events deemed necessary to control or develop this case.		DR 88 09 03306	
DATE	TIME	INVESTIGATION	
1/15/88	0810	8101 Sepulveda Bl. Det. Mayer responded to R/C for 9A9. "AMB 187"	
		Mayer first to arrive. Secured scene made notification to I/O.	
	0830	VNYS Station - Received phone call from Det. Mayer and was advised of 187	
		8101 Sepulveda. Vict was a female/white, 26 yrs old. Notified Lt. Durrer	

LAPD chrono for the Catherine Braley case, top of page 1

PART

Epilogue

FOUR

23

"We Do Not Condone Murder"

(2008–2012)

One day in late March 2008, more than twenty years after the murders of Sherri Rasmussen and Catherine Braley, a file box appeared, seemingly out of thin air, in the Van Nuys homicide squad room. Inside the box were the murder books for two cases, both still unsolved at that time: Rasmussen and Braley.

The brown corrugated cardboard file box was the same type used by the LAPD's Records and Identification Division, the arm of the department responsible for maintaining its vast collection of records. Given the volume of the official records the LAPD has to keep track of, the boxes were pre-printed on their sides with space to write where the box came from and what was in it. By necessity, R&I were sticklers about accepting any boxes that were unlabeled or that lacked a lid. Oddly, the file box that materialized at Van Nuys in 2008 had no markings on its sides and no lid.

A murder book may have more than one volume, but there is only ever one murder book for each case. Maintaining the murder book is the responsibility of the lead detective. Physical possession of the murder book and investigative responsibility for a case go hand in hand. It was common for cases to be transferred between divisions and detectives, but rare that it would happen without a heads-up of some kind, a meeting or at least a phone call, before the case arrived. Nor was there any sort of written report or letter inside the box, along with the Rasmussen and Braley murder books, to indicate where it came from, who dropped it off, and who was the intended recipient.

Whether by chance or fate, the detective who noticed the box and took ownership of it was Detective II Jim Nuttall of the Van Nuys homicide unit. Nuttall was thirty-eight years old at the time, with a scant three years of homicide experience, all at Van Nuys.

Nuttall was mildly irritated when he spotted the box, which someone had placed on the floor next to his desk. Nuttall felt he already had a lot on his plate at the time. In March 2008, the Van Nuys homicide unit was both in the process of moving offices and about to lose two of its longest-tenured detectives to retirement. Nuttall's wife was also eight and a half months pregnant with their first child. Nuttall had scheduled time off in April and had a long list of things he felt he needed to accomplish before he left on vacation so he could enjoy his time away in good conscience. He was not thrilled to add dealing with a mystery box, and the two unfamiliar cases in it, to his to-do list.

Nuttall could tell just by looking at the cases in the box that they were from an earlier era, long before he joined the LAPD. The murder books were in their original blue three-ring binders, the color and style used by LAPD detectives in the 1980s. The binders appeared rickety, their covers faded and peeling in places. The condition of the books was another clue that the cases had been somewhere else in the department, other than Van Nuys, for at least two years and possibly longer.

In 2006, a year after Nuttall joined the unit, the Detective III then in charge of Van Nuys Homicide tasked a team of civilian volunteers with repackaging the murder books for all their old unsolved cases. Each murder book was taken out of its timeworn blue binder and bound tightly inside an oversized heavy-duty folder. The idea was that it would conserve space and allow all the unsolveds to be stored, chronologically, in filing cabinets in the homicide squad room. In practice, Nuttall found that it made the old cases less accessible, since the squad room was already crowded with desks for four homicide and six sex crimes detectives. The desks faced each other in two rows of five, with the filing cabinets behind their chairs, against the wall. It was impossible to open a filing cabinet without making someone stand up from their desk. Nuttall also felt the folder-bound murder books were harder to page through than the binders he was accustomed to reading. The fact that the two sets of murder books in the box were in blue binders, rather than bound folders, told Nuttall that the cases had left Van Nuys sometime before 2006.

From the time Nuttall first joined the unit in 2005, as a rookie detective with zero homicide experience, it was drilled into him that if he wanted to learn how to work homicide, he should spend every single minute of his free time reading the old unsolveds. Nuttall's first homicide supervisor was an old-school detective with a reputation as a hard-ass. He liked to point at the library of old murder books and tell Nuttall, "Start reading. Get to work. That's how you're going to learn." The attitude was "Put your nose in a murder book and learn from it, kid."

Nuttall took the advice to heart. It was by reading old cases that Nuttall learned the basics, like the sections of the murder book and what reports belonged where, but also what to look for in the other cases he picked up.

It took Nuttall about a year of reading old cases, between working fresh homicides, before he felt ready to try his hand at actually investigating a cold case himself. Nuttall was fully humbled by the experience.

A bit like Rasmussen and Braley, the first cold case Nuttall attempted to solve picked him more than he picked it. In 2006, Nuttall answered a phone call from a citizen who wanted to know whatever happened with the murder of Sidney Fabricant. Fabricant, a biker and bookie who went by the nickname Sid the Squid, was beaten to death in 1984 inside his Van Nuys home. No one was ever arrested. Nuttall pulled the murder book and read it, then started digging into the case, tracking down long-lost witnesses and interviewing them. Nuttall believed the motive was the large amount of cash stolen from Fabricant's house. Nuttall ended up putting a lot of time into the case, whenever he could, and eventually identified a suspect, a fellow biker.

The problem Nuttall encountered, and could not find a way around, was that his case was entirely circumstantial. Nuttall had no physical evidence to put his suspect at the murder scene, twenty-two years earlier. Nuttall presented the case to the District Attorney's Office, which declined to file charges. The lesson Nuttall took from the Fabricant case was that it was nearly impossible to solve a cold case homicide without physical evidence.

Two years later, when the box with the Rasmussen and Braley murder books arrived in Van Nuys, Nuttall's batting average with cold cases remained .000, 0 for 1 with one strikeout.

All Nuttall did with the box on the day he found it was glance at the names and DR numbers on the covers of the murder books inside. Nuttall could tell from the DR numbers, the unique case number that invariably begins with the year of the crime, that the two cases dated from 1986 and 1988, more than twenty years earlier, when Nuttall was still in high school.

Nuttall made a mental note of the victims' names but neither one, Sherri Rasmussen or Catherine Braley, meant anything to him at the time.

Amid the tumult of the homicide unit's move to its new squad room, and the pressure Nuttall felt to get everything squared away before he went on paternity leave, he decided just to grab the box and stash it in their new office. The new homicide squad room, also on the third floor of the Van Nuys station, was a smaller space, but the unit had it all to itself. Nuttall placed the box with the Rasmussen and Braley murder books atop an unoccupied desk next to his own. Nuttall planned to read through the cases at some point after he got back to work, as time permitted between the fresh murder cases that were his primary responsibility as a detective. The open box with the two sets of murder books sat innocuously on the desk beside Nuttall's, untouched but in plain view, for the next several months.

Nuttall returned to work in May as a new father, and to a new detective partner, Pete Barba, who had just joined the Van Nuys unit. In getting their new digs set up, Nuttall and Barba discovered their shared antipathy for folder-bound murder books and their preference for the traditional three-ring binders. The two detectives took it upon themselves to reverse the job done a few years earlier by the team of civilian volunteers. Throughout 2008, whenever they had downtime, Nuttall and Barba plowed through Van Nuys's library of unsolved cases, one by one, removing each murder book from its folder and reassembling it inside a new white three-ring binder, neatly labeled on the front and spine with the victim's name, the DR number, and the date of the murder. If a page of a murder book was torn, they would photocopy it, write the date on the copy, and put it and the original page back in the book. The project was laborious, but they were motivated to do it, not just for themselves but for the Van Nuys homicide detectives who would inevitably succeed them. Nuttall and Barba wanted to give detectives ten or twenty years down the line something better to work with than murder books in inconvenient folders or old binders that were on the verge of falling apart.

Another benefit of the project was that it afforded Nuttall and Barba the opportunity to skim through and familiarize themselves with all the unsolved Van Nuys cases. By then, Nuttall had developed a standard practice when he picked up an unfamiliar murder book. He always flipped first to section 10, the follow-up report, sometimes called the "sixty-day report" in reference to its due date. Nuttall found reading the follow-up report usually gave him a good overview of the case and what he had to work with. After the follow-up report, Nuttall always turned next to section 5, the property and evidence reports, and section 6, the scientific reports. Nuttall had already learned the hard way, from all the time he had put into Fabricant, that without some physical evidence, a cold case was unlikely to go anywhere.

By the end of 2008, the Van Nuys homicide unit had gained another detective, Marc Martinez, and a new supervisor, Detective III Rob Bub, which brought the head count in their small squad room to four. Bub had transferred to Van Nuys from the Cold Case Homicide Unit, part of the Robbery-Homicide Division downtown. RHD was considered the LAPD's most prestigious detective assignment. By reputation at least, the LAPD's most experienced, talented, keen-eyed murder investigators were the detectives at RHD's Homicide Special Section. Homicide Special had citywide jurisdiction over particularly complex cases like serial killers or murders for hire, as well as any murder case that attracted intense media coverage or was otherwise deemed "high profile" by the LAPD.

The Van Nuys homicide squad room and RHD's downtown at Parker Center, LAPD headquarters, were only about fifteen miles apart, but psychically, the distance was greater. Van Nuys homicide was everything RHD was not. At the start of 2009, Van Nuys homicide had four detectives, one of whom, Bub, was the unit's supervisor. RHD's Homicide Special Section alone had upwards of twenty detectives, plus its own dedicated lieutenant. When RHD was in the news, a frequent occurrence given the nature of its caseload, the local media commonly referred to it, almost reflexively, as "the LAPD's elite Robbery-Homicide Division." Unlike their vaunted counterparts at RHD, the Van Nuys detectives were not accustomed to reading and hearing on a daily basis that they were the best of the best. The limelight, a fact of life at RHD, was seldom trained on the small, humble Van Nuys homicide unit.

By appearances, nothing about the file box that had sat next to Nuttall's desk for almost a year, or the two sets of murder books in it, Rasmussen and Braley, suggested that either case belonged anywhere but Van Nuys. Had Nuttall had the faintest sense that there was anything the least bit remarkable, let alone high profile, about either case, he would have attended to them sooner. Nuttall had no inkling that the homicide gods had delivered to him, with no warning whatsoever, the LAPD's version of Pandora's box, nor any foresight that he was about to open it, irreversibly.

None of the Van Nuys detectives knew what was in store for them when

Nuttall came to work on Monday morning, February 2, 2009, and decided that it was as good a day as any to finally tackle that box. The Friday before, Nuttall had finished trial in another of his cases, and no one was killed in Van Nuys over the weekend, so unlike many Mondays, there were no fresh cases to work. All Nuttall intended to do with the Rasmussen and Braley murder books was read them, transfer them to new white binders, shelve them, and move on.

Nuttall reached into the box and pulled out, purely by chance, the murder book for the Rasmussen case. As was his custom, Nuttall opened the binder to section 10, the follow-up report, written more than two decades earlier by Lyle Mayer, his predecessor at Van Nuys homicide. Mayer's report listed the motive for Sherri's murder as "residential burglary." The narrative described Sherri staying home from work on a weekday and surprising two burglars, one armed with a gun, inside the condo she shared with her husband, John. Shots were fired on the second floor and a vicious struggle ensued over the gun. The fight carried downstairs to the living room, where Sherri was knocked out and "executed," according to the report. Sherri's extensive injuries included the three fatal gunshot wounds and a "severe" bite mark on her forearm. The only suspects described in the follow-up report were two Latino men who attempted to burglarize a nearby condo, two months after Sherri's murder.

More than any details of the crime, what got Nuttall's attention as he read through the follow-up report was his impression of Sherri as a righteous victim. To Nuttall, and in the vernacular of LAPD homicide detectives, a "righteous victim" was someone who had not seemed to put themselves in harm's way. All homicide victims deserve justice and a thorough investigation, but righteous victims often inspire detectives to work harder, and dig a little deeper, than they otherwise might. Detectives are only human. A victim like Sherri struck a different emotional chord within Nuttall than, say, Sidney Fabricant, who was leading a criminal lifestyle when he was killed. The follow-up report described Sherri as "a pillar of the community," professionally successful, and happily married to John. There was a photo of Sherri, smiling, in the murder book. Nuttall looked at it and thought, "Here's an appealing young woman with the brightest of futures, murdered in her own home. If this was my sister, I'd want somebody to look at it. What happened to her? Who did this?" Before Nuttall knew anything else about Sherri's case, he already knew, innately, that he wanted to solve it.

Nuttall had a good feeling as he flipped to section 5 of the Rasmussen murder book in search of physical evidence. Nuttall knew from the follow-up report that it was an interior crime scene, which tend to be richer evidence environments than murders committed outdoors. Nuttall also knew that Sherri's murder was preceded by a ferocious struggle, which increased the odds of blood at the crime scene, some of it, Nuttall hoped, shed by the suspect. Nuttall found the original property report and was pleased to see that the detectives had picked up quite a bit of evidence in 1986, including several samples of blood from inside the condo.

Nuttall turned to section 6 of the murder book, the scientific reports, to see what evidence had already been tested by SID. The first report Nuttall read detailed the ABO blood type analysis performed in March 1986, just weeks after the murder. When Sherri was killed, there was no such thing as DNA analysis, which debuted the following year. In 1986, the most information the crime lab could extract from biological evidence was its source's blood type: A, B, AB, or O. The results helped detectives rule suspects in or out but rarely served as a smoking gun.

Nuttall saw that SID had analyzed, back in 1986, nearly a dozen items of crime scene evidence, plus a sample of Sherri's blood collected during her autopsy. The report stated that Sherri's blood type was O. About half the blood samples from the crime scene were type A, and the rest O or a mix of A and O, the 1986 report indicated.

Unbeknownst to Nuttall, Sherri had a very rare blood type that, when tested for ABO blood type, sometimes registered as A and sometimes as O. Nuttall leaped to the same understandable yet mistaken conclusion the detectives had in 1986, based on the ABO results. Nuttall believed he had blood at the crime scene from two different people: type O blood from the victim, and type A blood left there by someone else, presumably the killer. DNA analysis later established that all the blood collected at the crime scene was Sherri's. But when Nuttall first read the report, it made him sit up straight at his desk. Nuttall thought, "Damn, I've got a lot of the suspect's blood here. Now I've got something to work with."

Nuttall kept paging through section 6 until he came to another SID report, of much more recent vintage, detailing a DNA analysis completed in February 2005, just four years earlier. Nuttall couldn't believe his luck. He already felt as if he had a radar lock on the case, even before he saw the DNA report. Nuttall thought, "Not only do I have the suspect's blood, I've got DNA."

The 2005 report indicated that a criminalist at SID, Jennifer Francis, had performed DNA analysis on six pieces of evidence collected from the crime scene in 1986. Five of the six yielded a single DNA profile that matched the victim's, Sherri Rasmussen, Francis reported.

The sixth item Francis tested, item 30 on the LAPD's property log, was the swab of the bite mark on Sherri's arm. Francis developed two DNA profiles from the bite mark swab. In mixed-source DNA samples, whichever source contributed more DNA is referred to as the "major DNA profile," and the lesser source as the "minor DNA profile." Francis determined that the bite mark swab's minor DNA profile was consistent with Sherri's DNA profile. Francis's report stated, *"The major DNA profile obtained from item #30 is from a female. Sherri Rasmussen is excluded as the source of this major DNA profile."*

Nuttall recognized the significance of the four-year-old DNA report the moment he read it. Nuttall thought, "Oh, shit. Not only do I have DNA, I've got female DNA."

LAPD detectives don't get a lot of female-on-female homicides, nor many home invasions committed by women. The fact that Mayer's follow-up report, with its narrative centered on two male burglars, did not line up with the DNA report suggested to Nuttall that something was way off the mark. Nuttall's gut told him that he wasn't dealing with a botched burglary. The combination of a female DNA profile, and the duration and intensity of the struggle before the murder, made Nuttall suspect the motive was personal. The first theory that came to mind, when Nuttall thought of a woman killing another woman, was a love triangle.

Only hours earlier, Nuttall had been oblivious to Sherri Rasmussen, her fate in 1986, and the fate of her killer, who had gotten away with murder for more than twenty years. But just based on what he had read in the murder book, Nuttall felt a surge of confidence that he would be able to solve the case. Nuttall was a young detective, hungry to solve homicide cases. Nuttall had not forgotten his first big swing at a cold case, Fabricant, and how he had struck out. This felt different. Nuttall felt like he was back in the batter's box, and his newest case was a lazy fastball, belt-high and right over the plate. He thought, "I'm going to knock this out of the ballpark."

Nuttall briefed his three squad mates, Barba, Martinez, and Bub, the unit's supervisor, on the case and the female DNA profile. The SID report indicated that the major DNA profile was uploaded in 2005 to CODIS, the FBI's massive DNA database. The lack of a CODIS "hit" meant their suspect was not someone already in the database. The detectives would need to build from scratch their list of potential female suspects.

Nuttall also wanted to make sure he wasn't missing any documentation from the DNA analysis performed in 2005. Within days of reopening the Rasmussen case, Nuttall called SID and spoke with Nick Sanchez, a criminalist in the serology unit. When Nuttall mentioned what case he was calling about, Sanchez said there was a DNA analyst who had done a lot of work on the case, Jennifer Francis, whom Nuttall should speak to about it. Nuttall had never worked with Francis previously and did not know her even in passing.

Francis returned Nuttall's call the same day. One of the first things Francis said to Nuttall was, "Detective, I'm not telling you how to do your job, but I don't think this was a burglary." Nuttall was taken aback. Nuttall thought, "I know that. But how do you know that?"

Francis did not share the backstory with Nuttall that day, but the Rasmussen case had made a deep impression on her when she worked on it, starting in late 2004. At the time, Francis was newly authorized to perform DNA analysis, so unlike her more tenured colleagues, she had no backlog of other cases vying for her attention. Francis brought the number of criminalists in the serology unit to eleven, a number many times smaller than the number of DNA requests streaming in from detectives throughout the LAPD. In addition to DNA requests for recently committed homicide and rape cases, the LAPD had also established, in November 2001, a seven-detective Cold Case Homicide Unit within RHD.

RHD's cold case unit had its own epic caseload, the more than nine thousand unsolved murders committed citywide between 1960 and 1998, to start. The cold case unit was designed to harness the revolutionary investigative power of advances like DNA, and databases like CODIS, and bring them to bear on old cases and evidence. It took the seven detectives a solid year just to read all the murder books and whittle the nine thousand cases down to the fourteen hundred most promising, those cases in which there was physical evidence still available to test. Among the cases that made the cut was the 1986 murder of Sherri Rasmussen.

By 2003, the cold case unit had shifted its energies from screening cases to requesting analysis of evidence in individual cold cases. On September 19, 2003, RHD cold case detective Cliff Shepard submitted to SID's serology unit a request for DNA analysis of evidence from the Rasmussen case.

Given the volume of cases, there was a cap on the number of items per case that a detective could submit for DNA analysis. Shepard's request listed several items, mostly bloodstains at the crime scene, that he wanted tested. Shepard identified the items by their number on the case's property log. Submissions from the cold case unit were often accompanied by copies of the property log and, for background, any crime summaries in the murder book. Shepard included with his DNA request a copy of Mayer's follow-up report, plus a dot matrix printout of the Rasmussen property log, which included twenty-nine items. The bite mark swab collected in 1986 was not listed on the printout, an omission that did not escape Shepard's notice. Within the follow-up report, Shepard had highlighted in yellow the reference to the bite mark swab and jotted a note in the margin questioning where it was.

Shepard's request languished for more than a year, in line behind other cases, until October 2004, when Francis selected it as one of her first DNA cases to work. Francis had been offered her pick of cases from a stack of pending DNA requests on a colleague's desk. Francis chose Rasmussen mostly because Shepard wrote in his request that the victim's blood type was O, and foreign blood, type A, was also collected from the murder scene. Francis saw it as a simple, straightforward case for her to cut her teeth on. Francis figured that all she had to do was pick one of the type A blood stains, analyze it for the suspect's DNA profile, upload it to CODIS, analyze the victim's blood sample for her DNA profile, and she'd be done.

Francis already knew Shepard from having screened several DNA requests he'd made in other cold cases. Before Francis was authorized to perform DNA analysis, her primary responsibility in the unit was to screen cases. Screening involved testing an evidence sample to confirm it was the expected biological substance—for instance, blood, semen, or saliva. The screened evidence was then passed to a DNA-qualified criminalist, who did the DNA analysis.

Francis's impression of Shepard, from the cases she had screened for him, was that he was a very sharp, diligent, and dedicated detective. As with the bite mark swab missing from the Rasmussen property log, it seemed to Francis that nothing got past Shepard. Francis also felt that Shepard had excellent instincts, as good as any detective she had worked with, about which evidence items to submit for DNA analysis. Some detectives would request DNA analysis on a long list of items and leave it to the criminalist's discretion which of them they should test, that were likeliest to contain a suspect's DNA. Shepard, by contrast, seemed to know exactly which items to submit, right off the bat, usually the same ones Francis would have picked herself.

Francis started her DNA analysis in the Rasmussen case in early December 2004. She checked out from the LAPD's Property Division, next door to SID, the evidence items Shepard had requested. Francis was new at DNA, so she took her time and worked carefully. Each of the evidence items Francis analyzed matched the victim's DNA profile, which she had developed from Sherri's coroner's blood swatch. Francis was confused, because the DNA results contradicted the ABO blood type report from 1986.

Francis had seen Shepard's note in the follow-up report about the missing bite mark swab. Francis and Shepard had discussed where the swab might be. Shepard told Francis he would check with the coroner's office, since the follow-up report indicated a coroner's criminalist had collected it. Shepard also suggested that it was possible the bite mark swab had been stored inside the rape kit, a self-contained box of other swabs and slides taken at the crime scene.

Francis called Shepard and asked if she could see some of the crime scene photos from the Rasmussen murder book. Detectives commonly sent copies of crime scene photos and other reports from the murder book, upon request, to help the criminalist better understand the case and evidence they were being asked to analyze. Sometimes—if, for instance a detective did not know which items to submit for DNA analysis—they would bring the murder book to SID so the criminalist could help them decide. Because there was only one murder book per case, detectives usually had the analyst look at it in their presence and did not leave it behind at the crime lab.

Francis therefore was surprised when Shepard, in response to her request for crime scene photos, offered to bring her the Rasmussen murder book. Shepard told Francis there was no rush and she could keep the murder book as long as she needed. Francis hadn't asked for the murder book and didn't especially want the responsibility for it, since she knew it was irreplaceable. A few days later, however, Francis came back from lunch and was informed by a colleague that a detective had dropped something off for her. On the lab's center table was a blue three-ring binder, the Rasmussen murder book. Francis presumed it was Shepard who dropped it off, but she didn't know for sure, since she wasn't there when it was left.

Francis had seen murder books before, but she had never had an opportunity to read one without any time constraints. Francis showed it to a co-worker and said, "Check it out, a real-life murder book." The murder book seemed like an object of fascination because it genuinely was an object of fascination: between its covers was everything that was known about a single homicide case, with the exception of who did it.

Francis had not realized, until she started paging through the Rasmussen murder book, that murder books were organized by section, and what each section was for. For the first time in her career, Francis appreciated that there was a method to how LAPD homicide detectives investigated their cases.

Among the documents Francis stumbled across in the Rasmussen murder book, and read with interest, was a security report from Glendale Adventist Medical Center, Sherri's employer. The security report recounted Sherri's strained relationship with a nurse she had declined to promote. Francis read in the report that the hospital had disciplined the nurse and her doctor boyfriend for making harassing phone calls to Sherri.

At the same time Francis was absorbing all the information in the murder book, she proceeded with her DNA analysis of the remaining items Shepard had requested she test. By December 22, Francis had tested all of the evidence samples in Shepard's initial request. Frustratingly, the only DNA Francis had found matched Sherri's DNA profile.

Francis felt she'd done too much work in the case to have nothing to show for it but the victim's DNA profile. It occurred to her that if there was one piece of evidence in the case likely to contain the suspect's DNA, it was the bite mark swab, since people don't bite themselves. Francis thought, "That's the sample I need, the bite mark swab."

Francis returned to the Property Division, checked out the rape kit from the Rasmussen case, and opened it. No swabs or slides labeled "bite mark" were inside.

Tracking down physical evidence in homicide cases was ordinarily the detective's responsibility, and not within the purview of a civilian criminalist at SID. Although Francis had no contacts at the coroner's office, she decided to place a cold call anyway, figuring she had nothing to lose.

Francis called the coroner's office and a woman answered. Francis gave her name and said she was calling from the LAPD crime lab. Francis read off the coroner's case number for Rasmussen and explained she was looking for a bite mark swab. The woman asked Francis to hold a minute. About ten seconds later, the woman came back on the line and said she had no evidence booked under that case number. Francis thanked her and hung up.

Francis assumed the woman had typed the case number into a computer and nothing had come up. Francis thought, "What if she typed the number wrong? Like, switched a digit by mistake?" Francis discussed it with a colleague in the serology unit. Francis decided she would call back the next day and ask for the bite mark swab again. Francis hoped someone other than the woman she already spoke with would pick up the phone.

The next day, Francis dialed the coroner's office again and felt hopeful when a man answered. Francis gave him the same information and he gave her the same answer, that the coroner's office had no evidence in that case.

Francis thought if she called back and got someone else, maybe someone who had worked at the coroner's office longer, they might know where to find the bite mark swab. Francis ran the idea by her colleague, who told her, "You're done. You don't want to get the reputation of being a pain in the ass. You're brand new at this. You've already called twice. You can't keep calling back on every single case and say, 'Find the sample.'"

Francis knew her colleague was probably right. She went back to the follow-up report and read it again, on the faint hope she might find some other clue as to where the bite mark swab could be. Francis noted the name of the coroner's criminalist who had collected the swab in 1986: Lloyd Mahany. What were the odds Mahany was still on the job, almost twenty years later? Francis thought if Mahany was not retired, he might know how the bite mark swab was booked in 1986, since he had collected it himself. Francis decided to make one more last-ditch phone call.

Francis dialed the coroner's office and asked to speak with Lloyd Mahany. The next thing Francis knew, Mahany was on the line. Francis introduced herself and got right to the point. Francis asked Mahany, "If you swabbed a bite mark in 1986, what would you call it?"

"Bite mark swab," Mahany answered.

"Well, you swabbed it in eighty-six. Your guys say you don't have it. We don't have it either."

Mahany said he wasn't surprised Francis had been told the coroner's office didn't have it. Mahany explained that some old cases didn't make it into the computer when the coroner switched to its computer system. Mahany said he would have to pull the evidence log on microfiche. Mahany told Francis, "We would never get rid of a bite mark swab. We don't keep clothing forever. Bite mark swab, we wouldn't throw that away." Mahany said it would be a big undertaking to find it, and he was about to leave town on vacation.

Francis thanked Mahany and told him that there was no rush, as long as he didn't forget. Francis expected Mahany would look into it after he got back from vacation, whenever he had time. Francis thought she would hear back from Mahany in a few months, hopefully by springtime. Francis reminded Mahany before they hung up, "Don't forget about me."

A week later, Francis got a call from Dan Anderson, a supervisor at the coroner's office. Anderson told Francis, "We just spent six hours in the freezer. We found your bite mark swab."

Francis was so excited she called Shepard at the cold case unit. "We found the swab!" Francis told him.

Shepard asked, "How come when I called, they said they didn't have it?"

"That's what they told me, too. It's not in the computer system."

The bite mark swab was delivered to Francis at the crime lab in mid-January 2005. Francis was shocked by the tattered condition of the swab's original evidence envelope. Mahany's handwriting on the envelope was so faded that Francis could barely make out Rasmussen's name. Francis was amazed that the coroner's office had been able to find and identify it at all.

Francis started her analysis of the bite mark swab on January 27. Francis took a small cutting from the swab, extracted some cells from the sample, and examined the cells under a microscope. She saw nucleated epithelial cells, an indication that she was possibly looking at saliva, a good sign. Francis thought the cells looked pretty good and proceeded with DNA typing. The final step in the process was to run the raw data through a software program that produced the DNA profile, a string of numbers. As the software processed the data, which usually took about thirty minutes, the computer's screen displayed peaks that reflected the quality of the raw data. Smaller peaks meant the DNA sample was poor. Francis watched as the software rendered visible the raw data from the bite mark swab. Francis saw big spikes on the screen, another good sign.

Francis was still watching the screen when the software displayed its readings for the gender markers, the X and Y chromosomes. Only men have a Y chromosome. She saw a big peak for the X chromosome, which was normal, since everyone has an X chromosome.

Francis anticipated that she would see another big peak for the next marker, the Y chromosome, since most murders are committed by men.

She still assumed, based on what she'd read in the murder book, that it was a male burglar who bit Sherri. When the software reached the Y chromosome, however, there was no peak, but a flat reading. Francis initially assumed that the software was giving her Sherri's DNA profile, again, just as with the bloodstains. She thought it was possible the bite had broken the skin and the swab had picked up some of Sherri's blood. Only later, when Francis looked at the finished DNA profile and compared it to Sherri's, did she realize she had two different female DNA profiles.

Francis was stunned by the realization that it was a woman who bit Sherri. Francis immediately thought of the Glendale Adventist security report she had read in the murder book, about the nurse who was accused of harassing Sherri.

Francis typed up the DNA results and her scientific conclusions, minus any mention of her theory about the nurse. Francis's job was to analyze evidence. Criminalists were expected to stay in their lane and leave the investigative theories to the detectives. She submitted her DNA report to Shepard at the RHD cold case unit on February 8, 2005.

Given the rarity of female suspects, Francis expected Shepard to pounce on the DNA results. Francis, however, heard nothing. After a few weeks, Francis spoke to Shepard on the phone and asked him what was going on with Rasmussen. Shepard told her that he was looking at male-female burglary teams active in the Valley in the 1980s.

Francis thought that was an odd theory. "What about the other woman?" Francis asked Shepard. Francis meant the nurse she'd read about in the murder book.

According to Francis, Shepard replied, "Oh, you mean the LAPD detective? She was not a part of this." Shepard volunteered to Francis that the victim's husband had had an "on-again, off-again" relationship with an LAPD officer before the murder. Shepard did not tell Francis the ex-girlfriend's name. Nor did Shepard say what investigation he had done, or whom he had spoken with, to eliminate the ex-girlfriend as a murder suspect.

Francis was not aware of any police officer ex-girlfriend, since the only mention of her in the murder book was a single vague chrono entry that Francis had overlooked. Shepard also mentioned to Francis that the victim's husband, John, was remarried "to an Asian lady," a fact not noted within the murder book up to that time.

The first time they talked about it, Francis sensed Shepard was open to the possibility that Sherri was killed by someone she knew rather than in a botched burglary. Shepard mentioned to Francis that burglars usually do not carry guns, and that the victim's jewelry box was untouched. Nevertheless, by the end of the conversation, it was apparent to Francis that Shepard intended to focus his investigation on male-female burglary teams, not on any women with personal ties to Sherri Rasmussen.

Francis and Shepard discussed the Rasmussen case a few more times, later in 2005, both on the phone and via email. Francis did not fully grasp at the time why Shepard was so insistent on his theory. Francis thought it was far more likely that the motive was personal than that Sherri was killed by some latter-day San Fernando Valley Bonnie and Clyde. She was dumbfounded that Shepard appeared unwilling to even consider the possibility of a personal motive. But it seemed to Francis there was not much she could do. She was a criminalist, not a detective. Shepard controlled the investigation.

Francis moved on to other cases. She didn't forget the Rasmussen case, but it hadn't crossed her mind in some time, until Detective Nuttall called her from Van Nuys in February 2009. In their initial phone call, Francis and Nuttall both played their cards close to the vest, since they had never spoken before. For months after Nuttall reopened the Rasmussen case, Francis kept to herself what Shepard had told her in 2005.

The Van Nuys detectives' investigation moved quickly. On February 9, one week after Nuttall had first cracked the Rasmussen murder book, he contacted the current owner of the condo where Sherri was killed, to schedule a walk-through.

The next day, Nuttall called John Ruetten and interviewed him over the phone. Nuttall asked John if there were any women in his past with whom Sherri might have had a conflict, before her murder. John told Nuttall that before he and Sherri married, he was involved in a years-long, on-and-off intimate relationship with a woman named Stephanie Lazarus.

Nuttall had already seen in the murder book a chrono entry, written by the original detectives, which read, *"John Ruetten called—verified Stephanie Lazarus—P/O was former girlfriend."* Nuttall did not realize what "P/O" meant, however, until John mentioned that Stephanie was an LAPD officer. John said Stephanie had joined the LAPD before he met Sherri, and as far as he knew, she still worked there.

John recounted his relationship with Stephanie and how things changed between them after he met Sherri. John informed Nuttall that in 1985, Stephanie confronted Sherri at the hospital where she worked. John said the confrontation involved Stephanie telling Sherri that she loved John and he should be with her, not Sherri. John said he ended his relationship with Stephanie after Sherri told him about the encounter at Glendale Adventist. John said he gave Stephanie's name to the original detectives in 1986 and informed them that she was LAPD.

Although John was forthcoming about some of what transpired between him, Sherri, and Stephanie more than twenty years earlier, he did not volunteer that he and Stephanie had sex while he was engaged to Sherri, nor that Stephanie told Sherri that fact during their confrontation at the hospital in 1985.

None of the four Van Nuys detectives had heard of Stephanie or were acquainted with her. Martinez typed the name into the LAPD's online directory and found a listing for a Detective Stephanie Lazarus. The directory indicated that she was currently assigned to the Commercial Crimes Division at Parker Center, LAPD headquarters downtown.

Initially, the detectives found it difficult even to contemplate that a fellow cop might have murdered someone in cold blood and gotten away with it. At the same time, the detectives were increasingly certain that Sherri's murder was not a random act of violence. One clue was the bloody fingerprint on the video components left near the front door. This suggested to the detectives that they were moved there after the murder rather than before the bloodshed began, behavior that seemed more consistent with a suspect staging a crime scene than with an actual burglary. Another clue was that Sherri was already incapacitated when she was fatally shot, three times in the chest at close range. The execution-style manner of Sherri's death appeared consistent with the elimination of a witness who could have identified her killer.

The fact that Stephanie Lazarus was still active-duty LAPD raised the stakes significantly for the Van Nuys detectives. The only information they had at that time was what John had told Nuttall and what was in the murder book. John had said he told the original detectives about Stephanie, but there was no indication in the murder book that she was ever interviewed in 1986 or at any time since.

What Stephanie Lazarus might know about the murder was not the Van Nuys detectives' only concern. The fact that she was twenty-plus years on the job, and worked at Parker Center, suggested to them she probably knew a lot of people within the LAPD, and vice versa.

The four detectives had to make a fateful decision before they proceeded

Los Angeles Police Department

Detective
Stephanie Lazarus
Art Theft Detail

E-mail: 24270@lapd.lacity.org

FAX (213) 485-2524
(213) 628-4823
www.lapdonline.org/art_theft

Commercial Crimes Division
150 N. Los Angeles St. Rm 319
Los Angeles, CA 90012
artcop@lapd.lacity.org

Det. Stephanie Lazarus's LAPD Art Theft Detail business card (April 14, 2008)

any further with their investigation. LAPD policy required all employees to immediately report to either Internal Affairs or their own chain of command any possible misconduct by another officer. The strict responsibility to report misconduct as soon as it came to light had been drilled into them from their first days at the LAPD academy and throughout their careers.

At the same time, the detectives realized that if they hewed to policy and alerted the brass, they risked tipping Stephanie off. It also still seemed possible that she could be innocent. She had a motive, but at that point in time, the detectives had no physical evidence to tie her to the murder. If she didn't do it, reporting her to the brass or Internal Affairs would sully her good name.

Stephanie had a higher profile within the LAPD than the Van Nuys detectives knew, or likely could have imagined, when she came to their attention in February 2009. She had worked at Parker Center since January 2006, when she joined the LAPD's Art Theft Detail, a two-detective unit within the Commercial Crimes Division.

The LAPD was the only municipal police department in America with detectives assigned exclusively, full time, to the investigation of crimes involving fine art. Among LAPD detectives, the Art Theft Detail was not prestigious in the same way, professionally, as an assignment like RHD, but it was a cushier gig and closer to the limelight than most LAPD detectives ever got.

Unlike homicide detectives, art theft detectives were not routinely called to work in the middle of the night or on weekends and then expected to work around the clock for days. Art theft detectives did not have to deal with a murder victim's loved ones, their grief, and their expectations of swift justice. The hard-boiled satisfactions of homicide work—tracking down killers, slapping the cuffs on them, and putting them behind bars—were greater than the bloodless pursuit of stolen art, but so were the emotional costs.

Another perk Stephanie enjoyed as an art theft detective was increased visibility, both within the LAPD and beyond it. The idiosyncratic nature of her beat attracted a steady stream of media attention and interview requests from journalists. Stephanie freely granted interviews, including on camera. She also made presentations to the public, at museums like LACMA, about the inner workings of the LAPD's Art Theft Detail.

Stephanie's personal life was also thriving. In 2006, the same year she joined the Art Theft Detail, she and her husband, Scott Young, a fellow LAPD detective, adopted a baby girl.

As she had throughout her career, Stephanie mingled easily with the LAPD's top brass, including then LAPD chief of police William J. Bratton and other political figures.

Bratton, the high-profile former NYPD police commissioner, came to the LAPD in 2002, one year after the LAPD was placed under federal oversight for a long-standing "pattern or practice" of police misconduct. The cumulative weight of a succession of scandals, from the 1991 beating of Rodney King to the corruption exposed at the Rampart Division in the late 1990s, prompted the City of Los Angeles to sign a federal consent decree, essentially an admission that the LAPD could not be trusted to reform itself. The agreement committed the LAPD to implement a lengthy list of reforms within five years, under the supervision of a federal district court judge, Gary A. Feess. The consent decree went into effect on June 15, 2001.

Los Angeles Mayor Antonio Villaraigosa, Det. Stephanie Lazarus, and LAPD Chief Bill Bratton, circa 2006–2009

LAPD Chief Bill Bratton and Det. Stephanie Lazarus, circa 2006–2009

Within the LAPD, the consent decree was viewed as an unprecedented and humiliating loss of autonomy. In addition to the LAPD's wounded self-image, the consent decree required it to produce mountains of paperwork, including quarterly reports to Judge Feess detailing its progress toward full compliance. The reporting requirements alone were a significant, perpetual drain on the department's resources, tying up dozens of personnel who might otherwise be tasked with higher priorities, like fighting crime.

Bratton's overriding mission, from the day he was sworn in, was to bring the LAPD into compliance with the consent decree so that federal oversight could be lifted, department resources liberated, and the LAPD's pride and reputation restored. Bratton embraced the consent decree as a blueprint for remaking the department. At the same time, Bratton understood that as long as the consent decree remained in place, the LAPD would not be free of the stigma that it was incapable of running its own operations and could not be trusted by the public.

Although the five-year agreement was due to expire in June 2006, Feess had the power to extend it if he found the LAPD was not yet in full compliance with all its terms. During a hearing in March, with Bratton in the courtroom, Feess warned the city and LAPD, "There has been forty-plus years of debate in this community about how it is policed. And time after time after time, those reports were nodded to and nothing was ever done. This consent decree is going to affect real reform and it's not going to be extinguished until that happens."

By 2006, Bratton had been LAPD chief for more than three years. The LAPD had implemented many of the promised reforms, but far from all of them. Bratton nevertheless argued that the LAPD was sufficiently reformed and the consent decree should be lifted. In an op-ed for the *Los Angeles Times* headlined WE'VE CHANGED, Bratton wrote, *"This is a new LAPD . . . The LAPD has learned from the past and is ready to take on the mantle of accountability."*

The city proposed to Feess that federal oversight be extended for two years and narrowed in scope to only those reforms the LAPD had yet to enact. Feess stunned the city and LAPD by extending the full consent decree for three more years. The new expiration date, unless Feess decided at that time to extend it again, was June 15, 2009—coincidentally, just a few months after the Van Nuys detectives reopened the Rasmussen case.

Compared to the top brass downtown, for whom the consent decree and the LAPD's potential liberation from it were a preeminent preoccupation, rank-and-file homicide detectives were fairly well insulated from its effects. Most of the policy changes pertained to supervisors and patrol units rather than detectives. The Van Nuys detectives were not oblivious to the consent decree, but beyond a general awareness that it was costing the city and LAPD millions of dollars per year, whether and when federal oversight might be lifted was something they rarely if ever thought about as they investigated unsolved murder cases.

Faced with the decision in February 2009 whether to investigate Stephanie Lazarus themselves or to report what they had learned up the chain of command, the Van Nuys detectives gave no thought whatsoever to the consent decree deadline looming in June, three months away. Nor did they consider the possible political repercussions of their decision and how it might impact the LAPD's public image. The detectives' principal concerns at the time were who killed Sherri Rasmussen and how to protect the integrity of their investigation.

The detectives weighed their options and decided to make two pacts regarding the Rasmussen case. First, they agreed they would maintain total secrecy and would never speak or write Stephanie's name where anyone else might hear or see it. Second, they promised one another that they would follow the trail of evidence wherever it led.

By February 10, the detectives had compiled a list of five women in Sherri's life, people she knew well enough that if they rang her doorbell, she might open her front door to them. The first three names on the list were Sherri's mother, Loretta, her sister Teresa, and her friend and onetime roommate, Jayne. The fourth was Deborah Putnam, the nurse mentioned in the Glendale Adventist security report. Stephanie Lazarus was number 5, which was how the detectives solely referred to her, rather than by name, from then on.

The detectives also discussed how to prevent Stephanie from surveilling them as they investigated her. Every LAPD detective has access to a database called the Detective Case Tracking System. If Stephanie knew the DR number for the Rasmussen case, all she needed to do was run a search to see, for instance, if a new item of evidence had been booked. From that, she could surmise the investigation was active. She could then call the Property Division, provide the clerk with the DR number, and learn the name of the detective who had booked the evidence. For all they knew, Stephanie may have been keeping tabs on the Rasmussen case that way for years. To thwart any possible reconnaissance by her, and make it appear the Rasmussen case was dormant, Bub created a generic DR number for them to book evidence under.

Although the Van Nuys unit's countermeasures were intended to shield their murder investigation from only one officer, Stephanie Lazarus, they rendered it effectively invisible to the entire LAPD, from Chief Bratton on down. Only the four of them—Nuttall, Bub, Martinez, and Barba—had any idea what they were up to. Not even they knew what they might find.

On February 18, Nuttall called retired LAPD Detective Lyle Mayer and requested a meeting to discuss the Rasmussen case. Nuttall mentioned to Mayer on the phone the female DNA profile. Mayer told Nuttall that no female suspects were investigated, nor were there any leads generated in 1986 as to possible female suspects.

Mayer came to the Van Nuys station the next day and reviewed the murder book with Nuttall and Bub. Mayer said he could not recall what information the Rasmussens and John Ruetten provided in 1986. The four detectives and Mayer then went to the condo where Sherri was killed for a walk-through of the crime scene. The layout was virtually unchanged from the night of the murder, twenty-three years earlier.

In March 2009, the California Homicide Investigators' Association held its annual conference, a popular days-long event at which the LAPD is perennially well represented. The 2009 conference took place at the Silver Legacy Resort Casino in Reno, Nevada. Among the participants that year were Jennifer Francis, the SID criminalist, and Cliff Shepard, the RHD cold case detective. Four years had passed since Francis had completed her DNA analysis of the Rasmussen bite mark swab and sent Shepard her report pointing to a female suspect.

Francis and Shepard ran into each other at the conference and stopped to chat. Francis remembered the phone call she had received from Nuttall only a few weeks earlier. Francis informed Shepard that the Rasmussen case had been reopened by Van Nuys homicide. Francis felt excited about the possibility the case might be solved. To her surprise, Shepard seemed angry.

Shepard asked Francis which detective at Van Nuys had reopened the case. Shepard did not recognize Nuttall's name. Shepard asked Francis who else was working on Rasmussen. Francis mentioned Bub. According to Francis, Shepard replied, "Well, if Bub has that case, it'll never get solved."

Francis did not know what to make of Shepard's reaction. Francis later spoke to Nuttall and told him about her run-in with Shepard in Reno. Nuttall did not know what to make of it himself. Nuttall expected that Shepard would call him to discuss the Rasmussen case. Nuttall never heard from Shepard, however. Even more perplexing to Nuttall was that the Rasmussen chrono contained no record of any investigative activity between 1999 and 2008.

The Van Nuys detectives had no evidence of any animosity between Sherri and the first three women on their list, Loretta, Teresa, and Jayne. The detectives eliminated them as suspects for lack of motive. That left Deborah Putnam and Stephanie Lazarus, both of whom did have a possible motive. The detectives decided to focus on Putnam first, to try to confirm or eliminate her as a suspect, before they turned their attention to Stephanie.

Nuttall located Putnam living in Northern California and contacted her local law enforcement agency. Nuttall requested that a surreptitious DNA sample be collected from Putnam's trash. The DNA sample was obtained on March 20 and FedExed to Van Nuys homicide, then forwarded to SID for analysis.

Francis called Nuttall on April 16 and informed him that the evidence sample recovered from Putnam's trash did not match the suspect's DNA profile developed from the bite mark swab. Nuttall requested that Francis meet with the Van Nuys homicide unit in person to discuss the course and scope of the Rasmussen investigation.

A week later, on April 23, Francis went to the Van Nuys station and met with Nuttall, Bub, and Barba in the homicide squad room. The detectives gave Francis a complete briefing on the status of their investigation, including that Stephanie Lazarus, an LAPD detective, might have been involved in the murder of Sherri Rasmussen. Nuttall requested Francis's extraordinary discretion. Francis did not divulge to the Van Nuys detectives that she already knew about Stephanie Lazarus, if not by name, from her conversations with Shepard in 2005. Francis requested that the detectives brief her immediate supervisor at SID, Collin Yamauchi.

Nuttall spent the next week interviewing Sherri's friends and family. Nuttall spoke first with Jayne, Sherri's former roommate. Nuttall asked Jayne if Sherri had any troublesome relationships. Jayne told Nuttall she knew Sherri had problems with an ex-girlfriend of John's. Jayne said that in fall of 1985, the ex-girlfriend went to Sherri's work and told her that she was in love with John and would be waiting for him if the marriage failed. Jayne said Sherri told both her and John about the incident. Sherri had described it to Jayne as an "odd thing at work with a woman dressed real provocatively."

Nels and Loretta Rasmussen were in Washington State that week for their high school reunion. Loretta had thought about calling the LAPD in February, around Sherri's birthday and the date she was killed, but never did. Loretta figured it wouldn't do any good. Loretta decided to pray on it instead. Unbeknownst to the Rasmussens, Nuttall had reopened Sherri's case the same month. At their reunion, many of their old friends asked them, as they always did, "Have you heard anything on Sherri's case?" The Rasmussens said they hadn't. When they got home to Tucson, there was a message on their answering machine from Nuttall.

Nels returned the call and spoke with Nuttall for the first time on April 28. Nuttall informed Nels that his daughter's case was open and active. Nuttall said he had already talked to John but did not reveal anything else about the status of the investigation. Nuttall asked Nels, "Tell me what your feeling is about Sherri's case." Nels replied that he knew who was responsible for his daughter's murder, a female LAPD officer who had dated John Ruetten before he met Sherri. Nels also said Sherri had issues with a nurse and doctor she worked with. Nels told Nuttall that he had provided the same information to the LAPD in 1986. Nuttall asked Nels to give him a few days and said that he would be in touch again.

As the Van Nuys detectives ramped up their investigation into Stephanie, other pieces fell uncomfortably into place. Martinez recalled that in the 1980s, most LAPD officers carried a .38 as their backup gun, the same caliber as the bullets recovered during Sherri's autopsy. On April 30, Martinez ran Stephanie's name through a California database of registered firearms. The database indicated that she had five registered handguns. One of them, a .38 Smith & Wesson revolver, had been reported stolen in Santa Monica on March 9, 1986, thirteen days after the murder. For twenty-three years, the information about Stephanie's stolen gun had been available to any LAPD detective who bothered to search for it. No one had checked, apparently, until Martinez. Martinez contacted the Santa Monica Police Department and obtained a copy of the crime report, which stated that Stephanie had reported the gun stolen from her parked car. Nine days after that, she had purchased a new .38 Smith & Wesson revolver.

Nuttall emailed Francis on May 2, *"Candidate number five reported .38 cal. handgun stolen in Santa Monica within days of the 187. Working on obtaining the DNA for you."*

For all the detectives had learned about Stephanie, they still had no idea where she lived, nor how they might obtain a sample of her DNA to compare to the suspect's profile. Her home address was not easy to locate, almost as though she didn't want to be found. The first address Bub obtained, from Stephanie's LAPD emergency contact information, turned out to be her mother's. Bub cast a wider net, using other databases, and came up with three more addresses, all in Simi Valley. Bub and Nuttall drove up there early one morning and went to each address. Two were shuttered businesses and the third was a mailbox rental store. As they drove back to Van Nuys, Nuttall thought, "Damn, she's good. She kicked our asses today."

>>> JAMES NUTTALL 5/2/2009 3:13 PM >>>
Jennifer:

If your checking your e-mail I'm just keeping you informed. Candidate number five reported a .38 cal. handgun stolen in Santa Monica within days of the 187. Working on obtaining the DNA for you, I left a voicemail for your partner at the lab....hope all is well.....Jim

---

Det. Jim Nuttall's email to Jennifer Francis, May 2, 2009

On May 4, still on the hunt for Stephanie's home address, Barba identified her husband as Scott Young. A few database searches later, Barba was
stunned to discover that not only was Young also an LAPD detective, but
he was assigned to, of all possible places, the Van Nuys Division. Barba
informed Bub and Nuttall immediately. The detectives did not know Young
by name, but when they pulled up his driver's license photo, they recognized him. In the Van Nuys locker room, Nuttall and Young's lockers were
only a few apart. The stress level among the four detectives, already extraordinary, was ratcheted even higher.

Early the next morning, Bub drove back to Simi Valley and past another
possible address he had turned up for Stephanie Lazarus, a one-story
single family residence with an attached garage and an in-ground swimming pool. Parked in the driveway was a 1991 silver Toyota pickup truck
with the personalized license plate 5STEPH. Bub made no effort to initiate
contact with Stephanie, but they finally knew where she lived.

On May 6, Nuttall called Nels Rasmussen and reinterviewed him at
length, this time on a recorded phone line. Nuttall asked Nels to walk him
through everything from A to Z. Nels provided Nuttall with a step-by-step
account of his contacts with Sherri in the months leading up to her murder.
Nels also gave Nuttall a detailed account of events following the murder,
including all of his and Loretta's interactions with LAPD detectives in 1986
and in the years since. Nels said he informed Lyle Mayer of the ex-girlfriend
police officer the day after Sherri was killed, and many times thereafter,
throughout the first two years of the LAPD's original investigation.

Given the sensitivity of the unfolding investigation, Nuttall had to be
cautious about tipping his hand. Nuttall told Nels, "If one of our officers is
responsible for this, we're on the same page you are, Nels. It's an investigation that's moving forward. It will continue to move forward. There's a
handful of detectives working this, and the only thing we're waiting on now,
Nels, is to obtain what's called a DNA reference sample. That has to be done
with the utmost discretion, because as you can imagine, we can't walk
down, knock on someone's door, and say—"

"I realize that," Nels said.

Before they hung up, Nels told Nuttall, "If you want to make a hundred thousand dollars, bet me it's not her." Nuttall laughed.

The detectives initially toyed with the idea of trying to obtain a surreptitious DNA sample from Stephanie themselves, perhaps by collecting
and sifting through her trash. Nuttall called waste management in Simi

Valley and found out what day of the week garbage was picked up from her home. Ultimately, Bub decided there were too many variables and too much potential for a screw-up to justify the risk.

Bub knew that if Stephanie's DNA profile was a match, it was inevitable that investigative responsibility for the Rasmussen case would shift from the Van Nuys homicide unit to RHD downtown. Bub had worked at RHD for many years, and he was determined to deliver an ultra-professional package to whichever detectives at RHD took over the case from them.

If Stephanie's DNA profile was not a match, the Van Nuys detectives realized, the Rasmussen case would be designated "investigation continued" and shelved yet again, probably forever.

On May 12, Bub decided it was time to brief the brass on the status and focus of their investigation. Bub met with his lieutenant and the captain of the Van Nuys Division and updated them. The captain directed Bub to brief Deputy Chief Michel Moore, at that time the commanding officer of Valley Operations Bureau. Nine years later, in June 2018, Moore was sworn in as the LAPD's chief of police. Moore succeeded Chief Charlie Beck, who succeeded Bill Bratton.

Bub briefed Moore on the investigation and the circumstantial evidence his detectives had amassed against Stephanie Lazarus. Bub stressed to Moore that it could still turn out not to be her. Bub explained the only way to eliminate her definitively as a suspect was to obtain a DNA sample and compare her profile to the suspect's.

Moore authorized the deployment of the LAPD's Internal Surveillance Unit to obtain a surreptitious DNA sample from Stephanie. ISU is a secretive unit, separate from the Internal Affairs Group, within the department's Professional Standards Bureau. Officers assigned to the ISU are referred to within the LAPD as "operators."

Moore could have transferred responsibility for the Rasmussen investigation to RHD immediately. Moore warned Bub that if her DNA was a match, he and his detectives would probably lose the case. Moore told Bub that the case would remain with the Van Nuys unit until the DNA results were in.

On May 19, Bub, Nuttall, and Martinez met undercover officers from the ISU at a parking garage in Burbank. The three detectives were transported to an undisclosed location, where they met with a larger retinue of ISU operators and supervisors. Nuttall gave a detailed briefing on the Rasmussen investigation, from the time of the murder to the present day. The mood in the room grew tense and uncomfortable as Nuttall recounted how Stephanie had emerged as a suspect and ran down the circumstantial evidence against her. Even to the ISU operators jaded by repeated daily exposure to police misconduct allegations, the idea that one of their own might be responsible for a murder felt shocking and sickening. At the end of Nuttall's presentation, the captain in charge of the undercover unit directed the operation targeting Stephanie Lazarus to proceed.

Some of the ISU operators knew Stephanie personally, but not one person begged off the case. The consensus opinion was that while they hoped she hadn't done it, the facts suggested she probably had. With that realization came pressure to move quickly. If the murder allegation was true, Stephanie needed to be taken off the street.

Round-the-clock surveillance of Stephanie began the next day, May 20. Two teams of ISU operators alternated shadowing her, learning her habits and waiting for her to discard something that might have her DNA on it. ISU's reconnaissance report, a written summary of their activities on the case, directed, *The evidence is to be immediately transported to SID and Van Nuys homicide is to be notified, day or night.*

Among the challenges the surveillance team faced was that Stephanie lived in a very quiet neighborhood, with little pedestrian and vehicular activity outside her home, other than worker traffic. The ISU reconnaissance report noted, *"The location is difficult to surveil as the only parking is on the street across from the home. On a prior occasion, an off-duty LAPD Devonshire officer, who lives directly across the street . . . confronted [an ISU] unit and asked why he was there."* ISU's report also stated, *"TACTICAL NOTE: RHD CO Captain Cremins said the target is physically fit and takes training in Krav Magra [sic], the Israeli art of self defense."*

Every morning Stephanie worked, she came outside at 5:00 a.m. and got the newspaper from her driveway, then drove herself to the Simi Valley train station. Every day, she read the newspaper for the duration of her train ride downtown, then threw the newspaper out before she walked into Parker Center. The first several items the surveillance team collected were newspapers that she had discarded. A few days later, as Stephanie left Parker Center, she was observed eating a muffin straight from a cellophane wrapper. She brought the wrapper up to her mouth with each bite she took. After she threw out the wrapper, it, too, was collected. All the evidence items were booked and analyzed by SID, but none contained enough DNA to yield her profile.

Stephanie's husband, Scott, drove daily to and from work in Van Nuys. The surveillance team knew Stephanie was off duty on a given day if she didn't come outside at 5:00 a.m.

On Thursday morning, May 28, Scott drove off as usual. Stephanie did not appear until 8:00 a.m., when she stepped outside with her daughter, not yet three years old. Stephanie retrieved the newspaper and they went back inside. A few hours later, the surveillance team saw the garage door open and a van back out. Because they had not seen who got in the car when it was in the garage, they had to follow it to confirm who was inside. Stephanie was driving the van, and she had her daughter with her.

Stephanie drove to the Costco in Simi Valley. She first pulled into its gas station and filled up, then parked the van and walked into the Costco with her daughter in tow. The Costco had a food court with outdoor seating. Stephanie was watched as she ordered lunch.

After a week of trailing her, the ISU surveillance team recognized that this could be their shot. The undercover operators glided into place expertly around her, anticipating her next move. When Stephanie walked out to the courtyard, carrying pizza and soft drinks for herself and her daughter, she took no notice of the Latino man already seated outside, at a table right next to a trash bin. Stephanie and her daughter sat down about twenty feet away from him. Stephanie sipped repeatedly from her drink, a cardboard cup with a lid and straw. Minutes later, she stood up, cup in hand. Although there was another trash bin closer to her, she walked directly toward the undercover ISU operator. For a split second, he feared his cover was blown. Stephanie instead took a final sip through her straw and dropped the cup in the trash bin. She and her daughter then walked away.

Ten to fifteen seconds after Stephanie deposited it, the cup was fished carefully from the trash, placed in a manila envelope, and whisked to SID.

The next day, May 29, Bub and Nuttall were the first detectives notified by SID that Stephanie's DNA profile was a match. The DNA result made it a foregone conclusion that the district attorney would charge her with first-degree murder. Within hours, as Bub had anticipated, he and Nuttall were headed downtown with the Rasmussen murder book to brief the RHD detectives who would assume control of their four-month-old investigation.

The RHD Homicide Special squad room was on the third floor of Parker Center, just across the hall from Stephanie's desk in the Commercial Crimes Division. Many RHD detectives knew Stephanie either personally or as a familiar face, somebody they might literally chat with around the office water cooler. Commercial Crimes and RHD shared a water cooler located in the RHD squad room. Stephanie often popped in to refill her water bottle.

Nuttall and Bub met with and briefed the lieutenant at RHD, Gregg Strenk, and the two detectives who would take over the Rasmussen investigation, Dan Jaramillo and Greg Stearns. Strenk assigned the case to Stearns and Jaramillo because they were on call and neither knew Stephanie well. The task before the RHD detectives was not to solve the murder, since the Van Nuys unit had already accomplished that. Stearns and Jaramillo were to plan Stephanie's arrest, take her into custody, and then work with the DA's office to secure her conviction.

Stephanie presumably had not forgotten what happened between her and Sherri in 1986. As a detective, she surely also knew that the mandatory sentence in California for first-degree murder was twenty-five years to life. Not counting the gun that she reported stolen in 1986, she still owned four other registered handguns. There was no guarantee that Stephanie would not be tempted to take the easy way out when they confronted her, rather than face justice. For the same reasons, she had every incentive to flee if she were to get wind, even inadvertently, that a detective was being investigated for a cold case murder.

To maintain confidentiality, it was decided that the investigation would be run out of a conference room at the district attorney's Justice System Integrity Division, which handled criminal allegations against police officers. Two veteran prosecutors at JSID, Shannon Presby and Shelly Torrealba, were assigned to the Lazarus case. Torrealba and Detective Stearns were already friends from having worked together on previous cases. The detectives set up shop at JSID and briefed Presby and his supervisors on Friday night, the same day the DNA match was confirmed.

Several other RHD detectives were asked to report to work on Saturday morning, without being told why. Strenk interviewed each detective separately and asked them two questions: what relationships they had, if any, with detectives assigned to the Commercial Crimes Division, and whether they had any reservations about investigating a police officer. Once Strenk confirmed they did not know Stephanie and had no qualms about investigating a fellow cop, they were briefed on the case and added to the incipient task force at JSID. The additional detectives were to play a supporting role to Stearns and Jaramillo by handling smaller, discrete aspects of the investigation, grunt work and shoe leather tasks like tracking down departmental records and interviewing witnesses.

Later that morning, Nuttall met RHD detective Jay King at the Van Nuys station. Nuttall turned over to King all the investigative records from the Rasmussen case that remained at Van Nuys homicide. King copied to a thumb drive the "Rasmussen 1986" folder on the unit's P drive, which contained all the documents created by the Van Nuys detectives since they had reopened the case. King returned to RHD and gave all the materials to Stearns. Once Stearns had copied the computer files to his own thumb drive, King called Nuttall and instructed him to delete all the Rasmussen files from the Van Nuys unit's P drive. Stearns, whose last name matched his serious demeanor, assumed the role of de facto gatekeeper for all information the LAPD held about the murder of Sherri Rasmussen and the case against Stephanie Lazarus.

The same day, a supervisor in the SID Serology Unit, Harry Klann, emailed Jennifer Francis and other criminalists working on the Rasmussen case. Klann wrote that he had just received a call from RHD. *"All reports in this case are to go to Det. Jay King. **Do NOT send any reports through the RHD Cold Case Unit**,"* Klann emphasized. Klann's email suggests that as early as May 30, one day after Van Nuys handed over the case to RHD, questions were already being asked within RHD, and possibly higher up in the department, about why the case had not been solved in 2005, when Detective Cliff Shepard of the RHD Cold Case Homicide Unit was informed of the female DNA profile.

Bub returned to running the Van Nuys homicide unit after he and Nuttall briefed RHD and the prosecuters at JSID. Strenk told Bub that he wanted to keep Nuttall on the investigation. It was not uncommon for divisional detectives to move to RHD, sometimes permanently, if they were the lead investigator on a case that RHD took over. Bub wasn't thrilled, because he had only three detectives, counting Nuttall, in his unit. But there wasn't much Bub could do about it. RHD's profile within the department allowed it to pull detectives pretty much at will.

Strenk never explained to Nuttall his reasons for keeping him on the Rasmussen case, or whether the invitation was just a courtesy, given Nuttall's role in solving it. In any event, Nuttall was committed to seeing the case through and stood ready to do whatever was asked of him.

The following Monday, June 1, Nuttall reported for duty at JSID instead of Van Nuys. Nuttall was not well acquainted with any of the RHD detectives on the team, all of whom knew each other. Later that afternoon, Strenk, Nuttall, Stearns, Jaramillo, and the other detectives met at JSID with Presby and Torrealba to discuss the case and initial concerns raised by their higher-ups at both agencies. The prosecutors requested, among other things, that several witnesses be reinterviewed in person.

Strenk directed Nuttall and Lisa Sanchez-Padilla, an RHD detective on the team, to fly the next day to Sacramento to interview a hospital colleague of Sherri Rasmussen. From there, the detectives were to fly to Tucson to interview the Rasmussens and obtain elimination DNA samples from Sherri's female relatives.

Nuttall met Nels and Loretta in person for the first time on Tuesday night, June 2, at their home in Tucson. Nuttall could not reveal to the Rasmussens that, twenty-three years after Sherri's murder, an arrest was finally imminent.

Even as the detectives back at JSID worked to keep their investigation under wraps, the ongoing, unexplained absence of several Homicide Special Section detectives from the RHD squad room was noticed by other detectives at RHD who were still in the dark about what was unfolding. The extraordinary secrecy around the case heightened the sense that an uncommon suspect was being investigated for murder. The initial speculation in the squad room was that it had to be either a politician or a cop.

As the week went on, the rumors became more specific. One female RHD detective heard that it was a female detective being investigated for a cold case murder, and, supposedly, the last two digits of the suspect's LAPD serial number. The detective looked at RHD's roster and saw that another female RHD detective, someone she was friends with, had a serial number with the same last two digits. The detective never checked the Commercial Crimes Division roster, the one Stephanie was listed on. For the next few days, until Stephanie was arrested, the detective believed her friend at RHD was possibly a murderer.

The same week, a small group of RHD detectives were discussing the tension building in their squad room when one confessed he felt nervous.

"Do you remember committing a murder?" an older detective replied.

"No."

"Then what do you have to be nervous about?"

By midweek, Stearns and Jaramillo had devised a game plan for approaching Stephanie and taking her into custody. Chief Bratton did not want her to have a gun, or access to a gun, when the approach was made.

Stearns and Jaramillo decided to stage an interview in the Jail Division on the second floor of Parker Center, one below RHD and the Art Theft Detail. Firearms were not allowed in the jail, so it would not seem unnatural for them, including Stephanie, to surrender their guns before entering. The arrest was planned for that Friday morning, June 5.

Nuttall continued to report to work at JSID after he returned from Tucson. He expected that he would be involved in the operation to plan Stephanie's interrogation and arrest. Instead, he found himself watching from the sidelines. The tasks he was assigned, returning phone calls and making copies, struck him as nothing more than busywork. Nuttall was confident he knew the facts of the Rasmussen case as well as anyone. He and his squad mates in Van Nuys had lived and breathed the details for going on four months. Nuttall believed he could contribute to the game planning and wanted to be a part of it. But he was in no position to dictate his role to RHD.

On Thursday, Strenk informed Nuttall and Sanchez-Padilla that they would fly back to Tucson that night so the Rasmussens could be notified Friday morning of the arrest in person rather than learn of it via the news media.

Nuttall accepted the order without complaint. Still, it seemed odd to him that in the week since RHD had assumed the investigation, all he had been asked to do was travel. Nuttall wondered if the travel was meant to keep him away from Los Angeles, where all the key decisions in the investigation were being made. Suddenly, on the eve of the arrest, he was being sent out of town again, after just having returned from Tucson a day earlier.

Nuttall also was not particularly eager to get back on a plane with Sanchez-Padilla. He had a high opinion of her as a detective, and on their first trip, to Sacramento and Tucson, their working relationship was fine. Still, it was apparent to him, and perhaps to her as well, that they did not see eye to eye on the Rasmussen case.

Nuttall attributed the disconnect to the fact that none of the RHD detectives, including Sanchez-Padilla, knew what he and his Van Nuys squad mates had been through, investigating a fellow LAPD detective for murder, in total secrecy, for months. Only the four detectives in Van Nuys had experienced that excruciating pressure, all the while keeping their families, friends, and colleagues at arm's length. Not even their wives had known what they were grappling with at work. Coming to grips with the harrowing possibility that one of their own might be guilty of murder had been an emotional roller coaster, one that had made the Van Nuys detectives care deeply about the case and the Rasmussens. Sanchez-Padilla, by contrast, had been on the case for only a few days and had little emotional connection to it or to the Rasmussens.

Nuttall believed the Rasmussens deserved answers about why their concerns regarding John's ex-girlfriend were ignored. Nuttall sensed that Sanchez-Padilla did not share his perspective or feel the same responsibility to the Rasmussens. Nuttall thought that Sanchez-Padilla's priorities were the department first and the Rasmussens second. For Nuttall, it was the Rasmussens first, second, and third.

Nuttall thought it would have been better for the department to send him to Tucson with Bub, Barba, or Martinez, since they had solved the case and also had their own emotional connections to the Rasmussens. Nuttall did not even know yet what he wanted to say to Nels and Loretta, but he knew he did not want Sanchez-Padilla's input.

Nuttall was at JSID early Thursday afternoon, biding his time until his flight to Tucson, when he looked up and saw that Deputy Chief Charlie Beck, the LAPD's chief of detectives, had just walked through the door. Nuttall was caught off guard. No one had mentioned to him that Beck was coming to JSID for a high-level briefing. Up to that point, Nuttall had delivered every briefing on the case.

Beck came from a family of police officers. His father, George Beck, was a deputy chief who retired from the LAPD in 1980. The elder Beck was a longtime friend of Chief of Police Daryl Gates. The men were so close that when Charlie was born in 1953, Gates was made his godfather. At the time, Gates was so early in his LAPD career that he had yet to make sergeant.

Charlie grew up and joined the LAPD in 1977, a year before his godfather was named chief. In March 1984, Beck was assigned to the Hollywood Division when newly minted police officer Stephanie Lazarus reported there fresh from the academy. Beck and Stephanie overlapped at Hollywood station for the first three months of her police career, until June 1984, when Beck was promoted to sergeant and transferred out of the division. As young officers, both participated in LAPD athletics and were teammates on the LAPD's California Police Olympics team every year from 1984 to 1987. How well Beck and Stephanie knew each other is unknown.

As chief of detectives, Beck was squarely atop Nuttall's chain of command, but their positions in the department were separated by so many layers of brass that Nuttall had never met Beck previously. Nuttall was not sure if Beck even knew who he was, let alone his role in solving the Rasmussen case.

Beck and Nuttall made eye contact. For a moment, he thought Beck might come over to him and shake his hand, or even give him a pat on the back and say something like "Good job, detective." Beck stared right at Nuttall, and Nuttall at him. Beck said nothing and did not acknowledge his presence in any way. Nuttall's heart dropped.

The briefing held at JSID Thursday afternoon was for top LAPD and DA's office personnel. Beck was the highest-ranked LAPD official in attendance. The captain of RHD, Denis Cremins, also attended. Nuttall watched as Beck and the other brass disappeared into a meeting room, along with Strenk, Stearns, Jaramillo, and other detectives from RHD.

Nuttall sat in an adjacent room, by himself, while Stearns ran the briefing and recounted to the brass how the Rasmussen case was solved. Nuttall was flabbergasted that no one from the Van Nuys homicide unit was invited to participate in the briefing. The Van Nuys detectives had been knee-deep in the case for months. Not only weren't they handling the briefing, they weren't even in the room, denying them the credit and recognition they deserved and might have received for having solved the case.

Nuttall had his orders and returned to Tucson with Sanchez-Padilla that night. As they boarded their flight, the plan to arrest Stephanie seemed set to proceed Friday morning. There was still the possibility, however, that plans could change, and the LAPD brass or the DA's office could order the arrest team to stand down at the twenty-third hour.

Nuttall told Sanchez-Padilla that regardless of the outcome, he intended to spend Friday morning talking with Nels and Loretta. Nuttall believed the Rasmussens had waited long enough to know who killed their daughter, and for someone at the LAPD be one hundred percent truthful with them. Nuttall planned to answer, to the best of his ability, whatever questions the Rasmussens had. Sanchez-Padilla told Nuttall, "Those aren't our orders."

When they got to their hotel in Tucson, they parted company. Nuttall ate dinner by himself at the hotel restaurant. Nuttall called Nels and asked him if he and Loretta were available to meet the next morning. Nels said he had a doctor's appointment. Nuttall told Nels, "You may want to reschedule that."

Friday morning, Stephanie was placed under surveillance during her morning commute to work. Shortly after she sat down at her desk, Jaramillo approached her and used a ruse, a story involving a fictitious extortion suspect, to lure her down to the Jail Division. Jaramillo said the suspect had mentioned something about stolen art. "You can kind of talk to him. You can see if he's for real," Jaramillo bluffed. Stephanie said sure. As they entered the jail, Jaramillo checked his gun. Stephanie told Jaramillo that she'd left hers in her desk. Jaramillo walked her to an interview room, where Stearns, but no extortion suspect, was waiting.

Stearns and Jaramillo knew that Stephanie, a fellow detective, was well aware of her right to remain silent. The detectives expected she might clam up and demand an attorney as soon as they spoke John Ruetten's name. Stearns and Jaramillo intended to keep her talking for as long as possible, in the hope that she would incriminate herself. Whether or not Stephanie cooperated, she would be arrested the moment she ended the interview and left the room.

Remarkably, Stephanie answered Stearns and Jaramillo's questions for more than an hour. The detectives interviewed her in a way that kept her off balance about whether they considered her a witness or a suspect. Stephanie went off on various tangents, but the detectives always steered the conversation back to the murder of Sherri Rasmussen.

Jaramillo eventually asked Stephanie if she would voluntarily provide a DNA sample. Stephanie hemmed and hawed, then said, "Now, I'm thinking I probably need to talk to a lawyer . . . 'cause I know how this stuff works. Okay? Don't get me wrong. You're right. I have been doing this a long time." Stephanie got up and left the interview room. Once outside the room, she was immediately taken into custody.

The arrest of a female LAPD detective for a cold case murder was instant national and even international news. The initial details that leaked could hardly have been more sensational. Not only was the murder motivated by a love triangle, but the killer, a female police officer, had bitten her victim during the deadly struggle. In a karmic twist, DNA from the bite was what ultimately led to her arrest.

The intense media attention came at an extraordinarily sensitive moment for the LAPD's brass. On June 15, just ten days after Stephanie's arrest, the LAPD's long-running federal consent decree was due to expire. After eight years, the department was desperate for federal oversight to be lifted. The decision rested entirely with Judge Feess, who had already extended it once and had the power to do so again. Feess had vowed not to lift the consent decree until he was convinced that real reform had taken root and the LAPD could be trusted to run its own affairs without backsliding.

Friday afternoon, the LAPD held a press conference to announce Stephanie's arrest. Chief Bratton and Deputy Chief Beck addressed the media. Also in attendance was Assistant Chief Jim McDonnell, Bratton's chief of staff and second in command. Five years later, in 2014, McDonnell was elected Los Angeles County sheriff, a position he held until 2018.

LAPD press conference announcing Stephanie Lazarus's arrest, June 5, 2009 (left to right: Deputy Chief Charlie Beck, Assistant Chief Jim McDonnell, and LAPD Chief Bill Bratton)

During the press conference, Bratton misspoke and credited the RHD cold case unit with solving Sherri Rasmussen's murder. In reality, the RHD cold case unit had had the Rasmussen case since 2003, and a female DNA profile since 2005, but had failed to solve it.

Bratton told the media, "They did what was expected of Los Angeles police officers. They went where the truth and the facts as known to them took them. My compliments to the detectives involved in the investigation of this case. Painful for them to be reviewing a case, and then determine that the leads were leading to a current member of the police force." Bratton called the arrest "a very positive reflection on us, in the sense that we take our oath very seriously."

Beck acknowledged at the press conference that he had known Stephanie personally for many years. Beck, who knew better than Bratton, also credited RHD for the investigation. Beck said, "Commercial Crimes Division is right next door to it. These are folks on one side of the hallway investigating a member of the other. You know, this is very difficult. You can't know a person for that long, or their family, and not be affected by this."

Beck was asked if Lazarus received less scrutiny in the original investigation because she was an LAPD officer. "I don't know the answer to that, at this point. Many, many things are going to be looked at. That's one of them," Beck promised.

Within the LAPD, the news that a detective had been arrested for a cold case murder spread like wildfire. The allegations were so shocking that officers remembered where they were when they heard. Throughout the day Friday, Nuttall's and Bub's phones were blowing up with calls and messages from other officers, nearly all of whom had no idea that it was the Van Nuys homicide unit, working in secret, that had solved the case. One detective at

Van Nuys came into the homicide squad room and told Bub, "You're not going to believe this, but a female detective got arrested for doing one of your murders."

"Yeah, I know," Bub replied.

Stephanie's arraignment for first-degree murder was scheduled for Tuesday morning, June 9. The Rasmussens traveled from Tucson to attend in person. Monday at RHD, Nuttall mentioned that he planned to give Nels and Loretta a lift to the courthouse the next morning. In Nuttall's view, he was going to court anyway. Why not offer the Rasmussens a ride, so they didn't have to take a taxi? Nuttall felt the department should be rolling out the red carpet for the Rasmussens, given what they had been through.

Nuttall was directed, in no uncertain terms, that he was not to give the Rasmussens a ride to court. "That's not how we do things," Nuttall was told.

The next morning, the courtroom was packed for Stephanie's arraignment. The Rasmussens and Stephanie's husband both attended the arraignment. John Ruetten did not.

Afterward, the Rasmussens and their attorney, John Taylor, held a press conference on the courthouse plaza. Taylor spoke on behalf of Nels and Loretta, who stood over his shoulder. "The family has nothing but praise for the LAPD of 2009," Taylor said into a bouquet of TV and radio microphones. Taylor mentioned Bub and Nuttall by name and thanked them. Taylor went on, "The investigation in 1986 is a completely different story, and the family has numerous questions about what was done during that time period . . . The family has spent twenty-three years to get where they are now. The family would like a formal inquiry to go forward that looks at the activities and the investigation that was done by the LAPD during that time frame. We're hopeful that that will occur." No one from the LAPD attended the Rasmussens' press conference.

That afternoon, Nuttall and the RHD detectives who were assigned to the case were taken to lunch by Gregg Strenk, the RHD lieutenant. Afterward, Strenk told Nuttall that he needed to speak with him outside the restaurant. Strenk told Nuttall, "I've got to send you back," meaning to Van Nuys. Strenk offered no explanation for why Nuttall was off the case.

Shortly after Nuttall returned to his regular assignment, an RHD detective came to the Van Nuys homicide squad room and picked up the murder book for the unsolved 1988 homicide of Catherine Braley. Nuttall never even cracked the Braley murder book before RHD came to retrieve it.

On June 10, the day after Stephanie was arraigned, RHD cold case

```
Date:          6/10/2009 4:16 PM
Subject:       Promotion

Sorry I didn't contact you earlier to congratulate you, but belated congratulations. I owe you a toast or
two.  Also, obviously, to admit that you were on the right track with the love triangle theory.

Cliff
```

Det. Cliff Shepard's email to Jennifer Francis, June 10, 2009

detective Cliff Shepard emailed Jennifer Francis, the DNA analyst. Shepard wrote: *"Sorry I didn't contact you earlier to congratulate you, but belated congratulations. I owe you a toast or two. Also, obviously, to admit that you were on the right track with the love triangle theory. Cliff."*

Even before Francis read Shepard's email, she had been thinking back on her earlier conversations with him, in 2005, about the Rasmussen case. Ever since the DNA match to Lazarus, Francis saw those conversations in a new, more troubling light. At the time, Francis could not understand why Shepard was so intent on pursuing male-female burglary teams rather than female suspects Sherri knew. In hindsight, it seemed to Francis that Shepard had steered the investigation away from Lazarus. Francis knew of other LAPD officers who had been retaliated against by the department for failing to toe the line in a cover-up. Francis was afraid to tell anyone about her conversations with Shepard for several months.

In the weeks after the arrest, various details of the LAPD's secretive investigation of Lazarus began to leak to the media, including the names of the detectives who had solved the case. In mid-June, Bub received a voicemail from ABC News's *Nightline* requesting an interview with him or Nuttall. Following protocol, Bub relayed the interview request to the LAPD's Press Relations Unit. Bub was advised by Lt. John Romero that all media communications regarding the Lazarus case were to be run through the office of Charlie Beck, the LAPD's chief of detectives. In an email to Beck, Bub wrote, *"Detective Nuttall and I will make ourselves available (or not) based on your decision. I will wait to hear from you before returning the call."* Bub copied on his email to Beck several other high-ranking members of the LAPD brass, including the captains of the Van Nuys and Robbery-Homicide Divisions; the commanding officer of the department's Public Information Office; and from RHD, Lt. Strenk and detectives Stearns and Jaramillo.

When the *Nightline* report aired on July 10, the only LAPD interviewee was Deputy Chief Beck himself. Beck said of Stephanie Lazarus, "She had

Chief Beck,

  I was contacted (via voice mail) by Alicia (unknown last name) of ABC Nightline requesting an interview of myself and/or Detective Nuttall with regard to the Stephanie Lazarus case. I have not returned the call as of this morning. I contacted Lt. John Romero of Press Relations who advised me that all media communications was to be run through your office. Detective Nuttall and I will make ourselves available (or not) based on your decision.

  I will wait until I hear from you before returning the call.

Det III Robert Bub,
Serial No. 23603
LAPD -- Van Nuys Homicide Unit
(818) 374-1948

Occam's Razor: One should not increase, beyond what is necessary, the number of entities required to explain anything.

Det. Rob Bub's email to Deputy Chief Charlie Beck, June 2009

a good reputation. Hardworking, very energetic . . . What people have to recognize is that there are people that can hold very, very dark secrets and hold them very well . . . I think a lot of people are very, very shocked. She was a very outgoing, well-liked person that had a long, long history with a lot of people here. So I think a lot of people felt very bad, and are still coming to grips with it."

Judge Feess delayed his decision about whether to lift the LAPD's federal consent decree until mid-July. On July 9, the *Los Angeles Times* reported that Chief Bratton had placed his Los Angeles home on the market. The following week, on July 17, Judge Feess freed the LAPD from federal oversight. Bratton told the *Times* that Feess's ruling proved that the LAPD had regained its reputation.

On August 5, Bratton announced his surprise resignation as LAPD chief. Bratton was just a year and a half into his second five-year term. Deputy Chief Charlie Beck was selected as Bratton's successor, to be sworn in after Bratton stepped down that fall.

Despite the Rasmussens' public allegation of a cover-up, and their request for an investigation, the LAPD did not open one of its own accord. Although Stephanie was arrested for first-degree murder on June 5, no one at the LAPD, from Chief Bratton on down, initiated a personnel complaint against her for any misconduct until July 22, more than six weeks later.

In late September, the Rasmussens filed a legal claim against the City of Los Angeles, the precursor to a civil lawsuit. In the small space on the claim form for "*How did DAMAGE or INJURY occur? Please include as much* detail as possible," the Rasmussens' attorney wrote: *"LAPD Officer Stephanie Lazarus killed Claimants' daughter, Sherri Rasmussen, & used her position as a police officer to assist in committing the crime. LAPD subsequently committed fraud, negligence & other wrongful acts in an attempt to perpetuate a cover-up & otherwise protect Officer Lazarus from criminal prosecution."*

The Rasmussens' legal claim automatically triggered an Internal Affairs investigation into the allegations. LAPD policy compelled the department to open an official investigation whenever it was sued for police misconduct, a new reform it had agreed to adopt under the federal consent decree. The LAPD's investigation into the Rasmussens' allegations was opened on November 3, five months after Stephanie's arrest.

The LAPD itself, and not the complainant, gets to frame the specific allegations that Internal Affairs will investigate. Two allegations were enumerated, based on the Rasmussens' legal claim. Allegation 1 was that Stephanie, while off duty, killed Sherri Rasmussen. Allegation 2 stated, *"between February 24, 1986 and June 5, 2009, the LAPD attempted to cover-up [sic] the murder of Sherri Rasmussen."*

Each allegation also had to specify, by name, an accused employee. Stephanie was listed as the accused employee for allegation 1. For allegation 2, the accused employee was listed generically as *"Department."* Significantly, this framing of the Rasmussens' cover-up allegation meant that no individual officers, current or retired, other than Stephanie Lazarus, were named as subjects of the LAPD's Internal Affairs investigation.

On November 10, the LAPD's official investigation into the Rasmussens' allegations was assigned to a sergeant at Internal Affairs, Barbara Hodgin. Hodgin's first entry in her chronological log for the case stated,

LAPD Internal Affairs "face sheet" for the Rasmussens' complaint, CF #09-004314 (November 3, 2009)

"Received complaint of Claim for Damages. Per Captain Moriarty, toll case pending criminal investigation." Moriarty was LAPD Captain III Michael Moriarty, the commanding officer of the Administrative Investigation Division at Internal Affairs. Within Internal Affairs, Moriarty was outranked only by Commander Rick Webb, the commanding officer for the entire Internal Affairs Group.

In LAPD Internal Affairs investigations, the burden of proof to sustain an allegation of misconduct is "the preponderance of the evidence," meaning more likely than not. Because the burden of proof for a criminal case is "beyond a reasonable doubt," a far higher standard than a preponderance of the evidence, Internal Affairs would sometimes "toll" their own investigation—meaning suspend it—while related criminal charges were pending. If the accused officer was convicted criminally, the LAPD could sustain the allegation with minimal investigation, since the criminal burden of proof exceeded the LAPD's. The decision whether to toll an Internal Affairs investigation until criminal charges were resolved was entirely discretionary, however, not mandatory.

Although the LAPD's justification for tolling the Internal Affairs investigation pertained only to allegation 1, the Rasmussens' claim that Stephanie had killed Sherri, Moriarty's intervention also tolled Internal Affairs's investigation into allegation 2, the Rasmussens' claim of an LAPD cover-up.

For the next two years, until October 2011, the LAPD's investigation of the Rasmussens' allegation of a cover-up consisted of little more than periodic phone calls and emails between Hodgin at Internal Affairs and RHD Detective Greg Stearns about the status of Stephanie's criminal case. Other than with Stearns, the only contacts Hodgin documented in her chrono were communications with detectives in the LAPD's Legal Affairs Division and Risk Management Division, which were responsible for limiting the LAPD's legal liabilities.

Stephanie's preliminary hearing, a mini-trial to determine whether probable cause exists to sustain criminal charges, was scheduled for early December 2009.

Among the witnesses expected to testify at the preliminary hearing was Jennifer Francis of SID. As the prelim drew near, Francis became increasingly concerned that she could be questioned on the witness stand about her conversations with Shepard in 2005.

Francis did not know what the prosecutors and RHD detectives knew about Shepard's handling of the Rasmussen case in 2005. Shortly before the prelim, Francis informed Torrealba of her concerns about Shepard. Torrealba told Francis that she should talk to Stearns. Stearns told Francis that her role in the case was as a criminalist, not an investigator. Stearns also told Francis that any theories she had derived in the case were not relevant, and that she should not expect to be asked about them in court.

At the conclusion of Stephanie's preliminary hearing, she was ordered to stand trial for first-degree murder.

On May 4, 2010, Stephanie Lazarus retired from the LAPD on her fiftieth birthday. In the eleven months after she was arrested and jailed, the LAPD never moved to terminate her employment. Stephanie's retirement meant that she retained her full pension benefits as a twenty-five-year LAPD employee, twenty-two of which were after the murder. Stephanie's LAPD pension has paid her almost $400,000 since 2012, the year she was convicted of first-degree murder. The amount of Stephanie's pension, $66,949.50 in 2017, grows larger every year.

By the spring of 2010, no one from RHD or Internal Affairs had requested an interview from Jennifer Francis about Shepard, and their conversations in 2005.

On March 25, Francis met with her supervisor at SID, Harry Klann, in his office. Francis reported her concerns about Shepard's handling of the Rasmussen case five years earlier. Francis felt very nervous during her meeting with Klann, given the nature of what she was reporting. Francis also mentioned to Klann a dream she had in which she was shot, and a conversation she had with Nuttall in which Nuttall said he slept with his gun next to his bed.

Klann was more concerned about Francis's display of emotion than the possibility of a conspiracy and cover-up in the Rasmussen case. Klann refused to believe that a conspiracy existed. Klann sensed that Francis was looking to him for answers, but he did not know what to tell her, because he did not feel that there was a conspiracy. Klann suggested to Francis that she speak to a psychologist. Francis told Klann that she did not want to go to BSS, the Behavioral Sciences Section, which provides psychological counseling to LAPD personnel.

Klann subsequently told Jeffrey Thompson, his supervisor and the acting assistant lab director of SID, about Francis's concerns. Klann told Thompson, erroneously, that Nuttall had suggested to Francis that she get a gun and sleep with it close by, like maybe under her pillow. Klann also told Thompson that Francis had refused his suggestion to seek counseling at BSS.

Thompson met with Francis to discuss her concerns. Francis expressed the same concerns to Thompson as she had to Klann. Thompson felt what Francis reported about Shepard did not rise to the level of misconduct on Shepard's part. Thompson believed Francis was acting paranoid.

On May 26, Thompson summoned Francis to his office and asked her whether she would voluntarily seek counseling at BSS. Francis said no, because she did not believe there was anything wrong with her psychologically. Thompson ordered Francis to BSS for mandatory psychological counseling, to begin the following day. Within the LAPD, a "directed referral" to BSS can be a precursor to a departmental finding that someone is unfit for duty. According to Francis, Thompson refused to tell her why she was being sent to BSS, a requirement under the LAPD's policy on directed referrals. Thompson later claimed that his referral was based exclusively on Francis's emotional state and was not influenced in any way by her disclosures about Shepard and the Rasmussen case.

Francis attended her first mandatory counseling session the next day, with BSS psychologist Dr. Dorothy Tucker. Francis felt embarrassed to have been referred to BSS and did not believe her directed referral was appropriate. She asked Tucker why she was ordered there. According to Francis, Tucker said it was because Francis had made a statement that she slept with a gun under her pillow. Francis denied that she had made that statement. Francis informed Tucker that she did not even own a gun. Francis felt during the session that Tucker was interrogating her about what she knew rather than providing psychological counseling.

Francis was required to attend three more counseling sessions with Tucker. She completed her last session on June 17. According to Francis, Tucker told her during their last session that she was not properly ordered to BSS and should not have been. Francis believed Thompson had sent her to BSS as retaliation for the concerns that she had raised about Shepard's handling of the Rasmussen case in 2005.

A few days later, Francis asked RHD detective Dan Jaramillo for a meeting. She told Jaramillo that she did not want his partner at RHD, Stearns, to attend the meeting. The meeting was planned for June 30 at SID.

Stearns and Jaramillo decided to ask a supervisor at RHD, Detective Debra Winter, to attend the meeting with Jaramillo as a witness. Francis asked Nuttall to attend the meeting as her witness. According to Nuttall, the first thing Winter said to him when he walked into the conference room was "Detective, do you solve all your cases?" The meeting was acrimonious from the start. Francis expressed directly to Jaramillo and Winter her concerns about Shepard's 2005 investigation. Francis mentioned the email that she had received from Shepard after Stephanie's arrest.

Winter asked Francis whether she wanted to make a personnel complaint against Shepard. Francis said no. Francis had requested the meeting because she wanted to alert the prosecutors and RHD detectives on the Rasmussen case to a potential blind spot in the investigation so they would not be caught off guard if it came up at trial. Francis had already reported her concerns to Torrealba and her own supervisors at SID, Klann and Thompson. Jaramillo and Winter, by virtue of their rank, were also LAPD supervisors, with the responsibility to initiate an investigation if any misconduct was reported to them. Whether Francis wished to file a personnel complaint against Shepard had no bearing on their responsibilities as supervisors. Remarkably, not a single LAPD supervisor to whom Francis reported her concerns identified any possible misconduct or initiated an investigation, even to clear Shepard's name.

Afterward, Jaramillo discussed the Francis meeting with his partner, Stearns. Jaramillo told Stearns that Francis had made a statement along the lines of "I know things," which Francis denies she ever said. Jaramillo also told Stearns that Francis said during the meeting that she had an email from Shepard. Stearns took it upon himself to call Klann, Francis's supervisor at SID, and demand that Francis produce the email. According to Klann, Stearns told him, "You need to control your employees." Stearns also told Klann that he would not allow Francis to jeopardize the Rasmussen case.

Klann emailed Francis on July 8 and requested she turn over to him a copy of the email from Shepard. Francis initially told Klann that she was not comfortable providing the email to him. Francis wanted to give it to a different supervisor. Klann went to Thompson and told him that she had refused. Thompson instructed Klann to order Francis to provide the email. Klann summoned Francis to his office and told her he wanted the email. Francis returned to Klann's office fifteen minutes later and gave him a printout of the email. Klann told Francis, "RHD is not happy with you." Klann was referring to Stearns. Klann was unaware of any other RHD detective who was angry or upset with Francis besides Stearns.

In early July, Klann received a phone call from Deputy DA Beth Silverman, a prominent homicide prosecutor in the District Attorney's Major Crimes Division. Silverman asked Klann what was going on with Francis, because word had gotten around that "she was losing it." Francis had done some DNA analysis in the high-profile "Grim Sleeper" serial killer case, which Silverman was prosecuting. Among the detectives assigned to the RHD Grim Sleeper Task Force was Cliff Shepard. According to Klann, Silverman said that she would not allow Francis to affect the Grim Sleeper case and that she did not want Francis doing any further work on it, or testifying in any of Silverman's other cases.

Thompson received a similar phone call from Silverman. As she had informed Klann, Silverman told Thompson that she did not want Francis working on the Grim Sleeper case. According to Thompson, Silverman said she had heard from Stearns that Francis was making statements regarding a conspiracy, and he feared the department was going to be embarrassed. Silverman told Thompson that Francis would be a problematic and tainted witness and referred to her as "Defense Witness Number 1."

Francis heard that Silverman had a meeting with RHD detectives and told Thompson afterward that she did not want Francis working on the Grim Sleeper case or any of her other cases. Thompson confirmed to Francis that Silverman had a negative opinion of her. According to Francis, Thompson told her that maybe she needed to go back to BSS because it appeared to him the emotional side of her brain was overtaking the practical side. Thompson said Francis seemed obsessed with the Rasmussen case and that she needed a hobby. Thompson advised Francis that she could improve her relationship with the District Attorney's Office over time by doing her job well.

In July 2010, after the city declined the Rasmussens' legal claim, Nels and Loretta filed a civil rights and wrongful death lawsuit against the City of Los Angeles, the LAPD, Stephanie Lazarus, and as yet unidentified LAPD personnel responsible for the alleged cover-up. The Rasmussens' complaint alleged, *"Defendants acted to divert the investigation away from Lazarus so as to avoid scandal, disrepute, embarrassment, shame, and intense negative publicity that would otherwise result from investigating an LAPD officer for murder. At the time, the Chief of Police for the LAPD was Daryl Gates, who was fiercely protective of the reputation of his LAPD and went to great lengths to discredit any outsider who attempted to tarnish the department."*

The Rasmussens' lawsuit also highlighted the four-year gap between 2005, when the female DNA profile was obtained, and 2009, when Stephanie was arrested. The lawsuit stated, *"In 2005, the testing on the bite mark's DNA was performed. The results demonstrated that whoever bit Sherri in the violent struggle before her death was a female. This was a major break in the case. Plaintiffs were not told about this development until 2009."*

The lawsuit did not specify financial damages. Nels and Loretta's motivation for filing the lawsuit was to hold the LAPD accountable and to bring the truth to light. Nels and Loretta were financially secure and had no interest in profiting from Sherri's murder. The Rasmussens intended to endow a scholarship at Loma Linda's School of Nursing, Sherri's alma mater, with any monetary damages the lawsuit produced.

In early March 2011, the LAPD's murder book for the Catherine Braley cold case was returned from RHD to the Van Nuys homicide unit. Much as in March 2008, when the Rasmussen and Braley murder books first arrived in the Van Nuys squad room in a file box of mysterious origin, and again in June 2009, when RHD came to Van Nuys in the wake of Stephanie Lazarus's arrest and requisitioned the Braley murder book, no explanation was given as to why the Braley case had been sent back to Van Nuys.

Between June 2009 and March 2011, the nearly two-year period during which RHD had possession of the Braley murder book and investigative responsibility for her unsolved homicide, no activity whatsoever was documented in the LAPD's chrono for the Braley case. In fact, prior to March 2011, the last investigative activity documented in the Braley chrono dated to September 9, 1988, more than twenty years earlier and only eight months after Cathy's murder.

Van Nuys homicide detectives reopened the Braley case in March 2011. Two years later, new leads pointed away from the deputies to a previously unknown individual. On August 29, 2013, on what would have been Cathy Braley's fifty-second birthday, the individual was arrested for an unrelated crime. The LAPD presented the Braley case to the District Attorney's Office, which declined at that time to file charges.

On May 23, 2011, Jennifer Francis went to the LAPD's Inspector General, the investigative arm of the Los Angeles Police Commission, the civilian board that oversees the department. Francis initiated a personnel complaint against her supervisors at SID, Harry Klann and Jeffrey Thompson. Francis alleged that her directed referral to BSS was retaliation for her having reported to Klann her concerns about Shepard's handling of the Rasmussen case in 2005.

The following day, on May 24, Los Angeles Superior Court Judge Elizabeth Allen White dismissed the Rasmussens' civil lawsuit against the city and LAPD, primarily on the grounds of governmental immunity. Because their lawsuit was dismissed prior to the commencement of discovery, the Rasmussens were not given the opportunity to depose any witnesses or subpoena any police documents that might have shed light on whether there had been an LAPD cover-up of their daughter's murder. In contrast to Stephanie's arrest, the development received little media attention.

Francis's personnel complaint forced the LAPD to open a new Internal Affairs investigation focused on her allegations. The complaint was assigned to Internal Affairs Detective Mike Berretta of the Workplace Investigation Section. Berretta's investigation focused narrowly on whether Francis was retaliated against by her supervisors at SID. What went wrong in the Rasmussen murder investigation, and whether the LAPD perpetuated a cover-up between 1986 and 2009, were not part of Berretta's investigation. Between July 2011 and January 2012, Berretta interviewed fourteen witnesses. Berretta did not request an interview with RHD Detective Cliff Shepard or any other LAPD detectives responsible for the Rasmussen investigation before 2009.

Although the Rasmussens' civil lawsuit against the LAPD was dismissed in May, Internal Affairs did not learn of the dismissal until October 2011, five months later. On October 18, the Internal Affairs sergeant handling the Rasmussens' complaint, Barbara Hodgin, noted in her chrono, *"Contacted Det. Stearns, who advised trial not starting until Feb. 2012. Per Stearns, lawsuit was dismissed against the City."* A few hours later, Hodgin spoke to a detective in the LAPD's Risk Management Division, Lavita Jones, who confirmed the news.

The next activity Hodgin documented in the chrono was nine days later, on October 27. According to the chrono, Hodgin met with LAPD Commander Rick Webb, the commanding officer of the Internal Affairs Group.

The Internal Affairs investigation of the Rasmussens' allegations had been tolled since day one, in November 2009, almost two years earlier. In that time, zero witnesses had been interviewed and zero evidence collected or examined. The LAPD's original justification for tolling the entire Internal Affairs investigation was the criminal case pending against Stephanie Lazarus. The status of the Internal Affairs investigation did not change the following month, in December 2009, after Stephanie was ordered to stand trial for first-degree murder.

10/27/11 12:30 12:35 0.1 Met with Cmdr Webb, who adv'd to close case. Hodgin, Barbara

LAPD Internal Affairs chronological log for CF #09-004314 (October 27, 2011)

Stephanie was still awaiting trial in October 2011, when Hodgin met with Webb. The only thing that had changed was the dismissal of the Rasmussens' civil lawsuit, a legal decision based not on the facts of their case but as a matter of law, and which the Rasmussens had appealed. Nevertheless, on October 27, Webb advised Hodgin to close the Internal Affairs investigation into the Rasmussens' allegation of an LAPD cover-up. According to Hodgin's chrono, her meeting with Webb lasted all of five minutes.

Twelve days later, on November 8, Hodgin completed her report and submitted it to her supervisor at Internal Affairs. According to her chrono, Hodgin devoted a total of 6.8 hours, over the course of two years, to investigating the Rasmussens' allegations. Four of the 6.8 hours were spent writing the report.

Internal Affairs never contacted or interviewed Nels and Loretta Rasmussen before the LAPD closed its investigation into their allegations of a cover-up. Nor were any detectives involved in the LAPD's investigation of the Rasmussen case between 1986 and 2009 ever contacted or interviewed by Internal Affairs. There is also no indication that Internal Affairs ever examined the Rasmussen murder book, which has been in the possession of RHD since May 2009, when the case was transferred from Van Nuys.

LAPD Commander Rick Webb weighed in on the Rasmussens' complaint on November 22. Webb handwrote a "badge note," on his official letterhead used to issue orders. Webb wrote, *"A couple of issues: (1) The law suit is alleging that Lazarus killed the vict. That is sustained due to the burden of proof being preponderance of evid. (2) Ct. 2 also their lawsuit is alleging nexus between employment & vict. Also dept. culpability. That is unfounded. We do not condone murder. R."*

In mid-January 2012, Internal Affairs detective Jennifer Capa emailed Hodgin, Berretta, and two other IA investigators, inquiring about allegation 2 in the Rasmussens' complaint, the LAPD cover-up of their daughter's murder. Capa wrote, *"I do not believe that Allegation 2 was addressed."* Capa asked Hodgin, *"Barb: I'm guessing you had direction on this since it was such a high profile case . . . can you enlighten me as what you were directed to do . . . Thanks."*

Hodgin replied to Capa's email the following day. Hodgin wrote, *"Commander Webb directed me to 'Unfound' the allegation against the City since the judge released the LAPD of any wrong doing and to 'Sustain' the allegation against Lazarus due to the DA filed on her and the LAPD believes she committed crime; and close the case."*

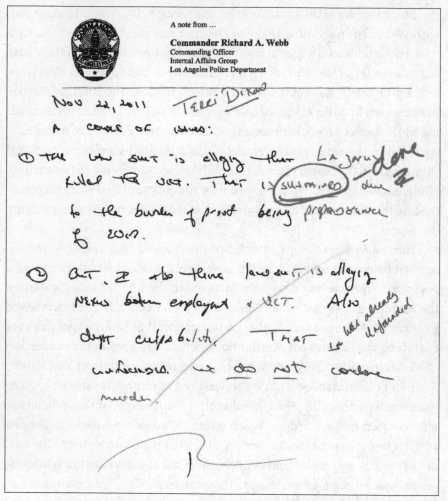

A note from ...

Commander Richard A. Webb
Commanding Officer
Internal Affairs Group
Los Angeles Police Department

LAPD Commander Rick Webb badge note re: IA CF 09-004314
(November 22, 2011)

On February 20, Berretta completed his investigation into Francis's allegation of retaliation and filed his report. The LAPD determined that Klann's and Thompson's actions did not rise to the level of misconduct. In 2013, Francis filed a civil lawsuit against the City of Los Angeles alleging retaliation and other claims. As of January 2019, the lawsuit remains active. Francis continues to work as a Criminalist III at the LAPD's Forensic Science Division, formerly SID.

Stephanie's trial for first-degree degree murder began on February 6, 2012. Stephanie pleaded not guilty. She did not testify in her own defense or make any public statements during her trial.

RHD Detective Cliff Shepard retired from the LAPD on February 23, in the middle of Stephanie Lazarus's murder trial.

On March 8, after a five-week trial, Stephanie was convicted of first-degree murder.

Two weeks later, on March 22, Commander Webb presented his penalty recommendation, the culmination of the Internal Affairs investigation of the Rasmussens' complaint, to Chief of Police Charlie Beck. Count 1, against Stephanie, was sustained. Because she had already retired from the LAPD in May 2010, no disciplinary penalty could be imposed. Count 2, the Rasmussens' allegation of an LAPD cover-up, was not addressed in the Penalty Recommendation form Commander Webb presented to Chief Beck on March 22.

The LAPD officially closed the Rasmussens' complaint six days later, on March 28.

Stephanie was sentenced on May 11. Victim impact statements were delivered in court by the Rasmussens and John Ruetten. John became emotional as he concluded his remarks, "The fact that Sherri's death occurred because she met and married me brings me to my knees. I do not know and fear I will never know how to cope with this appalling fact. I have resigned myself to praying for some measure of peace and trying to endure the daydreams about a world where Sherri is still with us and this pointless tragedy never occurred." Stephanie declined to make any statement before sentencing and expressed no regret or remorse. She was sentenced to twenty-seven years to life.

Stephanie maintains her innocence and has appealed her murder conviction. All her appeals to date have been denied.

On June 5, 2012, three years to the day after her arrest for murder, Stephanie arrived at the Central California Women's Facility in Chowchilla, a four-hour drive from Los Angeles, to begin her prison sentence. In her prison intake photo taken that day, Lazarus grinned like a Cheshire cat, the face of a woman and police officer who had escaped justice for twenty-three years, and nearly forever.

Since Stephanie Lazarus's conviction in 2012, the Rasmussen murder book and all of the LAPD's investigative records in the case have been stored securely in the RHD squad room under lock and key, in a special filing cabinet procured after the trial. The locked filing cabinet that holds the LAPD's Lazarus files has only two keys. Stearns has one key and Jaramillo the other.

For more than thirty years, the LAPD has consistently denied any

CDC# WE4479 Date: 06/05/2012

*Stephanie Lazarus's California Department
of Corrections prison intake photo,
June 5, 2012*

cover-up in the separate murder cases of Sherri Rasmussen, killed in Van Nuys in 1986, and Catherine Braley two years later. The LAPD has never acknowledged that either investigation was mishandled or influenced in any way by the possibility of malfeasance by law enforcement personnel.

Despite the proximity in time and distance between Sherri's and Cathy's murders, Nels and Loretta Rasmussen and Mary Postma were unaware of each other's cases in the 1980s, when their daughters were killed. For the next quarter century, neither the Rasmussens nor Mary had any idea that there was another family whose experience mirrored their own. To this day, the Ramsussens and Mary have never spoken or met. Nevertheless, the Rasmussen and Braley cases have shadowed each other for more than thirty years. For most of that time, both murders were unsolved.

To date, no one at the LAPD—detective or brass, active duty or retired—has been held accountable for any mistakes made in the LAPD's investigation of Sherri Rasmussen's homicide during the twenty-three years that Stephanie Lazarus got away with murder.

The murder of Catherine Braley remains an open investigation.

The individual who left the file box at the desk of Detective Jim Nuttall in 2008 has yet to step forward or be publicly identified.

Author's Note on Sources

This book is the product of nine years of investigative reporting.

My work on the book began on June 5, 2009, the day Stephanie Lazarus was arrested for murder. It was not merely the sensational nature of the allegations—a veteran LAPD detective accused of the cold case murder of a romantic rival—that drew me to the story on day one. In April 2008, about a year before she was arrested, I had actually met Lazarus at Parker Center, LAPD headquarters, and interviewed her at length for a book I was planning to write about art theft, Lazarus's beat at that time.

My chance encounter with Lazarus made me intensely curious to learn the truth. Did a respected police detective really commit murder and carry that secret for her entire career?

A few days after Lazarus's arrest, I attended her arraignment in a downtown L.A. courtroom. I returned to court for the next hearing, and the one after that. Over the next three years, I attended every court proceeding in the case, including every day of the monthlong trial in 2012, which ended in Lazarus's conviction for first-degree murder. Afterward, I obtained the complete court file, trial transcript, and copies of all the trial exhibits. These voluminous records included Lazarus's LAPD personnel file and many reports and documents from the original LAPD investigation of Sherri Rasmussen's murder. Additional documents were later entrusted to me by sources.

As I watched Lazarus's case unfold in real time, it became apparent that this story was not a whodunit. The evidence presented at trial proved

Lazarus's guilt beyond a reasonable doubt. The unanswered question that loomed over the trial and persisted in its wake was how Lazarus got away with murder for so long. Was it fate that protected her when the original investigators focused exclusively on burglary suspects? Or was she protected through the years by her fellow LAPD officers? Did she try to sabotage the investigation herself, from inside the LAPD? And to what extent did she succeed? When, decades after the murder, DNA analysis revealed that the killer was a woman, was justice further delayed because the LAPD refused to open its mind to the truth?

I had no preconceptions, let alone answers to any of these questions, when I first began digging into the story in June 2009. On the day of Lazarus's arraignment, the parents of the victim, Sherri Rasmussen, publicly alleged a long-running LAPD cover-up of their daughter's murder. The LAPD promised an investigation of the Rasmussens' allegation, but, as time passed, released no details about what its reinvestigation entailed or what it had uncovered. Three years later, shortly after Lazarus was convicted of first-degree murder, the LAPD proclaimed that its reinvestigation did not find evidence of an internal cover-up.

By then, I was more than three years into my own investigation and had begun to interview many people involved in the case. No one I spoke with had been interviewed or even contacted by the LAPD about the cover-up allegation. I wondered, How did the LAPD conclude that there was no evidence of a cover-up without apparently interviewing any witnesses? I was determined to try to get to the bottom of the story, even as its scope and depth continued to expand in ways that defied my expectations.

It was in 2011 that I learned about the unsolved murder of Catherine Braley, killed in Van Nuys in 1988, two years into the Rasmussen investigation. An old *Los Angeles Times* story described a wrongful death civil lawsuit filed a few months after the murder by Braley's mother, Mary Postma. Postma's lawsuit alleged that three L.A. County Sheriff's deputies were responsible for her daughter's death and accused the LAPD of a cover-up.

Once again guided primarily by my curiosity, I began investigating the Braley case in addition to Rasmussen. I learned that Postma's lawsuit went to trial in federal court in 1995, but ended with a hung jury. I obtained the complete court file, which included many reports and documents from the original LAPD investigation of Catherine Braley's murder. In late 2012, I provided the LAPD with a copy of the documents I had obtained.

This book is based wholly on information contained in these many thousands of documents from both cases, totaling tens of thousands of pages, as well as hundreds of hours of tape-recorded interviews that I conducted with witnesses, investigators, and other firsthand participants in these events. All interviews were tape-recorded with their permission and later transcribed. I have retained copies of all recordings, transcripts, and all other relevant records in my possession.

My ambition was to interview every person who knew Sherri Rasmussen or Catherine Braley while they were alive, as well as every person with knowledge relevant to their cases. Two of the people most central to the Rasmussen murder, whose perspectives I had hoped to include in this book, Stephanie Lazarus and John Ruetten, Sherri's husband, both declined my interview requests.

In my reporting on the Braley case, I proceeded cautiously, always mindful that her murder is unsolved and remains an open investigation. If I judged that contacting a witness posed a risk of interfering with the LAPD's investigation, I did not contact them and relied instead on other methods of reporting.

Wherever in the book I have attributed exact quotations or thoughts to a person, that information comes either directly from an interview I personally conducted with them; or from a tape-recorded interview, interview transcript, or statement they gave to the LAPD; or from their own sworn testimony on the witness stand.

Finally, it is worth noting that official chronologies, reports, notes, diaries, interviews, formal statements, and even sworn testimony are rarely coldly objective. Even well-documented information may in one way or another reflect the opinions, limited knowledge or perspective, and at times even the biases of their sources. While my aim was to present the facts as objectively as possible, the embedded opinions and perspectives of the sources I relied on could not always be avoided or eliminated. I wish to make clear that when it was necessary to present such subjective information in the book, whether to advance the narrative or describe what someone believed to be true at a particular in moment in time, the opinions and perspectives reported do not necessarily reflect my own.

My reporting on the story continues.

Acknowledgments

This book took far longer to report and write than I anticipated. I could not have stayed the course without the assistance, encouragement, and inspiration of many people.

First and foremost, I must thank Kathryn Busby, my wife, best friend, and the light of my life, for supporting our family and my work for the last nine years. Without her countless sacrifices, this book would not exist. No matter how dark the subject matter became or how distant the finish line appeared, I could count on her to lift my spirits.

I would also like to thank my sons Declan and Hudson, mere toddlers when I began writing what they knew only as my "police story," for always being more interested in basketball, soccer, and video games than my incremental progress on this book.

Thank you to the family and friends of Sherri Rasmussen and Catherine Braley, particularly Sherri's parents, Nels and Loretta, and Cathy's mother, Mary Postma. I could not have told their daughters' stories without their cooperation, openness, and inexhaustible patience in answering my endless questions.

Many other of Sherri's and Cathy's loved ones also shared invaluable insights and recollections, and I am grateful to them all. Among Sherri's friends, Jayne and Mike Goldberg, Peggy and Glenn Crabtree, and Donna Robison were particularly helpful. Among Cathy's loved ones, I would like to thank her brothers Danny and Joe Braley, as well as Jordan Weiner and Bonnie Harnden.

I was beyond blessed to have Serena Jones as my editor. As the scope of my reporting widened, and the manuscript grew to seemingly unpublishable dimensions, Serena never flinched. Her editorial instincts were impeccable, and her belief in me and the importance of the story never wavered. Thank you Serena for everything. I am grateful to everyone at Henry Holt who had a hand in this book's publication, particularly Gillian Blake, Patricia Eisemann, Paul Golob, and Madeline Jones, and Steve Rubin. Thank you to my agent Andrew Blauner for steering me to Serena and Henry Holt.

Everything I know about how to conduct a thorough investigation I learned from interviews with current and retired LAPD detectives. I could not have asked for better teachers. Detective Rick Jackson was an especially helpful and inspiring mentor.

I would like to thank Los Angeles Superior Court Judge Robert J. Perry and his courtroom staff for all their assistance. At the Los Angeles County District Attorney's Office, I'm grateful for the help of deputy DAs Shannon Presby and Paul Nunez.

For anyone who is interested in reading more about the 2012 murder trial of Detective Stephanie Lazarus, the definitive account was written by reporter Betsy Ross and is available online at her website Trials & Tribulations. Given her deep knowledge of the case and familiarity with the cast of characters, Betsy was my daily sounding board and the only person I trusted to read early drafts of each chapter.

At the *Atlantic* magazine, which in 2011 ran my initial article on the Rasmussen case, I would like to thank Geoff Gagnon, Christopher Orr, James Bennet, and Sue Parilla.

This project was influenced by many books, but most particularly: Joseph Wambaugh's *The Blooding*, Miles Corwin's *Homicide Special*, the Harry Bosch novels of Michael Connelly, Matthew Thomas's *We Are Not Ourselves*, and Susan Sheehan's *A Missing Plane*.

The roots of this project can be traced to Oslo, Norway, in 2005. I am grateful to Thor Wessel, Siri Ross, Berit Reiss-Andersen, and Gry Elise Jacobsen for their hospitality and for inadvertently setting me on this journey.

For their friendship, candor, and encouragement at key moments, I thank Jeff Alexander, Tom Bissell, R. J. Cutler, Keith Eisner, Wayne Federman, Dan Josefson, Jason Kolker, John Ortiz, Jonathan Ryland, Andy Walker, and David Wilcox.

I would like to close by thanking my mother, Rose McGough, and my mother-in-law, Rhona Busby.

About the Author

MATTHEW MCGOUGH's nonfiction writing has been published in *The Atlantic*, *The New York Times*, the *Los Angeles Times*, and more. His acclaimed memoir *Bat Boy: Coming of Age with the New York Yankees* was the basis of *Clubhouse*, a prime-time TV series on CBS, and his story about his first day with the Yankees was selected to lead off the pilot episode of *The Moth Radio Hour*. Formerly a legal consultant and writer for NBC's *Law & Order*, he lives in Los Angeles with his wife and children.